W9-BLB-235

Rick Steves'®

PARIS

Rick Steves, Steve Smith
& Gene Openshaw

2009

WEST PARIS*

1. Arc de Triomphe
2. Eiffel Tower
3. Grand & Petit Palais
4. Jacquemart-André Museum
5. Army Museum & Napoleon's Tomb
6. Opéra Garnier (Old Opera)
7. Orangerie Museum
8. Orsay Museum
9. Paris Sewer Tour
10. *Paris Story* Film
11. Quai Branly Museum
12. Rodin Museum
13. Tuileries Garden
14. American Church

* See key on next page.

KEY

- ▤ Pedestrian-Friendly Area
- ▤ Popular Shopping Area
- ═ ═ ═ Tunnel
- Ⓜ Ⓡ Metro Station, RER Station
- ⓣ Taxi Stand
- Ⓑ Batobus Boat Stops
- Ⓡ River Tour Boat Stops
- Ⓞ Open Bus Tour Stops
- 2ᴱ Arrondissement
- ■ Landmark or Point of Interest
- ⓘ Tourist Information Offices

0 km ———————————— 0.5 km

0 mi ———————————— 0.25 mi

EAST PARIS

1. Archaeological Crypt
2. Carnavalet Museum
3. Cluny Museum
4. Conciergerie
5. Deportation Memorial
6. Flower Market
7. Ile St. Louis
8. Louvre Museum
9. Luxembourg Garden
10. Museum of Jewish Art & History
11. Notre-Dame Cathedral
12. Opéra Bastille
13. Palais Royal Courtyards
14. Picasso Museum
15. Pompidou Center
16. To Promenade Plantée Park Entry
17. Sainte-Chapelle
18. St. Séverin Church
19. St. Sulpice Church
20. Victor Hugo's House

Rick Steves'

PARIS

2009

AVALON
TRAVEL

CONTENTS

INTRODUCTION   1
Planning. 3
Practicalities 6
Money. 8
Sightseeing 12
Transportation 14
Traveling as a Temporary Local 15
Back Door Travel Philosophy 16

ORIENTATION   17

SIGHTS   38

SELF-GUIDED WALKS AND TOURS

Historic Core
Historic Paris Walk. 74

Major Museums Neighborhood
Louvre Tour. 101
Orsay Museum Tour 130
Orangerie Museum Tour. 155

Eiffel Tower and Nearby
Rue Cler Walk. 164
Eiffel Tower Tour 172
Rodin Museum Tour 183
Army Museum and
    Napoleon's Tomb Tour 194
Bus #69 Sightseeing Tour 217
Marmottan Museum Tour. 225

Left Bank
Left Bank Walk. 233
Cluny Museum Tour. 244

Champs-Elysées and Nearby
Champs-Elysées Walk 251

Marais Neighborhood and Nearby
Marais Walk. 263
Pompidou Center Tour. 273
Carnavalet Museum Tour. 286
Picasso Museum Tour 301
Père Lachaise Cemetery Tour. 310

Montmartre
Montmartre Walk. 323

SLEEPING 338
Rue Cler Neighborhood 344
Marais Neighborhood 352
Luxembourg Garden Area 359
Near Place de la Republique 366
For Longer Stays 368

EATING 370
Rue Cler Neighborhood 380
Marais Neighborhood 385
Ile St. Louis 390
Luxembourg Garden Area 392
Elsewhere in Paris 395

Les Grands Cafés de Paris 397

PARIS WITH CHILDREN 401

SHOPPING 407

NIGHTLIFE 421

TRANSPORTATION CONNECTIONS 433

DAY TRIPS FROM PARIS 455
Versailles Day Trip 456
Chartres Cathedral Day Trip 482
Reims Day Trip 500
More Day Trips 511
Grand Châteaux near Paris 511
Impressionist Excursions 518
Disneyland Paris 525

FRENCH HISTORY AND CONTEMPORARY POLITICS 527

APPENDIX 535
Resources 535
Telephones, Email, and Mail 540
Holidays and Festivals 550
Conversions and Climate 552
Essential Packing Checklist 554
Hotel Reservation Form 555
French Pronunciation Guide for Paris 556
French Survival Phrases 559

INDEX 561

INTRODUCTION

Paris—the City of Light—has been a beacon of culture for centuries. As a world capital of art, fashion, food, literature, and ideas, it stands as a symbol of all the fine things human civilization can offer. Come prepared to celebrate, rather than judge the cultural differences, and you'll capture the romance and joie de vivre that Paris exudes.

Paris offers sweeping boulevards, chatty crêpe stands, chic boutiques, and world-class art galleries. Sip decaf with deconstructionists at a sidewalk café, then step into an Impressionist painting in a tree-lined park. Climb Notre-Dame and rub shoulders with the gargoyles. Cruise the Seine, zip up the Eiffel Tower, and saunter down avenue des Champs-Elysées. Master the Louvre and Orsay museums. Save some after-dark energy for one of the world's most romantic cities.

About This Book

Rick Steves' Paris 2009 is a personal tour guide in your pocket. Better yet, it's actually three tour guides in your pocket: The co-authors of this book are Steve Smith and Gene Openshaw. Steve has been traveling to France—as a guide, researcher, home owner, and devout Francophile—every year since 1985. Gene and I have been exploring the wonders of the Old World since our first "Europe through the gutter" trip together as high-school buddies in the 1970s. An inquisitive historian and lover of European culture, Gene wrote most of this book's self-guided museum tours and neighborhood walks. Together, Steve, Gene, and I keep this book up-to-date and accurate (though for simplicity, from this point "we" will shed our respective egos and become "I").

Here's what you'll find in the following chapters:

Orientation includes tourist information, specifics on public transportation, local tour options, and other helpful hints. The "Planning Your Time" section suggests a day-to-day schedule for how to best use your limited time.

Sights provides a succinct overview of the most important sights, arranged by neighborhood, with ratings:

▲▲▲—Don't miss.

▲▲—Try hard to see.

▲—Worthwhile if you can make it.

No rating—Worth knowing about.

The **Self-Guided Walks** cover six of Paris' most intriguing neighborhoods: Historic Paris (including Notre-Dame and Sainte-Chapelle), rue Cler (near the Eiffel Tower), the Left Bank, the Champs-Elysées, the Marais, and Montmartre.

The **Self-Guided Tours** lead you through Paris' most fascinating museums and sights: the Louvre, Orsay, Orangerie, Eiffel Tower, Rodin, Army Museum and Napoleon's Tomb, Marmottan, Cluny, Pompidou Center, Carnavalet, Picasso, and Père Lachaise Cemetery. The Bus #69 Sightseeing Tour gives an inexpensive overview of the city.

Sleeping describes my favorite hotels in four cozy neighborhoods, from budget deals to cushy splurges.

Eating offers good-value restaurants ranging from inexpensive eateries to romantic bistros, arranged by neighborhood, plus a listing of "Grand Cafés."

Paris with Children includes my top recommendations for keeping your kids (and you) happy in Paris.

Shopping gives you tips for shopping painlessly and enjoyably, without letting it overwhelm your vacation or ruin your budget. Read up on Paris' great department stores, neighborhood boutiques, flea markets, outdoor food markets, and arcaded, Old World shopping streets.

Nightlife is your guide to entertainment and evening fun, with music, bus and taxi tours, and the best night walks and river cruises. You'll also find information on how to easily translate *Pariscope,* the weekly entertainment guide.

Transportation Connections lays the groundwork for your smooth arrival and departure, covering connections by train and plane, with detailed information on Paris' two major airports (Charles de Gaulle and Orly), a minor airport (Beauvais), and Paris' six train stations.

Day Trips covers nearby sights: the great châteaux of Versailles (includes self-guided tour), Vaux-le-Vicomte, Fontainebleau, and Chantilly; Chartres' majestic cathedral (includes self-guided tour); the contemporary Champagne town of Reims; the Impressionist retreats of Claude Monet's Giverny and Vincent van Gogh's Auvers-sur-Oise; and, *finalement,* Disneyland Paris. For those who like to linger, I list accommodations near most of these sights.

French History and Contemporary Politics gives you a quick overview of France from the past to the present.

Major Holidays and Weekends

In 2009, be ready for unusually big crowds during these holiday periods: Easter weekend and the two weeks follow-ing it (April 10-24, busiest April 10-14); Labor Day (May 1-3); Ascension weekend (May 21-24); Pentecost weekend (May 29-June 1); Bastille Day (July 14) and the week during which it falls; Assumption weekend (Aug 14-16); and the winter holidays (Dec 20-Jan 4—note that Christmas week is quieter than the week of New Year's). These two holidays are usually quiet, but holidays nonetheless: All Saints' Day (Nov 1), and Armistice Day weekend (Nov 11). For information on festivals, see page 550 of the appendix.

The **appendix** is a traveler's tool kit, with a handy packing check-list, recommended books and films, instructions on how to use the telephone, useful French phone numbers, a climate chart, festival list, hotel reservation form, guide to pronouncing Parisian landmarks, and French survival phrases.

Throughout this book, when you see a ✪ in a listing, it means that the sight is covered in much more detail in one of my tours (a page number will tell you where to look to find more information).

Browse through this book and select your favorite sights. Then have a *fantastique* trip! Traveling like a temporary local, you'll get the absolute most out of every mile, minute, and euro. As you visit places I know and love, I'm happy you'll be meeting my favorite Parisians.

PLANNING

Trip Costs

Five components make up your trip costs: airfare, surface transportation, room and board, sightseeing/entertainment, and shopping/miscellany.

Airfare: A basic, round-trip flight from the US to Paris costs $800–1,600, depending on where you fly from and when (cheaper in winter). If your trip covers a wide area, consider saving time and money in Europe by flying "open jaw" (into one city and out of another—e.g., into Nice and out of Paris).

Surface Transportation: For a typical one-week visit, allow about $60 for Métro tickets and a couple of day trips. To budget the cost to get between Paris and either airport, add an additional $170 by taxi, $60 by shuttle, or around $25 for the airport bus or RER train.

Room and Board: You can thrive in Paris in 2009 on an overall average of $155 a day per person for room and board. This allows $15 for breakfast, $20 for lunch, $40 for dinner, and $80 for lodging (based on two people splitting the cost of a $160 double room). If you've got more money, I've listed great ways to spend it. Students and tightwads can enjoy Paris on $80 a day ($40 per bed, $40 for meals and snacks).

Sightseeing and Entertainment: Get the Paris Museum Pass, which covers most sights in the city (for more information, see page 38). You'll pay about $48 for a two-day pass (4 days/$72, 6 days/$96). While you can buy the pass through some US travel agents, it's easy and cheaper to buy in Paris. Without a Museum Pass, figure an average of $10–15 per major sight (Orsay $12, Louvre $14) and $10 for others. Assume that bus tours and splurge experiences (concerts in Sainte-Chapelle) cost about $40. An overall average of $30 a day works for most. Don't skimp here. After all, this category is the driving force behind your trip—you came to sightsee, enjoy, and experience Paris.

Shopping and Miscellany: Figure $5 per ice-cream cone, coffee, or soft drink. Shopping can vary in cost from nearly nothing to a small fortune. Good budget travelers find that this category has little to do with assembling a trip full of lifelong and wonderful memories.

When to Go

Late spring and fall have the best weather and the biggest crowds. May, June, September, and October are by far the toughest months for hotel-hunting. Summers are generally hot and dry; if you wilt in the heat, look for a room with air-conditioning. It's fairly easy to find rooms in summer, and though many French businesses close in August, you'll hardly notice. Paris makes a great winter getaway. Airfares are less, the cafés are cozy, and the city feels lively but not touristy. The only problem—weather—is fixed by dressing correctly. Expect cold and rain, but not snow. For specific temperatures, see the climate chart in the appendix (page 553).

Travel Smart

Your trip to Paris is like a complex play—easier to follow and really appreciate on a second viewing. While no one does the same trip twice to gain that advantage, reading this book in its entirety before your trip accomplishes much the same thing. Note the days when museums are closed (see page 20) or which days are the right ones for festivals (see page 550). You can wait in line at the Louvre, or—with a Paris Museum Pass—zip through without a sweat. Day-tripping to Versailles on Monday is bad, since it's closed—but it's not recommended on Tuesday either, when the Louvre is closed and tourist mobs storm the palace. A smart trip is a puzzle—a fun, doable, and worthwhile challenge.

Sundays have the same pros and cons as they do for travelers in the US. Special events and weekly markets pop up, sightseeing attractions are generally open, banks and many shops are closed, public transportation options are fewer, and there's no rush hour. Saturdays are virtually weekdays (without the rush hour).

Know Before You Go

Your trip is more likely to go smoothly if you plan ahead. Check this list of things to arrange while you're still at home.

Be sure that your **passport** is valid at least six months after your ticketed date of return to the US. If you need to get or renew a passport, it can take up to two months (for more on passports, see www.travel.state.gov).

Book your rooms well in advance if you'll be traveling during any major **holidays** (see "Major Holidays and Weekends," page 3).

Call your **debit and credit card companies** to let them know the countries you'll be visiting, so that they'll accept (and not deny) your international charges. Confirm what your daily withdrawal limit is; consider asking to have it raised so you can take out more cash at each ATM stop. Ask about international transaction fees.

If you'll be **traveling with children,** read over the list of pre-trip suggestions on page 401.

If you're bringing an iPod or other MP3 player, take advantage of our free downloadable **audiotours** of the Louvre, Orsay, Versailles, and Historic Paris (see page 536 for details).

If you're taking an **overnight train** (especially between Paris and Rome or Venice), and you need a *couchette* (overnight bunk) or sleeper—and you *must* leave on a certain day—consider booking it in advance through a US agent (such as www.raileurope.com), even though it may cost more. All high-speed trains in France require a seat reservation—book as early as possible, as these trains fill fast. (For more on train travel, see page 440 and www.ricksteves.com/rail.)

If you're planning on **renting a car** in France, you'll need your driver's license. It's recommended—but not required—that you carry an International Driving Permit (IDP), available at your local AAA office ($15 plus the cost of two passport-type photos; see www.aaa.com).

Since **airline carry-on restrictions** are always changing, visit the Transportation Security Administration's website (www.tsa.gov/travelers) for an up-to-date list of what you can bring on the plane with you...and what you have to check. Remember to arrive with plenty of time to get through security.

Be sure to mix intense and relaxed periods in your itinerary. Every trip (and every traveler) needs at least a few slack days. Pace yourself. Assume you will return.

Plan ahead for laundry, picnics, and Internet stops. Get online at Internet cafés or your hotel to research transportation connections, confirm events, and check the weather. Buy a phone card and use it for reservations, reconfirmations, and double-checking hours.

Just the FAQs, Please

Whom do I call in case of emergency?
Dial 17 for police help. In a medical emergency, call 15.

What if my credit card is stolen?
Act immediately. See "Damage Control for Lost Cards," page 10, for instructions.

How do I make a phone call to, within, and from Europe?
For detailed dialing instructions, refer to page 542.

How can I get tourist information about my destination?
This book is probably all the information you'll need for your trip; see page 23 for info on Paris' not-too-useful tourist information offices (abbreviated **TI** in this book). For the US office of France's national TI, see page 535.

What's the best way to pack?
Light. For a recommended packing list, see page 555.

Does Rick have other materials that will help me?
For info on Rick's guidebooks, public television series, free audio tours, public radio show, guided tours, travel bags, accessories, and railpasses, see page 536.

Are there any updates to this guidebook?
Check www.ricksteves.com/update for changes to the most recent edition of this book.

Can you recommend any good books or movies for my trip?
For suggestions, see pages 538.

Do I need to speak some French?
Be sure to learn the polite words: *bonjour, merci, s'il vous plait, pardon, au revoir*. Though many French people—especially those in the tourist trade, and in big cities—speak English, you'll get better treatment if you learn and use the French pleasantries. For

Connect with the culture. Set up your own quest for the best café, Eiffel Tower view, crêpe, or whatever. Enjoy the friendliness of your Parisian hosts. Slow down and be open to unexpected experiences. Ask questions—most locals are eager to point you in their idea of the right direction. Keep a notepad in your pocket for organizing your thoughts. Wear your money belt, and learn the local currency and how to estimate prices in dollars. Those who expect to travel smart, do.

PRACTICALITIES

Red Tape: You need a passport—but no visa or shots—to travel in France. Pack a photocopy of your passport in your luggage in case the original is lost or stolen. You are required to have proof of identity on you at all times in France.

background information on the language barrier, see page 548. For a list of survival phrases, see page 559.

Do you recommend any language or cooking schools?
See page 548 in the appendix for a list.

Do you have information on flights and train travel in France?
See the Transportation Connections chapter on page 433.

How much do I tip?
Relatively little. For tips on tipping, see page 10.

Are strikes common in France? How do travelers cope?
Strikes are typical in France, but usually short-lived. See "Coping with Strikes" on page 449 for more details.

Will I get a student or senior discount?
While discounts aren't listed in this book, seniors (age 60 and over), students with International Student Identification Cards, teachers with proper identification, and youths under 18 or even 26 can get discounts—but they have to ask. To inquire about a senior discount, ask, *"Réduction troisième âge?"* (ray-dook-see-ohn twah-zee-ehm ahzh). To get a teacher or student ID card, visit www.statravel.com or www.isic.org.

How can I get a VAT refund on major purchases?
See the details on page 11.

How do I calculate metric amounts?
Europe uses the metric system. A liter is about a quart, four to a gallon. A kilometer is six-tenths of a mile. I figure kilometers to miles by cutting them in half and adding back 10 percent of the original (120 km: 60 + 12 = 72 miles, 300 km: 150 + 30 = 180 miles). For more metric conversions, see page 552.

Time: In France—and in this book—you'll use the 24-hour clock. It's the same through 12:00 noon, then keep going: 13:00, 14:00, and so on. For anything over 12, subtract 12 and add p.m. (14:00 is 2:00 p.m.).

France, like most of continental Europe, is generally six/nine hours ahead of the East/West Coasts of the US. The exceptions are the beginning and end of Daylight Saving Time: Europe "springs forward" the last Sunday in March (two weeks after most of North America), and "falls back" the last Sunday in October (one week before North America). For a handy online time converter, try www.timeanddate.com/worldclock.

Business Hours: In France, most shops are open Monday through Saturday (10:00–12:00 & 14:00–19:00) and closed Sunday, though many small markets, *boulangeries* (bakeries), and street markets are open Sunday mornings until noon. On Mondays, some businesses are closed until 14:00, and possibly all day. Saturdays are like weekdays (but most banks are closed).

Cheap Tricks in Paris

Since hotels take the biggest bite out of your dollar, **book your room early** to land one of my great-value hotels. I list several well-located and comfortable hotels with rooms under €100, but you'll need to beat other travelers to the punch.

Enjoy picnic lunches and dinners regularly. You'll find tasty €4 sandwiches, to-go salads, quiches, and high-quality takeout at bakeries, *charcuteries,* and stands throughout Paris. Scenic picnic sites are everywhere.

Order only a *plat* (main course) for dinner on some nights. And at cafés (as opposed to restaurants), it's fine to order only a soup or salad for dinner.

Visit sights on free days (see "Affording Paris' Sights" sidebar on page 47).

Buy a Paris Museum Pass and use it wisely (see page 38 for advice). For stays of a week or longer, buy a weekly Métro pass (see page 26 for details).

Shopping: The Shopping chapter offers tips on how to enjoy Paris' plethora of shopping opportunities (page 407). Clothing-size conversions are on page 552. For customs regulations and VAT refunds, see page 11.

Watt's Up? Europe's electrical system is different from North America's in two ways: the shape of the plug (two round prongs) and the voltage of the current (220 volts instead of 110 volts). For your North American plug to work in Europe, you'll need an adapter, sold inexpensively at travel stores in the US. As for the voltage, most newer electronics or travel appliances (such as hair dryers, laptops, and battery chargers) automatically convert the voltage—if you see a range of voltages printed on the item or its plug (such as "110–220"), it'll work in Europe. Otherwise, you can buy a converter separately in the US (about $20).

News: Americans keep in touch via the *International Herald Tribune* (published almost daily throughout Europe). Every Tuesday, the European editions of *Time* and *Newsweek* hit the stands with articles of particular interest to European travelers. Sports addicts can get their daily fix online or from *USA Today*. Good websites include www.iht .com, http://news.bbc.co.uk, and www.europeantimes.com.

MONEY

Cash from ATMs

Throughout Europe, cash machines (ATMs) are the standard way for travelers to get local currency.

Bring plastic—credit and/or debit cards. As an emergency backup, bring several hundred dollars in hard cash. Avoid using currency exchange booths (lousy rates and/or outrageous fees); if you have currency to exchange, take it to a bank. Also avoid traveler's checks, which are a waste of time (long waits at banks) and a waste of money (in fees).

To use an ATM to withdraw money from your account, you'll need a debit card (ideally with a Visa or MasterCard logo for maximum usability), plus a PIN code. Know your PIN code in numbers; there are only numbers—no letters—on European keypads. It's smart to bring two cards, in case one gets demagnetized or eaten by a temperamental machine.

Before you go, verify with your bank that your cards will work overseas, and alert them that you'll be making withdrawals in Europe; otherwise, the bank may not approve transactions if it perceives unusual spending patterns. Also ask about international fees; see "Credit and Debit Cards," below.

French cash machines are labeled *point d'argent* or *distributeur des billets* (the French call them *D.A.B.*—day-ah-bay). You'll find these cash machines all over France—they're always open and provide quick transactions.

Try to take out large sums of money to reduce your per-transaction bank fees. If the machine refuses your request, try again and select a smaller amount (some cash machines won't let you take out more than about €150—don't take it personally). If that doesn't work, try a different machine.

To keep your cash safe, use a money belt—a pouch with a strap that you buckle around your waist like a belt, and wear under your clothes. Thieves target tourists. A money belt provides peace of mind, allowing you to carry lots of cash safely. Don't waste time every few days tracking down a cash machine—withdraw a week's worth of money, stuff it in your money belt, and travel!

Credit and Debit Cards

For purchases, Visa and MasterCard are more commonly accepted than American Express. Just like at home, credit or debit cards work easily at larger hotels, restaurants, and shops, but smaller businesses prefer payment in local currency (in small bills—break large bills at a bank or larger store). Your US credit and debit cards will not work in train- or Métro-ticket machines, at self-service gas pumps, or at freeway tollbooths.

Fees: Some credit and debit card transactions—whether purchases or ATM withdrawals—come with tacked-on "international transaction" fees of up to 3 percent plus $5 per transaction. To avoid unpleasant surprises, call your bank or credit-card company before your trip to ask about these fees.

Exchange Rate

1 euro (€) = about $1.50

To convert prices in euros to dollars, add about 50 percent: €20 = about $30, €50 = about $75. (To get the latest rate and print a cheat sheet, see www.oanda.com.) Just like the dollar, the euro is broken down into 100 cents. You'll find coins ranging from 1 cent to 2 euros, and bills from 5 euros to 500 euros.

Damage Control for Lost Cards

If you lose your credit, debit, or ATM card, you can stop people from using it by reporting the loss immediately to the respective global customer-assistance centers. Call these 24-hour US numbers collect: Visa (410/581-9994), MasterCard (636/722-7111), and American Express (623/492-8427). For another option (with the same results), you can call these toll-free numbers in France: Visa (08 00 90 11 79) and MasterCard (08 00 90 13 87). American Express has a Paris office, but the call isn't free (01 47 77 70 00, English spoken). Diners Club has offices in the US (702/797-5532, call collect) and Britain (from France, dial 00-44-1695-53760).

At a minimum, you'll need to know the name of the financial institution that issued you the card, along with the type of card (classic, platinum, or whatever). Providing the following information will allow for a quicker cancellation of your missing card: full card number, whether you are the primary or secondary cardholder, the cardholder's name exactly as printed on the card, billing address, home phone number, circumstances of the loss or theft, and identification verification (your birth date, your mother's maiden name, or your Social Security number—memorize this, don't carry a copy). If you are the secondary cardholder, you'll also need to provide the primary cardholder's identification-verification details. You can generally receive a temporary card within two or three business days in Europe.

If you promptly report your card lost or stolen, you typically won't be responsible for any unauthorized transactions on your account, although many banks charge a liability fee of $50.

Tipping

Tipping *(donner un pourboire)* in France isn't as automatic and generous as it is in the US, but for special service, tips are appreciated, if not expected. As in the US, the proper amount depends on your resources, tipping philosophy, and the circumstances, but some general guidelines apply.

Restaurants: At cafés and restaurants, a 15 percent service charge is generally included in the bill *(service compris)*, though it's good form to tip 5 percent extra for good service. When you hand your payment plus a tip to your waiter, you can say, *"C'est bon"* (say bohn), meaning, "It's good" (and you don't want any change back). If you order a meal at a counter, don't tip.

Taxis: To tip the cabbie, round up. For a typical ride, round up to the next euro on the fare (to pay a €13 fare, give €14); for a long ride, round to the nearest €10 (for a €75 fare, give €80). If the cabbie hauls your bags and zips you to the airport to help you catch your flight, you might want to toss in a little more. But if you feel like you're being driven in circles or otherwise ripped off, skip the tip.

Special Services: It's thoughtful to tip a couple of euros to someone who shows you a special sight and who is paid in no other way. Tour guides at public sites sometimes hold out their hands for tips (€1–2) after they give their spiel; if I've already paid for the tour, I don't tip extra, unless they really impressed me. I don't tip at hotels, but if you do, give the porter a euro for carrying bags and leave a couple of euros in your room at the end of your stay for the maid if the room was kept clean. In general, if someone in the service industry does a super job for you, a tip of a couple of euros is appropriate, but not required.

When in doubt, ask. If you're not sure whether (or how much) to tip for a service, ask your hotelier or the tourist information office; they'll fill you in on how it's done on their turf.

Getting a VAT Refund

Wrapped into the purchase price of your French souvenirs is a Value-Added Tax (VAT) of about 19.6 percent. If you purchase more than €175 (about $265) worth of goods at a store that participates in the VAT-refund scheme, you're entitled to get most of that tax back. Getting your refund is usually straightforward and, if you buy a substantial amount of souvenirs, well worth the hassle. If you're lucky, the merchant will subtract the tax when you make your purchase. (This is more likely to occur if the store ships the goods to your home.) Otherwise, you'll need to:

Get the paperwork. Have the merchant completely fill out the necessary refund document, *Bordereau de Vente a l'Exportation*, also called a "cheque." You'll have to present your passport at the store.

Get your stamp at the border or airport. Process your cheque(s) at your last stop in the EU (e.g., at the airport) with the customs agent who deals with VAT refunds. It's best to keep your purchases in your carry-on for viewing, but if they're too large or dangerous (such as knives) to carry on, track down the proper customs agent to inspect them before you check your bag. You're not supposed to use your purchased goods before you leave. If you show up at customs wearing your chic new French ensemble, officials might look the other way—or deny you a refund.

Collect your refund. You'll need to return your stamped document to the retailer or its representative. Many merchants work with a service, such as Global Refund (www.globalrefund.com) or Premier Tax Free (www.premiertaxfree.com), which have offices at major airports, ports, or border crossings. These services, which extract a 4 percent fee, can refund your money immediately in your currency of choice or credit your card (within two billing cycles). If the retailer handles VAT refunds directly, it's up to you to contact the merchant for your refund. You can mail the documents from home, or quicker, from your point of departure (using a stamped, addressed envelope you've prepared or one that's been provided by the merchant)—and then wait. It could take months.

Customs for American Shoppers

You are allowed to take home $800 worth of items per person duty-free, once every 30 days. The next $1,000 is taxed at a flat 3 percent. After that, you pay the individual item's duty rate. You can also bring in duty-free a liter of alcohol (slightly more than a standard-size bottle of wine; you must be at least 21), 200 cigarettes, and up to 100 non-Cuban cigars. You may take home vacuum-packed cheeses; dried herbs, spices, or mushrooms; canned fruits or vegetables including jams and vegetable spreads; and olive oil (many producers pack their oil in stainless steel canisters for easier transport). Red meats (even vacuum-packed or canned), and fresh fruits or vegetables are not permitted (canned pâtés allowed if goose, duck, or pork). Note that you'll need to carefully pack any bottles of wine and other liquid-containing items (jars of olives, etc.) in your checked luggage due to limits on liquids in carry-ons. To check customs rules and duty rates before you go, visit www.cbp.gov, and click on "Travel," then "Know Before You Go."

SIGHTSEEING

Sightseeing can be hard work. Use these tips to make your visits to Paris' finest sights meaningful, fun, fast, and painless.

Plan Ahead

Set up an itinerary that allows you to fit in all your must-see sights. For a one-stop look at opening hours, see "Paris at a Glance" (page 42). Most sights keep stable hours, but you can easily confirm the latest by picking up the booklet *Musées, Monuments Historiques, et Expositions* (available at most museums). Remember, the Louvre and other museums are closed on Tuesday, and many others are closed on Monday (see "Daily Reminder" on page 20). You can find good information on many of Paris' sights online at www.parisinfo.com.

Don't put off visiting a must-see sight—you never know when a place will close unexpectedly for a holiday, strike, or restoration. If you'll be visiting during a holiday, find out if a particular sight will be open by phoning ahead or visiting its website.

When possible, visit key museums first thing (when your energy is best) and save other activities for the afternoon. Hit the highlights first, then go back to other things if you have the stamina and time.

Going at the right time can also help you avoid crowds. This book offers tips on specific sights. Try visiting the sight very early, at lunch, or very late. The Louvre, Orsay, and Orangerie museums are open selected evenings, while the Pompidou Center is always open late, making for peaceful visits with fewer crowds.

To get the most out of the self-guided tours in this book, read the tour the night before your visit. When you arrive at the sight, use the overview map to get the lay of the land and the basic tour route.

Plan to buy a Paris Museum Pass, which can speed you through lines and saves you money (for details, see page 38). Also, some museums offer reduced prices on Sunday.

At the Sight

All sights have rules, and if you know about these in advance, they're no big deal.

Some important sights have metal detectors or conduct bag searches that will slow your entry.

At churches—most of which offer amazing art (usually free) and a welcome seat—a modest dress code (no bare shoulders or shorts) is encouraged.

Most museums require you to check daypacks and coats. They'll be kept safely. If you have something you can't bear to part with, stash it in a pocket or purse. If you don't want to check a small backpack, carry it (at least as you enter) under your arm like a purse. From a guard's point of view, a backpack is generally a problem while a purse is not.

If you check a bag, the attendant may ask you (in French) if it contains anything of value—e.g., camera, phone, money, passport—since these cannot be checked.

Photography is banned at most major sights. Look for signs or ask. If cameras are allowed, flashes or tripods are usually not. Flashes damage oil paintings and distract others in the room. Even without a flash, a handheld camera will take a decent picture (or buy postcards or posters at the museum bookstore). Video cameras are generally allowed.

Some museums have special exhibits in addition to their permanent collection. Some exhibits are included in the entry price; others come at an extra cost (which you may have to pay even if you don't want to see the exhibit).

Many sights rent audioguides, which offer dry-but-useful recorded descriptions in English (about €6). I have produced free

---

How Was Your Trip?

Were your travels fun, smooth, and meaningful? If you'd like to share your tips, concerns, and discoveries, please fill out the survey at www.ricksteves.com/feedback. I value your feedback. Thanks in advance—it helps a lot.

---

audioguides of my tours for the Louvre, Orsay Museum, Versailles, and Historic Paris (see page 536). If you bring along your own pair of headphones and a Y-jack, two people can sometimes share one audioguide and save. Guided tours in English (about €6 and widely ranging in quality) are most likely to occur during peak season.

Expect changes—paintings can be on tour, on loan, out sick, or shifted at the whim of the curator. To adapt, pick up any available free floor plans as you enter, and ask museum staff if you can't find a particular painting. Say the title or artist's name, or point to the photograph in this book and ask for its location by saying, *"Où est?"* (oo ay).

Most sights have an on-site café or cafeteria (usually a good place to rest and have a snack or light meal). The WCs at many sights are free and clean.

Key sights and museums have bookstores selling postcards and souvenirs. Before you leave, scan the postcards and thumb through the biggest guidebook (or skim its index) to be sure you haven't overlooked something that you'd like to see.

Most sights stop admitting people 30–60 minutes before closing time, and some rooms close early (generally about 45 minutes before the actual closing time). Guards usher people out, so don't save the best for last.

Every sight or museum offers more than what is covered in this book. Use these tours as an introduction—not the final word.

TRANSPORTATION

Transportation concerns within Paris are limited to the subway (Métro), buses, and taxis, all covered extensively in the Orientation chapter. Connections to day-trip destinations are covered in those chapters. You don't want to drive in Paris. If you have a car, stow it (for suggestions on parking, see page 453). For information on connecting Paris with the rest of France and with London on the Eurostar train, see page 451.

TRAVELING AS A TEMPORARY LOCAL

We travel all the way to Europe to enjoy differences—to become temporary locals. You'll experience frustrations. Certain truths that we find "God-given" or "self-evident," such as cold beer, ice in drinks, bottomless cups of coffee, hot showers, and bigger being better, are suddenly not so true. One of the benefits of travel is the eye-opening realization that there are logical, civil, and even better alternatives.

Paris is an understandably proud city. To enjoy its people, you need to celebrate the differences. A willingness to go local ensures that you'll enjoy a full dose of Parisian hospitality.

If there is a negative aspect to the image the French have of Americans (apart from our foreign policy), it's that we are big, loud, aggressive, impolite, rich, superficially friendly, and naive.

Europeans place a high value on speaking quietly in restaurants and on trains. Listen while on the bus, the Métro, or in a restaurant— the place can be packed, but the decibel level is low. Try to adjust your volume accordingly to show respect for their culture.

While the French look bemusedly at some of our Yankee excesses—and worriedly at others—they nearly always afford us individual travelers all the warmth we deserve. Judging from all the happy feedback I receive from travelers who have used this book, it's safe to assume you'll enjoy a great, affordable vacation—with the finesse of an independent, experienced traveler.

Thanks, and *bon voyage!*

BACK DOOR TRAVEL PHILOSOPHY
From *Rick Steves' Europe Through the Back Door*

Travel is intensified living—maximum thrills per minute and one of the last great sources of legal adventure. Travel is freedom. It's recess, and we need it.

Experiencing the real Europe requires catching it by surprise, going casual..."Through the Back Door."

Affording travel is a matter of priorities. (Make do with the old car.) You can travel—simply, safely, and comfortably—nearly any-where in Europe for $120 a day plus transportation costs (allow more for bigger cities). In many ways, spending more money only builds a thicker wall between you and what you came to see. Europe is a cultural carnival, and, time after time, you'll find that its best acts are free and the best seats are the cheap ones.

A tight budget forces you to travel close to the ground, meeting and communicating with the people, not relying on service with a purchased smile. Never sacrifice sleep, nutrition, safety, or cleanli-ness in the name of budget. Simply enjoy the local-style alternatives to expensive hotels and restaurants.

Extroverts have more fun. If your trip is low on magic moments, kick yourself and make things happen. If you don't enjoy a place, maybe you don't know enough about it. Seek the truth. Recognize tourist traps. Give a culture the benefit of your open mind. See things as different but not better or worse. Any culture has much to share.

Of course, travel, like the world, is a series of hills and valleys. Be fanatically positive and militantly optimistic. If something's not to your liking, change your liking. Travel is addictive. It can make you a happier American as well as a citizen of the world. Our Earth is home to six and a half billion equally important people. It's humbling to travel and find that people don't envy Americans. Europeans like us, but, with all due respect, they wouldn't trade passports.

Globe-trotting destroys ethnocentricity. It helps you understand and appreciate different cultures. Regrettably, there are forces in our society that want you dumbed down for their convenience. Don't let it happen. Thoughtful travel engages you with the world—more impor-tant than ever these days. Travel changes people. It broadens perspec-tives and teaches new ways to measure quality of life. Rather than fear the diversity on this planet, travelers celebrate it. Many travelers toss aside their hometown blinders. Their prized souvenirs are the strands of different cultures they decide to knit into their own character. The world is a cultural yarn shop, and Back Door travelers are weaving the ultimate tapestry. Join in!

ORIENTATION

Many people fall in love with Paris. Some see the essentials and flee, overwhelmed by the big city. With the proper approach and a measure of patience, you'll fall head over heels for Europe's capital city.

This orientation to the City of Light will illuminate your trip. The day plans—for visits of one to seven days—will help you prioritize the many sights. You'll tap into Paris' information sources for current events. Most importantly, you'll learn to navigate Paris by Métro, bus, taxi, or on foot.

Paris: A Verbal Map

Paris (population of city center: 2,170,000) is split in half by the Seine River, divided into 20 arrondissements (proud and independent governmental jurisdictions), circled by a ring-road freeway (the *périphérique*), and speckled with Métro stations. You'll find Paris easier to navigate if you know which side of the river you're on, which arrondissement you're in, and which Métro stop you're closest to. If you're north of the river (the top half of any city map), you're on the Right Bank (Rive Droite). If you're south of it, you're on the

Left Bank (Rive Gauche). The bull's-eye of your Paris map is Notre-Dame, which sits on an island in the middle of the Seine. Most of your sightseeing will take place within five blocks of the river.

Arrondissements are numbered, starting at the Louvre and moving in a clockwise spiral out to the

ring road. The last two digits in a Parisian zip code are the arrondissement number. The abbreviation for "Métro stop" is "Mo." In Parisian
jargon, the Eiffel Tower is on *la Rive Gauche* (the Left Bank) in the
7ème (7th arrondissement), zip code 75007, Mo: Trocadéro.

Paris Métro stops are used as a standard aid in giving directions, even for those not using the Métro. As you're tracking down
addresses, these words and pronunciations will help: Métro (may-
troh), *place* (plahs—square), *rue* (roo—road), *avenue* (ah-vuh-noo),
boulevard (boo-luh-var), and *pont* (pohn—bridge).

Paris by Neighborhood

Paris is a big, sprawling city, but its major sights cluster in convenient zones. Grouping your sightseeing, walks, dining, and shopping
thoughtfully can save you lots of time and money.

The **historic core** centers on the Ile de la Cité ("Island of the City"),
located in the middle of the Seine. On the Ile de la Cité, you'll find
Paris' oldest sights, from Roman ruins to the medieval Notre-Dame
and Sainte-Chapelle churches. Other sights in this area: Archaeological
Crypt, Deportation Memorial, Conciergerie, flower market, Paris
Plage, and the lovely island, Ile St. Louis, with appealing shops, cafés,
and restaurants. Paris' most historic riverside vendors, *les bouquinistes*,
line both sides of the Seine as it passes Ile de la Cité.

Just west of the historic core is the **major museums neighborhood,** where you'll find the Louvre, Orsay, and Orangerie. Other
sights: the Tuileries Garden, Palais Royal's courtyards, and shopping
at place de la Madeleine.

The **Champs-Elysées**—the greatest of many grand, 19th-century
boulevards on the Right Bank—runs northwest from the place de la
Concorde to the Arc de Triomphe. Other sights: the Petit and Grand
Palais, Opéra Garnier, Jacquemart-André museum and Fragonard
Perfume museum, La Défense and La Grande Arche, and shopping at
Galeries Lafayette and at Passages Choiseul and Ste. Anne.

South of the Champs-Elysées, the **Eiffel Tower** neighborhood, which is located in the shadow of that famous monument in
the Champ de Mars park, has colorful rue Cler (with many recommended hotels and restaurants), the Army Museum and Napoleon's
Tomb, the Rodin Museum, and the thriving outdoor market, Marché
boulevard de Grenelle (Wed and Sun mornings). Other sights: Quai
Branly Museum, National Maritime Museum, and Sewer Tour. The
Marmottan Museum is west of the Eiffel Tower on the Right Bank.

The **Left Bank** is home to...the Left Bank. Anchored by the large
Luxembourg Garden (with numerous nearby hotels and eateries listed
in this book), the Left Bank is the traditional neighborhood of Paris'
intellectual, artistic, and café life. Other sights: the Latin Quarter,
Cluny Museum, St. Germain-des-Prés and St. Sulpice churches,
Panthéon, Montparnasse Tower, Catacombs, Delacroix Museum, and

Paris Neighborhoods

ORIENTATION

the Jardin des Plantes park. This is also one of Paris' best shopping areas (see the Sèvres-Babylone to St. Sulpice shopping stroll on page 412).

The **Marais neighborhood** has lots of recommended restaurants and hotels, shops, the delightful place des Vosges, and artistic sights such as the Picasso and Pompidou museums. This area is alive with avant-garde boutiques (see page 415). Other Marais sights: Jewish Art and History and Carnavalet museums, Victor Hugo's House, Holocaust Memorial, Promenade Plantée park, Père Lachaise Cemetery, the traffic-free street market on rue Montorgueil, and markets at Bastille and place d'Aligre.

Finally, hovering on the northern fringes of your Paris map is the hilltop neighborhood of **Montmartre,** which still retains some of the untamed rural charm that once drew Impressionist painters and turn-of-the-century bohemians. Other sights: Sacré-Cœur basilica, Dalí and Montmartre museums, Moulin Rouge, Museum of Erotic Art, Pigalle, and nearby Puces St. Ouen flea market.

Planning Your Time

In the planning sections below, I've listed sights in descending order of importance. Therefore, if you have only one day, just do Day 1; for two days, add Day 2; and so on. When planning where to plug in Versailles, remember that the palace (Château) is closed on Mondays and especially crowded on Sundays and Tuesdays—try to avoid these days. For other itinerary considerations on a day-by-day basis, check the "Daily Reminder," next page.

ORIENTATION

Daily Reminder

Monday: These sights are closed today: Orsay, Rodin, Marmottan, Carnavalet, Catacombs, Petit Palais, Victor Hugo's House, Montmartre Museum, Quai Branly, and Paris Archaeological Crypt. Giverny and the Château at Versailles are also closed; the Louvre and Eiffel Tower are more crowded because of these closings. The Army Museum (and Napoleon's Tomb) is closed the first Monday of each month in winter (Oct–May). Some small stores don't open until 14:00. Street markets such as rue Cler and rue Mouffetard are dead today. Some banks are closed. It's discount night at many cinemas.

Tuesday: Many museums are closed today, including the Louvre, Orangerie, Cluny, Pompidou, Picasso, National Maritime, and Delacroix, as well as the Grand Palais and the châteaux of Chantilly and Fontainebleau. The Eiffel Tower, Orsay, Versailles, and Giverny are particularly busy today.

Wednesday: All sights are open (Louvre until 21:45). The weekly *Pariscope* magazine comes out today. Most schools are closed, so many kids' sights are busy, and in summer the Guignol puppet shows play in Luxembourg Garden. Some cinemas offer discounts.

Thursday: All sights are open except the Sewer Tour. The Orsay is open until 21:45. Some department stores are open late.

Friday: All sights are open (Louvre until 21:45) except the Sewer Tour. Vaux-le-Vicomte has candlelight visits (July–Aug).

Paris in One, Two, or Three Busy Days

If you want to fit in Versailles on a three-day visit, try the afternoon of the second day (easier) or the third day.

Day 1

Morning: Follow this book's Historic Paris Walk, featuring Ile de la Cité, Notre-Dame, the Latin Quarter, and Sainte-Chapelle.

Afternoon: Tour the Louvre.

Evening: Enjoy the Trocadéro scene and a twilight ride up the Eiffel Tower.

Day 2

Morning: Follow this book's Champs-Elysées Walk from the Arc de Triomphe down the grand avenue des Champs-Elysées to Tuileries Garden.

Midday: Cross the pedestrian bridge from the Tuileries Garden, then tour the Orsay Museum.

Afternoon: Tour the Rodin Museum, or the Army Museum and Napoleon's Tomb.

Afternoon trains and roads leaving Paris are crowded; TGV train reservation fees are higher.

Saturday: All sights are open except the Jewish Art and History Museum and the Holocaust Memorial. The fountains run at Versailles (April–Sept), and Vaux-le-Vicomte hosts candle-light visits (early-May–early-Oct); otherwise, avoid weekend crowds at area châteaux and Impressionist sights. Department stores are jammed. The Jewish Quarter is quiet and in summer the puppet shows play in Luxembourg Garden.

Sunday: Many sights are free the first Sunday of the month, including the Louvre, Orsay, Rodin, Cluny, Picasso, and Delacroix museums, the Arc de Triomphe (Oct–March only), and Pompidou Center. These free days at popular museums attract hordes of visitors.

Versailles is more crowded than usual on Sunday—but on the upside, the garden's fountains are running (April–Sept). Most of Paris' stores are closed on Sunday, but shoppers will find relief in the Marais neighborhood's lively Jewish Quarter, where many stores are open. Look for organ concerts at St. Sulpice and possibly other churches. Luxembourg Garden's summer puppet shows are on, and the American Church often hosts a free evening concert (generally Sept–June at 17:00—but not every week). Many recommended restaurants in the rue Cler neighborhood are closed for dinner.

Evening: Cruise the Seine River, take Paris Vision's night-time Illumination bus tour, or follow this book's Floodlit Paris Taxi Tour (see the Nightlife chapter; if you're staying more than two days, save this for your last-night finale).

Day 3

Morning: Ride the RER suburban train out to Versailles.

Afternoon: Take this book's Marais Walk.

Evening: Follow this book's Montmartre Walk, featuring the Sacré-Cœur basilica.

Paris in Five to Seven Days Without Going In-Seine

Day 1

Morning: Follow this book's Historic Paris Walk, featuring Ile de la Cité, Notre-Dame, the Latin Quarter, and Sainte-Chapelle. If you enjoy medieval art, visit the Cluny Museum.

Afternoon: Tour the Opéra Garnier (English tours available), consider the *Paris Story* film (for a video orientation), and end your day enjoying the glorious rooftop view at Galeries Lafayette department store.

Evening: Cruise the Seine River.

Day 2

Reversing the morning and afternoon activities on this day works well, because the Champs-Elysées Walk leaves you near the Louvre—but most people have more energy for museums in the morning.

Morning: Tour the Louvre (arrive 20 min before opening). Have coffee or lunch at Café le Nemours.

Afternoon: Follow this book's Champs-Elysées Walk from the Arc de Triomphe downhill along the incomparable avenue des Champs-Elysées to the Tuileries Garden, and possibly the Orangerie Museum.

Evening: Enjoy dinner on Ile St. Louis, then a floodlit walk by Notre-Dame.

Day 3

Morning: Tour the Orsay Museum (arrive 15 min before opening).

Midday: Tour the Rodin Museum (café lunch in gardens).

Afternoon: Visit the Army Museum and Napoleon's Tomb, then take this book's Rue Cler Walk and relax at Café du Marché.

Evening: Take this book's Montmartre Walk, featuring the Sacré-Cœur basilica.

Day 4

Morning: Catch the RER suburban train by 8:00 to arrive early at Versailles (before it opens at 9:00). Tour the palace's interior.

Midday: Have lunch in the Gardens at Versailles.

Afternoon: Spend the afternoon touring the Gardens and the Domaine de Marie-Antoinette.

Evening: Have dinner in Versailles town or return to Paris. For dessert, follow this book's Floodlit Paris Taxi Tour (in Nightlife chapter).

Day 5

Morning: Follow this book's Marais Walk and tour the Carnavalet Museum (free). Have lunch on place des Vosges or rue des Rosiers.

Afternoon: Depending on your interest, tour two of the following three sights—the Pompidou Center, Picasso Museum, or the Jewish Art and History Museum.

Evening: Enjoy the Trocadéro scene and a twilight ride up the Eiffel Tower.

Day 6

Morning: Take an Impressionist escape to Giverny or Auvers-sur-Oise.

ORIENTATION

Afternoon: Follow this book's Left Bank Walk (featuring art galleries, boutiques, historic cafés, and grand boulevards), mix in some shopping (see "Sèvres-Babylone to St. Sulpice" in the Shopping chapter, page 412), then relax in the Luxembourg Garden or at a nearby café (see "Les Grands Cafés de Paris," page 397).

Evening: Join the parade along the Champs-Elysées (which offers a different scene at night than the daytime walk you enjoyed on Day 2). If you haven't hiked to the top of the Arc de Triomphe yet, consider doing it by twilight.

Day 7
Choose from:
> More shopping and cafés
> Bus #69 tour followed by Père Lachaise Cemetery
> Montmartre and Sacré-Cœur (by day)
> Marmottan or Jacquemart-André museum
> Day trip to Chartres
> Day trip to Reims
> Day trip to Vaux-le-Vicomte and Fontainebleau
> Day trip to Disneyland Paris

Evening: Night bus or boat tour (whichever you have yet to do).

OVERVIEW

Tourist Information

Paris tourist offices (abbreviated as **TI** in this book) have long lines, offer little information, and may charge for maps. But all you really need are this book and one of the freebie maps available at any hotel (or in the front of this book). Paris' TIs share a single phone number: 08 92 68 30 00 (from the US, dial 011 33 8 92 68 30 00).

If you must visit a TI, you can do so at several locations, including **Pyramides** (daily 9:00–19:00, at Pyramides Métro stop between the Louvre and Opéra), **Gares de Lyon and Nord** (both Mon–Sat 8:00–18:00, closed Sun), and **Montmartre** (daily 10:00–19:00, place du Tertre). The official website for Paris' TIs is www.parisinfo.com. Both **airports** have handy information offices (called ADP) with long hours and short lines (see Transportation Connections chapter).

Pariscope: The weekly €0.40 *Pariscope* magazine (or one of its clones, available at any newsstand) lists museum hours, art exhibits, concerts, festivals, plays, movies, and nightclubs. Smart sightseers rely on this for the latest listings (see page 421).

Other Publications: Look for the *Paris Times*, which provides helpful English information and fresh insights into living in Paris (available at English-language bookstores, French-American establishments, the American Church, and online at www.theparistimes .com). *L'Officiel des Spectacles* (€0.35), which is similar to *Pariscope*, also lists goings-on around town (in French). The *Paris Voice*, with snappy reviews of concerts, plays, and current events, is available only online at www.parisvoice.com. For a schedule of museum hours and English museum tours, get the free *Musées, Monuments Historiques, et Expositions* booklet at any museum.

American Church and Franco-American Center: This interdenominational church—in the rue Cler neighborhood, facing the river between the Eiffel Tower and Orsay Museum—is a nerve center for the American émigré community. Worship services are at 9:00 and 11:00 on Sunday; the coffee hour after church and the free Sunday concerts (generally Sept–June at 17:00—but not every week) are a good way get a taste of émigré life in Paris (reception open Mon–Sat 9:00–12:00 & 13:00–22:00, Sun 14:30–19:00, 65 quai d'Orsay, Mo: Invalides, tel. 01 40 62 05 00, www.acparis.org). It's also a handy place to pick up free copies of *Paris Times* (described on previous page) and *France-USA Contacts* (an advertisement paper with info on housing and employment for the 30,000 Americans living in Paris, www.fusac .fr).

Arrival in Paris

For a comprehensive rundown of Paris' train stations and airports, see the Transportation Connections chapter.

Helpful Hints

Heightened Security *(Plan Vigipirate):* You may notice an abundance of police at monuments, on streets, and on the Métro, as well as security cameras at key sights. You'll go through quick and reassuring airport-like security checks at many major attractions. This is all part of Paris' anti-terror plan. The police are helpful, the security lines move quickly, and there are now fewer pickpocket problems on the Métro.

Theft Alert: Although the greater police presence has scared off some, troublesome thieves still thrive near famous monuments and on Métro and RER lines that serve high-profile tourist sights. Wear a money belt, put your wallet in your front pocket, loop your day bag over your shoulders, and keep a tight grip on your purse or shopping bag. Muggings are rare, but do occur. If you're out late, avoid the dark riverfront embankments and any place where the lighting is dim and pedestrian activity is minimal.

Tourist Scams: Be aware of the latest scams, including these current favorites. The "found ring" scam involves an innocent-looking person who picks up a ring on the ground, and asks if you dropped it. When you say no, the person examines the ring more closely, then shows you a mark "proving" that it's pure gold. He offers to sell it to you for a good price—several times more than he paid for it before dropping it on the sidewalk.

In the "friendship bracelet" scam, a vendor approaches you and asks if you'll help him with a demonstration. He proceeds to make a friendship bracelet right on your arm. When finished, he asks you to pay for the bracelet he created just for you. And since you can't easily take it off on the spot, he counts on your feeling obliged to pay up.

Distractions by "salesmen" can also function as a smoke-screen for theft—an accomplice picks your pocket as you try to wriggle away from a pushy vendor.

In popular tourist spots (such as in front of Notre-Dame) young ladies politely ask if you speak English, then pretend to beg for money while actually angling to pick your pocket.

Street Safety: Parisian drivers are notorious for ignoring pedestrians. Look both ways (many streets are one-way) and be careful of seemingly quiet bus/taxi lanes. Don't assume you have the right of way, even in a crosswalk. When crossing a street, keep your pace constant and don't stop suddenly. By law, drivers can miss pedestrians by up to just one meter—a little more than three feet (1.5 meters in the countryside). Drivers carefully calculate your speed and won't hit you, provided you don't alter your route or pace.

Paris' new "Vélib'" bike program, which offers short-term rentals to the French, means more bikes than ever are on the roads (see "Bike Freedom for Parisians" on page 33). When crossing streets, beware of this silent transportation.

Paris Museum Pass: This worthwhile pass, covering most sights in Paris, is sold at TIs and museums. For detailed information, see page 38.

Museum Strategy: When possible, visit key museums first thing (when your energy is best) and save other activities for the afternoon. Remember, most museums require you to check daypacks and coats, and important museums have metal detectors that will slow your entry. The Louvre, Orsay, and Pompidou are open on selected nights (see "Paris at a Glance," page 42), making for peaceful visits with fewer crowds.

Bookstores: There are many English-language bookstores in Paris, where you can pick up guidebooks (at nearly double their American prices). Most carry this book. My favorite is the friendly **Red Wheelbarrow Bookstore** in the Marais neighborhood, run by mellow Penelope (Mon–Sat 10:00–19:00, Sun 14:00–18:00, 22 rue St. Paul, Mo: St. Paul, tel. 01 48 04 75 08). Others include **Shakespeare and Company** (some used travel books, daily 12:00–24:00, 37 rue de la Bûcherie, across the river from Notre-Dame, Mo: St. Michel, tel. 01 43 26 96 50; see page 87 in Historic Paris Walk), **W. H. Smith** (Mon–Sat 10:00–19:00, closed Sun, 248 rue de Rivoli, Mo: Concorde, tel. 01 44 77 88

99), **Brentanos** (Mon–Sat 10:00–19:00, closed Sun, 37 avenue de l'Opéra, Mo: Opéra, tel. 01 42 61 52 50), and **Village Voice** (Mon 14:00–19:00, Tue–Sat 10:00–19:00, Sun 12:00–18:00, near St. Sulpice Church at 6 rue Princesse, tel. 01 46 33 36 47).

Public WCs: Public toilets are free (though it's polite to leave a small tip if there's an attendant). Modern, sanitary street-booth toilets provide both relief and a memory (don't leave small children inside unattended). The restrooms in museums are free and the best you'll find. Or walk into any sidewalk café like you own the place, and find the toilet in the back. Keep toilet paper or tissues with you, as some toilets are poorly supplied.

Parking: Most of the time, drivers must pay to park curbside (buy parking card at *tabac* shops), but not at night (19:00–9:00), all day Sunday, or anytime in August, when many Parisians are on vacation. There are parking garages under Ecole Militaire, St. Sulpice Church, Les Invalides, the Bastille, and the Panthéon; all charge about €27 per day (it's cheaper per hour the longer you stay). Some hotels offer parking for less—ask. See also "Parking in Paris" on page 453 in the Transportation Connections chapter.

Tobacco Stands *(Tabacs):* These little kiosks—usually just a counter inside a café—sell cards for parking meters, public-transit tickets (usually), postage stamps, and...oh yeah, cigarettes. For more on this slice of Parisian life, see page 171 in the Rue Cler Walk. To find one anywhere in Paris, just look for a *Tabac* sign and the red, cylinder-shaped symbol above some (but not all) cafés.

Getting Around Paris

Paris is easy to navigate. Your basic choices are Métro (in-city subway), RER (suburban rail tied into the Métro system), public bus, and taxi. (Also consider the hop-on, hop-off bus and boat tours, described under "Tours" on page 33.) You can buy tickets and passes at most *tabacs* (tobacco stands) and at Métro stations. While most Métro stations have staffed ticket windows, some smaller stations have only ticket-vending machines, for which you'll need coins (some take bills).

Public-Transit Tickets: The Métro, RER, and buses all work on the same tickets. (You can transfer between the Métro and RER on a single ticket, but combining a Métro or RER trip with a bus ride takes two tickets.) A **single ticket** costs €1.50. To save 25 percent, buy a *carnet* (kar-nay) of 10 tickets for €11.10 (that's €1.11 per ticket—€0.39 cheaper than a single ticket). It's less expensive for kids (ages 4–10 pay €5.50 for a *carnet*). *Carnets* can be shared between travelers.

Passes: The transit system has introduced a new chip-card, called the **Passe Navigo Découverte,** but for most tourists, *carnets* are still the better deal. The new Passe costs €21.50, runs Monday–Sunday (expires on Sun, even if you buy it on Fri), and requires a photo, which means it's not shareable. In contrast, two 10-packs of *carnets*—enough for most travelers staying a week—cost €22.50, are shareable, and don't expire until they're used.

If you do want the pass, ask for the "*Passe Navigo Découverte hebdo-madaire*" (pahs nah-vee-go day-koo-vairt ehb-doh-mah-dair) and supply a small postage-stamp-size photo of yourself (bring your own, or use the €4 photo booths in major Métro stations). You buy a chip-embedded card (€5 one-time cost), then "load" a weekly value onto it (€16.50); this gives you free run of the bus and Métro system. At the Métro/bus turnstile, you scan your Passe to enter, and you're on your way.

A month-long version costs about €54—request a Passe Navigo *mensuelle* (mahn-soo-ehl, good from the first day of the month to the last, also requires photo). The pass covers only central Paris. You can pay more for passes covering regional destinations (such as Versailles), but for most visitors, this is a bad value. Instead, buy individual tickets for longer-distance destinations.

The overpriced **Paris Visite** passes were designed for tourists and offer minor reductions at minor sights (1 day/€9, 2 days/€14, 3 days/€19, 5 days/€28), but you'll get a better value with a cheaper *carnet* of 10 tickets or a Passe Navigo Découverte.

By Métro

In Paris, you're never more than a 10-minute walk from a Métro station. Europe's best subway allows you to hop from sight to sight quickly and cheaply (runs daily 5:30–24:30 in the morning). Learn to use it. Begin by studying the color Métro map at the beginning of this book free at Métro stations, and included on freebie Paris maps at your hotel.

How the Métro Works: To get to your destination, determine the closest "Mo" stop and which line or lines will get you there. The lines have numbers, but they're best known by their end-of-the-line stops. (For example, the La Défense/Château de Vincennes line, also known as line 1, runs between La Défense in the west and Vincennes in the east.) Once in the Métro station, you'll see blue-and-white signs directing you to the train going in your direction (e.g., *direction: La Défense*). Insert your ticket in the automatic turnstile, pass through, reclaim your ticket, and keep it until you exit the system (some stations require you to pass your ticket through a turnstile to exit). *Fare inspec-*

tors regularly check for cheaters and accept absolutely no excuses, so keep that ticket!

Transfers are free and can be made wherever lines cross, providing you do so within 90 minutes. When you transfer, look for the orange *correspondance* (connection) signs when you exit your first train, then follow the proper direction sign.

Métro Basics

- The same tickets are good on the Métro, RER (within the city), and city buses (but not to transfer between Métro/RER and bus).
- Save money by buying a *carnet* of tickets.
- Find your train by its end-of-the-line stops.
- Insert your ticket into the turnstile (brown stripe down), retrieve it, and keep it until the end of your journey.
- Beware of pickpockets, and don't buy tickets from men roaming the stations.
- Transfers *(correspondances)* within the Métro or RER system are free.
- At the end of your trip, choose the right exit *(sortie)* to avoid extra walking.
- Dispose of used tickets after your ride is completed (not before), to avoid confusing them with fresh ones.
- On some trains you must activate the door by pushing a button (but most open automatically).

Key Words for the Métro and RER

French	Pronounced	English
direction	dee-rek-see-ohn	direction
ligne	leen-yuh	line
correspondance	kor-res-pohn-dahns	transfer
sortie	sor-tee	exit

Even though the Métro whisks you quickly from one point to another, be prepared to walk significant distances within stations to reach your platform (most noticeable when you transfer). Escalators are common, but they're often out of order. To limit excessive walking, avoid transferring at these sprawling stations: Montparnasse-Bienvenüe, Châtelet-Les Halles, Charles de Gaulle-Etoile, Gare du Nord, and Bastille.

Before taking the *sortie* (exit) to leave the Métro, check the helpful *plan du quartier* (map of the neighborhood) to get your bearings, locate your destination, and decide which *sortie* you want. At stops with several *sorties,* you can save lots of walking by choosing the best exit.

After you exit the system, toss or tear your used ticket so you don't confuse it with your unused ticket—they look virtually identical.

Beware of Pickpockets: Thieves dig the Métro. Be on guard. For example, if your pocket is picked as you pass through a turnstile, you end up stuck on the wrong side (after the turnstile bar has closed behind you) while the thief gets away. Stand away from Métro doors to avoid being a target for a theft-and-run just before the doors close. Any jostling or commotion—especially when boarding or leaving trains—is likely the sign of a thief or a team of thieves in action. Make

carnet	kar-nay	cheap set of 10 tickets
Pardon, madame/ monsieur.	par-dohn, mah-dahm/ mes-yur	Excuse me, ma`am/ sir.
Je descends.	juh day-sahn	I'm getting off.
Donnez-moi mon porte-monnaie!	duh-nay-mwah mohn port-moh-nay	Give me back my wallet!

ORIENTATION

Etiquette

- When waiting at the platform, get out of the way of those exiting the train. Board only once everyone is off.
- Avoid using the hinged seats near the doors of some trains when the car is jammed; they take up valuable standing space.
- In a crowded train, try not to block the exit. If you're blocking the door when the train stops, step out of the car and to the side, let others off, then get back on.
- Talk softly in the cars. Listen to how quietly Parisians communicate and follow their lead.
- On escalators, stand on the right and pass on the left.
- When leaving a station, hold the door for the person behind you.

any fare inspector show proof of identity (ask locals for help if you're not certain). Never show anyone your wallet.

By RER

The RER (Réseau Express Régionale; air-ay-air) is the suburban arm of the Métro, serving outlying destinations (such as Versailles, Disneyland Paris, and the airports). These routes are indicated by thick lines on your subway map and identified by the letters A, B, C, and so on. Some routes are operated by France's railroad (SNCF) and are called Transilien; they function the same way and use the same tickets as the RER. For all of these trains, you need to insert your ticket in a turnstile to exit the system.

Within the city center, the RER works like the Métro, but can be speedier (if it serves your destination directly) because it makes fewer stops. Métro tickets and the Passe Navigo Découverte card are good on the RER when traveling in the city center. (You can transfer between the Métro and RER systems with the same ticket.) But to travel outside the city (to Versailles or the airport, for example), you'll need to buy a separate, more expensive ticket at the station window (or, to save time, at a ticket-vending machine) before boarding. Also,

Key Buses for Tourists

Of Paris' many bus routes, these are some of the most scenic. They provide a great, cheap, and convenient introduction to the city.

Bus #69 runs east–west between the Eiffel Tower and Père Lachaise Cemetery by way of rue Cler (recommended hotels), quai d'Orsay, the Louvre, and the Marais (recommended hotels). For a self-guided tour, see Bus #69 Sightseeing Tour on page 217.

Bus #87 also links the Marais and rue Cler areas, but stays mostly on the Left Bank, connecting the Eiffel Tower, St. Sulpice, Luxembourg Garden (more recommended hotels and restaurants), St. Germain-des-Prés, the Latin Quarter, the Bastille, and Gare de Lyon.

Bus #24 runs east–west along the Seine riverbank from Gare St. Lazare to Madeleine, place de la Concorde, Orsay Museum, the Louvre, St. Michel, Notre-Dame, and Jardin des Plantes, all the way to trendy Bercy Village (cafés and shops).

Bus #63 is another good east–west route, connecting the Marmottan Museum, Trocadéro (Eiffel Tower), pont de l'Alma, Orsay Museum, St. Sulpice, Luxembourg Garden, Latin Quarter/Panthéon, and Gare de Lyon.

unlike the Métro, not every train stops at every station along the way; check the sign over the platform to see if your destination is listed as a stop ("*toutes les gares*" means it makes all stops along the way), or confirm with a local before you board.

By City Bus

Paris' excellent bus system is worth figuring out. Remember, even though buses use the same tickets as the Métro and RER, you can't use a single ticket to transfer between the systems—though you can transfer from one bus to another (within 90 minutes, though doesn't work with tickets bought on board). One ticket buys you a bus ride anywhere in central Paris—but if you leave the city center (shown as zone 1 on the diagram aboard the bus), you must validate a second ticket.

Buses don't seem as romantic as the famous Métro and are subject to traffic jams, but savvy travelers know that buses can have you swinging through the city like Tarzan in an urban jungle. Anywhere you are, you can generally see a bus stop, and every stop comes complete with all the information you need: a good city bus map, route maps showing exactly where each bus that uses this stop goes, a frequency chart and schedule, a *plan du quartier* map of the immediate neighborhood, and a *soirées* map explaining night service, if available. While the Métro shuts down about 24:30 in the

Key Bus Routes

LEGEND

#24 - - -   #69 —
#63 - - -   #87 ·····

morning, some buses continue much later (called *Noctilien* lines, www.noctilien.fr).

Enter buses through the front door. Punch your ticket in the machine behind the driver, scan your Passe Navigo Découverte, or pay the higher cash fare to get your ticket from the driver. (Remember: Tickets purchased from drivers do not allow transfers between buses.) When you reach your destination, push the red button to signal you want a stop, then exit through the rear door. Even if you're not certain you've figured out the system, do some joyriding (outside of rush hour: Mon–Fri 8:00–9:30 & 17:30–19:30). Be warned: Not all city buses are air-conditioned, so they can become rolling greenhouses on summer days. For information on some of Paris' most scenic and convenient routes, see "Key Buses for Tourists" on page 30. Handy bus-system maps *(plan des autobus)* are available in any Métro station (and in the €6 *Paris Pratique* map book sold at newsstands). Major stops are displayed on the side of each bus. I've also listed the handiest bus routes for each recommended hotel neighborhood (see Sleeping chapter).

By Taxi

Parisian taxis are reasonable, especially for couples and families. The meters are tamper-proof. Fares and supplements (described in English on the rear windows) are straightforward and tightly regulated.

A taxi can fit three people comfortably, and cabbies are legally required to accept four passengers at a time (you'll be charged €3 extra for the fourth person). Groups of up to five can use a *grand taxi,* which must be booked in advance—ask your hotelier to call. For a sample taxi tour of the city at night, see page 427.

Rates: All Parisian taxis charge a €5.20 minimum. A 10-minute ride (e.g., Bastille to Eiffel Tower) costs about €12 (versus €1.11 per person to get anywhere in town using a *carnet* ticket on the Métro or bus). Higher rates are charged at rush hour and at night (17:00–10:00), all day Sunday, and to any of the airports. Your first bag is free; additional pieces of luggage are €1 each. To tip, round up to the next euro (at least €0.50).

How to Catch *un Taxi:* You can try waving down a taxi, but it's often easier to ask someone for the nearest taxi stand (*"Où est une station de taxi?";* oo ay ewn stah-see-ohn duh "taxi"). Taxi stands are indicated by a circled "T" on good city maps, and on many maps in this book. When you summon a taxi by phone, the meter starts running as soon as the call is received, often adding €5 or more to the bill.

Taxis are tough to find during rush hour, when it's raining, and on Friday and Saturday nights, especially after the Métro closes (around 24:30 in the morning). If you need to catch a train or flight early in the morning, book a taxi the day before. Your hotelier can help.

Bike Freedom for Parisians

Those high-tech bike racks you see all over town are part of the city's innovative Vélib' program (from *vélo* + *liberté* or *libre* = "bike freedom" or "free bike"), which gives locals with a Vélib' card access to 20,000 bikes around the city. Parisians pay €30 per year for the card, which they swipe to unlock the nearest Vélib' bike. (Tourists can pay to ride one, but US credit cards are unlikely to work in the machine.) The first half-hour of each ride is free; after that, riders are billed the longer they have the bike checked out. The system is well-designed—racks show not only the location of other nearby racks, but how many bikes are available there. At night, bikes are redistributed by truck so that busy locations always have enough bikes. The program is also comprehensive, involving aggressive city-wide development of bike paths. Copenhagen tried a similar program, providing intentionally ugly and clumsy bikes to lower the risk of theft. Vélib's bikes, however, are great.

By Bike

Paris is surprisingly good by bicycle. Riders enjoy plenty of bike lanes, and the extensive parks have bike-friendly paths that enable anyone on two wheels to get around easily. I biked along the river from Notre-Dame to the Eiffel Tower in 15 minutes. The tourist board has a fine "Paris à Vélo" map showing all the dedicated bike paths.

Fat Tire Bike Tours (listed under "Tours," below) rents bikes *sans* tour for independent types (€2.50/hr, €15/24 hrs, includes helmets and locks, credit-card imprint required for deposit, €4 discount with book for daily rental, daily 9:00–18:00, ask for their map of suggested routes, 24 rue Edgar Faure, Mo: Dupleix, tel. 01 56 58 10 54, www.fattirebiketoursparis.com).

TOURS

By Bus

Bus Tours—Paris Vision offers bus tours of Paris, day and night (advertised in hotel lobbies). I'd consider a Paris Vision tour only for their night-time Illumination tour (see page 427) or for tricky-to-reach day trips (such as Vaux-le-Vicomte). During the day, the hop-on, hop-off bus tours (listed immediately below) and the Batobus (see "By Boat," next page)—which both provide transportation between sights as well as commentary—are a better value.

Hop-on, Hop-off Bus Tours—Double-decker buses connect Paris' main sights while providing a basic running commentary, allowing you to hop on and hop off along the way. You get a disposable set of ear plugs (dial English and listen to the so-so narration). You can get off at any stop, tour a sight, then catch a later bus. These are best in good weather, when you can sit up top. There are two companies: L'Open Tours and Les Cars Rouges; pick up their brochures showing routes and stops from any TI or on their buses. You can start either tour at just about any of the major sights, such as the Eiffel Tower, where both companies stop on avenue Joseph Bouvard.

L'Open Tours uses bright yellow buses and provides more extensive coverage (and slightly better commentary) on four different routes, rolling by most of the important sights in Paris. Their Paris Grand Tour (the green route) offers the best introduction. The same ticket gets you on any of their routes within the validity period. Buy your tickets from the driver (1 day-€29, 2 days-€32, kids 4–11 pay €15 for 1 or 2 days, allow 2 hours per tour). Two to four buses depart hourly from about 10:00 to 18:00; expect to wait 10–15 minutes at each stop (stops can be tricky to find—look for yellow signs; tel. 01 42 66 56 56, www.paris-opentour.com). A combo-ticket covers both the Batobus boats (described in "By Boat" below) and L'Open Tours buses (€44, kids under 12 pay €20, valid 3 days).

Les Cars Rouges' bright red buses offer largely the same service, with only one route and just nine stops, for less (recorded narration, adult-€24, kids 4–12 pay €12, good for 2 days, tel. 01 53 95 39 53, www.carsrouges.com).

Do-It-Yourself Bus Tour—Paris' cheapest "bus tour" is to simply hop on city bus #69 and follow my self-guided commentary (see Bus #69 Sightseeing Tour, page 217).

By Boat

Several companies run one-hour boat cruises on the Seine (by far best at night, see also "Dinner Cruises," page 396).

Two companies are convenient to the rue Cler hotels: **Bateaux-Mouches** departs from pont de l'Alma's right bank and has the biggest open-top, double-decker boats. But this company often has too many tour groups, causing these boats to get packed (€10, kids 4–12 pay €5, tel. 01 40 76 99 99, www.bateaux-mouches.com).

Bateaux Parisiens has smaller covered boats with handheld audioguides, fewer crowds, and only one deck (€11, kids 4–11 pay €5, discounted half-price if you have a valid France or France–Switzerland railpass—does not use up a day of a flexipass, leaves from right in front of the Eiffel Tower, tel. 08 25 01 01 01, www.bateauxparisiens.com). Both companies run daily year-round (April–Oct 10:00–22:30, 2–3/hr; Nov–March shorter hours, runs hourly).

Vedettes du Pont Neuf offers essentially the same one-hour tour as Bateaux Parisiens, but starts and ends at Pont Neuf, closer to recommended hotels in the Marais and Luxembourg Garden neighborhoods. The boats feature a live guide whose delivery (in English and French) is as stiff as a recorded narration—and as hard to understand, given the quality of their sound system (€11, kids 4–12 pay €6, tip requested, nearly 2/hr, daily 10:30–22:30, tel. 01 46 33 98 38).

Hop-on, Hop-Off Boat Tour—**Batobus** allows you to get on and off as often as you like at any of eight popular stops along the Seine: Eiffel Tower, Champs-Elysées, Orsay/place de la Concorde, the Louvre, Notre-Dame, St. Germain-des-Prés, Hôtel de Ville, and Jardin des Plantes. Safety-conscious glass enclosures turn the boats into virtual ovens on hot days (1 day-€12, 2 days-€14, boats run June–Aug 10:00–21:30, mid-March–May and Sept–Oct 10:00–19:00, Nov–early-Jan and Feb–mid-March 10:30–16:30, no service last three weeks in Jan, every 15–20 minutes, 45 min one-way, 90 min round-trip, worthless narration). If you use this for getting around—sort of a scenic, floating alternative to the Métro—this can be worthwhile. But if you just want a guided boat tour, Batobus is not as good a value as the regular tour boats described above. A special combo-ticket covers L'Open Tours buses (described on previous page) and Batobus boats (€40, kids under 12 pay €17, valid 3 days, www.batobus.com).

Low-Key Cruise on a Tranquil Canal—**Canauxrama** runs a lazy 2.5-hour cruise on a peaceful canal out of sight of the Seine. Tours start from place de la Bastille and end at Bassin de la Villette (near Mo: Stalingrad). During the first segment of your trip, you'll pass through a long tunnel (built at the order of Napoleon in the early 19th century, when canal boats were vital for industrial transport). Once outside, you glide—not much faster than you can walk—through sleepy Parisian neighborhoods and slowly climb through four double locks as a guide narrates the trip in French and English (€15, departs at 9:45 and 14:30 across from Opéra Bastille, just below boulevard de la Bastille, opposite #50—where the canal meets place de la Bastille, tel. 01 42 39 15 00). The same tour also goes in the opposite direction (from Bassin de la Villette to place de la Bastille). It's OK to bring a picnic on board.

On Foot

Paris Walks—This company offers a variety of two-hour walks, led by British and American guides. Tours are thoughtfully prepared and humorous. Don't hesitate to stand close to the guide to hear (€10–15, generally 2/day, private tours available, recorded English schedule tel. 01 48 09 21 40, www.paris-walks.com). Tours focus on the Marais (4/week), Montmartre (3/week), medieval Latin Quarter (Mon), Ile de la Cité/Notre-Dame (Mon), the "Two Islands" (Ile de la Cité and Ile St. Louis, Wed), *Da Vinci Code* sights (Wed), and Hemingway's Paris (Fri). Ask about their family-friendly tours. Call a day or two ahead to learn their schedule and starting point. Most tours don't require reservations, but specialty tours (such as the *Da Vinci Code* tour) require advance reservations and prepayment with credit card (not refundable if you cancel less than two days in advance).

Context Paris—These "intellectual by design" walking tours are led by docents (historians, architects, and academics) and cover both museums and neighborhoods, often with a fascinating theme (explained on their website). Try to book in advance, since groups are small and can fill up (limited to 6 participants, generally 3 hours long and €35–55 per person plus admissions, tel. 06 13 09 67 11, US tel. 888-467-1986, www.contextparis.com). They also offer private tours.

Classic Walks—If you'd prefer a more relaxed, low-brow walking tour, consider this outfit, run by Fat Tire Bike Tours (see "By Bike," below). Their 3.5-hour "Classic Walk" covers most major sights (€20, daily at 10:00, meet at office—see below). They also do two-hour walks on various themes and neighborhoods: Montmartre, French Revolution, World War II, *Da Vinci Code,* and Latin Quarter (€12, leave several times a week—see website for details, all walks get €2 discount with this book, 24 rue Edgar Faure, Mo: Dupleix, tel. 01 56 58 10 54, www.classicwalksparis.com).

Private Guides—For many, Paris merits hiring a Parisian as a personal guide. **Arnaud Servignat** is an excellent licensed local guide (€155/half-day, €260/day, also does car tours of the countryside around Paris for a little more, tel. 06 68 80 29 05, www.arnaud-servignat.com, arnotour@mac.com).

Elizabeth Van Hest is another highly likeable and capable guide (€175/half-day, €260/day, tel. 01 43 41 47 31, e.van.hest@erenis .fr). **Sylvie Moreau** is also good, and charges the same as Elizabeth (mobile 06 87 02 80 67, silvmor@gmail.com).

By Bike

Fat Tire Bike Tours—A hardworking gang of young American expats runs an extensive program of bike tours, Segway tours, and walking tours, and rents bikes as well.

Their high-energy guides run four-hour bike tours of Paris, by day and by night. Reservations aren't necessary—just show up. On the day tour, you'll pedal with a pack of 10–20 riders, mostly in parks and along bike lanes, with a lunch stop in the Tuileries Gardens (€26, show this book for a €4 per-person discount, maximum 2 discounts per book, English only, tours leave daily rain or shine at 11:00, April–Oct at 15:00 as well). Night tours are more lively, and include a boat cruise on the Seine (€28, €4 discount with this book, April–Oct daily at 19:00, March daily at 18:00, end of Feb and all of Nov Tue, Thu, and Sat–Sun at 18:00, no night tours Dec–mid-Feb). Both tours meet at the south pillar of the Eiffel Tower, where you'll get a short history lesson, then walk six minutes to the Fat Tire office to pick up bikes (helmets available upon request at no extra charge, office open daily 9:00–19:00, 24 rue Edgar Faure, Mo: Dupleix, tel. 01 56 58 10 54, toll-free from North America 866-614-6218, www.fattirebiketoursparis.com).

They also run bike tours to Versailles and Giverny (reservations required, see website for details). Their office has Internet access with English keyboards.

Fat Tire's pricey four-hour **City Segway Tours**—on stand-up motorized scooters—are novel in that you learn to ride a Segway while exploring Paris (you'll get the hang of it after about half an hour). These tours take no more than eight people at a time, so reservations are required (€75, daily at 9:30, March–Nov also at 14:00, April–Oct also at 18:30, www.citysegwaytours.com).

Excursions from Paris

Many companies offer bus tours to regional sights, including all of the day trips described in this book. **Paris Vision** runs mass-produced, full-size bus and minivan tours to several popular regional destinations, including the Loire Valley, Champagne region, D-Day beaches, and Mont St. Michel. Minivan tours are more expensive, but more personal and given in English, and most offer convenient pickup at your hotel (€90–190/person). Their full-size bus tours are multilingual and cheaper than the minivan tours—worthwhile for some travelers simply for the ease of transportation to the sights (about €70, destinations include Versailles and Giverny). Paris Vision's full-size buses depart from 214 rue de Rivoli (Mo: Tuileries, tel. 01 42 60 30 01, www.parisvision.com).

SIGHTS

The sights listed in this chapter are arranged by neighborhood for handy sightseeing. When you see a ✪ in a listing, it means the sight is covered in much more depth in one of my walks or self-guided tours. This is why Paris' most important attractions get the least coverage in this chapter—we'll explore them later in the book.

For tips on sightseeing, see page 4 in the Introduction. For advice on saving money, see "Affording Paris' Sights" on page 47. Best tip: Buy a Paris Museum Pass.

Paris Museum Pass

In Paris, there are two classes of sightseers—those with a Paris Museum Pass, and those who stand in line. Serious sightseers save time and money by getting this pass.

Buying the Pass

The pass pays for itself with four admissions in two days, and lets you skip the ticket line at most sights (2 days/€30, 4 days/€45, 6 days/€60, no youth or senior discount). It's sold at the participating museums, monuments, and TIs (even at airports). Try to avoid buying the pass at a major museum (such as the Louvre), where the supply can be spotty and lines long. For more info, call 01 44 61 96 60 or visit www.paris museumpass.com.

Tally up what you want to see from the list on page 40—and remember, an advantage of the pass is that you skip to the front of most lines, which can save hours of waiting, especially in summer. Note that at a few sights (including the Louvre, Sainte-Chapelle, and Notre-Dame's tower), everyone has to shuffle through the slow-moving baggage-check lines for security—but you still save time by avoiding the ticket line.

Paris Sights

SIGHTS

The pass isn't worth buying for children and teens, as most museums are free or discounted for those under 18 (teenagers may need to show ID as proof of age). Of the few museums that charge for children, some allow kids in for free if their parent has a Museum Pass, while others charge admission, depending on age (the cutoff age varies from 5 to 18). The free directory that comes with your pass lists the current hours of sights, phone numbers, and the price that kids pay. If a sight is free for kids, they can skip the line with their passholder parents. (Paris' museums don't offer discounts.)

Think ahead to make the most of your pass. Validate it only when you're ready to tackle the covered sights on consecutive days. Make sure the sights you want to visit will be open (Mondays and Tuesdays are big days for museums to be closed). The Paris Museum Pass even covers most of Versailles (your other option for Versailles is the Le Passeport pass; see Versailles Day Trip chapter). Keep in mind that sights such as the Arc de Triomphe and Pompidou Center are open later in the evening, and that the Louvre, Orsay, and Orangerie are open later on selected evenings, allowing you to stretch the day for your Paris Museum Pass. On days that you don't have pass coverage, visit free sights as well as sights that aren't covered by passes.

What the Paris Museum Pass Covers

Most of the sights listed in this chapter are covered by the pass (see below). The pass does not cover: the Eiffel Tower, Montparnasse Tower, Marmottan Museum, Opéra Garnier, Notre-Dame Treasury, Jacquemart-André Museum, Grand Palais, La Défense and La Grande Arche, Catacombs, *Paris Story* film, Montmartre Museum, Sacré-Cœur's dome, Dalí Museum, Museum of Erotic Art, and the ladies of Pigalle. The pass also does not cover these recommended sights outside of Paris: Vaux-le-Vicomte, Auvers-sur-Oise, or Giverny.

Here's a list of included sights and their admission prices without the pass:

In Paris

Louvre (€9)
Orsay Museum (€8)
Orangerie Museum (€7.50)
Sainte-Chapelle (€7.50)
Arc de Triomphe (€9)
Rodin Museum (€6)
Army Museum (€8)
Conciergerie (€6.50)
Panthéon (€7.50)
Sewer Tour (€4)

Notre-Dame Tower (€7.50)
Paris Archaeological Crypt (€3.50)
Picasso Museum (€6.50)
Cluny Museum (€6.50)
Pompidou Center (€10)
Jewish Art and History Museum (€7)
National Maritime Museum (€6.50)
Delacroix Museum (€5)
Quai Branly Museum (€8.50)

Outside Paris
Versailles (€22.50—€13.50 for Château; €9 for Domaine de Marie-Antoinette)
Château of Chantilly (€9)
Château of Fontainebleau (€8)

Activating and Using the Pass
The pass isn't activated until the first time you use it (write the starting date on the pass).

To use your pass at sights, boldly walk to the front of the ticket line, hold up your pass, and ask the ticket-taker: *"Entrez, pass?"* (ahn-tray pahs). You'll either be allowed to enter at that point or you'll be directed to a special entrance. For major sights, such as the Louvre and Orsay museums, we've identified passholder entrances on the maps in this book.

With the pass, you'll pop freely into sights that you're walking by (even for a few minutes) that otherwise might not be worth the expense (e.g., the Conciergerie or Paris Archaeological Crypt).

SIGHTS

Historic Core of Paris: Notre-Dame, Sainte-Chapelle, and More
✪ Many of these sights are covered in detail in the Historic Paris Walk (plus map) on page 74. If a sight is covered in the walk, I've listed only its essentials here.

▲▲▲**Notre-Dame Cathedral (Cathédrale Notre-Dame de Paris)**—This 700-year-old cathedral is packed with history and tourists. With a pair of 200-foot-tall bell towers, a facade studded

with ornate statuary, beautiful stained-glass rose windows, famous gargoyles, a picture-perfect Seine-side location, and textbook flying buttresses, there's a good reason that this cathedral of "Our Lady" *(Notre-Dame)* is France's most famous church.

Check out the facade: Mary with the baby Jesus (in rose window) above the 28 Kings of Judah (statues that were beheaded during the Revolution). Stroll the interior, echoing with history. Then wander around the exterior, through a forest of frilly buttresses, watched over by a fleet of whimsical gargoyles. The long line to the left is to climb the famous tower (see "Tower," page 44).

Cost, Hours, Location: Free, cathedral open daily 7:45–19:00; Treasury-€3, not covered by Museum Pass, daily 9:30–17:30;

Paris at a Glance

▲▲▲**Notre-Dame Cathedral** Paris' most beloved church, with towers and gargoyles. **Hours:** Cathedral daily 7:45–19:00; tower daily April–Sept 10:00–18:30—also June–Aug Sat–Sun until 23:00, daily Oct–March 10:00–17:30; Treasury daily 9:30–17:30. See page 41.

▲▲▲**Louvre** Europe's oldest and greatest museum, starring Mona Lisa and Venus de Milo. **Hours:** Wed–Mon 9:00–18:00, closed Tue. Most wings open Wed and Fri until 21:45. See page 46.

▲▲▲**Orsay Museum** Nineteenth-century art, including Europe's greatest Impressionist collection. **Hours:** Tue–Sun 9:30–18:00, Thu until 21:45, closed Mon. See page 49.

▲▲▲**Sainte-Chapelle** Gothic cathedral with peerless stained glass. **Hours:** Daily March–Oct 9:30–18:00, Nov–Feb 9:00–17:00. See page 45.

▲▲▲**Eiffel Tower** Paris' soaring exclamation point. **Hours:** Daily mid-June–Aug 9:00–24:45 in the morning, Sept–mid-June 9:30–23:45. See page 50.

▲▲▲**Arc de Triomphe** Triumphal arch with viewpoint, marking start of Champs-Elysées. **Hours:** Always viewable; inside daily April–Sept 10:00–23:00, Oct–March 10:00–22:30. See page 60.

▲▲▲**Versailles** The ultimate royal palace (Château), with a Hall of Mirrors, vast gardens, a grand canal, plus a queen's playground (Domaine de Marie-Antoinette). **Hours:** Château—April–Oct Tue–Sun 9:00–18:30, Nov–March Tue–Sun 9:00–17:30, closed Mon. Domaine—daily April–Oct 12:00–18:30, Nov–March 9:00–17:30. Gardens generally open daily 9:00 until sunset. See page 72.

▲▲**Orangerie Museum** Monet's water lilies, plus works by Utrillo, Cézanne, Renoir, Matisse, and Picasso, in a lovely setting. **Hours:** Wed–Mon 9:00–18:00, closed Tue. See page 49.

▲▲**Army Museum and Napoleon's Tomb** The emperor's imposing tomb, flanked by army museums. **Hours:** Daily April–Sept 10:00–18:00—mid-June–mid-Sept tomb stays open until 19:00, Oct–March 10:00–17:00, Oct–May closed first Mon of every month. See page 52.

▲▲**Rodin Museum** Works by the greatest sculptor since Michelangelo, with many sculptures in a peaceful garden. **Hours:** April–Sept Tue–Sun 9:30–17:45, Oct–March Tue–Sun 9:30–16:45, closed Mon. See page 53.

▲▲**Marmottan Museum** Untouristy art museum focusing on Monet. **Hours:** Tue 11:00–21:00, Wed–Sun 10:00–18:00, closed Mon. See page 53.

▲▲**Cluny Museum** Medieval art with unicorn tapestries. **Hours:** Wed–Mon 9:15–17:45, closed Tue. See page 54.

▲▲**Champs-Elysées** Paris' grand boulevard. **Hours:** Always open. See page 60.

▲▲**Jacquemart-André Museum** Art-strewn mansion. **Hours:** Daily 10:00–18:00. See page 64.

▲▲**La Défense and La Grande Arche** "Little Manhattan" business district and its colossal modern arch. **Hours:** Daily April–Sept 10:00–20:00, Oct–March until 19:00. See page 66.

▲▲**Pompidou Center** Modern art in colorful building with city views. **Hours:** Wed–Mon 11:00–21:00, closed Tue. See page 68.

▲▲**Jewish Art and History Museum** Displays history of Judaism in Europe. **Hours:** Mon–Fri 11:00–18:00, Sun 10:00–18:00, closed Sat. See page 68.

▲▲**Picasso Museum** World's largest collection of Picasso's works. **Hours:** closing for restoration In Sept 2009; until then April–Sept Wed–Mon 9:30–18:00, Oct–March Wed–Mon 9:30–17:30, closed Tue. See page 69.

▲▲**Carnavalet Museum** Paris' history wrapped up in a 16th-century mansion. **Hours:** Tue–Sun 10:00–18:00, closed Mon. See page 70.

▲▲**Sacré-Cœur** White basilica atop Montmartre with spectacular views. **Hours:** Daily 7:00–23:00. See page 71.

▲**Panthéon** Neoclassical monument celebrating the struggles of the French. **Hours:** Daily 10:00–18:30 in summer, until 18:00 in winter. See page 57.

▲**Opéra Garnier** Grand belle époque theater with a modern ceiling by Chagall. **Hours:** Daily 10:00–16:30, July–Aug until 18:00. See page 61.

▲**Père Lachaise Cemetery** Final home of Paris' illustrious dead. **Hours:** Mon–Sat 8:00–18:00, Sun 9:00–18:00. See page 71.

audioguide-€5, ask about free English tours—normally Wed and Thu at 12:00, Sat at 14:30; Mo: Cité, Hôtel de Ville, or St. Michel; tel. 01 42 34 56 10, www.cathedraledeparis.com.

For more on Notre-Dame (including information on weekday and Sun Mass, as well as organ performances and viewings of the Crown of Thorns), ✪ see page 76 in the Historic Paris Walk.

Tower: You can climb to the top of the facade between the towers, and then to the top of the south tower, 400 steps total, for a grand view (€7.50, covered by Museum Pass but no bypass line for passholders, daily April–Sept 10:00–18:30—also June–Aug Sat–Sun until 23:00, Oct–March 10:00–17:30, last entry 45 min before closing, arrive before 10:00 or after 17:00 to avoid long lines).

Paris Archaeological Crypt—This is a worthwhile 15-minute stop with your Museum Pass. You'll visit Roman ruins, trace the street plan of the medieval village, and see diagrams of how early Paris grew, all thoughtfully explained in English.

The first few displays put the ruins in historical context. Three models show the growth of Paris—from an uninhabited riverside plot to the Roman town of Lutèce, then to an early-medieval city with a church that preceded Notre-Dame. A fourth model shows the current Notre-Dame surrounded by buildings, along with the old, straight road—rue Neuve de Notre-Dame—that led up to the church, and ran right down what is now the center of the museum. The ruins in the middle of the museum are a confusing mix of foundations from all these time periods, including parts of the old rue Neuve de Notre-Dame.

Press the buttons on the display cases to light up a particular section, such as the oldest (Gallo-Roman) rampart. Along the far side of the museum, you'll see a medieval Foundling's Hospital, a well-preserved Gallo-Roman–paved room, and a Roman building with "hypocaustal" heating (narrow passages pumped full of hot air to heat the room).

Cost, Hours, Location: €3.50, covered by Museum Pass, Tue–Sun 10:00–18:00, closed Mon, enter 100 yards in front of cathedral.

▲Deportation Memorial (Mémorial de la Déportation)—Climb down the steps into this memorial dedicated to the 200,000 French victims of the Nazi concentration camps. As Paris disappears above you, this monument draws you into the victims' experience. Once underground, you enter a one-way hallway studded with tiny lights commemorating the dead, leading you to an eternal flame.

Cost, Hours, Location: Free, daily April–Sept 10:00–12:00 & 14:00–19:00, Oct–March 10:00–12:00 & 14:00–17:00. It's at the east tip of the island named Ile de la Cité, behind Notre-Dame and near Ile St. Louis (Mo: Cité, tel. 01 49 74 34 00).

For more on the Deportation Memorial, ✪ see page 85 in the Historic Paris Walk.

Ile St. Louis—The residential island behind Notre-Dame is known for its restaurants (see Eating chapter), great ice cream, and shops (along rue St. Louis-en-l'Ile).

✪ Also see page 86 in the Historic Paris Walk.

Cité Métropolitain Stop and Flower Market—On place Louis Lépine, between the Notre-Dame and Sainte-Chapelle cathedrals, you'll find an early-19th-century subway entrance and a flower market (that chirps with a bird market on Sun).

▲▲▲**Sainte-Chapelle**—The interior of this 13th-century chapel is a triumph of Gothic church architecture. Built to house Jesus' Crown of Thorns, Sainte-Chapelle is jam-packed with stained-glass windows, bathed in colorful light, and slippery with the drool of awestruck tourists. Ignore the humdrum exterior and climb the stairs into the sanctuary, where more than 1,100 Bible scenes—from the Creation to the Passion to Judgment Day—are illustrated by light and glass. There are tentative plans for Sainte-Chapelle to have a shared entrance with the Conciergerie (below), possibly sometime in 2009.

SIGHTS

Cost, Hours, Location: €7.50, €10 combo-ticket includes Conciergerie, both covered by Museum Pass, daily March–Oct 9:30–18:00, Nov–Feb 9:00–17:00, last entry 30 min before closing. Mo: Cité, www.monum.fr.

For a detailed tour of the cathedral's interior, ✪ see page 91 in the Historic Paris Walk.

▲**Conciergerie**—Marie-Antoinette was imprisoned here, as were Louis XVI, Robespierre, Danton, and many others on their way to the guillotine. Exhibits with good English descriptions trace the history of the building and give some insight into prison life. You can also relive the drama in Marie-Antoinette's cell on the day of her execution—complete with dummies and period furniture.

Cost, Hours, Location: €6.50, €10 combo-ticket includes Sainte-Chapelle, both covered by Museum Pass, daily April–Sept 9:30–18:00, Oct–March 10:00–17:00, last entry 30 min before closing, 4 boulevard du Palais, Mo: Cité, tel. 01 53 40 60 80, www.monum.fr.

✪ Also see page 97 in the Historic Paris Walk.

▲**Paris Plage (Beach)**—The Riviera it's not, but this fanciful faux beach—assembled in summer along a two-mile stretch of the Seine on the Right Bank—is a fun place to stroll, play, and people-watch on a sunny day. Each summer since 2002, the Paris city government has shut down the embankment's highway and trucked in potted palm trees, hammocks, lounge chairs, and 2,000 tons of sand to create a colorful urban beach. You'll also find "beach cafés," climbing walls, prefab pools, trampolines, *boules*, a library, beach volleyball, badminton, and Frisbee areas in three zones: sandy, grassy, and wood-tiled. As you take in the playful atmosphere, imagine how much has changed here since the Middle Ages, when this was a grimy fishing community. (Other less-central areas of town, such as Canal St. Martin and Bassin de la Vilette, now take part with their own *plages*.)

Cost, Hours, Location: Free, mid-July–mid-Aug daily 7:00–24:00, no beach off-season; on Right Bank of Seine, just north of Ile de la Cité, between pont des Arts and pont de Sully.

Skaters Gone Wild—Thousands of inline skaters take to the streets Fridays at 22:30 and all day on summer Sundays, when police close off various routes in different parts of downtown (ask at your hotel or a TI for locations). It's serious skaters only on Friday evenings, but anyone can roll with Paris on Sundays (when the expressways along the Right Bank of the Seine are closed for this rolling fun fest).

Major Museums Neighborhood

Paris' grandest park, the Tuileries Garden, was once the private property of kings and queens. Today, it links the museums of the Louvre, Orangerie, Jeu de Paume, and the Orsay. And across from the Louvre are the tranquil, historic courtyards of the Palais Royal.

▲▲▲**Louvre (Musée du Louvre)**—This is Europe's oldest, biggest, greatest, and second-most-crowded museum (after the Vatican). Housed in a U-shaped, 16th-century palace (accentuated by a 20th-century glass pyramid), the Louvre is Paris' top museum and one of its key landmarks. It's home to *Mona Lisa*, *Venus de Milo*, and hall after hall of Greek and Roman masterpieces, medieval jewels, Michelangelo statues, and paintings by the greatest artists from the Renaissance to the Romantics (mid-1800s).

Touring the Louvre can be overwhelming, so be selective. Focus on the Denon wing (south, along the river), with Greek sculptures, Italian paintings (by Raphael and da Vinci), and—of course—French paintings (Neoclassical and Romantic). For extra credit, tackle the Richelieu wing (north, away from the river), with works from ancient Mesopotamia (today's Iraq), as well as French, Dutch, and Northern art; or the Sully wing (connecting the other two wings), with Egyptian artifacts and more French paintings.

Cost: €9, €6 after 18:00 on Wed and Fri, free on first Sun of month, covered by Museum Pass. Tickets good all day and reentry allowed. Optional additional charges apply for temporary exhibits.

Hours: Wed–Mon 9:00–18:00, closed Tue. Most wings are open Wed and Fri until 21:45. Galleries start closing 30 minutes early. The last entry is 45 minutes before closing. Crowds worst on Sun, Mon, Wed, and mornings. Tel. 01 40 20 53 17, recorded info tel. 01 40 20 51 51, www.louvre.fr.

Affording Paris' Sights

Paris is an expensive city for tourists, with lots of pricey sights, but—fortunately—lots of freebies, too. Smart budget-minded travelers begin by buying and getting the most out of a **Paris Museum Pass** (see page 38), while considering these frugal sightseeing options.

Free Museums: Some museums are always free, including the Carnavalet, Petit Palais, Victor Hugo's House, and Fragonard Perfume Museum. Many of Paris' most famous museums offer free entry on the first Sunday of the month, including the Louvre, Orsay, Rodin, Cluny, Pompidou Center, Delacroix, and Picasso museums. You can also visit the Orsay Museum for free at 17:00, about 30 minutes before rooms start closing. One of the best everyday values is the Rodin Museum's garden, where you'll pay €1 to experience many of Rodin's finest works in a lovely outdoor setting.

Other Freebies: Many worthwhile sights don't charge entry, including the Notre-Dame Cathedral, Père Lachaise Cemetery, Deportation Memorial, Holocaust Memorial, Paris Plage (summers only), St. Sulpice Church (with organ recital), and La Défense (though there is a charge to enter La Grande Arche). And remember that the neighborhood walks described in this book are free unless you enter a sight (Historic Paris, Left Bank, Champs-Elysées, Marais, Rue Cler, and Montmartre).

Paris' glorious, entertaining parks are free, of course. These include Luxembourg Garden, Champ de Mars (under the Eiffel Tower), Tuileries Garden (between the Louvre and place de la Concorde), Palais Royal Courtyards, Jardin des Plantes, the Promenade Plantée walk, and Versailles' gardens (except on Fountain Spectacle weekends).

Reduced Price: Several museums offer a discount if you enter later in the day, including the Louvre (after 18:00 on Wed and Fri), Orsay (after 16:15), Army Museum and Napoleon's Tomb (after 17:00), and Versailles' Château (after 15:00) and Domaine de Marie-Antoinette (after 16:00).

Free Concerts: Venues offering free or cheap (€6–8) concerts include the American Church, Hotel des Invalides, Cluny Museum, St. Sulpice Church, La Madeleine Church, and Notre-Dame Cathedral. For a listing of free concerts, check *Pariscope* magazine (under "Musique and Concerts Classiques") and look for events marked entrée libre.

Good-Value Tours: At €10–15, Paris Walks' tours are a good value. The €10 Seine River cruises, best after dark, are also worthwhile. The Bus #69 Sightseeing Tour, which costs only the price of a transit ticket, could be the best deal of all.

Pricey... but worth it? Certain big-ticket items—primarily the Eiffel Tower, Louvre, and Versailles—are expensive and crowded, but offer once-in-a-lifetime experiences. Think of it like you would a spree in Vegas—budget in a little "gambling" money you expect to lose, then just relax...and enjoy.

Major Museums Neighborhood

Location: At Palais Royal–Musée du Louvre Métro stop. (The old Louvre Métro stop, called Louvre-Rivoli, is farther from the entrance.)

☻ See the Louvre Tour on page 101.

Palais Royal Courtyards—Across from the Louvre are the pleasant courtyards of the stately Palais Royal. Although the palace is closed to the public, the courtyards are open. As you enter, you'll pass through a whimsical courtyard filled with stubby, striped columns and playful fountains (with fun, reflective metal balls) into another, curiously peaceful courtyard. This is where in-the-know Parisians come to take a quiet break, walk their poodles, or enjoy a rendezvous—surrounded by a serene arcade and a handful of historic restaurants.

While tranquil today, this was once a hotbed of political activism. The palace was built in the 17th century by Louis XIII, and eventually became the headquarters of the powerful Dukes of Orléans. Because the Dukes' digs were off-limits to the police, some shocking free-thinking took root here. This was the meeting place for the debating clubs—the precursors to modern political parties. During the Revolution, palace resident Duke Phillip (nicknamed Phillip Egalité for his progressive ideas) advocated a constitutional monarchy, and voted in favor of beheading Louis XVI—his own cousin. Phillip hoped his liberal attitudes would spare him from the Revolutionaries, but he, too, was guillotined. His son, Louis-Phillippe, grew to become France's first constitutional monarch (r. 1830–1848). The palace's courtyards were a riotous social and political scene, filled with lively café culture, revolutionaries, rabble-rousers, scoundrels, and... Madame Tussaud's first wax shop (she used the severed heads of guillotine victims to model her sculptures).

Exiting the courtyard at the side facing away from the Seine brings you to the Galeries Colbert and Vivienne, good examples of shopping arcades from the early 1900s.

Cost, Hours, Location: Courtyards are free and always open. The Palais Royal is directly north of the Louvre on rue de Rivoli (Mo: Palais Royal–Musée du Louvre).

▲▲**Orangerie Museum (Musée de l'Orangerie)**—This Impressionist museum has recently reopened after years of renovation. Located in the Tuileries Garden and drenched by natural light from skylights, the Orangerie (oh-rahn-zheh-ree) is like an Impressionist painting come to life. Start with the museum's claim to fame: Monet's *Water Lilies*. Then head downstairs to enjoy the manageable collection of select works by Utrillo, Cézanne, Renoir, Matisse, and Picasso.

Cost, Hours, Location: €7.50, under 18 free, covered by Museum Pass, audioguide-€5, Wed–Mon 9:00–18:00, closed Tue, located in Tuileries Garden near place de la Concorde, Mo: Concorde, tel. 01 44 77 80 07, www.musee-orangerie.fr.

✪ See Orangerie Museum Tour on page 155.

▲▲▲**Orsay Museum (Musée d'Orsay)**—The Orsay boasts Europe's greatest collection of Impressionist works. It might be less important than the Louvre—but it's more purely enjoyable.

The Orsay, housed in an atmospheric old train station, picks up where the Louvre leaves off: the second half of the 19th century. This is art from the tumultuous time that began when revolutions swept across Europe in 1848, and ended with the outbreak of World War I in 1914. Begin on the ground floor, which features conservative art of the mid-1800s—careful, idealized Neoclassicism (with a few rebels mixed in). Then glide up the escalator to the late 1800s, when the likes of Manet, Monet, Degas, and Renoir jolted the art world with their colorful, lively new invention, Impressionism. (Somewhere in there, *Whistler's Mother* sits quietly.) You'll also enjoy the works of their artistic descendents, the post-Impressionists (Van Gogh and Cézanne) and the Primitives (Rousseau, Gauguin, Seurat, and Toulouse-Lautrec). On the mezzanine level, waltz through the Grand Ballroom, Art Nouveau exhibits, and Rodin sculptures.

Cost: €8, €5 after 16:15 and on Sun, free at exactly 17:00 (Thu at 21:00) and on first Sun of month, covered by Museum Pass. English-language tours usually run at 11:30 daily (except Sun), cost €7, and take 90 minutes. Audioguides are €6. Some tours are occasionally offered at other times (inquire when you arrive).

Hours: Tue–Sun 9:30–18:00, Thu until 21:45, last entry one hour before closing (45 min before on Thu), Impressionist galleries start closing 45 min early, closed Mon. Tel. 01 40 49 48 14, www.musee-orsay.fr.

Location: Above the RER-C stop called Musée d'Orsay; the nearest Métro stop is Solférino, three blocks southeast of the Orsay. From the Louvre, it's a lovely 15-minute walk through the Tuileries Garden and across the pedestrian bridge to the Orsay.

✪ See the Orsay Museum Tour on page 130.

Eiffel Tower and Nearby

▲▲▲**Eiffel Tower (La Tour Eiffel)**—Built a hundred years after the French Revolution (and in the midst of an industrial one), the tower served no function but to impress. For decades, it was the tallest structure the world had ever known, and though it's been eclipsed since, it's still the most visited monument. Ride the elevators to the top of its 1,063 feet for expansive views that stretch 40 miles. Then descend to the two lower levels, where the views are arguably even better, since the monuments are more recognizable. If you're going to Paris, you have to see the tower, so just brave the crowds, pay the money, and go up—if only to say you were there.

Cost, Hours, Location: €4.80 to go to the first level, €7.80 to the second, and €12 to go to the top, not covered by Museum Pass. Daily mid-June–Aug 9:00–24:45 in the morning, Sept–mid-June 9:30–23:45. Mo: Bir-Hakeim and Trocadéro or Champ de Mars-Tour Eiffel RER stop (each about a 10-min walk away). Tel. 01 44 11 23 23, www.tour-eiffel.fr. A new online reservation system may debut in 2009 allowing you to book a half-hour time slot for your visit—check the website.

✪ See the Eiffel Tower Tour (which also includes tips on avoiding lines) on page 172.

Eiffel Tower and Nearby

Quai Branly Museum (Museé du Quai Branly)—This is the best collection I've seen anywhere of so-called Primitive Art from Africa, Polynesia, Asia, and America. It's presented in a wild, organic, and strikingly modern building that's a sightseeing thrill in itself. This museum, opened in 2006, is still big news with locals. Masks, statuettes, musical instruments, clothes, voodoo dolls, and a variety of temporary exhibits and activities are artfully presented and exquisitely lit. It's not, however, accompanied by much printed English information—to really appreciate the exhibit, use the €5 audioguide. It's a 10-minute walk east (upriver) of the Eiffel Tower, along the river (€8.50, covered by Museum Pass, Tue–Sun 11:00–19:00, Thu–Sat until 21:00, closed Mon, 37 quai Branly, RER: Champ de Mars-Tour Eiffel or Pont de l'Alma, tel. 01 56 61 70 00, www.quaibranly.fr).

National Maritime Museum (Musée National de la Marine)—This extensive museum houses an amazing collection of ship models, submarines, torpedoes, cannonballs, *beaucoup* bowsprits, and naval you-name-it—including a small boat made for Napoleon.

You'll find limited English information on the walls, but kids like the museum anyway (adults-€6.50, kids-€4.50, more during special exhibits, covered by Museum Pass, Wed–Mon 10:00–18:00, closed Tue, on left side of Trocadéro Square with your back to Eiffel Tower, tel. 01 53 65 69 53, www.musee-marine.fr).

▲**Paris Sewer Tour (Les Egouts de Paris)**—Discover what happens after you flush. This quick, fascinating, and slightly stinky visit (a perfumed hanky helps) takes you along a few hundred yards of underground water tunnels in the world's first underground sewer system. Pick up the helpful English self-guided tour, then drop down into Jean Valjean's world of tunnels, rats, and manhole covers. (Victor Hugo was friends with the sewer inspector when he wrote *Les Misérables*.) You'll pass well-organized displays with helpful English information detailing the evolution of this amazing network. Over 1,500 miles of tunnels carry 317 million gallons of water daily through this underworld. It's the world's longest sewer system—so long, they say, that if it was laid out straight, it would stretch from Paris all the way to Istanbul.

It's enlightening to see how much work goes into something we take for granted. Sewage didn't always disappear so readily. In the Middle Ages, wastewater was tossed from windows to a center street gutter, then washed into the river. In castles, sewage ended up in the moat (enhancing the moat's defensive role). In the 1500s, French Renaissance King François I moved from château to château (he had several) when the moat muck became too much. Don't miss the slide show, fine WCs just beyond the gift shop, and occasional tours in English.

Cost, Hours, Location: €4, covered by Museum Pass, May–Sept Sat–Wed 11:00–17:00, Oct–April Sat–Wed 11:00–16:00, closed Thu–Fri, located where pont de l'Alma greets the Left Bank, Mo: Alma-Marceau, RER: Pont de l'Alma, tel. 01 53 68 27 81.

▲▲**Army Museum and Napoleon's Tomb (Musée de l'Armée)**—Europe's greatest military museum, in the Hôtel des Invalides, provides interesting coverage of several wars, particularly World Wars I and II. At the center of the complex, the emperor Napoleon lies majestically dead inside several coffins under a grand dome—a goose-bumping pilgrimage for historians. The dome overhead glitters with 26 pounds of thinly pounded gold leaf.

Cost, Hours, Location: €8, ticket covers Napoleon's Tomb and all museums within Les Invalides complex, includes audioguide for tomb, covered by Museum Pass, price drops to €6 an hour before closing time, always free for all military personnel with ID. Open daily April–Sept 10:00–18:00, mid-June–mid-Sept tomb stays open until 19:00, museum may be open Tue until 21:00; Oct–March until 17:00; last entry 30 min before closing, Oct–May closed first Mon of every month. The Hôtel des Invalides is at 129 rue de Grenelle; Mo: La Tour Maubourg, Varenne, or Invalides; tel. 01 44 42 38 77, www.invalides.org.

❂ See Army Museum and Napoleon's Tomb Tour on page 194.

▲▲Rodin Museum (Musée Rodin)—This user-friendly museum is filled with passionate works by the greatest sculptor since Michelangelo. You'll see *The Kiss, The Thinker, The Gates of Hell,* and many more. The entire museum is being gradually renovated over the next few years; pick up the essential museum map to guide you.

Well-displayed in the mansion where the sculptor lived and worked, exhibits trace Rodin's artistic development, explain how his bronze statues were cast, and show some of the studies he created to work up to his masterpiece (the unfinished *Gates of Hell*). Learn about Rodin's tumultuous relationship with his apprentice and lover, Camille Claudel. Mull over what makes his sculptures some of the most evocative since the Renaissance. And stroll the gardens, packed with many of his greatest works (including *The Thinker*). The beautiful gardens are ideal for artistic reflection.

Cost, Hours, Location: €6, free on first Sun of the month, covered by Museum Pass. You'll pay €1 to get into the gardens only—which may be Paris' best deal, as many works are on display there (also covered by Museum Pass). Audioguides are €4, and baggage check is mandatory. Open April–Sept Tue–Sun 9:30–17:45, gardens close 18:45; Oct–March Tue–Sun 9:30–16:45, gardens close 17:00, last entry 30 min before closing, closed Mon. It's near the Army Museum and Napoleon's Tomb, 79 rue de Varenne, Mo: Varenne, tel. 01 44 18 61 10, www.musee-rodin.fr.

○ See Rodin Museum Tour on page 183.

▲▲Marmottan Museum (Musée Marmottan Monet)—In this private, intimate, untouristy museum, you'll find the best collection anywhere of works by Impressionist headliner Claude Monet. Follow Monet's life through more than a hundred works, from simple sketches to the *Impression: Sunrise* painting that gave his artistic movement its start—and a name. You'll also enjoy large-scale canvases featuring the water lilies from his garden at Giverny.

Cost, Hours, Location: €8, not covered by Museum Pass, Tue 11:00–21:00, Wed–Sun 10:00–18:00, last entry 30 min before closing, closed Mon, 2 rue Louis Boilly, Mo: La Muette, tel. 01 44 96 50 33, www.marmottan.com. To get to the museum from the Métro stop, follow the brown museum signs six blocks down chaussée de la Muette through the park; pause to watch kids play on the old-time, crank-powered carousel.

○ See Marmottan Museum Tour on page 225.

Left Bank

○ For more information on these sights, see the Left Bank Walk on page 233, the Historic Paris Walk (which dips into the Latin Quarter) on page 74, and the "Sèvres-Babylone to St. Sulpice" shopping stroll on page 412.

▲Latin Quarter (Quartier Latin)—This Left Bank neighborhood, just opposite Notre-Dame, was the center of Roman Paris. But the

Latin Quarter's touristy fame relates to its intriguing, artsy, bohemian character. This was perhaps Europe's leading university district in the Middle Ages, when Latin was the language of higher education. The neighborhood's main boulevards (St. Michel and St. Germain) are lined with cafés—once the haunts of great poets and philosophers, now the hangouts of tired tourists. While still youthful and artsy, much of this area has become a tourist ghetto filled with cheap North African eateries. Exploring a few blocks up or down river from here gives you a better chance of feeling the pulse of what survives of Paris' classic Left Bank.

   ○ See Left Bank Walk on page 233.

▲▲Cluny Museum (Musée National du Moyen Age)—This treasure trove of Middle Ages (Moyen Age) art fills old Roman baths, offering close-up looks at stained glass, Notre-Dame carvings, fine goldsmithing and jewelry, and rooms of tapestries. The star here is the exquisite *Lady and the Unicorn* tapestry series: In five panels, a delicate, as-medieval-as-can-be noble lady introduces a delighted unicorn to the senses of taste, hearing, sight, smell, and touch.

   Cost, Hours, Location: €6.50, free on first Sun of month, covered by Museum Pass, Wed–Mon 9:15–17:45, closed Tue, near corner of boulevards St. Michel and St. Germain at 6 place Paul Painlevé; Mo: Cluny-La Sorbonne, St. Michel, or Odéon; tel. 01 53 73 78 16, www.musee-moyenage.fr.

   ○ See Cluny Museum Tour on page 244.

St. Germain-des-Prés—A church was first built on this site in A.D. 452. The church you see today was constructed in 1163 and is all that's left of a once sprawling and influential monastery. The colorful interior reminds us that medieval churches were originally painted in bright colors. The surrounding area hops at night with venerable cafés, fire-eaters, mimes, and scads of artists (free, daily 8:00–20:00, Mo: St. Germain-des-Prés).

▲St. Sulpice Church and Organ Concert—Since it was featured in *The Da Vinci Code,* this grand church has become a trendy stop for the book's many fans. But the real reason to visit is to see and hear its intimately accessible organ. For pipe-organ enthusiasts, this is one of Europe's great musical treats. The Grand Orgue at St. Sulpice Church has a rich history, with a succession of 12 world-class organists—including Charles-Marie Widor and Marcel Dupré—that goes back 300 years. Widor started the tradition of opening the loft to visitors after the 10:30 service on Sundays. Daniel Roth (or his understudy) continues to welcome guests in three languages while playing five keyboards. (See www.danielrothsaintsulpice.org for his exact dates and concert plans.)

Left Bank

(Map labels:) TO ORSAY MUSEUM · TO LOUVRE VIA PONT DES ARTS · ST. GERMAIN-DES-PRES · SAINTE-CHAPELLE · ILE DE LA CITE · NOTRE-DAME · CAFES DEUX MAGOTS + LA FLORE · DELACROIX MUSEUM · PLACE ST. MICHEL · SEINE · RUE DU FOUR · BLVD. MABILLON · ODEON · RUE ST. SEVERIN · RUE DE RENNES · BLVD. RASPAIL · SEVRES · VIEUX COLOMBIER · ST. SULPICE · CLUNY MUSEUM · GERMAIN · BON MARCHE · SEVRES-BAB. · RUE DE RENNES · SHOPPING AREA · THEATRE ODEON · SORBONNE · MAUBERT MUTUALITE · ECOLES · RENNES · VAUGIRARD · LUXEMBOURG GARDEN · POND · ST. ETIENNE DU MONT · CARD. LEMOINE · N.D. DES CHAMPS · KIDS' PLAY AREA · PANTHEON · SOUFFLOT · LUX · RUE ST. JACQUES · RUE MOUFFETARD · RUE MONGE · MONTPARNASSE TOWER · BLVD. MONTPARNASSE · LE SELECT CAFE · VAVIN · LA COUPOLE + LE DOME CAFES · PORT ROYAL · PLACE MONGE · TO CATACOMBS · 1/4 MILE · 400 METERS · DCH · LATIN QUARTER · METRO STATION · RER STOP

The 10:30–11:30 Sunday Mass (come appropriately dressed) is followed by a high-powered 25-minute recital. Then, just after noon, the small, unmarked door is opened (left of entry as you face the rear). Visitors scamper like 16th notes up spiral stairs, past the 19th-century StairMasters that five men once pumped to fill the bellows, into a world of 7,000 pipes. You can see the organ and visit with Daniel (or his substitute, who might not speak English). Space is tight; only a few can gather around him at a time, and you need to be quick to allow others a chance to meet him. You'll generally have 20–30 minutes to kill (church views are great and there's a small lounge) before watching the master play during the next Mass; you can leave at any time. If you're late or rushed, show up around 12:30 and wait at the little door. As someone leaves, you can slip in, climb up, and catch the rest of the performance (church open daily 7:30–19:30, Mo: St. Sulpice or Mabillon). Tempting boutiques surround the church (see Shopping chapter), and Luxembourg Garden is nearby.

For more on St. Sulpice, ✪ see page 240 in the Left Bank Walk.

Delacroix Museum (Musée National Eugène Delacroix)— This museum for Eugène Delacroix (1798–1863) was once his home and studio. A friend of bohemian artistic greats—including George Sand and Frédéric Chopin—Delacroix is most famous for the flag-waving painting *Liberty Leading the People,* which is displayed at the

The Da Vinci Code in Paris

Dan Brown's novel about a Harvard cryptologist on the hunt for the Holy Grail was an international bestseller, a pop-culture craze, and a hot conversation topic. This work of fiction—encrusted with real and invented historical information—has sold millions of copies and been translated into 44 languages, flooding bookstores from Paris to Beijing. The movie version (starring Tom Hanks and Audrey Tatou, a.k.a. Amélie) was filmed in Paris.

Since most of the book (and movie) is set in Paris, *Da Vinci Code* fans flock to the various sights described in the novel. Several tour companies (such as Paris Walks, see page 35) have even put together special walking tours to satisfy this curiosity. While *The Da Vinci Code* may be a good read, it's not accurate either as history or a good travel guide—there just isn't that much to see. Still, tours do their best to make something of these stops along the Grail trail:

The Louvre's Grand Gallery, near Leonardo's *Virgin of the Rocks:* "Renowned curator, Jacques Sauniere," the book begins, "staggered through the vaulted archway of the museum's Grand Gallery." He then falls to the parquet floor, smears a cryptic clue in his own blood, and dies. This starts the hunt, as protagonist Robert Langdon and police officer Sophie Neveu follow clues hidden in art, history, and religious lore to solve the murder and, ultimately, find the Holy Grail.

The Louvre's Salle des Etats: Langdon and Neveu find clues in Leonardo's *Mona Lisa*.

The Louvre Pyramid and Arc du Carrousel: Pursued by the police and fearing wrongful arrest, they escape the Louvre and drive off into the night.

The Ritz Hôtel on Place Vendôme: Langdon's address in Paris.

St. Sulpice Church: Home to the astrological clock—a line on the floor that calibrates sunbeams with the calendar—that Dan Brown incorrectly calls the "rose line." (For more on St. Sulpice, see the Left Bank Walk, page 233.)

Inverted Pyramid in the Carrousel du Louvre: The final stop on your quest is a shopping mall. You'll find the Holy Grail (says Brown) embedded in modern concrete under an inverted glass pyramid, just next to Virgin Records.

Louvre, not here (€5, covered by Museum Pass, free on first Sun of the month, Wed–Mon 9:30–17:00, last entry 30 min before closing, closed Tue, 6 rue de Furstenberg, Mo: St. Germain-des-Prés, tel. 01 44 41 86 50, www.musee-delacroix.fr).

For more on the Delacroix Museum, ✪ see page 237 in the Left Bank Walk.

▲**Luxembourg Garden (Jardin du Luxembourg)**—This lovely 60-acre garden is an Impressionist painting brought to life. Slip into a green chair and ponder pondside, enjoy the radiant flowerbeds, go jogging, or take in a chess game or puppet show (park open daily dawn until dusk, Mo: Odéon, RER: Luxembourg). Notice any pigeons? The story goes that a very poor Ernest Hemingway used to hand-hunt (read: strangle) them here.

✪ For more on the garden and nearby sights, see page 242 in the Left Bank Walk. Also see the kid-friendly activities in the garden (page 403), cafés listed in "Les Grands Cafés de Paris" (page 397), and the description of the Panthéon mausoleum (below).

If you enjoy the Luxembourg Garden and want to see more green spaces, you could visit the more elegant **Parc Monceau** (Mo: Monceau), the colorful **Jardin des Plantes** (Mo: Jussieu or Gare d'Austerlitz, RER: Gare d'Austerlitz), or the hilly and bigger **Parc des Buttes-Chaumont** (Mo: Buttes-Chaumont).

▲**Panthéon**—This dramatic Neoclassical monument celebrates France's illustrious history and people, balances Foucault's pendu-

lum, and is the final home of many French VIPs. In 1744, King Louis XV was gravely ill and prayed to St. Geneviève, the city's patron saint. Louis recovered, and thanked Geneviève by replacing her ruined church with a more fitting tribute. By the time the church was completed (1791), however, the secular-minded Revolution was in full swing, and the church was converted into a secular mausoleum honoring the "Champions of French liberty"—Voltaire, Rousseau, Descartes, and others. The Revolutionaries covered up the church's windows (as you can see from outside) to display grand, patriotic murals. On the entrance pediment (inspired by the ancient Pantheon in Rome), they carved the inscription, "To the great men of the Fatherland."

Step inside the vast building (360' by 280' by 270'). Working clockwise around the church-like space, you'll see monuments tracing the celebrated struggles of the French people.

The first mural along the left wall shows a martyred St. Denis picking up his head to carry on with his sermon (for background, see page 79). Next, the fledgling city of Paris is attacked by Attila the Hun (sixth century A.D.), but is saved by the calming influence of St. Geneviève. Farther along, "Saint" Louis IX ruled as a just king and fervent crusader. In the left transept is a wall dedicated to Joan of Arc. Scanning right to left, see her as a young girl having a vision of an angel, who gives her a sword to save her people from the English. Next, she's wearing a man's armor, leading troops in battle. In the third panel, she stands as the honorary flag-bearer as the French king is crowned. Finally, having been arrested by the English, she's tied to a stake and burned to death, clutching a cross. You'll find more French heroes on the church's right (south) wall, including the first king, Clovis, and the powerful medieval emperor, Charlemagne, King of the Franks.

Under the dome are four statue groups dedicated to more great Frenchmen: Jean-Jacques Rousseau (1712–1778), the philosopher who championed the idea of an equal Social Contract between government and the people; Diderot (1713–1784), whose *Encyclopédie* championed secular knowledge; orators and publicists (men in business suits) who served the state; and generals, including Napoleon on horseback.

At the far end of the nave stands an altar to liberty—the Monument to the National Convention. Dedicated to the political body that opposed the monarchy during the Revolution, it's inscribed with the familiar motto, "Live free or die."

Foucault's pendulum swings gracefully at the end of a 220-foot cable suspended from the towering dome. It was here in 1851 that the scientist Léon Foucault first demonstrated the rotation of the Earth. Stand a few minutes and watch the pendulum's arc (appear to) shift as you and the earth rotate beneath it.

Stairs in the back lead down to the crypt, where a pantheon of greats are buried. Rousseau is along the right wall as you enter. Head for the far left corner to find the French writers Victor Hugo *(Les Misérables, The Hunchback of Notre-Dame)*, Alexandre Dumas *(The Three Musketeers, The Count of Monte Cristo)*, and Emile Zola *(Les Rougon-Macquart)*, as well as Louis Braille, who invented the script for the blind. Elsewhere in the crypt are the discoverers of radium, Polish-born Marie Curie and her French husband, Pierre, along with many others. An exhibit explores the building's fascinating history (good English descriptions). And you can climb 206 steps to the dome gallery for fine views of the interior as well as the city (accessible only with an escort, who leaves for the top about every hour until 17:15—see schedule as you enter).

Cost, Hours, Location: €7.50, covered by Museum Pass, daily 10:00–18:30 in summer, until 18:00 in winter, last entry 45 min before closing (Mo: Cardinal Lemoine). Ask about occasional English tours or call ahead for schedule (tel. 01 44 32 18 00, www.monum.fr).

Montparnasse Tower (La Tour Montparnasse)—This 59-story superscraper—cheaper and easier to ascend than the Eiffel Tower—treats you to one of Paris' best views. (Some say it's the very best, as you can see the Eiffel Tower... and you can't see the Montparnasse Tower.) While there are plenty of dioramas identifying highlights of the star-studded vista, consider buying the €3 photo-guide, which makes a fun souvenir. As you zip up 56 floors in 38 seconds, watch the altimeter above the door. From

SIGHTS

the 56th floor, climb to the open terrace at the 59th floor to enjoy the surreal scene of a lonely man in a box, and a helipad surrounded by the window-cleaner track. Here, 690 feet above Paris, you can scan the city with the wind in your hair, noticing the lush courtyards hiding behind grand street fronts. Back inside and downstairs, you'll find a small, overpriced café, fascinating historic black-and-white photos, and a plush little theater playing a worthwhile video that celebrates the big views of this grand city (free, 12 min, shows continuously).

Cost, Hours, Location: €10, not covered by Museum Pass, daily April–Sept 9:30–23:30, Oct–March 9:30–22:30, disappointing after dark, entrance on rue de l'Arrivée, Mo: Montparnasse-Bienvenüe—from the Métro stay inside the station and simply follow the signs for "La Tour," tel. 01 45 38 52 56, www.tourmontparnasse56.com. The tower is an efficient stop when combined with a day trip to Chartres, which begins at the Montparnasse train station (see page 482 for details).

▲**Catacombs**—These underground tunnels contain the anonymous bones of six million permanent Parisians. In 1786, the Revolutionary government of Paris decided to relieve congestion and improve sanitary conditions by emptying the city cemeteries (which traditionally surrounded churches) into an official ossuary. They found the perfect locale in the many miles of underground tunnels from limestone quarries, which were, at that time, just outside the city. For decades, priests led ceremonial processions of black-veiled, bone-laden carts into the quarries, where the bones were stacked into piles five feet high and as much as 80 feet deep behind neat walls of skull-studded tibiae. Each transfer was complete when a plaque was placed, indicating the church and district where the bones came from and the date that they arrived.

From the entry, a spiral staircase leads 60 feet down. Then you begin a one-mile subterranean walk. After several blocks of empty passageways, you ignore a sign announcing: "Halt, this is the empire of the dead." Along the way, plaques encourage visitors to reflect on their destiny: "Happy is he who is forever faced with the hour of his death and prepares himself for the end every day." You emerge far from where you entered, with white-limestone-covered toes, telling anyone in the know you've been underground gawking at bones. Note to wannabe Hamlets: An attendant checks your bag at the exit for stolen souvenirs. A flashlight is handy. Being under 6'2" is helpful.

Cost, Hours, Location: €7, not covered by Museum Pass, Tue–Sun 10:00–17:00, ticket booth closes at 16:00, closed Mon, 1 place Denfert-Rochereau, tel. 01 43 22 47 63. Take the Métro to Denfert-Rochereau, then find the lion in the big traffic circle; if he looked left rather than right, he'd stare right at the green entrance to the Catacombs. You'll exit at 36 rue Remy Dumoncel, far from where you started. If you walk to the right, to avenue du Général Leclerc, you'll be equidistant from Métro stops Alésia (walk left) and Mouton Duvernet (walk right).

Champs-Elysées and Nearby

▲▲**Champs-Elysées**—This famous boulevard is Paris' backbone, with its greatest concentration of traffic. From the Arc de Triomphe down avenue des Champs-Elysées, all of France seems to converge on place de la Concorde, the city's largest square. While the Champs-Elysées has become as international as it is local, a walk here is still a must.

To reach the top of the Champs-Elysées, take the Métro to the Arc de Triomphe (Mo: Charles de Gaulle-Etoile) then saunter down the grand boulevard (Métro stops every few blocks, including: Charles de Gaulle-Etoile, George V, and Franklin D. Roosevelt).

○ See Champs-Elysées Walk on page 251.

▲▲▲**Arc de Triomphe**—Napoleon had the magnificent Arc de Triomphe commissioned to commemorate his victory at the battle of Austerlitz. The foot of the arch is a stage on which the last two centuries of Parisian history have played out—from the funeral of Napoleon to the goose-stepping arrival of the Nazis to the triumphant return of Charles de Gaulle after the Allied liberation. Examine the carvings on the pillars, featuring a mighty

Champs-Elysées and Nearby

Napoleon and excitable Lady Liberty. Pay your respects at the Tomb of the Unknown Soldier. Then climb the 284 steps to the observation deck up top, with sweeping skyline panoramas and a mesmerizing view down onto the traffic that swirls around the arch.

Cost, Hours, Location: Outside—free, always open. Interior—€9, free on first Sun of month Oct–March, free for kids under 18, covered by Museum Pass, daily April–Sept 10:00–23:00, Oct–March 10:00–22:30, last entry 30 min before closing, place Charles de Gaulle, use underpass to reach arch, Mo: Charles de Gaulle-Etoile, tel. 01 55 37 73 77, www.monum.fr.

✪ See Champs-Elysées Walk on page 251.

▲**Opéra Garnier**—This gleaming grand theater of the belle époque was built for Napoleon III and finished in 1875. From avenue de l'Opéra, once lined with Paris' most fashionable haunts, the recently restored facade suggests "all power to the wealthy." And Apollo, holding his lyre high above the building, seems to declare, "This is a temple of the highest arts."

While the building is huge, the auditorium itself seats only 2,000. The real show was before and after the performance, when the elite of Paris—out to see and be seen—strutted their elegant stuff in the extravagant lobbies. Think of the grand marble stairway as a theater. As you wander the halls and gawk at the decor, imagine the place filled with the beautiful people of its day. The massive foundations straddle an underground lake (inspiring the mysterious world of the

SIGHTS

Best Views over the City of Light

Your trip to Paris is played out in the streets, but the brilliance of the City of Light can only be fully appreciated by rising above it all. Invest time to marvel at all the man-made beauty, seen best in the early morning or around sunset. Many of the viewpoints I've listed are free or covered by the Museum Pass; otherwise, expect to pay about €8. Here are some prime locations for soaking in the views:

Eiffel Tower: It's hard to find a grander view of Paris than on the tower's second level. Go around sunset and stay after dark to see the tower illuminated; or go in the early morning to avoid the midday haze (not covered by Museum Pass, see page 50).

Arc de Triomphe: Without a doubt, this is the perfect place to see the glamorous Champs-Elysées (if you can manage the 284 steps). It's great during the day, but even greater at night, when the boulevard positively glitters (free with Museum Pass, see page 60).

La Défense and La Grande Arche: This is your best bet for a view of Paris from outside the center. Take the elevator up for a good perspective on the city, its suburbs, and the surrounding forests (not covered by Museum Pass, see page 66).

Notre-Dame's Tower: This viewpoint is brilliant—you couldn't be more central—but it requires climbing 400 steps and is usually crowded with long lines (try to arrive early). Up high on the tower, you'll get an unobstructed view of gargoyles, the river, the Latin Quarter, and the Ile de la Cité (covered by

Phantom of the Opera). Visitors can peek from two boxes into the actual red-velvet performance hall to view Marc Chagall's colorful ceiling (1964) playfully dancing around the eight-ton chandelier (guided tours take you into the performance hall). Note the box seats next to the stage—the most expensive in the house, with an obstructed view of the stage...but just right if you're here only to be seen.

The elitism of this place prompted President François Mitterrand to have a people's opera house built in the 1980s, symbolically on place de la Bastille, where the French Revolution started in 1789. This left the Opéra Garnier home only to ballet and occasional concerts (see next page). While the library/museum is of interest to opera buffs, anyone will enjoy the second-floor grand foyer and Salon du Glacier, iced with decor typical of 1900.

Cost, Hours, Location: €8, not covered by Museum Pass, daily 10:00–16:30, July–Aug until 18:00, closed during performances, 8 rue Scribe, Mo: Opéra, RER: Auber.

Tours: English tours of the building run during summer and off-season weekends, usually at 11:30 and 14:00; call to confirm schedule (€12, includes entry, 90 min, tel. 01 40 01 17 89).

Museum Pass, see page 44).

Steps of Sacré-Cœur in Montmartre: Join the party on Paris' only hilltop. Walk uphill or take the funicular (if it's running), then hunker down on the Sacré-Cœur's steps to enjoy the sunset and territorial views over Paris. Stay in Montmartre for dinner, then see the view again after dark (free, see page 71).

Galeries Lafayette in Opéra District: Take the elevator to the top floor of this department store for a stunning overlook of the old Opéra district (free, see page 410).

Montparnasse Tower: The top of this solitary skyscraper has some of the best views in Paris. Zip up 56 floors via elevator, then walk to the rooftop (not covered by Museum Pass, disappointing after dark, see page 59).

Pompidou Center: Take the escalator up and admire the beautiful cityscape along with the exciting modern art. There may be better views over Paris, but there are none better from a museum (covered by Museum Pass, see page 68).

Trocadéro Square: This is *the* place to see the Eiffel Tower. Come day or night (when the tower is lit up) for a look at Monsieur Eiffel's festive creation. Consider starting or ending your Eiffel Tower visit here (free, see page 174).

Bar at Hôtel Concorde-Lafayette: This otherwise unappealing hotel is noteworthy for its 33rd-floor bar, where you can sip wine and enjoy a stunning Parisian panorama (free elevator but pricey drinks, see page 66).

Ballet and Concert Tickets: Check the performance schedule at the information booth (inside entry), in *Pariscope* magazine (see page 421), or on the website to see the upcoming schedule (www.opera-de-paris.fr). To buy tickets by phone, call 08 92 89 90 90 (toll call, office closed Sun). There are usually no performances mid-July–mid-Sept. You can also go direct to the ticket office (open daily 11:00–18:00).

Nearby: The *Paris Story* film and Fragonard Perfume Museum (see below) are on the left side of the Opéra, and the venerable Galeries Lafayette department store (top-floor café with marvelous views, see page 410) is just behind. Across the street, the illustrious Café de la Paix has been a meeting spot for the local glitterati for generations. If you can afford the coffee, this spot offers a delightful break.

***Paris Story* Film**—Simultaneously cheesy, entertaining, and pricey, this film offers a painless overview of the city's turbulent and brilliant past, covering 2,000 years in 45 fast-moving minutes. The theater's wide-screen projection and cushy chairs provide a break from bad weather and sore feet, and the movie usually works for kids, but don't go out of your way to get here.

Cost, Hours, Location: €10, kids-€6, family of four-€26, not

SIGHTS

Baron Georges-Eugène Haussmann
(1809–1891)

The elegantly uniform streets that make Paris so Parisian are the work of Baron Haussmann, who oversaw the modernization of the city in the mid-19th century. He cleared out the cramped, higgledy-piggledy, unhygienic medieval cityscape and replaced it with broad, straight boulevards lined with stately buildings and linking modern train stations.

The quintessential view of Haussmann's work is from the pedestrian island immediately in front of the Opéra Garnier. You're surrounded by Paris, circa 1870, when it was the capital of the world. Spin slowly and find the Louvre in one direction, place Vendôme in another, and all the cohesiveness of the uniform buildings. Haussmann's buildings are all five stories tall, with angled, black slate roofs and formal facades. The balconies on the second and fifth floors match up with neighboring buildings to give strong lines of perspective, as the buildings stretch down the boulevard. Haussmann was so intent on putting the architecture at center-stage that he ordered no trees be planted along these streets.

But there was more than aesthetics to the plan. In pre-Haussmann Paris, angry rioters would take to the narrow streets setting up barricades (as made famous in Hugo's *Les Misérables*) to hold back government forces. With Haussmann's plan, government troops could circulate easily and fire cannons down the long, straight boulevards. A whiff of "grapeshot"—chains, nails, and buckshot-type people-busters—could clear out any revolutionaries in a hurry.

The 19th century was a great time to be wealthy—the city offered its fancy covered market halls, civilized sidewalks, and even elevators. With the coming of elevators, the wealthy took the higher floors and enjoyed the view.

covered by Museum Pass. Individuals get a 20 percent discount with this book in 2009 (no discount on family rate). The film shows on the hour daily 10:00–18:00. Next to Opéra Garnier at 11 rue Scribe, Mo: Opéra, tel. 01 42 66 62 06.

Fragonard Perfume Museum—Near Opéra Garnier, two perfume shops masquerade as museums. Either location will teach you a little about how perfume is made (ask for the English handout), but the one on rue Scribe smells even sweeter—and it's in a beautiful 19th-century mansion (both free, daily 9:00–18:00, at 9 rue Scribe and 30 rue des Capucines, tel. 01 47 42 04 56, www.fragonard.com).

▲▲Jacquemart-André Museum (Musée Jacquemart-André)—This thoroughly enjoyable museum (with an elegant café) showcases the lavish home of a wealthy, art-loving, 19th-century Parisian couple. After wandering the grand boulevards, get inside for an intimate look at the lifestyles of the Parisian rich and fabulous. Edouard André and his wife Nélie Jacquemart—who had no children—spent their lives and fortunes designing, building, and then decorating this sumptuous mansion. What makes the visit so rewarding is the excellent audioguide tour (in English, free with admission, plan on spending an hour with the audioguide). The place is strewn with paintings by Rembrandt, Botticelli, Uccello, Mantegna, Bellini, Boucher, and Fragonard—enough to make a painting gallery famous.

Cost, Hours, Location: €10, not covered by Museum Pass, daily 10:00–18:00, at 158 boulevard Haussmann, Mo: Miromesnil or Saint-Philippe de Roule, bus #80 makes a convenient connection to Ecole Militaire, tel. 01 45 62 11 59, www.musee-jacquemart-andre.com.

After Your Visit: Consider a break in the sumptuous museum tearoom, with delicious cakes and tea (daily 11:45–17:45). From here, walk north on rue de Courcelles to see Paris' most beautiful park, **Parc Monceau.**

▲**Petit Palais (and its Musée des Beaux-Arts)**—In this free museum, you'll find a broad collection of paintings and sculpture from the 1600s to the 1900s. It's a museum of second-choice art, but the building itself is impressive, and there are a few 19th-century diamonds in the rough, including pieces by Courbet and Monet.

Enter the museum, ask for a ticket to the permanent collection (free but required), and head toward the left wing. Soak up turn-of-the-century ambience, with Art Nouveau vases and portraits of well-dressed, belle époque era Parisians. The main hall features Romantics and Realists from the late 19th century. Midway down the main hall, Courbet's soft-porn *The Sleepers* (*Le Sommeil*, 1866) captures two women nestled in post-climactic bliss. His large, dark *Firefighters (Pompiers courant à un incendie)* is a Realist's take on an everyday scene—firefighters rushing to put out a blaze.

Turning the corner, you'll find artwork by Gustave Doré (1832–1883), the 19th-century's greatest book illustrator. In the enormous *La Vallée de larmes* (1883), Christ and the cross are the only salvation from this "vale of tears."

At the end of the main hall, enter the smaller room to find Claude Monet's *Sunset on the Seine at Lavacourt* (*Soleil couchant sur la Seine a Lavacourt*, 1880). Painted the winter after his wife died, it looks across the river from Monet's home to two lonely boats in the distance, with the hazy town on the far bank. The sun's reflection is a vertical smudge down the water. Nearby are works by the American painter Mary Cassatt and other Impressionists.

The Palais also has a pleasant garden courtyard and café (Wed–Sun 10:00–18:00, Tue 10:00–20:00 for temporary exhibits, closed Mon, across from Grand Palais on avenue Winston Churchill, just west of place de la Concorde, tel. 01 53 43 40 00, www.petitpalais.paris.fr).

Grand Palais—This grand exhibition hall, built for the 1900 World's Fair, is used for temporary exhibits. The building's Industrial Age, erector-set, iron-and-glass exterior is grand, but the steep entry price is only worthwhile if the exhibit interests you. Get details on the current schedule from the TIs, in *Pariscope* (see page 421), or from www.rmn .fr (usually €10, not covered by Museum Pass, Thu–Mon 10:00–20:00, Wed 10:00–22:00, last entry 45 min before closing, closed Tue and between exhibitions, avenue Winston Churchill, Mo: Rond Point or Champs-Elysées, tel. 01 44 13 17 17).

View from Hôtel Concorde-Lafayette—For a remarkable Parisian panorama and a suitable location for your next affair, take the Métro to the pedestrian-unfriendly Porte Maillot stop, then follow the *Palais de Congrés* signs to the glass-and-steel tower. (If you're strapped for time, the skies are clear, and the sun's about to set, spring for a taxi.) Take the free elevator in the rear of the lobby to the 33rd floor, walk up one flight, and enter a sky-high world of semicircular vinyl make-out booths, glass walls, pricey drinks, and jaw-dropping views (best before dark, not worth it in poor weather, bar open 17:30–2:00 in the morning, rooms start at €440, 3 place du General Koenig, tel. 01 40 68 50 68, www.concorde-lafayette.com).

▲▲**La Défense and La Grande Arche**—While Paris keeps its historic center classic and skyscraper-free, this district, nicknamed "le petit Manhattan," offers an impressive excursion into a side of Paris few tourists see: that of a modern-day economic superpower. La Défense was first conceived more than 60 years ago as a US-style forest of skyscrapers that would accommodate the business needs of the modern world. Today, La Défense is a thriving business and shopping center, home to 150,000 employees and 55,000 residents.

For an interesting visit, take the Métro to the La Défense stop and start with La Grande Arche—take the elevator to the top for great city views. Then stroll among the glass buildings to the Esplanade de la Défense Métro station, and return home from there.

La Grande Arche de la Fraternité is the centerpiece of this ambitious complex. Inaugurated in 1989 on the 200th anniversary of the French Revolution, it was, like the Revolution, dedicated to human rights and brotherhood. The place is big—Notre-Dame Cathedral could fit under its arch. The four-sided structure sits on enormous underground pillars and is covered with a veneer of Carrara marble. The arch is a 38-story office building for 30,000 people on more than 200 acres. The left side is government ministries, the right side is corporate offices, and the top is dedicated to human rights. The "cloud"—a huge canvas canopy under the arch—is an attempt to cut down on the wind-tunnel effect this gigantic building creates.

Wandering behind the arch, you can see a cemetery and peek at the Le Corbusier-style planning—separating motor traffic (the freeway and trains that tunnel underneath) from pedestrian traffic (the sky-bridges).

Glass capsule elevators whisk you scenically up to a grand open-air view, a thrilling 20-minute movie (with English subtitles) on the mammoth construction project, and models of the arch. You can also visit an exhibit on computer history, and take advantage of its free Internet access. Don't skip the fascinating set of digital portraits by French artist Dimitri, illustrating *remanence*—"after imagery." After staring at one of these colorful images for 30 seconds, close your eyes and see a clear image of the face...behind your eyelids.

Cost, Hours, Location: La Grande Arche elevator-€9, kids-€7.50, family deals, not covered by Museum Pass, daily April–Sept 10:00–20:00, Oct–March until 19:00, RER or Mo: La Défense, follow signs to *La Grande Arche*, tel. 01 49 07 27 57, www.grandearche.com.

The Esplanade: La Défense is much more than its eye-catching arch. Wander from the arch back toward the city center (and to the next Métro stop) along the Esplanade (a.k.a. "le Parvis"), the open area surrounded by skyscrapers. Take in the monumental buildings around you: Les Quatre Temps is a giant shopping mall of 250 stores. The Center of New Industries and Technologies (better known as CNIT), built in 1958 and now a congress center, is a feat of modern architecture: It's the largest concrete vault anywhere that rests on only three points. The Nexity Tower (nearest central Paris) looks old compared to the other skyscrapers. Dating from the 1960s, it was one of the first buildings at La Défense.

In France, getting a building permit often comes with a requirement to dedicate two percent of the construction cost to art. Hence the Esplanade is a virtual open-air modern art gallery, sporting pieces by Joan Miró (blue), Alexander Calder (red), and Yaacov Agam (the fountain with its colorful stripes and rhythmically dancing spouts), among others. *La Défense de Paris,* the statue that gave the area its name, recalls the 1871 Franco-Prussian war—it's a rare bit of old Paris out here in the 'burbs. Notice how the Wallace Fountain and *boules* courts are designed to integrate tradition into this celebration of modern commerce. Walking toward the Nexity Tower, you'll come to the Esplanade de la Défense Métro station, which zips you out of all this modernity and directly back into town.

Marais Neighborhood and Nearby

✪ To connect these sights with a fun, fact-filled stroll leading from place de la Bastille to the Pompidou Center, take the Marais Walk on page 263.

Don't waste time looking for the **Bastille,** the prison of Revolution fame. It's Paris' most famous non-sight. The building is long gone and just the square remains, good only for its nightlife and as a jumping-off point for the Marais Walk or Promenade Plantée Park (see page 263).

▲▲Pompidou Center (Centre Pompidou)—One of Europe's greatest collections of far-out modern art is housed in the Musée National d'Art Moderne, on the fourth and fifth floors of this colorful exoskeletal building. Created ahead of its time, the 20th-century art in this collection is still waiting for the world to catch up. After so many Madonnas-and-children, a piano smashed to bits and glued to the wall is refreshing.

The Pompidou Center and the square that fronts it are lively, with lots of people, street theater, and activity inside and out—a perpetual street fair. Kids of any age enjoy the fun, colorful fountain (called *Homage to Stravinsky*) next to the Pompidou Center. Ride the escalator for a great city view from the top (ticket or Museum Pass required), and consider eating at the good mezzanine-level café.

Cost, Hours, Location: €10, permanent collection covered by Museum Pass (but not special exhibitions), free on first Sun of month, Wed–Mon 11:00–21:00, ticket counters close at 20:00, closed Tue, Mo: Rambuteau or farther-away Hôtel de Ville, tel. 01 44 78 12 33, www.centrepompidou.fr.

○ See Pompidou Center Tour on page 273.

▲▲Jewish Art and History Museum (Musée d'Art et Histoire du Judaïsme)—This fine museum, located in a beautifully restored Marais mansion, tells the story of Judaism throughout Europe, from the Roman destruction of Jerusalem to the theft of famous artworks during World War II. Displays illustrate the cultural unity maintained by this continually dispersed population. You'll learn about the history of Jewish traditions from bar mitzvahs to menorahs, and see the exquisite traditional costumes and objects central to daily life. Don't miss the explanation of "the Dreyfus affair," a major event in early 1900s French politics. You'll also see photographs of and paintings by famous Jewish artists, including Marc Chagall, Amedeo Modigliani, and Chaim Soutine. A small but moving section is devoted to the deportation of Jews from Paris during World War II.

Helpful audioguides and many English explanations make this an enjoyable history lesson (red numbers on small signs indicate the number you should press on your audioguide). Move along at your own speed.

Marais Neighborhood and Nearby

Cost, Hours, Location: €7, more during special exhibits, includes audioguide, covered by Museum Pass, Mon–Fri 11:00–18:00, Sun 10:00–18:00, last entry one hour before closing, closed Sat, 71 rue du Temple, Mo: Rambuteau or Hôtel de Ville a few blocks farther away, tel. 01 53 01 86 60, www.mahj.org.

▲▲**Picasso Museum (Musée Picasso)**—Tucked into a corner of the Marais and worth ▲▲▲ if you're a Picasso fan, this museum contains the world's largest collection of Picasso's paintings, sculptures, sketches, and ceramics, and includes his small collection of Impressionist art. The art is well-displayed in a fine old mansion with a peaceful garden café. The room-by-room English introductions help make sense of Picasso's work—from the Toulouse-Lautrec–like portraits at the beginning of his career to his gray-brown Cubist period to his return-to-childhood, Salvador Dalí–like finish. The well-done English guidebook helps Picassophiles appreciate the context of his art and learn more about his interesting life. Most will be happy reading the posted English explanations while moving at a steady pace through the museum—the ground and first floors satisfied my curiosity.

Cost, Hours, Location: €6.50, covered by Museum Pass, additional fees for temporary exhibits, free on first Sun of month and for kids under 18 with ID; closing in Sept 2009—until then April–Sept Wed–Mon 9:30–18:00, Oct–March Wed–Mon 9:30–17:30; last entry 45 min before closing, closed Tue, 5 rue de Thorigny, Mo: St. Paul or Chemin Vert, tel. 01 42 71 25 21, www.musee-picasso.fr.

○ See Picasso Museum Tour on page 301.

▲▲**Carnavalet Museum (Musée Carnavalet)**—The tumultuous history of Paris—starring the Revolutionary years—is well portrayed in this converted Marais mansion. Explanations are in French only, but many displays are fairly self-explanatory. You'll see paintings of Parisian scenes, French Revolution paraphernalia, old Parisian store signs, a small guillotine, a model of the 16th-century Ile de la Cité (notice the bridge houses), and rooms full of 17th-century Parisian furniture.

Cost, Hours, Location: Free, Tue–Sun 10:00–18:00, closed Mon; avoid lunchtime (12:00–14:00), when many rooms close; 23 rue de Sévigné, Mo: St. Paul, tel. 01 44 59 58 58, www.carnavalet.paris.fr.

○ See Carnavalet Museum Tour on page 286.

Victor Hugo's House—France's literary giant lived in this house on place des Vosges from 1832 to 1848. After the phenomenal success of *The Hunchback of Notre Dame,* he moved into this nice address. You'll walk through the elegant and spacious rooms (all 10,000 square feet of them) where he wrote much of *Les Misérables* when he wasn't entertaining Paris' elite. Inside are posters advertising theater productions of his works, paintings of some of his most famous character creations, a few furnished rooms (including his bedroom and study), and fine views onto the square.

Cost, Hours, Location: Free, Tue–Sun 10:00–18:00, last entry 17:40, closed Mon, 6 place des Vosges, tel. 01 42 72 10 16, www.paris.fr/musees.

Holocaust Memorial (Mémorial de la Shoah)—Commemorating the lives of the more than 76,000 Jews deported from France in World War II, this memorial's focal point is underground, where victims' ashes are buried. Displaying original deportation records, the museum takes you through the history of Jews in Europe and France, from medieval pogroms to the Nazi era (free, Sun–Fri 10:00–18:00, Thu until 22:00, closed Sat and certain Jewish holidays, 17 rue Geoffroy l'Asnier, tel. 01 42 77 44 72, www.memorialdelashoah.org). For more on the Memorial, see page 270 in the Marais Walk.

▲**Promenade Plantée Park**—This two-mile-long, narrow garden walk on a viaduct was once used for train tracks and is now a joy on foot. Part of the park is elevated. At times, you'll walk along the street until you pick up the next segment. The shops below the viaduct's arches (a creative use of once-wasted urban space) make for entertaining window-shopping.

Cost, Hours, Location: Free, opens Mon–Fri at 8:00, Sat–Sun at 9:00, closes at sunset. It runs from place de la Bastille (Mo: Bastille) along avenue Daumesnil to Saint-Mandé (Mo: Michel Bizot). From place de la Bastille (follow signs for *Sortie Opéra* or *Sortie rue de Lyon* from Bastille Métro station), walk down rue de Lyon with the Opéra immediately on your left. Find the steps up the red brick wall a block after the Opéra.

▲**Père Lachaise Cemetery (Cimetière du Père Lachaise)**— Littered with the tombstones of many of the city's most illustrious dead, this is your best one-stop look at Paris' fascinating, romantic past residents. More like a small city, the cemetery is confusing, but maps and my self-guided tour will direct you to the graves of Frédéric Chopin, Molière, Edith Piaf, Oscar Wilde, Gertrude Stein, Jim Morrison, Héloïse and Abélard, and many more. Buy the helpful €2 map at the flower stores located near either entry.

Cost, Hours, Location: Free, Mon–Sat 8:00–18:00, Sun 9:00– 18:00, or until dusk if it falls before 18:00. It's down avenue du Père Lachaise from Mo: Gambetta (also across the street from the less-convenient Père Lachaise Métro stop and reachable via bus #69—see bus tour on page 217). Tel. 01 55 25 82 10.

✪ See Père Lachaise Cemetery Tour on page 310.

Montmartre

✪ Connect these sights with the Montmartre Walk on page 323.

▲▲**Sacré-Cœur and Montmartre**—This Byzantine-looking basilica, while only 130 years old, is impressive (church free, daily 7:00–23:00; €5 to climb dome, not covered by Museum Pass, daily June–Sept 9:00–19:00, Oct–May 10:00–18:00).

The neighborhood's main square (place du Tertre), one block from the church, was once the haunt of Henri de Toulouse-Lautrec and the original bohemians. Today, it's mobbed with tourists and unoriginal bohe-mians, but it's still fun (to beat the crowds, go early in the morning).

To get to Montmartre, take the Métro to the Anvers stop (one more Métro ticket buys your way up the funicular and avoids the stairs, but the funicular may be closed for repairs) or the closer but less scenic Abbesses stop. A taxi to the top of the hill saves time and avoids sweat (costs about €10, or €20 at night).

Dalí Museum (L'Espace Dalí)—The museum offers an entertain-ing look at some of Dalí's creations (€10, not covered by Museum Pass, daily 10:00–18:30, 11 rue Poulbot, tel. 01 42 64 40 10, www .daliparis.com).

Montmartre Museum (Musée de Montmartre)—This 17th-century home re-creates the traditional cancan and cabaret Montmartre scene, with paintings, posters, photos, music, and memorabilia (€7, includes audioguide, not covered by Museum Pass, Tue–Sun 11:00–18:00, closed Mon, 12 rue Cortot, tel. 01 49 25 89 39, www.museedemontmartre.fr).

Pigalle—Paris' red light district, the infamous "Pig Alley," is at the foot of Butte Montmartre. *Ooh la la.* It's more racy than dangerous. Walk from place Pigalle to place Blanche, teasing desperate barkers and fast-talking temptresses. In bars, a €150 bottle of cheap champagne comes with a friend. Stick to the bigger streets, hang onto your wallet, and exercise good judgment. Cancan can cost a fortune, as can con artists in topless bars. After dark, countless tour buses line the streets, reminding us that tour guides make big bucks by bringing their groups to touristy nightclubs like the famous Moulin Rouge (Mo: Pigalle or Abbesses).

Museum of Erotic Art (Musée de l'Erotisme)—Paris' sexy museum has five floors of risqué displays—mostly paintings and drawings—ranging from artistic to erotic to disgusting, with a few circa-1920 porn videos and a fascinating history of local brothels tossed in. It's in the center of the Pigalle red light district (€8, no... it's not covered by Museum Pass, daily 10:00–2:00 in the morning, 72 boulevard de Clichy, Mo: Blanche, tel. 01 42 58 28 73, www.musee-erotisme.com).

Near Paris: Versailles

▲▲▲**Versailles**—Every king's dream, Versailles was the residence of French kings and the cultural heartbeat of Europe for about 100 years—until the Revolution of 1789 ended the notion that God deputized some people to rule for him on earth. Louis XIV spent half a year's income of Europe's richest country turning his dad's hunting lodge into a palace fit for a divine monarch. Louis XV and Louis XVI spent much of the 18th century gilding Louis XIV's lily. In 1837, about 50 years after the royal family was evicted, King Louis-Philippe opened the palace as a museum. Today you can visit parts of the huge palace and wander through acres of manicured gardens sprinkled with fountains and studded with statues. Europe's next-best palaces are Versailles wannabes.

Cost and Hours: The **Château,** the main palace, costs €13.50 (€10 after 15:00, includes audioguide, under 18 free, covered by Museum Pass and Le Passeport pass). The **Domaine de Marie-Antoinette,** the queen's estate, costs €9 April–Oct (€5 after 16:00 and in Nov–March); under 18 always free, also covered by the Museum Pass and Le Passeport). The gardens are free (except for weekends April–Sept, when the fountains perform in the garden and it's €8), but there are extra charges for tours and audioguides.

The Château is open April–Oct Tue–Sun 9:00–18:30, Nov–March Tue–Sun 9:00–17:30, last entry one hour before closing, closed Mon. The Domaine de Marie-Antoinette is open daily April–Oct 12:00–18:30, Nov–March 9:00–17:30. The gardens are generally open daily from 9:00 to sunset, except on Sat in summer when they close at 18:00 to prepare for evening events. Tel. 08 10 81 16 14, www .chateauversailles.fr.

✪ See Versailles Day Trip on page 456.

HISTORIC PARIS WALK

Ile de la Cité and the Latin Quarter

Paris has been the cultural capital of Europe for centuries. We'll start where it did, on Ile de la Cité, with a foray onto the Left Bank, on a walk that laces together 80 generations of history: from Celtic fishing village to Roman city, bustling medieval capital, birthplace of the Revolution, bohemian haunt of the 1920s café scene, and the working world of modern Paris. Along the way, we'll step into two of Paris' greatest sights—Notre-Dame and Sainte-Chapelle.

ORIENTATION

Length of This Walk: Allow four hours to do justice to this three-mile walk.

Paris Museum Pass: Many sights in this walk that charge admission are covered by the Museum Pass. For many travelers, this is a great time- and money-saver (2 days/€30, 4 days/€45, or 6 days/€60, sold at participating sights, see page 38 for details).

Notre-Dame Cathedral: Free, daily 7:45–19:00. Treasury-€3, not covered by Museum Pass, daily 9:30–17:30. Audioguides cost €5. Ask about free English tours, normally Wed and Thu at 12:00, Sat at 14:30. The church's "no shorts" dress code is not strictly enforced, but inside you're expected to be quiet and respectful, if not worshipful. The cathedral hosts several Masses every morning, plus Vespers at 17:45. The international Mass is Sun at 11:30, with an organ concert at 16:30. Call or check the website for a full schedule (tel. 01 42 34 56 10, www.cathedraledeparis.com, Mo: Cité, Hôtel de Ville, or St. Michel). On Easter and the first Friday of the month at 15:00, the (physically underwhelming) relic known as Jesus' Crown of Thorns goes on display.

Tower Climb: The entrance for Notre-Dame's towers is outside of the cathedral, along the left side. It's 400 steps up, but it's worth

HISTORIC PARIS WALK

WALKING TOUR ROUTE

Ⓜ METRO STATION Ⓑ BATOBUS BOAT STOP

Ⓡ RER STOP 𝆢 VIEW   DCH

❶ Point Zero   ❾ Place St. Michel
❷ Deportation Memorial   ❿ Sainte-Chapelle
❸ Ile St. Louis   ⓫ Cité Métro Stop
❹ Left Bank Booksellers   ⓬ Conciergerie
❺ Medieval Paris   ⓭ Place Dauphine
❻ Shakespeare & Co. Bookstore ⓮ Statue of Henry IV
❼ St. Séverin   ⓯ Pont Neuf
❽ Place St. André-des-Arts

it for the gargoyle's-eye view of the cathedral, Seine, and city (€7.50, covered by Museum Pass, but no bypass line for pass-holders; daily April–Sept 10:00–18:30, also June–Aug Sat–Sun until 23:00, Oct–March 10:00–17:30, last entry 45 min before closing; to avoid crowds in peak season, arrive before 10:00 or after 17:00).

Paris Archaeological Crypt: €3.50, covered by Museum Pass, Tue–Sun 10:00–18:00, closed Mon, enter 100 yards in front of the cathedral.

Deportation Memorial: Free, daily April–Sept 10:00–12:00 & 14:00–19:00, Oct–March 10:00–12:00 & 14:00–17:00, Mo: Cité, tel. 01 49 74 34 00.

Shakespeare and Company Bookstore: Daily 12:00–24:00, 37 rue de la Bûcherie, across the river from Notre-Dame, Mo: St. Michel, tel. 01 43 26 96 50.

Sainte-Chapelle: €7.50, €10 combo-ticket with Conciergerie, covered by Museum Pass, daily March–Oct 9:30–18:00, Nov–Feb 9:00–17:00, last entry 30 min before closing, English tours most days at 10:45 and 14:45, 4 boulevard du Palais, Mo: Cité, tel. 01 53 40 60 80, www.monum.fr. Avoid the ticket line by buying from the *tabac* shop across the street from the security entrance.

Conciergerie: €6.50, €10 combo-ticket with Sainte-Chapelle, covered by Museum Pass, daily April–Sept 9:30–18:00, Oct–March 10:00–17:00, last entry 30 min before closing, 4 boulevard du Palais, Mo: Cité, www.monum.fr.

Audioguides: A free audioguide tour version of this walk is available for people with iPods and other MP3 players at www.ricksteves .com and on iTunes.

WCs: There's a free (often crowded) public WC in front of Notre-Dame. Find others at museums (Sainte-Chapelle and Conciergerie) and cafés.

THE WALK BEGINS

• *Start at Notre-Dame Cathedral on the island in the River Seine, the physical and historic bull's-eye of your Paris map. The closest Métro stops are Cité, Hôtel de Ville, and St. Michel, each a short walk away.*

NOTRE-DAME AND NEARBY

• *On the square in front of the cathedral, stand far enough back to take in the whole facade. Find the circular window in the center.*

For centuries, the main figure in the Christian "pantheon" has been Mary, the mother of Jesus. Catholics petition her in times of trouble to gain comfort, and to ask her to convince God to be compassionate with them. The church is dedicated to "Our Lady" *(Notre Dame),* and there she is, cradling God, right in the heart of the facade, surrounded by the halo of the rose window. Though the church is massive and imposing, it has always stood for the grace and compassion of Mary, the "mother of God."

Imagine the faith of the people who built this cathedral. They broke ground in 1163 with the hope that someday their great-great-great-great-great-great grand-children might attend the dedication Mass two centuries later, in 1345. Look up the 200-foot-tall bell towers and imagine a tiny medieval community mustering the money and energy for construction. Master masons supervised, but the people did much of the grunt work themselves for free—hauling the huge stones from distant quarries, digging a 30-foot-deep trench to lay the foundation, and treading like rats on a wheel designed to lift the stones up, one by one. This kind of backbreaking, arduous manual labor created the real hunchbacks of Notre-Dame.

• *"Walk this way" toward the cathedral, and view it from the bronze plaque on the ground (30 yards from the central doorway) marked...*

❶ Point Zero

You're standing at the center of France, the point from which all dis-tances are measured. It was also the center of Paris 2,300 years ago, when the Parisii tribe fished where the east–west river crossed a north–south road. The Romans conquered the Parisii and built their Temple of Jupiter where Notre-Dame stands today (52 B.C.). Then as now,

the center of religious power faced the center of political power (once the Roman military, today the police station, at the far end of the square). When Rome fell, the Germanic Franks sealed their victory by replacing the temple with the Christian church of St. Etienne in the sixth century. See the outlines of the former church in the pavement (in smaller gray stones), showing what were once walls and columns, angling out from Notre-Dame to Point Zero.

The grand equestrian statue (to your right, as you face the church) is of Charlemagne ("Charles the Great," 742–814), King of the Franks, whose reign marked the birth of modern France. He briefly united Europe and was crowned the first Holy Roman Emperor in 800, but after his death, the kingdom was divided into what would become

Paris Through History

250 B.C.	Small fishing village of the Parisii, a Celtic tribe.
52 B.C.	Julius Caesar conquers the Parisii capital of Lutetia (near Paris), and the Romans replace it with a new capital on the Left Bank.
A.D. 497	Rome falls to the Germanic Franks. King Clovis (482–511) converts to Christianity and makes Paris his capital.
885–886	Paris gets wasted in a siege by Viking Norsemen = Normans.
1163	Notre-Dame cornerstone laid.
c. 1250	Paris is a bustling commercial city with a university and new construction, such as Sainte-Chapelle and Notre-Dame.
c. 1600	King Henry IV beautifies Paris with buildings, roads, bridges, and squares.
c. 1700	Louis XIV makes Versailles his capital, while Parisians grumble.
1789	Paris is the heart of France's Revolution, which condemns thousands to the guillotine.
1804	Napoleon Bonaparte crowns himself emperor in a ceremony at Notre-Dame.
1830 & 1848	Parisians take to the streets again in revolutions, fighting the return of royalty.
c. 1860	Napoleon's nephew, Napoleon III, builds Paris' wide boulevards.
1889	The centennial of the Revolution is celebrated with the Eiffel Tower. Paris enjoys wealth and middle-class prosperity in the belle époque (beautiful age).
1920s	After the draining Great War, Paris is a cheap place to live, attracting expatriates like Ernest Hemingway.
1940–1944	Occupied Paris spends the war years under gray skies and gray Nazi uniforms.
2005	Lance Armstrong wins his seventh Tour de France.
2008	All bars, cafés, and restaurants in France become smoke-free, officially ending the era of the smoky Parisian café.

modern France and Germany.

Before its renovation 150 years ago, this square was much smaller, a characteristic medieval shambles facing a run-down church, surrounded by winding streets and higgledy-piggledy buildings. (Yellowed bricks in the pavement show the medieval street plan and even identify some of the buildings.) The church's huge bell towers rose above this tangle of smaller buildings, inspiring Victor Hugo's story of a deformed bell-ringer who could look down on all of Paris.

Looking two-thirds of the way up Notre-Dame's left tower, those with binoculars or good eyes can find Paris' most photographed gargoyle. Propped on his elbows on the balcony rail, he watches all the tourists in line.

• *Much of Paris' history is right under your feet. Some may consider visiting it in the...*

Archaeological Crypt

Two thousand years of dirt and debris have raised the city's altitude. In the crypt (entrance 100 yards in front of Notre-Dame's entrance), you can see cellars and foundations from many layers of Paris: a Roman building with central heating; a wall that didn't keep the Franks out; the main medieval road that once led grandly up the square to Notre-Dame; and even (wow) a 19th-century sewer. (For more info, see page 44.)

• *Now turn your attention to the...*

Notre-Dame Facade

• *Look at the left doorway (the Portal of Mary) and, to the left of the door, find the statue with his head in his hands.*

St. Denis

When Christianity began making converts in Roman Paris, the bishop of Paris (St. Denis) was beheaded as a warning to those forsaking the Roman gods. But those early Christians were hard to keep down. St. Denis got up, tucked his head under his arm, headed north, paused at a fountain to wash it off, and continued until he found just the right place to meet his maker. The Parisians were convinced by this miracle, Christianity gained ground, and a church soon replaced the pagan temple.

• *Above the central doorway, you'll find scenes from the Last Judgment.*

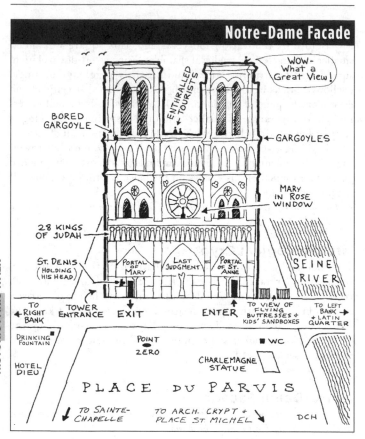

Notre-Dame Facade

WOW— What a Great View!

ENTHRALLED TOURISTS

BORED GARGOYLE

← GARGOYLES

MARY IN ROSE WINDOW

28 KINGS OF JUDAH

ST. DENIS (HOLDING HIS HEAD)

PORTAL OF MARY — LAST JUDGMENT — PORTAL OF ST. ANNE

SEINE RIVER

TO RIGHT BANK

TOWER ENTRANCE   EXIT   ENTER

TO VIEW OF FLYING BUTTRESSES + KIDS' SANDBOXES

TO LEFT BANK + LATIN QUARTER

DRINKING FOUNTAIN

POINT ZERO

■ WC

HOTEL DIEU

CHARLEMAGNE STATUE

PLACE DU PARVIS

↓ TO SAINTE-CHAPELLE

TO ARCH. CRYPT + PLACE ST MICHEL ↓

DCH

Central Portal

It's the end of the world, and Christ sits on the throne of judgment (just under the arches, holding both hands up). Below him, an angel and a demon weigh souls in the balance; the demon cheats by pressing down. The good people stand to the left, gazing up to heaven. The naughty ones to the right are chained up and led off to a six-hour tour of the Louvre on a hot day. Notice the crazy sculpted demons to the right, at the base of the arch. Find the flaming cauldron with the sinner diving into it headfirst. The lower panel shows Judgment Day, as angels with trumpets remind worshippers that all social classes will be judged—clergy, nobility, army, and peasants. Below that, Jesus stands between the 12 apostles—each barefoot and with his ID symbol (such as Peter with his keys).

• *Take 10 paces back. Above the arches is a row of 28 statues, known as...*

The Kings of Judah

In the days of the French Revolution (1789–1799), these Biblical kings were mistaken for the hated French kings, and Notre-Dame represented the oppressive Catholic hierarchy. The citizens stormed the church, crying, "Off with their heads!" Plop—they lopped off the crowned heads of these kings with glee, creating a row of St. Denises that wasn't repaired for decades.

But the story doesn't end there. A schoolteacher who lived nearby collected the heads and buried them in his backyard for safe-keeping. There they slept until 1977, when they were accidentally unearthed. Today, you can stare into the eyes of the original kings in the Cluny Museum, a few blocks away (see page 244).

• *Now let's head into the...*

Notre-Dame Interior

• *Enter the church at the right doorway (the Portal of St. Anne) and find a spot where you can view the long, high central aisle. (Be careful: Pickpockets attend church here religiously.)*

Nave

Remove your metaphorical hat and become a simple bareheaded peasant, entering the dim medieval light of the church. Take a minute to let your pupils dilate, then take in the subtle, mysterious light show that God beams through the stained-glass windows. Follow the slender columns up 10 stories to the praying-hands arches of the ceiling, and contemplate the heavens. Let's say it's dedication day for this great stone wonder. The priest intones the words of the Mass that echo through the hall: *Terribilis est locus iste...*"This place is *terribilis*," meaning awe-inspiring or even terrifying. It's a huge, dark, earthly cavern lit with an unearthly light.

This is Gothic. Taller and filled with light, this was a major improvement over the earlier Romanesque style. Gothic architects needed only a few structural columns, topped by crisscrossing pointed arches, to support the weight of the roof. This let them build higher than ever, freeing up the walls for windows.

Notre-Dame has the typical basilica floor plan shared by so many Catholic churches: a long central nave lined with columns and flanked by side aisles. It's designed in the shape of a cross, with the altar placed where the crossbeam intersects. The church can hold up to 10,000 faithful. And it's probably buzzing with visitors now, just as it was 600 years ago. The quiet, deserted churches we see elsewhere are in stark contrast to the busy, center-of-life places they were in the Middle Ages.

• *Walk up to the main altar.*

Notre-Dame Interior

AMBULATORY

❺

TO TREASURY

CHOIR

❾

N O R T H

S O U T H

❼

ALTAR

❽

T R A N S E P T

❻

N A V E

❹

COLUMNS

TO TOWERS

EXIT

❶

❷

❸

ENTER

TO VIEW OF FLYING BUTTRESSES

POINT ZERO ·

P L A C E   D U   P A R V I S

❶ St. Denis & Portal of Mary (exit)
❷ Last Judgment & Central Portal
❸ Portal of St. Anne (entrance)
❹ Glass-Walled Room for Confession
❺ Pietà Flanked by Louis XIII
   & Louis XIV

❻ Joan of Arc Statue
❼ North Rose Window
❽ Thomas Aquinas Painting
❾ Scenes of Life of Christ

HISTORIC PARIS WALK

Altar

This marks the place where Mass is said and the bread and wine of Communion are blessed and distributed. In olden days, there were no chairs. This was the holy spot for Romans, Christians...and even atheists. When the Revolutionaries stormed the church, they gutted it and turned it into a "Temple of Reason." A woman dressed like the Statue of Liberty held court at the altar as a symbol of the divinity of Man. France today, while nominally Catholic, remains aloof from Vatican dogmatism. Instead of traditional wooden confessional booths, there's an inviting **glass-walled room** (right aisle), where modern sinners seek counseling as much as forgiveness.

Just past the altar are the walls of the so-called "choir," the area where more intimate services can be held in this spacious building. Looking past the altar to the far end of the choir (under the cross), you'll see a fine **17th-century *pietà*,** flanked by two kneeling kings: Louis XIII (1601–1643, not so famous) and his son Louis XIV (1638–1715, very famous, also known as the Sun King; for more on this Louis, see the Versailles chapter).

Right Transept (and Beyond)

A statue of **Joan of Arc** (Jeanne d'Arc, 1412–1431), dressed in armor and praying, honors the French teenager who rallied her country's soldiers to try to drive English invaders from Paris before being burned at the stake for claiming to hear heavenly voices. Almost immediately, Parisians rallied to condemn Joan's execution, and finally, in 1909, here in Notre-Dame, the former "witch" was beatified.

Join the statue in gazing up to the blue-and-purple, **rose-shaped window** in the opposite transept—with teeny green Mary and baby Jesus in the center—the only one of the three rose windows still with its original medieval glass.

A large painting back down to your right shows portly **Thomas Aquinas** (1225–1274) teaching, while his students drink from the fountain of knowledge. This Italian monk did undergrad and master's work at the multicultural University of Paris, then taught there for several years while writing his theological works. His "scholasticism" used Aristotle's logic to examine the Christian universe, aiming to fuse faith and reason.

• *Continue toward the far end of the church, pausing at the top of the three stair steps.*

Circling the Choir

The back side of the choir walls feature **scenes of the resurrected Jesus** (c. 1350) appearing to his followers, starting with Mary Magdalene. Their starry robes still gleam, thanks to a 19th-century renovation. The niches below these carvings mark the tombs of centuries of archbishops. Just ahead on the right is the Treasury. It contains lavish robes and golden reliquaries, but lacks English explanations and probably isn't worth the €3 entry fee. Surrounding the choir are chapels, each dedicated to a particular saint and funded by a certain guild. One chapel displays models of the church and an exhibit on medieval construction techniques—pulleys, wagons, hamster-wheel cranes, and lots of elbow grease. The faithful can pause at any of the other chapels to light a candle as an offering, and meditate in the cool light of the stained glass.

· *Amble around the ambulatory, spill back outside, and make a slow U-turn left. Enter the park through the iron gates along the riverside.*

Notre-Dame Side View

Along the side of the church, you'll notice the flying buttresses. These 50-foot stone "beams" that stick out of the church were the key to the complex Gothic architecture. The pointed arches we saw inside cause the weight of the roof to push outward rather than downward. The "flying" buttresses support the roof by pushing back inward. Gothic architects were masters at playing architectural forces against each other to build loftier and loftier churches, with walls opened up for stained-glass windows.

Picture Quasimodo (the fictional hunchback) limping around along the railed balcony at the base of the roof among the "gargoyles."

These grotesque beasts sticking out from pillars and buttresses represent souls caught between heaven and earth. They also function as rainspouts (from the same French root as "gargle") when there are no evil spirits to battle.

The Neo-Gothic 300-foot spire is a product of the 1860 reconstruction of the dilapidated old church. Victor Hugo's book *The Hunchback of Notre-Dame* (1831) inspired a young architecture student named Eugène-Emmanuel Viollet-le-Duc to dedicate his career to a major renovation in Gothic style. Find Viollet-le-Duc himself at the base of the spire among the green apostles and evangelists (visible as you approach the back end of the church). The apostles look outward, blessing the city, while the architect (at top) looks up the spire, marveling at his fine work.

· *Behind Notre-Dame, cross the street and enter through the iron gate into the park at the tip of the island.*

Ile St. Louis

☆ View
Ⓜ Metro Station
Ⓑ Batobus Boat Stop

❶ Berthillon Ice Cream (3)
❷ Amorino Gelati
❸ Good Picnic Spot
❹ Rest. La Tour d'Argent
❺ Grocery Store

❷ Deportation Memorial (Mémorial de la Déportation)

This memorial to the 200,000 French victims of the Nazi concentration camps (1940–1945) draws you into their experience. France was quickly overrun by Nazi Germany, and Paris spent the war years under Nazi occupation. Jews and dissidents were rounded up and deported—many never returned.

As you descend the steps, the city around you disappears. Surrounded by walls, you have become a prisoner. Your only freedom is your view of the sky and the tiny glimpse of the river below. Enter the dark, single-file chamber up ahead. Inside, the circular plaque in the floor reads, "They went to the end of the earth and did not return."

The hallway stretching in front of you is lined with 200,000 lighted crystals, one for each French citizen who died. Flickering at the far end is the eternal flame of hope. The tomb of the unknown deportee lies at your feet. Above, the inscription reads, "Dedicated to the living memory of the 200,000 French deportees sleeping in the night and the fog, exterminated in the

Nazi concentration camps." The side rooms are filled with triangles—reminiscent of the identification patches inmates were forced to wear—each bearing the name of a concentration camp. Above the exit as you leave is the message you'll find at other Holocaust sites: "Forgive, but never forget."

• *Back on street level, look across the river (north) to the island called...*

❸ Ile St. Louis

If the Ile de la Cité is a tug laden with the history of Paris, it's towing this classy little residential dinghy, laden only with high-rent apartments, boutiques, characteristic restaurants, and famous sorbet shops.

This island wasn't developed until much later than the Ile de la Cité (17th century). What was a swampy mess is now harmonious Parisian architecture and one of Paris' most exclusive neighborhoods. Its uppity residents complain that the three local Berthillon ice-cream shops draw crowds until late into the night (one is at 31 rue St. Louis-en-l'Ile, another is across the street, and there's one more around the corner on rue Bellay—see map on page 85). Gelato-lovers head instead to Amorino Gelati (47 rue St. Louis-en-l'Ile).

Now look upstream (east) to the bridge that links the Ile St. Louis with the Left Bank (which is now on your right). Where the bridge meets the Left Bank, you'll find one of Paris' most exclusive restaurants, La Tour d'Argent. Because the top floor has floor-to-ceiling windows, your evening meal comes with glittering views—and a golden price (allow €200 minimum, though you get a free photo of yourself dining elegantly with Notre-Dame floodlit in the background).

• *From the Deportation Memorial, cross over to the Left Bank and turn right (west). Walk along the river, toward the front end of Notre-Dame. Stairs detour down to the riverbank if you need a place to picnic. This side view of the church from across the river is one of Europe's great sights and is best from river level.*

LEFT BANK

❹ Left Bank Booksellers

The Rive Gauche, or the Left Bank of the Seine—"left" if you were floating downstream—still has many of the twisting lanes and narrow buildings of medieval times. The Right Bank is more modern and business-oriented, with wide boulevards and stressed Parisians in suits. Here along the riverbank, the "big business" is secondhand books, displayed in the green metal stalls on the parapet. These literary entrepreneurs pride themselves on their easygoing style. With flexible hours and virtually no overhead, they run their businesses as they have since medieval times. For more information, see the "*Les Bouquinistes* (Riverside Vendors)" sidebar on page 409.

• *When you reach the bridge (pont au Double) that crosses over in front of Notre-Dame, veer to the left across the street to a small park (place Viviani; fill your water bottle from fountain on left).*

> *Angle across the square and pass by Paris' oldest inhabitant—an acacia tree nicknamed Robinier, after the guy who planted it in 1602. Imagine that this same tree might once have shaded the Sun King, Louis XIV. Just beyond the tree you'll find the small rough-stone church of St. Julien-le-Pauvre.*

❺ Medieval Paris (1000–1400)

Picture Paris in 1250, when the church of St. Julien-le-Pauvre was still new. Notre-Dame was nearly done (so they thought), Sainte-Chapelle had just opened, the university was expanding human knowledge, and Paris was fast becoming a prosperous industrial and commercial center. The area around the church gives you some of the medieval feel. From the door of the church, you can see plenty of the half-timbered and whitewashed architecture from that era. Looking along nearby rue Galande, you'll see a few old houses leaning every which way. In medieval days, people were piled on top of each other, building at all angles, as they scrambled for this prime real estate near the main commercial artery of the day—the Seine. The smell of fish competed with the smell of neighbors in this knot of humanity.

Narrow dirt (or mud) streets sloped from here down into the mucky Seine, until the 19th century, when modern quays and embankments cleaned everything up.

• *Return to the river and turn left on rue de la Bûcherie. At #37, drop into the...*

❻ Shakespeare and Company Bookstore

In addition to hosting butchers and fishmongers, the Left Bank has been home to scholars, philosophers, and poets since medieval times.

This funky bookstore—a reincarnation of the original shop from the 1920s—has picked up the literary torch. Sylvia Beach, an American with a passion for free thinking, opened Shakespeare and Company for the post-WWI Lost Generation, who came to Paris to find themselves. American writers flocked here for the cheap rent, fleeing the uptight, Prohibition-era United States. Beach's bookstore was famous as a meeting place for Paris' literary expatriate elite. Ernest Hemingway borrowed books from here regularly. James Joyce struggled to find a publisher for his now-classic novel *Ulysses*—until Sylvia Beach published it. George Bernard Shaw, Gertrude Stein, and Ezra Pound also got their English fix here.

Today, the bookstore carries on that literary tradition. Struggling writers are given free accommodations upstairs in tiny rooms with views of Notre-Dame. Downstairs, travelers enjoy a great selection of used English books.

Notice the green water fountain (1900) in front of the bookstore, one of the many in Paris donated by the English philanthropist Sir Richard Wallace. The hooks below the caryatids once held metal mugs for drinking the water.

• *Continue to rue du Petit-Pont (which becomes rue St. Jacques). This bustling north–south boulevard was the Romans' busiest street 2,000 years ago, with chariots racing in and out of the city. (Roman-iacs can view remains from the third-century baths, along with a fine medieval collection, at the nearby Cluny Museum, located near the corner of boulevards St. Michel and St. Germain; see page 244.)*

Walking away from the river for one block up a broad road that has cut straight through Paris since Roman times, turn right at the Gothic church of St. Séverin and walk into the Latin Quarter.

❼ St. Séverin

Don't ask me why, but it took a century longer to build this church than Notre-Dame. This is Flamboyant, or "flame-like," Gothic, and

you can see the short, prickly spires meant to make this building flicker in the eyes of the faithful. The church gives us a close-up look at gargoyles, the decorative drain spouts that also functioned to keep evil spirits away.

Inside you can see the final stage of Gothic, on the cusp of the Renaissance. The stained-glass windows favor the greens and reds popular in St. Séverin's heyday. In the apse, admire the lone twisted Flamboyant Gothic column and the fan vaulting. The impressive organ filling the back wall is a reminder that this church is a popular venue for evening concerts (see gate for information posters, buy tickets at door).

• *At #22 rue St. Séverin, you'll find the skinniest house in Paris, two windows wide. Rue St. Séverin leads right through...*

The Latin Quarter

While it may look more like the Greek Quarter today (cheap gyros abound), this area is the Latin Quarter, named for the language you'd have heard on these streets if you walked them in the Middle Ages. The University of Paris (founded 1215), one of the leading educational institutions of medieval Europe, was (and still is) nearby.

A thousand years ago, the "crude" or vernacular local languages were sophisticated enough to communicate basic human needs, but if you wanted to get philosophical, the language of choice was Latin. Medieval Europe's class of educated elite transcended nations and borders. From Sicily to Sweden, they spoke and corresponded in Latin. Now the most "Latin" thing about this area is the beat you may hear coming from some of the subterranean jazz clubs.

Along rue St. Séverin, you can still see the shadow of the medieval sewer system. The street slopes into a central channel of bricks. In the days before plumbing and toilets, when people still went to the river or neighborhood wells for their water, flushing meant throwing it out the window. At certain times of day, maids on the fourth floor would holler, *"Garde de l'eau!"* ("Watch out for the water!") and heave it into the streets, where it would eventually wash down into the Seine.

As you wander, remember that before Napoleon III commissioned Baron Haussmann to modernize the city with grand boulevards (19th century), Paris was just like this—a medieval tangle. The ethnic feel of this area is nothing new—it's been a melting pot and university district for almost 800 years.

• *Keep wandering straight, and you'll come to...*

Boulevard St. Michel

Busy boulevard St. Michel (or "boul' Miche") is famous as the main artery for Paris' café and artsy scene, culminating a block away (to the left) at the intersection with boulevard St. Germain. Although nowadays you're more likely to find pantyhose at 30 percent off, there are still many cafés, boutiques, and bohemian haunts nearby.

The Sorbonne—the University of Paris' humanities department—is also close, if you want to make a detour, though visitors are not allowed to enter. (Turn left on boulevard St. Michel and walk two blocks south. Gaze at the dome from the place de la Sorbonne courtyard.) Originally founded as a theological school, the Sorbonne began attracting more students and famous professors—such as St. Thomas Aquinas and Peter Abélard—as its prestige grew. By the time the school expanded to include other subjects, it had a reputation for bold new ideas. Nonconformity is a tradition here, and Paris remains a world center for new intellectual trends.

• *Cross boulevard St. Michel. Just ahead is...*

❽ Place St. André-des-Arts

This tree-filled square is lined with cafés. In Paris, most serious thinking goes on in cafés. For centuries, these have been social watering holes, where you can get a warm place to sit and stimulating conversation for the price of a cup of coffee. Every great French writer—from Voltaire and Jean-Jacques Rousseau to Jean-Paul Sartre and Jacques Derrida—had a favorite haunt.

Paris honors its writers. If you visit the Panthéon (described on page 57)—a few blocks up boulevard St. Michel and to the left—you will find French writers (Voltaire, Victor Hugo, Emile Zola, and Rousseau), inventors (Louis Braille), and scientists (including Marie and Pierre Curie) buried in a setting usually reserved for warriors and politicians.

• *Adjoining this square toward the river is the triangular place St. Michel, with a Métro stop and a statue of St. Michael killing a devil. Note: If you were to continue west along rue St. André-des-Arts, you'd find more Left Bank action.*

❾ Place St. Michel

You're standing at the traditional core of the Left Bank's artsy, liberal, hippie, bohemian district of poets, philosophers, and winos. Nearby, you'll find international eateries, far-out bookshops, street singers, pale girls in black berets, jazz clubs, and—these days—tourists. Small cinemas show avant-garde films, almost always in the *version originale* (v.o.). For colorful wandering and café-sitting, afternoons and evenings are best. In the morning, it feels sleepy. The Latin Quarter stays up late and sleeps in.

In less-commercial times, place St. Michel was a gathering point for the city's malcontents and misfits. In 1830, 1848, and again in 1871,

the citizens took the streets from the government troops, set up barricades *Les Miz*–style, and fought against royalist oppression. During World War II, the locals rose up against their Nazi oppressors (read the plaques under the dragons at the foot of the St. Michel fountain).

In the spring of 1968, a time of social upheaval all over the world, young students battled riot batons and tear gas, took over the square, and declared it an independent state. Factory workers followed their call to arms and went on strike, toppling the de Gaulle government and forcing change. Eventually, the students were pacified, the university was reformed, and the Latin Quarter's original cobblestones were replaced with pavement, so future scholars could never again use the streets as weapons. Even today, whenever there's a student demonstration, it starts here.

• *From place St. Michel, look across the river and find the spire of the Sainte-Chapelle church, with its weathervane angel nearby. Cross the river on pont St. Michel and continue north along the boulevard du Palais. On your left, you'll see the doorway to Sainte-Chapelle. You'll need to pass through a metal detector to get into the Sainte-Chapelle complex. This is more than a tourist attraction—you're entering the courtyard of France's Supreme Court (to the right of Sainte-Chapelle). Once you're past the extremely strict security, you'll find restrooms ahead on the left. The line into the church may be long (but you can bypass it with a Museum Pass).*

Enter the humble ground floor (pick up an English info flier and check the concert schedule if you're interested).

SAINTE-CHAPELLE AND NEARBY

⑩ Sainte-Chapelle

This triumph of Gothic church architecture is a cathedral of glass like no other. It was speedily built between 1242 and 1248 for King Louis IX—the only French king who is now a saint—to house the supposed Crown of Thorns (now kept at Notre-Dame and shown only on Good Friday and on the first Friday of the month at 15:00). Its architectural harmony is due to the fact that it was completed under the direction of one architect and in only five years—unheard of in Gothic times. Recall that Notre-Dame took over 200 years.

While the inside is beautiful, the exterior is basically functional. The muscular buttresses hold up the stone roof, so the walls are essentially there to display stained glass. The lacy spire is Neo-Gothic—added in the 19th century. Inside, the layout clearly shows an *ancien régime* approach to worship. The low-ceilinged basement was for staff and other

It takes 13 tourists to build a Gothic church: six columns, six buttresses, and one steeple.

Sainte-Chapelle

JESUS' PASSION SCENES

TO COURTYARD ENTRANCE + SECURITY CHECK

20 METERS
20 YARDS

ALTAR

ST. LOUIS' PEEK-A-BOO WINDOW

CAMPAIGN OF HOLOFERNES

MORE MOSES

STAINED GLASS

LIFE OF MOSES

BUTTRESSES

CAIN CLUBBING ABEL

HELENA IN JERUSALEM

ROSE WINDOW

SPIRAL STAIRCASE

SPIRAL STAIRCASE

TO WC →

DCH

ENTER BELOW (INTO LOWER CHAPEL)

common folks—worshipping under a sky filled with painted fleurs-de-lis, a symbol of the king. Royal Christians worshipped upstairs. The paint job, a 19th-century restoration, helps you imagine how grand this small, painted, jeweled chapel was. (Imagine Notre-Dame painted like this...) Each capital is playfully carved with a different plant's leaves.

• Climb the spiral staircase to the Chapelle Haute. Leave the rough stone of the earth and step into the light.

The Stained Glass

Fiat lux. "Let there be light." From the first page of the Bible, it's clear: Light is divine. Light shines through stained glass like God's grace shining down to earth. Gothic architects used their new technology to turn dark stone buildings into lanterns of light. The glory of Gothic shines brighter here than in any other church.

There are 15 separate panels of stained glass (6,500 square feet—two thirds of it 13th-century original), with more than 1,100 different scenes, mostly from the Bible. These cover the entire Christian history of the world, from the Creation in Genesis (first window on the left, as you face the altar), to the coming of Christ (over the altar), to the end of the world (the round "rose"-shaped window at the rear of the church). Each individual scene is interesting, and the whole effect is overwhelming. Allow yourself a few minutes to bask in the glow of the colored light before tackling the window descriptions below, then remember to keep referring to the map to find the windows.

• *Working clockwise from the entrance, look for these worthwhile scenes. (Note: The sun lights up different windows at various times of day. Overcast days give the most even light. On bright, sunny days, some sections are glorious, while others look like a sheet of lead.)*

Genesis—Cain Clubbing Abel (first window on the left, always dark because of a building butted up against it): On the bottom level in the third circle from the left, we see God create the round earth and hold it up. On the next level up, we catch glimpses of naked Adam and Eve. On the third level (far right circle), Cain, in red, clubs his brother Abel, creating murder.

Life of Moses (second window, the bottom row of diamond panels): The first panel shows baby Moses in a basket, placed by his sister in the squiggly brown river. Next, he's found by the pharaoh's daughter. Then he grows up. And finally, he's a man, a prince of Egypt on his royal throne.

More Moses (third window, in middle and upper sections): You'll see various scenes of Moses, the guy with the bright yellow horns—the result of a medieval mistranslation of the Hebrew word for "rays of light," or halo.

Jesus' Passion Scenes (over the altar): These scenes from Jesus' arrest and crucifixion were the backdrop for the Crown of Thorns (originally displayed on the altar), which was placed on Jesus' head when the Romans were torturing and humiliating him before his execution. Stand a few steps back from the altar to look through the canopy and find Jesus in yellow shorts, carrying his cross (fifth frame up from right bottom). A little below that, see Jesus being whipped (left) and—the key scene in this relic chapel—Jesus in purple, being fitted with the painful Crown of Thorns (right). Finally (as high as you can see), Jesus on the cross is speared by a soldier (trust me).

Campaign of Holofernes (window to the right of the altar wall): On the bottom row are four scenes of colorful knights (refer to map to get oriented). The second circle from the left is a battle scene

Stained Glass Supreme

Craftsmen made glass—which is, essentially, melted sand—using this recipe:

- Melt one part sand with two parts wood ash.
- Mix in rusty metals to get different colors—iron makes red; cobalt makes blue; copper, green; manganese, purple; cadmium, yellow.
- Blow glass into a cylinder shape, cut lengthwise, and lay flat.
- Cut into pieces with an iron tool, or by heating and cooling a select spot to make it crack.
- Fit pieces together to form a figure, using strips of lead to hold them in place.
- Place masterpiece so high on a wall that no one can read it.

(the campaign of Holofernes), showing three soldiers with swords slaughtering three men. The background is blue. The men have different-colored clothes—red, blue, green, mauve, and white. Examine some of the details. You can see the folds in the robes, the hair, and facial features. Look at the victim in the center—his head is splotched with blood. Details like the folds in the robes (see the victim in white, lower left) came about either by scratching on the glass or by baking on paint. It was a painstaking process of finding just the right colors, fitting them together to make a scene...and then multiplying by 1,100.

Helena in Jerusalem (first window on the right wall by entrance): This window tells the story of how Christ's Crown of Thorns found its way from Jerusalem to Constantinople to this chapel. Start in the lower-left corner, where the Roman emperor Constantine (in blue, on his throne) waves goodbye to his Christian mom, Helena. She arrives at the gate of Jerusalem (next panel to the right). Her men (in the two-part medallion above Jerusalem) dig through ruins and find Christ's (tiny) cross and other relics. She returns to Constantinople with a stash of holy relics, including the Crown of Thorns. Nine hundred years later, French Crusader knights (the next double medallion above) invade the Holy Land and visit Constantinople. Finally, King Louis IX, dressed in blue (in the panel up one and to the right of the last one) returns to France with the sacred relic.

Rose Window (above entrance): It's Judgment Day, with a tiny Christ in the center of the chaos and miracles. This window, from the Flamboyant period, is 200 years newer than the rest. Facing west and the sunset, it's best late in the day.

If you can't read much into the individual windows, you're not alone. (For some tutoring, a little book with color photos is on sale downstairs with the postcards.)

Altar

The altar was raised up high to better display the Crown of Thorns, the relic around which this chapel was built. Notice the staircase: Access was limited to the priest and the king, who wore the keys to the shrine around his neck. Also note that there is no high-profile image of Jesus anywhere—this chapel was all about the Crown.

King Louis IX, convinced he'd found the real McCoy, paid £135,000 for the Crown, £100,000 for the gem-studded shrine to display it in (destroyed in the French Revolution), and a mere £40,000 to build Sainte-Chapelle to house it. Today, the supposed Crown of Thorns is kept by the Notre-Dame Treasury (though it's occasionally brought out for display).

Lay your camera on the ground and shoot the ceiling. Those pure and simple ribs growing out of the slender columns are the essence of

Gothic structure.

• Exit Sainte-Chapelle. Back outside, as you walk around the church exterior, look down to see the foundation and take note of how much Paris has risen in the 750 years since Sainte-Chapelle was built.

Next door to Sainte-Chapelle is the...

Palais de Justice

Sainte-Chapelle sits within a huge complex of buildings that has housed the local government since ancient Roman times. It was the site of the original Gothic palace of the early kings of France. The only surviving medieval parts are Sainte-Chapelle and the Conciergerie prison.

Most of the site is now covered by the giant Palais de Justice, built in 1776, home of the French Supreme Court. The motto *Liberté, Egalité, Fraternité* (Liberty, Equality, Brotherhood) over the doors is a reminder that this was also the headquarters of the Revolutionary government. Here, they doled out justice, condemning many to imprisonment in the Conciergerie downstairs or to the guillotine.

Sainte-Chapelle Area

TO LOUVRE

PONT NEUF

CONCIERGERIE PRISON

PLACE DU CHATELET

RIVER CRUISES

PONT NEUF

QUAI DES

SEINE

CHATELET

GESVRES

HENRI IV

QUAI DE L'HOR-LOGE

CHANGE

PONT NOTRE DAME

B

PLACE DAUPHINE

OLD CLOCK

PALAIS DE JUSTICE

EXIT

CITE

PLACE

FLOWER MARKET

SAINTE-CHAPELLE

WC

ENTER COURT-YARD

RUE DE LUTECE

ST. MICHEL

TO NOTRE-DAME

BLVD DU PALAIS

RUE DE LA CITE

ST. MICHEL

→ ENTRANCES TO SIGHTS
M METRO STATION
R RER STOP
B BATOBUS BOAT STOP

ST. MICHEL

100 YARDS
100 METERS

• *Now pass through the big iron gate to the noisy boulevard du Palais. Cross the street to the wide, pedestrian-only rue de Lutèce and walk about half-way down.*

⓫ Cité "Metropolitain" Métro Stop

Of the 141 original early-20th-century subway entrances, this is one of only a few survivors—now preserved as a national art treasure. (New York's Museum of Modern Art even exhibits one.) It marks Paris at its peak in 1900—on the cutting edge of Modernism, but with an eye for beauty. The curvy, plantlike ironwork is a textbook example of Art Nouveau, the style that rebelled against the erector-set squareness of the Industrial Age. In Paris, only the stations here and at Abbesses and Porte Dauphine survive with their canopies.

The flower and plant market on place Louis Lépine is a pleasant detour. On Sundays, this square flutters with a busy bird market. And across the way is the Préfecture de Police, where Inspector Clouseau of *Pink Panther* fame used to work, and where the local resistance fighters took the first building from the Nazis in August of 1944, leading to the Allied liberation of Paris a week later.

• *Pause here to admire the view. Sainte-Chapelle is a pearl in an ugly architectural oyster. Double back to the Palais de Justice, turn right, and enter the Conciergerie (entrance on boulevard du Palais). Though pretty barren inside, the Conciergerie echoes with history (and is free with the Museum Pass).*

⑫ Conciergerie

Positioned next to the courthouse, the Conciergerie was the gloomy prison famous as the last stop for 2,780 victims of the guillotine, including France's last Old Regime queen, Marie-Antoinette. Before then, kings had used the building to torture and execute failed assassins. (One of its towers along the river was called "The Babbler," named for the pain-induced sounds that leaked from it.) When the Revolution (1789) toppled the king, the building kept its same function, but without torture. The progressive Revolutionaries proudly unveiled a modern and more humane way to execute people—the guillotine.

Inside, pick up a free map and breeze through. See the spacious, low-ceilinged Hall of Men-at-Arms (Room 1), used as the guards' dining room, with four large fireplaces (look up the chimneys). This big room gives a feel for the grandeur of the Great Hall (upstairs, not open to visitors), where the Revolutionary tribunals grilled scared prisoners on their political correctness. The raised area at the far end of the room (Room 4, today's bookstore) was notorious as the walkway of the executioner, who was known affectionately as "Monsieur de Paris."

Pass through the bookstore to find the Office of the Keeper, or "Concierge" of the place (who monitored torture...and recommended nearby restaurants). Next door is the *Toilette*, where condemned prisoners combed their hair or touched up their lipstick before their final public appearance—waiting for the open-air cart (tumbrel) to pull up outside. The tumbrel would carry them to the guillotine, which was on place de la Concorde.

Upstairs is a memorial room with the names of the 2,780 citizens condemned to death by the guillotine. Here are some of the people you'll find, in alphabetical order: Anne Elisabeth Capet, whose crime was being "sister of the tyrant"; Charlotte Corday *("dite d'Armais")*, a noblewoman who snuck into the bathroom of the revolutionary writer Jean-Paul Marat and stabbed him while he bathed; Georges Danton, a prominent revolutionary who was later condemned for being insufficiently liberal—a nasty crime. Louis XVI (called "Capet: last king of France"), who deserves only a modest mention, as does his wife, Marie-Antoinette (*veuve* means she's widowed). And finally—oh, the irony—Maximilien de Robespierre, the head of the Revolution, the man who sent so many to the guillotine. He was eventually toppled, humiliated, imprisoned here, and beheaded.

Head down the hallway. Along the way, you'll see some

reconstructed cells with mannequins that show how the poor slept on straw, while the wealthy got a cot.

After passing through a small museum, go back downstairs to a tiny chapel built on the site where Marie-Antoinette's prison cell originally stood. The chapel was made in Marie's honor by Louis XVIII, the brother of beheaded Louis XVI and the first king back on the throne after the Revolution. The chapel's paintings show Marie-Antoinette in her cell, receiving the Last Sacrament on the night before her beheading. The walls drip with silver-embroidered tears.

The tour continues outside in the courtyard, where female prisoners were allowed a little fresh air (notice the spikes still guarding from above). In the corner, a door leads to a re-creation of Marie-Antoinette's cell (Room 8). Imagine the queen spending her last days—separated from her 10-year-old son, and now widowed because the king had already been executed. Mannequins, period furniture, and the real cell wallpaper set the scene. The guard stands modestly behind a screen, while the queen psyches herself up with a crucifix. In the glass display case, see her actual crucifix, napkin, and small water pitcher. On October 16, 1793, the queen walked the corridor, stepped onto the cart, and was slowly carried to place de la Concorde, where she had a date with "Monsieur de Paris." Before you leave, check out the video in the next room, which gives a taste of prison life during the Reign of Terror.

• *Back outside, turn left on boulevard du Palais and head toward the river (north). On the corner is the city's oldest public clock. The mechanism of the present clock is from 1334, and even though the case is Baroque, it keeps on ticking.*

Turn left onto quai de l'Horloge and walk west along the river, past the round medieval tower called the babbler. The bridge up ahead is the pont Neuf, where we'll end this walk. At the first corner, veer left into a sleepy triangular square called...

⓮ Place Dauphine

It's amazing to find such coziness in the heart of Paris. This city of two million is still a city of neighborhoods, a collection of villages. The French Supreme Court building looms behind like a giant marble gavel. Enjoy the village-Paris feeling in the park. The **Caveau du Palais** restaurant is a nice spot for a drink or light meal. You may see lawyers on their lunch break playing *boules* (see sidebar on page 346).

• *Continue through place Dauphine. As you pop out the other end, you're face to face with a...*

⑭ Statue of Henry IV

Henry IV (1553–1610) is not as famous as his grandson, Louis XIV, but Henry helped make Paris what it is today—a European capital of elegant buildings and quiet squares. He built the place Dauphine (behind you), the pont Neuf (to the right), residences (to the left, down rue Dauphine), the Louvre's long Grand Gallery (downriver on the right), and the tree-filled square Vert-Galant (directly behind the statue, on the tip of the island). The square is one of Paris' make-out spots; its name comes from Henry's own nickname, the Green Knight, as Henry was a notorious ladies' man. The park is a great place to relax, dangling your legs over the concrete prow of this boat-shaped island.

• *From the statue, turn right onto the old bridge. Pause at the little nook halfway across.*

⑮ Pont Neuf

The pont Neuf, or "new bridge," is Paris' oldest standing bridge (built 1578–1607). Its 12 arches span the widest part of the river. Unlike other bridges, this one never had houses or buildings growing on it. The turrets were originally for vendors and street entertainers. In the days of Henry IV, who promised his peasants "a chicken in every pot every Sunday," this would have been a lively scene. From the bridge, look downstream (west) to see the next bridge, the pedestrian-only pont des Arts. Ahead on the Right Bank is the long Louvre Museum. Beyond that, on the Left Bank, is the Orsay. And what's that tall black tower in the distance?

The Seine

Our walk ends where Paris began—on the Seine River. From Dijon to the English Channel, the Seine meanders 500 miles, cutting through the center of Paris. The river is shallow and slow within the city, but still dangerous enough to require steep stone embankments (built 1910) to prevent occasional floods.

In summer, the roads that run along the river are replaced with acres of sand, as well as beach chairs and tanned locals, creating Paris Plage (see page 45). The success of the Paris Plage event has motivated some city officials to propose the permanent removal of vehicles from those fast lanes—turning them into riverside parks instead.

Any time of year, you'll see tourist boats and the commercial barges that carry 20 percent of Paris' transported goods. And on the banks, sportsmen today cast into the waters once fished by Paris' original Celtic inhabitants.

• *We're done. You can take a boat tour that leaves from near the base of pont Neuf on the island side (Vedettes du Pont Neuf, €11, tip requested, departs hourly on the hour, 2/hr after dark, has live guide with explanations in French and English).*

Or you could take the Left Bank Walk, which begins one bridge downriver (see page 233). You can also catch the Métro to anywhere in Paris (the nearest stop is Pont Neuf, across the bridge on the Right Bank) or hop on the #69 bus tour (cross pont Neuf, turn left on the quai du Louvre, and find the bus stop; see page 217 for the tour).

LOUVRE TOUR

Musée du Louvre

Paris walks you through world history in three world-class museums—the Louvre (ancient world to 1850), the Orsay (1848–1914, including Impressionism), and the Pompidou (20th century to today). Start your "art-yssey" at the Louvre. With more than 30,000 works of art, the Louvre is a full inventory of Western civilization. To cover it all in one visit is impossible. Let's focus on the Louvre's specialties—Greek sculpture, Italian painting, and French painting.

We'll see "Venuses" through history, from scrawny Stone Age fertility goddesses to the curvy *Venus de Milo*, from the wind-blown *Winged Victory of Samothrace* to placid medieval Madonnas, from *Mona Lisa* to the symbol of modern democracy. We'll see how each generation defined beauty differently, and gain insight into long-ago civilizations by admiring the things they found beautiful.

In addition, those with a little more time can visit some impressive chunks of stone from the "Cradle of Civilization," modern-day Iraq.

ORIENTATION

Cost: €9, €6 after 18:00 on Wed and Fri, free on first Sun of month, covered by Museum Pass. Tickets good all day; reentry allowed. Optional additional charges apply for temporary exhibits.

Hours: Wed–Mon 9:00–18:00, closed Tue. Most rooms stay open Wed and Fri until 21:45 (but not on holidays). Galleries start shutting down 30 minutes early. The last entry is 45 minutes before closing.

When to Go: Crowds are worst on Sun, Mon, Wed, and mornings. Evening visits are peaceful, and the glass pyramid glows after dark.

Getting There: You have a variety of options:

    By Métro: The Métro stop Palais Royal–Musée du Louvre is closer to the entrance than the stop called Louvre-Rivoli. From the Palais Royal–Musée du Louvre stop, you can stay underground to enter the museum, or exit above ground if you want to go in through the pyramid (more details below).

By Bus: Handy bus #69 runs every 10–20 minutes from the Marais and rue Cler neighborhoods to the Louvre. Buses headed west from the Marais drop off passengers next to the Palais Royal–Musée du Louvre Métro stop on rue de Rivoli. Buses headed east from rue Cler drop off along the Seine River. Note that bus #69 stops running after 21:30 and there is no service on Sundays.

By Taxi: A taxi stand is on rue de Rivoli, next to the Palais Royal–Musée du Louvre Métro station.

Getting In: There is no grander entry than through the main entrance at the pyramid in the central courtyard, but metal detectors (not ticket-buying) create a long line at times. There are several ways to avoid the line:

If you have a Museum Pass, you can use the group entrance in the pedestrian passageway (labeled *Pavilion Richelieu*) between the pyramid and rue de Rivoli. It's under the arches, a few steps north of the pyramid; find the uniformed guard at the entrance, with the escalator down.

Otherwise, you can enter the Louvre from its (usually less crowded) underground entrance, accessed through the Carrousel du Louvre shopping mall. Enter the mall at 99 rue de Rivoli (the door with the red awning) or directly from the Métro stop Palais Royal–Musée du Louvre (stepping off the train, exit at the end of the platform, following signs to *Musée du Louvre–Le Carrousel du Louvre*).

Information: Pick up the free *Plan/Information* in English at the information desk under the pyramid as you enter. Tel. 01 40 20 53 17, recorded info tel. 01 40 20 51 51, www.louvre.fr.

Buying Tickets: Located under the pyramid, the self-serve ticket machines are faster to use than the ticket windows (machines accept euro notes, coins, and Visa cards). The *tabac* in the underground mall at the Louvre sells tickets to the Louvre, Orsay, and Versailles, plus Paris Museum Passes, for the same prices as elsewhere.

Tours: There are 90-minute English-language **guided tours** that leave three times daily except Sun from the *Accueil des Groupes* area, under the pyramid between the Sully and Denon wings (normally at 11:00, 14:00, and 15:45; €5 plus your entry ticket, tour tel. 01 40 20 52 63). Digital **audioguides** provide eager students with commentary on about 130 masterpieces (€6, available at entries to the three wings, at the top of the escalators). I prefer the self-guided tour described below, which is also available as a free audio tour for people with iPods and other MP3 players (download from www.ricksteves.com or iTunes).

Louvre Overview

RIGHT PALAIS ROYAL BANK

CAFE LE NEMOURS →

PALAIS ROYAL MUSÉE DU LOUVRE

❷ RUE DE RIVOLI ←

RICHELIEU ORIENTAL ANTIQUITIES ❶ FRENCH SULLY

ARC DU CARROUSEL PEDESTRIAN PASSAGEWAY LOUVRE RIVOLI

TUILERIES GARDEN AXIS VIEW MAIN ENTRANCE → PYRAMID COUR CARREE RUE L'AMIRAL DE COLIGNY

FORMER TUILERIES PALACE LOUIS XIV ITALIAN + FRENCH GREEK

DENON WINGED VICTORY CAFES

QUAI DE F. MITTERAND

PONT ROYAL PONT CARROUSEL SEINE RIVER PONT DES ARTS DCH

QUAI VOLTAIRE

TO ORSAY MUSEUM (15 MIN. WALK) LEFT BANK TO LATIN QUARTER (15 MIN. WALK)

Ⓜ METRO STATION Ⓑ BUS #69 STOP 🄱 BATOBUS BOAT STOP
Ⓣ TAXI STAND → ONE-WAY STREET

❶ Museum Passholders' Entrance (In Passageway) ❷ To Underground Mall Entrance

LOUVRE

Length of This Tour: Allow at least two hours.

Baggage Check and WCs: Baggage storage and WCs are located under the escalators to the Denon and Richelieu wings (WCs are scarce once you're in the galleries). Purses and small day bags are okay, but large bags are not allowed. Check these (as well as any small bags to lighten your load) for free. The baggage storage *(Bagagerie)* will not take coats unless they're stuffed into bags. The cloakroom *(Vestiaire)* takes only coats and can have long lines (worst early in the morning and late afternoon). The baggage claim person might ask you in French, "Does your bag contain anything of value?" You can't check cameras, money, passports, or other valuables.

Cuisine Art: The Louvre has several cafés, including **Café Mollien,** located near the end of our tour (€11 for sandwich and drink on terrace overlooking pyramid; see page 120). A reasonably priced self-service **cafeteria** (€9 *plats du jour*) is just up the escalator from the pyramid in the Richelieu wing. But your best bet is in the underground shopping mall, the **Carrousel du Louvre** (daily

8:30–23:00), which has a dizzying assortment of decent-value, multiethnic fast-food eateries (west of the pyramid and up the escalator near the inverted pyramid). The mall also has glittering boutiques, a post office (after passing security), and the Palais Royal–Musée du Louvre Métro entrance. Stairs at the far end take you right into the Tuileries Garden, a perfect antidote to the stuffy, crowded rooms of the Louvre.

For a fine, elegant lunch near the Louvre, head to the venerable **Café le Nemours** (€11 salads, open daily; leaving the Louvre, cross rue de Rivoli and veer left to 2 place Colette, adjacent to Comédie Française; see Eating, page 399).

Photography: Photography without a flash is allowed. (Flash photography damages paintings and distracts viewers.)

Starring: *Venus de Milo*, *Winged Victory*, *Mona Lisa*, Leonardo da Vinci, Raphael, Michelangelo, the French painters, and many of the most iconic images of Western civilization.

Surviving the Louvre

Start by picking up a free map at the information desk and orienting yourself from underneath the glass pyramid.

The Louvre, the largest museum in the Western world, fills three wings of this immense, U-shaped palace. The **Richelieu wing** (north side) houses Oriental antiquities (covered in the second part of this tour), plus French, Dutch, and Northern art. The **Sully wing** (east side) has extensive French painting and ancient Egypt collections.

For this part of the tour, we'll concentrate on the Louvre's south side: the **Denon and Sully wings,** which hold many of the superstars, including ancient Greek sculpture, Italian Renaissance painting, and French Neoclassical and Romantic painting.

Expect changes—the sprawling Louvre is constantly in flux. Rooms are periodically closed for renovation, and their paintings and sculpture are moved to new places within the museum. In 2009, for example, the Greek section near *Venus de Milo* is being rearranged. To find the artwork you're looking for, ask the nearest guard for its new location. Point to the photo in your book and ask, *"Où est, s'il vous plaît?"* (oo ay see voo play).

You'll find English explanations throughout the museum to complement this tour. The bottom line: You could spend a lifetime here. Concentrate on seeing the biggies quickly, and try to finish the tour with enough energy left to browse.

The Louvre—Pre-Classical Greece

GREEK BARBIE DOLLS

DAME D'AUXERRE

COUROS■

TO ROMAN EGYPT

CORE■ ■

SALLE I. PRE-CLASSICAL GREECE

TO GOLDEN AGE GREECE

D E N O N

TICKET TAKER

|‖| = STAIRS

DCH

PYRAMID

LOUVRE

THE TOUR BEGINS

• *From inside the big glass pyramid, you'll see signs to the three wings. Head for the Denon wing.*

Escalate up one floor. After showing your ticket, take the first left you can, follow the signs that read Antiquités Grecques, *and climb a set of stairs to the brick-ceilinged Salle (room) 1: Grèce préclassique. Enter prehistory.*

GREECE (3,000 B.C–A.D. 1)

Pre-Classical Greek Statues

These statues are noble but crude. The Greek Barbie dolls (3000 B.C.) are older than the pyramids, as old as writing itself. These prerational

voodoo dolls whittle women down to their life-giving traits. Halfway down the hall, a woman *(Dame d'Auxerre)* pledges allegiance to stability. Another *(Core)* is essentially a column with breasts. A young, naked man *(Couros)* seems to have a gun to his back—his hands at his sides, facing front, with sketchy muscles and a mask-like face. "Don't move."

The early Greeks, who admired such statues, found stability more attractive than movement. Like their legendary hero, Odysseus, the

Greek people had spent generations wandering, war-weary, and longing for the comforts of a secure home. The noble strength and sturdiness of these works looked beautiful.

• *Exit Salle 1 at the far end, and climb the stairs one flight. At the top, veer left toward 10 o'clock, and continue into the Sully wing. After about 50 yards, turn right into Salle 7. You'll find* Venus de Milo *floating above a sea of worshipping tourists. It's been said that, among the warlike Greeks, this was the first statue to unilaterally disarm.*

Venus de Milo (*Aphrodite*, C. 100 B.C.)

The *Venus de Milo* (or goddess of love, from the Greek island of Melos) created a sensation when it was discovered in 1820. Europe was already

in the grip of a classical fad, and this statue seemed to sum up all that ancient Greece stood for. The Greeks pictured their gods in human form (meaning humans are godlike), telling us they had an optimistic view of the human race. *Venus'* well-proportioned body embodies the balance and orderliness of the Greek universe.

Split *Venus* down the middle from nose to toes and see how the two halves balance each other. *Venus* rests on her right foot (called *contrapposto*, or "counterpoise"), then lifts her left leg, setting her whole body in motion. As the left leg rises, her right shoulder droops down. And as her knee points one way, her head turns the other. *Venus* is a harmonious balance of opposites, orbiting slowly around a vertical axis. The twisting pose gives a balanced S-curve to her body (especially noticeable from the back view) that the Greeks and succeeding generations found beautiful.

Other opposites balance as well, like the smooth skin of her upper half that sets off the rough-cut texture of her dress (size 14). She's actually made from two different pieces of stone plugged together at the hips (the seam is visible). The face is realistic and anatomically accurate, but it's also idealized, a goddess, too generic and too perfect. This isn't any particular woman, but Everywoman—all the idealized features that appealed to the Greeks.

LOUVRE

The Louvre—Greek Statues

||| = STAIRS

1 Venus de Milo
2 Parthenon Frieze
3 Roman Detour
4 Winged Victory (upstairs)

SALLE 7

SALLE 6 (SALLE DE DIANE)

SALLE 22

SALLE 23

SALLE 24

SALLE 18

PYRAMID

START

UP

SALLE 30

DCH

LOUVRE

Most "Greek" statues are actually later Roman copies. This is a rare Greek original. This "epitome of the Golden Age" was actually sculpted three centuries after the Golden Age, though in a retro style.

What were her missing arms doing? Some say her right arm held her dress, while her left arm was raised. Others say she was hugging a male statue or leaning on a column. I say she was picking her navel.

• *Orbit Venus. This statue is interesting and different from every angle. Remember the view from the back—we'll see it again later. Now make your reentry to Earth. From Venus, browse around this gallery of Greek statues (in 2009, the collection may be in flux). Try to find even one that's not contrapposto. Now backtrack to Salle 6 (also known as Salle de Diane) and locate two carved panels on the wall.*

Parthenon Frieze
(*Les Sculptures du Parthenon*, c. 440 B.C.)

These stone fragments once decorated the exterior of the greatest Athenian temple, the Parthenon, built at the peak of the Greek Golden Age. The right panel shows a centaur sexually harassing a woman. It tells the story of how these rude creatures crashed a party of humans. But the Greeks fought back and threw the brutes out, just as Athens (metaphorically) conquered its barbarian neighbors and became civilized.

The other relief shows the sacred procession of young girls who marched up the hill every four years with an embroidered veil for

Golden Age Greece

The great Greek cultural explosion that changed the course of history unfolded over 50 years (starting around 450 B.C.) in Athens, a Greek town smaller than Muncie, Indiana. Having united the Greeks to repel a Persian invasion, Athens rebuilt, with the Parthenon as the centerpiece of the city. The Greeks dominated the ancient world through brain, not brawn, and their art shows their love of rationality, order, and balance. The ideal Greek was well-rounded—an athlete and a bookworm, a lover and a philosopher, a carpenter who played the piano, a warrior and a poet. In art, the balance between timeless stability and fleeting movement made beauty.

In a sense, we're all Greek. Democracy, mathematics, theater, philosophy, literature, and science were practically invented in ancient Greece. Most of the art that we'll see in the Louvre either came from Greece or was inspired by it.

the 40-foot-high statue of Athena, the goddess of wisdom. Though headless, the maidens speak volumes about Greek craftsmanship. Carved in only a couple of inches of stone, they're amazingly realistic—more so than anything we saw in the pre-Classical period.

They glide along horizontally (their belts and shoulders all in a line), while the folds of their dresses drape down vertically. The man in the center is relaxed, realistic, and *contrapposto*. Notice the veins in his arm. The maidens' pleated dresses make them look as stable as fluted columns, but their arms and legs

step out naturally—the human form is emerging from the stone.

• *Backtrack a few steps, then turn left into Salle 22, the Roman Antiquities room (Antiquités Romaines), for a...*

Roman Detour (Salles 22–30)

Stroll among the Caesars and try to see the person behind the public persona. Besides the many faces

of the ubiquitous Emperor *Inconnu* ("unknown"), you might spot Augustus (Auguste), the first emperor, and his wily wife, Livia (Livie). Their son Tiberius (Tibère) was the Caesar that Jesus Christ "rendered unto." Caligula was notoriously depraved, curly-haired Domitia murdered her husband,

Hadrian popularized the beard, Trajan ruled the Empire at its peak, and Marcus Aurelius (Marc Aurèle) presided stoically over Rome's slow fall.

The pragmatic Romans (500 B.C.–A.D. 500) were great conquerors but bad artists. One area in which they excelled was realistic portrait busts, especially of their emperors, who were worshipped as gods on earth. Fortunately for us, the Romans also had a huge appetite for Greek statues and made countless copies. They took the Greek style and wrote it in capital letters, adding a veneer of sophistication to their homes, temples, baths, and government buildings.

The Roman rooms take you past several sarcophagi, an impressive mosaic floor that fills a massive courtyard, and beautiful wall-mounted mosaics from the ancient city of Antioch. Weary? Kick back and relax with the statues in the Etruscan Lounge (in Salle 18).

• *Continue clockwise through the Roman collection, eventually spilling out at the base of the stairs leading up to the first floor and the dramatic...*

Winged Victory of Samothrace
(*Victoire de Samothrace*, c. 190 B.C.)

This woman with wings, poised on the prow of a ship, once stood on a hilltop to commemorate a naval victory. Her clothes are windblown and

sea-sprayed, clinging close enough to her body to win a wet T-shirt contest. (Look at the detail in the folds of her dress around the navel, curving down to her hips.) Originally, her right arm was stretched high, celebrating the victory like a Super Bowl champion, waving a "we're number one" finger.

This is the *Venus de Milo* gone Hellenistic, from the time after the culture of Athens was spread around the Mediterranean by Alexander the Great (c. 325 B.C.). As *Victory* strides forward, the wind blows her and her wings back. Her feet are firmly on the ground, but her wings (and missing arms) stretch upward. She is a pillar of vertical strength, while the clothes curve and whip around her. These opposing forces create a feeling of great energy, making her the lightest two-ton piece of rock in captivity.

The earlier Golden Age Greeks might have considered this statue ugly. Her rippling excitement is a far cry from the dainty Parthenon maidens and the soft-focus beauty of *Venus*. And the statue's off-balance pose, like an unfinished melody, leaves you hanging. But Hellenistic Greeks loved these cliff-hanging scenes of real-life humans struggling to make their mark.

In the glass case nearby is *Victory*'s open right hand with an outstretched finger, found in 1950, a century after the statue itself was unearthed. When the French discovered this was in Turkey, they negotiated with the Turkish government for the rights to it. Considering all the other ancient treasures that France had looted from Turkey in the past, the Turks thought it only appropriate to give the French the finger.

• *Enter the octagonal room to the left as you face the* Winged Victory, *with Icarus bungee-jumping from the ceiling. Find a friendly window and look out toward the pyramid.*

View from the Octagonal Room: The Louvre as a Palace

The former royal palace, the Louvre was built in stages over eight centuries. On your right (the eastern Sully wing) was the original medieval fortress. About 500 yards to the west, in the now-open area past the pyramid and the triumphal arch, the Tuileries Palace used to stand. Succeeding kings tried to connect these two palaces, each one adding another section onto the long, skinny north and south wings. Finally, in 1852, after three centuries of building, the two palaces were connected, creating a rectangular Louvre. Nineteen years later, the Tuileries Palace burned down during a riot, leaving the U-shaped Louvre we see today.

The glass pyramid was designed by the American architect I. M. Pei (1989). Many Parisians hated the pyramid, just as they hated another new and controversial structure 100 years ago—the Eiffel Tower.

In the octagonal room, a plaque at the base of the dome explains that France's Revolutionary National Assembly (the same people who brought you the guillotine) founded this museum in 1793. What could be more logical? You behead the king, inherit his palace and art collection, open the doors to the masses, and *voilà!* You have Europe's first public museum.

• *From the octagonal room, enter the Apollo Gallery (Galerie d'Apollon).*

Apollo Gallery

This gallery gives us a feel for the Louvre as the glorious home of French kings (before Versailles). Imagine a chandelier-lit party in this room, drenched in stucco and gold leaf, with tapestries of leading Frenchmen and paintings featuring mythological and symbolic themes. The inlaid tables made from marble and semiprecious stones, and many other art objects, show the wealth of France, Europe's number-one power for two centuries.

Stroll past glass cases of royal dinnerware to the far end of the room. In a glass case are the crown jewels, including the jewel-studded crown of Louis XV and the 140-carat Regent Diamond, which once graced crowns worn by Louis XV, Louis XVI, and Napoleon.

• *The Italian collection (Peintures Italiennes) is on the other side of* Winged Victory. *Cross back in front of* Winged Victory *to Salle 1, where you'll find…*

Two Botticelli Frescoes
Look at the paintings on the wall to the left. These pure maidens, like colorized versions of the Parthenon Frieze, give us a preview of how ancient Greece would be "reborn" in the Renaissance.
• *Continue into large Salle 3.*

THE MEDIEVAL WORLD (1200–1500)

Cimabue—*The Madonna of the Angels* (1280)

During the Age of Faith (1200s), most every church in Europe had a painting like this one. Mary was a cult figure—even bigger than the 20th-century Madonna—adored and prayed to by the faithful for

bringing baby Jesus into the world. After the collapse of the Roman Empire (c. A.D. 500), medieval Europe was a poorer and more violent place, with the Christian Church as the only constant in troubled times.

Altarpieces like this followed the same formula: somber iconic faces, stiff poses, elegant folds in the robes, and generic angels. Violating 3-D space, the angels at the "back" of Mary's throne are the same size as those holding the front. These holy figures are laid flat on a gold background like cardboard cutouts, existing in a golden never never land, as though the faithful couldn't imagine them as flesh-and-blood humans inhabiting our dark and sinful earth.

Giotto—*St. Francis of Assisi Receiving the Stigmata* (c. 1290–1295)

Francis of Assisi (c. 1181–1226), a wandering Italian monk of renowned goodness, kneels on a rocky Italian hillside, pondering the pain of Christ's torture and execution.
Suddenly, he looks up, startled, to see Christ himself, with six wings, hovering above. Christ shoots lasers from his wounds to burn marks on the hands, feet, and side of the empathetic monk. Francis went on to breathe the spirit of the Renaissance into medieval Europe. His humble love of man and nature inspired artists like Giotto to portray real human beings with real emotions, living in a physical world of beauty.

Like a good filmmaker, Giotto (c. 1266–1337, JOT-toh) doesn't just *tell* us what happened, he *shows* us in the present tense, freezing the scene at its most dramatic moment. Though the perspective is crude—Francis' hut is smaller than he is, and Christ is somehow shooting at Francis while facing us—Giotto creates the illusion of 3-D, with a foreground (Francis), middle ground (his hut), and background (the hillside). Painting a 3-D world on a 2-D surface is tough, and after a millennium of Dark Ages, artists were rusty.

In the *predella* (the panel of paintings below the altarpiece), birds gather at Francis' feet to hear him talk about God. Giotto catches the late arrivals in midflight, an aston-ishing technical feat for an artist more than a century before the Renaissance. The simple gesture of Francis' companion speaks volumes about his amazement. Breaking the stiff, iconic mold for saints, Francis bends forward at the waist to talk to his fellow creatures. The diversity of the birds—"red and yellow, black and white"—symbolizes how all humankind is equally precious in God's sight. Meanwhile, the tree bends down symmetrically to catch a few words from the beloved hippie of Assisi.

• *The long Grand Gallery displays Italian Renaissance painting, some masterpieces, some not.*

ITALIAN RENAISSANCE

The Grand Gallery

Built in the late 1500s to connect the old palace with the Tuileries Palace, the Grand Gallery displays much of the Louvre's Italian Renaissance art. From the doorway, look to the far end and consider this challenge: I hold the world's record for the Grand Gallery Heel-Toe-Fun-Walk-Tourist-Slalom, going end to end in one minute, 58 seconds, two injured. Time yourself. Along the way, notice some of the...

Features of Italian Renaissance Painting

- **Religious:** Lots of Madonnas, children, martyrs, and saints.
- **Symmetrical:** The Madonnas are flanked by saints, two to the left, two to the right, and so on.
- **Realistic:** Real-life human features are especially obvious in the occasional portrait.

The Louvre—Grand Gallery

1 BOTTICELLI – Frescoes

2 CIMABUE – The Madonna of the Angels

3 GIOTTO – St. Francis of Assisi

4 MANTEGNA – St. Sebastian

5 LEONARDO – Virgin, Child & St. Anne

6 RAPHAEL – La Belle Jardinière

7 LEONARDO – Mona Lisa

8 VERONESE – The Marriage at Cana

9 DAVID – The Coronation of Napoleon

10 INGRES – La Grande Odalisque

11 GERICAULT – The Raft of the Medusa

12 DELACROIX – Liberty Leading the People

13 MICHELANGELO – Slaves

- **Three-Dimensional:** Every scene gets a spacious setting with a distant horizon.
- **Classical:** You'll see some Greek gods and classical nudes, but even Christian saints pose like Greek statues, and Mary is a *Venus* whose face and gestures embody all that was good in the Christian world.

Andrea Mantegna—*St. Sebastian* (c. 1480)

This isn't the patron saint of acupuncture. St. Sebastian was a

Christian martyr, although here he looks more like a classical Greek statue. Notice the *contrapposto* stance (all of his weight resting on one leg) and the Greek ruins scattered around him. His executioners look like ignorant medieval brutes bewildered by this enlightened Renaissance man. Italian artists were beginning to learn how to create human realism and earthly beauty on the canvas. Let the Renaissance begin.

• *Look for the following masterpieces by Leonardo and Raphael in the Grand Gallery.*

Leonardo da Vinci—*Virgin, Child, and St. Anne* (*La Vierge à l'Enfant Jésus avec Sainte-Anne*, c. 1510)

Three generations—grandmother, mother, and child—are arranged in a pyramid, with Anne's face as the peak and the lamb as the lower right corner. Within this balanced structure, Leonardo sets the figures in motion. Anne's legs are pointed to our left. (Is Anne *Mona*? Hmm.) Her daughter Mary, sitting on her lap, reaches to the right. Jesus looks at her playfully while turning away. The lamb pulls away from him. But even with all the twisting and turning, this is still a placid scene. It's as orderly as the geometrically perfect universe created by the Renaissance god.

There's a psychological kidney punch in this happy painting. Jesus, the picture of childish joy, is innocently playing with a lamb—the symbol of his inevitable sacrificial death.

The Louvre has the greatest collection of Leonardos in the world—five of them. Look for the neighboring *Virgin of the Rocks* and *John the Baptist*. Leonardo was the consummate Renaissance man. Musician, sculptor, engineer, scientist, and sometimes painter, he combined knowledge from all areas to create beauty. If he were alive today, he'd create a Unified Field Theory in physics—and set it to music.

• *You'll likely find Raphael's art on the right side of the Grand Gallery, just past the statue of* Diana the Huntress.

Raphael—*La Belle Jardinière* (1507)

Raphael (roff-eye-ELL) perfected the style Leonardo pioneered. This configuration of Madonna, Child, and John the Baptist is also a balanced pyramid with hazy grace and beauty. Mary is a mountain of maternal tenderness (the title translates as "The Beautiful Gardener"), as she eyes her son with a knowing look and holds his hand in a

LOUVRE

Italian Renaissance
(1400–1600)

A thousand years after Rome fell, plunging Europe into the Dark Ages, the Greek ideal of beauty was reborn in 15th-century Italy. The Renaissance—or "rebirth" of the culture of ancient Greece and Rome—was a cultural boom that changed people's thinking about every aspect of life. In politics, it meant democracy. In religion, it meant a move away from Church dominance and toward the assertion of man (humanism) and a more personal faith. Science and secular learning were revived after centuries of superstition and ignorance. In architecture, it was a return to the balanced columns and domes of Greece and Rome.

In painting, the Renaissance meant realism, and for the Italians, realism was spelled "3-D." Artists rediscovered the beauty of nature and the human body. With pictures of beautiful people in harmonious, 3-D surroundings, they expressed the optimism and confidence of this new age.

gesture of union. Jesus looks up innocently, standing *contrapposto* like a chubby Greek statue. Baby John the Baptist kneels lovingly at Jesus' feet, holding a cross that hints at his playmate's sacrificial death. The interplay of gestures and gazes gives the masterpiece both intimacy and cohesiveness, while Raphael's blended brushstrokes varnish the work with an iridescent smoothness.

With Raphael, the Greek ideal of beauty—reborn in the Renaissance—reached its peak. His work spawned so many imitators who cranked out sickly sweet, generic Madonnas that we often take him for granted. Don't. This is the real thing.

• *The* Mona Lisa (La Joconde) *is near the statue of* Diana, *in Salle 6—the Salle des Etats—midway down the Grand Gallery on the right. After several years and a €5 million renovation,* Mona *is alone behind glass on her own false wall. Six million heavy-breathing people crowd in each year to glimpse the most ogled painting in the world. (You can't miss her. Just follow the signs and the people…it's the only painting you can hear. With all the groveling crowds, you can even smell it.)*

Leonardo da Vinci—*Mona Lisa* (1503-1506)

Leonardo was already an old man when François I invited him to France. Determined to pack light, he took only a few paintings with him. One was a portrait of a Lisa del Giocondo, the wife of a wealthy Florentine merchant. When Leonardo arrived, François immediately fell in love with the painting, making it the centerpiece of the small collection of Italian masterpieces that would, in three centuries, become the Louvre museum. He called it *La Gioconda (La Joconde* in French)—both her last name and a play on the Italian word for "happy woman." We know it as a contraction of the Italian for "my lady Lisa"—*Mona Lisa.*

Mona may disappoint you. She's smaller than you'd expect, darker, engulfed in a huge room, and hidden behind a glaring pane of glass. So, you ask, "Why all the hubbub?" Let's take a closer look. Like any lover, you've got to take her for what she is, not what you'd like her to be.

The famous smile attracts you first. Leonardo used a hazy technique called *sfumato,* blurring the edges of *Mona*'s mysterious smile. Try as you might, you can never quite see the corners of her mouth. Is she happy? Sad? Tender? Or is it a cynical supermodel's smirk? All visitors read it differently, projecting their own mood onto her enigmatic face. *Mona* is a Rorschach inkblot...so, how are you feeling?

Now look past the smile and the eyes that really do follow you (most eyes in portraits do) to some of the subtle Renaissance elements that make this painting work. The body is surprisingly massive and statue-like, a perfectly balanced pyramid turned at an angle, so we can see its mass. Her arm is resting lightly on the chair's armrest, almost on the level of the frame itself, like she's sitting in a window looking out at us. The folds of her sleeves and her gently folded hands are remarkably realistic and relaxed. The typical Leonardo landscape shows distance by getting hazier and hazier.

Though the portrait is most likely of Lisa del Giocondo, the 20-something wife of a Florentine businessman, there are many hypotheses, including the idea that it's Leonardo himself. Or she might be the Mama Lisa. A recent infrared scan revealed that she has a barely visible veil over her dress, which may mean (in the custom of the day) that she had just had a baby.

The overall mood is one of balance and serenity, but there's also an element of mystery. *Mona*'s smile and long-distance beauty are subtle and elusive, tempting but always just out of reach, like strands of a street singer's melody drifting through the Métro tunnel. *Mona* doesn't knock your socks off, but she winks at the patient viewer.

• *Before leaving* Mona, *stand back and just observe the paparazzi scene. The huge canvas opposite* Mona *is...*

Paolo Veronese—*The Marriage at Cana* (1562–1563)

Stand 10 steps away from this enormous canvas to where it just fills your field of vision, and suddenly...you're in a party! Help yourself to a glass of wine. This is the Renaissance love of beautiful things gone hog-wild. Venetian artists like Veronese painted the good life of rich, happy-go-lucky Venetian merchants.

In a spacious setting of Renaissance architecture, colorful lords and ladies, decked out in their fanciest duds, feast on a great spread of food and drink, while the musicians fuel the fires of good fun. Servants prepare and serve the food, jesters play, and animals roam. In the upper left, a dog and his master look on. A sturdy line-backer in yellow pours wine out of a jug (right foreground). The man in white samples some wine and thinks, "Hmm, not bad," while nearby a ferocious cat battles a lion. The wedding couple at the far left is almost forgotten.

Believe it or not, this is a religious work showing the wedding celebration where Jesus turned water into wine. And there's Jesus in the dead center of 130 frolicking figures, wondering if maybe wine coolers might not have been a better choice. With true Renaissance optimism, Venetians pictured Christ as a party animal, someone who loved the created world as much as they did.

Now, let's hear it for the band! On bass—the bad cat with the funny hat—Titian the Venetian! And joining him on viola—Crazy Veronese!

• *Exit behind* Mona *into the Salle Denon. The dramatic Romantic room is to your left, and the grand Neoclassical room is to your right (see the map on page 113). These two rooms feature the most exciting French canvases in the Louvre. In the Neoclassical room (Salle Daru), kneel before the largest canvas in the Louvre.*

FRENCH NEOCLASSICISM (1780–1850)

Jacques-Louis David—*The Coronation of Napoleon* (1806–1807)

Napoleon holds aloft an imperial crown. This common-born son of immigrants is about to be crowned emperor of a "New Rome." He has just made his wife, Josephine, the empress, and she kneels at his feet. Seated behind Napoleon is the pope, who journeyed from Rome to place the imperial crown on his head. But Napoleon feels that no one is worthy of the task. At the last moment, he shrugs the pope aside, grabs the crown, holds it up for all to see...and crowns himself. The pope looks p.o.'d.

After the French people decapitated their king during the Revolution (1793), their fledgling democracy floundered in chaos. France was united by a charismatic, brilliant, temperamental, upstart general who kept his feet on the ground, his eyes on the horizon, and his hand in his coat—Napoleon Bonaparte. Napoleon quickly conquered most of Europe and insisted on being made emperor (not merely king). The painter David (dah-VEED) recorded the coronation for posterity.

The radiant woman in the gallery in the background center wasn't actually there. Napoleon's mother couldn't make it to see her boy become the most powerful man in Europe, but he had David paint her in anyway. (There's a key on the frame telling who's who in the picture.)

The traditional place of French coronations was the ultra-Gothic Notre-Dame cathedral. But Napoleon wanted a setting that would reflect the glories of Greece and the grandeur of Rome. So, interior decorators erected stage sets of Greek columns and Roman arches to give the cathedral the architectural political correctness you see in this painting. (The *pietà* statue on the right edge of the painting is still in Notre-Dame today.)

David was the new emperor's official painter and propagandist, in charge of color-coordinating the costumes and flags for public ceremonies and spectacles. (Find his self-portrait with curly gray hair in the *Coronation*, way up in the second balcony, peeking around the tassel directly above Napoleon's crown.) His "Neoclassical" style influenced French fashion. Take a look at his *Madame Juliet Récamier* portrait on the opposite wall, showing a modern Parisian woman in ancient garb and Pompeii hairstyle reclining on a Roman couch. Nearby paintings, such as *The Oath of the Horatii (Le Serment des Horaces)*, are fine examples of Neoclassicism, with Greek subjects, patriotic sentiment, and a clean, simple style.

• *As you double back toward the Romantic room, stop at...*

Jean-Auguste-Dominique Ingres—
La Grande Odalisque (1819)

Take *Venus de Milo*, turn her around, lay her down, and stick a hash pipe next to her, and you have the *Grande Odalisque*. OK, maybe you'd have to add a vertebra or two.

Using clean, polished, sculptural lines, Ingres (ang-gruh, with a soft "gruh") exaggerates the S-curve of a standing Greek nude. As in the *Venus de Milo*, rough folds of cloth set off her smooth skin. The face, too, has a touch of *Venus'* idealized features (or like Raphael's kindergarten teacher), taking nature and improving on it. Contrast the cool colors of this statue-like nude with Titian's golden girls. Ingres preserves *Venus'* backside for posterior—I mean, posterity.

• *Cross back through the Salle Denon (where you might spot a painting high up titled* The Death of Walter Mondale) *and into a room gushing with...*

FRENCH ROMANTICISM (1800–1850)

Théodore Géricault—*The Raft of the Medusa* (*Le Radeau de la Méduse,* 1819)

In the artistic war between hearts and minds, the heart style was known as Romanticism. Stressing motion and emotion, it was the flip side of

cool, balanced Neoclassicism, though they both flourished in the early 1800s.

What better setting for an emotional work than a ship-wreck? Clinging to a raft is a tangle of bodies and lunatics sprawled over each other. The scene writhes with agitated, ominous motion— the ripple of muscles, churning clouds, and choppy seas. On the right is a deathly green corpse dangling overboard. The face of the man at left, cradling a dead body, says it all—the despair of spending weeks stranded in the middle of nowhere.

This painting was based on the actual sinking of the ship *Medusa* off the coast of Africa in 1816. About 150 people packed onto the raft. After floating in the open seas for 12 days—suffering hardship and hunger, even resorting to cannibalism—only 15 survived. The story was made to order for a painter determined to shock the public and arouse its emotions. That painter was young Géricault (ZHAIR-ee-ko). He interviewed survivors and honed his craft, sketching dead bodies in the morgue and the twisted faces of lunatics in asylums, capturing the moment when all hope is lost.

But wait. There's a stir in the crowd. Someone has spotted something. The bodies rise up in a pyramid of hope, culminating in a flag wave. They signal frantically, trying to catch the attention of the tiny ship on the horizon, their last desperate hope...which did finally save them. Géricault uses rippling movement and powerful colors to catch us up in the excitement. If art controls your heart-beat, this is a masterpiece.

LOUVRE

Eugène Delacroix—*Liberty Leading the People* (*La Liberté Guidant le Peuple*, 1830)

The year is 1830. King Charles has just issued the 19th-century equivalent of the "Patriot Act," and his subjects are angry. The Parisians take to the streets once again, *Les Miz*–style, to fight royalist oppressors. The people triumph—replacing the king with Louis-Philippe, who is happy to rule within the constraints of a modern constitution. There's a hard-bitten proletarian with a sword (far left), an intellectual with a top hat and a sawed-off shotgun, and even a little boy brandishing pistols.

Leading them on through the smoke and over the dead and dying is the figure of Liberty, a strong woman waving the French flag. Does this symbol of victory look familiar? It's the *Winged Victory*, wingless and topless.

To stir our emotions, Delacroix (del-ah-kwah) uses only three major colors—the red, white, and blue of the French flag. France is the symbol of modern democracy, and this painting has long stirred its citizens' passion for liberty. The French weren't the first to adopt democracy (Americans were), nor are they the best working example of it, but they've had to try harder to achieve it than any other country. No sooner would they throw one king or dictator out

then they'd get another. They're now working on their fifth republic.

This symbol of freedom is a fitting tribute to the Louvre, the first museum ever opened to the common rabble of humanity. The good things in life don't belong only to a small wealthy part of society, but to everyone. The motto of France is *Liberté, Egalité, Fraternité*—liberty, equality, and the brotherhood of all.

• *Exit the room at the far end (past a café) and go downstairs, where you'll bump into the bum of a large, twisting male nude looking like he's just waking up after a thousand-year nap.*

MORE ITALIAN RENAISSANCE

Michelangelo—*Slaves* (1513–1515)

These two statues by earth's greatest sculptor are a fitting end to this museum—works that bridge the ancient and modern worlds. Michelangelo, like his fellow Renaissance artists, learned from the Greeks. The perfect anatomy, twisting poses, and idealized faces appear as if they could have been done 2,000 years earlier.

The so-called *Dying Slave* (also called the *Sleeping Slave*, looking

LOUVRE

like he should be stretched out on a sofa) twists listlessly against his T-shirt-like bonds, revealing his smooth skin. Compare the polished detail of the rippling, bulging left arm with the sketchy details of the face and neck. With Michelangelo, the body does the talking. This is probably the most sensual nude ever done by the master of the male body.

The *Rebellious Slave* fights against his bondage. His shoulders rotate one way, while his head and leg turn the other. He looks upward, straining to get free. He even seems to be trying to free himself from the rock he's made of. Michelangelo said that his purpose was to carve away the marble to reveal the figures God put inside. This slave shows the agony of that process and the ecstasy of the result.

• *Tour over! These two may be slaves of the museum, but you are free to go. You've seen the essential Louvre. To leave the museum, head for the end of the hall, turn right, and follow signs down the escalators to the* Sortie.

But, of course, there's so much more. After a break (or on a second visit), consider a stroll through a few rooms of the Richelieu wing, which contain some of the Louvre's oldest and biggest pieces. Bible students, amateur archaeologists, and Iraq War vets may find the collection especially interesting.

RICHELIEU WING

Oriental Antiquities (Antiquités Orientales)

Saddam Hussein is only the latest iron-fisted, palace-building conqueror to fall in Iraq's long history, which stretches back to the dawn of civilization. Civilization began 6,000 years ago in Iraq, between the Tigris and Euphrates Rivers, in the area called the Fertile Crescent.

In the Richelieu wing, you can sweep quickly through 2,000 years of Iraq's ancient history, enjoying some of the Louvre's biggest and oldest artifacts. See how each new civilization toppled the previous one—pulling down its statues, destroying its palaces, looting its cultural heritage, and replacing it with victory monuments of its own...only to be toppled again by the next wave of history.

• *From under the pyramid, enter the Richelieu wing. Show your ticket, then take the first right. Go up one flight of stairs and one escalator to the ground floor* (rez-de-chaussée)*, where you'll find the* Antiquites Orientales. *Walk straight off the escalator, enter Salle 1-a (Mesopotamie Archaïque), and come face-to-face with fragments of the broken...*

Stela of the Vultures (Stele de victoire d'Eannatum, roi de Lagash, c. 2450 B.C.)

As old as the pyramids, this stela (ceremonial stone pillar) may be the oldest depiction of a historical event—the battle between the city of Lagash (100 miles north of modern Basra) and its archrival, Umma.

Bearded King Eannatum waves the eagle flag of Lagash with one hand, while with the other he clubs a puny enemy soldier trapped in a battle net, making his enemies pledge allegiance to Lagash's gods.

Circle around to the flip side of the stela for the rest of the story, "reading" from top to bottom. Top level: Behind

a wall of shields, a phalanx of helmeted soldiers advances, trampling the enemy underfoot. They pile the corpses (right), while vultures swoop down from above to pluck the remains. Middle level: The king waves to the crowd from his chariot in the victory parade. Bottom level: They dig a mass grave—one of 20 for the 36,000 enemy dead—while a priest (top of the fragment) gives thanks to the gods. A tethered ox (see his big head tied to a stake) is about to become a burnt sacrifice.

The inscription on the stela is in cuneiform, the world's first written language, invented by the Sumerians.

• *Continue into Salle 1-b, with the blissful statue of...*

Ebih-il, The Superintendent of Mari (c. 2400 B.C.)

Bald, bearded, blue-eyed Ebih-il (his name is inscribed on his shoul-

der) sits in his fleece skirt, folds his hands reverently across his chest, and gazes rapturously into space, dreaming of...Ishtar. Ebih-il was a priest in the goddess Ishtar's temple, and the statue is dedicated to her.

Ishtar was the chief goddess of many Middle Eastern peoples. As goddess of both love and war, she was a favorite of horny soldiers. She was a giver of life (this statue is dedicated "to

The Louvre—Oriental Antiquities

1. Stela of the Vultures
2. Ebih-il
3. Various Gudea Statues
4. Stela of Naram-Sin
5. Law Codex of Hammurabi
6. Winged Bulls
7. King Sargon II & a Dignitary
8. Transport of the Cedars of Lebanon
9. Scenes of Court Life

ROOM 3

ROOM 2

ROOM 4

ROOM 1-A   ROOM 1-B

FROM ESCALATOR

||| = STAIRS

PYRAMID

DCH

Ishtar the virile"), yet also miraculously a virgin. She was also a great hunter with bow and arrow, and a great lover ("Her lips are sweet...her figure is beautiful, her eyes are brilliant...women and men adore her," sang the *Hymn to Ishtar*, c. 1600 B.C.).

Ebih-il adores her eternally with his eyes made of seashells and lapis lazuli. The smile on his face reflects the pleasure the goddess has just given him, perhaps through one of the sacred prostitutes who resided in Ishtar's Temple.

• *Go up the five steps behind* Ebih-il, *and turn left into Salle 2, containing a dozen statues, all of a man named...*

Gudea, Prince of Lagash (c. 2125–2110 B.C.)

Gudea (r. 2141–2122 B.C.), in his wool stocking cap, folds his hands and prays to the gods to save his people from invading barbarians. One of Sumeria's last great rulers, the peaceful and pious Gudea (his name means "the destined") rebuilt temples (where these statues once stood) to thank the gods for their help.

• *Behind you, find the rosy-colored...*

Stela of Naram-Sin (*Stele de victoire de Naram-Sin, roi d'Akkad*, c. 2230 B.C.)

After a millennium of prosperity, Sumeria was plundered (c. 2250 B.C.), and Akkadia became the new king of the mountain. Here, King Naram-Sin climbs up to the sunny heavens, crowned with the horned helmet of a god. His soldiers look up to admire him as he tramples his enemies. Next to him, a victim tries to remove a spear from his neck, while another pleads to the conqueror for mercy.

• *Exit Salle 2 at the far end and enter Salle 3, with the large black stela of Hammurabi.*

Law Codex of Hammurabi, King of Babylon (c. 1760 B.C.)

Hammurabi (r. c. 1792–1750 B.C.) established the next great civilization, ruling as King of Babylon (50 miles south of modern-day Baghdad). He proclaimed 282 laws,

all inscribed on this eight-foot black basalt stela—one of the first formal legal documents, four centuries before the Ten Commandments. Stelas such as this likely dotted Hammurabi's empire, and this one may have stood in Babylon before being moved to Susa, Iran.

At the top of the stela, Hammurabi (standing and wearing Gudea's hat of kingship) receives the scepter of judgment from the god of justice and the sun, who radiates flames from his shoulders. The inscription begins, "When Anu the Sublime...called me, Hammurabi, by name...I did right, and brought about the well-being of the oppressed."

Next come the laws, scratched in cuneiform down the length of the stela, some 3,500 lines reading right to left. The laws cover very specific situations, everything from lying, theft, and trade to marriage and medical malpractice. The legal innovation was the immediate retribution for wrongdoing, often with poetic justice. Here's a sample:

#1: If any man ensnares another falsely, he shall be put to death.

#57: If your sheep graze another man's land, you must repay 20 gur of grain.

#129: If a couple is caught in adultery, they shall both be tied up and thrown in the water.

#137: If you divorce your wife, you must pay alimony and child support.

#218: A surgeon who bungles an operation shall have his hands cut off.

Just Enough Geography and History for This Tour

The northern half of Iraq is mountainous, and the southern half is the delta of the Tigris and Euphrates Rivers. Baghdad sits roughly in between north and south, along the Tigris. The Sumerians inhabited the south, the Assyrians the north, and the Akkadians and Babylonians the center, around Baghdad.

Here's a brief timeline:

3500–2400 B.C. Sumerian city-states flourish between the Tigris and Euphrates Rivers. Sumerians invent writing.

2300 B.C. Akkadians invade Sumer.

1750 B.C. Hammurabi establishes first Babylonian empire.

710 B.C. Sargon II rules over a vast Assyrian-controlled empire, encompassing modern Iraq, Israel, Syria, and Egypt.

612 B.C. Babylonians revolt against the Assyrians and destroy the Assyrian capital of Nineveh (300 miles north of Baghdad), then build their own near Baghdad.

#282: If a slave shall say, "You are not my master," the master can cut off the slave's ear.

The most quoted laws—summing up the spirit of ancient Middle Eastern justice—are #196 ("If a man put out the eye of another man, his eye shall be put out") and #200 (a tooth for a tooth).

• *Make a U-turn to the right, entering the large Salle 4, dominated by colossal winged bulls with human heads. These sculptures—including five winged bulls and many relief panels along the walls—are from the...*

Palace of Sargon II

Sargon II, the Assyrian king (r. 721–705 B.C.), spared no expense on his palace (see various reconstructions of the palace on plaques around the room). In Assyrian society, the palace of the king—not the temple of the gods—was the focus of life, and each ruler demonstrated his authority with large residences.

Sargon II actually built a whole new city for his palace, just north of the traditional capital of Nineveh (modern-day Mosul). He called it Dur Sharrukin ("Sargonburg"), and the city's vast dimensions were 4,000 cubits by—oh, excuse me—it covered about 150 football fields pieced together. The whole city was built on a raised, artificial mound, and the 25-acre palace itself sat even higher, surrounded by walls, with courtyards, temples, the king's residence, and a wedding cake–shaped temple (called a ziggurat) dedicated to the god Sin.

• *Start with the two big bulls supporting a (reconstructed) arch.*

Winged Bulls (C. 710 B.C.)

These 30-ton, 14-foot alabaster bulls with human faces once guarded the entrance to the throne room of Sargon II. A visitor to the palace back then could have looked over the bulls' heads and seen a 15-story ziggurat (stepped-pyramid temple) towering overhead. The winged bulls were guardian spirits to keep out demons and intimidate liberals.

Between their legs are cuneiform inscriptions such as: "I, Sargon, King of the Universe, built palaces for my royal residence.... I had winged bulls with human heads carved from great blocks of mountain stone, and I placed them at the doors facing the four winds as powerful divine guardians.... My creation amazed all who gazed upon it."

• *We'll see a few relief panels from the palace, working counterclockwise around the room. Start with the panel just to the left of the two big bulls (as you face them). Find the bearded, earringed man in whose image the bulls were made.*

The Assyrians

This Semitic people from the agriculturally challenged hills of northern Iraq became traders and conquerors, not farmers. They conquered their southern neighbors and dominated the Middle East for 300 years (c. 900–600 B.C.).

Their strength came from a superb army (chariots, mounted cavalry, and siege engines), a policy of terrorism against enemies ("I tied their heads to tree trunks all around the city," reads a royal inscription), ethnic cleansing and mass deportations of the vanquished, and efficient administration (roads and express postal service). They have been called "The Romans of the East."

King Sargon II and a Dignitary
(*Le roi Sargon II et un haut dignitaire*, c. 710 B.C.)

Sargon II, wearing a fez-like crown with a cone on the top and straps down the back, cradles his scepter and raises his staff to receive a for-

eign ambassador who's come to pay tribute. Sargon II controlled a vast empire, consisting of modern-day Iraq and extending westward to the Mediterranean and Egypt.

Before becoming emperor, Sargon II was a conquering general who invaded Israel (2 Kings 17:1–6). After a three-year siege, he took Jerusalem and deported much of the population, inspiring the legends of the "Lost" Ten Tribes. The prophet Isaiah saw him as God's tool to punish the sinful Israelites, "to seize loot and snatch plunder, and to trample them down like mud in the streets" (Isaiah 10:6).

• *On the wall to the left of Sargon are four panels depicting the...*

Transport of the Cedars of Lebanon
(*Transport du bois de cèdre du Liban*)

Boats carry the finest quality logs for Sargon II's palace, crossing a wavy sea populated with fish, turtles, crabs, and mermen. The transport process is described in the Bible (1 Kings 5:9): "My men will haul them down from Lebanon to the sea, and I will float them in rafts to the place you specify."

LOUVRE

Ancient Places in Today's Iraq

Lagash, the ancient city of Prince Gudea (see page 123), is near modern **Shatra,** in southeast Iraq. In March of 2003, American invasion forces met some of their stiffest resistance in Shatra (before the fall of Baghdad). "Chemical Ali"—Saddam's cousin and the Ace of Spades in America's deck of most-wanted Iraqis—was thought to be holed up in the city; he eluded capture for a few more months. After shelling Shatra with planes, helicopters, and tanks, US Marines took the town and were met by Iraqis with signs saying *Welcome to Iraq.*

The Stela of the Vultures (on page 122) depicts battles between Lagash and Umma, near modern **An Nasiriyah.** It was there that, in March of 2003, a US convoy took a wrong turn and was ambushed by Iraqis, and Pfc. Jessica Lynch was captured. Nine days later, a US helicopter full of soldiers stormed the An Nasiriyah hospital, and Lynch was airlifted away to a hero's welcome. Later reports revealed that she'd suffered wounds from the crash of her truck during the attack, and that she was being tended to in the Iraqi hospital.

Though discovered in Iran, *Hammurabi's Code* may once have stood in ancient Babylon, 50 miles south of Baghdad in **Al Hillah.** On February 28, 2005, a suicide car bomb detonated in a crowd of Iraqi police officers, killing 125, the deadliest such blast yet. On March 6, 2007, another 114 people died here when two suicide bombers blew themselves up in a crowd of pilgrims—examples of the new tactic of warfare that emerged in the Iraq War.

Sargon II built his palace outside **Mosul,** now an oil-rich Kurdish center in northern Iraq. After US soldiers drove insurgents from Fallujah in the fall of 2004, many resettled in Mosul. In May of 2008, a US-backed offensive called Operation Lion's Roar was launched against this stronghold of insurgents.

• *Continue counterclockwise around the room—past more big winged animals, past the huge hero Gilgamesh crushing a lion—until you reach more relief panels. These depict...*

Scenes of Court Life

The brown, eroded gypsum panels we see were originally painted and varnished. Placed side by side, they would have stretched over a mile. The panels read like a comic strip, showing the king's men parading in to serve him.

First, soldiers *(Guerrier en armée)* sheathe their swords and fold their hands reverently. A winged spirit prepares them to enter the king's presence by shaking a pine cone to anoint them with holy perfume. Next, servants (see photo on previous page) hurry to the throne room with the king's dinner, carrying his table, chair, and bowl. Other servants ready the king's horses and chariots.

From Sargon to Saddam

Sargon II's palace remained unfinished and was later burned and buried. Sargon's great Assyrian empire dissolved over the next few generations. When the Babylonians revolted and conquered their northern neighbors (612 B.C.), the whole Middle East applauded. As the Bible put it: "Nineveh is in ruins—who will mourn for her?.... Everyone who hears the news claps his hands at your fall, for who has not felt your endless cruelty?" (Nahum 3:7, 19).

The new capital was Babylon (50 miles south of modern Baghdad), ruled by King Nebuchadnezzar, who conquered Judea (586 B.C., the Bible's "Babylonian Captivity") and built a palace with the Hanging Gardens, one of the Seven Wonders of the World.

Over the succeeding centuries, Babylon/Baghdad fell to Persians (539 B.C.), Greeks (Alexander the Great, 331 B.C.), Persians again (second century B.C.), Arab Muslims (A.D. 634), Mongol hordes (Genghis Khan's grandson, 1258), Iranians (1502), Ottoman Turks (1535), British-controlled kings (1921), and military regimes (1958), the most recent headed by Saddam Hussein (1979).

After toppling Saddam Hussein in 2003, George W. Bush declared, "Mission accomplished!" Five thousand years of invasions, violence, and regime change, as well as current events, suggest otherwise.

LOUVRE

ORSAY
MUSEUM TOUR

Musée d'Orsay

The Musée d'Orsay (mew-zay dor-say) houses French art of the 1800s and early 1900s (specifically, 1848–1914), picking up where the Louvre's art collection leaves off. For us, that means Impressionism, the art of sun-dappled fields, bright colors, and crowded Parisian cafés. The Orsay houses the best general collection anywhere of Manet, Monet, Renoir, Degas, Van Gogh, Cézanne, and Gauguin. If you like Impressionism, visit this museum. If you don't like Impressionism, visit this museum. I personally find it a more enjoyable and rewarding place than the Louvre. Sure, ya gotta see the *Mona Lisa* and *Venus de Milo*, but after you get your gottas out of the way, enjoy the Orsay.

ORIENTATION

Cost: €8, €5 after 16:15 and on Sun, free first Sun of month, covered by Museum Pass. Tickets are good all day.

Hours: Tue–Sun 9:30–18:00, Thu until 21:45 year-round, last entry one hour before closing (45 min before on Thu), closed Mon. The Impressionist galleries begin closing 45 minutes early, frustrating unwary visitors. Tuesdays are particularly crowded, since the Louvre is closed.

Free Entry near Closing Time: Right when the ticket booth stops selling tickets (Tue–Wed and Fri–Sun at 17:00, Thu at 21:00), you're welcome to scoot in free of charge. (They won't let you in much after that, however.) Remember that the Impressionist galleries upstairs start shutting down first, so go there right away.

Getting There: The museum sits above the RER-C stop called Musée d'Orsay. The nearest Métro stop is Solférino, three blocks southeast of the Orsay. Bus #69 from the Marais neighborhood stops at the museum on the river side (quai Anatole France); from the rue Cler area, it stops behind the museum on the rue du Bac. From

Orsay Ground Floor—Overview

TO LOUVRE
(15 MIN. WALK)

BUS #69
FROM RUE CLER
TO LOUVRE + MARAIS

Ⓑ

PONT ← ROYAL

← RUE DU BAC

SEINE RIVER

Ⓑ

🄱

QUAI ANATOLE FRANCE

ESCALATOR UP TO
IMPRESSIONISM
↓

MANET

REALISM

CONSERVATIVE ART

START

BOOKSTORE

← TICKET TAKER

BOOKS

SECURITY ↘

DCH

ENTRANCE

← FOR PASS HOLDERS

FOR NON-PASS HOLDERS

BUS #69
FROM MARAIS
TO
RUE CLER +
EIFFEL
TOWER

Ⓑ

Ⓣ

MUSÉE D'ORSAY

Ⓡ

RUE DE LA
LÉGION D'HONNEUR

RUE DE
BELLECHASSE

SOLFERINO
PED. BRIDGE

← TO
ORANGERIE

→
TO Ⓜ SOLFERINO
(5 MIN. WALK)
+ RODIN MUSEUM

Ⓑ Bus #69 Stop   🄱 Batobus Boat Stop
Ⓜ Metro Station   Ⓣ Taxi Stand
Ⓡ RER Stop   → One-Way Street

ORSAY MUSEUM

the Louvre, catch bus #69 along rue de Rivoli; otherwise, it's a lovely 15-minute walk through the Tuileries Garden and across the river on the pedestrian bridge. The museum is at 1 rue de la Légion d'Honneur. A taxi stand is in front of the entrance on quai Anatole France. The Batobus boat also makes a stop here (see page 35).

Getting In: As you face the front of the museum from rue de la Légion d'Honneur (with the river on your left), passholders enter on the right side of the museum (Entrance C), and ticket purchasers enter along the river side (Entrance A).

Information: The booth inside the entrance provides free floor plans in English. Tel. 01 40 49 48 14, www.musee-orsay.fr.

Tours: Audioguides cost €6. English guided tours usually run daily (except Sun) at 11:30 (€7/90 min). Some tours are occasionally offered at other times (inquire when you arrive). I recommend the self-guided tour described below, which is also available as a free audioguide tour for people with an iPod or other MP3 player (download from www.ricksteves.com or iTunes).

Length of This Tour: Allow two hours.

Cloakroom *(Vestiaire):* Checking bags or coats is free. Day bags (but nothing big) are allowed in the museum. No valuables can be stored in checked bags. The cloakroom clerk might ask you in French not to check cameras, passports, or anything particularly precious.

Cuisine Art: There's a pricey but *très* elegant restaurant on the second floor, with affordable tea and coffee served 15:00–17:30 (daily except Thu). A simple fifth-floor café is sandwiched between the Impressionists; above it is an easy self-service place with sandwiches and drinks.

Photography: Photography without a flash is allowed.

Starring: Manet, Monet, Renoir, Degas, Van Gogh, Cézanne, and Gauguin.

THE TOUR BEGINS

Gare d'Orsay: The Old Train Station

• *Pick up a free English map upon entering, buy your ticket, and check your bag. Belly up to the stone balustrade overlooking the main floor, and orient yourself.*

Trains used to run right under our feet down the center of the gallery. This former train station, or *gare,* barely escaped the wrecking ball in the 1970s, when the French realized it'd be a great place to house the enormous collections of 19th-century art scattered throughout the city.

The main floor has early 19th-century art—as usual, Conservative on the right, Realism on the left. Upstairs (not visible from here) is the core of the collection— the Impressionist rooms. If you're pressed for time, go directly there (see directions following "Opéra Exhibit" on page 138). We'll start with the Conservatives and early rebels on the ground floor, then head upstairs to see how a few visionary young artists bucked the system and revolutionized the art world, paving the way for the 20th century. We'll end the tour with the "other" Orsay on the mezzanine level. Clear as Seine water? *Bien.*

If a painting isn't where I say it is, it's probably on loan (a common occurrence) or being restored—though it's wise to ask a museum guard if it's been moved to another location within the Orsay.

• *Walk down the steps to the main floor, a gallery filled with statues.*

CONSERVATIVE ART

Main Gallery Statues

No, this isn't ancient Greece. These statues are from the same era as the Theory of Relativity. It's the Conservative art of the French schools that was so popular throughout the 19th century. It was well-liked for its beauty. The balanced poses, perfect anatomy, sweet faces, curving lines, and gleaming white stone—all of this is very appealing. (I'll bad-mouth it later, but for now appreciate the exquisite craftsmanship of this "perfect" art.)

• *Take your first right into the small Room 1, marked "Ingres et l'Ingrisme." Look for a nude woman with a pitcher of water.*

❶ Jean-Auguste-Dominique Ingres— *The Source (La Source, 1856)*

Let's start where the Louvre left off. Ingres (ang-gruh, with a soft "gruh"), who helped cap the Louvre collection, championed a Neoclassical style. *The Source* is virtually a Greek statue on canvas. Like *Venus de Milo*, she's a balance of opposite motions—her hips tilt one way, her breasts the other; one arm goes up, the other down; the water falling from the pitcher matches the fluid curve of her body. Her skin is porcelain-smooth, painted with seamless brushstrokes.

ORSAY MUSEUM

Ingres worked on this painting over the course of 35 years and considered it his "image of perfection." Famous in its day, *The Source* influenced many artists whose classical statues and paintings are in this museum.

In this and the next few rooms, you'll see more of these visions of idealized beauty—nude women in languid poses, Greek myths, and so on. The Romantics, like Eugène Delacroix, added bright colors, movement, and emotion to the classical coolness of Ingres.

• *Walk uphill (quickly, this is background stuff) to the last room (Room 3), and find a pastel blue-green painting.*

The Orsay's "19th Century"
(1848–1914)

Einstein and Geronimo. Abraham Lincoln and Karl Marx. The train, the bicycle, the horse and buggy, the automobile, and the balloon. Freud and Dickens. Darwin's *Origin of Species* and the Church's Immaculate Conception. Louis Pasteur and Billy the Kid. Ty Cobb and V. I. Lenin.

The 19th century was a mix of old and new, side by side. Europe was entering the modern Industrial Age, with cities, factories, rapid transit, instant communication, and global networks. At the same time, it clung to the past with traditional, rural—almost medieval—attitudes and morals.

According to the Orsay, the "19th century" began in 1848 with the socialist and democratic revolutions (Marx's *Communist Manifesto*). It ended in 1914 with the pull of an assassin's trigger, which ignited World War I and ushered in the modern world. The museum shows art that is also both old and new, conservative and revolutionary.

❷ Alexandre Cabanel—
The Birth of Venus (*La Naissance de Vénus*, 1863)

Cabanel lays Ingres' *The Source* on her back. This goddess is a perfect fantasy, an orgasm of beauty. The Love Goddess stretches back seductively, recently birthed from the ephemeral foam of the wave. This is art of a pre-Freudian society, when sex was dirty and mysterious and had to be exalted into a more pure and divine form. The sex drive was channeled into an

acute sense of beauty. French folk would literally swoon in ecstasy before these works of art.

The art world of Cabanel's day was dominated by two conservative institutions: the Academy (the state-funded art school) and the Salon, where works were exhibited to the buying public. The public loved Cabanel's *Venus* (and Napoleon III purchased it).

Get a feel for the ideal beauty and refined emotion of these Greek-style works. (Out in the gallery, you'll find a statue of another swooning Venus.) Go ahead, swoon. If it feels good, enjoy it. Now, take a mental cold shower, and let's cross over to the "wrong side of the tracks," to the art of the early rebels.

• *Exit Room 3 into the main gallery, turn left, and head back toward the entrance, turning right into Room 4, marked* Daumier *(opposite the Ingres room).*

ORSAY MUSEUM

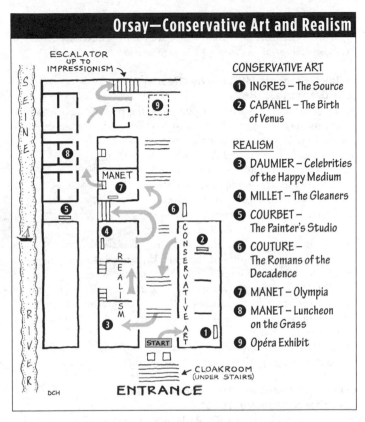

Orsay—Conservative Art and Realism

ESCALATOR
UP TO
IMPRESSIONISM

CONSERVATIVE ART

❶ INGRES – The Source

❷ CABANEL – The Birth of Venus

REALISM

❸ DAUMIER – Celebrities of the Happy Medium

❹ MILLET – The Gleaners

❺ COURBET – The Painter's Studio

❻ COUTURE – The Romans of the Decadence

❼ MANET – Olympia

❽ MANET – Luncheon on the Grass

❾ Opéra Exhibit

CLOAKROOM (UNDER STAIRS)

ENTRANCE

REALISM—EARLY REBELS

❸ Honoré Daumier—*Celebrities of the Happy Medium* (*Célébrités du juste milieu*, 1832–1835)

This is a liberal's look at the stuffy bourgeois establishment that controlled the Academy and the Salon. In these 36 bustlets, Daumier, trained as a political cartoonist, exaggerates each subject's most distinct characteristic to capture with vicious precision the pomposity and self-righteousness of these self-appointed arbiters of taste. The labels next to the busts give the name of the person being caricatured, his title or job (most were members of the French parliament), and an insulting nickname (like "gross, fat, and satisfied" or Monsieur "Platehead"). Give a few nicknames yourself. Can you find Reagan, Clinton, Yeltsin, Thatcher, Kerry, and Rumsfeld?

These people hated the art you're about to see. Their prudish faces tightened as their fantasy world was shattered by the Realists.

• *Go uphill four steps and through a leafy room to the final room, #6.*

❹ Jean-François Millet—*The Gleaners* (*Les Glaneuses*, 1867)

Millet (mee-yay) shows us three gleaners, the poor women who pick up the meager leftovers after a field has already been harvested by the wealthy. Millet grew up on a humble farm. He didn't attend the Academy and despised the uppity Paris art scene. Instead of idealized gods, goddesses, nymphs, and winged babies, he painted simple rural scenes. He was strongly affected by the socialist revolution of 1848, with its affirmation of the working class. Here he captures the innate dignity of these stocky, tanned women who bend their backs quietly in a large field for their small reward.

This is "Realism" in two senses. It's painted "realistically," unlike the prettified pastels of Cabanel's *Birth of Venus*. And it's the "real" world—not the fantasy world of Greek myth, but the harsh life of the working poor.

• *Exit Room 6 into the main gallery and make a U-turn to the left, climbing the steps to a large alcove with two huge canvases. On the left is...*

❺ Gustave Courbet—*The Painter's Studio* (*L'Atelier du Peintre*, 1855)

The Salon of 1855 rejected this dark-colored, sprawling, monumental painting of..."What's it about?" In an age when "Realist painter" was equated with "bomb-throwing Socialist," it took courage to buck the system. Dismissed by the so-called experts, Courbet (coor-bay) held his own one-man exhibit. He built a shed in the middle of Paris, defiantly hung his art out, and basically mooned the shocked public.

Courbet's painting takes us backstage, showing us the gritty reality behind the creation of pretty pictures. We see Courbet himself in his studio, working diligently on a Realistic landscape, oblivious to the confusion around him. Milling around are ordinary citizens, not Greek heroes. The woman who looks on is not a nude Venus but a naked artist's model. And the little boy with an adoring look on his face? Perhaps it's Courbet's inner child, admiring the artist who sticks to his guns, whether it's popular or not.

• *Return to the main gallery. Back across "the tracks," the huge canvas you see is...*

❻ Thomas Couture—*The Romans of the Decadence* (*Les Romains de la Décadence*, 1847)

We see a *fin de siècle* (end-of-century) society that looks like it's packed

in a big hot tub. It's stuffed with too much luxury, too much classical beauty, too much pleasure; it's wasted, burned out, and in decay. The old, backward-looking order was about to be slapped in the face.
• *Continue up the gallery, then left into Room 14 (Manet). Find the reclining nude.*

❼ Edouard Manet—*Olympia* (1863)

"This brunette is thoroughly ugly. Her face is stupid, her skin cadaverous. All this clash of colors is stupefying." So wrote a critic when Edouard Manet's nude hung in the Salon. The public hated it, attacking Manet (man-ay) in print and literally attacking the canvas.

Think back on Cabanel's painting, *The Birth of Venus:* an idealized, pastel, Vaseline-on-the-lens beauty. It's basically soft-core pornography, the kind you see selling lingerie and perfume.

Manet's nude doesn't gloss over anything. The pose is classic, used by Titian, Goya, and countless others. But this is a Realist's

take on the classics. The sharp outlines and harsh, contrasting colors are new and shocking. Her hand is a clamp, and her stare is shockingly defiant, with not a hint of the seductive, heysailor look of most nudes. This prostitute, ignoring the

flowers sent by her last customer, looks out as if to say, "Next." Manet replaced soft-core porn with hard-core art.

Edouard Manet (1832–1883) had an upper-class upbringing and some formal art training, and he had been accepted by the Salon. He could have cranked out pretty nudes and been a successful painter. Instead, he surrounded himself with a group of young artists experimenting with new techniques. Because of his reputation and strong personality, he was their master, though he learned equally from them.
• *Climb the small set of stairs in Room 14. Across the hall (and slightly to the right) is Room 19, where you'll find...*

❽ Edouard Manet—*Luncheon on the Grass* (*Le Déjeuner sur l'Herbe*, 1863)

A shocked public looked at this and wondered: What are these scantily clad women doing with these men? Or rather, what will they be doing

after the last baguette is eaten? It isn't the nudity, but the presence of the men in ordinary clothes, that suddenly make the nudes look naked. Once again, the public judged the painting on moral rather than artistic terms.

You can see that a new revolutionary movement was starting to bud—Impressionism. Notice the background: the messy brushwork of trees and leaves, the play of light on the pond, and the light that filters through the trees onto the woman who stoops in the haze. Also note the strong contrast of colors (white skin, black clothes, green grass). This is a true out-of-doors painting, not a studio production. Let the Impressionist revolution begin.

• *Get a sneak peak of that revolution in the adjoining Room 20, with a fine collection of works by Monet. Otherwise, continue to the far end of the gallery, where you'll walk on a glass floor over a model of Paris.*

❾ Opéra Exhibit

Expand to 100 times your size and hover over this scale-model section of the city. In the center sits the 19th-century Opéra Garnier, with its green-domed roof.

Nearby, you'll also see a cross-section model of the Opéra. You'd enter from the right end, buy your ticket in the foyer, then move into

the entrance hall with its grand staircase, where you could see and be seen by *tout* Paris. At curtain time, you'd find your seat in the red-and-gold auditorium, topped by a glorious painted ceiling. (The current ceiling, painted by Marc Chagall, is even more wonderful than the one in the model.) Notice that the stage, with elaborate riggings to raise and lower scenery, is as big as the seating area. Nearby, there are models of set designs from some famous productions. These days, Parisians enjoy their Verdi and Gounod at the modern opera house at place de la Bastille.

• *To the left of the Opéra model, a covered escalator leads up to the often-crowded Impressionist rooms. (To read ahead, consider wandering to the quiet far-left corner of the ground floor, where you'll find a huge painting of a hot-air-balloonist's-eye view of pre–Eiffel Tower Paris, c. 1855).*

Ride the escalator to the top floor. Take your first left for a commanding view of the Orsay. *The second left takes you past a bookshop and a giant "backwards" clock (with great city views) to the art, starting in Room 29. The Impressionist collection is scattered somewhat randomly through the next few rooms. Shadows dance and the displays mingle. You'll find nearly all of the following paintings, but exactly where they're hung is a lot like their brushwork... delightfully sloppy. (If you don't see a described painting, ask a guard or just move on. It's either hanging farther down or it's on vacation.)*

IMPRESSIONISM

Rooms 29–34: Manet, Degas, Monet, Renoir, and More

Light! Color! Vibrations! You don't hang an Impressionist canvas—you tether it. Impressionism features bright colors, easygoing open-air scenes, spontaneity, broad brushstrokes, and the play of light.

The Impressionists made their canvases shimmer by using a simple but revolutionary technique. Let's say you mix red, yellow, and green together—you'll get brown, right? But Impressionists didn't bother to mix them. They'd slap a thick brushstroke of yellow down, then a stroke of green next to it, then red next to that. Up close, all you see are the three messy strokes, but as you back up...*voilà!* Brown! The colors blend in the eye, at a distance. But while your eye is saying "bland old brown," your subconscious is shouting, "Red! Yellow! Green! Yes!"

There are no lines in nature, yet someone in the classical tradition (Ingres, for example) would draw an outline of his subject, then fill it in with color. Instead the Impressionists built a figure with dabs of paint...a snowman of color.

• *In Room 30, find the non-Impressionist but equally famous...*

James Abbott McNeill Whistler—*Portrait of the Artist's Mother* (*Portrait de la Mère de l'Auteur*, 1871)

Why's it so famous? I don't know either. Perhaps because it's by an American, and we see in his mother some of the monumental solidity of our own ancestral moms, who were made tough by pioneering the American wilderness.

Or perhaps because it was so starkly different for its day. In a roomful of golden goddesses, it'd stand out like a fish in a tree. The alternate title is *Arrangement in Gray and Black, No. 1,* and the whole point is the subtle variations of dark shades softened by the rosy tint of her cheeks. Nevertheless, the critics kept waiting for it to come out in Colorization.

• *In Room 31, on the left side, is work by...*

Edgar Degas—*The Dance Class* (*La Classe de Danse*, c. 1873–1875)

Clearly, Degas loved dance and the theater. (Catch his statue, *Tiny Dancer, 14 Years Old,* in the glass case.) The play of stage lights off his

dancers, especially the halos of ballet skirts, is made to order for an Impressionist. In *The Dance Class*, bored, tired dancers scratch their backs restlessly at the end of a long rehearsal. And look at the bright green bow on the girl with her back to us. In the Impressionist style, Degas slopped green paint onto her dress and didn't even say, *"Excusez-moi."*

Edgar Degas (1834–1917, day-gah) was a rich kid from a family of bankers who got the best classical-style art training. Adoring Ingres' pure lines and cool colors, he painted in the Academic style. His work was exhibited in the Salon. He gained success and a good reputation, and then...he met the Impressionists.

Degas blends classical lines with Impressionist color, spontaneity, and everyday subjects from urban Paris. Degas loved the unposed "snapshot" effect, catching his models off guard. Dance students, women at work, and café scenes are approached from odd angles that aren't always ideal, but make the scenes seem more real.

Edgar Degas—*In a Café*, or *The Glass of Absinthe* (*Au Café, dit L'Absinthe*, 1876)

Degas hung out with low-life Impressionists, discussing art, love, and life in the cheap cafés and bars in Montmartre. Here, a weary lady

ORSAY MUSEUM

Impressionism

The camera threatened to make artists obsolete. Now a machine could capture a better likeness faster than you could say, "Etch-a-Sketch."

But true art is more than just painting reality. It gives us reality from the artist's point of view, with the artist's personal impressions of the scene. Impressions are often fleeting, so you have to work quickly.

The Impressionist painters rejected camera-like detail for a quick style more suited to capturing the passing moment. Feeling stifled by the rigid rules and stuffy atmosphere of the Academy, the Impressionists took as their motto, "Out of the studio, into the open air." They grabbed their berets and scarves and went on excursions to the country, where they set up their easels (and newly invented tubes of premixed paint) on riverbanks and hillsides, or they sketched in cafés and dance halls. Gods, goddesses, nymphs, and fantasy scenes were out; common people and rural landscapes were in.

The quick style and everyday subjects were ridiculed and called childish by the "experts." Rejected by the Salon, the Impressionists staged their own exhibition in 1874. They brashly took their name from an insult thrown at them by a critic who laughed at one of Monet's "impressions" of a sunrise. During the next decade, they exhibited their own work independently. The public, opposed at first, was slowly won over by the simplicity, the color, and the vibrancy of Impressionist art.

of the evening meets morning with a last, lonely, coffin-nail drink in the glaring light of a four-in-the-morning café. The pale green drink at the center of the composition is the toxic substance absinthe, which fueled many artists and burned out many more.

• *The next few rooms (32–34) feature works by two Impressionist masters at their peak, Monet and Renoir. You're looking at the quintessence of Impressionism. The two were good friends, often working side by side, and their canvases now hang side by side in these rooms.*

Pierre-Auguste Renoir—*Dance at the Moulin de la Galette* (*Bal du Moulin de la Galette*, 1876)

On Sunday afternoons, working-class folk would dress up and head for the fields on butte Montmartre (near Sacré-Cœur basilica) to dance, drink, and eat little crêpes *(galettes)* till dark. Pierre-Auguste

Renoir (1841–1919, ren-wah) liked to go there to paint the common Parisians living and loving in the afternoon sun. The sunlight filtering through the trees creates a kaleidoscope of colors, like the 19th-century equivalent of a mirror ball throwing darts of light onto the dancers.

He captures the dappled light with quick blobs of yellow staining the ground, the men's jackets, and the sun-dappled straw hat (right of center). Smell the powder on the ladies' faces. The painting glows with bright colors. Even the shadows on the ground, which should be gray or black, are colored a warm blue. Like a photographer who uses a slow shutter speed to show motion, Renoir paints a waltzing blur.

Renoir's work is lighthearted, with light colors, almost pastels. He seems to be searching for an ideal, the pure beauty we saw on the ground floor. In later years, he used more and more red tones, as if trying for even more warmth. If you love Renoir, you'll likely find more of his work farther along, in Room 39.

Camille Pissarro, Alfred Sisley, and Others

The Orsay features some of the "lesser" pioneers of the Impressionist style. Browse around and discover your own favorites. Pissarro (Room 32) is one of mine. His grainy landscapes are more subtle and subdued than those of the flashy Monet and Renoir, but, as someone said, "He did for the earth what Monet did for the water."

Claude Monet—*The Cathedral of Rouen* (*La Cathédrale de Rouen*, 1893)

Claude Monet (1840–1926, mo-nay) is the father of Impressionism. He fully explored the possibilities of open-air painting and tried to

faithfully reproduce nature's colors with bright blobs of paint.

Monet went to Rouen, rented a room across from the cathedral, set up his easel...and waited. He wanted to catch "a series of differing impressions" of the cathedral facade at various times of day and year. He often had several canvases going at once. In all, he did 30 paintings of the cathedral, and each is unique. The time-lapse series shows the sun passing slowly across the sky, creating different-colored light and shadows. The labels next to the art describe the conditions: in gray weather, in the morning, morning sun, full sunlight, etc.

As Monet zeroes in on the play of colors and light, the physical subject—the cathedral—is dissolving. It's only a rack upon which to hang the light and color. Later artists would boldly throw away the rack, leaving purely abstract modern art in its place.

Claude Monet—Paintings from Monet's Garden at Giverny

One of Monet's favorite places to paint was the garden he landscaped at his home in Giverny, west of Paris (and worth a visit, provided you like Monet more than you hate crowds—see day trip on page 518). The Japanese bridge and the water lilies floating in the pond were his two favorite subjects. As Monet aged and his eyesight failed, he made bigger canvases of smaller subjects. The final water lilies are monumental smudges of thick paint surrounded by paint-splotched clouds reflected on the surface of the pond.

Monet's most famous water lilies are in full bloom at the Orangerie Museum, across the river in the Tuileries Garden (see page 221). You can see more Monet at the Marmottan Museum (see Marmottan Museum Tour, page 225).

• *Notice the skylight above you: These Impressionist rooms are appropriately illuminated by ever-changing natural light. Then carry on to Room 35.*

POST-IMPRESSIONISM

❿ Vincent van Gogh

Impressionists have been accused of being "light"-weights. The colorful style lends itself to bright country scenes, gardens, sunlight on the water, and happy crowds of simple people. It took a remarkable genius to add profound emotion to the Impressionist style.

Like Michelangelo, Beethoven, Rembrandt, Wayne Newton, and a select handful of others, Vincent van Gogh (1853–1890, van-go, or van-HOCK by the Dutch and the snooty) put so much of himself into his work that art and life became one. In this room, you'll see both Van Gogh's painting style and his life unfold.

Orsay—Post-Impressionism

47 · 17 · 46 · 45 · 44 · 43 · 42 · 41 · 40

48 · 16 · 15 · 14 · 13

39 · 12

WC

ESCALATOR DOWN TO LEVEL ("NIVEAU") 2

38
37 CAFE

10 Van Gogh
11 Cézanne
12 Monet & Renoir
13 Redon
14 Rousseau
15 Gauguin
16 Pointillism
17 Toulouse-Lautrec

11 36 TERRACE

10 35

SEINE RIVER

DCH

ORSAY MUSEUM

Vincent van Gogh—*Peasant Woman near the Hearth* (*Paysanne près de l'Atre*, 1885)

As the son of a Dutch minister, Van Gogh too feels drawn to a religious vocation, and he spreads the gospel among the poorest of the poor—peasants and miners in overcast Holland and Belgium. He paints these hardworking, dignified folks in a crude, dark style reflecting the oppressiveness of their lives...and the loneliness of his own as he roams northern Europe in search of a calling.

Vincent van Gogh—*Self-Portrait, Paris* (*Portrait de l'Artiste*, 1887)

Encouraged by his art-dealer brother, Van Gogh moves to Paris, and *voilà!* The color! He meets Monet, drinks with Paul Gauguin and Henri de Toulouse-Lautrec, and soaks up the Impressionist style. (See how he builds a bristling brown beard using thick strokes of red, yellow, and green side by side.)

At first, he paints like the others, but soon he develops his own style. By using thick, swirling brushstrokes, he even infuses life into inanimate objects. Van Gogh's brushstrokes curve and thrash like a garden hose pumped full of wine.

Vincent van Gogh—*Midday (La Méridienne,* 1890, based on a painting by Millet)

The social life of Paris becomes too much for the solitary Van Gogh. He moves to the South of France. At first, in the glow of the bright spring sunshine, he has a period of incredible creativity and happiness, as he is overwhelmed by the bright colors,

landscape vistas, and common people—an Impressionist's dream.

Vincent van Gogh—*Van Gogh's Room at Arles (La Chambre de van Gogh à Arles,* 1889)

But being alone in a strange country begins to wear on him. An ugly

man, he finds it hard to get a date. The close-up perspective of this painting makes his tiny rented room look even more cramped. He invites his friend Gauguin to join him, but after two months together arguing passionately about art, nerves get raw. Van Gogh threatens Gauguin with a knife, which drives his friend back to Paris. In crazed despair, Van Gogh mutilates his own ear.

The people of Arles realize they have a madman on their hands and convince Van Gogh to seek help. He enters a mental hospital.

Vincent van Gogh—*The Church at Auvers-sur-Oise (L'Eglise d'Auvers-sur-Oise,* 1890)

Van Gogh's paintings done in the peace of the mental hospital are more meditative—fewer bright landscapes, more closed-in scenes with deeper and almost surreal colors. The sky is cobalt blue and the church's windows are also blue, as if we're looking right through the building to an infinite sky. There's a road that leads from us to the church, then splits to go behind it. A choice must be made. Which way?

Van Gogh, the preacher's son, saw painting as a calling, and he approached it with a spiritual intensity.

Vincent van Gogh—*Self-Portrait, St. Rémy* (1889)

Van Gogh wavers between happiness and madness. He despairs of ever being sane enough to continue painting.

This self-portrait shows a man engulfed in a confused background of brushstrokes that swirl and rave, setting in motion the waves of the jacket. But in the midst of this rippling sea of mystery floats a still, detached island of a face with probing, questioning, yet wise eyes.

Do his troubled eyes know that only a few months on, he will take a pistol and put a bullet through his chest?

• *Vincent van Gone. Continue to Room 36.*

⓫ Paul Cézanne

Paul Cézanne (1839–1906, say-zahn) brought Impressionism into the 20th century. After the color of Monet, the warmth of Renoir, and Van Gogh's passion, Cézanne's rather impersonal canvases can be difficult to appreciate. Bowls of fruit, landscapes, and a few portraits were Cézanne's passion. Because of his style (not the content), he is often called the first modern painter.

Paul Cézanne—*Self-Portrait* (*Portrait de l'Artiste*, c. 1873–1876)

Cézanne was virtually unknown and unappreciated in his lifetime.

He worked alone, lived alone, and died alone, ignored by all but a few revolutionary young artists who understood his efforts. Cézanne's brush was a blunt instrument. With it, he'd bludgeon reality into submission, drag it across a canvas, and leave it there to dry. But Cézanne, the mediocre painter, was a great innovator. His work spoke for itself—which is good because, as you can see here, he had no mouth.

Paul Cézanne—*Landscape* (*Rochers près des Grottes au-dessus de Château-Noir*, 1904)

Cézanne used chunks of green, tan, and blue paint as building blocks to construct this rocky brown cliff. Where the Impressionists built a figure out of a mosaic of individual brushstrokes, Cézanne used blocks of paint to give it a more solid, geometrical shape. A block of paint forming part of a rock in the foreground is the same size as one in the background, flattening the scene into a wall of brushstrokes.

These chunks are like little "cubes." It's no coincidence that his experiments in reducing forms to their geometric basics influenced the...Cubists.

Paul Cézanne—*The Card Players*
(*Les Joueurs de Cartes*, c. 1890–1895)

These aren't people. They're studies in color and pattern. The subject matter—two guys playing cards—is less important than the pleasingly

balanced pattern they make on the canvas, two sloping forms framing a cylinder (a bottle) in the center. Later, abstract artists would focus solely on the shapes and colors.

The jacket of the player to the right is a patchwork of tans, greens, and browns. Even the "empty" space between the men—painted with fragmented chunks

of color—is almost as tangible as they are. As one art scholar puts it: "Cézanne confused intermingled forms and colors, achieving an extraordinarily luminous density in which lyricism is controlled by a rigorously constructed rhythm." Just what I said—chunks of color.

• *Exit to the café and consider a well-deserved break. From the café, continue ahead, walking under the large green beam, following signs to* Salles 39–48. *The hallway leads past WCs to Room 39, which often displays* **work by Monet and Renoir (⑫)**, *and may include paintings covered earlier in this tour. Then continue into dark Room 40 in the right corner...*

⓭ Odilon Redon

Flip out the lights and step into Odilon Redon's mysterious *fin de siècle* world. If the Orsay's a zoo, this is the nocturnal house. Prowl around. This is wild, wild stuff. It's intense—imagine Richard Nixon on mushrooms playing sax.

If the Impressionists painted by sunlight, Odilon Redon (1840–1916) painted by moonlight. His pastels (protected by dim lighting) portray dream imagery and mythological archetypes. Classed as Symbolism, Redon's weird work later inspired the Surrealists.

• *Coming out of the darkness, pass into the gallery lined with metal columns, containing the primitive art of Rousseau and Gauguin. Start in the first alcove to the left.*

PRIMITIVES

⓮ Henri Rousseau—*War*
(*La Guerre*, or *La Chevauchée de la Discorde*, 1894)

War, in the form of a woman with a sword, flies on horseback across the battlefield leaving destruction in her wake: broken bare trees, burning clouds in the background, and heaps of corpses picked at by the birds. Some artists, rejecting the harried, scientific, and rational world, remembered a time before "isms," when works of art weren't scholarly "studies in form and color," but voodoo dolls full of mystery and magic power. They learned from the art of primitive tribes in Africa and the South Seas, trying to re-create a primal Garden of Eden of peace and wholeness. In doing so, they created another "ism": Primitivism.

Henri Rousseau (1844–1910), a man who painted like a child, was an amateur artist who palled around with all the great painters—but they never took his naive style of art seriously. Like a child's drawing of a nightmare, the images are primitive—flat and simple, with unreal colors—but the effect is both beautiful and terrifying.

· *Farther along this columned gallery, you'll find work by...*

⓯ Paul Gauguin—*Arearea*, or *Joyousness* (*Joyeusetés*, 1892)

Paul Gauguin (1848–1903, go-gan) got the travel bug early in childhood and grew up wanting to be a sailor. Instead, he became a stock-

broker. In his spare time, he painted, and he was introduced to the Impressionist circle. He learned their bright clashing colors but diverged from this path about the time Van Gogh waved a knife in his face. At the age of 35, he got fed up with it all, quit his job, abandoned his wife (her stern portrait bust may be nearby) and family, and took refuge in his art. He traveled to the South Seas in search of the exotic, finally settling on Tahiti.

In Tahiti, Gauguin found his Garden of Eden. He simplified his life into a routine of eating, sleeping, and painting. He simplified his painting still more, to flat images with heavy black outlines filled in with bright, pure colors. He painted the native girls in their naked innocence (so different from Cabanel's seductive *Venus*). But this simple style had a deep undercurrent of symbolic meaning.

Arearea shows native women and a dog. In the "distance" (there's no attempt at traditional 3-D here), a procession goes by with a large pagan idol. What's the connection between the idol and the foreground figures, who are apparently unaware of it? In primitive

societies, religion permeates life. Idols, dogs, and women are holy.
• *Farther along, find...*

⓰ Pointillist Paintings (Lots of Dots)

Pointillism, as illustrated by many paintings in the next rooms, brings
Impressionism to its logical conclusion—little dabs of different colors

placed side by side to blend in the
viewer's eye. In works such as *The
Circus* (*Le Cirque*, 1891), Georges
Seurat (1859–1891) uses only red,
yellow, blue, and green points of
paint to create a mosaic of colors
that shimmers at a distance, capturing the wonder of the dawn of
electric lights.

• *In darkened Room 47 are pastels by...*

⓱ Henri de Toulouse-Lautrec—
The Clownesse Cha-U-Kao (1895)

Henri de Toulouse-Lautrec (1864–1901) was the black sheep of a noble
family. At age 15 he broke both legs, which left him disabled. Shunned

by his family, a freak to society, he felt
more at home in the underworld of other
outcasts—prostitutes, drunks, thieves,
dancers, and actors. He painted the lowlife
in the bars, cafés, dance halls, and brothels he frequented. Toulouse-Lautrec died
young of alcoholism.

The Clownesse Cha-U-Kao is one of his
fellow freaks, a fat lady clown who made
her living by being laughed at. She slumps
wearily after a performance, indifferent
to the applause, and adjusts her dress to
prepare for the curtain call.

Toulouse-Lautrec was a true impression-ist, catching his models in candid poses. He worked spontaneously, never correcting his
mistakes, as you can see from the blotches on her dark skirt and the
unintentional yellow sash that hangs down. Can you see a bit of Degas
here, in the subject matter, snapshot pose, and colors?

Henri de Toulouse-Lautrec—*Jane Avril Dancing*
(*Jane Avril dansant*, 1891)

Toulouse-Lautrec hung out at the Moulin Rouge dance hall in
Montmartre. One of the most popular dancers was this slim, graceful,
elegant, and melancholy woman, who stood out above the rabble of
the Moulin Rouge. Her legs keep dancing while her mind is far away.

Toulouse-Lautrec, the aristocrat, might have identified with her noble face—sad and weary of the nightlife, but immersed in it.

• *You've seen the essential Orsay and are permitted to cut out (the exit is directly below you). But there's an "other" Orsay I think you'll find entertaining.*

To reach Level 2 ("niveau 2"), go down three flights (escalator nearby), turn left, and cross to the other side of the gallery.

Along the way, on niveau 2, peek into "Le Restaurant." This was part of the original hotel that adjoined the sta-

tion—built in 1900, abandoned after 1939, condemned, and restored to the elegance you see today. The restaurant is pricey, but there's affordable coffee and tea (daily 15:00–17:30 except Thu).

Now find the palatial Room 51, with mirrors and chandeliers, marked Salle des Fêtes *(Grand Ballroom).*

THE "OTHER" ORSAY—LEVEL 2

The beauty of the Orsay is that it combines all the art from 1848–1914, both modern and classical, in one building. The classical art, so popular in its own day, has been maligned and was forgotten in the 20th century. It's time for a reassessment. Is it as gaudy and gawd-awful as we've been led to believe? From our 21st-century perspective, let's take a look at the opulent *fin de siècle* French high society and its luxurious art.

⓲ The Grand Ballroom (Salle des Fêtes)

When the Orsay hotel was here, this was one of France's poshest

nightspots. You can easily imagine gowned debutantes and white-gloved dandies waltzing the night away to the music of a chamber orchestra. Notice:

- The interior decorating: raspberry marble-ripple ice-cream columns, pastel-colored ceiling painting, gold work, mirrors, and leafy garlands of chandeliers.
- The statue *Bacchante Couchée* sprawled in the middle of the room.
- *La Nature*, a statue of a woman dressed in multicolored marble.
- The statue *Aurore*, with her canopy of hair,

The "Other" Orsay—Level 2

18 Grand Ballroom

19 Art worth a second look

20 Art NOT worth a second look

21 CHARPENTIER - Dining Room of Adrien Benard

22 RODIN - The Walking Man

23 CLAUDEL - Maturity

24 RODIN - The Gates of Hell

25 RODIN - Balzac

hide-and-seek face, and silver-dollar nipples, looking like a shampoo ad.

- The large painting *The Birth of Venus (La Naissance de Vénus)* by William Bouguereau. Van Gogh once said, "If I painted like Bouguereau, I could make money. But the public will never change—they only love sweet things."

Is this stuff beautiful or merely gaudy? Divine or decadent?

• *Exit the Salles des Fêtes and turn left, then left again onto the mezzanine overlooking the main gallery. Enter the first room on the left (#55), labeled* Naturalism.

⑲ Art Worth a Second Look

We've seen some great art; now let's see some not-so-great art—at least, that's what modern critics tell us. This is realistic art with a subconscious kick.

• *Working clockwise, you'll see...*

Cain

The world's first murderer, with the murder weapon still in his belt, is exiled with his family. Archaeologists had recently discovered a Neanderthal skull, so the artist makes the family part of a prehistoric hunter/gatherer tribe.

The Dream (Le Rêve)

Soldiers lie still, asleep without beds, while visions of Gatling guns dance in their heads.

Payday (La Paye des Moissonneurs)

Called "the grandson of Courbet and Millet," Leon L'Hermitte depicts peasants getting paid. The subtitle of the work could be, "Is this all there is to life?" (Or, "The Paycheck...After Deductions.")

The Excommunication of Robert le Pieux

The bishops exit after performing the rite. The king and queen are stunned, the scepter dropped. The ritual candle has been snuffed out; it falls, fuming, echoing through the huge hall.... Is this art, or only cheap theatrics?

• *Continue down the mezzanine. Skip the next room, then go left into Room 59.*

❷⓪ Art Not Worth a Second Look

The Orsay's director once said, "Certainly, we have bad paintings. But we have only the greatest bad paintings." And here they are.

Serenity

An idyll in the woods. Three nymphs with harps waft off to the right. These people are stoned on something.

The School of Plato (L'Ecole de Platon)

Subtitled "The Athens YMCA." A Christ-like Plato surrounded by adoring, half-naked nubile youths gives new meaning to the term "Platonic relationship."

Will the pendulum shift so that one day art like *The School of Plato* becomes the new, radical avant-garde style?

• *Return to the mezzanine and continue to the far end. Enter Room 61* (Art Nouveau) *and browse through several rooms of curvaceous furniture on your way to the far left corner, Room 66.*

ART NOUVEAU

㉑ Alexandre Charpentier—*Dining Room of Adrien Benard* (*Boiserie de la Salle à Mangér de la Propriété Benard*)

The Industrial Age brought factories, row houses, machines, train stations, geometrical precision—and ugliness. At the turn of the 20th century, some artists reacted against the unrelieved geometry of harsh, prag- matic, iron-and-steel Eiffel Tower art with a "new art"—Art Nouveau. (Hmm. I think I had a driver's ed teacher by that name.) This wood-paneled dining room, with its carved vines, leafy garlands, and tree- branch arches, is one of the finest examples of Art Nouveau.

Like nature, which also abhors a straight line, Art Nouveau artists used the curves of flowers and vines as their pattern. They were convinced that "practical" didn't have to mean "ugly" as well. They turned everyday household objects into art. (Another well-known example of Art Nouveau is the curvy, wrought-ironwork of some of Paris' early Métro entrances, commis- sioned by the same man who ordered this dining room for his home.)

• *Return to the mezzanine and grab a seat in front of the Rodin statue of a man missing everything but his legs.*

㉒ Auguste Rodin—*The Walking Man* (*L'Homme Qui Marche*, c. 1900)

Like this statue, Auguste Rodin (1840–1917) had one foot in the past,

while the other was stepping into the future. Rodin combined classical solidity with Impressionist surfaces to become the greatest sculptor since Michelangelo.

This muscular, forcefully striding man could be a symbol of the Renaissance man with his clas- sical power. With no mouth or hands, he speaks with his body. Get close and look at the statue's surface. This rough, "unfinished" look reflects light like the rough Impressionist brushwork, making the statue come alive, never quite at rest in the viewer's eye.

• *Near the far end of the mezzanine, you'll see a small bronze statue of a couple.*

㉓ Camille Claudel—*Maturity* (*L'Age Mûr*, 1899–1903)

Camille Claudel, Rodin's student and mistress, may have portrayed their doomed love affair here. A young girl desperately reaches out to an older man, who is led away reluctantly by an older woman. The center of the composition is the empty space left when their hands separate. In real life, Rodin refused to leave his wife, and Camille (see her head sticking up from a block of marble nearby) ended up in an insane asylum.

㉔ Auguste Rodin—*The Gates of Hell* (*La Porte de l'Enfer*, 1880–1917)

Rodin worked for decades on these doors depicting Dante's hell, and they contain some of his greatest hits—small statues that he later executed in full size. Find *The Thinker* squatting above the doorway, contemplating Man's fate. And in the lower left is the same kneeling man eating his children *(Ugolin)* that you'll see in full size nearby. Rodin paid models to run, squat, leap, and spin around his studio however they wanted. When he saw an interesting pose, he'd yell, "freeze" (or "statue maker") and get out his sketch pad. (For more on *The Gates of Hell* and Rodin, see the Rodin Museum Tour, page 183.)

㉕ Auguste Rodin—*Honoré de Balzac* (1897)

The great French novelist is given a heroic, monumental ugliness. Wrapped in a long cloak, he thrusts his head out at a defiant angle, showing the strong individualism and egoism of the 19th-century Romantic movement. Balzac is proud and snooty—but his body forms a question mark, and underneath the twisted features we can see a touch of personal pain and self-doubt. This is hardly camera-eye realism—Balzac wasn't that grotesque—but it captures a personality that strikes us even if we don't know the man.

From this perch, look over the main floor at all the classical statues between you and the big clock and realize how far we've come—not in years, but in style changes. Many of the statues below—beautiful, smooth, balanced, and idealized—were done at the same time as Rodin's powerful, haunting works. Rodin is a good place to end this tour. With a stable base of 19th-century stone, he launched art into the 20th century.

ORSAY MUSEUM

ORANGERIE MUSEUM TOUR

Musée de l'Orangerie

This Impressionist museum—lovely as a water lily—has reopened after an extensive renovation. Step out of the tree-lined, sun-dappled Impressionist painting that is the Tuileries Garden, and into the Orangerie (oh-rahn-zhay-ree), a little bijou of select works by Monet, Renoir, Matisse, Picasso, and others.

On the main floor you'll find the main attraction, Monet's *Water Lilies (Nymphéas),* floating dreamily in the oval-shaped rooms Monet intended for them. Downstairs are select works from the personal collection of Paris' trend-spotting art dealer of the 1920s, Paul Guillaume. The museum is small enough to enjoy in a short visit, but complete enough to show the bridge from Impressionism to the Moderns. And it's all beautiful.

ORIENTATION

Cost: €7.50, under 18 free, covered by Museum Pass.

Hours: Wed–Mon 9:00–18:00, closed Tue (galleries shut down 15 minutes before closing time).

Getting There: It's in the Tuileries Garden near place de la Concorde (Mo: Concorde).

Information: Tel. 01 44 77 80 07, www.musee-orangerie.fr.

Audioguide Tours: The €5 audioguide is a bit skimpy on the *Water Lilies,* but adds good detail about individual canvases in the Walter-Guillaume collection.

Length of This Tour: Allow one hour.

Starring: Claude Monet's water lilies and select works by the pioneers of Modern painting.

THE TOUR BEGINS

• *Monet's* Water Lilies *float serenely in two pond-shaped rooms on the main floor. Examine them up close to see Monet's technique; stand back to take in the whole picture.*

MAIN FLOOR

Claude Monet (1840–1926)

Hall (Salle) I

Like Beethoven going deaf, a nearly blind Claude Monet wrote his final symphonies on a monumental scale. Even as he struggled with cata-racts, he planned a series
of huge six-foot-tall can-vases of water lilies to hang
in special rooms at the
Orangerie. (For more on
Monet, see the Marmottan
Museum Tour, page 225,
and Giverny Day Trip,
page 518.)

These eight mammoth, curved panels immerse you in Monet's garden. We're looking at the pond in his garden at Giverny—dotted with water lilies, surrounded by foliage, and dappled by the reflections of the sky, clouds, and trees on the surface. The water lilies (*nymphéas* in French) range from plain green lily pads to flowers of red, white, yellow, lavender, and various combos.

The effect is intentionally disorienting; the different canvases feature different parts of the pond from different angles, at different times of day, with no obvious chronological order. Monet mingles the pond's many elements and lets us sort it out.

• *Start with the long wall on your right (as you enter) and work counter-clockwise.*

It's *Morning* on the pond at Giverny. The blue pond is the center of the composition, framed by the green, foliage-covered banks at
either end. Lilies float in the
foreground, and the pond
stretches into the distance.

The sheer scale of the
Orangerie project was daunt-ing for an artist in his twi-light years. This vast painting
is made from four separate
canvases stitched together,
and spans 6 feet 6 inches by 55 feet—it could cover an entire Paris hotel room. Altogether, Monet painted 1,950 square feet of canvas

ORANGERIE MUSEUM

to complete the *Water Lilies* series. Working at his home in Giverny, Monet built a special studio with skylights and wheeled easels to accommodate the canvases.

The panel at the far end, called *Green Affections,* looks deep into the dark water. Green willow branches are reflected on the water in a vertical pattern, while lily pads stretch horizontally.

Along the other long wall *(Clouds)*, green lilies float among lavender clouds reflected in blue water. Staring into Monet's pond, we see the intermingling of the four classical elements—earth (foliage), air (the sky), fire (sunlight), and water—the primordial soup of life.

The true subject of these works is the play of reflected light off the surface of the pond. Monet would work on several canvases at once, each dedicated to a different time of day. He'd move with the sun from one canvas to the next. Pan slowly around this hall. Watch the pond turn from pre-dawn darkness (far end) to clear morning light *(Morning)* to lavender late afternoon *(Clouds)* to glorious sunset.

In *Sunset* (near end), the surface of the pond is stained a bright yellow. Get close and see how Monet worked. Starting from the gray of blank canvas (lower right), he'd lay down big, thick brushstrokes of a single color, weaving them in a (mostly) horizontal and vertical pattern to create a dense mesh of foliage. Over this, he'd add more color for the dramatic highlights, until (in the center of the yellow) he got a dense paste of piled-up paint. Up close, it's a mess—but back up, and the colors begin to resolve into a luminous scene. There are no clearly identifiable objects in this canvas—no lilies, no trees, no clouds—just pure reflected color.

• *Continue into Room II, starting with the long wall on your right and working counterclockwise.*

Hall (Salle) II

In this room, Monet frames the pond with pillar-like tree trunks and overhanging foliage. The compositions are a bit more symmetrical

and the color schemes more muted, with blue and lavender and green-brown. Monet is often thought of as a lightweight, but his paintings almost always deal with the foundation of life—unspoiled nature.

In *Willows on a Clear Morning* (on the long wall to the right), we seem to be standing on the bank of the pond, looking out through overhanging trees at the water. The swirling branches and horizontal ripples on the pond suggest it's windy.

The Two Willows (far end) frame a wide expanse of water dotted with lilies and the reflection of gray-pink clouds.

The Renovation of the Orangerie

The Orangerie reopened in May 2006 after undergoing six long years of renovation. The refurbished museum was constructed around the two original *Water Lilies* rooms, which dated from 1927 and were custom-designed for the paintings. During the reconstruction, the Monet rooms and the paintings themselves were hermetically sealed in a big box while jackhammers blasted away around them.

The former upper floor (which previously held the Walter-Guillaume collection) has been transformed into a tall skylight, drenching the lilies in natural light. The Guillaume paintings are now displayed in a new underground gallery dug beneath the *Water Lilies*.

Designers kept intact the exterior shell of the Neoclassical building (built to hold orange trees in the 1850s, later housing soldiers in World War I) while reconfiguring the gallery space. Reconstruction was delayed by years of red tape after excavators struck a historically valuable 16th-century wall, which was eventually preserved and incorporated into the Orangerie's design.

Get in close in front of *Morning Willows* (long left wall). Notice how a "brown" tree is a tangled Impressionist beard of purple, green, blue, and red. Each leaf is a long brushstroke, and each lily pad a dozen smudges.

At the near end, *Reflections of Trees* is a mess of blue-purple paint brightened only by the lone rose lilies in the center. Each lily is made of many Impressionist brushstrokes, and each brushstroke is itself a mix of red, white, and pink paints. Monet demonstrates both his mastery of color and his ability to render it with paint, applied generously and deftly. He wanted the vibrant colors to keep firing your synapses.

With this last canvas, darkness descends on the pond. The room's large, moody canvases, painted by an 80-year-old man in the twilight of his life, invite meditation.

For 12 years (1914–1926), Monet worked on these paintings obsessively. A successful eye operation in 1923 gave him new energy. Monet completed all the planned canvases, but never lived to see them installed here. In 1927, the year after Monet's death, these rooms were completed and the canvases were put in place. Some call this the first "art installation"—a space specially designed for the art it displays in order to enhance the experience.

Monet's final work was more "modern" than Impressionist. Each

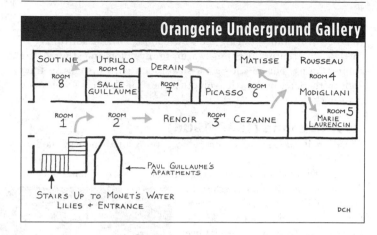

Orangerie Underground Gallery

SOUTINE
ROOM 8

UTRILLO
ROOM 9

SALLE
GUILLAUME

DERAIN

ROOM 7

PICASSO

MATISSE

ROOM 6

ROUSSEAU

ROOM 4

MODIGLIANI

ROOM 1

ROOM 2

RENOIR

ROOM 3

CEZANNE

ROOM 5
MARIE
LAURENCIN

← PAUL GUILLAUME'S
APARTMENTS

↑
STAIRS UP TO MONET'S WATER
LILIES + ENTRANCE

DCH

canvas is fully saturated with color, the distant objects as bright as the close ones. Monet's mosaic of brushstrokes forms a colorful design that's beautiful even if you just look "at" the canvas, like wallpaper. He wanted his paintings to be realistic and three-dimensional, but with a pleasant, two-dimensional pattern. As the subjects become fuzzier, the colors and patterns predominate. Monet builds a bridge between Impressionism and modern, abstract art.

UNDERGROUND GALLERY

Walter-Guillaume Collection

These paintings—Impressionist, Fauvist, and Cubist—were amassed by the art dealer Paul Guillaume. They're a snapshot of what was hot in the world of art, circa 1920. The once-revolutionary Impressionists had become completely old-school, though their paintings—now classics—commanded a fortune. The bohemian Fauvists and Cubists, who invented Modern art atop Butte Montmartre (c. 1900–1915), had suddenly become the darlings of the art world. But they refused to be categorized, and their work in the 1920s branched in dozens of new directions. Browse through the gallery, and watch the various "isms" unfold.

• *Descend the stairs to the lower floor. Turn right and find several Renoir canvases midway down the gallery.*

Pierre-Auguste Renoir (1841–1919)

Renoir loved to paint *les femmes*—women and girls—nude and innocent, taking a bath or practicing the piano, all with rosy red cheeks and a relaxed grace. We get

ORANGERIE MUSEUM

a feel for the happy family life of middle-class Parisians (including Renoir's own family) during the belle époque—the beautiful age of the late 19th century. Renoir's warm, sunny colors (mostly red) are Impressionist, but he adds a classical touch with his clearer lines and, in the later nudes, the voluptuousness of classical statues and paintings.

Paul Cézanne (1839–1906)

These small canvases of simple subjects reinvented the way modern artists painted.

The fruit of Cézanne's still lifes are "built" out of patches of color.

There's no traditional shading to create the illusion of 3-D, but these fruit bulge out like cameos from the canvas. The fruit are clearly at eye level, yet they're also clearly placed on a table seen from above. Picasso was fascinated with Cézanne's strange new world that showed multiple perspectives at once.

In his landscapes, Cézanne the Impressionist creates "brown" rocks out of red, orange, and purple; and "green" trees out of green, lime, and purple. Cézanne the proto-Cubist builds the rocks and trees with blocks of thick brushstrokes.

Henri Rousseau (1812–1867)

Rousseau, a simple government official, never traveled outside France, but he created an exotic, dreamlike, completely unique world. A Parisian wedding is set amid tropical trees. Figures are placed in a 3-D world, but the lines of perspective recede so steeply into the distance that everyone is in danger of sliding down the canvas. The way he put familiar images in bizarre settings influenced the Surrealists. Enjoy France's biggest collection of Rousseaus.

Amedeo Modigliani (1884–1920)

In his short, poverty-stricken, drug-addled life, Modigliani produced timeless-looking portraits of modern people. Born in Italy, Modigliani moved to Paris, where he hung around the fringes of the avant-garde in-crowd in Montmartre. He gained a reputation for his alcoholic excesses and outrageous behavior.

Turning his back on the prevailing Fauvist/Cubist ambience of the times, Modigliani developed a unique style, influenced by primitive tribal masks. His canvases feature stylized heads, almond eyes, long necks, and puckered mouths. *Novo Pilota* (1915) portrays Paul

Paul Guillaume
(1891–1934)

For the first three decades of the 20th century, Paris was the center of the art world, and the center of Paris' art scene was Paul Guillaume. An art dealer, promoter of "modern" art, and friend of out-there artists, Guillaume rose from humble beginnings to become wealthy and famous.

In his early days, this self-made businessman struggled alongside struggling painters in Montmartre—Picasso, Modigliani, Derain, Laurencin, and many others. When the art market boomed in the 1920s (along with the stock market), he and his fellow bohemians became the toasts of high society. With his flamboyant wife Domenica (also called Juliette), Guillaume hosted exotic parties featuring what we would now call "performance art" to shock and titillate the buying public.

Many of their artist friends honored Paul and Domenica by painting their portraits. In Modigliani's *Novo Pilota*, young Paul strikes a pose as the dapper man-of-the-world he was soon to become. The title of the painting is Italian for "new helmsman," reflecting Paul's growing status as a champion of Modernism. Marie Laurencin's portrait captures the winsome beauty of Domenica, whose charm helped establish the nouveau riche couple in social circles. Andre Derain's and Kees Van Dongen's portraits feature Paul and Domenica when they were older, more confident, and fully sophisticated.

The Orangerie displays Guillaume's personal collection of favorite paintings. After Paul's death, Domenica married Jean Walter and took her husband's last name, which is why it's officially called the "Walter-Guillaume" collection.

Guillaume as a cool dandy, suavely cradling a cigarette. Modigliani died young, just as his work was gaining recognition.

Marie Laurencin (1883–1956)
As the girlfriend of the poet and art critic Guillaume Apollinaire, Laurencin was right at the heart of the Montmartre circle when Modern art was born. Her work spreads a pastel sheen over this rough time, featuring women and cuddly animals intertwined in pink, blue, and gray tones.

Henri Matisse (1869–1954)

After World War I, Matisse moved to the south of France. He aban-

doned his fierce Fauvist style, and painted languid women in angular rooms with arabesque wallpaper. These paler tones evoke the sunny luxury of the Riviera. Traditional 3-D perspective is thrown out the occasional hotel window as the women and furnishings in the "foreground" blend with the wall-paper "background" to become part of the decor.

Pablo Picasso (1881–1973)

Picasso is a shopping mall of 20th-century artis-tic styles. In this room alone, he passes through his "Blue" Period (sad and tragic), "Rose" Period (red-toned nudes with timeless, masklike faces), Cubism (flat planes of interwoven perspec-tives), and his Classical Period, with massive, sculptural nudes—warm blow-up dolls with substance. If all roads lead to Paris, all art styles flowed through Picasso.

Andre Derain (1880–1954)

This former wild beast *(fauve)* tamed his colors in the 1920s. He and Picasso rode the rising wave of Classicism that surfaced after the chaos of the war years. With sharp outlines and studied realism, Derain painted still lifes, nudes, harlequins, por-traits, and landscapes—all of them in odd, angular poses.

Maurice Utrillo (1883–1955)

This hard-drinking, streetwise bohemian artist is known for his post-card views of Montmartre—whitewashed buildings under perennially cloudy skies.

Chaim Soutine (1893–1943)

When his friend Modigliani died (and Modigliani's widow com-mitted suicide), Soutine went into a tailspin of depression that drove him to paint. The subjects are ordinary—landscapes, portraits, and a fine selection of your favorite cuts of meat—but the style is deformed and Expressionistic. It shows a warped world in a funhouse mirror, smeared onto the canvas with thick, lurid colors. The never-cheerful Soutine was known to destroy work that did not satisfy him. Stand and ponder why these made the cut.

Did I say that the Orangerie's collection was as beautiful as an Impressionist painting? Well, Soutine's misery is so complete, it's almost a thing of beauty.

RUE CLER WALK

The Art of Parisian Living

Paris is changing quickly, but a stroll down this street introduces you to a thriving, traditional Parisian neighborhood and offers insights into the local culture. While this is a wealthy district (as reflected in the elegance of its shops), rue Cler retains a certain workaday charm still found in small neighborhoods throughout Paris.

Shopping for groceries is an integral part of everyday life here. Parisians shop almost daily for three good reasons: Refrigerators are small (tiny kitchens), produce must be fresh, and it's an important social event. Shopping is a chance to hear about the butcher's vacation plans, see photos of the florist's new grandchild, relax over *un café*, and kiss the cheeks of friends (the French standard is twice for regular acquaintances, three times for friends you haven't seen in a while).

Rue Cler—traffic-free since 1984—offers plenty of space for tiny stores and their patrons to spill into the street. It's an ideal environment for this ritual to survive and for you to explore. The street is lined with the essential shops—wine, cheese, chocolate, bread—as well as a bank and a post office. And the shops of this community are run by people who've found their niche: boys who grew up on quiche, girls who know a good wine. The people in uniform you might see are likely from the Ecole Militaire (military school, Napoleon's alma mater, two blocks away).

For those learning the fine art of living Parisian-style, rue Cler provides an excellent classroom. And if you want to assemble the ultimate French picnic, there's no better place. The Rue Cler Walk is the only tour in this guidebook you should start while hungry.

ORIENTATION

Length of This Walk: Allow an hour to browse and café-hop along this short walk of two or three blocks.

When to Go: Visit rue Cler when its market is open and lively (Tue–Sat 8:30–13:00 or 15:00–19:30, Sun 8:30–12:00, dead on Mon). Remember that these shops are busy serving regular customers. Be polite (say *"Bonjour, Madame/Monsieur"* as you enter and *"Au revoir, Madame/Monsieur"* when you leave), and be careful not to get in the way.

Getting There: Start your walk where the pedestrian section of rue Cler begins, at rue de Grenelle (Mo: Ecole Militaire or bus #69 stop).

THE WALK BEGINS

❶ Café Roussillon

This place, a neighborhood fixture, recently dumped its old-fashioned, characteristic look for the latest café style—warm, natural wood tones, easy lighting, and music. The sign on the window next to the door makes the pricing clear: Drinks at the bar *(comptoir)* are about a third the price of drinks at the tables *(salles)*. Also displayed are various *chèque déjeuner* decals, advertising that this café accepts lunch "checks." In France, an employee lunch subsidy program is an expected perk. Employers—responding to strong tax incentives designed to keep the café culture vital—issue a voucher check (worth about €8) for each day an employee works in a month. Sack lunches are rare, since a good lunch is sacred.

Inside, the bar is always busy. The blackboard lists wines sold by the little (7-centiliter) glass.

Next door, the little late-night grocery is one of countless corner shops nicknamed *dépanneurs* ("to help you out of difficulty"). Open nightly until midnight, these stores are often run by hardworking North Africans willing to keep crazy hours. Locals happily pay the higher prices for the convenience *dépanneurs* provide.

• *If you're shopping for designer baby clothes, you'll find them across the street at...*

❷ Petit Bateau

The French spend at least as much on their babies as they do on their dogs—dolling them up with designer jammies. This store is one in a popular chain. Babies-in-the-know just aren't comfortable unless they're making a fashion statement (such as underwear with sailor stripes). In the last generation, an aging and shrinking population has been a serious problem for Europe's wealthier nations. But France now has one of Europe's biggest baby populations—the fertile French average two children per family, compared to 1.6 for the rest of

Rue Cler Walk

TO RIVER

CAFE ROUSSILLON EMERGENCY STORE

1

TO EIFFEL TOWER

PETIT BATEAU **2**

RUE DE GRENELLE

3

FRANPRIX

TOP HALLES FRUIT + VEG.

ASIE TRAITEUR

HOTEL LEVEQUE

4 WINE BACCHUS

POISSONNERIE **6**

5 FROMAGERIE

HORSE MEAT SIGN **7**

FLEURS

8 PHARMACY

CHARCUTERIE **9** DAVIOLI

8 OLDEST BUILDING

CHOCOLATS

FROMAGERIE

WINE NICHOLAS

CAFE DU MARCHE

L'EPICERIE FINE

LEADER PRICE BULK SHOPPING

LOANER BIKES

11 **10**

RUE DU CHAMP DE MARS

HOTEL DU CHAMP DE MARS

12 BOULANGERIE

13 ← JAPANESE RESTAURANT

14

OLIVIERS **15** + CO.

↖ CHOCOLATS CONFISERIES "LA MERE DE FAMILLE"

RUE BOSQUET

CITY INFO POST

DCH

16

POST

TO ARMY + RODIN MUSEUMS

RUE DE LA MOTTE PICQUET

METRO "ECOLE MILITAIRE" Ⓜ

17

↗ TABAC "LA CAVE A CIGARES"

TO EIFFEL TOWER

NOTE: NOT TO SCALE- RUE CLER IS ABOUT 250 YARDS LONG

Europe. Babies are trendy today, and the government rewards parents with substantial tax deductions for their first two children—and then doubles the deductions after that. Making babies is good business.

• *Cross rue de Grenelle to find...*

❸ Top Halles Fruits and Vegetables

Each morning, fresh produce is trucked in from farmers' fields to Paris' huge Rungis market—Europe's largest, near Orly Airport—and

then dispatched to merchants with FedEx-like speed and precision. Good luck finding a shopping bag—locals bring their own two-wheeled carts or reusable bags. Also, notice how the earth-friendly French resist excessive packaging.

Parisians—who know they eat best by being tuned into the seasons—shop with their noses. Try it. Smell the cheap foreign strawberries. One sniff of the torpedo-shaped French ones *(garriguettes)* in June, and you know which is better. Locals call those from Belgium "plastic strawberries"—red on outside, white on inside. Find the herbs in the back. Is today's delivery in? Look at the price of those melons. What's the country of origin? (It must be posted.) If they're out of season, they come from Guadeloupe. Many people buy only local products.

The Franprix across the street is a small Safeway-type store. Opposite Grand Hôtel Lévêque is Asie Traiteur. Fast Asian food to go is popular in Paris. These shops—about as common as bakeries now—are making an impact on Parisian eating habits.

• *Just past Grand Hôtel Lévêque is...*

❹ Wine Bacchus

Shoppers often visit the neighborhood wine shop last, once they've assembled their meal and are able to pick the appropriate wine. The wine is classified by region. Most "Parisians" (born elsewhere) have an affinity for the wines of their home region. Check out the great prices. Wines of the month—in the center—sell for as little as €6–8. You can get a fine bottle for €10. The clerk is a counselor who works with your needs and budget, and he can put a bottle of white in the fridge for you to pick up later (open until 20:00 except Sun).

• *Next door, smell the...*

❺ Fromagerie

A long, narrow, canopied cheese table brings the *fromagerie* into the street. Wedges, cylinders, balls, and miniature hockey pucks are all powdered white, gray, and burnt marshmallow—it's a festival of mold.

The street cart and front window feature both cow and goat cheeses. Locals know the shape indicates the region of origin (for example, a pyramid shape indicates a cheese from the Loire). And this is important. Regions create the *terroir* (physical and magical union of sun, soil, and generations of farmer love) that gives the production—whether wine or cheese—its personality. *Ooh la la* means you're impressed. If you like cheese, show greater excitement with more *la*s. *Ooh la la la la.* My local friend once held the stinkiest glob close to her nose, took an orgasmic breath, and exhaled, "Yes, it smells like zee feet of angels." Go ahead...inhale.

Step inside and browse through more than 400 types of French cheese. A cheese shop—lab-coat-serious but friendly, and known as a "BOF" for *beurre, oeuf,* and *fromage*—is where people shop for butter, eggs, and cheese. In the back room, they store *les meules,* the big, 170-pound wheels of cheese (made from 250 gallons of milk). The "hard" cheeses are cut from these. Don't eat the skin of these big ones...they're rolled on the floor. But the skin on most smaller

cheeses—the Brie, the Camembert—is part of the taste. "It completes the package," says my local friend.

At dinner tonight, you can take the cheese course just before or instead of dessert. On a good cheese plate, you have a hard cheese (like Emmentaler—a.k.a. "Swiss cheese"), a flowery cheese (maybe Brie or Camembert), a bleu cheese, and a goat cheese—ideally from different regions. Because it's strongest, the goat cheese is usually eaten last.

• *Across the street, find the fish shop, known as the...*

❻ Poissonnerie

Fresh fish is brought into Paris daily from ports on the English Channel, 110 miles away. In fact, fish here is likely fresher than in many towns closer to the sea, because Paris is a commerce hub (from here, it's shipped to outlying towns). Anything wiggling? This *poissonnerie,* like all such shops, has been recently upgraded to meet the new Europe-wide hygiene standards.

• *Next door at the Ulysse en Gaule Crêperie (under the awning—get close to see) is a particularly tempting rue Cler storefront.*

❼ No More Horse Meat

The stones and glass set over the doorway advertise horse meat: *Boucherie Chevaline.* While today this store serves souvlaki and crêpes, the classy old storefront survives from the previous occupant. Created in the 1930s and signed by the artist, it's a work of art fit for a museum—but it belongs right here. Notice that the door is decorated with lunch coupon decals for local workers. (Say hi to Marcos happily baking crêpes.)

• *A few steps farther along is a flower shop. (When visiting friends, French people give a gift of flowers. It's classiest to have them delivered before you show up.) Across the street is the...*

❽ Pharmacy and Oldest Building

In France, the pharmacist makes the first diagnosis and has the authority to prescribe certain drugs. If it's out of his league, he'll recommend a doctor.

Next to the pharmacy is rue Cler's oldest building (with the two garret windows on the roof). It's from the early 1800s, when this street was part of a village near Paris, and was lined with structures like this. Over the years, Paris engulfed these surrounding villages—and now the street is a mishmash of architectural styles.

• *Across the street from this oldest house is...*

❾ Charcuterie Davoli

A charcuterie sells mouthwatering deli food to go. Because Parisian kitchens are so small, these gourmet delis are handy, even for those who cook. It lets the hosts concentrate on creating the main course, and then buy beautifully prepared side dishes to complete a fine dinner. Each day, the charcuteries cook up *plats du jour* (specials of the day), advertised on the board outside. Note the system: Order, take your ticket to the cashier to pay, and return with the receipt to pick up your food.

• *A few doors down is...*

❿ Café du Marché and More

Café du Marché, on the corner, is *the* place to sit and enjoy the action. It's rue Cler's living room, where locals gather before heading home, many staying for a relaxed and affordable dinner. The owner priced his menu so that locals could afford to dine out on a regular basis, and it worked—many patrons eat here five days a week. For a reasonable meal, grab a chair and check the chalk menu listing the *plat du jour*. For details on this restaurant, see page 381 in the Eating chapter. Notice how the new no-smoking-indoors laws have made outdoor seating and propane heaters a huge hit.

The shiny, sterile Leader Price grocery store (across the street) is a Parisian Costco, selling bulk items. Because storage space is so limited in most Parisian apartments, bulk purchases are unlikely to become a big deal here. The latest trend is to stock up on non-perishables by shopping online, pick up produce three times a week, and buy fresh bread daily. The awful exterior of this store suggests a sneaky bending of the rules. Normally any proposed building modification on rue

Cler must undergo a rigorous design review in order for the owner to obtain the required permit.

• *From Café du Marché, hook right and side-trip a couple doors down rue du Champ du Mars to visit...*

⓫ L'Epicerie Fine

This fine-foods boutique stands out from the rest because of its gentle owners, Pascal and Joanna. Their mission in life is to explain to travelers, in fluent English, what the French fuss over food is all about. Say *bonjour* to Pascal and company. Let them help you assemble a picnic and tempt you with fine gourmet treats, Berthillon ice cream, and generous tastes of caramel, balsamic vinegar, and French and Italian olive oil (Tue–Fri 9:30–13:00 & 15:00–19:30, Sat 10:00–13:30, Sun 10:00–13:00, closed Mon, tel. 01 47 05 98 18).

• *Return to rue Cler. On the corner, the neighborhood bakery is often marked by a line of people waiting to pick up their daily baguette.*

⓬ Boulangerie

Since the French Revolution, the government has regulated the cost of a basic baguette. Locals debate the merits of Paris' many *boulangeries*. It's said that a baker cannot be both good at bread and good at pastry. At cooking school, they major in one or the other. Here, the baker makes good bread, and another baker does the tasty little pastries for him.

• *Next door is a strangely out-of-place...*

⓭ Japanese Restaurant

Sushi is for sale everywhere in Paris these days. Locals explain that the phenomenon is the same as when Chinese restaurants were spreading like gastronomic weeds. Real French restaurants found it hard to compete with these inexpensive places, and in some areas, local authorities actually forbid giving business permits to Chinese restaurants.

• *A bit farther along is...*

⓮ La Mère de Famille Gourmand Chocolats Confiseries

This shop has been in the neighborhood for 30 years. The wholesalers wanted the owner to take the new products, but she kept the old traditional candies, too. "The old ladies, they want the same sweets that made them so happy 80 years ago," she says. You can buy "naked bonbons" right out of the jar and chocolate by the piece (about €0.75 each). You're welcome to assemble a small assortment,

Until a few years ago, the chocolate was dipped and decorated right on the premises. As was the tradition in rue Cler shops, the merchants resided and produced in the back and sold in the front.

• *Across the street, you'll find...*

ⓕ Oliviers & Co. Olive Oils

This shop, typical of an upscale neighborhood like this, sells fine gourmet goodies from the south of France and olive oil from around the Mediterranean. They are happy to give visitors a taste test. Try the tapenade. Use their tiny spoons to sample three distinct oils. Melanie speaks English and enthusiastically teaches all about their products.

• *Walk on to the end of rue Cler (where it hits a busy street).*

ⓖ City Info Post

This electronic signpost directs residents to websites for local information—transportation changes, surveys, employment opportunities, community events, and so on. Also notice the big green recycling stations and see-through green garbage sacks. In the 1990s, Paris suffered a rash of trash-can bombings. Bad guys hid rigged-up camp stove canisters in metal garbage cans, which broke into deadly "shrapnel" when they exploded. Local authorities solved this by replacing the metal cans with these see-through plastic bags.

• *Across the busy street is a* tabac *(tobacco shop).*

ⓗ Tabac La Cave a Cigares

Just as the US has liquor stores licensed to sell booze, the only place for people over 16 to buy tobacco legally in France is at a *tabac* (tah-bah) counter. Tobacco counters like this one are a much-appreciated fixture of each neighborhood, offering lots of services (and an insight into the local culture).

Even non-smokers enjoy perusing the wares at a *tabac*. Notice how European laws require a bold warning sign on cigarettes—about half the size of the package—that says, bluntly, *fumer tué* (smoking kills). Even so, you may not be able to resist the temptation to pick up a *petit Corona*—your chance to buy a fine Cuban cigar for €6 without breaking US law.

Tabacs also serve their neighborhoods as a kind of government cash desk. All sell stamps and most sell public-transit tickets (for the same price you'd pay at Métro stations—but they pocket a five percent profit). Locals pay for parking meters in *tabacs* by buying a card (see page 26)...or pay fines if they don't. Like back home, the LOTO is a big deal—and a lucrative way for the government to tax poor and less-educated people.

• *Rue Cler ends at the post office. The Ecole Militaire Métro stop is just down the street. If you bought a picnic along this walk, head for the nearby benches and gardens: From the post office, avenue de la Motte-Picquet leads to two fine parks—turn left for the Army Museum or right for the Eiffel Tower.*

EIFFEL TOWER TOUR

La Tour Eiffel

It's crowded, expensive, and there are probably better views in Paris, but this 1,000-foot-tall ornament is worth the trouble. Visitors to Paris may find *Mona Lisa* to be less than expected, but the Eiffel Tower rarely disappoints, even in an era of skyscrapers. This is a once-in-a-lifetime, I've-been-there experience. Making the trip gives you membership in the exclusive society of 240 million other humans who have made the Eiffel Tower the most visited monument in the modern world.

ORIENTATION

Cost: €4.80 to go up to the first level, €7.80 to the second, and €12 to the top (not covered by Museum Pass). You can skip the elevator line and climb the stairs to the first or second level for €4.50, or for €3 if you're under 25. (Elevators and stairs are both free going down.)

    If you climb the stairs, or buy a ticket only to one of the lower levels, you can buy your way up once you're in the tower—ticket booths and machines on the first and second levels sell supplements to go higher (with no penalty).

Hours: Daily mid-June–Aug 9:00–24:45 in the morning, last ascent to top at 23:30 and to lower levels at 24:00; Sept–mid-June 9:30–23:45, last ascent to top at 22:30 and to lower levels via elevator at 23:00 or by stairs at 18:30. During windy weather, the top level may close to tourists.

When to Go: For the best of both worlds, arrive with enough light to see the views, then stay as it gets dark to see the lights. The views are grand whether you ascend or not. At the top of the hour, a five-minute lighting display features thousands of sparkling lights (best viewed from Trocadéro Square or the grassy park below).

Avoiding Lines: Go early (get in line by 8:45, before it opens) or late

EIFFEL TOWER

Eiffel Tower Area

TO ARC DE TRIOMPHE

AVE KLEBER

Iéna Ⓜ

AVE PRES. WILSON

Alma → Marceau Ⓜ

RIVER CRUISES

TROCADERO Ⓜ

RIVER CRUISES

R I V E R

QUAI D'ORSAY

SEWER TOUR

AMERICAN CHURCH

MARITIME MUSEUM

Ⓝ

AVE BRANLY

Pont de l'Alma

Quai BRANLY MUSEUM

AVE RAPP

RUE BOSQUET

ST. DOMINIQUE

AVE D'IENA

QUAI

EIFFEL TOWER

DE LA BOURDONNAIS

RUE

GRENELLE

Ⓑ

RUE CLER

S E I N E

BIR-HAKEIM

Ⓡ

CHAMP DE MARS

AVE BOUVARD

C H A M P

AVE J.

Ⓑ

KIDS' PLAY AREA + PUPPETS

Ⓑ

D E

M A R S

AVE DE LA MOTTE PICQUET

Ⓟ

AVE

Ⓜ TOUR.

Bir-Hakeim

SUFFREN

DCH

KIDS' PLAY AREA

Ecole Militaire

AVE DE SUFFREN

ECOLE MILITAIRE

Ⓜ METRO STATION
Ⓡ RER STOP
Ⓑ START OF BUS #69 TOUR
Ⓑ BATOBUS BOAT STOP
Ⓟ PARKING
⋗ VIEW

¼ MILE

400 METERS

(after 20:00 May–Aug, after 18:00 off-season—see "Hours," previous page, for last ascent times). Weekends and holidays are worst. Weekdays off-season are not as crowded.

There's less of a line for the stairs. You can bypass the elevator line if you have a reservation at either of the tower's view restaurants (see "Cuisine Art" on next page).

A new online reservation system may debut in 2009, allowing you to book a half-hour time slot for your visit—check the website for details: www.tour-eiffel.fr.

Pickpockets: The crowded elevators are like fish in a barrel for predatory thieves. *En garde.*

Getting There: The Bir-Hakeim and Trocadéro Métro stops, and the Champ de Mars Tour Eiffel RER stop, are each about a 10-minute walk away. The Ecole Militaire Métro stop in the rue Cler area is 20 minutes away. Bus #69 stops nearby on avenue Joseph Bouvard in the Champ de Mars park.

Information: A tourist information office/ticket booth is between the north and east pillars. Each level has displays pointing out the landmarks and monuments visible below. Tel. 01 44 11 23 23, www.tour-eiffel.fr.

Length of This Tour: Budget three hours to wait in line, get to the top, and sightsee your way back down. With no crowds, it's 90 minutes to the top and back. If you're in line to buy tickets, estimate about 20 minutes for every 100 yards, plus 30 minutes more after you reach the security check near the ticket booths.

Once you've toured the tower and are ready to leave, it's quickest and most memorable to use the stairs to descend the last two levels.

Baggage Check: Bags larger than 19" x 8" x 12" are not allowed and there is no baggage check. All bags are subject to a security search.

Services: There are free WCs at the base of the tower, behind the east pillar. Inside the tower itself, WCs are on all levels, but they're small, with long lines.

Cuisine Art: The first and second levels have small sandwich-and-coffee-type cafés. The tower's two classy restaurants offer great views. **Altitude 95** is on the first level (€35 lunches, €65 dinners, daily 12:00–21:45, bar open until 23:00, dinner seatings nightly at about 19:00 and 21:00, reserve a month in advance for view table—less for non-view, tel. 01 45 55 20 04, fax 01 47 05 94 40, desk.altitude95@restaurants-toureiffel.com). The expensive **Jules Verne Restaurant** is on the second level (€75 lunch *menu*, €190 dinner *menu*, daily 12:15–13:45 & 19:15–21:45, reserve 3 months in advance, tel. 01 45 55 61 44, fax 01 47 05 29 41, www.lejulesverne -paris.com). Dining at either the Jules Verne or Altitude 95 lets you skip the long elevator line and ride for free.

Near the tower, there's not much besides the burger-and-fries stands at the base. Rue Cler, with many options, is a 20-minute walk away (see page 164). The Quai Branly Museum's **Garden Café** is in a pleasant courtyard setting, a 10-minute walk east along the Seine (27 Quai Branly, tel. 01 47 53 68 00).

Your tastiest option may be to assemble a picnic beforehand (several handy shops near Métro stop Ecole Militaire) and picnic on the Champ de Mars.

Photography: All photos and videos are allowed.

Best Views: The best place to view the tower is from Trocadéro Square to the north. It's a 10-minute walk across the river, a happening scene at night, and especially fun for kids. Consider arriving at the Trocadéro Métro stop for the view, then walking toward the tower. Another delightful viewpoint is the long, grassy park—Champ de Mars—to the south (great for dinner picnics).

Starring: All of Paris... and beyond.

OVERVIEW

There are three observation platforms, at 200, 400, and 900 feet; the higher you go, the more you pay. While being on the windy top of

the Eiffel Tower is a thrill you'll never forget, the view is actually better from the second level, where you can actually see Paris' monuments. The first level also has nice views and more tourist-oriented sights. All three levels have some displays, WCs (usually with long lines), souvenir stores, and a few other services.

To get to the top, you need to take two different elevators. The first takes you to the first or second level. (Note: If you bought a ticket to either the second or third levels, you must bypass the first level on the way up and see it on your way back down.) A separate elevator—with another line—shuttles between the second and third levels.

For the hardy, stairs lead from the ground level up to the first and second levels—and rarely have a long line. It's 360 stairs to the first level and another 360 to the second. The staircase is enclosed with a wire cage, so you can't fall, but those with vertigo issues may still find them dizzying.

To see the entire tower, from top to bottom, then see it...from top to bottom. Ride the elevator to the second level, then immediately line up for the other elevator to the top. Enjoy the views on top, then ride back down to the second level. Frolic there for a while and take in some more views. When you're ready, head to the first level by taking the stairs (no line) or lining up for the elevator. Explore the shops and exhibits on the first level, have a snack, then take the stairs (best) or elevator back to earth.

THE TOUR BEGINS

Find the various entrances at the base of the tower's four *piliers* (pillars), named for their compass points: *nord* (north), *sud* (south), *est*

(east), and *ouest* (west). The various ticket offices can move around from time to time, so make sure you get in the right line. Avoid lines selling tickets only for *groupes*. Follow signs for *individuels* or *visiteurs sans tickets*. If you want to climb the stairs, pay the fee at the ticket office at the south pillar, next to

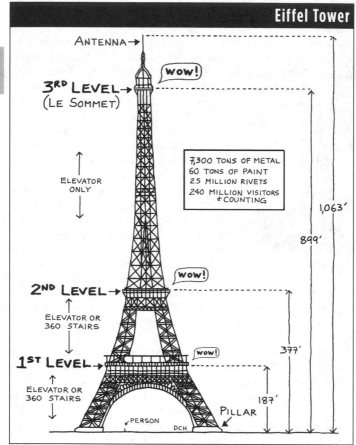

the Jules Verne Restaurant entrance.

To pass the time in line, read the following background information, or pick up whatever free reading material is available at the ground-level tourist stands. Look up at the tower towering above you, and don't even think about what would happen if someone dropped a coin from the top.

Exterior

Delicate and graceful when seen from afar, the Eiffel tower is massive—even a bit scary—close up. You don't appreciate its size until you walk toward it; like a mountain, it seems so close but takes forever to reach.

The tower, including its antenna, stands 1,063 feet tall, or slightly higher than the 77-story Chrysler Building in New York. Its four support pillars straddle an area of 3.5 acres. Despite the tower's 7,300 tons of metal and 60 tons of paint, it is so well-engineered that it weighs no more per square inch at its base than a linebacker on tiptoes.

Once the world's tallest structure, it's now eclipsed by a number of skyscrapers (e.g., the Sears Tower, Chicago, 1,730 feet); towers (CN Tower, Toronto, 1,815 feet); and radio antennae (KVLY-TV Mast, North Dakota, 2,063 feet).

The long green lawn stretching south of the tower is the Champ de Mars, originally the training ground for troops and students of the nearby Military School (Ecole Militaire) and now a park. On the north side, across the Seine, is the curved palace colonnade framing a square called the Trocadéro, site of the 1878 World's Fair.

History

In 1889, the first visitor to Paris' Universal Exposition walked

beneath the "arch" formed by the newly built Eiffel Tower and entered the fair grounds. The World's Fair celebrated both the centennial of the French Revolution and France's position as a global superpower. Bridge-builder Gustave Eiffel (1832–1923) won the contest to build the fair's centerpiece by beating out such rival proposals as a giant guillotine.

Gustave deserved to have the tower named for him. He not only designed it, but he oversaw the entire work, personally financed it, and was legally responsible if the project floundered. His factory produced the iron beams, he designed the cranes and apparatus, his workers built it, and—working on a deadline for the World's Fair—he brought in the project on time and under budget.

The tower was nothing but a showpiece, with no functional purpose except to demonstrate to the world that France had the wealth, knowledge, and can-do spirit to erect a structure far taller than anything the world had ever seen. The original plan was to dismantle the tower as quickly as it was built after the celebration ended, but it was kept by popular demand.

To a generation hooked on technology, the tower was the marvel of the age, a symbol of progress and human ingenuity. Not all were so impressed, however; many found it a monstrosity. The writer Guy de Maupassant (1850–1893) routinely ate lunch in the tower just so he wouldn't have to look at it.

In subsequent years, the tower has come to serve many

functions: as a radio transmitter (1909–present), a cosmic-ray observatory (1910), a billboard (spelling "Citroën" in lights, 1925–1934), a broadcaster of Nazi TV programs (1940–1944), a fireworks launch pad (numerous times), and as a framework for dazzling lighting displays, including the current arrangement, designed in 2000 for the Millennium celebration.

• *To reach the top, ride the elevator—bypassing the first level—to the second level. From there, get in line for the next elevator and continue to the top. Pop out 900 feet above the ground.*

Third Level *(Le Sommet)*

The top level, called *le sommet*, is tiny. (It can close temporarily without warning when it reaches capacity.) All you'll find here are wind and grand, sweeping views. The city lies before you, with a panorama guide. On a good day, you can see for 40 miles. Do a 360-degree tour of Paris. (Note that the following compass points are only approximate; in fact, what the tower's displays call "west" is more like southwest, etc.)

Looking west *(ouest):* The Seine runs east to west (though at this point it's flowing more southwest). At the far end of the skinny "island" in the river, find the tiny copy of the Statue of Liberty, looking 3,633 miles away to her big sister in New York. Gustave Eiffel, a man of many talents, also designed the internal supports of New York's Statue of Liberty, which was cast in copper by fellow Frenchman Frederic Bartholdi (1886).

The sharp-eyed might spy on the Left Bank a round green patch amid all the buildings—Paris' heliport.

Looking north *(nord):* The vast, forested expanse is the Bois de Boulogne, the three-square-mile park that hosts joggers and *boules* players by day and prostitutes by night. The track with bleachers is Paris' horseracing track, the Hippodrome de Longchamp. At your feet is the curved arcade of the Trocadéro. Beyond, in the far distance, are the skyscrapers of La Defense. Find the Arc de Triomphe, to the right. The lone skyscraper between the Arc and the Trocadéro is the Palais des Congrès, a complex that hosts international conferences and major concerts.

Looking east *(est):* At your feet are the Seine and the pont Alexandre bridge, with its four golden statues. Looking upstream, find the Orsay Museum, the Louvre, and the twin towers and steeple of Notre-Dame.

On the Right Bank (which is to your left), find the Grand Palais, next to the pont Alexandre. Beyond the Grand Palais is the bullet-shaped dome of Sacré-Coeur atop Butte Montmarte.

Looking south *(sud):* In a line, find the Champ de Mars, the Ecole Militaire, the Y-shaped UNESCO building, and the 689-foot Montparnasse Tower skyscraper. To the left is the golden dome of Les Invalides, and beyond that, the state capitol-shaped dome of the Pantheon.

Building the Tower

As you ascend through the metal beams, imagine being a worker, perched high above nothing, riveting this thing together. It was a massive project, and it took all the ingenuity of the Industrial Age—including mass production, cutting-edge technology, and capitalist funding.

The foundation was the biggest obstacle. The soil, especially along the river, was too muddy to support big pillars. Gustave Eiffel drew on his bridge-building experience, where support piers needed to be constructed underwater. He sunk heavy compartments (caissons) into the wet soil. These were water-tight and injected with breathable air, so workers could dig out the mud beneath them, allowing the caisson to sink

further. When the workers were done, the hole was filled in with cement 20 feet thick and capped with stone. The massive iron pillars were sunk into the ground at an angle, anchored in the subterranean stone.

The tower went up like an 18,000-piece erector set, made of 15-foot iron beams held together with 2.5 million rivets. The pieces were mass-produced in factories in the suburbs and brought in on wagons. For two years, 300 workers assembled the pieces, the tower rising as they went. First, they used wooden scaffolding to support the lower (angled) sections, until the pillars came together and the tower could support itself. Then the iron beams were lifted up with steam-powered cranes, including cranes on tracks (creeper cranes) that inched up the pillars as the tower progressed. There, daring workers dangled from rope ladders, balanced on beams, and tightroped their way across them as they put the pieces in place. The workers then hammered in red-hot rivets made on-site by blacksmiths. As the rivets cooled, they solidified the structure.

After a mere year and a half of work, the tower already surpassed the previous tallest building in the world—the Washington Monument (555 feet)—which had taken 36 years to build.

The tower was painted a rusty red. (Since then, it's sported several colors, including mustard and the current brown-gray, and is repainted every seven years.) Two years, two months, and five days after construction began, the tower was done. On May 15, 1889, a red, white, and blue beacon was lit on the top, the World's Fair began, and the tower carried its first astounded visitor to the top.

The tippy top: Ascend another short staircase to the open-air top. Look up at all the satellite dishes and communications equipment (and around to find the tiny WC). You'll see the tiny apartment given to the builder of the tower, Gustave Eiffel, now represented by a mannequin (he's the one with the beard).

The mannequins re-create the moment during the 1889 Exhibition when the American Thomas Edison paid a visit to his fellow techie, Gustave (and Gustave's daughter Claire), presenting them with his new invention, a phonograph. (Then they cranked it up and blasted The Who's "I Can See for Miles".)

• *Catch the elevator down to the...*

Second Level

The second level (400 feet) has the best views because you're closer to the sights, and the monuments are more recognizable. (The best views are up the short stairway, on the platform without the wire-cage barriers.) This level has souvenir shops, public telephones to call home, and a small stand-up café.

The head chef at Jules Verne Restaurant on this level is currently Alain Ducasse, who operates restaurants around the world. Hopefully, his three-star brand of haute cuisine matches the 400-foot *haute* of the restaurant.

• *Catch the elevator or take the stairs (5 minutes, 360 steps, free) down to the...*

First Level

The first level (200 feet) has more great views, all well-described by the tower's panorama displays. There are a number of photo exhibits on the tower's history, a post office (daily 10:00–19:00, cancellation stamp will read "Eiffel Tower"), WCs, a conference hall (closed to tourists), an ATM, and souvenirs. There's a small café (€6 sandwich or pizza, outdoor tables in summer) and the Altitude 95 restaurant. (In wintertime, part of the first level is set up as an ice-skating rink.)

Up and Down

The tower—which was designed from the start to accom-modate hordes of visitors—has always had elevators. Today's elevators are modern replacements. Back in the late 19th cen-tury, elevator technology was so new that this was the one job that Gustave Eiffel subcontracted to other experts (including an American company).

They needed a special design to accommodate the angle of the tower's pillars. Today's elevators make about 100 round-trip journeys a day.

There are 1,665 stairs up to the top level, though tourists can only climb 720 of them, up as far as the second level. During a race in 1905, a gentleman climbed from the ground to the second floor—elevation gain 400 feet—in 3 minutes, 12 seconds.

Videos shown in the small theater (some permanent, some rotat-ing) document the tower's construction, paint job, place in pop culture, and a century of fireworks, capped by the entire millennium blast.

A display on weather shows how the sun warms the metal, caus-ing the top to expand and lean about five inches away from the sun. Nearby, a small model of the tower oscillates slightly, simulating the tower's real-time movement in the wind and sun. Because of its lacy design, even the strongest of winds could never blow the tower down, only cause it to sway back and forth a few inches. In fact, Eiffel designed the tower primarily with wind resistance in mind, wanting a structure seemingly "molded by the action of the wind itself." Many modern skyscrapers follow the mathematics pioneered by Eiffel.

Watch the original hydraulic pump (1889) at work. This once pumped water from this level to the second level to feed the machin-ery powering the upper elevator. Then look at the big wheels that wind and unwind heavy cables to lift the elevators.

• *Consider a drink or a sandwich overlooking all of Paris, then take the elevator or stairs (5 minutes, 360 steps, free) to the ground.*

The Tour Ends

Welcome back to earth. Nearby, you can catch the Bateaux Parisiens boat for a Seine cruise (near the base of Eiffel Tower, see page 34 for details). Also nearby are the Quai Branly Museum (page 51), the rue Cler area (page 164), Army Museum and Napoleon's Tomb (page 52), and the Rodin Museum (page 52).

Once you've climbed the tower, you come to appreciate it even more from a distance. For a final look, stroll across the river to Trocadéro Square or to the end of the Champ de Mars and look back for great views. However impressive it may be by day, the tower is an awesome thing to see at twilight, when it becomes engorged with light, and virile Paris lies back and lets night be on top. When darkness fully envelops the city, the tower seems to climax with a spectacular light show at the top of each hour...for five minutes.

RODIN MUSEUM TOUR

Musée Rodin

Auguste Rodin (1840–1917) was a modern Michelangelo, sculpting human figures on an epic scale, revealing through the body their deepest thoughts and feelings. Like many of Michelangelo's unfinished works, Rodin's statues rise from the raw stone around them, driven by the life force. With missing limbs and scarred skin, these are prefab classics, making ugliness noble. Rodin's people are always moving restlessly. Even the famous *Thinker* is moving. While he's plopped down solidly, his mind is a million miles away. The museum presents a full range of Rodin's work, housed in a historic mansion where he once lived and worked.

ORIENTATION

Cost: €6, free on the first Sun of the month, €1 for garden only, both museum and garden covered by Museum Pass, temporary exhibits in the entrance hall cost extra (not covered by Museum Pass). Museum Pass–holders can bypass lines for temporary exhibits to quickly get into the permanent collection.

Hours: April–Sept Tue–Sun 9:30–17:45, gardens close at 18:45; Oct–March Tue–Sun 9:30–16:45, gardens close at 17:00; last entry 30 minutes before closing, closed Mon.

Getting There: It's at 79 rue de Varenne, near the Army Museum and Napoleon's Tomb (Mo: Varenne). Bus #69 stops at Grenelle-Bellechasse.

Information: The entire museum is being gradually renovated over the next few years; expect some changes to this tour. Pick up the museum map. Tel. 01 44 18 61 10, www.musee-rodin.fr.

Audioguide Tours: €4, covering the museum and gardens.

Length of This Tour: Allow one hour.

Baggage Check: Even a fairly small bag must be checked, unless you tuck it under your arm like a purse.

Cuisine Art: There's a peaceful café in the gardens behind the museum. For better options, leave the museum, cross the esplanade des Invalides, and find many recommended cafés and restaurants in the rue Cler area (a 10-min walk, see page 380).

Photography: Photography without a flash is allowed.

THE TOUR BEGINS

Enter and buy tickets in the new, modern entrance hall. There's a bookstore, a gallery for temporary exhibits, and WCs. Pick up the museum map—this tour is keyed to its room numbers. The permanent collection is located outside this hall, in the mansion and the gardens.

• *Exit the entrance hall, walk across the courtyard, and enter the mansion. Turn left (baggage-check here), and walk to the first room to start a circular tour of the ground floor.*

Room 1

Rodin's early works match the belle époque style of the time—noble busts of bourgeois citizens, pretty portraits of their daughters, and classical themes. Born of working-class roots, Rodin taught himself art by sketching statues at the Louvre and then sculpting copies.

The Man with the Broken Nose (*L'Homme au nez cassé*, 1865)—a deliberately ugly work—was 23-year-old Rodin's first break from the norm. He meticulously sculpted this deformed man (one of the few models the struggling

sculptor could afford), but then the clay statue froze in his unheated studio, and the back of the head fell off. Rodin loved it! Art critics hated it. Rodin persevered. (Note: The museum rotates the display of two different versions—the broken-headed one and another, repaired version Rodin made later that critics accepted.)

See the painting of Rodin's future wife, Rose Beuret *(Portrait de Madame Rodin)*, who suffered with him through obscurity and celebrity.

Room 2

To feed his new family, Rodin cranked out small-scale works with his boss' name on them—portraits, ornamental vases, nymphs, and

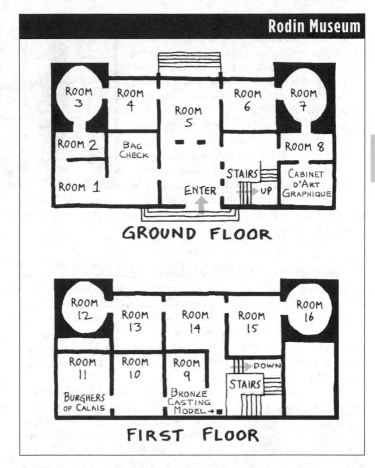

Rodin Museum

ROOM 3 · ROOM 4 · ROOM 5 · ROOM 6 · ROOM 7

ROOM 2 · BAG CHECK · ROOM 8

ROOM 1 · STAIRS UP · CABINET D'ART GRAPHIQUE

ENTER

GROUND FLOOR

ROOM 12 · ROOM 13 · ROOM 14 · ROOM 15 · ROOM 16

ROOM 11 · ROOM 10 · ROOM 9 · STAIRS DOWN

BURGHERS OF CALAIS · BRONZE CASTING MODEL →

FIRST FLOOR

RODIN MUSEUM

knickknacks to decorate buildings. Still, the series of mother-and-childs (Rose and baby Auguste?) allowed him to experiment on a small scale with the intertwined twosomes he'd do later.

His job gave him enough money to visit Italy, where he was inspired by Michelangelo's boldness, monumental scale, restless figures, and "unfinished" look. Rapidly approaching middle age, Rodin was ready to rock.

Room 3

Rodin moved to Brussels, where his first major work, *The Bronze Age* (*L'âge d'airain*, 1877), brought controversy and the fame that surrounds it. This nude youth perhaps inspired by Michelangelo's *Dying Slave* (in the Louvre—see page 120), awakens to a new world. It was so lifelike that Rodin was accused of not sculpting it himself, but simply casting it directly from a live body. The boy's left hand looks like he should be leaning on a spear, but it's just that missing element that makes the pose more tenuous and interesting.

The art establishment still snubbed Rodin as an outsider, and no wonder. Look at his ultra-intense take on the winged symbol of France *(La Défense)*—this Marseillaise screams, "Off with their heads!" at the top of her lungs. Rodin was a slave to his muses, and some of them inspired monsters.

Room 4

Like the hand of a sculptor, *The Hand of God* (*La Main de Dieu*, 1896) shapes Adam and Eve from the mud of the earth to which they will return. Rodin himself worked in "mud," using his hands to model clay figures, which were then reproduced in marble or bronze, usually by his assistants. Spin this masterpiece on its turntable. (I'm serious, give it a turn.) Rodin wants you to see it from every angle. He first worked from the front view, then checked the back and side profiles, then filled in the in-between.

In *The Kiss* (1888–1889), a passionate woman twines around a solid man for their first, spontaneous kiss. In their bodies, we can almost read the thoughts, words, and movements that led up to this meeting of lips. *The Kiss* was the first Rodin work the public loved. Rodin came to despise it, thinking it simple and sentimental.

Other works in this room show embracing couples who seem to emerge from the stone just long enough to love. Rodin left many works "unfinished," reminding us that all creation is a difficult process of dragging a form out of chaos.

Room 5

The two hands that form the arch of *The Cathedral* (*La Cathédrale*, 1908) are actually two right hands (a man's and a woman's?).

In the room's center, a bronze man strides forward, as bold as the often-controversial Rodin. The armless and headless *The Walking Man* (*L'Homme Qui Marche*, 1900–1907) plants his back foot forcefully, as though he's about to step, while his front foot already has stepped. Rodin—who himself had one foot in the classical past, one in the modernist future—captures two poses at once.

Rodin worked with many materials—he chiseled marble (though not often), modeled clay, cast bronze, worked plaster, painted, and sketched. He often created different versions of the same subject in different media.

Room 6

This room displays works by Camille Claudel, mostly in the style of her master. The 44-year-old Rodin took 18-year-old Camille as his pupil, muse, colleague, and lover. We can follow the arc of their relationship:

Rodin was inspired by young Camille's beauty and spirit, and he often used her as a model. (See several versions of her head.)

As his student, "Mademoiselle C" learned from Rodin, doing portrait busts in his lumpy, molded-clay style. Her bronze bust of

Rodin (which might not be on display) shows the steely-eyed sculptor with strong front and side profiles, barely emerging from the materials they both worked with.

Soon they were lovers. *The Waltz* (*La Valse*, 1892) captures the spinning exuberance the two must have felt as they embarked together on a new life. The couple twirls—hands so close but not touching—in a delicate balance.

But Rodin was devoted as well to his lifelong companion, Rose (see her face emerging from a block of marble). Camille's *Maturity* (*L'Age Mûr*, 1895–1907, also in Orsay Museum) shows the breakup. A young woman on her knees begs the man not to leave her, as he's led away reluctantly by an older woman. The statue may literally depict a scene from real life, in which a naked, fragile Camille begged Rodin not to return to his wife. In the larger sense, it may also be a metaphor for the cruel passage of time, as Youth tries to save Maturity from the clutches of Old Age.

Rodin did leave Camille. Talented in her own right but tormented by grief and jealousy, Camille became increasingly unstable and spent her final years in an institution. Camille's *The Wave* (*La*

Vague, 1900), carved in green onyx in a very un-Rodin style, shows tiny, helpless women huddling together as a tsunami is about to engulf them.

Room 7 and Room 8

What did Rodin think of women? Here are many different images from which you can draw your own conclusions.

Eve (1881) buries her head in shame, hiding her nakedness. But she can't hide the consequences—she's pregnant.

Rodin became famous, wealthy, and respected, and society ladies all wanted him to do their portraits. In Room 8, you'll see a sculpture of his last mistress *(La Duchesse de Choiseul),* an American who lived with him here in this mansion. Rodin purposely left in the metal base points (used in the sculpting process), placed suggestively.

Cabinet d'Art Graphique/Temporary Exhibits

This dimly lit room may contain Rodin's sketches (though temporary exhibits often occupy this space). The first flash of inspiration for a huge statue might be a single line sketched on notepaper. Rodin wanted nude models in his studio at all times—walking, dancing, and squatting—in case they struck some new and interesting pose. Rodin thought of sculpture as simply "drawing in all dimensions."

• *Upstairs, you'll find a glass display case on the mezzanine that tries hard to explain…*

The Bronze Casting Process

Rodin made his bronze statues not by hammering sheets of metal, but by using the classic "lost wax" technique. He'd start by shaping the figure out of wet plaster. This figure becomes a model that's covered with a form-fitting mold. Pour molten bronze into the narrow space between the model and the mold around it, let it cool, remove the mold, and—*voilà!*—you have a hollow bronze statue ready to be polished and varnished. With a mold, you could produce other copies, which is why there are many authorized bronze versions of Rodin's masterpieces all over the world.

RODIN'S "THE QUACKER"

PINS   WAX

ROUGH COPY   OUTER MOLD

TUBES (TO DRAIN THE WAX)

DCH

As the display case teaches, there are actually a number of additional steps involving two models and two molds. Rodin used the original plaster model to make a first mold, which was used to make a heat-resistant clay copy of the original plaster model. He sanded down the clay copy, coated it with a wax skin, and then touched up the wax to add surface details. He used this touched-up copy to make the more detailed, final mold. He fitted the mold with ventilation tubes and started pouring in the molten bronze. The wax melted away—the "lost wax" technique—and the bronze cooled and hardened in its place, thus forming the final bronze statue.

Room 9

The Thinker was to have been the centerpiece of a massive project that Rodin wrestled with for decades—a doorway encrusted with characters from Dante's *Inferno*. These *Gates of Hell* were never completed (we'll later see the partly finished piece in the garden), but the studies for it (scattered throughout this room and in a display cabinet) are some of Rodin's masterpieces.

These figures struggle to come into existence. Rodin was fascinated by the theory of evolution—not Darwin's version of the survival of the fittest, but the Frenchman Jean-Baptiste Lamarck's. His figures survive not by the good fortune of random mutation (Darwin), but by their own striving (Lamarck). They are driven by the life force, a restless energy that animates and shapes dead matter (Lamarck and Henri-Louis Bergson). Rodin must have felt that force even as a child, when he first squeezed soft clay and saw a worm emerge.

Room 10

Rodin's feverish attempts to capture a portrait of the novelist Balzac ranged from a pot-bellied Bacchus to a headless nude cradling an erection (the display changes, showing various versions). In a moment of inspiration, Rodin threw a plaster-soaked robe over a nude and watched it dry. This became the proud, final, definitive version.

Room 11

A virtual unknown until his mid-30s, Rodin slowly began receiving major commissions for public monuments. *The Burghers of Calais* (*Bourgeois de Calais*, in the center of the room, described below in garden section) depicts the actual event in 1347, when, in order to save their people, the city fathers surrendered the keys of the city—and their own lives—to the king of England. Rodin portrays them not in some glorious pose drenched in pomp and allegory, but as a simple example of men sacrificing their lives together. As they head to the gallows, with ropes already around their necks, each body shows a distinct emotion, ranging from courage to despair. Compare the small plaster model in this room with the final, life-size bronze group outside the window in the garden (near the street).

• Double back past the bronze-casting display, to the rooms overlooking the gardens in the back.

Room 14

Here you'll see studies of the female body in its different forms—crouching, soaring, dying, open, closed, wrinkled, intertwined. Newsreel footage of Rodin is often on display in this room or nearby.

Room 15

Legendary lovers kiss, embrace, and intertwine in yin-yang bliss. In a display case, dancers stretch, pose, and leap.

Room 16

For the 1900 World's Fair, Paris considered building a huge monument honoring common workers, who were powering the Industrial Revolution (and demanding bathroom breaks and overtime pay). Rodin submitted this model of a Tower of Labor *(La Tour du Travail)*. A column wrapped in a corkscrew symbolizes the march of progress. At the base, statues of Day and Night remind everyone that factories operated 24/7. Reliefs spiraling up the column honored workers: workers at the base doing manual labor, then climbing the career ladder to desk jobs and the arts. Crowning the monument are the fruits of man's labor—the spinning angels of Love and Joy. Rodin's model was much admired but never built.

• Backtrack through Room 14 to reach...

Room 13

See Rodin's portrait busts of celebrities and some paintings by (yawn, are we through yet?) Vincent van Gogh, Claude Monet, and Pierre-Auguste Renoir. Rodin enjoyed discussions with Monet and other artists and incorporated their ideas in his work. Rodin is often considered an Impressionist because he captured spontaneous "impressions" of figures and created rough surfaces that catch reflected light.

Room 12

Get a sense of Rodin's working process by comparing the small plaster "sketches" (in the glass case) with the final, large-scale marble versions that line the walls. Rodin employed and mentored many artists who executed these designs. By the end of his long, productive life, Rodin was more famous than his works.

THE GARDENS

Rodin lived and worked in this mansion, renting rooms alongside Henri Matisse, the poet Rainer Maria Rilke (Rodin's secretary), and the dancer Isadora Duncan. He loved placing his creations in the overgrown gardens. These are his greatest works, Rodin at his most expansive. The epic human figures are enhanced, not dwarfed, by nature.

• *Leaving the house, you've got five more stops: two on the left and three on the right. Beyond these stops is a big, breezy garden ornamented with statues, a cafeteria, and a WC.*

The Thinker (*Le Penseur,* 1906)

Leaning slightly forward, tense and compact, every muscle working toward producing that one great thought, Man contemplates his fate. No constipation jokes, please.

This is not an intellectual, but a linebacker who's realizing there's

more to life than frat parties. It's the first man evolving beyond his animal nature to think the first thought. It's anyone who's ever worked hard to reinvent himself or to make something new or better. Said Rodin: "It is a statue of myself."

There are 29 other authorized copies of this statue, one of the most famous in the world.

• *To the left of* The Thinker, *you'll find...*

Balzac (1898)

The iconoclastic novelist turns his nose up at the notion he should be honored with a statue. This final version also stands in the Musée d'Orsay, and on a street median in Montparnasse. When the statue was unveiled, the crowd booed, a fitting tribute to both the defiant novelist and the bold man who sculpted him.

• *Along the street opposite the ticket booth are...*

The Burghers of Calais (1889)

The six city fathers trudge to their execution, and we can read in their

faces and poses what their last thoughts are. They mill about, dazed, as each one deals with the decision he's made to sacrifice himself for his city.

• *Circling counterclockwise...*

The man carrying the key to the city tightens his lips in determination. The bearded man is weighed down with grief. Another buries his head in his hands. One turns, seeking reassurance from his friend, who turns

Rodin Museum Gardens

away and gestures helplessly. The final key-bearer (in back) raises his hand to his head.

Each is alone in his thoughts, but they're united by their mutual sacrifice, by the base they stand on, and by their weighty robes—gravity is already dragging them down to their graves.

Pity the poor souls; view the statue from various angles (you can't ever see all the faces at once); then thank King Edward III, who, at the last second, pardoned them.

• *Follow* The Thinker's *gaze across the gardens. Standing before a tall white backdrop is a big dark door...*

The Gates of Hell (*La Porte de l'Enfer,* 1880–1917)

These doors (never meant to actually open) were never finished for a museum that was never built. But the vision of Dante's trip into hell gave Rodin a chance to explore the dark side of human experience. "Abandon all hope ye who enter here," was hell's motto. The three Shades at the top of the door point down—that's where we're going.

Beneath the Shades, pondering the whole scene from above, is Dante as the Thinker. Below him, the figures emerge from the darkness just long enough to tell their sad tale of depravity. There are Paolo and Francesca (in the center of the right door), who were driven into an illicit love affair that brought them here. Ugolino (left door, just below center) crouches in prison over his kids. This poor soul was so driven by hunger that he ate the corpses of his own children. On all fours like an animal, he is the dark side of natural selection. Finally, find what some say is Rodin himself (at the very bottom, inside the right doorjamb, where it just starts to jut out), crouching humbly.

You'll find some of these figures writ large in the garden. *The Thinker* is behind you, *The Shades* (c. 1889) are 30 yards to the right, and *Ugolino* (1901–1904) dines in the fountain at the far end.

It's appropriate that the *Gates*—Rodin's "cathedral"—remained unfinished. He was always a restless artist for whom the process of discovery was as important as the finished product.

• *To the right of* The Gates of Hell *is a glassed-in building, the...*

Gallery of Marbles

Unfinished, these statues show human features emerging from the rough stone. Imagine Rodin in his studio, working to give them life.

Victor Hugo (at the far end of the Gallery), the great champion of progress, and author of *Les Misérables* and *The Hunchback of Notre-Dame*, leans back like Michelangelo's nude *Adam*, waiting for the spark of creation. He tenses his face and cups his ear, straining to hear the call from the blurry Muse above him. Once inspired, he can bring the idea to life (just as Rodin did) with the strength of his powerful arms. It's been said that all of Rodin's work shows the struggle of mind over matter, of brute creatures emerging from the mud and evolving into a species of thinkers.

ARMY MUSEUM AND NAPOLEON'S TOMB TOUR

Musée de l'Armée

If you've ever considered being absolute dictator of a united Europe, come here first. Hitler did, but still went out and made the same mistakes as his role model. (Hint: Don't invade Russia.) Napoleon's tomb rests beneath the golden dome of Les Invalides church.

In addition to the tomb, the complex of Les Invalides—a former veterans' hospital built by Louis XIV—has various military museums, collectively called the Army Museum. Visiting the different sections, you can watch the art of war unfold from stone axes to Axis powers. See medieval armor, Napoleon's horse stuffed and mounted, Louis XIV–era uniforms and weapons, and much more. The best part is the section dedicated to the two World Wars, especially World War II.

The Army Museum's section on French military history ("Louis XIV to Napoleon III") is closed for renovation but is slated to reopen in the spring of 2009...in *théorie*.

ORIENTATION

Cost: €8, ticket covers all museums within Les Invalides complex—including Napoleon's Tomb, includes audioguide for tomb; covered by Museum Pass, free for all military personnel with ID, €6 within an hour of closing time.

Hours: Daily April–Sept 10:00–18:00 (tomb closes 15 min earlier), mid-June–mid-Sept tomb stays open until 19:00, museum might be open Tue until 21:00; Oct–March closes at 17:00; last entry 30 min before closing, Oct–May closed first Mon of every month.

Getting There: The museum and tomb are at Hôtel des Invalides, with its hard-to-miss golden dome (129 rue de Grenelle, near Rodin Museum; Mo: La Tour Maubourg, Varenne, or Invalides). Bus #69 from the Marais and rue Cler area is also handy. The museum is a 10-minute walk from rue Cler. There are two entrances: one from the grand esplanade des Invalides (river side) and the other from behind the gold dome on avenue de Tourville.

Information: A slim English map/guide is available at the ticket office. Pick up the included audioguide when you enter the tomb. Tel. 01 44 42 38 77, www.invalides.org.

Length of This Tour: Women—two hours, men—three hours.

Cuisine Art: A reasonable cafeteria is next to the ticket office, the rear gardens are picnic-perfect, and rue Cler is a 10-minute walk away (see page 380).

Nearby: You'll likely see the French playing *boules* on the esplanade (as you face Les Invalides, look for the dirt area to the upper right; for the rules of *boules*, see page 346).

THE TOUR BEGINS

• *Start at Napoleon's Tomb, underneath the golden dome. The entrance is from the back end (farthest from the Seine) of this vast complex of churches and museums.*

NAPOLEON'S TOMB

Enter the church, gaze up at the dome, then lean over the railing and bow to the emperor lying inside the scrolled, red porphyry tomb

(see photo on opposite page). If the lid were opened, you'd find an oak coffin inside, holding another ebony coffin, housing two lead ones, then mahogany, then tinplate...until finally, you'd find Napoleon himself, staring up, with his head closest to the door. When his body was exhumed from the original grave and transported here (1840), it was still perfectly preserved, even after 19 years in the ground.

Born of humble Italian heritage on the French-owned isle of Corsica, Napoleon Bonaparte (1769–1821) went to school at Paris' Ecole Militaire, quickly rising through the ranks amid the chaos of the Revolution. The charismatic "Little Corporal" won fans by fighting for democracy at home and abroad. In 1799, he assumed power and, within five short years, conquered most of Europe. The great champion of the Revolution had become a dictator, declaring himself emperor of a new Rome.

Napoleon's red tomb on its green base stands 15 feet high in the center of a marble floor. It's exalted by the dome above, where dead Frenchmen cavort with saints and angels, forming a golden halo over Napoleon.

Napoleon is surrounded by family. After conquering Europe,

ARMY MUSEUM

Overview of the Army Museum and Napoleon's Tomb

The Army Museum and Napoleon's Tomb are in the Invalides complex (or should I say "Napoleon complex"?). The buildings house several noteworthy sights, with different entrances. All are included in your ticket price. The tomb is on the back (south) side, while the various museums surround the main courtyard on the north side. For their exact loca-

tions, see the map in this chapter and the free English map/guide available at the ticket office. Be prepared for considerable renovation work—this museum is in the middle of a major overhaul.

Pick your favorite war. With limited time, visit only Napoleon's Tomb and the excellent World War I and World War II Wings. Most other displays consist of dummies in uniforms and endless glass cases full of muskets without historical context.

Of the various sights scattered about, these are the best, rated in order of importance (the first four are described more fully in self-guided tours in this chapter):

▲▲▲**Napoleon's Tomb**—The emperor's final resting place, under the golden dome of Les Invalides church (at the back of the complex, farthest from the river).

he installed his big brother, Joseph, as king of Spain (turn around to see Joseph's black-and-white marble tomb in the alcove to the left of the door); his little brother, Jerome, became king of the German kingdom of Westphalia (tucked into the chapel to the right of the door); and his baby boy, Napoleon II (downstairs), sat in diapers on the throne of Rome.

In other alcoves, you'll find more dead war heroes, including Marshal Ferdinand Foch, the commander in chief of the multinational Allied forces in World War I, his tomb lit with otherworldly blue light. These heroes, plus many painted saints, make this the French Valhalla in the Versailles of churches.

• *The stairs behind the altar (with the corkscrew columns) take you down to crypt level for a closer look at the tomb.*

The Crypt

Wandering clockwise, read the names of Napoleon's battles on the floor around the base of the tomb. Rivoli marks the battle where the rookie 26-year-old general took a ragtag band of "citizens" and

▲▲▲**World War II Wing**—Interesting coverage of this critical war (entrance at southwest corner of courtyard).

▲▲**World War I Wing**—A manageable-sized series of rooms setting the stage for World War II (same entrance as World War II Wing, at southwest corner of courtyard).

▲**Louis XIV to Napoleon III** (East Wing)—French military history (c. 1670–1870), with a focus on Napoleon (entrance on east side of courtyard). This museum is scheduled to reopen in the spring of 2009, after extensive renovation. (I have included a self-guided tour in this chapter, just in case they've finished in time for your visit—but be aware that the displays may have changed.)

Charles de Gaulle Museum—New museum (in the basement of the East Wing) with 25-minute film plus high-tech display of photos tracing the life of France's towering 20th-century figure. An audioguide leads you through his youth in the era of the hot-air balloon, two world wars, his rebuilding of France as president, and the social unrest of the 1960s that toppled him. The museum helps bring France's history of war into the modern age.

Arms and Armour (West Wing)—Weapons from the 13th–17th centuries (entrance on west side of courtyard). Connoisseurs of cannons, swords, suits of armor, crossbows, and early guns will love it; others can browse a few rooms and move on.

The Rest—Your ticket is good for all the exhibits in the complex (consult your free museum map), including the St. Louis Church, the Museum of Relief Maps (town models used by strategists to plan defenses), and the Museum of the Order of Liberation (honoring heroes of the WWII Resistance).

thrashed the professional Austrian troops in Italy, returning to Paris a celebrity. In Egypt *(Pyramides)*, he fought Turks and tribesmen to a standstill. The exotic expedition caught the public eye and he returned home a legend.

Napoleon's huge victory over Austria at Austerlitz on the first anniversary of his coronation made him Europe's top dog. At the head of the million-man Great Army *(La Grande Armée),* he made a three-month blitz attack through Germany and Austria. As a general, he was daring, relying on top-notch generals and a mobile force of independent armies. His personal charisma on the battlefield was said to be worth 10,000 additional men.

Pause in the battles to gaze at the grand statue of Napoleon the emperor in the alcove at the head of the tomb—royal scepter and orb of Earth in his hands. By 1804, all of Europe was at his feet. He held an elaborate ceremony in Notre-Dame, where he proclaimed his wife, Josephine, an empress, and himself—the 35-year-old son of humble immigrants—as emperor. The laurel wreath, the robes, and the Roman eagles proclaim him the equal of the Caesars. The floor

Napoleon Bonaparte
(1769–1821)

Born to Italian parents on the French-ruled isle of Corsica, Napoleon attended French schools, although he spoke the language with an Italian accent to the end of his days. After graduating from Paris' Ecole Militaire (trained in the latest high-tech artillery), his military career took an unexpected turn when the Revolution erupted (1789), and he chose to return to Corsica to fight royalist oppression.

In 1793, as commander of artillery, he besieged Toulon, forcing the royalists to surrender, and earning his first great victory. He later defended the Revolutionary government from royalist mobs in Paris by firing a "whiff of grapeshot" into the crowd (1795). Such daring military exploits and personal charisma earned him promotions and the nickname "The Little Corporal"—not for his height (he was an average 5'6") but as a term of endearment from the rank and file. When he married the classy socialite Josephine Beauharnais, Napoleon became a true celebrity. In 1798, having conquered Italy, Austria, and Egypt, Napoleon returned to Paris, where the weak government declared him First Consul—ostensibly as the champion of democracy, but in fact, a virtual dictator of much of Europe. He was 29 years old.

Over the next years, he solidified his reign with military victories over Europe's kings—now allied against France. Under his rule, France sold the Louisiana Purchase to America, and legal scholars drew up the Code of Napoleon, a system of laws still used by many European governments today. In 1804, his power peaked when he crowned himself emperor in a ceremony in Notre-Dame blessed by the pope. The Revolutionary general was now, paradoxically, part of Europe's royalty. Needing an heir to the throne, he divorced barren Josephine and married an Austrian duchess, Marie Louise, who bore him the boy known to historians as "The King of Rome."

In 1812, Napoleon decided to invade Russia, and the horrendous losses from that failed venture drained his power. It was time to pig-pile on France, and Europe's nations toppled Napoleon, sending him to exile on the isle of Elba (1814). Napoleon escaped long enough to raise an army for a final hundred-day campaign before finally being defeated by British and Prussian forces at the Battle of Waterloo (1815). Guilty of war crimes, he was sentenced to exile on the remote South Atlantic island of St. Helena, where he talked to his dog, studied a little English, penned his memoirs, spoke his final word—"Josephine"—and died.

at the statue's feet marks the grave of his son, Napoleon II (*Roi de Rome*, 1811–1832).

Around the crypt are relief panels showing Napoleon's constructive side. Dressed in toga and laurel leaves, he dispenses justice, charity, and pork-barrel projects to an awed populace.

• *In the first panel to the right of the statue...*

He establishes an Imperial University to educate naked boys throughout "*tout l'empire.*" The roll of great scholars links modern France with those of the past: Plutarch, Homer, Plato, and Aristotle. Three panels later, his various building projects (canals, roads, and so on) are celebrated with a list and his quotation, "Everywhere I passed, I left durable benefit" *("Partout où mon regne à passé...").*

Hail Napoleon. Then, at his peak, came his fatal mistake.

• *Turn around and look down to* Moscowa *(the Battle of Moscow).*

Napoleon invaded Russia with 600,000 men and returned to Paris with 60,000 frostbitten survivors. Two years later, the Russians marched into Paris, and Napoleon's days were numbered. After a brief exile on the isle of Elba, he skipped parole, sailed to France, bared his breast, and said, "Strike me down or follow me!" For 100 days, they followed him, finally into Belgium, where the British hammered the French at the Battle of Waterloo (conspicuously absent on the floor's decor). Exiled again by a war tribunal, he spent his last years in a crude shack on the small South Atlantic island of St. Helena.

• *To get to the Courtyard of Honor and the various military museums, exit the same way you entered, make a U-turn right, and march past the cafeteria and ticket hall. Pause halfway down the long hallway. On the right through the glass, you'll see...*

Napoleon's Tombstone (Pierre Tombale)

This bare stone slab, surrounded by shrubs and weeping willows, once rested atop Napoleon's grave on the island of St. Helena. The epitaph was never finished, since the French and British wrangled over what to call the hero/tyrant. The stone simply reads, "Here lies..."

• *Continuing to the end of the hallway, you'll find the entrance to the World War I and World War II Wings (in the southwest corner of the main courtyard). Go upstairs, following blue-banner signs reading* Les Deux Guerres Mondiales, 1871–1945. *The museum is laid out so that you first see the coverage of World War I, though some may choose to skip ahead to the more substantial WWII section.*

ARMY MUSEUM

Army Museum and Napoleon's Tomb

GRAND ESPLANADE
DES INVALIDES

TO LA TOUR-MAUBOURG Ⓜ

TICKETS & INFO

ENTER

TO SEINE, BUS #69 & INVALIDES Ⓜ

ARMY MUSEUM (WEST WING)

ARMS & ARMOUR

COURT-YARD OF HONOR

ARMY MUSEUM (EAST WING)

❷ ❸

LOUIS XIV TO NAPOLEON III

VARENNE Ⓜ

BLVD. DES INVALIDES

R. VARENNE

❶

NAPOLEON'S TOMBSTONE

SOLDIERS' CHURCH (ST. LOUIS)

RODIN MUSEUM

WC

INFO & TICKETS

GILDED DOME

CAFÉ

ENTER

NAPOLEON'S TOMB

GARDENS

TO ECOLE MILITAIRE Ⓜ & RUE CLER

50 YARDS

50 METERS

Ⓜ METRO STATION

DCH

❶ Entrance to WWI & WWII Wings
❷ East Wing scheduled to reopen in spring of 2009
❸ Charles de Gaulle Museum (in basement)

WORLD WAR I WING

World War I (1914–1918) introduced modern technology to the age-old business of war. Tanks, chemical weapons, monstrous cannons, rapid communication, and airplanes made their debut, conspiring to kill nearly 10 million people. In addition, the war ultimately seemed senseless: It started with little provocation, raged on with few decisive battles, and ended with nothing resolved, a situation that sowed the seeds of World War II.

This 20-room museum leads you chronologically through the background, causes, battles, and outcome. There's good English information, but the displays themselves are lackluster and low-tech; move quickly and don't burn out before World War II. Even a quick walk-through gives you the essential background for the next World War. (For a better understanding of World War I, take the fast TGV train from Paris' Gare de l'Est station to Verdun and spend a day touring the battlefields where 700,000 soldiers died.)

Room 1: "Honour to the Unfortunate Bravery"

Paintings of dead and wounded soldiers from the Franco-Prussian War make it clear that World War I actually "began" in 1871, when Germany thrashed France. Suddenly, a recently united Germany was the new bully in Europe.

ARMY MUSEUM

Rooms 2–3: France Rebounds

Snapping back from its loss, France began re-arming itself, with spiffy new **uniforms** and weapons like the American-invented **Gatling gun** (early machine gun).

The French replaced the humiliation of defeat with a proud and extreme nationalism. A **video** shows how fanatic patriots hounded a (Jewish) officer named Alfred Dreyfus on trumped-up treason charges (1890s). They convicted and imprisoned him (after ceremonially breaking his sword in the Invalides courtyard), before he was finally acquitted.

Rooms 4–6: Tensions Rise

France, Germany, and the rest of Europe were in a race for wealth and power, jostling to acquire lucrative colonies in Africa and Asia (**map, video, exotic uniforms**). In a climate of mutual distrust, nations allied with their neighbors, vowing to protect each other if war ever erupted. A **map in room 6** shows France, Britain, and Russia (the Allies) teaming up against Germany, Austria-Hungary, and Italy (the Central Powers). Meanwhile, the Ottoman Empire (Turkey and the Balkans) was breaking apart, creating a tense and unstable Western world. Europe was ready to explode, but the spark that would set it off had nothing to do with Germany or France.

Room 7: Assassination, War Begins

Bang. On June 28, 1914, an Austrian archduke was shot to death (see **video** of the political mood, assassination, and mobilization). It happened in Serbia—a region not all that central, but very politically charged. One by one, Europe's nations were dragged into the regional dispute by their webs of alliances. All of Europe mobilized its troops. The **1914** stone on the floor is the first of the museum's year-stones. The Great War had begun.

Room 8: The Battle of the Marne

In September, German forces swarmed into France, hoping for a quick knockout blow. Germany brought its big guns (photo and model of

Big Bertha). The **projection map** shows how the armies tried to outflank each other along a 200-mile battlefront. As the Germans (gray-brown arrows) zeroed in on Paris, the French scrambled to send 6,000 crucial reinforcements, shuttled to the front lines in 670 Parisian **taxis.** The German tide was stemmed, and the two sides faced off, expecting to duke it out and get this war over quick. It didn't work out that way.

• *The war continues upstairs.*

Rooms 9–10: The War in the Trenches

By **1915,** they'd reached a stalemate, and the two sides settled into a long war of attrition—French and Britons on one side, Germans on the other. A **map** shows the battle line, known as the Western Front: a long line snaking 450 miles across Europe from the North Sea to the Alps. For protection against flying bullets, the soldiers dug **trenches,** which soon became home—24 hours a day, 7 days a week—for millions of men.

Life in the trenches was awful—cold, rainy, muddy, disease-ridden, and most of all, boring. Every so often, generals waved their swords and ordered their men "over the top" and into "no man's land." Armed with rifles and bayonets, they advanced into a hail of machine gun fire. In a number

La guerre des tranchées

of battles, France lost 70,000 men in a single day. The "victorious" side often won only a few hundred yards of meaningless territory that was lost the next day after still more deaths.

The war pitted 19th-century values of honor, bravery, and chivalry against 20th-century **weapons:** grenades, machine guns, tanks, and gas masks. To shoot over the tops of trenches while staying hidden, they even invented **crooked and periscope-style guns.**

Rooms 11–13: "World" War

Besides the Western Front, the War extended elsewhere, including the colonies, where many natives joined the armies of their mother countries. On the Eastern Front, Russia and Germany wore each other down. (Finally, the Russians had enough; they killed their czar, brought the troops home, and fomented a revolution that put Communists in power.)

• *Down a short hallway, enter...*

Room 14: The Allies

By 1917, the Allied forces were beginning to outstrip the Central Powers, thanks to help from around the world. Britain drew heavily from its Commonwealth nations, like Canada and Australia.

And when Uncle Sam said **"I Want You,"** five million Americans answered the call to go "Over There" (in the words of a popular song) and fight the Germans. Though the US didn't enter the War until April 1917 (and was never an enormous military factor), its very presence was one more indication that the Allies seemed destined to prevail.

Room 15: Armistice

Under the command of the French Marshal Ferdinand Foch, the Allies undertook a series of offensives that, by **1918,** would prove decisive. At the eleventh hour of the eleventh day of the eleventh month (November 11, 1918), the guns fell silent. Europeans celebrated with **victory parades.**

Room 16: A Costly Victory

Weary soldiers returned home to be honored (painting of **Arc de Triomphe** parade). After four years of battle, the war had left 9.5 million dead and 21 million wounded (see plaster casts of **disfigured faces**). Three out of every four French soldiers had been either killed or wounded. A generation was lost.

ARMY MUSEUM

Rooms 17–19: From 1918 to 1938

The Treaty of Versailles (1919), signed in the Hall of Mirrors, officially ended the war. A **map** shows how it radically redrew Europe's borders. Germany was punished severely, leaving it crushed, humiliated, stripped of crucial land, and saddled with demoralizing war debts. Marshal Foch said of the Treaty: "This is not a peace. It is an armistice for 20 years."

France, one of the "victors," was drained, trying to hang onto its prosperity and its **colonial empire.**

But by the 1930s—swamped by the Great Depression and a stagnant military (**dummy on horseback**)—France was reeling, unprepared for the onslaught of a retooled Germany seeking revenge.

• *World War II is covered directly across the hall, in the rooms marked 1939–1942.*

WORLD WAR II WING

World War II was the most destructive of Earth's struggles. In this exhibit, the war unfolds in photos, displays, and newsreels, with special emphasis on the French contribution. You may never have realized that it was Charles de Gaulle who won the war for us.

The free museum map is helpful for locating the displays we'll see. Climb to the top floor and work back down, from Germany's quick domination (third floor), to the Allies turning the tide (second floor), to the final surrender (first floor).

There are fine English descriptions throughout. Be ready—rooms come in rapid succession—and treat the following text as just an overview.

Third Floor—Axis Aggression (1939–1941)
Room 1: The Phony War (La Drôle de Guerre)

On September 1, 1939, Germany, under Adolf Hitler, invaded Poland,

starting World War II. But in a sense the war had really begun in 1918, when the "war to end all wars" ground to a halt, leaving 9.5 million dead, Germany defeated, and France devastated (if victorious). For the next two decades, Hitler fed off German resentment over the Treaty of Versailles, which humiliated and ruined Germany.

After Hitler's move into Poland, France and Britain mobilized. For the next six months, the two sides faced off, with neither actually doing battle—a tense time known to historians as the "phony" war.

Room 2: The Defeat of 1940 (La Défaite de 1940)

Then, in spring 1940, came the Blitzkrieg ("lightning war"), and Germany's better-trained and better-equipped soldiers and tanks (see **turret**) swept west through Belgium. France was immediately overwhelmed, and British troops barely escaped across the English Channel from Dunkirk. Within a month, Nazis were goose-stepping down the Champs-Elysées, and Hitler was on his way to Napoleon's tomb. Hitler made a three-hour blitz tour of the city, after which he said, "It was the dream of my life to be permitted to see Paris. I cannot say how happy I am to have that dream fulfilled today."

Room 3: The Appeal of June 18, 1940

Just like that, virtually all of Europe was dominated by Fascists. During those darkest days, as France fell and Nazism spread across the Continent, one Frenchman—an obscure military man named **Charles de Gaulle**—refused to admit defeat. He escaped to London, made inspiring speeches over the radio, and slowly convinced a small audience of French expatriates that victory was still possible.

• *Through the small door to your right is...*

Room 4: Charles de Gaulle (1890–1970)

This 20th-century John of Arc had an unshakable belief in his mission to save France. He was born into a literate, upper-class family, raised

Our War Album.—44. France's Voice in London

in military academies, and became a WWI hero and POW. (After the war, he helped administer the occupied Rhineland.) When World War II broke out, he was only a minor officer (the title of "Brigadier General" was hastily acquired during the invasion). He had limited political experience, and was virtually unknown to the French public. But he rallied France, became the focus of French patriotism, and later guided the country in the postwar years.

Room 5 and Room 6: France After the Armistice

After the surrender, Germany ruled northern France, including Paris—see the **photo** of Hitler as tourist at the Eiffel Tower. The Nazis allowed the French to administer the south and the colonies (North Africa). This puppet government, centered in the city of Vichy, was right-wing and traditional, bowing to Hitler's demands as he looted

France's raw materials and manpower for the war machine. (The movie *Casablanca,* set in Vichy-controlled Morocco, shows French officials following Nazi orders while French citizens defiantly sing "The Marseillaise.")

Room 7: The Battle of Britain—June 1940–June 1941

Facing a "New Dark Age" in Europe, British Prime Minister Winston Churchill pledged, "We will fight on the beaches....We will fight in the hills. We will never surrender."

In June 1940, Germany mobilized to invade Britain across the Channel. From June to September, they paved the way, sending bombers—up to 1,500 planes a day—to destroy military and industrial sites. When Britain wouldn't budge, Hitler concentrated on London and civilian targets. This was "The Blitz" of the winter of 1940, which killed 30,000 and left London in ruins. But Britain hung on, armed with newfangled radar, speedy Spitfires, and an iron will.

They also had the Germans' secret "Enigma" code. The **Enigma machine** (in display case), with its set of revolving drums, allowed

German commanders to scramble orders in a complex code that could safely be broadcast to their troops. The British (with crucial help from Poland) captured a machine, broke the code (in a project called "Ultra"), then monitored German airwaves. For the rest of the war, they had advance knowledge of many top-secret plans. (Occasionally, Britain even let Germany's plans succeed—sacrificing its own people—to avoid suspicion.)

By spring 1941, Hitler had given up any hope of invading the Isle of Britain. Churchill said of his people: "This was their finest hour."

Room 10: Germany Invades the Soviet Union— June 1941

Perhaps hoping to one-up Napoleon, Hitler sent his state-of-the-art tanks speeding toward Moscow (betraying his former ally, Joseph

Stalin). By winter, the advance had stalled at the gates of Moscow and was bogged down by bad weather and Soviet stubbornness. The Third Reich had reached its peak. From now on, Hitler would have to fight a two-front war. The French Renault **tank** (displayed) was downright puny compared to

the big, fast, high-caliber German Panzers. This war was often a battle of factories, to see who could produce the latest technology fastest and in the greatest numbers. And what nation might that be...?

Room 12: The United States Joins the War

"On December 7, 1941, a date which will live in infamy" (as FDR put it), Japanese planes made a sneak attack on the US base at Pearl Harbor, Hawaii, and destroyed the pride of the Pacific fleet in two hours.

The US quickly entered the fray against Japan and her ally, Germany. In two short years, America had gone from isolationist observer to supplier of Britain's arms to full-blown war ally against fascism. The US now faced a two-front war—in Europe against Hitler, and in Asia against Japan's imperialist conquest of China, Southeast Asia, and the South Pacific.

America's first victory came when Japan tried a sneak attack on the US base at Midway Island (June 3, 1942). This time—thanks to the Allies who cracked the Enigma code—America had the aircraft carrier **USS *Enterprise*** (see model) and two of her buddies lying in wait. In five minutes, three of Japan's carriers (with valuable planes) were fatally wounded, their major attack force was sunk, and Japan and the US were dead even, settling in for a long war of attrition.

Though slow to start, America eventually had an army of 16 million strong, 80,000 planes, the latest technology, $250 million a day, unlimited raw materials, and a population of Rosie the Riveters fighting for freedom to a boogie-woogie beat.

• *Continue downstairs to the second floor.*

Second Floor—The Tide Turns (1942-1944)

In 1942, the Continent was black with fascism, and Japan was secure on a distant island. The Allies had to chip away on the fringes.

Room 13: Battle of the Atlantic

German U-boats (short for *Unterseeboot*, see model) and battleships such as the *Bismarck* patrolled Europe's perimeter, where they laid spiky mines and kept America from aiding Britain. (Until long-range transport planes were invented near war's end, virtually all military transport was by ship.) The Allies traveled in convoys with air cover, used sonar and radar, and dropped depth charges, but for years, they endured the loss of up to 60 ships per month.

• *Don't bypass Room 14, tucked in the corner.*

Room 14: The War Turns—El-Alamein, Stalingrad, and Guadalcanal

Three crucial battles in autumn of 1942 put the first chink in the Fascist armor. Off the east coast of Australia, 10,000 US Marines (see kneeling soldier in glass case 14D) took an airstrip on Guadalcanal, while 30,000 Japanese held the rest of the tiny, isolated island. For the next six months, the two armies were marooned together, duking it out in thick jungles and malaria-infested swamps while their countries struggled to reinforce or rescue them. By February 1943, America had won and gained a crucial launch pad for bombing raids.

A world away, German tanks under General Erwin Rommel rolled across the vast deserts of North Africa. In October 1942, a well-equipped, well-planned offensive by British General Bernard ("Monty") Montgomery attacked at El-Alamein, Egypt, with 300 tanks. (See **British tank soldier** with headphones.) Monty drove "the Desert Fox" west into Tunisia for the first real Allied victory against the Nazi *Wehrmacht* war machine.

Then came Stalingrad. (See kneeling **Soviet soldier** in heavy coat.) In August 1942, Germany attacked the Soviet city, an industrial center and gateway to the Caucasus oil fields.

By October, the Germans had battled their way into the city center and were fighting house-to-house, but their supplies were running low, the Soviets wouldn't give up, and winter was coming. The snow fell, their tanks had no fuel, and relief efforts failed. Hitler ordered them to fight on through the bitter cold. On the worst days, 50,000 men died. (America lost a total of 58,000 in Vietnam.) Finally, on January 31, 1943, the Germans surrendered, against Hitler's orders. The six-month totals? Eight hundred thousand German and other Axis soldiers dead, 1.1 million Soviets dead. The Russian campaign put hard miles on the German war machine.

Also in 1942, the Allies began long-range bombing of German-held territory, including saturation bombing of civilians. It was global war and total war.

Room 15: The Allies Land in North Africa

Winston Churchill and US President **Franklin D. Roosevelt** (see photo with de Gaulle), two of the 20th century's most dynamic and

strong-willed statesmen, decided to attack Hitler indirectly by invading Vichy-controlled Morocco and Algeria. On November 8, 1942, 100,000 Americans and British—under the joint command of an unknown, low-key problem-solver named General Dwight ("Ike")

Eisenhower—landed on three separate beaches (including Casablanca). More than 120,000 Vichy French soldiers, ordered by their superiors to defend the Fascist cause, confronted the Allies and...gave up. (See display of some standard-issue **weapons:** Springfield rifle, Colt 45, Thompson machine gun, hand grenade.)

The Allies moved east, but bad weather, their own inexperience, and the powerful Afrika Korps under Rommel stopped them in Tunisia. But with flamboyant General George S. ("Old Blood-and-Guts") Patton punching from the west, and Monty pushing from the south, they captured the port town of Tunis on May 7, 1943. The Allies now had a base from which to retake Europe.

Room 17: The French Resistance
(also see displays in Room 20)

ARMY MUSEUM

Inside occupied France, other ordinary heroes fought the Nazis—the "underground," or Resistance. Bakers hid radios within loaves of bread to secretly contact London. Barmaids passed along tips from tipsy Nazis. Communists in black berets cut telephone lines. Farmers hid downed airmen in haystacks. Housewives spread news from the front with their gossip. Printers countered Nazi propaganda with pamphlets.

Jean Moulin (see photo in museum), de Gaulle's assistant, secretly parachuted into France and organized these scattered heroes into a unified effort. In May 1943, Moulin was elected chairman of the National Council of the Resistance. A month later, he was arrested by the Gestapo (Nazi secret police), imprisoned, tortured, and sent to Germany, where he died in transit. Still, Free France now had a (secret) government again, rallied around de Gaulle, and was ready to take over when liberation came.

Room 18: The Red Army

Monty, Patton, and Ike were certainly heroes, but the war was won on the Eastern Front by Soviet grunts, who slowly bled Germany dry. Maps show the shifting border of the Eastern Front.

Rooms 21 and 22: The Italian Campaign

On July 10, 1943, the assault on Hitler's European fortress began. More than 150,000 Americans and British sailed from Tunis and landed on the south shore of Sicily. (See **maps** and **video clips** of the campaigns.) Speedy Patton and methodical Monty began a "horse race" to take the city of Messina (the US won the friendly competition by a few hours). They met little resistance from 300,000 Italian soldiers, and were actually cheered as liberators by the Sicilian people. Their real enemies were the 50,000 German troops sent by Hitler to bolster his ally, Benito Mussolini. By September, the island was captured. On the mainland, Mussolini was arrested by his own people and Italy surrendered to the Allies. Hitler quickly poured troops into Italy (and reinstalled Mussolini) to hold off the Allied onslaught.

In early September, the Allies launched a two-pronged landing onto the beaches of southern Italy. Finally, after four long years of war, free men set foot on the European continent. Lieutenant General Mark Clark, leading the slow, bloody push north to liberate Rome, must have been reminded of the French trenches he'd fought in during World War I. As in that bloody war, the fighting in Italy was a war of attrition, fought on the ground by foot soldiers and costing many lives for just a few miles.

In January 1944, the Germans dug in between Rome and Naples at Monte Cassino, a rocky hill topped by the monastery of St. Benedict. Thousands died as the Allies tried inching up the hillside. In frustration, the Allies air-bombed the historic **monastery** to smithereens (see photo), killing many noncombatants...but no Germans, who dug in deeper. Finally, after four months of vicious, sometimes hand-to-hand combat by the Allies (Americans, Brits, Free French, Poles, Italian partisans, Indians, etc.), a band of Poles stormed the monastery, and the German back was broken.

Meanwhile, 50,000 Allies had landed on Anzio (a beach near Rome) and held the narrow beachhead for months against massive German attacks. When reinforcements arrived, Allied troops broke out and joined the two-pronged assault on the capital. Without a single bomb threatening its historic treasures, Rome fell on June 4, 1944.

• *Room 23 (with chairs) shows a film on...*

Room 23: D-Day—June 6, 1944, "Operation Overlord"

Three million Allies and six million tons of material were massed in England in preparation for the biggest fleet-led invasion in history—across the Channel to France, then eastward to Berlin. The Germans, hunkered down in northern France, knew an invasion was imminent, but the Allies kept the details top secret. On the night of June 5, 150,000 soldiers boarded ships and planes without knowing where they were headed until they were under way. Each one carried a note from General Eisenhower: "The tide has turned. The free men of the world are marching together to victory."

At 6:30 in the morning on June 6, 1944, Americans spilled out of troop transports into the cold waters off a beach in Normandy, code-named Omaha. The weather was bad, seas were rough, and the prep bombing had failed. The soldiers, many seeing their first action, were dazed and confused. Nazi machine guns pinned them against the sea. Slowly, they crawled up the beach on their stomachs. A thousand died. They held on until the next wave of transports arrived.

All day long, Allied confusion did battle with German indecision;

the Nazis never really counterattacked, thinking D-Day was just a ruse, instead of the main invasion. By day's end, the Allies had taken several beaches along the Normandy coast and began building artificial harbors, providing a tiny port-of-entry for the reconquest of Europe. The stage was set for a quick and easy end to the war. Right.

• *Go downstairs to the...*

First Floor—The War Ends...Very Slowly (June 1944–August 1945)

Rooms 24 and 25: Battle of Normandy and Landing in Provence, August 1944

For a month, the Allies (mostly Americans) secured Normandy by taking bigger ports (Cherbourg and Caen) and amassing troops and supplies for the assault on Germany. In July, they broke out and sped eastward across France, with Patton's tanks covering up to 40 miles a day. They had "Jerry" on the run.

On France's Mediterranean coast, American troops under General Alexander Patch landed near Cannes (see **parachute** photo), took Marseilles, and headed north to meet up with Patton.

Room 26: "Les Maquis"

French Resistance guerrilla fighters helped reconquer France from behind the lines. (Don't miss the **folding motorcycle** in its parachute case.) The liberation of Paris was started by a Resistance attack on a German garrison.

Room 27: Liberation of Paris

As the Allies marched on Paris, Hitler ordered his officers to torch the city—but they sanely disobeyed and prepared to surrender. On August 26, 1944, General Charles de Gaulle walked ramrod-straight down the Champs-Elysées, followed by Free French troops and US GIs passing out chocolate and Camels. Two million Parisians went ape.

Room 28: Towards Berlin—Offensive from the West

The quick advance through France, Belgium, and Luxembourg bogged down at the German border in autumn of 1944. Patton outstripped supply lines, a parachute invasion of Holland (the Battle of Arnhem) was disastrous, and bad weather grounded planes and slowed tanks.

On December 16, the Allies met a deadly surprise. An enormous, well-equipped, energetic German army appeared from nowhere, punched a "bulge" deep into Allied lines, and demanded surrender. General Anthony McAuliffe sent a one-word response—"Nuts!"—and the momentum shifted. The Battle of the Bulge was Germany's last great offensive.

ARMY MUSEUM

The Germans retreated across the Rhine River, blowing up bridges behind them. The last bridge, at Remagen, was captured by the Allies just long enough for them to cross and establish themselves on German soil. Soon, US tanks were speeding down the autobahns and Patton could wire the good news back to Ike: "General, I have just pissed in the Rhine."

Soviet soldiers did the dirty work of taking fortified Berlin by launching a final offensive in January 1945, and surrounding the city in April. German citizens fled west to surrender to the more-benevolent Americans and Brits. Hitler, defiant to the end, hunkered in his underground bunker. (See photo of **ruined Berlin.**)

On April 28, 1945, Mussolini and his girlfriend were killed and hung by their heels in Milan. Two days later, Adolf Hitler and his new bride, Eva Braun, avoided similar humiliation by committing suicide (pistol in mouth), and having their bodies burned beyond recognition. Germany formally surrendered on May 8, 1945.

In Corridor to the Left of Room 28: Concentration Camps

Lest anyone mourn Hitler or doubt this war's purpose, gaze at photos from Germany's concentration camps. Some camps held political enemies and prisoners of war, including two million French. Others were expressly built to exterminate peoples considered "genetically inferior" to the "Aryan master race"—particularly Jews, Gypsies, homosexuals, and the mentally ill. The criminals who perpetrated these acts were tried and sentenced in an international court—the first of its kind—held in Nuremburg, Germany.

Room 29: War of the Pacific

Often treated as an afterthought, the final campaign against Japan was a massive American effort, costing many lives, but saving millions of others from Japanese domination.

Japan was an island bunker surrounded by a vast ring of fortified Pacific islands. America's strategy was to take one island at a time, "island-hopping" until close enough for B-29 Superfortress bombers to attack Japan itself. The war spread across thousands of miles. In a new form of warfare, ships carrying planes led the attack and prepared tiny islands for troops to land and build an airbase. While General Douglas MacArthur island-hopped south to retake the Philippines ("I have returned!"), others pushed north toward Japan.

In February 1945, marines landed on Iwo Jima, a city-size island-volcano close enough to Japan (800 miles) to launch air raids. Twenty thousand Japanese had dug in on the volcano's top and were picking off the advancing Americans. On February 23, several US soldiers raised the Stars and Stripes on the mountain (that famous photo), which inspired their mates to victory at a cost of nearly 7,000 men.

ARMY MUSEUM

Japan Surrenders

On March 9, Tokyo was firebombed, and 90,000 were killed. Japan was losing, but a land invasion would cost hundreds of thousands of

lives. The Japanese had a reputation for choosing death over the shame of surrender—they even sent bomb-laden "kamikaze" planes on suicide missions.

America unleashed its secret weapon, an atomic bomb (originally suggested by German-turned-American Albert Einstein). On August 6,

a B-29 dropped one (named **"Little Boy,"** see the replica dangling overhead) on the city of Hiroshima and instantly vaporized 100,000 people and four square miles. Three days later, a second bomb fell on Nagasaki. The next day, Emperor Hirohito unofficially surrendered. The long war was over, and US sailors returned home to kiss their girlfriends in public places.

The Closing Chapter

The death toll for World War II (September 1939–August 1945) totaled 80 million soldiers and civilians. The Soviet Union lost 26 million, China 13 million, France 580,000, and the US 340,000.

World War II changed the world, with America emerging as the dominant political, military, and economic superpower. Europe was split in two. The western half recovered, with American aid. The eastern half remained under Soviet occupation. For 45 years, the US and the Soviet Union would compete—without ever actually doing battle—in a "Cold War" of espionage, propaganda, and weapons production that stretched from Korea to Cuba, from Vietnam to the moon.

• *Return to the large Courtyard of Honor, where Napoleon honored his troops, Dreyfus had his sword broken, and de Gaulle once kissed Churchill. Two Army Museums—one in the East Wing and one in the West Wing—flank the courtyard. The West Wing contains "Arms and Armour" (see "Overview of the Army Museum and Napoleon's Tomb," earlier in this tour, for a short description). The East Wing covers French military history from "Louis XIV to Napoleon III," including the Revolution and Napoleon Bonaparte), and is scheduled to reopen in the spring of 2009 after renovation.*

LOUIS XIV TO NAPOLEON III (EAST WING)

This museum traces uniforms and weapons through French history, from Louis XIV to World War I, with emphasis on Napoleon. As you circle the second floor, you'll follow the history and art of

French warfare from about 1700 to 1850: Pre-Revolution, Revolution, Napoleon, and Restoration. Most rooms have some English info posted. Notice how many of the room names have been given to Métro stops.

Note: This renovated exhibit is slated to reopen in the spring of 2009. I've included the information below as background material (though the order of the displays may be quite different from what I've indicated here).

• *Enter the East Wing under the golden letters, and go up to the second floor (the third floor, to us North Americans) to reach the main core of the exhibits (elevator available, WC downstairs). Skip the first room and enter the...*

Salle Louis XIV

Louis XIV unified the army as he unified the country, creating the first modern nation-state with a military force. In these first dozen rooms, you'll see how gunpowder was quickly turning swords, pikes, and lances to pistols, muskets, and bayonets. Uniforms became more uniform, and everyone got a standard-issue flintlock.

• *Browse the first dozen or so rooms, turn the corner and pass beneath a lighted sign:* Première République. *Enter the...*

Salle Guerres de la République

With the Revolution, the king's Royal Army became the people's National Guard, protecting their fledgling democracy from Europe's monarchies, while spreading revolutionary ideas by conquest. At the Battle of Lodi (1796, see the model with tiny toy soldiers), the French and Austrians faced off on opposites sides of a northern Italian river, trying to capture the crucial bridge and using cannons to clear the way for a cavalry charge. Young, relatively obscure Bonaparte personally sighted the French cannons on the enemy—normally the job of a lesser officer—which turned the tide of battle and earned him a reputation and a nickname, "The Little Corporal."

• *A couple of rooms farther along is the...*

Salle Boulogne

See General Bonaparte's hat, sword, and medals. The tent (behind screen) shows his bivouac equipment: a bed with mosquito netting, a director's chair, and a table that you can imagine his generals hunched over as they made battle plans.

• *Continue, turning the corner to the...*

Salle Austerlitz

Now at the peak of his power, Emperor Napoleon (in the famous portrait by Jean-Auguste-Dominique Ingres) stretches his right arm to supernatural lengths.

Salle Eylau

Behold Napoleon's beloved Arabian horse, Le Vizir, who weathered many a campaign and grew old with him in exile (stuffed, in a glass case).

Salle Montmirail

A portrait catches a dejected

Napoleon after his first abdication in 1814. A glass case is dedicated to Napoleon's son, the "King of Rome" *(Roi de Rome)*. His little soldier boots are there, and an engraving shows the child king in a royal carriage. When he grew up (miniature portrait in the center), he looked a lot like his dad—a fact that kept French Royalists wary until his death. Junior's mother (engraving to the left) was Marie Louise, whom Napoleon married after divorcing barren Josephine.

• *Turn the corner into a long, faded blue corridor, the...*

ARMY MUSEUM

Corridor de Tarascon

Napoleon's big white dog (in a glass case to left), his companion in exile on Elba, suffered the same fate as the horse. On the wall to the left of the dog hang proclamations of thanks and good-byes (announcing the surrender at Waterloo) that Napoleon sent to his soldiers and the French people. Directly behind the dog (other side of the wall), a shining breastplate shows the effectiveness of British artillery in the battle of Waterloo.

A dozen steps farther along, you'll find Napoleon's death mask. It's opposite the blue drapes that hide a reconstruction of a room in his final home on St. Helena (step inside the drapes). Picture a lonely man suffering from ulcers sitting here in his nightcap and slippers, playing chess, not war.

Exit the long blue corridor, and you'll see an American flag (in a glass case) along with the French tricolor flag, honoring the Marquis de Lafayette of France, the general who helped George Washington take Yorktown.

• *Turn right before the American flag to exit.*

The Musée des Plans Reliefs (on the top floor of the East Wing) has 17th- and 18th-century models (1:1,600 scale) of France's cities, used by the French to devise strategies to thwart enemy attacks (see English flier at the door). Survey a city, and ponder which hillside you'd use to launch an attack. Big models of Mont-Saint-Michel and Antibes lie at either end. Other floors of this wing are filled with temporary exhibits.

ARMY MUSEUM

BUS #69 SIGHTSEEING TOUR

From the Eiffel Tower to Père Lachaise Cemetery

Why pay €25 for a tour company to give you an overview of Paris, when city bus #69 can do it for €1.50? Get on the bus and settle in for a ride through some of the city's most interesting neighborhoods. Or hop on and off using this tour as a fun way to lace together many of Paris' most important sightseeing districts (your ticket gives you 90 minutes). On this ride from the Eiffel Tower to Père Lachaise Cemetery, you'll learn how great the city's bus system is—and you'll wonder why you've been tunneling by Métro under this gorgeous city. And if you're staying in the Marais or rue Cler neighborhoods, line #69 is a useful route for just getting around town (except on Sun, when it doesn't run).

You'll find that the bus goes faster than you can read. It's best to look through this chapter ahead of time, then ride with an eye out for the various sights described here.

ORIENTATION

Cost: €1.50 (one Métro ticket) per one-way ride.

When to Go: You can hop on Monday through Saturday, but avoid Sunday (no service), weekday rush hours (8:00–9:30 & 17:30–19:30), and hot days (no air-conditioning). Evening bus rides are magical in months when it gets dark early enough to see the flood-lit monuments before the bus stops running (last trip at 21:15).

Getting There: Eastbound line #69 leaves from the Eiffel Tower on avenue Joseph Bouvard (the street that becomes rue St. Dominique as it crosses the Champ de Mars). The first stop is at the southwestern end of the avenue, across from the Eiffel Tower (with the tower at your back, walk through the grassy park; avenue Joseph Bouvard is the second street you'll cross). You may want to start on the eastern end of avenue Joseph Bouvard (second stop, just before avenue de la Bourdonnais). Stops are located about every three blocks along the route shown on the map in this chapter. At whatever stop you plan to catch the bus, check if "#69" is posted at the stop to make sure you're on the right route.

Bus Tips: Use a ticket purchased at a Métro station or *tabac*—it works on buses and gives you 90 minutes to complete your one-way trip, jumping on and off buses as often as you like. (Note that you can't use the same ticket to transfer between the bus and Métro.) Don't buy a ticket from the bus driver—tickets bought on the bus don't allow the 90-minute privilege. All tickets must be validated in the machine behind the driver. Board through the front door and exit through the rear door. Push a red button to signal that you want to get off at the next stop. Buses run every 10–15 minutes (7:30–21:15).

Length of This Tour: Allow one hour.

Overview

BUS #69 TOUR

Handy line #69 crosses the city east–west, running between the Eiffel Tower and Père Lachaise, and passing these great monuments and neighborhoods: Eiffel Tower, Ecole Militaire, rue Cler, Les Invalides (Army Museum and Napoleon's Tomb), Louvre Museum, Ile de la Cité, Ile St. Louis, Hôtel de Ville, Pompidou Center, Marais, Bastille, and Père Lachaise. You don't have to do the whole enchilada; get on and off wherever you like.

This tour is best done in the direction it's written (east from the Eiffel Tower to Père Lachaise Cemetery), since one-way streets change the route in the other direction. Grab a window seat—right side is best. If you get on at one of the first stops, you're most likely to secure a good seat.

Many find the Bastille a good ending point (where you can begin my walking tour of the Marais, page 263). This ride also ties in well after a visit to the Eiffel Tower or on your way to visiting Père Lachaise Cemetery. Think of this as an overview. The sights you'll survey are written up in more depth elsewhere in the book. Okay—let's roll.

THE TOUR BEGINS

Champ de Mars and Eiffel Tower

Your tour begins below this 1,000-foot, reddish-brown hood ornament. While you're waiting for the bus, read up on the Eiffel Tower (page 50). The park surrounding you is called Champ de Mars (named for the god of war). It served as a parade ground for the military school, Ecole Militaire, that seals the park at the right end. Napoleon Bonaparte is the school's most famous graduate.

In 1889, the Champ de Mars was covered with a massive

Bus #69 Tour

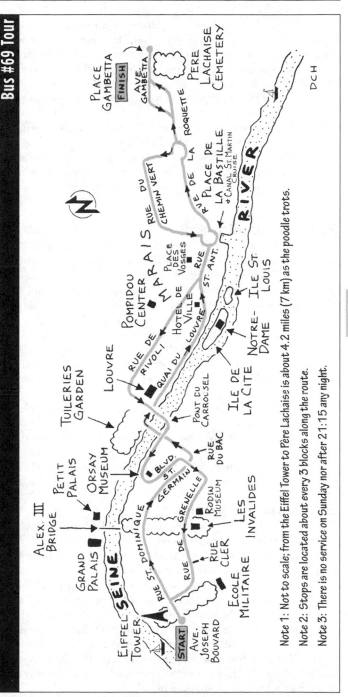

Note 1: Not to scale; from the Eiffel Tower to Père Lachaise is about 4.2 miles (7 km) as the poodle trots.

Note 2: Stops are located about every 3 blocks along the route.

Note 3: There is no service on Sunday nor after 21:15 any night.

temporary structure to house exhibitions of all sorts; it was a celebration of the Centennial World's Fair, the same event for which the Eiffel Tower was built. The apartments surrounding the park are among the most exclusive in Paris, and the grass that runs down the center of the park was strictly off-limits—until the new mayor made a change. Now the neighborhood has discovered the joys of picnic dinners. Warm evenings are grand social affairs, as friends share candlelit dinners on the grass. Soccer balls fly past and dogs scavenge for leftovers, all within the glow of the Eiffel Tower.

• *Leaving the Champ de Mars, the bus slices through the 7th arrondissement along its primary shopping street. As you head onto rue St. Dominique, notice how well your driver navigates past delivery trucks and illegally parked cars.*

Rue St. Dominique

Paris functions as a city of hundreds of small neighborhoods. This area, which was once the village of Grenelle (before it was consumed by Paris), is a case in point. Shops and cafés line the streets, topped by several floors of apartments, giving the district a liveliness not found in less-vibrant commercial districts. You can shop for anything you need on rue St. Dominique (but not at any hour). Many locals never leave the area, and neighbors trust each other. The dry cleaner knows that if his customer forgets her wallet, she'll return to pay him another time. If the plumber can only come during work hours, locals can leave their apartment keys with the nearest shop owner, who will make sure the plumber gets them.

This area has long been popular with Americans—the American Church (two blocks to the left), American Library, American University, and lots of my readers (in recommended hotels) call this area home.

• *After crossing boulevard de la Tour Maubourg, you'll enter the open world of esplanade des Invalides.*

Esplanade des Invalides

This sprawling esplanade links the **river** (to the left) and Europe's first veteran's hospital, **Les Invalides** (right), built by Louis XIV (✪ see Army Museum and Napoleon's Tomb Tour, page 194). Napoleon lies powerfully dead under the brilliant golden dome.

Afternoon *boules* (lawn bowling), near the Invalides building under the trees on the far right, is an engaging spectator sport. I spend more time watching the player's mannerisms than the game itself (see sidebar on page 346). In summer, American football games are played on the grassy esplanade with teams composed of Franco-American friends. They even have a league and drink beer after the games. The Rodin Museum lies just beyond the esplanade, left of Les Invalides (✪ see Rodin Museum Tour, page 183).

BUS #69 TOUR

Look left and see the **pont d'Alexandre III (Alexander III Bridge)** crossing the Seine. Spiked with golden statues and ironwork lamps, the bridge was built to celebrate a turn-of-the-20th-century treaty between France and Russia. Just across the bridge are the glass-and-steel-domed **Grand and Petit Palais** exhibition halls, built for the 1900 World's Fair. Like the bridge, they are fine examples of belle époque architecture. Impressive temporary exhibits fill the huge Grand Palais, while the smaller Petit Palais houses a permanent collection of 19th-century paintings, starring works by Courbet and Monet (among others). The **Air France building** (just this side of the river) is an airport shuttle stop (4/hr).

• *Leaving Les Invalides, you'll reenter narrow streets lined with...*

Government Buildings

Many of France's most important ministries occupy the golden-hued buildings (look for police guarding doorways, heavily barred windows, and people in suits speaking in hushed tones). Opposite the **frilly Gothic church** (on right) sprawls the **Ministry of Defense,** originally the mansion of Napoleon's mother.

• *You'll emerge from the government ghetto onto the stylish and leafy...*

Boulevard St. Germain

Along this stretch, colorful furniture stores tempt the neighborhood's upper-crust residents. Notice the fine Haussmann architecture. Several blocks farther down are the boulevard's famous cafés, once frequented by existentialists Albert Camus and Jean-Paul Sartre. But we turn left onto **rue du Bac,** and cross streets (to the right) filled with antiques, art galleries, and smart hotels. The Orsay Museum is a few blocks to the left (if you need an art break, the best stop for this museum is at Pont Royal, just before the river; ❂ see Orsay Museum Tour on page 130).

• *Next, you'll cross the river (see the Orsay Museum behind on the left) and enter the Right Bank.*

Tuileries Garden and Louvre Museum

The Tuileries Garden (Jardin des Tuileries) lies straight ahead as you cross the Seine. This was the royal garden of the Louvre palace—come here after touring the Louvre to clear your mind (❂ see Louvre Tour, page 101). There are several cafés scattered among these pretty gardens, ponds with toy boats for rent, and trampolines for jumping. After turning right along the river, you'll follow the immense Grand Gallery of the **Louvre,** dominating the left side of the street, and **café-boats** on the right. (There are about 2,000 barges docked on the Seine in Paris.)

The U-shaped Louvre, once the biggest building in the world, now houses 12 miles of galleries wallpapered with thousands of the world's greatest paintings. Various kings added new wings, marking their contributions with their initials and medallions carved into the decor. The statues put on a stony toga fashion show as you roll by.

Just before the end of the Louvre building on the right is the view-perfect pedestrian bridge **pont des Arts** (described at the beginning of the ❂ Left Bank Walk, page 233). That curved **building with a dome** on the other side is where the Académie Française has met since the 1600s to defend the French language from corrupting influences (like English), and to compose the official French dictionary.

• *Next on the right is the island where Paris was founded. Get ready for quick right-left-right head movements.*

Ile de la Cité

The river splits around this island where Paris began over 2,000 years ago. The first bridge you see dates from about 1600. While it's called **pont Neuf,** meaning "new bridge," it's Paris' oldest. Pont Neuf leads to an equestrian statue of King Henry IV, who doesn't face a tiny and romantic tip-of-the-island park from which Seine tour boats depart (see listing for Vedettes du Pont Neuf on page 34).

On your left is Paris' primary **department-store shopping district.** Next along this street are sidewalk **pet stalls**—a hit with local children, who dream of taking home a turtle, canary, or rabbit. Back across the river, find the squat and round medieval towers (wearing pointy black cone hats) of the **Conciergerie,** named for the *concierge* (or caretaker) who ran these offices when the king moved to the Louvre. The towers guard the Ile de la Cité's law courts, the Palais de Justice, the prison famous as the last stop for those about to be guillotined. That intricate needle—the **spire of Sainte-Chapelle**—marks the most beautiful Gothic interior in Paris. You'll see the substantial twin towers and thin spire of **Notre-Dame Cathedral** soon after the Conciergerie. Back to the left, the grand **Hôtel de Ville** (Paris' city hall) stands proudly behind playful fountains. Each of the 20 arrondissements (governmental areas) in Paris has its own city hall, and this one is the big daddy of them all. In the summer, the square in front of Hôtel de Ville hosts sand volleyball courts and at Christmas time, a big ice-skating rink. It's beautifully lit after dark all year. Take a quick look through the trees back across the river to see the gray steel **modern pedestrian bridge** that connects Paris' two islands.

• *The bus leaves the river after city hall, and angles through the Marais.*

Le Marais

This is jumbled, medieval Paris at its finest. It's been a swamp, an aristocratic district, and a bohemian hangout. Today, classy stone mansions sit alongside trendy bars, keeping the antiques shops and fashion-conscious boutiques company. The Picasso Museum, Carnavalet Museum, Victor Hugo's House, Jewish Art and History

Museum, and Pompidou Center all have Marais addresses. On your left, a couple of blocks past city hall, you'll see the **oldest houses** in Paris—tall, skinny, and half-timbered—clustered around #13.

The narrow street soon merges into **rue St. Antoine,** the main street through the Marais and the main street of Paris in medieval times. The small-but-grand **Church of St. Paul and St. Louis** (on the right, with classical columns) is the only Jesuit church in Paris. It was the neighborhood church of Victor Hugo.

• *Rue St. Antoine leads straight into the place de la Bastille, marked with a giant pillar in the center. If your trip ends here, get off 30 yards before entering place de la Bastille. Options if you get off: Marais Walk (page 263), canal boat tour (page 34), Promenade Plantée Park (page 70), and Marais eateries (page 385).*

Place de la Bastille

The namesake of this square, a fortress-turned-prison that symbolized royal tyranny, is long gone. But for centuries, the fortress that stood here was used to defend the city, mostly from its own people. On July 14, 1789, angry Parisians swarmed the Bastille, released its prisoners, and kicked off the French Revolution. Since then, the French celebrate their Independence Day on July 14 (a.k.a. Bastille Day) as enthusiastically as Americans commemorate July 4.

In the middle of the square, you'll actually cross over **Canal St. Martin** (look to the right), which runs from the Seine underneath the tree-lined boulevard Richard Lenoir (on the left) to northern Paris. You'll curve in front of the reflecting-glass **Opéra Bastille**.

• *Leaving place de la Bastille, you'll angle left up rue de la Roquette all the way to Père Lachaise.*

Rue de la Roquette

This street begins at the Bastille in a hip, less touristed neighborhood. Here you'll find a fun mix of galleries, seedy bars, and trendy, cheap eateries. The first street to the right is **rue de Lappe** (described on page 426). One of the wildest nightspots in Paris, rue de Lappe is filled with a dizzying array of wacky bistros, bars, and dance halls.

• *The bus eventually turns left onto boulevard de Ménilmontant (which locals happily associate with a famous Maurice Chevalier tune) and rumbles past the Père Lachaise Cemetery. While the bus stops at the front gate of the vast cemetery, I'd recommend staying on to place Gambetta, where bus #69 ends its trip through the heart of Paris. Place Gambetta's centerpiece is another grandiose City Hall (this one for the 20th arrondissement). You'll also see some inviting cafés and avenue du Père Lachaise (opposite City Hall). Follow this street 100 yards, past flower shops selling cyclamen, heather, and chrysanthemums—the standard flowers for funerals and memorials—to the gate of the cemetery. Take a short stroll through the evocative home of so many permanent Parisians (Mo: Gambetta or Père Lachaise).*

Père Lachaise Cemetery

Navigating the labyrinthine rows is a challenge, but maps and my walking tour (❂ see Père Lachaise Cemetery Tour, page 310) will help you find the graves of greats such as Frédéric Chopin, Oscar Wilde, Gertrude Stein, and Jim Morrison. The tour is over. What better place for your final stop?

MARMOTTAN MUSEUM TOUR

Musée Marmottan Monet

The Marmottan has the best collection of works by the master Impressionist, Claude Monet. In this mansion on the fringe of urban Paris, you can walk through Monet's life, from black-and-white sketches to colorful open-air paintings to the canvas that gave Impressionism its name. The museum's highlights are scenes of his garden at Giverny, including larger-than-life water lilies.

Since the layout of the museum changes often, this chapter is best as a general background on Monet. Read it before you go, then let the museum surprise you.

ORIENTATION

Cost: €8, not covered by Museum Pass.

Hours: Tue 11:00–21:00, Wed–Sun 11:00–18:00, last entry 30 min before closing, closed Mon.

Getting There: It's in southwest Paris at 2 rue Louis Boilly. The Métro, RER, and buses all work:

Take the Métro to La Muette, then walk six blocks (10 min), following the brown signs down chaussée de la Muette through the delightful park with its old-time kiddy carousel, to the museum.

Or you could take the RER-C from the rue Cler area (Invalides or Pont de l'Alma), get off at the Boulainvilliers stop, and follow signs to *sortie Singer*. Turn left on rue Singer, turn right up rue Boulainvilliers, then turn left down chaussée de la Muette to get to the museum.

Bus #63 is handy from rue Cler and St. Sulpice (buses #32, #22, and #52 also serve the museum).

Post-Museum Stroll: Wander down one of Paris' most pleasant (and upscale) shopping streets, rue de Passy (2 blocks up chaussée de la Muette, opposite direction from La Muette Métro stop). After rue de Passy ends, you can continue straight—on boulevard Delessert—all the way to the Eiffel Tower. It takes one full hour of walking, without stops, to get from the Marmottan Museum to the Eiffel Tower.

Information: Tel. 01 44 96 50 33, www.marmottan.com.

Length of This Tour: Allow one hour.

Photography: Not allowed.

Starring: Claude Monet, including: *Impression: Sunrise* (shown at the top of this chapter); paintings of Rouen Cathedral, Gare St. Lazare, and Houses of Parliament; scenes from Giverny; and water lilies.

Overview

The museum traces Monet's life chronologically, but in a way that's as rough and fragmented as a Monet canvas. The collection is reorganized periodically and some paintings go on road shows, so have patience and hold on to the big picture.

Basement: Entirely devoted to Monet, with works from throughout his life—many from his gardens at Giverny.

Ground Floor: Bookstore, a timeline of Monet's life, and some Monet memorabilia. The rest is an eclectic collection of non-Monet objects—period furnishings, a beautifully displayed series of illuminated manuscript drawings, and non-Monet paintings done in the seamless-brushstroke style that Monet rebelled against.

First Floor (upstairs): Often devoted to special exhibits. Otherwise, paintings by Impressionist colleagues Pierre-Auguste Renoir, Camille Pissarro, Berthe Morisot, and more.

THE TOUR BEGINS

• *Turn left after entering the ground floor, and walk to the end of the hall where you'll find a timeline on the wall.*

Claude Monet (1840–1926)

Claude Monet was the leading light of the Impressionist movement that revolutionized painting in the 1870s. Fiercely independent and dedicated to his craft, Monet gave courage to Renoir and others in the face of harsh criticism.

Timeline, Memorabilia, and Portraits of Monet and His Family

Though the timeline is in French, you can follow the **pictures** to survey Monet's long life:

Born in Paris in 1840, Monet began his art career sketching **caricatures** of local townspeople. Baby **Jean** was born to Monet and his partner **Camille** in 1867, the year his work was rejected by the Salon. They moved to the countryside of **Argenteuil,** where he developed his open-air, Impressionist style. *Impression: Sunrise* was his landmark work at the breakthrough 1874 Impressionist Exhibition. He went on to paint several series of scenes, such as *Gare Saint-Lazare*, at different times of day.

After the birth of **Michel,** Camille's health declined, and she later died. Monet traveled a lot, painting landscapes **(Bordighera),** people **(Portrait de Poly),** and more series, including the famous **Cathedral of Rouen.** In 1890, he settled down at his farmhouse in **Giverny** and married **Alice Hoschede.** He traveled less, but visited London to paint the **Halls of Parliament.** Mostly, he painted his own **water lilies** and **flowers** in an increasingly messy style. He died in 1926 a famous man.

Nearby, you'll often find some Monet memorabilia: letters, an actual palette, or portraits and photos of Monet and his family.

• *Drop downstairs to the basement level and trace the stages of Monet's life in (very) condensed form. This tour follows the general outline of the often changing displays. The basement is one big space divided into three "rooms." Start with Monet's black-and-white drawings in a glass case, then work clockwise around the first "room."*

Room 1: From Le Havre to London (1857–1900)

Growing Up in Le Havre (1840–1860): Caricature Drawings (c. 1858)

Teenage Monet's first works—black-and-white, meticulously drawn, humorous sketches of small-town celebrities—are as different as can be from the colorful, messy oils that would make him famous. Still, they show his gift for quickly capturing an overall impression with a few simple strokes.

The son of a grocer, Monet defied his family, insisted he was an artist, and sketched the world around him— beaches, boats, and small-town life. A fellow artist, Eugène Boudin, encouraged him to don a scarf, set up his easel outdoors, and paint the scene exactly as he saw it. Today, we say, "Well, duh!" But "open-air" painting was unorthodox for artists trained to study their subjects thoroughly in the perfect lighting of a controlled studio setting.

At 19, Monet went to Paris but refused to enroll in the official art schools. Letters in the glass case (unless they're out on loan) from Monet asking for survival money from his friends show the price he paid for his early bohemian lifestyle.

The 1870s: Pure Impressionism

Monet teamed up with Renoir and Alfred Sisley, leading them on open-air painting safaris to the countryside. Inspired by the realism of Edouard Manet, they painted everyday things—landscapes, seascapes, street scenes, ladies with parasols, family picnics—in bright, basic colors.

In 1870, Monet married his girlfriend, Camille (the dark-haired woman in many of his paintings), and moved just outside Paris to the resort town of Argenteuil. Playing host to Renoir, Manet, and others, he perfected the Impressionist style—painting nature as a mosaic of short brushstrokes of different colors placed side by side, suggesting shimmering light.

First, he simplified. In *On the Beach at Trouville* (*Sur la Plage à Trouville*, 1870–1871), a lady's dress is a few thick strokes of paint.

Monet gradually broke things down into smaller dots of different shades. If you back up from a Monet canvas, the pigments blend into one (for example, red plus green plus yellow equals a brown boat). Still, they never fully resolve, creating the effect of shimmering light. Monet limited his palette to a few bright basics—cobalt blue, white, yellow, two shades of red, and emerald green abound. But no black—even shadows are a combination of bright colors.

Monet's constant quest was to faithfully reproduce nature in blobs of paint. His eye was a camera lens set at a very slow shutter speed to admit maximum light. Then

he "developed" the impression made on his retina with an oil-based solution. Even as the heartbroken Monet watched Camille die of tuberculosis in 1879, he was (he admitted later) intrigued by the changing colors in her dying face.

Impression: Sunrise (*Impression Soleil Levant,* 1873)

Here's the painting that started the revolution—a simple, serene view of boats bobbing under an orange sun (see photo on page 225). At the first public showing by Monet, Renoir, Degas, and others in Paris in

Monet's Family

You'll likely see portraits of Monet's wife and children. Monet's first wife, Camille, died in 1879, leaving Monet to raise 12-year-old Jean and babe-in-arms Michel. (Michel would grow up to inherit the family home and many of the paintings that ended up here.) But Monet was also involved with Alice Hoschede, who had recently been abandoned by her husband. Alice moved in with her six kids and took care of the dying Camille, and the two families made a Brady Bunch merger. Baby Michel became bosom buddies with Alice's baby, Jean-Pierre, while teenage Jean Monet and stepsister Blanche fell in love and later married.

1874, critics howled at this work and ridiculed the title. "Wallpaper," one called it. The sloppy brushstrokes and ordinary subject looked like a study, not a finished work. The style was dubbed "Impressionist"—an accurate name.

The misty harbor scene obviously made an "impression" on Monet, who faithfully rendered the fleeting moment in quick strokes of paint. The waves are simple horizontal brushstrokes. The sun's reflection on the water is a few thick, bold strokes of orange tipped with white. They zigzag down the canvas, the way a reflection shifts on moving water.

Monet the Traveler

In search of new light and new scenes, Monet traveled throughout France and Europe. As you enjoy landscapes painted in all kinds of weather, picture Monet at work—hiking to a remote spot; carrying an easel, several canvases, brushes (large-size), a palette, tubes of paint (an invention that made open-air painting practical), food and drink, a folding chair, and an umbrella; and wearing his trademark hat, with a cigarette on his lip. He weathered the elements, occasionally putting himself in danger by clambering on cliffs to get the shot.

The key was to work fast, before the weather changed and the light shifted, completely changing the colors. Monet worked "wet-in-wet," applying new paint before the first layer dried, mixing colors on the canvas, and piling them up into a thick paste.

The 1890s: Series

Monet often painted the same subject several times under different light (such as one of Paris' train stations, the Gare St. Lazare, 1870s). In the 1890s, he conceived of a series of paintings to be shown as a group, giving a time-lapse view of a single subject.

He rented several rooms offering different angles overlooking the Rouen Cathedral and worked on up to 14 different canvases at a time,

MARMOTTAN MUSEUM

shuffling the right one onto the easel as the sun moved across the sky. The cathedral is made of brown stone, but at sunset it becomes gold and pink with blue shadows, softened by thick smudges of paint. The true subject is not the cathedral, but the full spectrum of light that bounces off it.

These series—of the cathedral, of haystacks, poplars, and mornings on the Seine—were very popular. Monet, poverty-stricken until his mid-40s, was slowly becoming famous, first in America, then London, and finally in France.

• *Just before leaving the first room, you'll see...*

The 1900s: London

Turning a hotel room into a studio, Monet—working on nearly a hundred different canvases simultaneously—painted the changing light on the River Thames. The *London Houses of Parliament, Reflected in the Thames* (*Londres, Le Parlement, Reflets sur la Tamise*, 1905) stretch and bend with the tide. *Charing Cross Bridge* is only a few smudgy lines enveloped in fog.

London's fog epitomized Monet's favorite subject—the atmosphere that distorts distant objects. That filtering haze gives even different-colored objects a similar tone, resulting in a more harmonious picture. When the light was just right and the atmosphere glowed, the moment of "instantaneity" had arrived, and Monet worked like a madman.

In truth, many of Monet's canvases were begun quickly in the open air, and then painstakingly perfected later in the studio. He composed his scenes with great care—clear horizon lines give a strong horizontal axis, while diagonal lines (of trees or shorelines) create solid triangles. And he wasn't above airbrushing out details that might spoil the composition—such as Cleopatra's Needle near Charing Cross.

• *Continue into the next room.*

Room 2: Paintings Of Giverny (1883-1926)

Rose Trellises (*L'Allée des Rosiers,* several versions) and the Japanese Bridge (*Le Pont Japonais*)

In 1883, Monet's brood settled into a farmhouse in Giverny (50 miles west of Paris). Financially stable and domestically blissful, he turned Giverny into a garden paradise and painted nature without the long commute.

In 1890, Monet started work on his Japanese garden, inspired by tranquil scenes from the Japanese prints he collected. He diverted a river to form a pond, planted willows and bamboo on the shores, filled the pond with water lilies, then crossed it with this wooden footbridge. As years passed, the bridge became overgrown with wisteria. Compare several different versions. He painted it at different times of day and year, exploring different color schemes.

Monet uses the bridge as the symmetrical center of simple, pleasing designs. The water is drawn with horizontal brushstrokes that get shorter as you move up the canvas (farther away), creating the illusion of distance. The horizontal water contrasts with the vertical willows, while the bridge "bridges" the sides of the square canvas and laces the scene together.

In 1912, Monet began to go blind. Cataracts distorted his perception of depth and color, and sent him into a tailspin of despair. The (angry?) red paintings date from this period.

Early Water Lilies (*Nymphéas*, several versions)

As his vision slowly failed, Monet concentrated on painting close-ups of the surface of the pond and its water lilies—red, white, yellow, and lavender. Some lilies are just a few broad strokes on a bare canvas (a study), while others are piles of paint formed with overlapping colors.

But more than the lilies, the paintings focus on the changing reflections on the surface of the pond. Pan slowly around the room and watch the pond go from predawn to bright sunlight to twilight.

Early lily paintings (c. 1900) show the shoreline as a reference

point. But increasingly, Monet cropped the scene ever closer, until there was no shoreline, no horizon, no sense of what's up or down. Stepping back from the canvas, you see the lilies just hang there on the museum wall, suspended in space. The surface of the pond and the surface of the canvas are one. Modern abstract art—a colored design on a flat surface—is just around the corner.

• *Enter the final, round room and find the big tree trunk.*

Room 3: *Nympheas* and Large-Scale Canvases

Big Weeping Willow (*Le Saule Pleureur,* 1918–1919)

Get close—Monet did—and analyze the trunk. Rough "brown" bark is made of thick strokes (an inch wide and four inches long) of pink, purple, orange, and green. Impressionism lives. But to get these colors to resolve in your eye, you'd have to back up all the way to Giverny.

Later Water Lilies (*Nymphéas,* 1915–1926)

In the midst of the chaos of World War I, Monet began a series of large-scale paintings of water lilies. They were installed at the Orangerie (**☉** see Orangerie Museum Tour, page 155). Here at the Marmottan are smaller-scale studies for that series.

Some lilies are patches of thick paint circled by a squiggly "caricature" of a lily pad. Monet simplifies in a way that Henri Matisse and Pablo Picasso would envy. But getting close, you can see that the simple smudge of paint that composes the flower is actually a complex mix of different colors. The sheer size of these studies (and his Orangerie canvases) is impressive.

When Monet died in 1926, he was a celebrity. Starting with meticulous line drawings, he had evolved into an open-air realist, then Impressionist color analyst, then serial painter, and finally master of reflections. In the latter half of his life, Monet's world shrank—from the broad vistas of the world traveler to the tranquility of his home, family, and garden. But his artistic vision expanded as he painted smaller details on bigger canvases and helped invent modern abstract art.

LEFT BANK WALK

From the Seine to Luxembourg Garden

The Left Bank is as much an attitude as it is an actual neighborhood. But this walk, which is a little over a mile—from the Seine to St. Germain-des-Prés to Luxembourg Garden—captures some of the artistic, intellectual, and countercultural spirit long associated with the south side of the river. We'll pass through an upscale area of art galleries, home-furnishing boutiques, antiques dealers, bookstores, small restaurants, classic cafés, evening hot spots, and the former homes of writers, painters, and composers. Though trendy now, the area still has the offbeat funkiness that has always defined the Rive Gauche. (*Gauche*, or left-handed, has come to imply social incorrectness, like giving a handshake with the wrong—left—hand.)

Use this walk as a series of historical markers as you explore the Left Bank of today. The walk dovetails perfectly with a shopping stroll (see "Sèvres-Babylone to St. Sulpice" in Shopping, page 412). It also works well after a visit to the Louvre or after the Historic Paris Walk (see page 74), and it's ideal for connoisseurs of contemporary art galleries.

ORIENTATION

Length of This Walk: Allow two hours.

Delacroix Museum: €5, covered by Museum Pass, free first Sun of month, Wed–Mon 9:30–17:00, last entry 30 min before closing, closed Tue, tel. 01 44 41 86 50, www.musee-delacroix.fr.

St. Germain-des-Prés: Free, daily 8:00–20:00.

St. Sulpice Church and Organ Concert: Free, daily 7:30–19:30, Sun morning organ concerts (see page 54).

Luxembourg Garden: Free, daily dawn until dusk.

THE WALK BEGINS

• *Start on the pedestrian-only bridge across the Seine, the pont des Arts (next to Louvre, Mo: Pont Neuf or Louvre-Rivoli).*

❶ Pont des Arts

Before dozens of bridges crossed the Seine, the two riverbanks were like different cities—royalty on the right, commoners on the left. This bridge has always been a pedestrian bridge...and long a popular meeting point for lovers.

Under the dome of the Institut de France (the building the pont des Arts leads to), 40 linguists meet periodically to decide whether it's acceptable to call mail *"le mail"* (as the French commonly do), or whether it should be the French word *courriel* (which linguists prefer). The Académie Française, dedicated to halting the erosion of French culture, is wary of new French terms with strangely foreign sounds—like *le week-end, le marketing, le fast-food,* and *c'est cool.* In 2008, France's entry in the Eurovision Song Contest was (controversially) sung in English.

Besides the Académie Française, the Institut houses several other Académies, such as the Académie des Beaux-Arts, which is dedicated to subjects like music and painting, appropriate for the Left Bank.

• *Circle around the right side of the Institut de France building to the head of rue de Seine. You're immediately met by a statue in a street-corner garden.*

❷ Statue of Voltaire

"Jesus committed suicide." The mischievous philosopher Voltaire could scandalize a party with a wicked comment like that, delivered with an enigmatic smile and a twinkle in the eye (meaning if Christ is truly God, he could have prevented his crucifixion). Voltaire—a commoner more sophisticated than the royalty who lived across the river—introduces us to the Left Bank.

Born François-Marie Arouet (1694–1778), he took up Voltaire as his one-word pen name. Although Voltaire mingled with aristocrats, he was constantly in trouble for questioning the ruling class and for fueling ideas that would soon spark a revolution. He did 11 months in the Bastille prison, then spent 40 years in virtual exile from his beloved Paris. Returning as an old man, he got a hero's welcome so surprising it killed him.

Left Bank Walk

1. Pont des Arts
2. Statue of Voltaire
3. Roger-Viollet Shop
4. Oscar Wilde's Hotel
5. George Sand's House
6. La Palette Café
7. Toy Store
8. Richard Wagner's House
9. Delacroix Museum
10. Abbey Mansion
11. Heart of the Left Bank
12. Café le Procope
13. Odéon Cinemas
14. St. Germain-des-Prés
15. Les Deux Magots Café & Le Café de Flore
16. Rue des Canettes
17. Marché St. Germain Mall
18. St. Sulpice
19. Luxembourg Garden
20. To Bon Marché Dept. Store

The rue de Seine and adjoining streets are lined with art galleries and upscale shops selling lamps, sconces, vases, bowls, and statues for people who turn their living rooms into art.

• *From here, we'll head south down rue de Seine to boulevard St. Germain, making a few detours along the way. The first stop is at 6 rue de Seine...*

❸ Roger-Viollet

Look in the windows at black-and-white photos from Paris' history—a half-built Eiffel Tower, Hitler in Paris, and so on (the display changes often). This humble shop is the funky origin of a worldwide press agency dealing in historic photographs. The family of photographer Henri Roger expanded his photographs into an archive of millions of photos, chronicling Paris' changes through the years.

• *At the first intersection, a half-block detour to the right leads to 13 rue des Beaux-Arts and...*

❹ Oscar Wilde's Hotel

Oscar Wilde (1854–1900), the Irish playwright with the flamboyant clothes and outrageous wit, died in this hotel on November 30, 1900 (don't blame the current owners).

Just five years before, he'd been at his peak. He had several plays running simultaneously in London's West End and had returned to London triumphant from a lecture tour through America. Then, news of his love affair with a lord leaked out, causing a scandal, and he was sentenced to two years in prison for "gross indecency." Wilde's wife abandoned him, refusing to let him see their children again.

After his prison term, a poor and broken Wilde was exiled to Paris, where he succumbed to an ear infection and died here in a (then) shabby hotel room. Among his last words in the rundown place were: "Either this wallpaper goes, or I do."

Wilde is buried in Paris (see Père Lachaise Cemetery Tour, page 310).

• *Return to rue de Seine and continue south. A plaque at 31 rue de Seine marks...*

❺ George Sand's House

George Sand (1804–1876) divorced her abusive husband, left her children behind, and moved into this apartment, determined to become a writer. In the year she lived here (1831), she wrote articles for *Le Figaro* while turning her real-life experiences with men into a sensational novel, *Indiana*. It made her a celebrity and allowed her to afford a better apartment.

George Sand is known for her novels, her cross-dressing (men's suits, slicked-down hair, and cigars), and for her complex love affair with a sensitive pianist from Poland, Frédéric Chopin.

• *At 43 rue de Seine is...*

❻ Café La Palette

Though less famous than more historic cafés, this is a "real" one, where a *café crème*, beer, or glass of wine at an outdoor table costs less than €5. Inside, the 100-year-old, tobacco-stained wood paneling and faded Art Nouveau decor exude Left Bank chic. Toulouse-Lautrec would have liked it here. Have something to drink at the bar, and examine your surroundings; notice the artist palettes above the bar. Nothing seems to have changed since it was built in 1903, except the modern espresso machine (open daily, tel. 01 43 26 68 15).

• *At the fork, you could follow rue de Seine straight down to boulevard St. Germain. But we'll branch off, veering right down small rue de l'Echaudé. Four doors up, at 6 rue de l'Echaudé, is a...*

❼ Toy Store

French and American kids share many of the same toys and storybook characters: Babar the Elephant, Maisy Mouse, Tintin, the Smurfs, Madeline, and the Little Prince.

In *The Little Prince* (1943), written by Antoine de Saint-Exupéry, a pilot crashes in the Sahara, where a mysterious little prince takes him to various planets, teaching him about life from a child's wise perspective.

"Saint-Ex" (1900–1944) was himself a daring aviator who had survived wrecks in the Sahara. After France fell to the Nazis, he fled to America, where he wrote and published *The Little Prince*. A year later, he returned to Europe, then disappeared while flying a spy mission for the Allies. Lost for six decades, his plane was recently found off the coast of Marseille. The cause of the crash remains a mystery, part of a legend as enduring in France as Amelia Earhart's in the US.

• *A half-block detour to the right down rue Jacob (to #14) leads to...*

❽ Richard Wagner's House

Having survived a storm at sea on the way here, the young German composer (1813–1883) spent the gray winter of 1841–1842 in Paris in this building writing *The Flying Dutchman*, an opera about a ghost ship. It was the restless young man's lowest point of poverty. Six months later, a German company staged his first opera *(Rienzi)*, plucking him from obscurity and leading to a production of *The Flying Dutchman* that launched his career.

Now the premises are occupied by a hip-looking bar.

• *Backtrack along rue Jacob, then turn right and continue south on rue de Furstemberg to #6, the...*

❾ Delacroix Museum

The painter Eugène Delacroix (1798–1863) lived here on this tiny, quiet square. Today, his home is a museum with paintings and memorabilia. It's delightful for his fans, skippable for most, and free with the Museum Pass.

You start in an anteroom with a chronology of his life. An ambassador's son, Delacroix moved to Paris and studied at the Beaux-Arts. By his early 20s, he had exhibited at the Salon. His *Liberty Leading the People* (1831, see page 120) was an instant classic, a symbol of French democracy. Trips to North Africa added exotic Muslim elements to his palette. He hobnobbed with aristocrats and bohemians like George Sand and Frédéric Chopin (whom he painted). He painted large-scale murals for the Louvre, Hôtel de Ville, and Luxembourg Palace.

In 1857, his health failing, Delacroix moved here, seeking a quiet home/studio where he could concentrate on his final great works for the Church of St. Sulpice (which we'll see later).

Next comes the living room, decorated with a few pieces of original furniture, along with portraits and memorabilia. To the left is the bedroom (with fireplace) where Delacroix died in 1863, nursed by his long-time servant, Lucile-Virginie "Jenny" Le Guillou (her portrait is on display). You'll also see a haunting painting of Mary Magdalene and Delacroix's painting table (where he kept his paints). Backtracking, you pass through the library, then go outside and down some stairs to his studio *(atelier)* in the pleasant backyard.

Delacroix built the studio to his own specifications, with high ceilings, big windows, and a skylight, ideal for an artist working prior to electric lights. See his easel and some more paintings, including a small-scale study for *The Death of Sardanapalus,* which hangs in the Louvre. Some of Delacroix's most popular works were book illustrations (lithographs for Goethe's *Faust,* Revolutionary history, and Shakespeare). Admire Delacroix's artistic range—from messy, colorful oils to meticulously detailed lithographs. This room has frequent temporary exhibits.

Finally, in the peaceful backyard, soak up the meditative atmosphere that inspired Delacroix's religious paintings in St. Sulpice.

• *Rue de Furstemberg runs directly into the Abbey Mansion* ❿. *This building (1586) was the administrative center for the vast complex of monks gathered around the nearby church of St. Germain-des-Prés.*

Facing the mansion, turn left on rue de l'Abbaye and work your way two blocks east to the intersection of rue de Seine and rue de Buci. This intersection is, arguably, the...

⓫ Heart of the Left Bank

Explore. The rue de Buci hosts *pâtisseries* and a produce market by day, and bars by night. Mixing earthiness and elegance, your Left Bank is here. A right on rue de Buci leads to boulevard St. Germain. A left on rue de Buci leads to place St. Michel and the Latin Quarter.

• *Wherever you wander, we'll meet up a block south of here on boulevard St. Germain. But first, I'm making a several-block detour to find Voltaire's favorite café. Head east (left) on rue de Buci, which becomes rue St. André-des-Arts in a few blocks. Turn right onto rue de l'Ancienne Comédie and find #13 on the left side of the street.*

⑫ Café le Procope

Le Procope (at 13 rue de l'Ancienne Comédie) is just one of many eating options in this pleasant restaurant mall. Founded in 1686, Le Procope is one of the world's oldest continuously operating restaurants, and was one of Europe's first places to sample an exotic new stimulant—coffee—recently imported from the Muslim culture.

In the 1700s, Le Procope caffeinated the Revolution. Voltaire reportedly drank 30 cups a day, fueling his intellectual passion (his favorite table bears his carved initials). Benjamin Franklin recounted old war stories about America's Revolution. Robespierre, Danton, and Marat plotted coups over cups of double-short-two-percent-frappuccinos. And a young lieutenant named Napoleon Bonaparte ran up a tab he never paid.

Located midway between university students, royalty, and the counterculture Comédie Française, Le Procope attracted literary types who loved the free newspapers, writing paper, and quill pens. Today, the coffeehouse is an appealing restaurant (affordable if mediocre *menus*, open daily). If you're discreet, you can wander the ground floor, with its memorabilia-plastered walls.

• *Exit through Café le Procope's back door to the pedestrian-only passageway called the cour du Commerce. Follow it to the right as it spills out onto boulevard St. Germain at an intersection (and Métro stop) called...*

⑬ Odéon Cinemas

Paris' many lovers of film converge here for the latest releases at several multiplexes in the area. Looking south up rue de l'Odéon, you can see the classical columns of the front of Théâtre de l'Odéon, the descendant of the original Comédie Française (now housed in Palais Royal).

• *Walk to the right (west) along busy boulevard St. Germain for six blocks, passing Café Vagenande (famous for its plush Art Nouveau interior) and other fashionable, noisy cafés with outdoor terraces. You'll reach the large stone church and square of...*

⑭ St. Germain-des-Prés

Paris' oldest church, dating from the 11th century (the square bell tower is original), stands on a site where a Christian church has stood since the fall of Rome. (The first church was destroyed by Vikings in the 885–886 siege.)

The restored interior is still painted in the medieval manner, as were Notre-Dame and others. The church is in the Romanesque style, with round—not pointed—arches over the aisles of the nave.

The square outside is one of Paris' great gathering spots on warm evenings. Musicians, mimes, and fire-eaters entertain café patrons. The church is often lit up and open late. This is where the rich come to see and be seen, and the poor come for a night of free spectacle.

• *Note that Métro stop St. Germain-des-Prés is here, and the Mabillon stop is just a couple of blocks east. On place St. Germain-des-Prés, you'll find...*

ⓕ Les Deux Magots Café and Le Café de Flore

Since opening in 1885, "The Two Chinamen Café" (wooden statues inside) has taken over Le Procope as the café of ideas. From Oscar Wilde's Aestheticism (1900) to Picasso's Cubism (1910s) to Hemingway's spare prose ('20s) to Sartre's Existentialism (with his girlfriend Simone de Beauvoir and Albert Camus, 1930s and '40s) to rock singer Jim Morrison ('60s), worldwide movements have been born in the simple atmosphere of these two cafés. Le Café de Flore, once frequented by Picasso, is more hip, but Deux Magots, right next door, is more inviting for just coffee. Across the street is Brasserie Lipp, a classic brasserie where Hemingway wrote much of *A Farewell to Arms*. (See also "Les Grands Cafés de Paris," page 397.)

• *From place St. Germain-des-Prés, cross boulevard St. Germain and head south toward the Montparnasse Tower skyscraper (in the distance) on rue Bonaparte (not rue de Rennes). Turn left on busy rue du Four, then right on...*

ⓖ Rue des Canettes

Small, midpriced restaurants, boutique shops, and comfortable brewpubs make this neighborhood a pleasant nightspot. It's easy to find a *plat du jour* or a two-course *formule* for under €20. Chez Georges (at #11) is the last outpost of funkiness (and how!) in an increasingly gentrified neighborhood (see page 394).

• *A one-block detour left down rue Guisarde leads to more restaurants, shops, and pubs, and the* ⓗ *Marché St. Germain shopping mall, a former farmers' market where fish and produce have been replaced by the Gap and other chain stores.*

Continue south on rue des Canettes to the church of...

ⓘ St. Sulpice

The impressive Neoclassical arcaded facade, with two round, half-finished towers, is modeled on St. Paul's in London. It has a remarkable organ and offers Sunday-morning concerts (see page 54). The lone café on the square in front (Café de la Mairie) is always lively and perfectly located for a break.

The Da Vinci Code in St. Sulpice

In Dan Brown's novel (see page 56), this church is supposedly where a secret society, the Priory of Sion, held mysterious rituals. In fact, there's a stained-glass window (above the door in the north transept) with the letters P and S intertwined, but the church has posted a bilingual sign (by the gnomon) refuting the claims of "a recently written novel." In the novel, Silas the murderous monk seeks the "keystone" under a pavement stone in St. Sulpice's astrological clock (which Brown embellishes into a mysterious "rose line"). Sister Sandrine watches from the church's interior balcony, and later has a nasty encounter here with Silas.

Inside, circle the church counterclockwise, making a few stops. In the first chapel on the right, find **Delacroix's three murals** (on the chapel's ceiling and walls) of fighting angels, completed during his final years fighting illness. They sum up his long career, from Renaissance/Baroque roots to furious Romanticism to proto-Impressionism.

The most famous is the agitated *Jacob Wrestling the Angel*. The two grapple in a leafy wood that echoes the wrestlers' rippling energy. Jacob fights the angel to a standstill, bringing him a well-earned blessing for his ordeal. The shepherd Laban and his daughter Rachel (Jacob's future wife) hover in the background. Get close and notice the thick brushwork that influenced the next generation of Impressionists—each leaf is a single brushstroke, often smudging two different colors in a single stroke. The "black" pile of clothes in the foreground is built from rough strokes of purple, green, and white. (Too much glare? Take a couple of steps to the right to view it. Also, there are three light buttons nearby.)

On the opposite wall, *Heliodorus Chased from the Temple* has the smooth, seamless brushwork of Delacroix's prime. The Syrian Heliodorus has killed the king, launched a coup, and has now entered the sacred Jewish Temple in Jerusalem trying to steal the treasure. Angry angels launch themselves at him, sending him sprawling. The vibrant, clashing colors, swirling composition, and over-the-top subject are trademark Delacroix Romanticism. On the ceiling, *The Archangel Michael* drives demons from heaven.

Notice the **unmarked door** at the foot of the three steps leading to Delacroix's chapel. On Sundays just after noon, this door opens, and you can go upstairs to the organ loft to hear music played for the Mass.

Walking up the right side of the church, pause at the **fourth chapel,** with a statue of Joan of Arc and wall plaques listing hundreds upon hundreds of names. These are France's WWI dead—from this congregation alone. In the chapel at the far end of the church, ponder the cryptic symbolism of Mary and Child lit by a sunburst, standing on an orb, and trampling a snake, while a stone cloud tumbles down to a sacrificial lamb.

Continue clockwise around the church. On the wall of the north transept is an Egyptian-style obelisk used as a **gnomon,** or part of a

sundial. At Christmas Mass, the sun shines into the church through a tiny hole—it's opposite the obelisk, high up on the south wall (in the upper-right window pane). The sunbeam strikes a mark on the obelisk that indicates the winter solstice. Then, week by week, the sunbeam moves down the obelisk and across the bronze rod in the floor, until, at midsummer, the sun lights up the area near the altar.

In the final chapel before the exit, you may see a display on the **Shroud of Turin.** This burial cloth (which is in Turin, Italy) is purported to have wrapped the body of Christ, who left it with a mysterious, holy stain in his image.

• *Turning left out of the church, continue south on rue Férou, which leads directly to the fenced-in Luxembourg Garden. Enter the garden through the gate ahead of you (or, if it's closed, turn right on busy rue de Vaugirard, then left on rue Guynemer, where you'll find another entrance gate).*

⑲ Luxembourg Garden

Paris' most beautiful, interesting, and enjoyable garden/park/recreational area, Jardin du Luxembourg, is a great place to watch Parisians at rest and play. These 60-acre private gardens, dotted with fountains and statues, are the property of the French Senate, which meets here in the Luxembourg Palace.

The palace was begun in 1615 by Marie de Médici. Recently widowed (by Henry IV) and homesick for Florence, she built the palace as a re-creation of her girlhood home, the Pitti Palace. When her son grew to be Louis XIII, he drove his mother from the palace, exiling her to Germany.

Luxembourg Garden has special rules governing its use (for example, where cards can be played, where dogs can be walked, where joggers can run, and when and where music can be played). The brilliant flower beds are completely changed three times a year, and the boxed trees are brought out of the orangerie in May. Children enjoy the rentable toy sailboats, pony rides, and marionette shows (Les Guignols, or Punch and Judy; see page 403).

Luxembourg Garden

Challenge the card and chess players to a game (near the tennis courts), or find a free chair near the main pond and take a well-deserved break, here at the end of our Left Bank Walk.

Nearby

The grand Neoclassical-domed Panthéon, now a mausoleum housing the tombs of great Frenchmen, is three blocks away and worth touring (see page 57). The historic cafés of Montparnasse are a few blocks from the southwest-corner exit of the park (on rue Vavin, see "Les Grands Cafés de Paris," page 397).

• *Getting home: The Luxembourg Garden is ringed with Métro stops (all a 10-min walk away). North of the garden, the two closest Métro stops are St. Sulpice and Odéon. A convenient RER stop (Luxembourg) is at the park's east entry.*

CLUNY MUSEUM TOUR

Musée National du Moyen Age

The National Museum of the Middle Ages doesn't sound quite so boring as I sink deeper into middle age myself. Aside from the solemn religious art, there is some lively stuff here.

Paris emerged on the world stage in the Middle Ages, the time between ancient Rome and the Renaissance. Europe was awakening from a thousand-year slumber. Trade was booming, people actually owned chairs, and the Renaissance was moving in like a warm front from Italy.

ORIENTATION

Cost: €6.50, free on first Sun of the month, covered by Museum Pass.

Hours: Wed–Mon 9:15–17:45, closed Tue.

Getting There: The museum, a five-minute walk from the Ile de la Cité, is a block above the intersection of boulevards St. Germain and St. Michel at 6 place Paul Painlevé (Mo: Cluny-La Sorbonne, St. Michel, or Odéon; bus #63 from rue Cler or #86 from the Marais).

Information: Pick up the free and handy museum map. Tel. 01 53 73 78 16, www.musee-moyenage.fr.

Length of This Tour: Allow one hour, though you could spend far more time here. While this self-guided tour covers the museum's greatest hits, there's much more to the underrated Cluny (such as medieval altarpieces, weaponry, eighth-century Visigothic crowns, a wonderful chapel with an elaborate stone ceiling, and a medieval garden). For details, see the museum's free map.

Baggage Check: Required and free.

Photography: OK without flash.

Cuisine Art: Just a few blocks away, the charming place de la Sorbonne has several good cafés (see page 393; walk up boulevard St. Michel toward the Panthéon).

THE TOUR BEGINS

• *The museum hosts occasional special exhibits that can affect the permanent collection described below (especially in the first few rooms). Start in the second room after the bookshop...*

Room 2: Tapestries

The first art you see is not some grim, gray crucifixion, but six colorful wool-and-silk tapestries that celebrate the secular pleasures of life on a country estate. The humans mingle harmoniously with the trees, flowers, and animals of the glorious physical world. (Note that it's not unusual for a tapestry to be missing from the six described here.)

Reading clockwise: 1) A lady with a puppy spins wool, while her husband relaxes with the morning paper. 2) A naked woman takes

a chilly bath and enjoys fruit, jewels, and music—the good things of a material world becoming increasingly less sinful. 3) The family picks fruit from their plentiful orchards. 4) Out in the garden, the sexes mingle unchaperoned by the Church. A lady takes a breath mint while a troubadour puts the moves on her servant. 5) A lord goes hunting with his falcon, dog, and servant. 6) A lady embroiders a pillow.

Having survived their Y1K crisis, these people realize the world won't end, and they turn their attention to the beauty of their surroundings.

Room 3: Fabrics Brought Back by Crusaders

Colorful woven fabrics were brought back to France by Crusaders, who went off to conquer barbarian infidels but returned with tales of enlightened peoples on the fringes of Europe.

Room 6: Stained Glass

Enter the Dark Ages, when life was harsh and violent, angels and demons made regular appearances, and the Church was your only refuge. This room offers a rare close-up look at stained glass, which gave poor people a glimpse of the glories of heaven. These panels (many from the basilica of light, Sainte-Chapelle) give us a window into the magical, supernatural, miraculous—and often violent—medieval mind.

Read clockwise around the room, all at eye level (the bottom): 1) The angel Gabriel blasts his horn on Resurrection morning, rousting the grateful dead from their coffins. Notice that Gabriel's royal robe is made up of several different pieces of glass—purples, whites, blues—held together with lead. 2) Naked Christ is baptized in the squiggly River Jordan. 3) A red-faced, horned, horny demon, accompanied

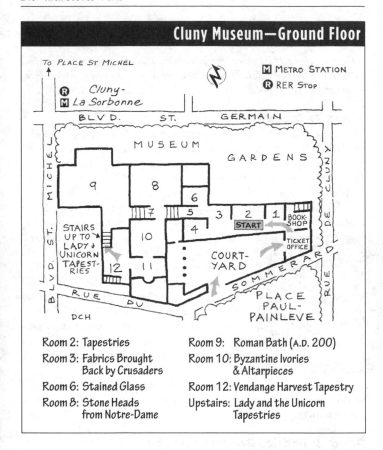

Cluny Museum—Ground Floor

To Place St Michel

Ⓡ Ⓜ Cluny-La Sorbonne

BLVD.   ST.   GERMAIN

Ⓜ METRO STATION
Ⓡ RER STOP

MUSEUM

GARDENS

RUE   DE   CLUNY

9   8   6

7   5   3   2   1

START

BOOK-SHOP

STAIRS UP TO LADY & UNICORN TAPEST-RIES

10   4

TICKET OFFICE

12   11

COURT-YARD

SOMMERARD

RUE   DU   DCH

PLACE PAUL-PAINLEVE

RUE

Room 2: Tapestries
Room 3: Fabrics Brought Back by Crusaders
Room 6: Stained Glass
Room 8: Stone Heads from Notre-Dame

Room 9: Roman Bath (A.D. 200)
Room 10: Byzantine Ivories & Altarpieces
Room 12: Vendange Harvest Tapestry
Upstairs: Lady and the Unicorn Tapestries

by an equally lascivious wolf and henchman, carries off a frightened girl in red on a date from Hell. 4) Blond, pious Joseph is sold into slavery to camel merchants by his plotting brothers.

Next wall: 5) Samson is about to pull down the temple... 6) Then he has his eyes gouged out by Philistines. 7) Slaughter on the

battlefield. Men with bloodstained hands and faces hack at each other with golden swords. 8) Aaron, disobeying God and Moses, worships a golden calf. 9) A king on a throne closes his eyes to all this wickedness.

Next wall (with some panels from the first Gothic church, St. Denis): 10) Two monks with prayer books gaze up, as one of their brothers disappears into heaven. The Latin inscription, "*hec est via,*" means "This is the way." 11) Seated Jesus, in a royal purple robe, is consoled by two angels. 12) Theophilus ("Lover of God") has struck a Faustian deal—shaking hands with the red-faced devil, yet feeling buyer's remorse. 13) Sleeping St. Martin is visited by a heavenly vision. 14) Angels in Rock-and-Roll Heaven.

Last wall: Four apostles—John (Ioannes), James (with his scallop shell), Paul, and Peter (Petrus, with key).

Before leaving, turn around and take in all the narrative medieval glass.

Room 8: Stone Heads from Notre-Dame

This room has occasional exhibits, as well as the permanent displays, so be prepared to search for the objects described.

The 21 stone heads (sculpted 1220–1230) of the Biblical kings of Judah once decorated the front of Notre-Dame. In 1793, an angry mob of Revolutionaries mistook the kings of Judah for the kings of France and abused and decapitated the statues. (Today's heads on the Notre-Dame statues are reconstructions.) Someone gathered up the heads and buried them in his backyard near the present-day Opéra Garnier. There they slept for two centuries, unknown and noseless, until 1977, when some diggers accidentally unearthed them and brought them to an astounded world. Their stoic expressions accept what fate, time, and liberals have done to them.

The statue of Adam (nearby) is also from Notre-Dame. He's scrawny and flaccid by Renaissance standards. And it will be another 200 years before naked Adam can step out from behind that bush.

Room 9: Roman Bath

This echoing cavern was a Roman *frigidarium*. Pretty cool. The museum is located on the site of a Roman bathhouse, which was in the center of town during the Roman years. After hot baths and exercise in adjoining rooms, ordinary Romans would take a cold dip in the sunken pool (in the alcove), then relax cheek to cheek with such notables as Emperor Julian the Apostate (see his statue), who lived right next door. As the empire decayed in the fourth century, Julian avoided the corrupt city of Rome and made Paris a northern power base.

The 40-foot-high ceiling is the largest Roman vault in France, and it took the French another 1,000 years to improve on that crisscross-arch technology. The sheer size of this room—constructed in A.D. 200, when Rome was at its peak—gives an idea of the epic scale on which the Romans built, and it inspired Europeans to greatness during the less civilized Middle Ages.

The four square column fragments *(Le Pilier des Nautes)* are the oldest man-made objects you'll see from Paris. Using the small model (in glass case) you can see how these pillars once fit together to support a 20-foot-high altar to the king of the gods in the Temple of Jupiter, where Notre-Dame now stands. The fragment labeled *Pierre de la dedicace* is inscribed "TIB. CAESARE," announcing that the altar was built in the time of the Emperor Tiberius (A.D. 14–37), and was paid for by the Parisian boatmen's union (see them holding their shields). On the column labeled *Pierre aux quatre divinites*, find the horned Celtic god Cernunnos, who is also known as the Stag Lord and god of the hunt. The eclectic Romans allowed this local "druid" god to support the shrine of Jupiter, in league with their own Vulcan, who hammers, and Castor and Pollux, who pet their horses.

Room 10: Byzantine Ivories and Altarpieces

Rome lived on after the fall of the empire. The finely carved Byzantine ivories (first glass case) show how pagan gods, emperors, and griffins became Christian saints, gargoyles, and icons. Constantinople—the eastern half of the empire that survived the fall—preserved Roman tastes and imagery. In painting, Byzantine gold-background icons inspired medieval altarpieces, like some in this room. Study the exquisite detail. (Adam and Eve, in the tiny double panel, are not really "sword fighting.")

Rome also lived on in the "Roman"-esque grandeur of Christian churches such as St. Germain-des-Prés (see the 12 column capitals). In the central capital, Christ sits in robes on a throne, ruling the world like a Roman emperor. These capitals were originally painted, much like the painted wooden statues across the room.

Don't leave this room before eyeing the tusk of a narwhal (on the wall), which must have convinced superstitious folk to believe in unicorns.

Room 12: Vendange Harvest Tapestry

The large tapestry shows grape-stomping peasants during the *vendange,* the annual autumn harvest and wine celebration. A peasant man treads grapes in a vat, while his wife collects the juice. A wealthy man gives orders. Above that, a peasant with a big wart turns a new-fangled mechanical press. On the right, you'll see the joy of picking—pawns, knights, and queens all working side by side.

• *Go upstairs to...*

Room 13 (upstairs): The Lady and the Unicorn Tapestries

As Europeans emerged from the Dark Ages, they rediscovered the beauty of the world around them.

These six mysterious tapestries were designed by an unknown (but probably French) artist before A.D. 1500 and were woven in Belgium out of wool and silk. Loaded with symbols—some serious, some playful—they have been interpreted many ways, but, in short, the series deals with each of the five senses (hand-held English explanations that you can pick up from slots hanging on the wall add more detail).

In medieval lore, uni-corns were enigmatic, solitary creatures that could only be tamed by a virgin. In secular society, they symbolized how a feral man was drawn to his lady love. Religiously, the unicorn was a symbol of Christ—radiant, pure, and somewhat remote—who is made acces-sible to humankind by the Virgin Mary. These tapestries likely draw inspiration from all these traditions.

• *Moving clockwise around the room...*

Taste: A blonde lady takes candy from a servant's dish to feed it to her parakeet. A unicorn and a lion look on. At the lady's feet, a monkey also tastes something, while the little white dog behind her wishes he had some. This was the dawn of the Age of Discovery, when overseas explorers spiced up Europe's bland gruel with new fruits, herbs, and spices.

The lion (symbol of knighthood?) and unicorn (symbol of "bour-geois nobility," purity, or fertility?) wave flags with the coat of arms of the family that commissioned the tapestries—three silver crescents in a band of blue.

Hearing: Wearing a stunning dress, the lady plays sweet music on an organ, which soothes the savage beasts around her. The pattern and folds of the tablecloth are lovely. Humans and their fellow crea-tures live in harmony in an enchanted blue garden filled with flowers, all set in a red background.

Sight: The unicorn cuddles up and looks at himself in the lady's mirror, pleased with what he sees. The lion turns away and snickers. As the Renaissance dawns, vanity is a less-than-deadly sin.

Admire the great artistic skill in some of the detail work, such as the necklace and the patterns in her dress. This tapestry had quality control in all its stages: the drawing of the scene, its enlargement and transfer to a cartoon, and the weaving. Still, the design itself is crude by Renaissance 3-D standards. The fox and rabbits, supposedly in the distance, simply float overhead, as big as the animals at the lady's feet.

Smell: The lady picks flowers and weaves them into a sweet-smelling wreath. On a bench behind, the monkey apes her. The flowers, trees, and animals are exotic and varied. Each detail is exquisite alone, but step back, and they blend together into pleasing patterns.

Touch: This is the most basic and dangerous of the senses. The lady "strokes the unicorn's horn," if you know what I mean, and the lion gets the double entendre. Unicorns, a species extinct since the Age of Reason, were so wild that only the purest virgins could entice and tame them. Medieval Europeans were exploring the wonders of love and the pleasures of sex.

Tapestry #6: The most talked-about tapestry gets its name from the words on our lady's tent: *A Mon Seul Désir* (To My Sole Desire). What *is* her only desire? Is it jewelry, as she grabs a necklace from the jewel box? Or is she putting the necklace away and renouncing material things in order to follow her only desire?

Our lady has tried all things sensual and is now prepared to follow the one true impulse. Is it God? Or love? Her friends the unicorn and lion open the tent doors. Flickering flames cover the tent. Perhaps she's stepping out from the tent. Or is she going in to meet the object of her desire? Human sensuality is awakening, an old dark age is ending, and the Renaissance is emerging.

CHAMPS-ELYSEES WALK

From the Arc de Triomphe to the Place de la Concorde

Don't leave Paris without a stroll along avenue des Champs-Elysées (shahnz ay-lee-zay). This is Paris at its most Parisian: monumental sidewalks, stylish shops, elegant cafés, glimmering showrooms, and proud Parisians on parade. It's a great walk day or night, making you feel a part of an increasingly global scene.

ORIENTATION

Length of This Walk: This two-mile walk takes three hours, including a one-hour visit to the Arc de Triomphe. Métro stops are located every few blocks along the Champs-Elysées.

Arc de Triomphe: Outside—free and always open. Interior—€9, free for children under 18, free the first Sun of month Oct–March, covered by Museum Pass. Daily April–Sept 10:00–23:00, Oct–March 10:00–22:30, last entry 30 min before closing. It's at place Charles de Gaulle (tel. 01 55 37 73 77, www.monum.fr). The arch's elevator, only for people with disabilities, runs to the museum level, but not to the top (which requires a 40-step climb).

Getting There: To reach the Arc de Triomphe, take the Métro to Charles de Gaulle-Etoile. Then follow the *Sortie #1, Champs-Elysées/Arc de Triomphe* signs.

Services: There are WCs underground, south of the Arc de Triomphe, across the Champs-Elysées from the start of this walk. A small WC is inside the Arc de Triomphe, near the top, but it's often crowded.

Cuisine Art: See "Eating near the Champs-Elysées" (page 254).

Starring: Grand boulevards, grander shops, and grandiose monuments.

THE WALK BEGINS

Start at the Arc de Triomphe at the top of the Champs-Elysées. Take the underground pedestrian walkway in front of you to reach the arch. (Don't try to cross in the traffic—there are no crosswalks on the roundabout.) It's worthwhile to get to the base of the arch even if you don't climb it; there's no charge to wander around.

• *Cross through the tunnel, take the first left up a few steps and buy your ticket (skip the ticket line if you have a Museum Pass or aren't ascending), then walk up to the arch. Stroll around left toward the Champs-Elysées, turn around, and face the arch.*

The Arc de Triomphe
Exterior

Construction of the 165-foot-high arch began in 1809 to honor Napoleon's soldiers, who, in spite of being vastly outnumbered by the Austrians, scored a remarkable victory at the Battle of Austerlitz. Patterned after the ceremonial arches of ancient Roman conquerors (but more than twice the size), it celebrates Napoleon as emperor of a "New Rome." On the arch's massive left pillar, a relief sculpture shows a toga-clad Napoleon posing confidently, while an awestruck Paris—crowned by her city walls—kneels at his imperial feet. Napoleon died prior to the Arc's completion, but it was finished in time for his 1840 funeral procession to pass underneath, carrying his remains (19 years dead) from exile in St. Helena to Paris.

On the right pillar is the Arc's most famous relief, *La Marseillaise* (*Le Départ des Volontaires de 1792*, by François Rude). Lady Liberty—looking like an ugly reincarnation of Joan of Arc—screams, "Freedom is this way!" and points the direction with a sword. The soldiers below her are tired, naked, and stumbling, but she rallies them to carry on the fight against oppression.

Today, the Arc de Triomphe is dedicated to the glory of all French armies. Walk to its center and stand directly beneath it on the faded eagle. You're surrounded by the lists of French victories since the Revolution—19th century on the arch, 20th century in the pavement. On the columns, you'll see lists of generals (with a line under the names of those who died in battle). Nearby, stand on the bronze plaque at the foot of the Tomb of the Unknown Soldier (from World War I). Every day at 18:30 since just after World War I, the flame has been rekindled and new flowers set in place.

Like its Roman ancestors, this arch has served as a parade gateway

Champs-Elysées Walk

400 YARDS
400 METERS

TO LOUVRE
TO ORSAY

TUILERIES GARDEN
Orangerie

FAUCHON
MADELEINE →

ST. FLOR
CONCORDE
R. ROYALE
R. BOISSY
ST. HONORÉ

RUE
RIVOLI
QUAI TUILERIES

PLACE DE LA
CONCORDE
END
SEINE

NAT'L. ASSEMBLY

PONT
CONC.

PALAIS DE L'ELYSÉE
MARIGNY

PETIT PALAIS

R I V E R

TO ARMY MUSEUM

1 Arc de Triomphe
2 Comptoir de L'Arc Rest.
3 Qatar Embassy
4 McDonald's & Peugeot
5 Mercedes-Benz & Lido
6 Louis Vuitton
7 Fouquet's Café-Rest.
8 Ladurée Tea Salon
9 Thomas Jefferson Plaque
10 Arcades des Champs-Elysées, Sephora, Guerlain, & English Pharmacy
11 Renault
12 Virgin Music, Disney, Gap & Quiksilver
13 De Gaulle Statue, Grand & Petit Palais
14 Obelisk of Luxor
15 Hôtel Crillon
16 US Embassy
17 Pont de la Concorde
18 US Consulate
19 W. H. Smith Books
20 Monte Carlo Cafeteria
21 Café Lateral

CHURCHILL
PONT ALEX. III
COURS DE LA REINE

FRANKLIN
GRAND PALAIS

MATIGNON AVE.
ROND POINT
ROOSEVELT
COLISÉE
IGN
R. BOÉTIE
R. DE BERRI
R. WASH
#92
BALZAC
FRIEDLAND
ARSENE
HOCHE

MONTAIGNE
F.D.R.

CHAMPS
AVE. DES CHAMPS

GEORGE V
GEORGE V
MARCEAU
IENA

START
METRO:
CHARLES DE GAULLE ETOILE

WAGRAM
PED. UNDER-PASS
WC
RUE DE PRESBOURG
KLEBER →
TO EIFFEL TOWER

ARC DE TRIOMPHE

RUE DE TILSITT
MACMAHON
CARNOT
AVE. DE LA GRANDE ARMÉE
TO LA DÉFENSE

VIEW
M METRO STATION
B BATOBUS BOAT STOP

DCH

Eating near the Champs-Elysées

Good eating options on the Champs-Elysées are slim. Most sit-down restaurants have lazy service, mediocre food, and inflated prices. For a better value, try one of these places:

Within a Block of the Arc de Triomphe
Comptoir de L'Arc, a block from the Arc toward the Eiffel Tower, is a bustling place dishing out good €11 salads and *plats du jour* to locals just beyond the tourist flow (Mon–Fri 7:00–24:00, closed Sat–Sun, 73 avenue Marceau, tel. 01 47 20 72 04).

Café Lateral is a stylish corner café popular with the local business crowd at lunch. It serves €12 salads and traditional French fare, and has a great weekday two-course €16 lunch *menu* (daily 7:00–24:00, 4 avenue Mac Mahon, tel. 01 43 80 20 96).

Monte Carlo Cafeteria has a surprisingly nice ambience, with reasonably priced daily specials, salads, desserts, and *menu* combos for about €10 (open daily 11:00–23:00, 9 avenue de Wagram, tel. 01 43 80 02 20).

On the Place de la Concorde
The **Tuileries Garden** has several café and sandwich-stand options, and, of course, ice-cream vendors everywhere in good weather.

for triumphal armies (French or foe) and important ceremonies. From 1940 to 1944, a large swastika flew from here as Nazis goose-stepped down the Champs-Elysées. In August 1944, Charles de Gaulle led Allied troops under this arch as they celebrated liberation. Today, national parades start and end here with one minute of silence.

Interior and View from the Top
Ascend the Arc de Triomphe via the 284 steps inside the north pillar (the one closest to the ticket office). Catch your breath two-thirds of the way up in the small exhibition area (WC also on this mezzanine level). It hosts rotating exhibits about the arch and its founder, Napoleon.

From the top, you have an eye-popping view of *tout Paris*. You're gazing at the home of 11 million people, all crammed into an area the size of an average city in the US (the city center has 2,170,000 residents and covers 40 square miles). Paris has the highest density of any city in Europe, about 20 times greater than that of New York City.

Looking East: Look down the Champs-Elysées to the Tuileries Garden and the Louvre. Scan the cityscape of downtown Paris. That lonely hill to the left is Montmartre, topped by the white dome of Sacré-Cœur; until 1860, this hill town was a separate city. To the right, find the blue top of the modern Pompidou Center, then the distant twin towers of Notre-Dame, the "state-capitol-dome" of the Panthéon, a block of small skyscrapers on a hill (the Quartier d'Italie), the golden dome of Les Invalides, and the lonely-looking Montparnasse Tower, standing like the box the Eiffel Tower came in. It served as a wake-up call in the early 1970s to preserve the building height restrictions and strengthen urban design standards. Aside from the Montparnasse Tower, notice the symmetry. Each corner building surrounding the arch is part of an elegant grand scheme. The beauty of Paris—basically a flat basin with a river running through it—is man-made. There's a harmonious relationship between the width of its grand boulevards and the standard height and design of the buildings.

Looking West: Cross the arch and look to the west. In the distance, the huge, white, rectangular Grande Arche de la Défense, standing amid skyscrapers, is the final piece of a grand city axis—from the Louvre, up the Champs-Elysées to the Arc de Triomphe, continuing on to a forest of skyscrapers at La Défense, three miles away. Former French president François Mitterrand had the Grande Arche built as a centerpiece of this mini-Manhattan (see page 66). Notice the contrast between the skyscrapers of La Défense and the more uniform heights of the buildings closer to the Arc de Triomphe. Below you, the wide boulevard lined with grass and trees angling to your left is avenue Foch (named after the WWI hero), which ends at the huge Bois de Boulogne park. Avenue Foch is the best address to have in Paris. Nicknamed the "Avenue of Millionaires," it was home to the Shah of Iran and Aristotle Onassis. Today many fabulously rich Arabs call it home. While Parisians pride themselves on being discreet, not-so-discreet Homes-of-the-Stars-type tours are offered here.

The Etoile: Gaze down at what appears to be a chaotic traffic mess. The 12 boulevards that radiate from the Arc de Triomphe (forming an *étoile*, or star) were part of Baron Haussmann's master plan for Paris: the creation of a series of major boulevards intersecting at diagonals, with monuments (such as the Arc de Triomphe) as centerpieces of those intersections (see sidebar in Sights, page 64). Haussmann's plan did not anticipate the automobile—obvious when you watch the traffic scene below. But see how smoothly it functions. Cars entering the circle have the right of way (the only roundabout in France with this rule); those in the circle must yield. Still, there are plenty of accidents, often caused by tourists oblivious to the rules. Tired of disputes, insurance companies split the fault and damages of any Arc de Triomphe accident 50/50. The trick is to make a parabola—get to the center ASAP, and then begin working your way out two avenues before you want to exit.

• *We'll start our stroll down the Champs-Elysées at the Charles de Gaulle-Etoile Métro stop, on the north (sunnier) side of the street where the tunnel deposits you. Look straight down the Champs-Elysées to the Tuileries Garden at the far end.*

The Champs-Elysées

You're at the top of one of the world's grandest and most celebrated streets, home to big business, celebrity cafés, glitzy nightclubs, high-fashion shopping, and international people-watching. People gather here to celebrate Bastille Day (July 14), World Cup triumphs, the finales of famous bike races, and the ends of wars.

In 1667, Louis XIV opened the first section of the street as a short extension of the Tuileries Garden. This year is considered the birth of Paris as a grand city. The Champs-Elysées soon became *the* place to cruise in your carriage. (It still is today; traffic can be gridlocked even at midnight.) In the late 1700s, the café scene arrived. From the 1920s until the 1960s, this boulevard was pure elegance. Parisians actually dressed up to come here. It was mainly residences, rich hotels, and cafés. Then, in 1963, the government pumped up the neighborhood's commercial metabolism by bringing in the RER (commuter train). Suburbanites had easy access, and *pfft*—there went the neighborhood.

• *Start your descent, pausing at the first tiny street you cross, rue de Tilsitt. This street is part of a shadow ring road—an option for drivers who'd like to avoid the chaos of the Arc, complete with stoplights.*

Half a block down rue de Tilsitt is a building now housing the **Qatar Embassy.** It's one of the few survivors of a dozen uniformly U-shaped buildings from Haussmann's original 1853 grand design. Peek into the foyer for a glimpse of 19th-century Champs-Elysées classiness.

Back on the main drag, look across to the other side of the Champs-Elysées at the big, gray, concrete-and-glass "Publicis" building. Ugh. In the 1960s, venerable old buildings (similar to the Qatar Embassy building) were leveled to make way for new commercial operations like Publicis. Then, in 1985, a law prohibited the demolition of the old building fronts that gave the boulevard a uniform grace. Today, many modern businesses hide behind preserved facades. Consider dashing to the center of the Champs for a great Arc view (from a crosswalk, of course), then come back.

The coming of **McDonald's**—a hundred yards farther down on the left at #140—was a shock to the boulevard. At first, it was allowed to have only white arches painted on the window. Today, it spills out legally onto the sidewalk—provided it offers café-quality chairs and flower boxes—and dining at *chez MacDo* has become typically Parisian. A €4 Big Mac here buys an hour of people-watching. (There's a WC inside.)

The *nouveau* Champs-Elysées, revitalized in 1994, has new benches and lamps, broader sidewalks, all-underground parking, and a fleet of green-suited workers who drive motorized street cleaners. Blink away the modern elements, and it's not hard to imagine the boulevard pre-1963, with only the finest structures lining both sides all the way to the palace gardens.

Glitz

Fancy car dealerships include **Peugeot,** at #136 (showing off its futuristic concept cars, often alongside the classic models), and **Mercedes-Benz,** a block down at #118. In the 19th century, this was an area for horse stables; today, it's the district of garages, limo companies, and car dealerships. If you're serious about selling cars in France, you must have a showroom on the Champs-Elysées.

Next to Mercedes is the famous **Lido,** Paris' largest cabaret (and a multiplex cinema). You can walk all the way inside until 18:00 without a ticket. Check out the perky photos in the entryway, the R-rated videos, and the shocking prices. Paris still offers the kind of burlesque-type spectacles combining music, comedy, and scantily clad women that have been performed here since the 19th century. Moviegoing on the Champs-Elysées provides another kind of fun, with theaters showing the very latest releases. Check to see if there are films you recognize, then look for the showings *(séances).* A "v.o." *(version originale)* next to the time indicates the film will be shown in its original language.

• *Now cross the boulevard. Look up at the Arc de Triomphe, its rooftop bristling with tourists. Notice the variety of architecture along this street—old and elegant, new, and new–behind–old–facades.*

Continue to #101...

Louis Vuitton

The flagship store of this famous producer of leather bags may be the largest single-brand luxury store in the world. Step inside. The store insists on providing enough salespeople to treat each customer royally—if there's a line, it means shoppers have overwhelmed the place. The vintage suitcase/trunks hanging all around (there are 101 of them, since the address is 101 Champs-Elysées) were Vuitton's claim to fame back in 1854. That's when he came up with this flat, hard-sided, stackable alternative to the standard, rounded trunks of that earlier age.

• *Across the street is a Paris institution.*

Café Culture

Fouquet's café-restaurant (#99), under the red awning, is a popular spot among French celebrities, serving the most expensive shot of espresso I've found in downtown Paris (€6). Opened in 1899 as a coachman's bistro, Fouquet's gained fame as the hangout of France's

WWI biplane fighter pilots—those who weren't shot down by Germany's infamous "Red Baron." It also served as James Joyce's dining room. Since the early 1900s, Fouquet's has been a favorite of French actors and actresses. The golden plaques at the entrance honor winners of France's Oscar-like film awards, the Césars (one is cut into the ground at the end of the red carpet). There are plaques for Gérard Depardieu, Catherine Deneuve, Roman Polanski, Juliette Binoche, and many famous Americans (but not Jerry Lewis). Recent winners are shown on the floor just inside. While the hushed interior is at once classy and intimidating, it's a grand experience if you dare (the outdoor setting is also great, and more relaxed). Fouquet's was recently saved from foreign purchase and eventual destruction when the government declared it a historic monument. For his election-night victory party in 2007, the flamboyant President Sarkozy celebrated at Fouquet's, along with France's glitterati—including the "French Elvis," Johnny Hallyday.

Ladurée (two blocks downhill at #75, with green-and-purple awning) is a classic 19th-century tea salon/restaurant/*pâtisserie*. Its interior is right out of the 1860s. Non-patrons can discreetly wander in through the door farthest downhill and peek into the cozy rooms upstairs. A coffee here is *très élégant* (only €3.50). The bakery sells traditional macaroons, cute little cakes, and gift-wrapped finger sandwiches to go (your choice of four mini-macaroons for €7.20).

• *Cross back to the lively (north) side of the street.*

At #92 (next to Triomphe cinema), a wall plaque marks the place Thomas Jefferson lived (with his 14-year-old slave, Sally Hemings) while serving as minister to France (1785–1789). He replaced the popular Benjamin Franklin but quickly made his own mark, extolling the virtues of America's Revolution to a country approaching its own.

French Shopping

Stroll into the **Arcades des Champs-Elysées** mall at #76 (not the unappealing Galerie des Champs). With its fancy lamps, mosaic floors, glass skylight, and classical columns (try to ignore the Starbucks), it captures faint echoes of the *années folles*—the "crazy years," as the roaring '20s were called in France. Architecture buffs can observe how flowery Art Nouveau became simpler, more geometrical Art Deco. Down the street at #74, the Galerie du Claridge building sports an old facade. Its ironwork awning, balconies, *putti*, and sculpted fantasy faces disguise an otherwise new building. The current tenant is FNAC, a large French chain that sells electronics, CDs, and concert tickets.

Take your nose sightseeing at #72 and glide down **Sephora's** ramp into a vast hall of cosmetics and perfumes. Grab a disposable white strip from a lovely clerk, spritz it with a sample, and sniff. The store is thoughtfully laid out: The entry hall is lined with new products. In the main showroom, women's perfumes line the right wall and men's line the left—organized alphabetically by company, from Armani to Versace. The mesmerizing music, carefully chosen just for Sephora, makes you crave cosmetics. Here, you can have your face made over and your nails fixed like new. You can also get the advice of a "skin consultant."

While Sephora seems to be going all out to attract the general public, the venerable **Guerlain** perfume shop next door is more elegant and retains a bit of the Champs-Elysées' old gold-leaf elegance. Notice the 1914 details. Climb upstairs. It's *très* French.

At the intersection with rue la Boëtie, the English **pharmacy** is open until midnight. Map-lovers can detour one block down this street to shop at **Espace IGN**, France's version of the National Geographic Society (Institut Géographique National).

Car buffs and *Star Trek* fans should detour across the Champs and park themselves at the space-age bar in the **Renault** store (open until midnight, cheap espresso). The car exhibits change regularly, but the high-backed leather chairs looking down onto the Champs-Elysées are permanent.

International Shopping

Back on earth, a half block farther down on the north side, the **Virgin Megastore** (#52–60)—the biggest music store in Paris—sells a world of music. Nearby, the Disney, Gap, and Quiksilver stores are reminders of global economics—the French may live in a world of their own, but they love these places as much as Americans do.

Rond-Point and Beyond

At the Rond-Point des Champs-Elysées, the shopping ends and the park begins. This round, leafy traffic circle is always colorful, lined with flowers or seasonal decorations (thousands of pumpkins at Halloween, hundreds of decorated trees at Christmas). Avenue Montaigne, cutting off to the right, is lined by the most exclusive shops in town—places where you need to make an appointment to buy a dress.

A long block past the Rond-Point, at avenue de Marigny, look to the other side of the Champs-Elysées to find a statue of Charles de Gaulle—ramrod-straight and striding out as he did the day Paris was liberated in 1944.

Grand and Petit Palais

From the statue of de Gaulle, a grand boulevard (avenue Winston Churchill) passes through the site of the 1900 World's Fair, leading past the glass-and-steel-domed Grand and Petit Palais exhibition halls, and across the river over the ornate bridge called pont Alexander III. Imagine pavilions like the two you see today lining this street all the way to the golden dome of Les Invalides—examples of the "can-do" spirit that ran rampant in Europe at the dawn of the 20th century.

Today, the huge Grand Palais (on the right side and pricey) houses impressive temporary exhibits (described on page 66). Classical columns and giant, colorful mosaics running the length of the Palais' facade wowed fairgoers. The Petit Palais (left side and free) houses a permanent collection of lesser paintings by Courbet, Claude Monet, and other 19th-century masters. It's a breathtaking building and worth a quick detour (see page 65).

The exquisite pont Alexander III, spiked with golden statues and ironwork lamps, was built to celebrate a turn-of-the-20th-century treaty between France and Russia. Les Invalides was built by Louis XIV as a veterans' hospital for his battle-weary troops (see Army Museum and Napoleon's Tomb Tour on page 194). The esplanade leading up to Les Invalides—possibly the largest patch of accessible grass in Paris—gives soccer balls and Frisbees a rare-in-Paris welcome.

• *Return to the Champs-Elysées. From here, it's a straight shot to the finish line. The plane trees that you'll see are a kind of sycamore, with peeling bark that does well in big-city pollution. They're reminiscent of the big push made by Napoleon III—who ruled as president/emperor from 1849 to 1870—when he had 600,000 trees planted to green up the city. Finally, you reach the 21-acre place de la Concorde. View it from the obelisk in the center.*

Place de la Concorde

During the Revolution, this was the place de la Révolution. The guillotine sat on this square, and many of the 2,780 beheaded during the Revolution lost their bodies here during the Reign of Terror. A bronze plaque in the ground in front of the obelisk memorializes the place where Louis XVI, Marie-Antoinette, Georges Danton, Charlotte Corday, and Maximilien de Robespierre, among about 1,200 others, were made "a foot shorter on top." Three people worked the guillotine: One managed the blade, one held the blood bucket, and one caught the head, raising it high to the roaring crowd. (In 1981, France abolished the death penalty—one of many preconditions for membership in today's European Union.)

The 3,300-year-old, 72-foot, 220-ton, red granite, hieroglyph-inscribed obelisk of Luxor now forms the centerpiece of place de la Concorde. Here—on the spot where Louis XVI was beheaded—his brother (Charles X) honored the executed with this obelisk. (Charles became king when the monarchy was restored after Napoleon.) The obelisk was carted here from Egypt in the 1830s. The gold pictures on the pedestal tell the story of the obelisk's incredible two-year journey: pulled down from the entrance to Ramses II's Temple of Amon in Luxor; encased in wood; loaded onto a boat built to navigate both shallow rivers and open seas; floated down the Nile, across the Mediterranean, along the Atlantic coast, and up the Seine; and unloaded here, where it was re-erected in 1836. Its glittering gold-leaf cap is a recent addition (1998), replacing the original, which was stolen 2,500 years ago.

The obelisk also forms a center point along a line that locals call the "royal perspective." You can hang a lot of history along this straight line (Louvre–obelisk–Arc de Triomphe–Grande Arche de la Défense). The Louvre symbolizes the old regime (divine right rule by kings and queens). The obelisk and place de la Concorde symbolize the people's revolution (cutting off the king's head). The Arc de Triomphe calls to mind the triumph of nationalism (victorious armies carrying national flags under the arch). And the huge modern arch in the distance, surrounded by the headquarters of multinational corporations, heralds a future in which business entities are more powerful than nations.

Near the Place de la Concorde

Your guided walk is over. From here, the closest Métro stop is Concorde (entrance on the Tuileries Gardens side of the square, away from the river). But, of course, Paris offers so much more.

The beautiful Tuileries Gardens (with a public WC just inside on the right) are through the iron gates. Pull up a chair next to a pond or at one of the cafés in the gardens. From these gardens, you can access the Orangerie Museum (see page 155) and, farther in, the Louvre (page 101).

On the north side of place de la Concorde is Hôtel Crillon, Paris' most exclusive hotel. Of the twin buildings that guard the entrance to rue Royale (which leads to the Greek-style Church of the Madeleine), it's the one on the left. This hotel is so fancy that one of its belle époque rooms is displayed in New York's Metropolitan Museum of Art.

Eleven years before Louis XVI lost his head on this square, he met with Benjamin Franklin in this hotel to sign a treaty recognizing the US as an independent country. (Today's low-profile, heavily fortified American Embassy is located next door.) For a memorable splurge, consider high tea at the Crillon (see "Les Grands Cafés de Paris," page 397).

North of place de la Concorde, you can go to a fancy shopping area near place de la Madeleine (see page 413).

South of the place de la Concorde (across the river) stands the building where the French National Assembly (similar to the US Congress) meets. If you walk toward it, you'll cross a bridge, the pont de la Concorde, over a freeway underpass. This stretch of road is similar to the one at the pont de l'Alma, three bridges downstream, where Princess Diana lost her life in a 1997 car accident. The pont de la Concorde, built of stones from the Bastille prison (which was demolished by the Revolution in 1789), symbolizes that, with good government, *concorde* (harmony) can come from chaos.

Stand mid-bridge and gaze upriver (east). Using an imaginary clock as a compass, the Orangerie hides behind the trees at 10 o'clock, and the tall building with the skinny chimneys at 11 o'clock is the architectural caboose of the sprawling Louvre palace. The thin spire of Sainte-Chapelle is dead center at 12 o'clock, with the twin towers of Notre-Dame to its right. The Orsay Museum (see page 130) is closer on the right, connected with the Tuileries Garden by a sleek pedestrian bridge (the next bridge upriver). Paris awaits.

MARAIS WALK

*From Place Bastille to the
Pompidou Center*

This walk takes you through one of Paris' most characteristic quarters, the Marais, and finishes in the artsy Beaubourg district. When in Paris, you naturally want to see the big sights—but to experience the city, you also need to visit a vital neighborhood.

The Marais, containing more pre-Revolutionary lanes and buildings than anywhere else in town, is more atmospheric than touristy. It's medieval Paris, and the haunt of the old nobility. After the aristocrats left, the Marais became a dumpy bohemian quarter so sordid it was nearly slated for destruction. But today this thriving, trendy, real community is a joy to explore. It looks the way much of the city did until the mid-1800s, when Napoleon III had Baron Georges-Eugène Haussmann blast out the narrow streets to construct broad boulevards (wide enough for the guns and ranks of the army, too wide for revolutionary barricades), thus creating modern Paris. A big Haussmann-type boulevard was planned to slice efficiently through the Marais, but World War I got in the way.

ORIENTATION

Length of This Walk: Allow about two hours for this two-mile walk. Figure on an additional hour for each museum you visit along the way (listed below).

Victor Hugo's House: Free, Tue–Sun 10:00–18:00, last entry 17:40, closed Mon, 6 place des Vosges, tel. 01 42 72 10 16. For more information, see page 268.

Carnavalet Museum: Free, Tue–Sun 10:00–18:00, closed Mon. Avoid lunchtime (12:00–14:00), when many rooms close. It's at 23 rue de Sévigné (Mo: St. Paul, tel. 01 44 59 58 58). ✪ See tour on page 286.

Marais Walk

1. Place de la Bastille
2. Hôtel de Sully
3. Place des Vosges & Victor Hugo's House
4. Rue des Francs Bourgeois
5. Carnavalet Museum
6. Rue Pavée
7. Jewish Quarter
8. Holocaust Memorial
9. Rue Ste. Croix de la Bretonnerie
10. Pompidou Center

Picasso Museum: €6.50, covered by Museum Pass, additional fees for temporary exhibits, free on first Sun of month and for kids under 18 with ID, April–Sept Wed–Mon 9:30–18:00, Oct–March Wed–Mon 9:30–17:30, last entry 45 min before closing, closed Tue, 5 rue de Thorigny, Mo: St. Paul or Chemin Vert, tel. 01 42 71 25 21, www.musee-picasso.fr. ✪ See tour on page 301.

Holocaust Memorial: Free, Sun–Fri 10:00–18:00, Thu until 22:00, closed Sat and certain Jewish holidays, 17 rue Geoffroy l'Asnier, tel. 01 42 77 44 72, www.memorialdelashoah.org.

Jewish Art and History Museum: €7 but more during special exhibits, includes audioguide, covered by Museum Pass, Mon–Fri 11:00–18:00, Sun 10:00–18:00, last entry 1 hour before closing, closed Sat, 71 rue du Temple, Mo: Rambuteau, or Hôtel de Ville a few blocks farther away, tel. 01 53 01 86 60, www.mahj.org. See page 68.

Pompidou Center: €10, covered by Museum Pass, free on first Sun of month, Wed–Mon 11:00–21:00, ticket counters close at 20:00, closed Tue, Mo: Rambuteau, or Hôtel de Ville farther away, tel. 01 44 78 12 33, www.centrepompidou.fr. ✪ See tour on page 273.

Private Tours: Paris Walks offers guided tours of this area (4/week, see page 35).

Starring: The grand place des Vosges, the Jewish Quarter, several museums, and the boutiques and trendy lifestyle of today's Marais.

THE WALK BEGINS

• *Start at the west end of place de la Bastille. From the Bastille Métro, exit following signs to* rue St. Antoine *(not the signs to* rue du Faubourg St. Antoine*). Ascend onto a noisy square dominated by the bronze Colonne de Juillet (July Column). The bronze god on the top is, like you, headed west.*

❶ Place de la Bastille

There are more Revolutionary images in the Métro station murals than on the square. While place de la Bastille is famous for its part in the French Revolution of 1789, little from that time remains. The Bastille itself, a royal-fortress-turned-prison that once symbolized old-regime tyranny and now symbolizes the Parisian emancipation, is long gone. Only a brick outline of the fortress' round turrets survives (under the traffic where rue St. Antoine hits the square), though the story of the Bastille is indelibly etched into the city's psyche.

For centuries, the Bastille was used to defend the city (mostly from its own people). On July 14, 1789, the people of Paris stormed the prison, releasing its seven prisoners and hoping to find arms. They demolished the stone fortress and decorated their pikes with the heads of a few bigwigs. By shedding blood, the leaders of the gang made sure it would

Bastille Day in France

Bastille Day—July 14, the symbolic kickoff date of the French Revolution—became the French national holiday in 1880. Traditionally, Parisians celebrate at place de la Bastille starting at 20:00 on July 13, but the best parties are on the numerous smaller squares, where firefighter units sponsor dances. At 10:00 on the morning of the 14th, a grand military parade fills the Champs-Elysées. Then, at 22:30, there's a fireworks display at the Eiffel Tower (arrive by 20:30 to get a seat on the grass). *Vive la France!*

be tough to turn back the tides of revolution. Ever since, the French have celebrated July 14 as their independence day—Bastille Day.

The monument on the square—with its gilded statue of liberty—is a symbol of France's long struggle to establish democracy, commemorating the revolutions of 1830 and 1848. In 1830, the conservative king Charles X—who forgot all about the Revolution of the previous generation—needed to be tossed out. In 1848, a time of social unrest throughout Europe, the streets of Paris were barricaded by the working class, as dramatized in *Les Misérables*. Today, winged Mercury carries the torch of freedom into the future.

The southeast corner of the square is dominated (some say overwhelmed) by the flashy, curved, glassy gray facade of the controversial **Opéra Bastille.** In a symbolic attempt to bring high culture to the masses, former French president François Mitterrand chose this square for the building that would become Paris' main opera venue, edging out Paris' earlier "palace of the rich," the Garnier-designed opera house (see page 61).

Designed by the Canadian architect Carlos Ott, this grand Parisian project was opened with fanfare by Mitterrand on the 200th Bastille Day, July 14, 1989. While tickets are heavily subsidized to encourage the unwashed masses to attend, how much high culture they have actually enjoyed here is a subject of debate. (For opera ticket information, see page 424.)

You'll now turn your back on this Haussmann-style grandeur and walk down what was—before the Revolution—one of the grandest streets in Paris: rue St. Antoine. In 1350, there was a gate to the city here, Porte St. Antoine, defended by a drawbridge and fortress—a *bastille*.

• *Passing the Banque de France, head west down rue St. Antoine about four blocks into the Marais. At the intersection with rue de Birague, old hippies may wish to make a 100-yard detour to the left, down rue Beautrellis to #17, the nondescript apartment where rock star Jim Morrison died. (For more on Jim, see page 316.) Otherwise, continue down rue St. Antoine, and at 62 rue St. Antoine, enter the grand courtyard of Hôtel de Sully (open until 19:00, fine bookstore inside). If the building is closed, you'll need to backtrack one block to rue de Birague to reach the next stop, place des Vosges.*

❷ Hôtel de Sully

During the reign of Henry IV, this area—originally a swamp *(marais)*—became the hometown of the French aristocracy. In the 17th century, big shots built their private mansions *(hôtels)*, like this one, close to Henry's stylish place des Vosges. *Hôtels* that survived the Revolution now house museums, libraries, and national institutions.

The first of two courtyards is carriage-friendly and elegant, separating the mansion from the noisy and very public street. Look up at statues of Autumn (carrying grapes from the harvest), Winter (a feeble old man), and the four elements.

Continue into a passageway with a bookstore with skillfully carved and painted ceilings. Exit into the back courtyard, where noisy Paris disappears. Use the bit of Gothic window tracery (on the right) for a fun framed photo of your travel partner as a Madonna. At the far end, the French doors are part of a former *orangerie*, or greenhouse, for homegrown fruits and vegetables through the winter; these days, it warms office workers.

• *Continue through the small door at the far right corner of the second courtyard, and pop out into one of Paris' finest squares.*

❸ Place des Vosges

Walk to the center, where Louis XIII on horseback gestures, "Look at this wonderful square my dad built." He's surrounded by locals enjoy-

ing their community park. Children frolic in the sandbox, lovers warm benches, and pigeons guard their fountains while trees shade this retreat from the glare of the big city. (Or is it raining?)

Study the architecture: nine pavilions (houses) per side. The two highest—at the front and back—were for the king and queen (but were never used). Warm red brickwork—some real, some fake—is topped with sloped slate roofs, chimneys, and another quaint relic of a bygone era: TV antennas. Beneath the arcades are cafés, art galleries, and restaurants—it's a romantic place for dinner (see page 385).

Henry IV (r. 1589–1610) built this centerpiece of the Marais in 1605 and called it "place Royal." As he'd hoped, it turned the Marais into Paris' most exclusive neighborhood. Just like Versailles 80 years later, this was a magnet for the rich and powerful of France. With the Revolution, the aristocratic splendor of this quarter passed. To encourage the country to pay its taxes, Napoleon promised naming rights to the district that paid first—the Vosges region (near Germany).

In the 19th century, the Marais became a working-class quarter, filled with gritty shops, artisans, immigrants, and a Jewish community. The insightful writer **Victor Hugo** lived at #6—at the southeast corner of the square—from 1832–1848. This was when he wrote much of his most important work, including his biggest hit, *Les Misérables*. Inside, you'll wander through eight plush rooms and enjoy a fine view of the square (marked by the French flag in the corner closest to the Bastille; see page 70).

• *Sample some of the upscale art galleries ringing the place, then exit the square at the northwest (far left) corner. Head west on...*

❹ Rue des Francs Bourgeois

From the Marais of yesteryear, immediately enter the lively neighborhood of today. Stroll down a block of cafés and clothing boutiques with the latest fashions. A few doorways (including #8 and #13) lead into courtyards with more shops.

• *Continue west one block along rue des Francs Bourgeois, and turn right on rue Sévigné to reach the entrance (at #23) of the...*

❺ Carnavalet Museum

Housed inside a Marais mansion, this museum focuses on the history of Paris, particularly the Revolution years. Since this is the best possible look at the elegance of the neighborhood back when place des Vosges was place Royal—and the museum is free—it's worthwhile to interrupt this walk and splice in a trip to the Carnavalet. ✪See Carnavalet Museum Tour on page 286.

• *From the Carnavalet, continue west one block down rue des Francs Bourgeois to the post office. From here, you can detour to the right to the Picasso Museum, located two blocks north (page 301). But we'll turn left onto...*

❻ Rue Pavée

At #24, you'll pass the 16th-century **Paris Historical Library** (Bibliothèque Historique de la Ville de Paris). Step into the courtyard of this rare Renaissance mansion to see the clear windows, clean classical motifs, and settling stones. Because the neighborhood is built upon a swamp (*marais* means swamp), many buildings in this area have foundation problems.

Farther down the street on your right, a funky bookstore at #17 bis has more inside than meets the eye (it's called Mona Lisait, which means "Mona was reading").

Continue along rue Pavée, overshooting the rue des Rosiers turnoff, to the Agoudas Hakehilos **synagogue** with its fine Art Nouveau facade (c. 1913, closed to public, at 10 rue Pavée). It was designed by Hector Guimard, the same architect who designed Paris' Art Nouveau Métro stations.

• *Backtrack a few steps and turn onto rue des Rosiers (named for the roses that once lined the city wall), which runs straight for three blocks through Paris' Jewish Quarter—lively every day except Saturday.*

❼ Jewish Quarter

Once the largest in Western Europe, Paris' Jewish Quarter is much smaller today but is still colorful. Notice the sign above #4, which says *Hamam* (Turkish bath). Although still bearing the sign of an

old public bath, it's now a furniture showroom. Next door, at #4 bis, the Ecole de Travail (trade school) has a plaque on the wall remembering the headmaster, staff, and students arrested here during World War II and killed at Auschwitz.

The size of the Jewish population here has fluctuated. It expanded in the 19th century when Jews arrived from Eastern Europe, escaping pogroms (surprise attacks on villages). The numbers swelled during the 1930s as Jews fled Nazi Germany. Then, during World War II, 75 percent of the Jews here were taken to concentration camps (for more information, visit the Holocaust Memorial, described later in this tour). And, most recently, Algerian exiles, both Jewish and Muslim, have settled in— living together peacefully here in Paris. (Nevertheless, much of the street has granite blocks on the sidewalk—an attempt to keep out any terrorists' cars.) Currently the district's traditional population is being squeezed out by the trendy boutiques of modern Paris.

The intersection of rue des Rosiers and rue des Ecouffes marks the heart of the small neighborhood that Jews call the Pletzl ("little place"). Lively rue des Ecouffes, named for a bird of prey, is a derogatory nod to the moneychangers' shops that once lined this lane. Rue des Rosiers features kosher *(cascher)* restaurants and fast-food places selling falafel, *shawarma, kefta,* and other Mediterranean dishes. Bakeries specialize in braided challah, bagels, and strudels. Delis offer gefilte fish, piroshkis, and blintzes. Art galleries exhibit Jewish-themed works, and store windows post flyers for community events. Looking for a menorah? This is a great place to buy one. You may see Jewish men in yarmulkes, a few bearded Orthodox Jews, and Hasidic Jews with black coat and hat, beard, and earlocks.

Lunch: This is a fine place for a lunch break. You'll be tempted by kosher pizza and plenty of cheap fast-food joints selling falafel "to go" *(emporter)*. The best falafel is at **L'As du Falafel,** with a bustling New York deli atmosphere (at #34, sit-down or to go). The **Sacha Finkelsztajn Yiddish bakery** at #27 is also good (Polish and Russian cuisine, pop in for a tempting treat, sit for the same price as takeaway). **Chez Marianne** cooks up traditional Jewish meals (at corner of rue des Rosiers and rue des Hospitalieres St. Gervais; see page 389 in Eating).

• *Rue des Rosiers dead-ends at rue Vieille du Temple. Here you have two choices; you can continue the walk, or detour to the Holocaust Memorial.*

To continue the walk: Turn left on rue Vieille du Temple from rue des Rosiers, then take your first right onto rue Ste. Croix de la Bretonnerie (and skip down to ❾, *next page).*

To detour to the Holocaust Memorial: To better understand the Jewish suffering during World War II, take this 10-block round-trip detour. From rue des Rosiers, turn left on rue Vieille du Temple and continue straight, crossing rue de Rivoli. Make your second left after rue de Rivoli onto the cobbled passageway, Allée des Justes. At rue L'Asnier, turn right to find the entrance to the stark...

❽ Holocaust Memorial (Mémorial de la Shoah)

Opened in 2005, the Holocaust Memorial serves several functions: a WWII deportation memorial, a museum on the Holocaust, and a Jewish resource center. Pass through airport-like security. The entry courtyard contains a cylinder evoking concentration camp smokestacks. Large stone walls are engraved with the names of the 76,000 French Jews deported during the war. Enter the building (with an information desk, bookstore, café, and exhibits) and pick up a brochure. Go downstairs one floor to the crypt, which has a large Star of David in black marble. Ashes from some of the six million victims of Nazi brutality are buried underneath the star, in soil brought from Israel. Behind you, you'll find a small corridor containing the original French police files from the arrest, internment, and deportation of Paris' Jews. (Since 1995, the French—thanks to President Chirac's leadership—have acknowledged the Vichy government's complicity in the Nazis' local ethnic cleansing.)

Go downstairs another floor to the permanent exhibition. Photos and videos (most with English explanations) present an introduction to Judaism and the history of Jews in Europe (including pogroms) and in France (including the notorious Dreyfus affair, described on page 201). The displays trace the rise of Nazism, the deportations (including 12,884 Parisians rounded up in a single day), the death camps, and the liberation at the end of the war. The moving finale is a brightly lit collage of children lost to the terror of the Holocaust.

• *Head back the way you came. After crossing rue de Rivoli, take your second left onto...*

❾ Rue Ste. Croix de la Bretonnerie

Gay Paree's openly gay main drag is lined with cafés, lively shops, and crowded bars at night. Check the posters at #7, Le Point Virgule theater, to see what form of edgy musical comedy is showing tonight (most productions are in French). At #38, peruse real estate prices in the area—€400,000 for a one-bedroom flat?!

At rue du Temple, some may wish to detour half a block to the right to The Studio (41 rue du Temple), a dance school wonderfully located in a 17th-century courtyard. At the restaurant in the courtyard, you can sip a *café crème*—or have a Tex-Mex meal—surrounded by ballet, tap dance, and tango.

A block beyond the dance school is the Jewish Art and History Museum (see page 68).

• *Continue west on rue Ste. Croix (which changes names to rue St. Merri). Up ahead, you'll see the colorful pipes of the...*

❿ Pompidou Center

Survey this popular spot from the top of the sloping square. Tubular escalators lead up to a great view and the modern art museum. ❷ See

Pompidou Center Tour on page 273.

The Pompidou Center subscribes with gusto to the 20th-century architectural axiom, "form follows function." To get a more spacious and functional interior, the guts of this exoskeletal building are draped on the outside and color-coded: vibrant red for people lifts, cool blue for air ducts, eco-green for plumbing, don't-touch-it yellow for electrical stuff, and white for bones. (Compare the Pompidou Center to another exoskeletal building, Notre-Dame.)

Enjoy the adjacent *Homage to Stravinsky* fountains. Jean Tinguely and Niki de Saint-Phalle designed these as a tribute to the composer: Every fountain represents one of his hard-to-hum scores. For low-stress meals, try the lighthearted Dame Tartine, which overlooks the *Homage to Stravinsky* fountains and serves good, inexpensive food, or walk up to the lively rue Montorgueil market street (read on).

Beyond the Marais

From the Pompidou, continue west along the cobbled pedestrian mall, crossing the busy boulevard de Sébastopol to the ivy-covered pavilions of Les Halles. Paris' down-and-dirty central produce market of 800 years was replaced by a glitzy but soulless shopping center in the late 1970s. The mall's most endearing layer is its grassy rooftop park. (The Gothic St. Eustache Church overlooking this contemporary scene has a famous 8,000-pipe organ.)

For a more soulful shopping experience (similar to that of rue Cler), find your way behind St. Eustache Church and cross rue Montmartre onto the delightfully traffic-free rue Montorgueil (mohn-tor-go-ee). This street is the site of a flourishing market (open daily throughout the week except Sun afternoon, Mon, and lunchtime—13:00–15:00). If you've walked here all the way from place Bastille, you deserve a break at one of the street's lively cafés.

POMPIDOU CENTER TOUR

Centre Pompidou

Some people hate Modern art. But the Pompidou Center contains what is possibly Europe's best collection of 20th-century art. After the super-serious Louvre and Orsay, finish things off with this artistic kick in the pants. You won't find classical beauty here, no dreamy Madonnas-and-children—just a stimulating, offbeat, and, if you like, instructive walk through nearly every art style of the wild and crazy last century.

The Pompidou's "permanent" collection...isn't. It changes so often that a painting-by-painting tour is impossible. So, this chapter is more a general overview of the major trends of 20th-century art, with emphasis on artists you're likely to find in the Pompidou. Read this chapter ahead of time for background, or take it with you to the museum to look up specific painters as you stumble across their work.

ORIENTATION

Cost: A €10 combo-ticket gets you into all of the building's various exhibits—both the permanent collection (which we'll see) and the temporary exhibits that make this place so edgy. The Museum Pass only gets you into the permanent collection, known as the *Musée National d'Art Moderne: Collection Permanente*. Buy tickets on the ground floor. If lines are long, use the red ticket machines (credit cards only). The museum is free on the first Sunday of the month.

Hours: Wed–Mon 11:00–21:00, ticket counters close at 20:00, closed Tue.

Getting There: Métro stop Rambuteau or, a few blocks farther away, Hôtel de Ville. Bus #69 from the Marais and rue Cler also stops a few blocks away at Hôtel de Ville. The wild, color-coded exterior makes it about as hard to locate as the Eiffel Tower.

Information: Tel. 01 44 78 12 33, www.centrepompidou.fr. Parisians call the complex the "Centre Beaubourg" (sahn-truh boh-boor), but official publications call it the "Centre Pompidou." Once inside, most rooms have informative English explanations.

Length of This Tour: Allow one hour.

Cloakroom: Ground floor, free, and required for large bags.

Shopping: There's a terrific museum store with zany gift ideas on the mezzanine overlooking the main floor.

Cuisine Art: You'll find a sparse, sandwich-and-coffee café on the mezzanine and a fancier view restaurant on Level 6. Outside the museum, the neighborhood abounds with cheap, hip bistros and crêpe stands. My favorite places are to the right of the museum, lining the playful fountain, *Homage to Stravinsky*. **Dame Tartine** and **Crêperie Beaubourg** both have reasonable prices.

View Art: The sixth floor (where the pricey restaurant is) has stunning views of the Paris cityscape.

Starring: Matisse, Picasso, Chagall, Dalí, Warhol, and contemporary art.

THE TOUR BEGINS

That slight tremor you may feel comes from Italy, where Michelangelo has been spinning in his grave ever since 1977, when the Pompidou Center first revolted Paris. Still, it's an appropriate modern temple for the controversial art it houses.

The building itself is "exoskeletal" (like Notre-Dame or a crab), with its functional parts—the pipes, heating ducts, and escalator—on the outside, and the meaty art inside. It's the epitome of Modern architecture, where "form follows function."

The *Musée National d'Art Moderne: Collection Permanente* (what we'll see) is on the fourth and fifth floors. But there's plenty more art scattered all over the building. Ask at the ground-floor information booth, or just wander.

• *Buy your ticket on the ground floor, then ride up the escalator (or run up the down escalator to get in the proper mood). When you see the view, your opinion of the Pompidou's exterior should improve a good 15 percent. Find the permanent collection—the entrance is either on the fourth or fifth floor (it varies).*

Enter, show your ticket, and get the current floor plan (plan du musée). *Generally, art from 1905–1960 is on the fifth floor, while the fourth floor contains more recent art. But 20th-century art resents being put in chronological order, and the Pompidou's collection is rarely in any neat-and-*

tidy arrangement. Use the museum's map to find select artists, and don't hesitate to ask, "Où est Kandinsky?"

Remember, the following text is not a "tour" of the museum—it's a chronological overview of Modern art.

MODERN ART 1905–1960

A.D. 1900: A new century dawns. War is a thing of the past. Science will wipe out poverty and disease. Rational Man is poised at a new era of peace and prosperity....

Right. This cozy Victorian dream was soon shattered by two world wars and rapid technological change. Nietzsche murdered God. Freud washed ashore on the beach of a vast new continent inside each of us. Einstein made everything merely "relative." Even the fundamental building blocks of the universe, atoms, were behaving erratically.

The 20th century—accelerated by technology and fragmented by war—was exciting and chaotic, and the art reflects the turbulence of that century of change.

Cubism: Reality Shattered (1907–1912)

I throw a rock at a glass statue, shatter it, pick up the pieces, and glue them onto a canvas. I'm a Cubist.

Pablo Picasso (1881–1973) and Georges Braque (1882–1963)

Born in Spain, Picasso moved to Paris as a young man, settling into a studio (the Bateau-Lavoir) in Montmartre (see page 332). He worked

with next-door neighbor Georges Braque in poverty so dire they often didn't know where their next bottle of wine was coming from. They corrected each other's paintings (it's hard to tell whose is whose without the titles), and they shared ideas, meals, and girlfriends while inventing a whole new way to look at the world.

They show the world through a kaleidoscope of brown and gray. The subjects are somewhat recognizable (with the help of the titles), but they are broken into geometric shards (let's call them "cubes," though there are many different shapes), then pieced back together.

Cubism gives us several different angles of the subject at once—say, a woman seen from the front and side angles simultaneously, resulting in two eyes on the same side of the nose. This involves showing three dimensions, plus Einstein's new fourth dimension, the time it takes to walk around the subject to see other angles. Newfangled motion pictures could capture this moving, 4-D world, but how to do it on a 2-D canvas? The Cubist "solution" is a kind of Mercator projection, where the round world is sliced up like an orange peel and then laid as flat as possible.

Notice how the "cubes" often overlap. A single cube might contain both an arm (in the foreground) and the window behind (in the background), both painted the same color. The foreground and the background are woven together, so that the subject dissolves into a pattern.

Picasso: Synthetic Cubism (1912–1915) and Beyond

If the Cubists were as smart as Einstein, why couldn't they draw a picture to save their lives? Picasso was one Modern artist who could draw exceptionally well (see his partly finished *Harlequin*). But he constantly explored and adapted his style to new trends, and so became the most famous painter of the century. Scattered throughout the museum are works from the many periods of Picasso's life.

Picasso soon began to use more colorful "cubes" (1912–1915). Eventually, he used curved shapes to build the subject, rather than the straight-line shards of early Cubism.

Picasso married and had children. Works from this period (the 1920s) are more realistic, with full-bodied (and big-nosed) women and children. He tries to capture the solidity, serenity, and volume of classical statues.

As his relationships with women deteriorated, he vented his sexual demons by twisting the female body into grotesque balloon-animal shapes (1925–1931).

All through his life, Picasso explored new materials. He made collages, tried his hand at making "statues" out of wood, wire, or whatever, and even made statues out of everyday household objects. These multimedia works, so revolutionary at the time, have become stock-in-trade today.

Marc Chagall (1887–1985)

Marc Chagall, at age 22, arrived in Paris with the wide-eyed wonder of a country boy. Lovers are weightless with bliss. Animals smile and wink at us. Musicians, poets, peasants, and dreamers ignore gravity, tumbling in slow-motion circles high above the rooftops. The colors are deep, dark, and earthy—a pool of mystery with figures bleeding through below the surface. (Chagall claimed his early poverty forced him to paint over used canvases, inspiring the overlapping images.)

Chagall's very personal style fuses many

influences. He was raised in a small Belarus village, which explains his "naive" outlook and fiddler-on-the-roof motifs. His simple figures are like Russian Orthodox icons, and his Jewish roots produced Old Testament themes. Stylistically, he's thoroughly Modern—Cubist shards, bright Fauve colors, and Primitive simplification. This otherworldly style was a natural for religious works, and so his murals and stained glass, which feature both Jewish and Christian motifs, decorate buildings around the world—including the ceiling of Paris' Opéra Garnier (Mo: Opéra).

Georges Rouault (1871–1958)

Young Georges Rouault was apprenticed to a stained-glass-window-maker. Enough said?

The paintings have the same thick, glowing colors, heavy black outlines, simple subjects, and (mostly) religious themes. The style is Modern, but the mood is medieval, solemn, and melancholy. Rouault captures the tragic spirit of those people—clowns, prostitutes, and sons of God—who have been made outcasts by society.

Henri Matisse (1869–1954)

Matisse's colorful "wallpaper" works are not realistic. A man is a few black lines and blocks of paint. The colors are unnaturally bright.

There's no illusion of the distance and 3-D that were so important to Renaissance Italians. The "distant" landscape is as bright as things close up, and the slanted lines meant to suggest depth are crudely done.

Traditionally, the canvas was like a window that you looked "through" to see a slice of the real world stretching off into the distance. Now, a camera could do that better. With Matisse, you look "at" the canvas, like wallpaper. Voilà! What was a crudely drawn scene now becomes a sophisticated and decorative pattern of colors and shapes.

Though fully "Modern," Matisse built on 19th-century art—the bright colors of Vincent van Gogh, the primitive figures of Paul Gauguin, the colorful designs of Japanese prints, and the Impressionist patches of paint that only blend together at a distance.

Primitive Masks and Statues

Matisse was one of the Fauves ("wild beasts") who, inspired by African and Oceanic masks and voodoo dolls, tried to inject a bit of the jungle into bored French society. The result? Modern art that looked primitive: long, mask-like faces with almond eyes; bright, clashing colors; simple figures; and "flat," two-dimensional scenes.

POMPIDOU CENTER

Abstract Art

Abstract art simplifies. A man becomes a stick figure. A squiggle is a wave. A streak of red expresses anger. Arches make you want a cheeseburger. These are universal symbols that everyone from a caveman to a banker understands. Abstract artists capture the essence of reality in a few lines and colors, and they capture things even a camera can't—emotions, abstract concepts, musical rhythms, and spiritual states of mind. Again, with abstract art, you don't look *through* the canvas to see the visual world, but *at* it to read the symbolism of lines, shapes, and colors.

Wassily Kandinsky (1866–1944)

The bright colors, bent lines, and lack of symmetry tell us that Kandinsky's world was passionate and intense.

Notice titles like *Improvisation* and *Composition*. Kandinsky was inspired by music, an art form that's also "abstract," though it still packs a punch. Like a jazz musician improvising a new pattern of notes from a set scale, Kandinsky plays with new patterns of related colors as he looks for just the right combination. Using lines and color, Kandinsky translates the unseen reality into a new medium...like lightning crackling over the radio. Go, man, go.

Piet Mondrian (1872–1944)

Like blueprints for Modernism, Mondrian's T-square style boils paint-

ing down to its basic building blocks (black lines, white canvas) and the three primary colors (red, yellow, and blue), all arranged in orderly patterns.

(When you come right down to it, that's all painting ever has been. A schematic drawing of, say, the *Mona Lisa* shows that it's less about a woman than about the triangles and rectangles of which she's composed.)

Mondrian started out painting realistic landscapes of the orderly fields in his native Netherlands. Increasingly, he simplified them into horizontal and vertical patterns. For Mondrian, who was heavy into Eastern mysticism, "up vs. down" and "left vs. right" were the perfect metaphors for life's dualities: "good vs. evil," "body vs. spirit," "man vs. woman." The canvas is a bird's-eye view of Mondrian's personal landscape.

Constantin Brancusi (1876–1957)

Brancusi's curved, shiny statues reduce things to their essence. A bird is a single stylized wing, the one feature that sets it apart from other animals. He rounds off to the closest geometrical form, so a woman's head becomes a perfect oval on a cubic pedestal.

Humans love symmetry (maybe because our own bodies are roughly symmetrical) and find geometric shapes restful, even worthy of meditation. Brancusi follows the instinct for order that has driven art from earliest times, from circular Stonehenge and Egyptian pyramids, to Greek columns and Roman arches, to Renaissance symmetry and the Native American "medicine wheel."

Paul Klee (1879–1940)

Paul Klee's small and playful canvases are deceptively simple, containing shapes so basic they can be read as universal symbols. Klee thought a wavy line, for example, would always suggest motion, while a stick figure would always mean a human—like the psychiatrist Carl Jung's universal dream symbols, part of our "collective unconscious."

Klee saw these universals in the art of children, who express themselves without censoring or cluttering things up with learning. His art has a childlike playfulness and features simple figures painted in an uninhibited frame of mind.

Klee also turned to nature. The same forces that cause the wave to draw a line of foam on the beach can cause a meditative artist to draw a squiggly line of paint on a canvas. The result is a universal shape. The true artist doesn't just paint nature, he becomes Nature.

Design: Chairs by Gerrit Rietveld and Alvar Aalto

Hey, if you can't handle Modern art, sit on it! (Actually, don't.) The

applied arts—chairs, tables, lamps, and vases—are as much a part of the art world as the fine arts. (Some say the first art object was the pot.) As machines became as talented as humans, artists embraced new technology and mass production to bring beauty to the masses.

Fernand Léger (1881–1955)

Fernand Léger's style has been called "Tubism"—breaking the world down into cylinders, rather than cubes. (He supposedly got his inspiration during World War I from the gleaming barrel of a cannon.) Léger captures the feel of the encroaching Age of Machines, with all the world looking like an internal-combustion engine.

Robert Delaunay (1885–1941) and Sonia Delaunay (1885–1979)

This husband and wife both painted colorful, fragmented canvases (including a psychedelic Eiffel Tower) that prove the Modern style doesn't have to be ugly or puzzling.

World War I: The Death of Values

Ankle-deep in mud, a soldier shivers in a trench, waiting to be ordered "over the top." He'll have to run through barbed wire, over fallen comrades, and into a hail of machine-gun fire, only to capture a few hundred yards of meaningless territory that will be lost the next day. This soldier was not thinking about art.

World War I left nine million dead. (During the war, France sometimes lost more men in a single month than America lost in all of the Vietnam War.) The war also killed the optimism and faith in mankind that had guided Europe since the Renaissance. Now, rationality just meant schemes, technology meant machines of death, and morality meant giving your life for an empty cause.

Expressionism: Ernst Ludwig Kirchner, Max Beckmann, George Grosz, Chaïm Soutine, Otto Dix, and Oskar Kokoschka

Cynicism and decadence settled over postwar Europe. Artists "expressed" their disgust by showing a distorted reality that emphasized the ugly. Using the lurid colors and simplified figures of the Fauves, they slapped paint on in thick brushstrokes and depicted a hypocritical, hard-edged, dog-eat-dog world that had lost its bearings. The people have a haunted look in their eyes, the fixed stare of corpses and those who have to bury them.

Dada: Marcel Duchamp's Urinal (1917)

When people could grieve no longer, they turned to grief's giddy twin: laughter. The war made all old values a joke, including artistic ones. The Dada movement, choosing a purposely childish name, made art that was intentionally outrageous: a moustache on the *Mona Lisa*, a shovel hung on a wall, or a modern version of a Renaissance "fountain"—a urinal (by either Marcel Duchamp or I. P. Freeley, 1917). It was a dig at all the pompous prewar artistic theories based on the noble intellect of Rational Women and Men. While the experts ranted on, Dadaists sat in the back of the class and made cultural fart noises.

Hey, I love this stuff. My mind says it's sophomoric, but my heart belongs to Dada.

POMPIDOU CENTER

Surrealism: Salvador Dalí, Max Ernst, and René Magritte (1920–1940)

Greek statues with sunglasses, a man as a spinning top, shoes becoming feet, and black ants as musical notes...Surrealism. The world was moving fast, and Surrealists caught the jumble of images. The artist scatters seemingly unrelated things on the canvas, which leaves us to trace the links in a kind of connect-the-dots without numbers. If it comes together, the synergy of unrelated things can be pretty startling. But even if the juxtaposed images don't ultimately connect, the artist has made you think, rerouting your thoughts through new neural paths. If you don't "get" it...you got it.

Complicating the modern world was Freud's discovery of the "unconscious" mind that thinks dirty thoughts while we sleep. Many a Surrealist canvas is an uncensored, stream-of-consciousness "landscape" of these deep urges, revealed in the bizarre images of dreams.

In dreams, sometimes one object can be two things at once: "I dreamt that you walked in with a cat...no, wait, maybe you *were* the cat...no...." Surrealists paint opposites like these and let them speak for themselves.

Salvador Dalí (1904–1989)

Salvador Dalí could draw exceptionally well. He painted "unreal" scenes with photographic realism, thus making us believe they could really happen. Seeing familiar objects in an unfamiliar setting—like a grand piano adorned with disembodied heads of Lenin—creates an air of mystery, the feeling that anything can happen. That's both exciting and unsettling. Dalí's images—crucifixes, political and religious figures, naked bodies—pack an emotional punch. Take one mixed bag of reality, jumble in a blender, and serve on a canvas...Surrealism.

Abstract Surrealists: Joan Miró, Alexander Calder, and Jean Arp

Abstract artists described their subconscious urges using color and shapes alone, like Rorschach inkblots in reverse.

The thin-line scrawl of Joan Miró's work is like the doodling of a three-year-old. You'll recognize crudely drawn birds, stars, animals, and strange cell-like creatures with whiskers ("Biological Cubism"). Miró was trying to express the most basic of human emotions using the most basic of techniques.

Alexander Calder's mobiles hang like Mirós in the sky, waiting for a gust of wind to bring them to life.

And talk about a primal image! Jean Arp builds human beings out of amoeba-like shapes.

Decorative Art: Pierre Bonnard, Balthus, and Later Picasso and Braque

Most 20th-century paintings are a mix of the real world ("representation") and the colorful patterns of "abstract" art. Artists purposely distort camera-eye reality to make the resulting canvas more decorative. So, Picasso flattens a woman into a pattern of colored shapes, Bonnard makes a man from a shimmer of golden paint, and Balthus turns a boudoir scene into colorful wallpaper.

Patterns and Textures: Jean Dubuffet, Lucio Fontana, and Karel Appel

Increasingly, you'll have to focus your eyes to look *at* the canvases, not *through* them.

Enjoy the lines and colors, but also a new element: texture. Some works have very thick paint piled on, and so you can see the brushstroke clearly. Some have substances besides paint applied to the canvas, such as Dubuffet's brown, earthy rectangles of real dirt and organic waste. Fontana punctures the canvas so that the fabric itself (and the hole) becomes the subject. Artists show their skill by mastering new materials. The canvas is a tray, serving up a delightful array of different substances with interesting colors, patterns, shapes, and textures.

Alberto Giacometti (1901–1966)

Giacometti's skinny statues have the emaciated, haunted, and faceless look of concentration camp survivors. The simplicity of the figures may be "primitive," but these aren't stately, sturdy, Easter Island heads. Here, man is weak in the face of technology and the winds of history.

Abstract Expressionism

America emerged from World War II as the globe's superpower. With Europe in ruins, New York replaced Paris as the art capital of the world. The trend was toward bigger canvases, abstract designs, and experimentation with new materials and techniques. It was called "Abstract Expressionism"—expressing emotions and ideas using color and form alone.

Jackson Pollock (1912–1956)

"Jack the Dripper" attacks convention with a can of paint, dripping and splashing a dense web onto the canvas. Picture Pollock in his

studio, as he jives to the hi-fi, bounces off the walls, and throws paint in a moment of enlighten- ment. Of course, the artist loses some control this way—control over the paint flying in midair and over himself, now in an ecstatic trance. Painting becomes a whole- body activity, a "dance" between the artist and his materials.

The act of creating is what's important, not the final product. The canvas is only a record of that moment of ecstasy.

Big, Empty Canvases: Barnett Newman and Robert Rauschenberg

All those big, empty canvases with just a few lines or colors—what reality are they trying to show?

In the modern world, we find ourselves insignificant specks in a vast and indifferent universe. Every morning, each of us must con- front that big, blank, existentialist canvas and decide how we're going to make our mark on it. Like, wow.

Another influence was the simplicity of Japanese landscape paint- ing. A Zen master studies and meditates for years to achieve the state of mind in which he can draw one pure line. These canvases, again, are only a record of that state of enlightenment. (What is the sound of one brush painting?)

On more familiar ground, postwar painters were following in the footsteps of artists such as Mondrian, Klee, and Kandinsky (whose work they must have considered "busy"). The geometrical forms here reflect the same search for order, but these artists painted to the 5/4 asymmetry of Dave Brubeck's "Take Five."

If you are on the fifth floor, descend to the fourth floor, where you'll usually find "contemporary" art, from the last 50 years.

THE CONTEMPORARY COLLECTION 1960–PRESENT

Pop Art: Andy Warhol (1928–1987)

America's postwar wealth made the consumer king. Pop art is created from the "pop"-ular objects of that throwaway society—a soup

can, a car fender, mannequins, tacky plastic statues, movie icons, advertising posters. Take something out of Sears and hang it in a museum, and you have to think about it in a wholly different way.

Is this art? Are all these mass-produced objects beautiful? Or crap? If they're not art, why do we work so hard to acquire them? Pop art, like Dada, questions our society's values.

Andy Warhol (who coined the idea of everyone having "15 minutes of fame" and became a pop star) concentrated on another mass-produced phenomenon: celebrities. He took publicity photos of famous people and repeated them. The repetition—like the constant bombardment we get from repeated images on television—cheapens even the most beautiful things.

New Media for a New Century

The "modern" world is history. Picasso and his ilk are now gathering dust and boring art students everywhere. Minimalist painting and abstract sculpture are old-school. Enter the "postmodern" world, as seen through the eyes of current artists.

You'll see fewer traditional canvases or sculptures. Artists have traded paintbrushes for blowtorches (Miró said he was out to "murder" painting), and blowtorches for computer mouses. Mixed media work is the norm, combining painting, sculpture, photography, welding, photography/video, computer programming, new resins, plastics, industrial techniques, and lighting and sound systems.

Here are some of the trends:

Installations: An entire room is given to an artist to prepare. Like entering an art funhouse, you walk in without quite knowing what to expect. (I'm always thinking, "Is this safe?") Using the latest technology, the artist engages all your senses, by controlling the lights, sounds, and sometimes even smells.

Assemblages: Artists raid Dumpsters, recycling junk into the building blocks for larger "assemblages." Each piece is intended to be interesting and tell its own story, and so is the whole sculpture. Weird, useless, Rube Goldberg machines make fun of technology.

Natural Objects: A rock in an urban setting is inherently interesting.

The Occasional Canvas: This comes as a familiar relief. Artists of the New Realism labor over painstaking, hyper-realistic canvases to re-create the glossy look of a photo or video image.

Interaction: Some exhibits require your participation, whether you push a button to get the contraption going, touch something, or just walk around the room. In some cases, the viewer "does" art, rather than just staring at it. If art is really meant to change, it has to move you, literally.

Deconstruction: Late-20th-century artists critiqued (or "deconstructed") society by examining our underlying assumptions. One way to do it is to take a familiar object (say, a crucifix) out of its normal context (a church), and place it in a new setting (a jar of urine). Video and film can deconstruct something by playing it over and over, ad nauseam. Ad copy painted on canvas deconstructs itself.

Conceptual Art: The *concept* of which object to pair with another to produce maximum effect is the key. (Crucifix + urine = million-dollar masterpiece.)

Performance Art: This is a kind of mixed media of live performance. Many artists—who in another day would have painted canvases—have turned to music, dance, theater, and performance art. This art form is often interactive, by dropping the illusion of a performance and encouraging audience participation. When you finish with the Pompidou Center, go outside for some of the street theater.

Playful Art: Children love the art being produced today. If it doesn't put a smile on your face, well, then you must be a jaded grump like me, who's seen the same repetitious s#%t passed off as "daring" since Warhol stole it from Duchamp. I mean, it's *so* 20th-century.

CARNAVALET
MUSEUM TOUR

Musée Carnavalet

At the Carnavalet Museum, French history unfolds in a series of stills—like a Ken Burns documentary, except you have to walk. The Revolution is the highlight, but you get a good overview of everything, from Louis XIV–period rooms, to Napoleon, to the belle époque.

ORIENTATION

Cost: Free.

Hours: Tue–Sun 10:00–18:00, closed Mon. Avoid lunchtime (12:00–14:00), since many rooms close then.

Getting There: It's in the heart of the Marais district at 23 rue de Sévigné (Mo: St. Paul), and on the Marais Walk (page 263). There is a second, larger entrance on rue des Francs Bourgeois, but this tour begins from the courtyard on rue de Sévigné.

Information: Get the free (necessary) map at the information desk *(accueil)*. Tel. 01 44 59 58 58, www.carnavalet.paris.fr.

Length of This Tour: Allow two hours. You could do the Revolution in an hour.

Starring: François I, Louis XIV, Louis XV, Louis XVI, the Bastille, Robespierre, the guillotine, Napoleon, Napoleon III, the Paris Commune, and the belle époque.

Overview

The museum is housed in two Marais mansions connected by a corridor. The first half of the museum (pre-Revolution) is difficult to follow—rooms numbered out of order, no English descriptions, and sections closed due to understaffing. See this part quickly, so you can concentrate your energy on the Revolution and beyond. If you get lost or frustrated, we'll meet up again in Room 45 (on the first floor), where the Revolution begins.

To do this whole tour is a major course in French history. Consider limiting your visit to just the Revolution, located on the second floor (accessed from Room 45 on the first floor). The Revolution section starts on page 290.

THE TOUR BEGINS
MAIN BUILDING—1500-1789

• *Begin outside in the...*

Courtyard

You're surrounded by the in-your-face richness of the *ancien régime*—back when people generally accepted the notion that some were born to rule, and most were born to be ruled. And the embodiment of that age stands atop the statue in the center: Louis XIV, the ultimate divine monarch.

Notice the date: July 14, 1689, exactly 100 years before the French Revolution ended all that. This statue is a rare surviving pre-Revolutionary bronze. In 1792, nearly all of them were melted down to make weapons, as Revolutionary France took on the rest of Europe in an all-out war. Notice the relief below—a great piece of counter-Reformation propaganda. France (the angel with the royal shield) and heaven (portrayed by the angel protecting the Communion Host) are literally stomping the snakes and reformers of Protestantism (Hus, Calvin, Wycliffe, and Luther). Subtle.

• *Now find Room 7 on the ground floor. It's not obvious where it is—grab a free map and ask a guard ("Où est salle sept?"; oo ay sahl set). Once again, if you get lost or rooms are closed, we'll meet up again in Room 45, on the first floor (next page).*

1500s—Renaissance and Reformation
Room 7

A model of Ile de la Cité (made by a monk around 1900) shows the medieval city in about 1520 before France became a world power—crowded, narrow-laned, and steeple-dotted, with houses piled even on top of bridges. There's Notre-Dame on the east end, and Sainte-Chapelle, with its royal palace and gardens, on the west. The only straight road in town was the old Roman road that splits the island north–south and is still used today.

King François I (1494–1547, r. 1515–1547) brought Paris into the modern world. Handsome, athletic François—a writer of poems, leader of knights, and lover of women—

embodied the optimism of the Italian Renaissance. "*Le grand roi François*" (it rhymes) centralized the government around his charismatic self and made a rebuilt Louvre his home. He affirmed his absolute right to rule every time he ordered something done: "For such is our pleasure!"

Rooms 8 and 9

Renaissance open-mindedness brought religious debate, leading to open warfare between Catholics and Protestants (called Huguenots in France). You'll find paintings here of the Catholic **King Charles IX** (1550–1574, r. 1560–1574) and his mother, **Catherine de Médicis,** who plotted to assassinate several prominent Protestants. Their plan quickly snowballed into the slaughter of thousands of Parisian Huguenots on St. Bartholomew's Day in 1572. Paintings in both of these rooms show events organized by the **Catholic League:** parades, Bible studies, and the occasional Protestant barbecue to keep the faithful in good spirits.

Room 10

King Henry IV (1553–1610, r. 1589–1610, Louis XIV's grandfather) was perhaps France's most popular king. His **bust** depicts him with a faint smile and smile lines around the eyes, capturing his reputation as a witty conversationalist and friend of commoners. Henry helped reconcile Catholics and Protestants and rebuilt Paris. Still, that didn't stop a Revolutionary mob from tearing his equestrian statue to pieces *(Fragment du monument)*. See **engravings** of Henry's second wife, Marie de Médicis, and of some of Henry's building projects. The grotesque **stone faces** are four of the 300 that adorn Henry's greatest creation, the pont Neuf.

• *Head upstairs to the first floor.*

FIRST FLOOR

The Luxury of Louis XIV, XV, and XVI

Browse around the furnished rooms, getting a feel for the luxurious life of France's kings and nobles before the Revolution. In fact, several rooms are straight out of the mansions lining the nearby place des Vosges. Use the following material as background.

• *See you in Room 45, located in the far right corner.*

Louis XIV (1638–1715, r. 1643–1715)

The flowery walls, Greek-myth ceiling paintings, and powdered-wig portraits give a tiny glimpse of the opulence of Louis XIV and his greatest monument, the palace at Versailles. You'll see luxurious wallpaper, tables, chairs, parquet floors, clocks, gaming tables, statues, paintings, and even a doghouse that costs more than a peasant hut. Versailles was the physical symbol of Louis' absolute power over the largest, most populous, and richest nation in Europe.

Louis XIV Style: Baroque. In rooms from this period, ceilings are decorated with curved ornamental frames (cartouches) that hold paintings of Greek myths, and furnishings are gilded. The heavy tables and chairs have thick, curved legs, animal feet, and bronze corner-protectors.

Louis XV (1710–1774, r. 1715–1774)

Louis XV ascended the throne of Europe's most powerful nation when his great-grandfather, the Sun King, died after reigning for 72 years. Only five years old at the time, he was for many years a figurehead, while the government was run by his mentors: a regent during his childhood, his teacher during his youth, one of his many mistresses (Madame de Pompadour) during his middle age, and bureaucrats by the end. Louis was intelligent and educated, and he personally embraced the budding democratic ideals of the Enlightenment, but he spent his time at Versailles, where he gamed and consorted with Europe's most cultured and beautiful people. Meanwhile, France's money was spent on costly wars with Austria and England (including the American "French and Indian War"). Louis, basking in the lap of luxury and the glow of the Enlightenment, looked to the horizon and uttered his prophetic phrase: *"Après moi—le déluge!"* ("After me—the flood!").

Louis XV Style: Rococo. The rooms are decorated in pastel colors, with lighter decoration and exotic landscapes. The chairs are made of highly polished, rare woods, with delicate curved legs and padded seats and backs. Note the Chinese decor and objects such as the Ming vase.

Louis XVI (1754–1793, r. 1774–1792)

With a flood watch in effect, the next Louis stubbornly clung to the rules of the *ancien régime* (the traditional chessboard society with king on top, pawns on bottom, and bishops that walk diagonally).

While peasants groaned in the fields, the rich enjoyed their mansions: parties lit by chandeliers glimmering off mirrors, the sound of a string quartet, exotic foods from newly colonized lands, billiards in one room and high-stakes card games in another, a Molière comedy downstairs, dangerous ideas by radicals like Voltaire and Jean-Jacques Rousseau, and dangerous liaisons among social butterflies—male and female—dressed in high heels, makeup, wigs, and perfume.

Louis XVI Style: Neoclassical. Influenced by recently excavated Pompeii, the rooms are simpler—with classical motifs—and the furniture is straighter. The chairs' straight legs taper to a point.

• *From Room 45, walk down three steps, following signs reading* La Révolution, 19e et 20e siècle. *A long corridor (of mostly 19th-century paintings and sketches of Paris) leads to the next building. Hike up the hardwood stairs to the second floor and* La Révolution Française.

SECOND FLOOR

The Revolution: 1789-1799

No period of history is as charged with the full range of human emotions and actions as the French Revolution: bloodshed, martyrdom, daring speeches, murdered priests, emancipated women, backstabbing former friends—all done in the name of government "by, for, and of the people." Common people with their everyday concerns were driving the engine of history. Or perhaps they were only foam bubbles swept along in the shifting tides of vast socioeconomic trends.

Room 101: The Estates-General

It's 1789, France is bankrupt from wars and corruption, and the people want change. The large allegorical painting *L'espoir du bonheur* shows King Louis XVI in the boat of France, navigating stormy seas. Lady Truth is trying to light the way, but the winged demon of tyranny keeps nagging at the king. Above shines the fleur-de-lis, whose petals are labeled with the three social groups that held all power in France: clergy, king, and nobles. Now they are laced together by the new power... the people.

In May, the king called each sector of society together at Versailles to solve the financial crisis. But in a bold and unheard-of move, the Third Estate (the people), tired of being outvoted by the clergy and nobility, split and formed their own National Assembly (see *The Oath of the Jeu-de-Paume* on the opposite wall, a preparatory painting by Jacques-Louis David for a huge canvas that was never painted). Amid the chaos of speeches, debate, and deal-making, they raised their hands, bravely pledging to stick together until a new constitution was written. Vacillating between democratic change and royalist repression, **Louis XVI** (see his pink-faced portrait to the left) ordered the Assembly to dissolve (they refused), sent 25,000 Swiss mercenary soldiers to Paris, and fired his most popular, liberal minister.

Room 102: The Bastille (July 14, 1789)

The Bastille (see the **model**) was a medieval fortress turned prison. With its eight towers and 100-foot-high walls, it dominated the Parisian skyline, a symbol of oppression. (See the series of **paintings** that illustrate some of the following events.)

On the hot, muggy morning of July 14, Paris' citizens waited on edge, listening to reports of attacks on the populace by the king's Swiss guards. A crowd formed, marched on the Invalides armory, and seized 30,000 rifles...but no gunpowder. Word spread that it was stored across town at the Bastille. The mob grew bigger and angrier as it went. By noon, they stood at the foot of the walls of the Bastille and demanded gunpowder. They captured the fort's gov-

ernor, then two citizens managed to scale the wall and cut the chains. The drawbridge crashed down and the mob poured through. Terrified guards opened fire, killing dozens and wounding hundreds. At the battle's peak, French soldiers in red and blue appeared on the horizon...but whose side were they on?

A loud cheer went up as they pointed their cannons at the Bastille and the fort surrendered. The mob trashed the Bastille, opened the dark dungeons, and brought seven prisoners into the light of day. They then stormed City Hall (Hôtel de Ville) and arrested the mayor, who was literally torn apart by the hysterical crowd. His head was stuck on a stick and carried through the city. The Revolution had begun.

Today, the events of July 14 are celebrated every Bastille Day with equally colorful festivities. The Bastille itself was soon dismantled, stone by stone—nothing remains but the open space of place de la Bastille—but the memory became a rallying cry throughout the Revolution: *"Vive le quatorze juillet!"* ("Long live July 14th!").

Room 103: The Celebration (La Fête de la Fédération, 1790)

Imagine the jubilation! To finally be able to shout out things formerly whispered in fear.

The large painting of *La Fête de la Fédération* shows the joy and exuberance of the people as they celebrate the first anniversary

of Bastille Day (July 14, 1790). Liberty! Equality! Fraternity! Members of every social class (even including, it appears, three women) hugged, kissed, and mingled on the Champ de Mars, where the Eiffel Tower stands today. The crowd built an artificial mound for heroes of the Revolution to ascend while a choir sang. Women dressed to symbolize Truth, Freedom, Justice, and other capital-letter virtues were worshipped in a new kind of secular religion. Public demonstrations like these must have infuriated the king, queen, bishops, and nobles, who were now quarantined in their palaces, fuming impotently.

The **Declaration** ("Tables") *of the Rights of Man and the Citizen* (see two different versions) made freedom the law. The preamble makes it clear that "*Le Peuple Français*" (the French people)—not the king—were the ultimate authority. "Men are born free and equal," it states, possessing "freedom of the individual, freedom of conscience, freedom of speech."

Room 104: Louis XVI Quietly Responds (De la Monarchie à la République, 1789–1792)

Louis XVI (see the bust)—studious, shy, aloof, and easily dominated—was stunned by the ferocious summer of 1789. The Bastille's violence spread to the countryside, where uppity peasants tenderized their masters with pitchforks. The Assembly was changing France with lightning speed: abolishing Church privileges, nationalizing nobles' land, and declaring the king irrelevant. Louis accepted his role as a rubber-stamp monarch, hoping the furor would pass and trying to appear idealistic and optimistic.

But looming on the horizon was...***Le docteur Joseph-Ignace Guillotin*** (see portrait, opposite the window). The progressive Assembly abolished brutal, medieval-style torture and executions. In their place, Dr. Guillotin proposed a kinder, gentler execution device that would make France a model of compassion. The guillotine—also known as "the national razor" or simply "The Machine"—could instantly make someone "a head shorter at the top." (In 1977, it claimed its last victim; capital punishment is now abolished in France.)

Room 105: Royalty Loses Its Head (La Famille Royale, 1793)

Louis' wife, **Queen Marie-Antoinette** (several portraits), became the focus of the citizens' disgust. Reports flew that she spent extravagantly and plunged France into debt. More decisive than her husband, she steered him toward repressive measures meant to snuff out the Revolution. Worst of all, she was foreign-born, known simply as "The Austrian," and soon Austria was trying to preserve the monarchy by making war on the French. A rumor spread—one that had been common among the poor in France for over a decade—that when Marie was informed that the Parisians had no bread to eat, she had sneered, "Let them eat cake!" ("Cake" was the term for the burnt crusts peeled off the oven and generally fed only to the cattle.) Historians today find no evidence Marie ever said it.

Enraged and hungry, 6,000 Parisian women (backed by armed

men) marched through the rain to Versailles to demand lower bread prices. On the night of October 5, 1789, a small band infiltrated the palace, burst into the Queen's room, killed her bodyguards, and chased her down the hall. The royal family was kidnapped and taken to Paris, where—though still monarchs—they were under house arrest in the Tuileries Palace (which once stood where the Louvre today meets the Tuileries Garden).

Three years later, the royal family became actual prisoners (see the reconstructed and rather cushy **Prison du Temple** in Room 106) after trying to escape to Austria to begin a counterrevolution. One of their servants pretended to be a German baroness, while Louis dressed up as her servant (the irony must have been killing him). When a citizen recognized Louis from his portrait on a franc note, the family was captured, thrown into prison, and soon put on trial as traitors to France. The National Convention (the Assembly's successor) declared the monarchy abolished.

The royal family—Louis, Marie-Antoinette, and their eight-year-old son—was tearfully split up (see the painting *Les adieux de Louis XVI à sa famille* in Room 105), and Marie-Antoinette was imprisoned in the Conciergerie.

On January 21, 1793 (see **execution painting**), King Louis XVI (excuse me, that's "Citizen Capet") was led to place de la Concorde and laid face down on a slab, and then—*shoop!*—a thousand years of monarchy that dated back before Charlemagne was decapitated. On October 16, 1793 (see **painting**), Marie-Antoinette also met her fate on place de la Concorde. Genteel to the end, she apologized to the

executioner for stepping on his foot. The blade fell, the blood gushed, and her head was shown to the crowd on a stick—an exclamation point for the new rallying cry: *Vive la nation!*

Little **Louis XVII** (portrait in corner) died in prison at age 10. Rumors spread that the boy-king had escaped, fueled by Elvis-type sightings and impersonators. But recent DNA evidence confirms that the *dauphin* (heir to the throne) did indeed die in prison in 1795.

Room 108: The Reign of Terror
(La Convention—La Terreur, 1793–1794)

Here are **portraits** of key players in the Revolutionary spectacle. Some were moderate reformers, some radical priest-killers. With Europe ganging up on the Revolution, they all lived in fear that any backward step could tip the delicate balance of power back to the *ancien* *régime.* Enemies of the Revolution were everywhere—even in their own ranks.

By the summer of 1793, the left-of-center Jacobin party took control of France's fledgling democracy. Pug-faced but silver-tongued **Georges Danton** (see portrait of this Newt Gingrich look-alike) drove the Revolution with his personal charisma and bold speeches: "To conquer the enemies of the fatherland, we need daring, more daring, daring now, always daring." He led the Committee of Public Safety to root out and execute those enemies, even moderates opposed to the Jacobins.

More radical still, **Jean-Paul Marat** (the "Friend of the People," portrait next to Danton) dressed and burped like a man of the street, but he wrote eloquently against all forms of authority. Wildly popular with the commoners, he was seen by others as a loose cannon. A beautiful 25-year-old noblewoman named **Charlotte Corday** decided it was her mission in life to save France by silencing him. On July 11, 1793, she entered his home under the pretext of giving him names of counterrevolutionaries. Marat, seated in a bathtub to nurse a skin condition, wrote down the names and said, "Good. I'll have them all guillotined." Corday stood up, whipped a knife out from under her dress, and stabbed him through the heart. Corday was guillotined, and Marat was hailed as a martyr to the cause.

Marat's death was further "proof" that counterrevolutionaries were everywhere. For the next year (summer of 1793 to summer of 1794, see **paintings of guillotine scenes**), the Jacobin government arrested, briefly tried, and then guillotined everyone suspected of being "enemies of the Revolution": nobles, priests, the rich, and many true Revolutionaries who simply belonged to the wrong political party. More than 2,500 Parisians were beheaded, 18,000 were executed by

other means, and tens of thousands died in similar violence throughout the country. The violence begun at the **Bastille** in July of 1789 would climax in July of 1794.

Master of the Reign of Terror was **Maximilien de Robespierre** (the portrait next to Danton's), a 35-year-old lawyer who promoted the Revolution with a religious fervor. By July of 1794, the guillotine was slicing 30 necks a day. In Paris' main squares, grim executions alternated with politically correct public spectacles that honored "Liberty," "Truth," and the heroes of France. As the death toll rose, so did public cynicism. Finally, Robespierre even sentenced to death his old friend Danton, who had spoken out against the bloodshed. As Danton knelt under the blade, he joked, "My turn." The people had had enough.

Room 109: Terror Ends (Thermidor—Le Directoire, July 1794)

Engravings show the chaos—riots, assassinations, food shortages, inflation—that fueled Robespierre's meteoric fall from power. Robespierre's own self-righteousness made him an easy target. On July 27, 1794, as Robespierre prepared to name the daily list of victims, his fellow committee members started yelling "Tyrant!" and shouted him down. Stunned by the sudden fall from grace, Robespierre unsuccessfully attempted suicide by shooting himself in the mouth.

The next day, he walked the walk he'd ordered thousands to take. Hands tied behind his back, he was carried through the streets on a two-wheeled cart, while citizens jeered and spat on him. At the guillotine, the broken-down demagogue had no last words, thanks to his wounded jaw. When the executioner yanked off the bandage, Robespierre let out a horrible cry, the blade fell, and the Reign of Terror came to an end.

From 1795–1799, France caught its breath, ruled by the Directory, a government so intentionally weak and decentralized (two houses of parliament, five executives, and no funding) that it could never create another Robespierre.

Room 110: France vs. Europe (La Guerre)

The blade that dropped on Louis XVI rattled royal teacups throughout Europe. Even as early as 1792, France had to defend its young democracy against Austria and Prussia. France's new army was composed of ordinary citizens from a universal draft and led by daring young citizen-officers, who sang a stirring, bloodthirsty new song, "La Marseillaise." Surprisingly, they quickly defeated the apathetic mercenaries they faced. France vowed to liberate all Europe from tyranny. Europe feared that, by "exporting Revolution," France would export democracy...plus senseless violence and chaos.

A young Corsican named **Napoleon Bonaparte** (see the bust) rose quickly through the ranks and proved himself by fighting royalists in Italy, Egypt, and on the streets of Paris. In 1799, the 29-year-old general returned to Paris as a conquering hero. Backed by an adoring public, he dissolved the Directory, established order, and gave himself the Roman-style title of "first consul."

French National Anthem: "La Marseillaise"

The genteel French have a gory past.

Allons enfants de la Patrie,	Let's go, children of the motherland,
Le jour de gloire est arrivé.	The day of glory has arrived.
Contre nous de la tyrannie	The blood-covered flag of tyranny
L'étendard sanglant est levé.	Is raised against us.
L'étendard sanglant est levé.	Is raised against us.
Entendez-vous dans les campagnes	Do you hear these ferocious soldiers
Mugir ces féroces soldats?	Howling in the countryside?
Qui viennent jusque dans nos bras	They're coming nearly into our grasp
Egorger vos fils et vos compagnes.	To slit the throats of your sons and your women.
Aux armes, citoyens,	Grab your weapons, citizens,
Formez vos bataillons,	Form your battalions,
Marchons, marchons,	We march, we march,
Qu'un sang impur	So that their impure blood
Abreuve nos sillons.	Will fill our trenches.

Room 111: The Revolution vs. Religion (Vandalisme et Conservation)

Three-fourths of France's churches were destroyed or vandalized during the Revolution, a backlash against the wealthy and politically repressive Catholic Church. In Notre-Dame, Christ was mothballed, and a woman dressed as "Dame Reason" was worshipped on the altar.

Room 113: Souvenirs of Revolution

After the Reign of Terror, *Liberté, Egalité, Fraternité* was just a slogan, remembered fondly on commemorative **plates and knickknacks.** The Revolution was history.

• *The visit continues down four flights of stairs—or down the elevator—on the ground floor.*

Room 115: Napoleon Conquers Europe (Le Premier Empire, 1799–1815)

Here's **Napoleon I** at the peak of power, master of Western Europe (see **portrait, breastplate, pistols,** and **death mask** in glass case). Dressed in his general's uniform, he's checking the maps to see who's left to conquer. Behind him is a throne with his imperial seal. This Corsican-born commoner (1769–1821, ruled as emperor 1804–1815), educated in Paris' military schools, became a young Revolutionary and a daring general, rising to prominence as a champion of democracy. Once in power, he preached revolution, but in fact became a dictator and crowned himself emperor (1804).

During the Empire, all things classical became popular. Wealthy socialites such as **Juliette Récamier** (see painting) donned robes and lounged on couches, while Paris was rebuilt with Neoclassical monuments, such as the Arc de Triomphe, to make it the "New Rome."

In 1812, Napoleon foolishly invaded Russia, thus starting a downward spiral that ended in defeat by allied Europe at the Battle of Waterloo in Belgium (1815). Napoleon was exiled. He died in 1821 on the island of St. Helena, off the coast of Africa.

Room 118: The Monarchy Restored (La Restauration, 1815–1830)

After almost 25 years in exile, royalty returned. **Louis XVIII** (see the crowd scene of *Entrée du Louis XVIII à Paris, le 3 mai 1814*) was the younger brother of headless Louis XVI. He returned to Paris with the backing of Europe's royalty and reclaimed the crown as a constitutional monarch.

The next king, **Charles X** (youngest brother of Louis XVI), dressed in glorious coronation robes, revived the fashion and oppression of the *ancien régime* as he plotted to dissolve the people's Assembly. But the French people were not about to turn back the clock.

Room 119: Revolution of 1830 (Juillet 1830)

Parisians again blocked off the narrow streets with barricades to fight the king's red-coated soldiers (see various **street battle paintings**). After "Three Glorious Days" of fighting, order was restored by Louis-Philippe (see **model of Hôtel de Ville**), an unassuming nobleman who appeared on the balcony of the Hôtel de Ville and was cheered by royalists, the middle class, and peasants alike. They made him king.

Room 120: Constitutional Monarchy (La Monarchie de Juillet, 1830–1848)

King Louis-Philippe (1773–1850, r. 1830–1848, see black bust with epaulettes)—a former lieutenant turned banker, with a few drops of royal blood—was a true constitutional monarch, harmlessly presiding over an era of middle-class progress fueled by the Industrial Revolution. Still, liberal reforms came too slowly. New factories brought division between wealthy employers and poor workers, and only 200,000 out of 30 million French citizens (1/150) could vote.

Room 121: Revolution of 1848 (La Deuxième République)

In February of 1848—a time of Europe-wide depression and socialist strikes—Parisians took to the streets again **(battle scenes)**. They battled at the Bastille, Palais-Royal, Panthéon, and place de la Concorde, and they toppled the king. After five decades of dictators (including Napoleon), retread Bourbons (the Restoration), and self-proclaimed monarchs (Louis-Philippe), France was back in the hands of the people—the Second Republic.

Room 122: Romanticism (Le Romantisme)

Freedom of expression, the uniqueness of each person, the glories of the human spirit and the natural world—these values from the 1789 Revolution were extolled by artists of the 1800s known as Romantics.

You'll see **caricature busts** of many famous Frenchmen and visitors to Paris, the center of European culture. There's Victor Hugo (author of *Les Misérables* and *The Hunchback of Notre-Dame*), Frédéric Chopin (Polish pianist who charmed Parisian society), Giuseppe Verdi (composer of stirring operas, such as *Aida*), and Gioacchino Rossini (*Lone Ranger* theme).

There are also **paintings** of the glamorous pianist Franz Liszt and his mistress, Marie d'Agoult—the ultimate Romantic. She left her husband and children to follow the dynamic Liszt on a journey of self-discovery in Italy and Switzerland—"the years of pilgrimage."

• *Journey upstairs and to the left toward* Paris: Du Second Empire à nos jours—*From the Second Empire to Today.*

Room 128: Napoleon III and the Second Empire (Le Deuxième Empire, 1852–1870)

Louis-Napoleon Bonaparte (1808–1873, ruled as emperor 1852–1871; in the big painting, with red pants and sash, waxed moustache, and goatee) was the nephew of the famous Emperor Napoleon I. He used his well-known name to get elected president by a landslide in 1848, and then combined democracy with monarchy to be voted "Emperor Napoleon III." He suppressed opposition while promoting liberal reforms as well as economic and colonial expansion.

Here he hands an order to **Baron Georges Haussmann** (mutton-chop sideburns) to modernize Paris. Haussmann cut the wide, straight boulevards of today to move goods, open up the crowded city...and prevent barricades in future revolutions. Parks, railroad stations, and the Opéra Garnier made Paris the model for world capitals. (Room 129 shows building projects.)

The **boat-like cradle** (Room 128) is a copy of the famous cradle of Napoleon II (1811–1832, known to history as the King of Rome), the only son of Napoleon I, who died at 21 of tuberculosis before ever ruling anything.

Napoleon III pursued popular wars (the **model** in Room 129 celebrates Crimean War vets, 1855) and unpopular ones (backing Austrian Emperor Maximilian in Mexico). In the summer of 1870, he personally led a jubilant French Army to crush upstart Prussia—"On to Berlin!" Uh-oh.

Room 130: The Franco-Prussian War (Le Siège de Paris, 1870–1871)

Within weeks, the overconfident French were surrounded, Napoleon III himself was captured, and he surrendered. Paris was stunned. (See the big **painting of a crowd** hearing the news on the legislature steps.) The Germans quickly put a stranglehold on Paris, and a long, especially cold winter settled in.

Some would not give up. Without an emperor, they proclaimed yet another democratic republic (France's third in a century), and sent minister Léon Gambetta in a newfangled balloon **(painting)** over the Germans' heads to rally the countryside to come save Paris. The Parisians themselves held out bravely (**painting of Tuileries** as army camp), but German efficiency and modern technology simply overwhelmed the French.

Room 131: The Paris Commune (La Commune, Spring 1871)

The Republic finally agreed to a humiliating surrender. Paris' liberals—enraged at the capitulation after such a brave winter and fearing a return of monarchy—rejected the surrender and proclaimed their own government, the Paris Commune. **Portraits** honor the proud idealists, who barricaded themselves inside Paris' neighborhoods, refusing to bow to the German emperor.

Then, in one "bloody week" in May **(battle scenes)**, French troops backing the Republic stormed through Paris, leaving 15,000 dead, 5,000 jailed, and 8,000 deported. The Commune was snuffed out, but the memory was treasured by generations of liberals in popular **souvenirs:** a jar of bread from the hungry winter, a carrier pigeon's feather, a box reading *"Vive la Commune!"*

The church of Sacré-Cœur (see **painting** way up high) was built after the war as a form of national penance for the sins of liberalism.

Rooms 132–142: The Beautiful Age (La Belle Epoque, 1871–1914)

The Third Republic restored peace to a prosperous middle-class society. The **Eiffel Tower** (Room 132) marked the 1889 centennial of the Revolution, and the **Statue of Liberty** (Room 133) honored America's revolution.

Paris was a capital of world culture in the era known as the belle époque (beautiful age). It was a city of **Impressionist painters** (Room 135), and of writers and actors, including the actress **Sarah Bernhardt** (Room 136), called the world's first international star ("a force of nature, a fiery soul, a marvelous intelligence, a magnificent creature of the highest order," raved one of the smitten).

And it was the city of Art Nouveau (see two delightful **Art Nouveau** rooms, 141–142).

Room 145: World War I (1914–1918)

Three costly wars with Germany—the Franco-Prussian War, World War I, and World War II—drained France's resources. Although **Marshal Foch** (big painting above the elevator) is hailed as the man who coordinated the Allied armies to defeat Germany in World War I, France was hardly a winner. More than 1.5 million Frenchmen died, a generation was lost, and the country would be a pushover when Hitler invaded in 1940. France's long history as a global superpower was over.

Room 147: Remembrance of Things Past (La Vie Littéraire du XXe Siècle)

The last room is filled with portraits of Paris' 20th-century literary greats. By producing such figures as the writer **Marcel Proust** (see his reconstructed bedroom) and the dreamy writer/filmmaker **Jean Cocteau,** France has remained a cultural superpower.

PICASSO MUSEUM TOUR

Musée Picasso

The 20th century's most famous and—okay, I'll say it—greatest artist was the master of many styles (Cubism, Surrealism, Expressionism, etc.) and of many media (painting, sculpture, prints, ceramics, and assemblages). Still, he could make anything he touched look unmistakably like "a Picasso."

The Picasso Museum walks you through the evolution of the artist's long life and many styles. The women he loved and the global events he lived through appear in his canvases, filtered through his own emotional response. You don't have to admire Picasso's lifestyle or like his modern painting style. But a visit here might make you appreciate the sheer vitality and creativity of this hardworking and unique man.

ORIENTATION

Cost: €6.50, covered by Museum Pass, additional fees for temporary exhibits, free on first Sun of month and for kids under 18 with ID.

Hours: Closing in Sept 2009 for restoration; until then April–Sept Wed–Mon 9:30–18:00, Oct–March Wed–Mon 9:30–17:30, last entry 45 min before closing, closed Tue.

Getting There: 5 rue de Thorigny, Mo: St. Paul or Chemin Vert (see Marais map on page 264).

Information: The well-done English guidebook sold at the museum helps Picasso-philes appreciate the context of his art, but most will be satisfied with reading this tour and the English explanations posted throughout the museum. Tel. 01 42 71 25 21, www. musee-picasso.fr. Garden café open in summer.

Length of This Tour: Allow one hour.

Photography: Permitted.

Overview

The museum presents Picasso's life and art in roughly chronological order. The first part of this chapter is designed to provide a room-by-room tour, but be warned that the collection changes regularly. Much of this chapter is thematic, touching on motifs found in Picasso's work. This explanation may be most useful if you read it as background material before your visit. Once there, make use of the museum's excellent information in English.

• *Start upstairs on the first floor.*

THE TOUR BEGINS

Pablo Picasso (1881–1973)

Born in Spain, Picasso was the son of an art teacher. As a teenager he quickly advanced beyond his teachers. He mastered camera-eye realism but also showed an empathy for the people he painted that was insightful beyond his years. (Unfortunately, the museum has very few early works. Many doubters of Picasso's genius warm to him somewhat after seeing his excellent draftsmanship and facility with oils from his youth.) As a teenager in Barcelona, he fell in with a bohemian crowd that mixed wine, women, and art.

In 1900, Picasso set out to make his mark in Paris, the undisputed world capital of culture. He rejected the surname his father had given him (Ruíz) and chose his mother's instead, making it his distinctive one-word brand: Picasso.

Room 1: Early Years and Blue Period (1895–1903)

The brash Spaniard quickly became a poor, homesick foreigner, absorbing the styles of many painters (especially Henri de Toulouse-Lautrec) while searching for his own artist's voice. He found companionship among fellow freaks and outcasts on Butte Montmartre, painting jesters, circus performers, and garish cabarets. When his best friend committed suicide (*Death of Casagemas*, 1901), Picasso plunged into a "Blue Period," painting emaciated beggars, hard-eyed pimps, and himself, bundled up against the cold, with eyes all cried out (*Autoportrait*, 1901; see photo on page 301).

Room 2: Rose Period (1904–1907)

In 1904, Picasso moved into his Bateau-Lavoir home/studio on Montmartre (see Montmartre Walk, page 323), got a steady girlfriend, and suddenly saw the world through rose-colored glasses (the Rose Period, though the museum has very few works from this phase).

Rooms 2 and 3: Primitive Masks and Cubist Experiments (1907–1909)

Only 25 years old, Picasso reinvented painting. Fascinated by the primitive power of African and Iberian tribal masks, he sketched human faces with simple outlines and almond eyes (*Autoportrait*, 1906). Intrigued by the body of his girlfriend, Fernande Olivier, he sketched it from every angle (see various nude studies), then experimented with showing several different views on the same canvas.

A hundred paintings and nine months later, Picasso gave birth to a monstrous canvas of five nude, fragmented prostitutes with mask-

like faces—*Les Demoiselles d'Avignon* (1907). The painting hangs in New York's Museum of Modern Art, but you'll observe similar techniques in Room 3. His friends were speechless over the bold new style, his enemies reviled it, and almost overnight, Picasso was famous.

Picasso went to the Louvre for a special exhibit on Cézanne, then returned to the Bateau-Lavoir to expand on Cézanne's chunky style and geometric simplicity—oval-shaped heads, circular breasts, and diamond thighs. Picasso rejected traditional 3-D. Instead of painting, say, a distant hillside in dimmer tones than the trees in the bright foreground, Picasso did it all bright, making the foreground blend into the background, and turning a scene into an abstract design. Modern art was being born.

PICASSO MUSEUM

Room 4: Cubism (1910–1917)

With his next-door neighbor, Georges Braque, Picasso invented Cubism, a fragmented, "cube"-shaped style. He'd fracture a musician (*Man with a Mandolin*, 1911) into a barely recognizable jumble of facets, and facets within facets. Even empty space is composed of these "cubes," all of them the same basic color, that weave together the background and foreground. Picasso sketches reality from every angle, then pastes it all together, a composite of different views. The monochrome color (mostly gray or brown) is less important than the experiments with putting the 3-D world on a 2-D canvas in a modern way. (For more on Cubism, see the Pompidou Center Tour, page 273.)

In a few short years, Picasso had turned painting in the direction it would go for the next 50 years.

Room 4b: Synthetic Cubism

Analytic Cubism (1907–1913) broke the world down into small facets, to "analyze" the subject from every angle. Now it was time to "synthesize" it back together with the real world.

These "constructions" are still-life paintings (a 2-D illusion) augmented with glued-on, real-life materials—wood, paper, rope, or chair caning (the real 3-D world). The contrast between real objects and painted objects makes it clear that while traditional painting is a mere illusion, art can be more substantial.

Rooms 5 and 6: Family Life, Classicism (1920s)

Personally, Picasso's life had fragmented into a series of relationships with women. He finally met (1917) and married a graceful Russian dancer with the Ballet Russes, Olga Kokhlova (*Portrait of Olga in an Armchair*, 1917).

Soon he was a financially secure husband and father (see the portrait of his three-year-old son, *Paul en Harlequin*, 1924). With the

disastrous Great War over, Picasso took his family for summer vacations on the Riviera. There, he painted peaceful scenes of women and children at the beach.

A trip to Rome inspired him to emulate the bulky mass of ancient statues, transforming them into plump but graceful women, with Olga's round features. Picasso could create the illusion of a face or body bulging out from the canvas, like a cameo or classical

bas-relief. Watching kids drawing in the sand with a stick, he tried drawing a figure without lifting the brush from the canvas.

Picasso had an encyclopedic knowledge of art history and a caricaturist's ability to easily "quote" another artist's style, which he would adapt to his own uses. Clever students of art can spot some of Picasso's sources, from Pierre-Auguste Renoir's plump women to Paul Cézanne's chunky surfaces to the simple outlines and bright colors of Henri Matisse.

• *From here, the collection is less chronological and more thematic. Use the following material on Picasso as background for what you'll see. There are often temporary exhibits in Room 7 and in rooms upstairs. Otherwise, the permanent collection continues downstairs.*

Multi-Media

It's so common in the 21st century for artists to explore new materials

that we forget how revolutionary it was when Picasso pioneered it. Ceramics, papier-mâché, statuettes, metal-working, mobiles—Picasso tried his hand in all of these.

The minute Picasso discovered ceramics (1947), the passion consumed him. Working in a small, family-owned ceramics factory in the south of France, he shaped wet clay, painted it, and fired

Marie-Thérèse Walter

In 1927, a middle-aged Picasso stopped a 17-year-old girl out-side the Galeries Lafayette department store (by the Opéra

Garnier) and said, "Mademoiselle, you have an interesting face. Can I paint it? I am Picasso." She said, "Who?"

The two had little in common, but the unsophisticated Marie-Thérèse Walter and the short, balding artist developed a strange attraction for each other. Soon, Marie-Thérèse moved into the house next door to Picasso and his wife, and they began an awkward three-wheeled relation-ship. Worldly Olga was jealous, young Marie-Thérèse was insecure and clingy, and Picasso the workaholic artist faith-fully chronicled the erotic/neurotic experience in canvases of twisted, screaming nudes.

Young and athletic, Marie-Thérèse had a classic profile—big chin and long nose with a straight bridge. Picasso would never tire of portraying her prominent features, often seen in paintings and sculpture simply titled *Head of a Woman*. In 1935, Marie-Thérèse gave birth to their daughter, Maya.

up a dozen or more pieces a day—2,000 in a single year. He created plates with faces, bird-shaped vases, woman shaped bottles, bull-shaped statues, and colorful tiles. Working in this timeless medium, he gives a Modernist's take on classic motifs: red-and-black Greek vases, fauns, primitive goddesses, Roman amphorae, and so on.

One of Picasso's most famous creations was a bicycle seat with handlebar horns that becomes the *Head of a Bull* (1942). This is quint-essential Picasso—a timeless motif (the minotaur) made of 20th-century materials and done with a twinkle in his eye.

Picasso and Spain

Though he lived in France, Picasso remained a Spaniard at heart, incorporating Spanish motifs into his work.

Unrepentantly macho, he loved bullfights, seeing them as a metaphor for the timeless human interaction between the genders. Me bull, you horse, I gore you.

The Minotaur (a bull-headed

Picasso's Residences

The Spaniard lived almost all of his adult life in France, mostly in Paris and the South of France. Over the years, Picasso had 13 different studios in Paris, mainly in the Montmartre and Montparnasse neighborhoods. Picasso liked both France and Spain, but after 1936, he vowed never again to set foot in Fascist-controlled Spain, and he never did.

man) symbolized man's warring halves: half rational human (Freud's superego) and half raging beast (the id). Picasso could be both tender and violent with women, thus playing out both sides of this love/war duality.

Spanish imagery—bulls, screaming horses, a Madonna—appears in Picasso's most famous work, *Guernica* (1937, on display in Madrid). The monumental canvas of a bombed village summed up the pain of Spain's brutal Civil War (1936–1939) and foreshadowed the onslaught of World War II.

Sculpture Garden

Picture Picasso with goggles and a blowtorch, creating 3-D Cubist statues out of scrap metal. A master of many media, he turned 20th-century industrial junk into art. A true scavenger, Picasso took what he found, played with it, and transformed it into something interesting. Among the statues, find the distinctive features of Marie-Thérèse.

Picasso's Women

Women were Picasso's main subject. As an artist, Picasso used women both as models and as muses. Having sex with his model allowed him to paint not just the woman's physical features, but also the emotional associations of their relationship. At least, that's what he told his wife.

In today's psychobabble, Picasso was an egotistical and abusive male, a sex addict fueled by his own insecurities and inability to connect intimately with women.

In the lingo of Picasso's crowd—steeped in the psychoanalysis of Freud and Jung—relations with women allowed him to express primal urges, recover repressed memories, confront his relationship with his mother, discover hidden truths, connect with his anima (female side), and re-create the archetypal experiences lived since the beginning of time.

Borrowing from the Surrealist style, Picasso let the id speak in his paintings. His women—a jumble of clashing colors and twisted limbs—

open their toothy mouths and scream their frustration (*Large Nude on a Red Armchair*, 1929). The artist and his model often became hopelessly entangled. Picasso needed a big ego to keep his big id out of trouble.

After about 1910, Picasso almost never painted (only sketched) from a posed model. His "portraits" of women were often composites of several different women from his large catalog of memories, filtered through emotional associations.

In Rooms 13–18, you'll likely see somewhat-recognizable portraits of some of Picasso's models/mistresses/muses:

María Picasso y López—his mom—wrote him a letter almost every day until her death. In childhood, Picasso was raised as a lone boy among the many women of his extended family.

Dark-haired **Fernande Olivier,** an artist's model who'd lived a wild life, was Picasso's first real love. They lived together (1904–1909) in Montmartre (with a dog and a 10-year-old street urchin they'd taken in) when Picasso was inventing Cubism, and her features are seen in *Les Demoiselles d'Avignon*. Fernande claimed that Picasso locked her in or hid her shoes so she couldn't go out while he was gone.

In May 1913, Fernande left him for good, his father died, and **Eva Gouel** moved in. Picasso launched into Synthetic Cubism. Eva died two years later of tuberculosis.

Elegant **Olga Kokhlova** (1896–1955, see image at right) gave Picasso a son (Pablo Jr.) and 10 years of stability. They lived high class, hobnobbing with the international set surrounding the Ballet Russes.

Blonde, athletic **Marie-Thérèse Walter** (1910–1977) knew nothing of art and never mixed with Picasso's sophisticated crowd. But even as she put on weight, Picasso found her figure worthy to paint. They had a daughter together named Maya (b. 1935). Also see the sidebar on page 305.

Sparkly-eyed **Dora Maar** (1909–1998) was the anti-Marie-Thérèse—an artsy, sophisticated woman who could converse with Picasso about his art. He met the photographer over coffee at Les Deux Magots in 1936. She photographed him in his studio working on *Guernica*, and they became romantically involved.

Picasso still kept ties with Marie-Thérèse while also working out a complicated divorce from Olga.

In portraits, dark-haired Dora is slender, with long red nails and sparkling, intelligent eyes. She's often pictured crying. Go figure. She's attached to a physically abusive married man who refuses to leave his other mistress.

Françoise Gilot (b. 1921), a painter herself, is often depicted with a flower, perhaps symbolizing the new life (and two children) she gave to an aging Picasso. She stubbornly forced Picasso to sever ties with Dora Maar before she'd settle in. When he dumped her for his next conquest (1954), she went on to write a scathing tell-all book. Their children, Claude and Paloma, grew up amid lawsuits over whether they could use their father's famous last name.

Jacqueline Roque (1927–1986) married the god of painting when he was 80 and she was 33. She outlived him, but later took her own life.

So, I guess Picasso's ideal model would be a composite—a brainy but tubercular dancer with a curvaceous figure, as well as a youthful flower-child who could pose like a slut but remind him of his mother.

World War II (1940–1945)

In 1940, Nazi tanks rolled into Paris. Picasso decided to stay for the duration and live under gray skies and gray uniforms. Not only did he suffer from wartime shortages, condescending Nazis, and the grief of having comrades killed or deported, he had girl trouble. "The worst time of my life," he said. His beloved mother had died, and he endured the endless, bitter divorce from Olga, all the while juggling his two longtime, feuding mistresses—as well as the occasional fling.

Still, he continued working, and many canvases from this period are gray and gloomy.

The South of France (1948–1954)

Sun! Color! Water! Spacious skies! Freedom!

At war's end, he left Paris and all that emotional baggage behind, finding fun in the sun in the South of France. Sixty-five-year-old Pablo Picasso was reborn, enjoying worldwide fame and the love of a beautiful 23-year-old painter named Françoise Gilot. She soon offered him a fresh start at fatherhood, giving birth to son Claude and daughter Paloma.

Picasso spent mornings swimming in the Mediterranean, days painting, evenings partying with friends, and late nights painting again, like a madman. Dressed in rolled-up white pants and a striped sailor's shirt, bursting with pent-up creativity, he often cranked out more than a painting a day. Ever-restless Picasso had finally found his Garden of Eden and rediscovered his joie de vivre.

He palled around with Henri Matisse, his rival for the title of

Century's Greatest Painter. Occasionally they traded masterpieces, letting the other pick out his favorite for his own collection.

Picasso's Riviera works set the tone for the rest of his life—sunny, light-hearted, childlike, experimenting in new media, and using motifs of the sea, of Greek mythology (fauns, centaurs), and animals (birds, goats, and pregnant baboons). His childlike doves became an international symbol of peace. These joyous themes announce Picasso's newfound freedom in a newly liberated France.

The Last Years (1961–1973)

He was fertile to the end, still painting with bright thick colors at age 91. With no living peers in the world of art, the great Picasso dialogued with dead masters, reworking paintings by Edouard Manet, Diego de Velázquez, and others. Oh yes, also in this period he met mistress number...um, whatever: 27-year-old Jacqueline Roque, whom he later married.

Throughout his long life, Picasso was intrigued by portraying people—always people, ignoring the background—conveying their features with a single curved line and their moods with colors. These last works have the humor and playfulness of someone much younger. As it has been said of Picasso, "When he was a child, he painted like a man. When he was old, he painted like a child."

PICASSO MUSEUM

PÈRE LACHAISE CEMETERY TOUR

Cimetière du Père Lachaise

Enclosed by a massive wall and lined with 5,000 trees, the peaceful, car-free lanes and dirt paths of Père Lachaise cemetery encourage parklike meandering. Named for Father *(Père)* La Chaise, whose job was listening to Louis XIV's sins, the cemetery is relatively new, having opened in 1804 to accommodate Paris' expansion. Today, this city of the dead (pop. 70,000) still accepts new residents, but real estate prices are very high.

The 100-acre cemetery is big and confusing, with thousands of graves and tombs crammed every which way, and only a few pedestrian pathways to navigate by. The maps available from any of the nearby florists help guide your way. But better still, take my tour and save lots of time as you play grave-hunt with the cemetery's other visitors. This walk takes you on a one-way tour between two convenient Métro/bus stops (Gambetta and Père Lachaise), connecting a handful of graves from some of this necropolis' best-known residents.

ORIENTATION

Cost: Free.

Hours: Mon–Sat 8:00–18:00, Sun 9:00–18:00. If it gets dark before 18:00, the cemetery closes at dusk.

Getting There: Catch bus #69 to the end of the line (see Bus #69 Sightseeing Tour chapter) or take the Métro to the Gambetta stop. If you're arriving on bus #69, it will stop at place Gambetta on avenue du Père Lachaise, two blocks from the cemetery. If you're taking the Métro, exit at Gambetta Métro (not the Père Lachaise stop, which is less convenient for this tour), take *sortie* #3 (Père Lachaise exit), turn left, and follow signs to Père Lachaise. Either way, it's two short blocks up avenue du Père Lachaise, which ends at the cemetery. Along the route, you'll pass flower shops selling €2 maps (not necessary for this tour, but helpful for finding additional graves) and a WC just inside the Porte Gambetta entrance to Père Lachaise.

Information: Tel. 01 55 25 82 10.

Length of this Tour: Allow 90 minutes to do this walk, and another 30 minutes for your own detours. Bring good walking shoes for the rough, cobbled streets.

Cuisine Art: As you approach the cemetery, there are several cafés near Métro stop Gambetta and along avenue du Père Lachaise.

Starring: Oscar Wilde, Edith Piaf, Gertrude Stein, Molière, Jim Morrison, Frédéric Chopin, Héloïse and Abélard, Colette, and Rossini.

Overview

From the Porte Gambetta entrance, we'll walk roughly southwest (mostly downhill) through the cemetery. At the end of the tour,

we'll exit Porte Principale onto boulevard Ménilmontant, near the Père Lachaise Métro entrance and another bus #69 stop. (You can follow the tour heading the other direction, but it's not recommended, since it's confusing—and almost completely uphill.)

Remember to keep referring to the map on page 312 (note that north is not up on the map), and follow street signs posted at intersections. The layout of the cemetery makes an easy-to-follow tour impossible. Be patient, make a few discoveries of your own, and ask passersby for graves you can't locate.

THE TOUR BEGINS

• *Entering the cemetery at the Porte Gambetta entrance, walk straight up avenue des Combattants past World War memorials, cross avenue Transversale No. 3, pass the first building, and look left to the...*

❶ Columbarium/Crematorium

Marked by a dome with a gilded flame and working chimneys on top, the Columbarium sits in a courtyard surrounded by about 1,300 niches, small cubicles for cremated remains, often decorated with real or artificial flowers.

Beneath the courtyard (steps leading underground) are about 12,000 smaller niches, including one for Maria Callas (1923–1977), an American-born opera diva known for her versatility, flair for drama, and affair with Aristotle Onassis (niche #16258, down aisle J).

PÈRE LACHAISE

Père Lachaise Cemetery Tour

PORTE GAMBETTA ENTRANCE
START

100 YARDS
100 METERS

GAMBETTA

RONDEAUX

RUE DE

AVENUE CIRCULAIRE

W.C.

AVENUE TRANSVERSALE

PORTE DE LA REUNION

NO. 3

NO. 2

AVENUE

AVE.

TRANSVER-SALE

AVE. TRANSV. MARRONIERS

NO. 1

AVE. CIRCULAIRE

AVENUE GAMBETTA

CHAPEL

BASSIN MOLIERE

ROND POINT

La Bedoyere

LESSEPS

CHAPELLE

DENON

CASIMIR PERIER

SERRE

CH.

DCH

PORTE DU REPOS

W.C.

PORTE PRINCIPALE
FINISH

BOULEVARD

PORTE DES AMANDIERS ENTRANCE

PHILIPPE AUGUSTE

DE MENILMONTANT

← RUE DE LA ROQUETTE

M METRO STATION
B BUS #69 STOP

PERE LACHAISE

TOUR
1. Columbarium/Crematorium
2. Oscar Wilde
3. Gertrude Stein
4. Mur des Fédérés
5. Edith Piaf
6. Molière
7. Jim Morrison
8. Frédéric Chopin
9. Héloïse & Abélard
10. Colette
11. Gioacchino Rossini
12. Baron Haussmann

OTHER NOTABLE TOMBS
A. Jacques-Louis David
B. Théodore Géricault
C. Eugène Delacroix
D. J. A. D. Ingres
E. Georges Seurat
F. Amadeo Modigliani
G. Marcel Proust
H. Sarah Bernhardt
J. Yves Montand & Simone Signoret

• *Turn around and walk back to the intersection with avenue Transversale No. 3. Turn right, heading southeast on avenue Transversale No. 3. Turn left on avenue Carette and walk half a block to the block-of-stone tomb (on the left) with heavy-winged angels trying to fly.*

❷ Oscar Wilde (1854–1900)

The writer and martyr to homosexuality is mourned by "outcast men"

(as the inscription says) and by wearers of heavy lipstick, who cover the tomb and the angels' emasculated privates with kisses. Despite Wilde's notoriety, an inscription says "He died fortified by the Sacraments of the Church." There's a short résumé scratched (in English) into the back side of the tomb. For more on Wilde and his death in Paris, see page 236.

"Alas, I am dying beyond my means."

—Oscar Wilde

• *Continue along avenue Carette and turn right (southeast) down avenue Circulaire. A block and a half down, you'll reach Gertrude Stein's unadorned, easy-to-miss grave (on the right just before a yellow stone structure).*

❸ Gertrude Stein (1874–1946)

While traveling through Europe, the twentysomething American dropped out of med school and moved to Paris, her home for the rest of her life. She shared an apartment at 27 rue de Fleurus (a couple of blocks west of Luxembourg Garden) with her brother Leo and, later, with her life partner, Alice B. Toklas (who's also buried here, see gravestone's flipside). Every Saturday night, Paris' brightest artistic lights converged *chez vingt-sept* for dinner and intellectual stimulation. Picasso painted her portrait, Hemingway sought her approval, and Virgil Thompson set her words to music.

America discovered "Gerty" in 1933 when her memoirs, the slyly titled *Autobiography of Alice B. Toklas*, hit the bestseller list. After 30 years away, she returned to the United States for a triumphant lecture tour. Her writing is less well-known than her persona, except for the oft-quoted "A rose is a rose is a rose."

Stein's last words: When asked, "What is the answer?" she replied, "What is the question?"

• *Ponder Stein's tomb again and again and again, and continue southeast on avenue Circulaire to where it curves to the right. Emaciated statues remember victims of the concentration camps and Nazi resistance heroes. Pebbles on the tombstones represent Jewish prayers. At the corner of the*

PÈRE LACHAISE

cemetery, veer left off the road a few steps, to the wall marked Aux Morts de la Commune.

❹ Mur des Fédérés

The "Communards' Wall" marks the place where the quixotic Paris Commune came to a violent end.

In 1870, Prussia invaded France, and the country quickly collapsed and surrendered—all except the city of Paris. For six months, through a bitter winter, the Prussians laid siege to the city. Defiant Paris held out, even opposing the French government, which had fled to Versailles and was collaborating with the Germans. Parisians formed an opposition government that was revolutionary and socialist, called the Paris Commune.

The Versailles government sent French soldiers to retake Paris. In May of 1871, they breached the west walls and swept eastward. French soldiers fought French citizens, and tens of thousands died during a bloody week of street fighting (La Semaine Sanglante). The last resisters holed up inside the walls of Père Lachaise and made an Alamo-type last stand before they were finally overcome.

At dawn on May 28, 1871, the 147 Communards were lined up against this wall and shot by French soldiers. They were buried in a mass grave where they fell. With them, the Paris Commune died, and the city entered five years of martial law.

• *Return to the road, continue to the next (unmarked) street, avenue Transversale No. 3, and turn right. A half-block uphill, Edith Piaf's grave is on the right. It's not directly on the street, but one grave in, behind a white tombstone with a small gray cross. Edith Gassion-Piaf rests among many graves. Hers is often adorned with photos, fresh flowers, and love notes.*

❺ Edith Piaf (1915–1963)

A child of the Parisian streets, she was raised in her grandma's bordello and her father's traveling circus troupe. The teenager sang in Paris' streets for spare change, where a nightclub owner discovered her. Waif-like and dressed in black, she sang in a warbling voice under the name "La Môme Piaf" (The Little Sparrow). She became the toast of pre-WWII Paris society.

Her offstage love life was busy and often messy, including a teenage pregnancy (her daughter is buried along with her, in a grave marked *Marcelle Dupont, 1933–1935),* a murdered husband, and a heartbreaking affair with costar Yves Montand.

With her strong but trembling voice, she buoyed French spirits under the German occupation, and her most famous song, "La Vie en Rose" (The Rosy Life) captured the joy of postwar Paris. Her personal life declined into ill health, alcohol, and painkillers, while onstage she sang, *"Non, je ne regrette rien"* ("No, I don't regret anything").

• *From Edith Piaf's grave, continue up along avenue Transversale No. 3, and turn left on avenue Greffulhe. Follow Greffulhe straight (even when it narrows), until it dead-ends at avenue Transversale des Marronières No. 1. Continue ahead 20 paces on a dirt path, where you reach chemin Molière et La Fontaine. Turn right. Molière lies 30 yards down, on the right side of the street, just beyond the highest point of this lane.*

❻ Molière (1622–1675)

In 1804, the great comic playwright was the first to be reburied in Père Lachaise, a publicity stunt that gave instant prestige to the new cemetery.

Born in Paris, Molière was not of noble blood, but as the son of the king's furniture supervisor, he had connections. The 21-year-old Molière joined a troupe of strolling players, who ranked very low on the social scale, touring the provinces. Twelve long years later, they returned to Paris to perform before Louis XIV. Molière, by now an accomplished comic actor, cracked the king up. He was instantly famous—writing, directing, and often starring in his own works. He satirized rich nobles, hypocritical priests, and quack doctors, creating enemies in high places.

On February 17, 1675, an aging Molière went on stage in the title role of his latest comedy, *The Imaginary Invalid*. Though ill, he insisted he had to go on, concerned for all the little people. His role was of a hypochondriac who coughs to get sympathy. The deathly ill Molière effectively faked coughing fits...which soon turned to real convulsions. The unaware crowd roared with laughter while his fellow players fretted in the wings.

In the final scene, Molière's character becomes a doctor himself in a mock swearing-in ceremony. The ultimate trouper, Molière finished his final line—*"Juro"* ("I accept")—and collapsed while coughing blood. The audience laughed hysterically. He died shortly after.

Irony upon irony for the master of satire: Molière—a sick man whose doctors thought he was a hypochondriac—dies playing a well man who is a hypochondriac, succumbing onstage while the audience cheers.

Molière lies next to his friend and fellow writer, La Fontaine (1621–1695), who wrote a popular version of Aesop's Fables.

"We die only once, and for such a long time."

—Molière

• *Continue downhill on chemin Molière (which becomes the paved chemin du Bassin), and turn left on avenue de la Chapelle. It leads to the Rond Point roundabout intersection.*

    Cross Carrefour Rond Point and continue straight (opposite where you entered, on unmarked chemin de la Bédoyère). Just a few steps along, veer to the right onto chemin Lauriston. Keep to the left on chemin de Lesseps, and look (immediately) for the temple on the right with three wreaths. Jim lies just behind, often with a personal security guard. You can't miss the commotion.

❼ Jim Morrison (1943–1971)

An American rock star has perhaps the most visited tomb in the cemetery. An iconic, funky bust of the rocker, which was stolen by fans, was replaced with a more toned-down headstone. Even so, his faithful still gather here at all hours. The headstone's Greek inscription reads: "To the spirit (or demon) within." Graffiti-ing nearby tombs, fans write: "You still Light My Fire" (referring to Jim's biggest hit), "Ring my bell at the Dead Rock Star Hotel," and "Mister Mojo Risin'" (referring to the legend that Jim faked his death and still lives today, age 66).

Jim Morrison—singer for the popular rock band The Doors (named for the "Doors of Perception" they aimed to open)—arrived in Paris in the winter of 1971. He was famous; notorious for his erotic onstage antics; alcoholic; and burned-out. Paris was to be his chance to leave celebrity behind, get healthy, and get serious as a writer.

Living under an assumed name in a nondescript sublet apartment near place Bastille (head west down rue St. Antoine, and turn left to 17 rue Beautrellis), he spent his days as a carefree artist. He scribbled in notebooks at Le Café de Flore and Les Deux Magots (❂ see Left Bank Walk, page 233), watched the sun set from the steps of Sacré-Cœur, visited Baudelaire's house, and jammed with street musicians. He drank a lot, took other drugs, gained weight, and his health declined.

In the wee hours of July 3, he died in his bathtub at age 27, officially of a heart attack, but likely from an overdose. (Any police investigation was thwarted by Morrison's social circle of heroin users, leading to wild rumors surrounding his death.)

Jim's friends approached Père Lachaise Cemetery about burying the famous rock star there, in accordance with his wishes. The director refused to admit him, until they mentioned that Jim was a writer. "A writer?" he said, and found a spot.

> *"This is the end, my only friend, the end."*
>
> —Jim Morrison

• *Return to Rond Point, cross it, and retrace your steps—sorry, but there are no straight lines connecting these dead geniuses. Retrace your steps up avenue de la Chapelle. At the intersection with the small park and chapels, turn left onto avenue Laterale du Sud. Walk down two sets of stairs and turn left onto narrow chemin Denon. "Fred" Chopin's grave—usually with flowers and burning candles—is halfway down on the left.*

❽ Frédéric Chopin (1810–1849)

Fresh-cut flowers and geraniums on the gravestone speak of the emotional staying power of Chopin's music, which still connects souls across the centuries. A muse sorrows atop the tomb and a carved relief of Chopin in profile captures the delicate features of this sensitive artist.

The 21-year-old Polish pianist arrived in Paris, fell in love with the city, and never returned to his homeland (which was occupied by an increasingly oppressive Russia). In Paris, he could finally shake off the "child prodigy" label and performance schedule he'd lived with since age seven. Cursed with stage fright ("I don't like concerts. The crowds scare me, their breath chokes me, I'm paralyzed by their stares..."), and with too light a touch for big venues, Chopin preferred playing at private parties for Paris' elite. They were wowed by his technique, his ability to make a piano sing, and his melodic, soul-stirring compositions. Soon he was recognized as a pianist, composer, and teacher, and even idolized as a brooding genius. He ran in aristocratic circles with fellow artists, such as pianist Franz Liszt, painter Delacroix, novelists Victor Hugo and Balzac, and composer Rossini. (All but Liszt lie in Père Lachaise.)

Chopin composed nearly 200 pieces, almost all for piano, in many different styles—from lively Polish dances, to the Bach-like counterpoint of his *Preludes,* to the moody, romantic *Nocturnes.*

In 1837, the quiet, refined, dreamy-eyed genius met the scandalous, assertive, stormy novelist George Sand (see page 236 in the Left Bank Walk). Sand was swept away by Chopin's music and artistic nature. She pursued him, and sparks flew. Though the romance faded quickly, they continued living together for nearly a decade in an increasingly bitter love-hate relationship. When Chopin developed tuberculosis, Sand nursed him for years (Chopin complained she was killing him). Sand finally left, Chopin was devastated, and he died two years later at age 39. At the funeral, they played perhaps Chopin's most famous piece, the *Funeral March* (it's that 11-note dirge that everyone knows). The grave contains Chopin's body, but his heart lies in Warsaw, embedded in a church column.

> *"The earth is suffocating. Swear to make them cut me open, so that I won't be buried alive."*
>
> —Chopin, on his deathbed

• *Continue walking down chemin Denon, as it curves down and to the right. Stay left at the* chemin du Coq *sign and walk down to avenue Casimir Perier. Turn right and walk downhill 30 yards, looking to the left, over the tops of the graves, for a tall monument that looks like a church with a cross perched on top. Under this stone canopy lie...*

❾ Héloïse (c. 1101–1164) and Abélard (1079–1142)

Born nearly a millennium ago, these are the oldest residents in Père Lachaise, and their story is timeless.

In an age of faith and Church domination of all aspects of life, the independent scholar Peter Abélard dared to say, "By questioning, we learn truth." Brash, combative, and charismatic, Abélard shocked and titillated Paris with his secular knowledge and reasoned critique of Church doctrine. He set up a school on the Left Bank (near today's Sorbonne) that would become the University of Paris. Bright minds from all over Europe converged on Paris, including Héloïse, the brainy niece of the powerful canon of Notre-Dame.

Abélard was hired (c. 1118) to give private instruction to Héloïse. Their intense intellectual intercourse quickly flared into physical passion and a spiritual bond. They fled Paris and married in secret, fearing the damage to Abélard's career. After a year, Héloïse gave birth to a son (named Astrolabe), and the news was out, soon reaching Héloïse's uncle. The canon exploded, sending a volley of thugs to Abélard's bedroom in the middle of the night, where they castrated him.

Disgraced, Abélard retired to a monastery, and Héloïse to a convent, never again to live as man and wife. But for the next two decades, the two remained intimately connected by the postal service, exchanging letters of love, devotion, and intellectual discourse that survive today. (The dog at Abélard's feet symbolizes their fidelity to each other.) Héloïse went on to become an influential abbess, and Abélard bounced back with some of his most critical writings. (He was forced to burn his *Theologia* in 1121 and was on trial for heresy when he died.) Abélard used logic to analyze Church pronouncements—a practice that would flower into the "scholasticism" accepted by the Church a century later.

When they died, the two were buried together in Héloïse's convent and were later laid to rest here in Père Lachaise. The canopy tomb we see today (1817) is made from stones from Héloïse's convent and Abélard's monastery.

> *"Thou, O Lord, brought us together, and when it pleased Thee, Thou hast parted us."*
>
> —From a prayer of Héloïse and Abélard

• *Continue walking downhill along avenue Casimir Perier, until it crosses avenue Principale, the street at the cemetery's main entrance. Cross Principale to find Colette's grave (third grave from corner on right side).*

⓾ Colette (1873–1954)

France's most honored female writer led an unconventional life—thrice married and often linked romantically with other women—and wrote about it in semi-autobiographical novels. Her first fame came from a series of novels about naughty teenage Claudine's misadventures. In her thirties, she went on to a career as a music hall performer, scandalizing Paris by pulling a Janet Jackson onstage. Her late novel, *Gigi* (1945)—about a teenage girl groomed to be a professional mistress who blossoms into independence—became a musical film starring Leslie Caron and Maurice Chevalier (1958). Thank heaven for little girls!

> *"The only misplaced curiosity is trying to find out here, on this side, what lies beyond the grave."*
>
> —Colette

• *Retrace your steps to avenue Principale and go uphill a half block. On the left, find Rossini, with Haussmann a few graves up.*

⓫ Gioacchino Rossini (1792–1868)

Dut. Dutta-dut. Dutta dut dut dut dut dut dut dut, dut dut dut dut dut dut dut....

The composer of the *William Tell Overture* (a.k.a. the *Lone Ranger* theme) was Italian, but he moved to Paris (1823) to bring his popular comic operas to France. Extremely prolific, he could crank out

Other Notable Residents

Though not along our walking tour, the following folks can be found on our map, as well as the €2 map you get from the florists.

Ⓐ Jacques-Louis David (1748–1825)—Section 56
The Neoclassical painter David chronicled the heroic Revolution and the Napoleonic Era. See his *Coronation of Napoleon* in the Louvre (page 117).

Ⓑ Théodore Géricault (1791–1824)—Section 12
Géricault was the master of painting extreme situations (ship-wrecks, battles) and extreme emotions (noble sacrifice, cour-age, agony, insanity) with Romantic realism. See his *Raft of the Medusa* in the Louvre (page 119).

Ⓒ Eugène Delacroix (1798–1863)—Section 49
For more on this Romantic painter, see his *Liberty Leading the People* in the Louvre (page 120) or visit the Delacroix Museum (see Left Bank Walk, page 237).

Ⓓ Jean-August-Dominique Ingres (1780–1867)—Section 23
Often considered the anti-Delacroix, Ingres was a painter of placid portraits and bathing nudes, using curved outlines and smooth-surfaced paint. Despite his deliberate distortions (see his beautifully deformed *La Grande Odalisque* in the Louvre, page 118), he was hailed as the champion of traditional Neoclassical balance against the furious Romantic style (see his *The Source* in the Orsay, page 133).

Ⓔ Georges Seurat (1859–1891)—Section 66
Georges spent Sunday afternoons in the park with his easel, cap-turing shimmering light using tiny dots of different-colored paint. See his Pointillist canvas *The Circus* in the Orsay (page 149).

Ⓕ Amadeo Modigliani (1884–1920)—Section 96, not far from Edith Piaf
Poor, tubercular, and strung out on drugs and alcohol in Paris, this young Italian painter forged a distinctive style. His portraits and nudes have African mask–like faces, and elongated necks and arms.

a three-hour opera in literally weeks, including the highly success-ful *Barber of Seville* (based on a play by Pierre Beaumarchais, who is also buried in Père Lachaise). When *Guillaume Tell* debuted (1829), Rossini, age 37, was at the peak of his career as an opera composer.

Then he stopped. For the next four decades, he never again wrote an opera and scarcely wrote anything else. He moved to Italy, went through a stretch of bad health, and then returned to Paris, where his health and spirits revived. He even wrote a little music in his old age. Rossini's impressive little sepulcher is empty, as his remains were

⑨ Marcel Proust (1871–1922)—Section 85

Some who make it through the seven volumes and 3,000 pages of Proust's autobiographical novel, *Remembrance of Things Past*, close the book and cry, "Brilliant!" Others get lost in the meandering, stream-of-consciousness style, and forget that the whole "Remembrance" began with the taste of a *madeleine* (a type of cookie) that triggered a flashback to Proust's childhood, as relived over the last 10 years of his life, during which he labored alone in his apartment on boulevard Haussmann—midway between the Arc de Triomphe and Gare de l'Est—penning his life story with reflections on Time (as we experience it, not clock time) and Memory, in long sentences.

⑩ Sarah Bernhardt (1844–1923)—Section 44

The greatest actress of her generation, she conquered Paris and the world. Charismatic Sarah made a triumphant tour of America and Europe (1880–1881) starring in *La Dame aux Camélias*. No one could die onstage like Sarah, and in the final scene—when her character succumbs to tuberculosis—she had cowboys and railroad workers sniffling in the audience. Of her hundred-plus stage roles and many silent films, perhaps her most memorable role may have been playing...Hamlet (1899). Offstage, her numerous affairs and passionate, capricious personality set a standard for future divas to aspire to.

⑪ Yves Montand (1921–1991) and
Simone Signoret (1921–1985)—Section 44

Yves Montand was a film actor and nightclub singer with blue-collar roots, left-wing politics, and a social conscience. Montand's career was boosted by his lover, Edith Piaf, when they appeared together at the Moulin Rouge during World War II. Yves went on to stardom throughout the world (except in America, thanks partly to a 1960 flop film with Marilyn Monroe, *Let's Make Love*). In 1951, he married actress Simone Signoret, whose on-screen persona was the long-suffering lover. They remain together still, despite rumors of Yves' womanizing. After their deaths, their eternal love was tested in 1998, when Yves' body was exhumed to take a DNA sample for a paternity suit (it wasn't him).

PÈRE LACHAISE

moved to Florence.

• *Four graves uphill, find...*

⑫ Baron Georges-Eugène Haussmann (1809–1891)

(Look through the green door long enough for your eyes to dilate.) Love him or hate him, Baron Haussmann made the Paris we see today. In the 1860s, Paris was a construction zone, with civil servant Haussmann overseeing the city's modernization. Narrow medieval lanes were widened and straightened into broad, traffic-carrying boulevards. Historic buildings were torn down. Sewers, bridges, and water systems were repaired. Haussmann blew the boulevard St. Michel through the formerly quaint Latin Quarter (as part of Emperor Napoleon III's plan to prevent revolutionaries from barricading narrow streets). The Opéra Garnier, Bois de Boulogne park, and avenues radiating from the Arc de Triomphe were all part of Haussmann's grand scheme, which touched 60 percent of the city. How did he finance it all? That's what the next government wanted to know when they canned him.

Thank God You Can Leave

• *Have you seen enough dead people? To leave the cemetery, return downhill on avenue Principale and exit onto boulevard de Ménilmontant. The Père Lachaise Métro stop is one long block to the right. To find the bus #69 stop heading west to downtown, cross boulevard de Ménilmontant and walk down the right side of rue de la Roquette; the stop is four blocks down, on the right-hand side.*

MONTMARTRE WALK

*From Sacré-Cœur
to the Moulin Rouge*

Stroll along the hilltop of Butte Montmartre amid traces of the people who've lived here—monks stomping grapes (1200s), farmers grinding grain in windmills (1600s), dust-coated gypsum miners (1700s), Parisian liberals (1800s), Modernist painters (1900s), and all the struggling artists, poets, dreamers, and drunkards who came here for cheap rent, untaxed booze, rustic landscapes, and cabaret nightlife.

While many tourists make the almost obligatory trek to the top of Paris' Butte Montmartre, eat an overpriced crêpe, and marvel at the view, most miss out on the neighborhood's charm and history—both uncovered in this stroll.

We'll start at the radiant Sacré-Cœur church, wander through the hilltop village, browse affordable art, ogle the Moulin Rouge nightclub, and catch echoes of those who once partied to a bohemian rhapsody during the belle époque. We'll end by going through part of a red light district (once adored by American GIs) and finally down a lively neighborhood market street.

ORIENTATION

Length of This Walk: Allow more than two hours for this two-mile uphill/downhill walk.

When to Go: To avoid crowds at Sacré-Cœur, come on a weekday or by 9:30 on a weekend. Sunny weekends are the busiest—especially on Sunday, when Montmartre becomes a pedestrian-only zone and shops stay open. If crowds don't get you down, come for the sunset and stay for dinner (see page 395 of the Eating chapter). This walk is best under clear skies, when views are sensational. Regardless of when you go, prepare for more seediness than you're accustomed to in Paris.

Getting There: Nearby Métro stops include Anvers, Abbesses, and

Pigalle). You have a couple of options to avoid climbing the hill to Sacré-Cœur: The simplest approach is to take the Métro to Anvers, then take the funicular (mentioned in walk, below). Or, from place Pigalle, you can take the tiny electric Montmartrobus, which drops you right by place du Tertre, near Sacré-Cœur (costs one Métro ticket, 4/hr). A taxi from the Seine or the Bastille to Sacré-Cœur costs about €12 (figure on €20 at night).

Sacré-Cœur: Church interior-free, open daily 7:00–23:00; climbing dome-€5; not covered by Museum Pass, daily June–Sept 9:00–19:00, Oct–May 10:00–18:00.

Dalí Museum (L'Espace Dalí): €10, not covered by Museum Pass, daily 10:00–18:30, 11 rue Poulbot, tel. 01 42 64 40 10, www.dali paris.com.

Montmartre Museum: €7 (includes audioguide), not covered by Museum Pass, Tue–Sun 11:00–18:00, closed Mon, 12 rue Cortot, tel. 01 49 25 89 39, www.museedemontmartre.fr.

Museum of Erotic Art (Musée de l'Erotisme): €8, definitely not covered by Museum Pass, daily 10:00–2:00 in the morning, 72 boulevard de Clichy, Mo: Blanche, tel. 01 42 58 28 73, www.musee-erotisme.com.

Cuisine Art: See page 395 of the Eating chapter.

Starring: Cityscape views, Sacré-Cœur, postcard scenes brought to life, a charming market street, and boring buildings where interesting people once lived.

THE WALK BEGINS

To reach Sacré-Cœur by Métro, get off at Métro stop Anvers. The **Elysées Montmartre** theater across the street is the oldest cancan dance hall in Paris. Today, it's a rowdy dance club and concert hall, signaling this area's transition. (The famous Chat Noir—or Black Cat—cabaret was half a block down, in the peeling and neglected building at #80.) Historically, people have moved to this neighborhood for cheap rents. While it still feels neglected, urban gentrification is underway, as young professionals restore dilapidated apartments, hotels renovate for a more upscale clientele, and rents increase.

Walk two blocks up rue de Steinkerque (the street to the right of Elysées Montmartre), through a bizarre, low-rent urban bazaar, past bolts of fabric, cheap clothing, and souvenir shops (pick up inexpensive postcards and €3 blue jeans). You'll reach a grassy park way below the white Sacré-Cœur church. The terraced hillside was once dotted with openings to gypsum mines, the source of the white "plaster of Paris" that plastered Paris' buildings for centuries.

• *Hike up to the church, or ride the funicular (station to your left, costs one Métro ticket). At the top, find a good viewing spot at the steps of the church.*

Montmartre Walk

1. Sacré-Cœur Basilica
2. Church of St. Pierre, Bus & Taxi Stop
3. Cabaret de Patachou
4. Place du Tertre
5. Rue Norvins
6. Dalí Museum & Rest. Chez Plumeau
7. Boulangerie & View
8. Montmartre Mus. & Satie's House
9. La Maison Rose Restaurant
10. Clos Montmartre Vineyard
11. Au Lapin Agile Cabaret
12. Renoir's House
13. St. Denis Statue
14. Le Bateau-Lavoir (Picasso's Studio)
15. Moulin de la Galette
16. Toulouse-Lautrec's House
17. Van Gogh's House
18. Café des Deux Moulins
19. Moulin Rouge
20. Museum of Erotic Art
21. Pig Alley
22. Rue des Martyrs
23. To Notre-Dame-de-Lorette Church & Métro
24. To Rest. L'Eté en Pente Douce

MONTMARTRE WALK

❶ Sacré-Cœur Basilica and View

From Paris' highest point (420 feet), the City of Light fans out at your feet. Pan from left to right. The big triangular roof on your left is the Gare du Nord train station. The blue-and-red Pompidou Center is straight ahead, and the skyscrapers in the distance define the southern limit of central Paris. Next is the domed Panthéon, atop Paris' other (and far smaller) butte. Then comes the modern Montparnasse Tower, and finally (if you're in position to see this far to the right), the golden dome of Les Invalides.

Now face the church. The Sacré-Cœur (Sacred Heart) basilica's exterior, with its onion domes and bleached-bone pallor, looks ancient, but was built only a century ago by Parisians humiliated by German invaders. Otto von Bismarck's Prussian army laid siege to Paris for more than four months in 1870. Things got so bad for residents that urban hunting for dinner (to cook up dogs, cats, and finally rats) became accepted behavior. Convinced they were being punished for the country's liberal sins, France's Catholics raised money to build the church as a "praise the Lord anyway" gesture. Some say the church was also built as a kind of penitence by the French. Many were disgusted that in 1871 their government actually shot their own citizens, the Communards, who held out here on Montmartre after the French leadership surrendered to the Prussians.

The five-domed, Roman-Byzantine–looking basilica took 44 years to build (1875–1919). It stands on a foundation of 83 pillars sunk 130 feet deep, necessary because the ground beneath was honeycombed with gypsum mines. The exterior is laced with gypsum, which whitens with age.

Interior: In the impressive mosaic high above the altar, Christ exposes his sacred heart, burning with love and compassion for humanity. Christ is flanked by biblical figures on the left and French

figures on the right. Among the French are Jeanne d'Arc (in her trademark armor, at Jesus' feet), clergymen (who offer a model of this church to the Lord), government leaders (in business suits), and French saints (including St. Bernard, above, with his famous dog; and St. Louis, with the crown of thorns). The centerpiece of the mosaic is the Holy Trinity: Jesus, a dove representing the Holy Spirit, and God the father high above. Right now, in this church, at least one person is praying for Christ to be understanding of the world's sins—part of a tradition that's been carried out here, day and night, 24/7, since Sacré-Cœur's completion.

• *Find the first pillar to the left (as you face the altar), across from the statue of St. Thérèse.*

A plaque on the pillar ("*L'an 1944...*") shows where the 13 WWII bombs that hit Paris fell—all in a line, all near the church—killing no one. This fueled local devotion to the Sacred Heart and to this church.

Walking clockwise around the ambulatory, find a scale model of the church. Since the church's original windows were broken by the concussion of WWII bombs, all the glass you see is post-1945. Continuing behind the altar, notice the colorful mosaics of the Stations of the Cross. At the far end of the church, rub St. Peter's bronze foot and look up to the heavens.

Continue your circuit around the church. As you approach the entrance, you'll walk straight toward three stained-glass windows dedicated to Joan of Arc (Jeanne d'Arc, 1412–1431). See the teenage girl as she hears the voice of the Archangel Michael (right panel, at bottom), and later (above, on right) as she takes up the Archangel's sword. Next, she kneels to take communion (central panel), then kneels before the bishop to tell him she's been sent by God to rally France's soldiers and save Orléans from English invaders. However, French forces allied with England arrest her, and she's burned at the stake as a heretic (above, on left), dying with her eyes fixed on a crucifix and chanting, "Jesus, Jesus, Jesus...."

• *Exit the church. Once outside, a public WC is to your left, down 50 steps. To your right is the entrance to the church's...*

Dome and Crypt: For an unobstructed panoramic view of Paris, climb 260 feet up the tight and claustrophobic spiral stairs to the top of the **dome** (especially worthwhile if you have kids with excess energy). The crypt is just a big empty basement.

• *Leaving the church, turn right and walk west along the ridge, following tree-lined rue Azaïs. At rue St. Eleuthère, turn right and walk uphill a block to the Church of St. Pierre-de-Montmartre (at top on right).*

The small square in front of the church has a convenient taxi stand and a bus stop for the Montmartrobus to and from place Pigalle (bus costs one Métro ticket).

❷ Church of St. Pierre-de-Montmartre

This church was the center of Montmartre's first claim to fame, a sprawling abbey of Benedictine monks and nuns. The church is one of Paris' oldest (1147)—some say Dante prayed here; founded by King Louis VI and his wife, Adelaide. Find Adelaide's tombstone *(pierre tombale)* midway down on the left wall. Older still are the four gray columns—two flank the entrance, and two others are behind the altar. These may have stood in a temple of Mercury or Mars in Roman times. The name "Montmartre" comes from the Roman "Mount of Mars," though later generations—thinking of their beheaded patron St. Denis—preferred a less pagan version, "Mount of Martyrs."

Along the right wall, rub St. Peter's toe (again), look up, and ask for *déliverance* from the tourist mobs outside. Now step back outside, where a sign for the *Café and Cabaret la Bohème* reminds visitors that in the late 19th and early 20th centuries, this was the world capital of bohemian life. The artist-filled place du Tertre awaits.

• *Before entering the square, a short detour to the right leads to 13 rue du Mont-Cenis, the former...*

❸ Cabaret de Patachou

This building, now a pleasant art gallery, is where singer Edith Piaf (1915–1963) once trilled "La Vie en Rose." Piaf—a destitute teenager who sang for pocket change in the streets of pre-WWII Paris—was discovered by a nightclub owner and became a star. Her singing inspired the people of Nazi-occupied Paris. In the heady days after the war, she sang about the joyous, rosy life in the city. For more on this warbling-voiced singer, see page 314.

• *Head back to the always-lively square, and stand on its cusp for the best perspective of...*

❹ Place du Tertre—Bohemian Montmartre

Lined with cafés, shaded by acacia trees, and filled with artists, hucksters, and tourists, the scene mixes charm and kitsch in ever-changing proportions. The place du Tertre has been the town square of the small village of Montmartre since medieval times. (*Tertre* means "stepped lanes" in French.)

In 1800, a wall separated Paris from this hilltop village. To enter Paris, you had to pass tollbooths that taxed anything for sale. Montmartre was a mining community where the wine flowed cheap (tax-free) and easy. Life here was a working-class festival of cafés, bistros, and dance halls. Painters came here for the ruddy charm, the light, and the low rents. In 1860, Montmartre was annexed into the growing city of Paris. The "bohemian" ambience survived, and it attracted sophisticated Parisians ready to get down and dirty in the belle époque of cancan.

The Restaurant Mère Catherine is often called the first bistro, since this is where Russian soldiers first coined the word by saying, "I'm thirsty, bring my drink *bistro!*" (meaning "right away").

The square's artists, who at times outnumber the tourists, are the great-great-grandkids of the Renoirs, Van Goghs, and Picassos who once roamed

Maurice Utrillo
(1883–1955)

Born to a free-spirited single mom and raised by his grand-mother, Utrillo had his first detox treatment at age 18. Encouraged by his mother and doctors, he started painting as occupational therapy. That, plus guidance from his mother (and later, from his wife), allowed him to live productively into his seventies, becoming wealthy and famous, despite occasional relapses into drink and mental problems.

Utrillo grew up in Montmartre's streets. He fought, broke street lamps, and haunted the cafés and bars, buying drinks with masterpieces. A very free spirit, he's said to have exposed himself to strangers on the street, yelling, "I paint with this!"

His simple scenes of streets, squares, and cafés in a vaguely Impressionist style became popular with common-ers and scholars alike. He honed his style during his "white period" (c. 1909–1914), painting a thick paste of predomi-nantly white tints—perfect for capturing Sacré-Cœur. In later years, after he moved out of Montmartre, he still painted the world he knew in his youth, using postcards and photographs as models.

Utrillo's mom, Suzanne Valadon, was a former trapeze performer and artist's model who posed for Toulouse-Lautrec, slept with Renoir, studied under Degas, and went on to become a notable painter in her own right. Her partner, a Spanish artist named André Utter, gave Maurice his family name (Utrillo = little Utter).

here—poor, carefree, seeking inspiration, and occasionally cursing a world too selfish to bankroll their dreams.

• *Plunge headfirst into the square. The tourist office (Syndicat d'Initiative) across the square sells good maps (daily 10:00–19:00). Just south of the square is the quiet, tiny place du Calvaire, with the recommended café Chez Plumeau (closed Wed). But for now, continue west along the main drag, called...*

❺ Rue Norvins

Montmartre's oldest and main street is still the primary commercial artery, serving the current trade—tourism.

• *If you're a devotee of Dalí, take a detour left on rue Poulbot, leading to the...*

❻ Dalí Museum (L'Espace Dalí)

This beautifully lit black gallery (well-described in English) offers a walk through statues, etchings, and paintings by the master of Surrealism. The Spaniard found fame in Paris in the 1920s and '30s, hanging with the Surrealist crowd in Montparnasse, and shocking the world with his dreamscape paintings and experimental films. Don't miss the printed interview on the exit stairs.

• *Return to rue Norvins and continue west a dozen steps to the intersection with rue des Saules, where you'll find a...*

❼ Boulangerie with a View

The venerable *boulangerie* (bakery) on the left, dating from 1900, is one of the last surviving bits of the old-time community, made famous in a painting by the artist Maurice Utrillo (see sidebar).

From the *boulangerie*, look back up rue Norvins, then backpedal a few steps to catch the classic view of the dome of Sacré-Cœur rising above the rooftops.

• *Let's lose the tourists. Follow rue des Saules downhill (north) onto the back side of Montmartre. A block downhill, turn right on rue Cortot to the...*

❽ Montmartre Museum and Satie's House

In what is now the museum (at 12 rue Cortot), Pierre-Auguste Renoir once lived while painting his best-known work, *Bal du Moulin de la Galette* (pictured on page 333). Every day, he'd lug the four-foot-by-six-foot canvas from here to the other side of the butte to paint in the open air *(en plein aire)* the famous windmill ballroom, which we'll see later.

A few years later, Utrillo lived and painted here with his mom, Suzanne Valadon. In 1893, she carried on a torrid six-month relationship with the lonely, eccentric man who lived two doors up at #6—composer Erik Satie *(Trois Gymnopédies),* who was eking out a living playing piano in Montmartre nightclubs.

The Montmartre Museum fills several floors in this creaky 17th-century manor house with paintings, posters, old photos, music, and memorabilia to re-create the traditional cancan and cabaret Montmartre scene. An audioguide is free with admission. Highlights include several original Toulouse-Lautrec posters for the Moulin Rouge, a few paintings by Utrillo and Valadon, the original *Lapin Agile* sign, and displays on Montmartre's history, from gypsum mining to the Paris Commune to the Chat Noir cabaret.

• *Return to rue des Saules and walk downhill to...*

❾ La Maison Rose Restaurant

The restaurant, made famous by a Utrillo painting, was once frequented by Utrillo, Pablo Picasso, and Gertrude Stein. Today, it serves lousy food to nostalgic tourists.

• *Just downhill from the restaurant is Paris' last remaining vineyard.*

❿ Clos Montmartre Vineyard

What originally drew artists to Montmartre was country charm like this. Ever since the 12th century, the monks and nuns of the large abbey produced wine here. With vineyards, wheat fields, windmills, animals, and a village tempo of life, it was the perfect escape from grimy Paris. In 1576, puritanical laws taxed wine in Paris, bringing budget-minded drinkers to Montmartre. Today's vineyard is off-limits to tourists except during the annual grape-harvest fest (first Sat in Oct), when a thousand costumed locals bring back the boisterous old days. The vineyard's annual production of 300 liters is auctioned off at the fest to support local charities.

• *Continue downhill to the intersection with rue St. Vincent.*

⓫ Au Lapin Agile Cabaret

The poster above the door gives the place its name. A rabbit *(lapin)* makes an agile leap out of the pot while balancing the bottle of wine that he can now drink—rather than be cooked in. This was the village's hot spot. Picasso and other artists and writers (Renoir, Utrillo, Paul Verlaine, Aristide Bruant, Amedeo Modigliani, etc.) would gather for "performances" that ranged from serious poetry, dirty limericks, sing-alongs, and parodies of the famous to anarchist manifestos. Once, to play a practical joke on the avant-garde art community, patrons tied a paintbrush to the tail of the owner's donkey and entered the "abstract paint-

ing" that resulted in the Salon. Called *Sunset over the Adriatic,* it won critical acclaim and sold for a nice price.

The old Parisian personality of this cabaret survives. Every night except Monday, a series of performers take a small, French-speaking audience on a wistful musical journey back to the good old days (for details, see Nightlife chapter, page 421).

• *Before heading back uphill on rue des Saules to the* boulangerie *(at the intersection with rue Norvins), some may wish to make a detour (an extra 15 min) to see a more residential part of Montmartre. If you're pooped, we'll meet you back at the* boulangerie.

Detour to ⓬ Renoir's House and ⓭ St. Denis Statue

• *Walk up rue des Saules and turn right at La Maison Rose, heading west one block on rue de l'Abreuvoir. At the busty bust of singer/actress Dalida*

(1933–1987, who popularized disco in France), continue straight (west) along the small walkway called allée des Brouillards. You'll pass another of **Renoir's homes** *(at #6). Walk down the steps at the walkway's end, then stroll up through the small, fenced, multilevel park called Square Suzanne Buisson.*

In the park, find the stone statue of headless **St. Denis.** This early Christian bishop was sentenced to death by the Romans for spreading Christianity. As they marched him up to the top of Montmartre to

be executed, the Roman soldiers got tired, and just beheaded him near here. But Denis popped right up, picked up his head, and carried on another three miles north before he finally died. The statue of Denis cradles his head in his hands, looks over a regulation-size *boules* court...and gets ready to play ball.

• *At the top of the park, turn left onto avenue Junot, which turns into rue Norvins. (Don't you wish you could just walk right through these darn hills? You'll pass a statue that looks like it could do it.) The* boulangerie *is at the top of rue Norvins.*

Once reunited at the boulangerie, *we all go downhill (south). Don't curve right on car-filled rue Lepic; instead, go straight, down the pedestrian-only place J. B. Clement, hugging the buildings on the left. Turn right on rue Ravignan and follow it down to the leafy little square with the TIM Hôtel. Just right of the hotel, at 13 place Emile Goudeau, is...*

⓮ Le Bateau-Lavoir (Picasso's Studio)

A humble facade marks the place where Modern art was born. Here, in a lowly artists' abode (destroyed by fire in 1970, rebuilt a few years

later), as many as 10 artists lived and worked. This former piano factory, converted to cheap housing, was nicknamed the "Laundry Boat" for its sprawling layout and crude facilities (sharing one water tap). It was "a weird, squalid place," wrote one resident, "filled with every kind of noise: arguing, singing, bedpans clattering, slamming doors, and

suggestive moans coming from studio doors."

In 1904, a poor, unknown Spanish émigré named Pablo Picasso (1881–1973) moved in. He met dark-haired Fernande Olivier, his first real girlfriend, in the square outside. She soon moved in, lifting him out of his melancholy Blue Period into the rosy Rose Period. *La belle Fernande* posed nude for him, inspiring a freer treatment of the female form.

In 1907, Picasso started on a major canvas. For nine months, he produced hundreds of preparatory sketches, working long into the night. When he unveiled the work, even his friends were shocked. *Les Demoiselles d'Avignon* showed five nude women in a brothel (Fernande claimed they were all her), with primitive mask-like faces and fragmented bodies. Picasso had invented Cubism.

For the next two years, he and his neighbors Georges Braque and Juan Gris revolutionized the art world. Sharing paints, ideas, and girlfriends, they made Montmartre "The Cubist Acropolis," attracting free-thinking "Moderns" from all over the world to visit their studios—the artists Modigliani and Henri Rousseau, the poet Guillaume Apollinaire, and the American expatriate writer Gertrude Stein. By the time Picasso moved to better quarters (and dumped Fernande), he was famous. Still, Picasso would later say, "I know one day we'll return to Bateau-Lavoir. It was there that we were really happy—where they thought of us as painters, not strange animals."

• *Walk back half a block uphill and turn left on rue d'Orchampt. (Notice the north-facing windows of another studio.) Walk the length of this short street and into a tiny alley, which squirts you out the other end at the intersection with rue Lepic, where you're face-to-face with a wooden windmill.*

⓫ Moulin de la Galette

Only two windmills *(moulins)* remain on a hill that was once dotted with 30 of them. Originally, they pressed monks' grapes and farmers' grain, and crushed gypsum rocks into powdery plaster of Paris. When the gypsum mines closed (c. 1850) and the vineyards sprouted apartments, this windmill turned into the ceremonial centerpiece of a popular outdoor dance hall. Renoir's *Bal du Moulin de la Galette* (in the Orsay) shows it in its heyday—a sunny Sunday afternoon in the acacia-shaded gardens with working-class people dancing, laughing, drinking, and eating the house crêpes, called *galettes*. Some call Renoir's version the quintessential Impressionist work and the painting that best captures—on a large canvas in bright colors—the joy of the Montmartre lifestyle.

• *Follow rue Lepic as it winds down the hill. The green-latticed building on the right side was also part of the Moulin de la Galette (the second surviving windmill is just above, through the trees). Rounding the bend, look to the right down rue Tourlaque. The building one block down rue Tourlaque was...*

⑯ Henri de Toulouse-Lautrec's House

Find the building on the southwest corner with the tall, brick-framed art-studio windows under the heavy mansard roof. Every night, Toulouse-Lautrec (1864–1901, see page 149)—a nobleman turned painter, whose legs were deformed in a horse-riding accident during his teenage years—would dress up here and then journey down rue Lepic to the Moulin Rouge. One of Henri's occasional drinking buddies and fellow artists lived nearby.

• *Continue down rue Lepic and, at #54, find...*

⑰ Vincent van Gogh's House

Vincent van Gogh lived here with his brother, enjoying a grand city view from his top-floor window from 1886 to 1888. In those two short years, Van Gogh transformed from a gloomy Dutch painter of brown and gray peasant scenes into an inspired visionary with wild ideas and Impressionist colors.

• *Follow rue Lepic downhill as it makes a hard right at #36 and becomes a lively market street. Enjoy the small shops and neighborhood ambience. Two blocks down, on the corner to your right (at #15), you'll find...*

⑱ Café des Deux Moulins

This café has become a site of pilgrimage for movie buffs worldwide, since it was featured in the quirky film *Amélie*. Today, it's just another funky place with unassuming ambience, frequented by another generation of real-life Amélies who ignore the movie poster on the back wall (daily 7:00–24:00, 15 rue Lepic, tel. 01 42 54 90 50).

• *Now continue downhill on rue Lepic to place Blanche. On busy place Blanche is the...*

⑲ Moulin Rouge

Ooh la la. The new Eiffel Tower at the 1889 World's Fair was nothing compared to the sight of pretty cancan girls kicking their legs at the newly opened "Red Windmill." The nightclub seemed to sum up the belle époque—the age of elegance, opulence, sophistication, and worldliness. The big draw was amateur night, when working-class girls in risqué dresses danced "Le Quadrille" (dubbed "cancan" by a Brit). Wealthy Parisians slummed it by coming here.

On most nights, you'd see a small man in a sleek black coat, checked pants, a green scarf, and a bowler hat peering through his pince-nez glasses at the dancers and making sketches of them—Henri de Toulouse-Lautrec. Perhaps he'd order an absinthe, the dense green liqueur (evil ancestor of today's pastis) that was the toxic muse for so many great (and so many forgotten) artists. Toulouse-Lautrec's sketches of dancer Jane Avril and comic La Goulue hang in the Orsay (see reproductions in the entryway).

After its initial splash, the Moulin Rouge survived as a venue for all kinds of entertainment. In 1906, the novelist Colette kissed her female lover onstage, and the authorities closed the "Dream of Egypt" down. Yves Montand opened for Edith Piaf (1944), and the two fell in love off-stage. It has hosted such diverse acts as Ginger Rogers, Dalida, and the Village People—together on one bill (1979). Mikhail Baryshnikov strode across its stage (1986). And the club celebrated its centennial (1989) with Ray Charles, Tony Curtis, Ella Fitzgerald, and...Jerry Lewis.

Tonight they're showing...well, find out yourself: Walk into the open-air entryway or step into the lobby to mull over the photos, show options, and prices.

• *Turn left out of the Moulin Rouge. The Blanche Métro stop is here in place Blanche, a good place to end if you are tired. (Plaster of Paris from the gypsum found on this mount was loaded sloppily at place Blanche...the white square.) Others may want to sully themselves by continuing east to the...*

⑳ Museum of Erotic Art (Musée de l'Erotisme)

Basically a sexy art gallery, this museum has five floors of displays—mostly paintings and drawings—ranging from artistic to erotic to disgusting. They also toss in a few circa-1920 porn videos and a fascinating history of local brothels (see page 72).

• *Outside, farther down the boulevard, you'll find...*

㉑ Pig Alley

The stretch of the boulevard de Clichy from place Blanche eastward (toward Sacré-Cœur) to place Pigalle is the den mother of all iniquities. Today, sex shops, peep shows, live sex shows, chatty pitchmen, and hot dog stands line the busy boulevard. Dildos abound.

It's raunchy now, but the area has always been the place where bistros had tax-free status, wine was cheap, and prostitutes roamed freely. In World War II, GIs nicknamed Pigalle "Pig Alley." While the government is cracking down on prostitution, and the ladies of the night are being driven deeper into their red-velvet bars as the area is being gentrified, very few think of the great French sculptor Pigalle when they hear the district's name.

Bars lining the streets downhill from place Pigalle (especially rue Pigalle) are lively with working girls eager to share a drink with anyone passing by. Escape home via the fine Art Nouveau Métro stop, Pigalle. After all that, the Métro system seems cleaner.

• *While you can pop into the Métro from here, the next (optional) leg of this walk starts a block away and takes you downhill six blocks through a lively market street to another Métro station. Continue walking down boulevard de Clichy to the next street, where you turn right on...*

㉒ Rue des Martyrs

As they race from big museum to big museum, it's easy for visitors to miss the market streets and village-like charm that give Paris a warm and human vibrancy. Rue Cler remains my favorite market street (see walk on page 164), but many of its down-and-dirty shops are being replaced by trendy restaurants with crowds of tourists. For a rougher market street serving village Paris, stroll down rue des Martyrs.

Boulevard de Clichy runs where the town wall once did (*boulevard* literally means "road that replaced a wall"); the reason Montmartre is so cozy is that it was outside the walls. Entering rue des Martyrs, you pass into a finer neighborhood with broader streets, richer buildings...and signs of the reality of raising a family in an urban setting. Security can be a concern. The school has barriers to keep possible car bombs at a distance. (Since terrorist attacks rocked Paris decades ago, there's been no parking in front of schools or near buildings that serve a predominantly Jewish clientele.) Several side streets are "*voie privée*"—private lanes or high-rise, gated communities.

Slalom past people strolling dogs and babies. Goods spill out onto the sidewalk. Banners across the street announce *vide grenier* ("empty your attic") street-market days, neighborhood picnics, concerts, and so on.

People know their butcher and baker as if they lived in a village. Locals willingly pay more in a shop that's not part of a chain. At #58, the traditional charcuterie still sells various meats, but it's morphed with the times into a "*traiteur*" with more variety, food to eat in as well as to go, and prepared dishes sold by the weight.

Across the street, you'll see one of the countless late-night groceries. These are generally run by North African immigrants who are willing to work the night shift for the convenience of others. Pay attention: Produce with rip-off prices is often priced by the half-kilo.

At #50, a favorite cheesemonger has been serving the neighborhood ever since it actually had goats and cows grazing out back.

Notice the marble shelves, old milk jugs, and small artisanal cheeses.

The baker at #39 proudly displays his "best baguette in Paris" award from 2007. Nearby, at #46, the Rose Bakery serves a young, affluent, and health-conscious crowd with top-quality organic and vegetarian breakfasts and lunches.

If you're homesick and looking for barbecue chicken or a banana split, head half a block away, opposite #36, for the first African American restaurant in Paris—established by Leroy Haynes in 1939.

Continuing your stroll, take a look at the traditional butcher at #21. You know he's good because the ceiling hooks—where butchers once hung sides of beef—now display a red medallion that certifies the slaughtered cow's quality.

The *pâtisserie* at #22 is worth popping in to see the typically French works of art. Bakers often make special treats in synch with the season: Easter, Christmas, First Communion, and so on.

Nearby, the tobacco shop/café at #20 is coping well with the new smoking ban by putting out heaters (in cool weather) and as many tables as will fit on the sidewalk. Shops like this—once run by rural people from what was then France's poorest region, Auvergne—are now generally managed by Chinese immigrants.

At #10, Eat Sushi delivers its food like a pizzeria—notice the motorbikes parked outside. A step above fast food, these places are trendy, serving modern professionals who don't want to cook after a long day of work.

Just before rue des Martyrs ends at the neighborhood church— the Neoclassical Notre-Dame-de-Lorette (circa 1836)—it reaches a commercial climax.

• *Our walk is over. The Métro station Notre-Dame-de-Lorette awaits.*

SLEEPING

I've focused most of my recommendations in three safe, handy, and colorful neighborhoods: the village-like rue Cler (near the Eiffel Tower), the artsy and trendy Marais (near place de la Bastille), and the lively and Latin yet classy Luxembourg (on the Left Bank).

For each neighborhood, I list good hotels, helpful hints, and a selection of restaurants (see Eating chapter). Before choosing a hotel, read the descriptions of the neighborhoods closely. Each offers different pros and cons, and your neighborhood is as important as your hotel for the success of your trip. Less expensive and less central accommodations are also listed in other chapters—Versailles Day Trip, Chartres Cathedral Day Trip, Reims, and More Day Trips (Fontainebleau, Giverny, Auvers-sur-Oise, and Disneyland Paris). For accommodations near the two major airports, see the Transportation Connections chapter.

Reserve ahead for Paris—the sooner, the better. Conventions clog Paris in September (worst), October, May, and June (very tough). There are unusually large crowds during holiday periods (see "Holidays and Festivals" on page 550), so book your accommodations well in advance. In August, when Paris is quiet, some hotels offer lower rates to fill their rooms. For advice on booking rooms, see "Making Reservations" on page 343.

Paris is a good hotel city. A comfortable hotel in Paris costs less than a comparable hotel in London, Amsterdam, or Rome. I like places that are clean, small, central, traditional, friendly, and a good value. Most places I list have at least four of these six virtues.

In this book, the price for a double room will normally range from €55 (very simple, toilet and shower down the hall) to €450 (grand lobbies, maximum plumbing, and the works), with most clustering around €100–150.

As you look over the listings, you'll notice that some hotels promise special prices to my readers who book direct (without using a room-finding service or hotel-booking website, which take a commission). To get these rates, mention this book when you reserve (for online reservations, you may be asked to type in a special code listed with the hotel description), then show the book upon arrival.

TYPES OF ACCOMMODATIONS

Hotels

The French have a simple hotel rating system based on amenities (zero through four stars, indicated in this book by * through ****). One star is modest, two has most of the comforts, and three is generally just a two-star with a fancier lobby and more elaborately designed rooms. Four stars offer more luxury than you have time to appreciate. Two- and three-star hotels are required to have an English-speaking staff, though virtually all hotels I recommend have someone who speaks English (unless I note otherwise in the listing).

Generally, the number of stars does not reflect room size or guarantee quality. Some two-star hotels are better than many three-star hotels. One- and two-star hotels are inexpensive, but some three-star (and even a few four-star hotels) offer good value, justifying the extra cost. Unclassified hotels (no stars) can be bargains or depressing dumps.

Old, characteristic, budget Parisian hotels have always been cramped. Retrofitted with toilets, private showers, and elevators (as most are today), they are even more cramped. Recommended hotels have an elevator unless otherwise noted.

Most hotels have lots of doubles and a few singles, triples, and quads. Traveling alone can be expensive, as singles (except for the rare closet-type rooms that fit only one twin bed) are simply doubles used by one person—so they cost about the same as a double. Room prices vary within each hotel depending on size, and whether the room has a bath or shower, and twin beds or a double bed (tubs and twins cost more than showers and double beds). A triple and a double are often the same room, with a double or queen-size bed plus a sliver-sized single. Quad rooms usually have two double beds. Hotels cannot legally allow more in the room than what's shown on their price list. Modern hotels generally have a few family-friendly rooms that open up to each other *(chambres communiquantes)*.

If you're on a budget, ask for a cheaper room or a discount (mention this book). Ask if staying for three or more nights will reduce the price. People traveling off-season can show up without reservations and find substantial discounts.

French hotels must charge a daily room tax *(taxe du séjour)* of about €1 per person per day. While some hotels include it in the price list, most add it to your bill.

Types of Rooms

Study the price list on the hotel's website or posted at the desk, so you know your options. Receptionists often don't mention the cheaper rooms—they assume you want a private bathroom or a bigger room. Here are the types of rooms and beds:

une chambre sans douche et WC	room without a private shower or toilet (uncommon these days)
une chambre avec cabinet de toilette	room with a toilet but no shower (some hotels charge for down-the-hall showers)
une chambre avec bain et WC	room with private bathtub and toilet
une chambre avec douche et WC	room with private shower and toilet
chambres communiquantes	connecting rooms (ideal for families)
un grand lit	double bed (55 inches wide)
deux petits lits	twin beds (30–36 inches wide)
un lit single	a true single room
un lit de cent-soixante	queen-size bed (literally 160 centimeters, or 63 inches wide)
le king size	king-size bed (usually two twins pushed together)
un lit pliant	folding bed
un bérceau	baby crib
un lit d'enfant	child's bed

You can save as much as €20–25 by finding the rare room without a private shower or toilet. A room with a bathtub costs €10–15 more than a room with a shower and is generally larger. Hotels often have more rooms with tubs than showers and are inclined to give you a room with a tub (which the French prefer).

A double bed is €10–15 cheaper than twins, though rooms with twin beds tend to be larger, and French double beds are smaller than American double beds. Many hotels have queen-size beds (a bed that's 63 inches wide—most doubles are 55). To see if a hotel has queen-size beds, ask, *"Avez-vous des lits de cent-soixante?"* (ah-vay-voo day lee duh sahn-swah-sahnt). Some hotels push two twins together under king-size sheets and blankets to make *le king size*.

If you prefer a double bed (instead of twins) and a shower (instead of a tub), you need to ask for it—and you'll save up to €30 at more expensive hotels. If you'll take either twins or a double, ask generically

Sleep Code

(€1 = about $1.50, country code: 33)

To help you easily sort through these listings, I've divided the rooms into three categories based on the price for a standard double room with bath:

  $$$ Higher Priced: Most rooms €150 or more.
   $$ Moderately Priced: Most rooms between €100–150.
    $ Lower Priced: Most rooms €100 or less.

To give maximum information in a minimum of space, I use the following code to describe the accommodations. Prices listed are per room, not per person. When a price range is given for a type of room (such as "Db-€140–180"), it means the price fluctuates with the season, size of room, or length of stay.

  S = Single room (or price for one person in a double).
  D = Double or twin room.
  T = Triple (generally a double bed with a single).
  Q = Quad (usually two double beds).
  b = Private bathroom with toilet and shower or tub.
  s = Private shower or tub only (the toilet is down the hall).
  * = French hotel rating system, ranging from zero to four stars.

  According to this code, a couple staying at a "Db-€140" hotel would pay a total of €140 (about $210) for a double room with a private bathroom. You can assume a hotel takes credit cards unless you see "cash only" in the listing. Unless otherwise noted, hotel staff speak basic English and breakfast is not included (but is usually optional).

for *une chambre pour deux* (room for two) to avoid being needlessly turned away.

Hotels lobbies, halls, and breakfast rooms are now off-limits to smokers, though smokers can light up in their rooms. Still, I rarely smell any smoke in my rooms. Some hotels have non-smoking rooms or floors—ask about them if this is important to you.

Most hotels offer some kind of breakfast (see page 370 for details). Only a few hotels include it the room rates (I've indicated this in the listings)—pay attention when comparing rates between hotels. While hotels hope you'll buy their breakfast, it's optional unless otherwise noted; to save money, head to a bakery and/or café instead.

Rooms are safe. Still, keep cameras and money out of sight. Towels aren't routinely replaced every day; drip-dry and conserve. If that French Lincoln Log of a pillow isn't your idea of comfort, American-style pillows (and extra blankets) are sometimes in the

Keep Cool

If you're planning to visit Paris in the summer, the extra expense of an air-conditioned room can be money well-spent. Most hotel rooms with air-conditioners come with a control stick (like a TV remote) that generally has the same symbols and features: fan icon (click to toggle through wind power, from light to gale); louver icon (choose steady airflow or waves); snowflake and sunshine icons (cold air or heat, depending on season); clock ("O" setting: run *X* hours before turning off; "I" setting: wait *X* hours to start); and the temperature control (20 or 21 degrees Celsius is comfortable; also see thermometer diagram on page 553).

closet or available on request. To get a pillow, ask for *"Un oreiller, s'il vous plaît"* (uhn oh-ray-yay, see voo play).

If pushing the power button on your TV remote doesn't turn it on, try pressing the channel-up or channel-down button. If it still doesn't work, see if there's a power button on the TV itself, then press the up or down button again.

Get advice from your hotel for safe parking. Consider long-term parking at either airport—Orly is closer and much easier for drivers to navigate than Charles de Gaulle. Garages are plentiful (€20–30/day, with special rates through some hotels). Curb parking is free at night (19:00–9:00), all day Sunday, and throughout the month of August. (For more information, see "Parking in Paris," page 453.)

Your hotelier, a good source of advice, can direct you to the nearest Internet café (*café internet*, kah-fay an-ter-net) and self-service launderette (*laverie automatique,* lah-vay-ree oh-to-mah-teek). To avoid the time-wasting line at the reception desk in the morning, ask if you can settle up your bill the evening before you leave.

All hotels in these listings have elevators, air-conditioning, Internet access (usually a computer available to guests in their lobbies), and Wi-Fi, unless otherwise noted. "Wi-Fi only" means there's no public computer available (but you can get online if you have your own).

Hostels

Parisian hostels charge about €22–34 per bed. Travelers of any age are welcome if they don't mind dorm-style accommodations and meeting other travelers. Cheap meals are sometimes available, and kitchen facilities are usually provided for do-it-yourselfers. Hostelling International hostels (also known as official hostels) require a hostel membership and charge a few extra euros for non-members. If you'll be staying for several days in an official hostel, consider buying a membership card before you go (www.hihostels.com). Hostels that have no such requirements are called independent hostels.

Apartments

It's easy, though not necessarily cheaper, to rent a furnished apartment in Paris. Consider this option if you're either traveling with a family or staying two weeks or longer. For listings, see "For Longer Stays" at the end of this chapter.

PRACTICALITIES

Phoning

To call France, you'll need to know its country code: 33. To call France from the US or Canada, dial 011-33-local number (without the initial 0). If calling France from another European country, dial 00-33-local number (without the initial 0). For more information on telephoning, see page 540.

Making Reservations

Remember, it's important to reserve ahead for Paris. Note that some national holidays jam things up and merit your making reservations far in advance (for a list of holidays, see page 550). To make a reservation, contact hotels directly by email, phone, or fax.

The recommended hotels are accustomed to English-only travelers. Email is the clearest and most economical way to make a reservation. In addition, many hotel websites now have online reservation forms. If phoning from the US, be mindful of time zones (see page 7). To ensure you have all the information you need for your reservation, use the form in this book's appendix (also at www.ricksteves.com/reservation). If you don't get a response within a few days, call to follow up.

When you request a room for a certain time period, use the European style for writing dates: day/month/year. Hoteliers need to know your arrival and departure dates. For example, a two-night stay in July would be "2 nights, 16/07/09 to 18/07/09." Think ahead about how long you'll stay; if you have to guess, guess long (it's hard to add days at the last minute), then cancel the extra days as soon as you know the real length of your stay. (But be warned that if you don't give the hotel plenty of advance warning, you might be billed for the entire visit; for more on cancellation policies, see below).

If the hotel's response tells you its room availability and rates, it's not a confirmation. You must tell them that you want that room at the given rate.

Some travelers make reservations as they travel, calling hotels a few days to a week before their visit. If you prefer the flexibility of traveling without any reservations at all, you'll have greater success snaring rooms if you arrive at your destination early in the day. When you anticipate crowds, call hotels around 9:00 on the day you plan to arrive, when the hotel clerk knows which rooms will be available. If you encounter a language barrier, ask the fluent receptionist at your current hotel to call ahead for you.

Whether you're reserving from home or on the road, the hotelier will sometimes request your credit-card number for a one-night deposit. While you can email your credit-card information (I do), it's safer to share that personal info via phone call, fax, or secure online reservation form (if the hotel has one on its website).

If you must cancel your reservation, it's courteous to do so with as much advance notice as possible (three days is standard in France—simply make a quick phone call or send an email). Hotels, which are often family-run, lose money if they turn away customers while holding a room for someone who doesn't show up.

Be warned that some hotels have strict cancellation policies. Some hotels require seven days' notice, while most want three days; otherwise, you might lose a deposit. Ask about cancellation policies before you book.

Always reconfirm your room reservation a few days in advance from the road. If you'll be arriving after 17:00, let them know.

On the small chance that a hotel loses track of your reservation, bring along a hard copy of their emailed or faxed confirmation.

IN THE RUE CLER NEIGHBORHOOD

(7th arrondissement, Mo: Ecole Militaire, La Tour Maubourg, or Invalides)

Rue Cler, lined with open-air produce stands six days a week, is a safe, tidy, village-like pedestrian street. It's so French that when I step out of my hotel in the morning, I feel like I must have been a poodle in a previous life. How such coziness lodged itself between the high-powered government district and the wealthy Eiffel Tower and Les Invalides areas, I'll never know. This is a neighborhood of wide, tree-lined boulevards, stately apartment buildings, and lots of Americans. The American Church, American Library, American University, and many of my readers call this area home. Hotels here are relatively spacious and a good value, considering the elegance of the neighborhood and the higher prices of the more cramped hotels in other central areas. And for sightseeing, you're within walking distance of the Eiffel Tower, Army Museum, Seine River, and Orsay and Rodin museums.

Become a local at a rue Cler café for breakfast, or join the afternoon crowd for *une bière pression* (a draft beer). On rue Cler, you can eat and browse your way through a street full of pastry shops, delis, cheese shops, and colorful outdoor produce stalls. Afternoon *boules* (outdoor bowling) on the esplanade des Invalides is a relaxing spectator sport (look for the dirt area to the upper right as you face the front of Les Invalides; see sidebar on page 346). The manicured gardens behind the golden dome of the Army Museum are free, peaceful, and filled with flowers (at southwest corner of grounds, closes at about 19:00).

While hardly a happening nightlife spot, rue Cler offers many low-impact after-dark activities. Take an evening stroll above the river through the parkway between pont de l'Alma and pont des Invalides. For an after-dinner cruise on the Seine, it's a 15-minute walk to the river and the Bateaux-Mouches (see page 34 in Orientation chapter). For a post-dinner cruise on foot, saunter into Champ de Mars park to admire the glowing Eiffel Tower. For more ideas on Paris after hours, see the Nightlife chapter.

The American Church and Franco-American Center is the community center for Americans living in Paris. They host interdenominational worship services (every Sun at 9:00 and 11:00) and occasional concerts (most Sun at 17:00 Sept–June—but not every week), and distribute the useful *France-USA Contacts* (reception open Mon–Sat 9:00–12:00 & 13:00–22:00, Sun 14:30–19:00, 65 quai d'Orsay, Mo: Invalides, tel. 01 40 62 05 00, www.acparis.org).

Services: There's a large **post office** at the end of rue Cler on avenue de la Motte-Picquet, and a handy **SNCF train office** at 78 rue St. Dominique (Mon–Sat 8:30–19:30, closed Sun, get there when it opens to avoid a long wait). At both of these offices, take a number and wait your turn. A smaller post office is closer to the Eiffel Tower on avenue Rapp, one block past rue St. Dominique toward the river.

Markets: Cross Champ de Mars park to mix it up with bargain-hunters at the twice-weekly open-air market, **Marché Boulevard de Grenelle,** under the Métro, a few blocks southwest of Champ de Mars park (Wed and Sun until 12:30, between Mo: Dupleix and Mo: La Motte-Picquet-Grenelle). Two grocery stores, both on rue de Grenelle, are open until midnight: **Epicerie de la Tour** (at #197) and **Alimentation** (at corner with rue Cler). **Rue St. Dominique** is the area's boutique-browsing street.

Internet Access: Two Internet cafés compete in this neighborhood: **Com Avenue** is best (about €5/hr, shareable and multi-use accounts, Mon–Sat 10:00–20:00, closed Sun, 24 rue du Champ de Mars, tel. 01 45 55 00 07); **Cyber World Café** is more expensive but open later (about €7/hr, Mon–Sat 12:00–22:00, Sun 12:00–20:00, 20 rue de l'Exposition, tel. 01 53 59 96 54).

Laundry: Launderettes are omnipresent; ask your hotel for the nearest. Here are three handy locations: on rue Auguer (between rue St. Dominique and rue de Grenelle), on rue Amélie (between rue St. Dominique and rue de Grenelle), and at the southeast corner of rue Valadon and rue de Grenelle.

Métro Connections: Key Métro stops are Ecole Militaire, La Tour Maubourg, and Invalides. The RER-C line runs from the pont de l'Alma and Invalides stations, serving Versailles to the west; Auvers-sur-Oise to the north; and the Orsay Museum, Latin Quarter (St. Michel stop), and Austerlitz train station to the east.

The Rules of *Boules*

Throughout Paris—and particularly on Les Invalides' big "front lawn" near the rue Cler neighborhood—you'll see citizens playing *boules*.

Each player starts with three iron balls, with the object of getting them close to the target, a small wooden ball called a *cochonnet*. The first player tosses the *cochonnet* about 30 feet, then throws the first of his iron balls near the target. The next player takes a turn. As soon as a player's ball is closest, it's the other guy's turn. Once all balls have been lobbed, the score is tallied—the player with the closest ball gets one point for each ball closer to the target than his opponent's. The loser gets zero. Games are generally to 15 points.

A regulation *boules* field is 10 feet by 43 feet, but the game is played everywhere—just scratch a throwing circle in the sand, toss the *cochonnet*, and you're off. Strategists can try to knock the opponent's balls out of position, knock the *cochonnet* itself out of position, or guard their best ball with the other two.

Bus Routes: Smart travelers take advantage of these helpful bus routes (see map on the next page for stop locations): Line #69 runs east–west along rue St. Dominique and serves Les Invalides, Orsay, Louvre, Marais, and Père Lachaise Cemetery (Mon–Sat only—no Sun service; see Bus #69 Sightseeing Tour, page 217). Line #63 runs along the river (the quai d'Orsay), serving the Latin Quarter along boulevard St. Germain to the east (ending at Gare de Lyon), and Trocadéro and the Marmottan Museum to the west. Line #92 runs along avenue Bosquet, north to the Champs-Elysées and Arc de Triomphe (far better than the Métro) and south to the Montparnasse Tower and Gare Montparnasse. Line #87 runs on avenue de la Bourdonnais and serves St. Sulpice, Luxembourg Garden, the Sèvres-Babylone shopping area, the Bastille, and Gare de Lyon (also more convenient than Métro for these destinations). Line #28 runs on boulevard de la Tour Maubourg and serves Gare St. Lazare.

In the Heart of Rue Cler

Many of my readers stay in the rue Cler neighborhood. If you want to disappear into Paris, choose a hotel elsewhere. The first six hotels listed below are within Camembert-smelling distance of rue Cler; the others are within a five- to 10-minute stroll. All hotels listed in the rue Cler area have elevators, air-conditioning, Internet access, and Wi-Fi unless noted ("Wi-Fi only" means there's no computer available, but they do have Wi-Fi).

$$$ Hôtel Relais Bosquet*** is a professional place with

Rue Cler Hotels

- Ⓜ METRO STATION
- Ⓑ BUS STOP w/ ROUTE #
- Ⓟ PARKING
- Ⓣ TAXI STAND

5 MIN. WALK TO SEINE RIVER & AMERICAN CHURCH

RUE DE L'UNIVERSITE

ST. PIERRE

TO EIFFEL TOWER

GRENELLE

ST. JEAN

La Tour Maubourg

ARMY MUSEUM & NAPOLEONS TOMB

Ecole Militaire

TO EIFFEL TOWER

CHAMP DE MARS

KIDS' PLAY AREA

AVE DE TOURVILLE

200 YARDS
200 METERS

❶ Hôtel Relais Bosquet
❷ Hôtel Beaugency
❸ Grand Hôtel Lévêque
❹ Hôtel du Champ de Mars
❺ Hôtel de la Motte Picquet
❻ Hôtels le Tourville & de Turenne
❼ Hôtel Duquesne Eiffel
❽ Hôtel La Bourdonnais
❾ Hôtel de Londres Eiffel
❿ Hôtel Eber Mars
⓫ Hôtel de la Tulipe
⓬ Hôtel Royal Phare
⓭ Hôtel Les Jardins d'Eiffel

⓮ Hôtel Muguet
⓯ Hôtel de l'Empereur
⓰ Hôtel du Cadran
⓱ Best Western Eiffel Park
⓲ Hôtel Kensington
⓳ Hôtel Prince
⓴ Hôtel St. Dominique
㉑ Hôtel de la Tour Eiffel
㉒ SNCF Office
㉓ Com Avenue Internet Café
㉔ Cyber World Internet Café
㉕ Late-Night Groceries (2)
㉖ Launderettes (3)

SLEEPING

generous public spaces and comfortable rooms that feature effective darkness blinds. The staff are politely formal and offer free breakfast (good buffet, including eggs and sausage) to anyone booking direct with this book in 2009 (standard Db-€170, bigger Db-€190, check website for special discounts, extra bed-€25, 19 rue du Champ de Mars, tel. 01 47 05 25 45, fax 01 45 55 08 24, www.relaisbosquet.com, hotel@relaisbosquet.com).

$$$ Hôtel du Cadran***, perfectly located a *boule* toss from rue Cler, welcomes you with a smart lobby, efficient staff, and stylish rooms featuring cool colors, mood lighting, and every comfort (Db-€205–230, 10 percent discount and free breakfast by entering the code "RickSteves" when you book by email or via their website, discount not valid for promotional rates on website; 10 rue du Champ de Mars, tel. 01 40 62 67 00, fax 01 40 62 67 13, www.hotelducadran.com, info@cadranhotel.com).

$$$ Hôtel de la Motte Picquet***, at the corner of rue Cler and avenue de la Motte-Picquet, is an intimate little place with plush rooms at fair prices (Sb-€150, standard Db-€160, bigger Db-€200, 30 avenue de la Motte-Picquet, tel. 01 47 05 09 57, fax 01 47 05 74 36, www.hotel mottepicquetparis.com, book@hotelmottepicquetparis.com).

$$ Hôtel Beaugency***, a solid value on a quieter street a short block off rue Cler, has 30 small rooms with standard furnishings and a lobby you can stretch out in (Sb-€105–115, Db-€115–155, Christelle and Amel promise a 20 percent discount with this book in 2009 if you reserve through the website and enter code word "RICK," 21 rue Duvivier, tel. 01 47 05 01 63, fax 01 45 51 04 96, www.hotel-beaugency .com, infos@hotel-beaugency.com).

Warning: The next two hotels are super values, but very busy with my readers (reserve long in advance).

$$ Grand Hôtel Lévêque** faces rue Cler with red and gray tones, a singing maid, and a sliver-sized slow-dance elevator. This busy hotel has a convivial breakfast/hangout room and four floors. Half the rooms have been renovated and cost more (S-€69–74, Db-€99–109, Tb-€139–144, first breakfast free—a €9 value—with this book in 2009, 29 rue Cler, tel. 01 47 05 49 15, fax 01 45 50 49 36, www.hotel-leveque.com, info@hotel-leveque.com, helpful Christophe and Lidwine).

$ Hôtel du Champ de Mars**, with adorable pastel rooms and serious owners Françoise and Stephane, is a cozy rue Cler option. This plush little hotel has a small-town feel from top to bottom. The rooms are snug but lovingly kept, and single rooms can work as tiny doubles. It's an excellent value despite the lack of air-conditioning. This popular hotel receives an overwhelming number of reservations, so please be patient with them (Sb-€89, Db-€95, Tb-€119, 30 yards off rue Cler at 7 rue du Champ de Mars, tel. 01 45 51 52 30, fax 01 45 51 64 36, www .hotelduchampdemars.com, reservation@hotelduchampdemars.com).

Rue Cler Musts for Temporary Residents

- Watch *boules* action in the afternoon on the Esplanade des Invalides (see sidebar on page 346).
- Relax in the flowery park at the southwest corner of Les Invalides, where avenue de Tourville meets boulevard de la Tour Maubourg.
- See the Eiffel Tower at night, from the park below and from across the river on Trocadéro Square (dinner picnics are best).
- Linger at a rue Cler café and observe daily life.
- Take a Bateaux-Mouches cruise after dark (see page 34).
- Stroll the paths along the river between the d'Alma and Invalides bridges.

Near Rue Cler, Close to Ecole Militaire Métro Stop

The following listings are a five-minute walk from rue Cler, near Métro stop Ecole Militaire or RER: Pont de l'Alma.

$$$ Hôtel le Tourville********, despite its four official stars, is really a top-notch three-star place. It's intimate and classy, from its living-room lobby and vaulted breakfast area to its pretty pastel rooms (small standard Db-€190, superior Db-€250, Db with private terrace-€290, junior suite for 3–4 people-€450, 16 avenue de Tourville, tel. 01 47 05 62 62, fax 01 47 05 43 90, www.hoteltourville.com, hotel@tourville.com).

$$$ Hôtel Duquesne Eiffel*****, a few blocks farther from the action, is hospitable. It offers handsome rooms, a welcoming lobby, and a big, hot breakfast (Db-€170–210, price grows with room size, Tb-€230, breakfast-€13, 23 avenue Duquesne, tel. 01 44 42 09 02, fax 01 44 42 09 08, www.hde.fr, julie@hde.fr).

$$$ Hôtel La Bourdonnais***** is *très* Parisian, mixing an Old World feel with creaky, comfortable rooms and generous public spaces. Its mostly spacious rooms are traditionally decorated (Sb-€140, Db-€175, Tb-€195, Qb-€220, Sophie promises a 10 percent discount with this book through 2009, 111 avenue de la Bourdonnais, tel. 01 47 05 45 42, fax 01 45 55 75 54, www.hotellabourdonnais.fr, hlb@hotel labourdonnais.fr).

$$ Hôtel Prince****, across from the Ecole Militaire Métro stop, has a spartan lobby, ugly halls, and plain-but-acceptable rooms for the price (Sb-€83, Db with shower-€105, Db with tub-€120, Tb-€130, no Internet access, 66 avenue Bosquet, tel. 01 47 05 40 90, fax 01 47 53 06 62, www.hotelparisprince.com, paris@hotel-prince.com).

$$ Hôtel Eber Mars**** has larger-than-most rooms with weathered furnishings, oak-paneled public spaces, and a beam-me-up-Jacques, coffin-sized elevator. Air-conditioning is planned for 2009 (Sb-€100, Db-€118–138, Tb-€170, Qb-€190, 20 percent cheaper Nov–March and July–Aug, first breakfast free with this book in 2009, 117 avenue de la Bourdonnais, tel. 01 47 05 42 30, fax 01 47 05 45 91, www.hotel ebermars.com, reservation@hotelebermars.com, manager Mr. Eber is a wealth of information for travelers).

$ **Hôtel de Turenne**** is modest, with the cheapest air-conditioned rooms I've found and a colorful, open lobby. While the halls are frumpy and the rooms are *très* simple, the price is right. There are five true singles and several connecting rooms good for families (Sb-€69, Db-€79–92, Tb-€112, extra bed-€10, Wi-Fi only, 20 avenue de Tourville, tel. 01 47 05 99 92, fax 01 45 56 06 04, hotel.turenne .paris7@wanadoo.fr).

Near Rue Cler, Closer to Rue St. Dominique (and the Seine)

$$$ **Hôtel de Londres Eiffel***** is my closest listing to the Eiffel Tower and Champ de Mars park. A good value, it offers immaculate, warmly decorated rooms, cozy public spaces, and a service-oriented staff. Show them this book in 2009 for a free Seine cruise (inquire upon arrival). It's less convenient to the Métro (10-min walk) but handy to bus #69 and RER-C: Pont de l'Alma (Sb-€165, Db-€185, Db with Eiffel Tower view-€195–215, Tb-€245, check website for special rates, 1 rue Augerau, tel. 01 45 51 63 02, fax 01 47 05 28 96, www .londres-eiffel.com, info@londres-eiffel.com). The owners also have a good two-star hotel (Hôtel Apollon Montparnasse) in the Montparnasse area, with much lower rates—see www.londres-eiffel.com for details.

$$$ **Hôtel de la Tulipe*****, three blocks from rue Cler toward the river, is pricey but unique. The 20 small but artistically decorated rooms—each one different—come with stylish little bathrooms and surround a seductive, wood-beamed lounge and a peaceful, leafy courtyard (Db-€160, Tb-€180, two-room suite for up to five people-€280, friendly staff, no air-con, no elevator, 33 rue Malar, tel. 01 45 51 67 21, fax 01 47 53 96 37, www.paris-hotel-tulipe.com, hoteldelatulipe@wanadoo.fr).

$$ **Hôtel St. Dominique**** has fair rates, an inviting lobby, a small courtyard, and traditionally decorated rooms—most with minibars and floral wallpaper (Db-€140–160, extra bed-€20, no air-con, no elevator, Wi-Fi only, 62 rue St. Dominique, tel. 01 47 05 51 44, fax 01 47 05 81 28, www.hotelstdominique.com, saint-dominique.reservations @wanadoo.fr).

$ **Hôtel de la Tour Eiffel**** is a terrific two-star value on a quiet street near several of my favorite restaurants. The rooms are well-designed, spotless, and comfortable (snug Db-€79, bigger Db-€105–115, no air-con, no elevator, Wi-Fi only, 17 rue de l'Exposition, tel. 01 47 05 14 75, fax 01 47 53 99 46, www.hotel-toureiffel.com, hte7 @wanadoo.fr).

$ Hôtel Kensington** is a fine budget value close to the Eiffel Tower and run by elegant Daniele. It's an unpretentious place with mostly small, simple, but well-kept rooms (Sb-€62, Db-€79, big Db on back side-€94, Eiffel Tower views for those who ask, no air-con, no Internet access, 79 avenue de la Bourdonnais, tel. 01 47 05 74 00, fax 01 47 05 25 81, www.hotel-kensington.com, hk@hotel-kensington.com).

Near La Tour Maubourg Métro Stop

The next three listings are within two blocks of the intersection of avenue de la Motte-Picquet and boulevard de la Tour Maubourg.

$$$ Hôtel Les Jardins d'Eiffel*,** on a quiet street, feels like the modern motel it is, with professional service, its own parking garage (€24/day), and a spacious lobby. The 81 rooms are all designed for double occupancy (Sb/Db-€170–230; 15 percent Rick Steves discount when you book direct through 2009, or check website for special discounts; 8 rue Amélie, tel. 01 47 05 46 21, fax 01 45 55 28 08, www.hoteljardinseiffel.com, paris@hoteljardinseiffel.com).

$$ Hôtel Muguet,** a peaceful, stylish, immaculate refuge, gives you three-star comfort for a two-star price. This delightful spot offers 43 tasteful rooms, a greenhouse lounge, and a small garden courtyard. The hands-on owner, Catherine, gives her guests a restful and secure home in Paris (Sb-€105, Db with one big bed-€135, twin Db-€135, small Db with view-€160, big Db with view and balcony-€190, Tb-€190, 11 rue Chevert, tel. 01 47 05 05 93, fax 01 45 50 25 37, www.hotelmuguet.com, muguet@wanadoo.fr, gentle Jacqueline runs reception).

$$ Hôtel de l'Empereur** lacks intimacy, but it's spacious and a fair value. Its 38 pleasant rooms come with real wood furniture and views but some noise; fifth-floor rooms have small balconies and Napoleonic views (Db-€108, Tb-€135, Qb-€155, 2 rue Chevert, tel. 01 45 55 88 02, fax 01 45 51 88 54, www.hotelempereur.com, contact@hotelempereur.com).

Lesser Values in the Rue Cler Area

Given how fine this area is, these are acceptable last choices.

$$$ Best Western Eiffel Park** is a dead-quiet concrete business hotel with all the comforts, a relaxing lobby, 36 pleasant if unexceptional rooms, and a rooftop terrace (Db-€240, bigger "luxe" Db-€260, check online for promotional rates, 17 bis rue Amélie, tel. 01 45 55 10 01, fax 01 47 05 28 68, www.eiffelpark.com, reservation@eiffelpark.com).

$ Hôtel Royal Phare,** facing the busy Ecole Militaire Métro stop, is humble and ideal for backpackers. The 34 basic, pink-pastel rooms are unimaginative but sleepable. Rooms on the courtyard are quietest, with peek-a-boo views of the Eiffel Tower from the fifth floor up (Sb-€76, Db with shower-€80–95, Db with tub-€100,

Tb-€105, fridges in rooms, 40 avenue de la Motte-Picquet, tel. 01 47 05 57 30, fax 01 45 51 64 41, www.hotel-royalphare-paris.com, hotel-royalphare@wanadoo.fr, friendly manager Hocin).

IN THE MARAIS NEIGHBORHOOD

(4th arrondissement, Mo: Bastille, St. Paul, and Hôtel de Ville)
Those interested in a more SoHo/Greenwich Village locale should make the Marais their Parisian home. Once a forgotten Parisian backwater, the Marais now is one of Paris' most popular residential, tourist, and shopping areas. This is jumbled, medieval Paris at its finest, where classy stone mansions sit alongside trendy bars, antiques shops, and fashion-conscious boutiques. The streets are a fascinating parade of artists, students, tourists, immigrants, and baguette-munching babies in strollers. The Marais is also known as a hub of the Parisian gay and lesbian scene. This area is *sans doute* livelier (and louder) than the rue Cler area.

In the Marais, you have these major sights close at hand: Picasso Museum, Carnavalet Museum, Victor Hugo's House, the Jewish Art and History Museum, and the Pompidou Center. You're also a manageable walk from Paris' two islands (Ile St. Louis and Ile de la Cité), home to Notre-Dame and Sainte-Chapelle. The Opéra Bastille, Promenade Plantée park, place des Vosges (Paris' oldest square), Jewish Quarter (rue des Rosiers), and nightlife-packed rue de Lappe are also walkable. (For Marais sight descriptions, see page 67; for the Opéra, see page 266.)

Most of my recommended hotels are located a few blocks north of the Marais' main east–west drag, rue St. Antoine/rue de Rivoli.

Tourist Information: The nearest TI is in Gare de Lyon (Mon–Sat 8:00–18:00, closed Sun, all-Paris TI tel. 08 92 68 30 00).

Services: Most banks and other services are on the main street, rue de Rivoli, which becomes rue St. Antoine. Marais **post offices** are on rue Castex and at the corner of rue Pavée and rue des Francs Bourgeois. There's a busy **SNCF Boutique** where you can take care of all train needs on rue St. Antoine at rue de Turenne (Mon–Sat 8:30–20:30, closed Sun). A quieter SNCF Boutique is nearer Gare de Lyon at 5 rue de Lyon (Mon–Sat 8:30–18:00, closed Sun).

Markets: The Marais has two good open-air markets: the sprawling **Marché de la Bastille,** around place de la Bastille (Thu and Sun until 12:30); and the more intimate, untouristy **Marché de la place d'Aligre** (Tue–Sun 9:00–12:00, closed Mon, cross place de la Bastille and walk about 10 blocks down rue du Faubourg St. Antoine, turn right at rue de Cotte to place d'Aligre; or, easier, take Métro line 8 from Bastille in the direction of Créteil-Préfecture, get off at the Ledru-Rollin stop, and walk a few blocks southeast). A small **grocery shop** is open until 23:00 on rue St. Antoine (near intersection with rue Castex). To shop at a Parisian Sears, find the **BHV** next to Hôtel de Ville.

Marais Musts for Temporary Residents

- Have dinner or a drink on place du Marché Ste. Catherine.
- Dine or enjoy a drink on place des Vosges.
- Take a late-night art gallery stroll around place des Vosges.
- Stroll the Promenade Plantée elevated park (see page 70).
- Mix it up with local shoppers one morning at the Marché de la place d'Aligre.
- Walk the Ile St. Louis after dark and enjoy the floodlit view of Notre-Dame (see page 425).

Bookstore: The Marais is home to the friendliest English-language bookstore in Paris, **Red Wheelbarrow.** Penelope sells most of my guidebooks at good prices, and carries a great collection of other books about Paris and France for both adults and children (Mon–Fri 10:00–19:00, Sat 10:00–12:00 & 14:00–19:00, Sun 14:00–18:00, 22 rue St. Paul, Mo: St. Paul, tel. 01 48 04 75 08).

Internet Access: Try **Paris CY** (Mon–Sat 8:00–20:00, Sun 13:00–20:00, 8 rue de Jouy, Mo: St. Paul, tel. 01 42 71 37 37), or **Cyber Cube** (daily 10:00–22:00, 12 rue Daval, Mo: Bastille, tel. 01 49 29 67 67).

Laundry: There are many launderettes; ask your hotelier for the nearest. Here are four you can count on: on impasse Guéménée (north of rue St. Antoine), on rue du Plâtre (just west of rue du Temple), on rue du Petit Musc (south of rue St. Antoine), and on rue Daval (near Cyber Cube).

Métro Connections: Key Métro stops in the Marais are, from east to west: Bastille, St. Paul, and Hôtel de Ville (Sully-Morland, Pont Marie, and Rambuteau stops are also handy). Métro service to the Marais neighborhood is excellent, with direct service to the Louvre, Champs-Elysées, Arc de Triomphe, and La Défense (all on line 1); the rue Cler area and Opéra Garnier (line 8 from Bastille stop); and four major train stations: Gare de Lyon, Gare du Nord, Gare de l'Est, and Gare d'Austerlitz (all accessible from Bastille stop).

Bus Routes: Line #69 on rue St. Antoine takes you eastbound to Père Lachaise Cemetery and westbound to the Louvre, Orsay, and Rodin museums, plus the Army Museum, ending at the Eiffel Tower (Mon–Sat only—no Sun service; see Bus #69 Sightseeing Tour, page 217). Line #86 runs down boulevard Henri IV, crossing Ile St. Louis and serving the Latin Quarter along boulevard St. Germain. Line #87 follows a similar route, but also serves Gare de Lyon to the east and the Eiffel Tower and rue Cler neighborhood to the west. Line #96 runs on rues Turenne and François Miron and serves the Louvre and boulevard St. Germain (near Luxembourg Garden), ending at Gare

SLEEPING

Marais Hotels

1. Hôtel Castex
2. Hôtel Bastille Spéria
3. Hôtel Daval
4. Hôtel Saint-Louis Marais
5. Grand Hôtel Jeanne d'Arc
6. Hôtel Lyon-Mulhouse
7. Hôtel Sévigné
8. Hôtel du 7ème Art
9. Hôtel du Sully
10. MIJE Hostels (3)
11. Hôtel de la Bretonnerie
12. Hôtel Caron de Beaumarchais
13. Hôtel du Vieux Marais
14. Hôtel Beaubourg
15. Hôtel de Nice
16. Hôtel du Loiret
17. BHV Department Store
18. Red Wheelbarrow Books
19. SNCF Boutique (Train Tickets)
20. Late-Night Grocery
21. Cyber Cube Internet Café & Launderette
22. Paris CY Internet Café
23. Launderettes (3)

200 YARDS
200 METERS

PICASSO MUSEUM

JEWISH MUSEUM

NAT'L ARCHIVES

PLACE DE THORIGNY

CARNAVALET MUSEUM

PLACE DES VOSGES

POMPIDOU CENTER

PLACE STRAVINSKY

ST. MERRI

HOTEL DE VILLE

HOLOCAUST MEM.

ST. PAUL

PLACE DE LA BASTILLE

OPERA BASTILLE

BOAT DOCK

SEINE RIVER

to Ile St-Louis

to Notre-Dame

PONT MARIE

QUAI DES CELESTINS

QUAI DE L'HOTEL DE VILLE

to Louvre

M   METRO STATION
T   TAXI STAND
P   PARKING
B   BUS STOP W/ ROUTE #

Montparnasse. Line #65 runs from Gare de Lyon up rue de Lyon, around place de la Bastille, and then up boulevard Beaumarchais to Gare de l'Est and Gare du Nord.

Taxis: You'll find taxi stands on place de la Bastille (where boulevard Richard Lenoir meets the square), on the south side of rue St. Antoine (in front of St. Paul Church), and a quieter one on the north side of rue St. Antoine (where it meets rue Castex).

Near Place des Vosges

$$$ Hôtel Castex*,** a well-managed place with tiled floors and dark wood accents, is well-situated on a quiet street near place de la Bastille. A clever system of connecting rooms allows families total privacy between two rooms, each with its own bathroom. The 30 rooms are narrow but tasteful; it's a good value year-round. Your fourth night is free in August and from November through February, except around New Year's (Sb–€120, Db–€150, Tb–€220, 5 percent discount and free buffet breakfast with this book through 2009, just off place de la Bastille and rue St. Antoine at 5 rue Castex, Mo: Bastille, tel. 01 42 72 31 52, fax 01 42 72 57 91, www.castexhotel.com, info@castexhotel.com).

$$ Hôtel Bastille Spéria*,** a short block off place de la Bastille, offers business-type service. The walls are thin, but the 42 well-configured rooms are modern and comfortable, with big beds (Sb-115, Db–€140–178, child's bed-€20, good buffet breakfast-€13, 1 rue de la Bastille, Mo: Bastille, tel. 01 42 72 04 01, fax 01 42 72 56 38, www .hotel-bastille-speria.com, info@hotel-bastille-speria.com).

$$ Hôtel Saint-Louis Marais** is a little hotel on a quiet residential street between the river and rue St. Antoine. The lobby is inviting and the 19 rooms have character (a few are at street level), but there's no air-conditioning, no elevator, and no Internet access (small Db–€115, standard Db–€140, Tb–€160, parking–€20, 1 rue Charles V, Mo: Sully Morland, tel. 01 48 87 87 04, fax 01 48 87 33 26, www .saintlouismarais.com, slmarais@noos.fr).

$$ Hôtel du 7ème Art,** two blocks south of rue St. Antoine toward the river, is a young, carefree, Hollywood-nostalgia place with a full-service café-bar and Charlie Chaplin murals (but no elevator and pay Wi-Fi). Its 23 good-value rooms have brown 1970s decor, but are comfortable enough. The large rooms are American-spacious (small Db–€93, standard Db–€105, large Db–€120–150, Tb–€140–170, extra bed–€20, 20 rue St. Paul, Mo: St. Paul, tel. 01 44 54 85 00, fax 01 42 77 69 10, www.paris-hotel-7art.com, hotel7art@wanadoo.fr).

$ Grand Hôtel Jeanne d'Arc,** a lovely little hotel with thoughtfully appointed rooms, is ideally located for (and very popular with) connoisseurs of the Marais. It's a fine value and worth booking way ahead (three months in advance, if possible). Sixth-floor rooms have views, and corner rooms are wonderfully bright in the City of Light—though no rooms have air-conditioning and there's no Internet access.

SLEEPING

Rooms on the street can be noisy until the bars close (Sb-€62–89, Db-€89, larger twin Db-€116, Tb-€146, good Qb-€160, 3 rue de Jarente, Mo: St. Paul, tel. 01 48 87 62 11, fax 01 48 87 37 31, information @hoteljeannedarc.com).

$ Hôtel Lyon-Mulhouse**, well-managed by gregarious Nathalia, is located on a busy street barely off place de la Bastille. While less intimate than some, it is a solid deal, with pleasant, relatively large rooms—five are true singles with partial Eiffel Tower views (Sb-€70, Db-€100, Tb-€130, Qb-€150, pay Wi-Fi, 8 boulevard Beaumarchais, Mo: Bastille, tel. 01 47 00 91 50, fax 01 47 00 06 31, www.1-hotel-paris.com, hotelyonmulhouse@wanadoo.fr).

$ Hôtel Daval**, an unassuming place with good rates on the lively side of place de la Bastille, is ideal for night owls. Ask for a quieter room on the courtyard side (Sb-€72, Db-€85, Tb-110, Qb-€125, 21 rue Daval, Mo: Bastille, tel. 01 47 00 51 23, fax 01 40 21 80 26, www.hoteldaval.com, hoteldaval@wanadoo.fr, Didier).

$ Hôtel Sévigné**, run by straight-faced owner Monsieur Mercier, is a snappy little hotel with lavender halls and 30 tidy, comfortable rooms at good prices (Sb-€68, Db-€81–92, Tb-€104; one-night, no-refund policy for any cancellation; no Internet access, 2 rue Malher, Mo: St. Paul, tel. 01 42 72 76 17, fax 01 42 78 68 26, www .le-sevigne.com, contact@le-sevigne.com).

$ Hôtel du Sully, sitting right on rue St. Antoine, is nothing fancy, but it is cheap. The entry is long and narrow, and the rooms are dimly lit but sleepable (Db-€65, Tb-€80, no elevator, no air-con, no Internet access, 48 rue St. Antoine, Mo: St. Paul, tel. 01 42 78 49 32, fax 01 44 61 76 50, www.sullyhotelparis.com, sullyhotel@orange.fr, run by friendly Monsieur Zeroual).

$ *MIJE Youth Hostels:* The Maison Internationale de la Jeunesse et des Etudiants (MIJE) runs three classy old residences that make a budget traveler's dream come true. Each is well-maintained, with simple, clean, single-sex (unless your group takes a whole room), one- to four-bed rooms for travelers of any age. The hostels are **MIJE Fourcy** (biggest and loudest, €11 dinners available with a membership card, 6 rue de Fourcy, just south of rue de Rivoli), **MIJE Fauconnier** (no elevator, 11 rue du Fauconnier), and **MIJE Maubisson** (smallest and quietest, no outdoor terrace, 12 rue des Barres). None has double beds or air-conditioning; all have private showers in every room (all prices per person: Sb-€49, Db-€36, Tb-€32, Qb-€30, credit cards accepted, includes breakfast but not towels, required membership card-€2.50 extra/person, 7-day maximum stay, rooms locked 12:00–15:00, curfew at 1:00 in the morning). They all share the same contact information (tel. 01 42 74 23 45, fax 01 40 27 81 64, www.mije.com, info@mije .com) and Métro stop (St. Paul). Reservations are accepted (six weeks ahead online, 10 days ahead by phone)—though you must show up by noon, or call the morning of arrival to confirm a later arrival time.

Near the Pompidou Center

These hotels are farther west, closer to the Pompidou Center than to place de la Bastille. The Hôtel de Ville Métro stop works well for all of these hotels, unless a closer stop is noted.

$$$ Hôtel Caron de Beaumarchais*** feels like a fluffy folk museum with 20 sweet little rooms and a lobby cluttered with bits from an elegant 18th-century Marais house. Short antique collectors should sleep here (small Db in back-€152, larger Db facing the front-€170, Wi-Fi only, 12 rue Vieille du Temple, tel. 01 42 72 34 12, fax 01 42 72 34 63, www.carondebeaumarchais.com, hotel@caronde beaumarchais.com).

$$ Hôtel de la Bretonnerie***, three blocks from the Hôtel de Ville, makes a fine Marais home. It has a warm, welcoming lobby, chic decor, and 29 tastefully appointed rooms with an antique, open-beam warmth (perfectly good standard "classic" Db-€130, bigger "charming" Db-€160, Db suite-€190, Tb/Qb-€190, Tb/Qb suite-€210, no air-con, between rue Vieille du Temple and rue des Archives at 22 rue Ste. Croix de la Bretonnerie, tel. 01 48 87 77 63, fax 01 42 77 26 78, www.bretonnerie.com, hotel@bretonnerie.com).

$$ Hôtel du Vieux Marais**, with a quirky owner and modern rooms that should all be renovated by the time you get here, is tucked away on a quiet street two blocks east of the Pompidou Center. Say *bonjour* to friendly bulldog Leelou, who runs the small lobby (Sb-€100–115, Db-€120–155, extra bed-€23, Wi-Fi only, just off rue des Archives at 8 rue du Plâtre, Mo: Rambuteau or Hôtel de Ville, tel. 01 42 78 47 22, fax 01 42 78 34 32, www.vieuxmarais.com, hotel@vieux marais.com).

$$ Hôtel Beaubourg*** is a good three-star value on a quiet street in the shadow of the Pompidou Center. The lounge is inviting, and the 28 rooms are wood-beam comfy (standard Db-€140, bigger twin Db-€160, rates vary wildly by season, 11 rue Simon Le Franc, Mo: Rambuteau, tel. 01 42 74 34 24, fax 01 42 78 68 11, www.hotel beaubourg.com, htlbeaubourg@hotelleric.net).

$$ Hôtel de Nice**, on the Marais' busy main drag, is a turquoise-and-fuchsia "Marie-Antoinette-does-tie-dye" spot. Its narrow halls are littered with paintings and layered with carpets, and its 23 Old World rooms have thoughtful touches and tight bathrooms. Twin rooms, which cost the same as doubles, are larger and on the street side—but have effective double-paned windows (Sb-€85, Db-€115, Tb-€140, extra bed-€20, no Internet access, reception on second floor, 42 bis rue de Rivoli, tel. 01 42 78 55 29, fax 01 42 78 36 07, www.hoteldenice.com, contact@hoteldenice.com, laissez-faire management).

$ Hôtel du Loiret* is a centrally located (some noise) and rare Marais budget hotel. If you can get past the lobby, you'll be surprised at how much better the rooms are (S with WC across hall-€50, Db-€70–90, Tb-€100, no air-con, 8 rue des Mauvais Garçons, tel.

01 48 87 77 00, fax 01 48 04 96 56, www.hotel-loiret.fr, hotelduloiret @hotmail.com).

In the Historic Core, on Ile St. Louis

The peaceful, residential character of this river-wrapped island, its brilliant location, and its homemade ice cream have drawn Americans for decades, allowing hotels to charge dearly. There are no budget values here, but the island's coziness and proximity to the Marais, Notre-Dame, and the Latin Quarter help compensate for higher rates. All of the following hotels are on the island's main drag, rue St. Louis-en-l'Ile, where I list several restaurants (see page 390 in the Eating chapter). Use Mo: Pont Marie or Sully-Morland.

$$$ Hôtel du Jeu de Paume**,** occupying a 17th-century tennis center, is the most expensive hotel I list in Paris. When you enter its magnificent lobby, you'll understand why. Greet Scoop, *le chien*, then take a spin in the glass elevator for a half-timbered-tree-house experience. The 30 quite comfortable rooms are carefully designed and *très* tasteful, though small for the price (you're paying for the location and public spaces—check for deals on their website). Most rooms face a small garden; all are pin-drop peaceful (standard Db-€285, larger Db-€370, deluxe Db-€450, 54 rue St. Louis-en-l'Ile, tel. 01 43 26 14 18, fax 01 40 46 02 76, www.jeudepaumehotel.com, info@jeudepaumehotel.com).

$$$ Hôtel de Lutèce*** charges top euro for its island address but comes with a sit-awhile wood-paneled lobby, a fireplace, and warmly designed rooms. Twin rooms are larger and the same price as double rooms (Db-€195, Tb-€235, 65 rue St. Louis-en-l'Ile, tel. 01 43 26 23 52, fax 01 43 29 60 25, www.hoteldelutece.com, info @hoteldelutece.com).

$$$ Hôtel des Deux-Iles*** is bright and colorful, with marginally smaller rooms (Db-€180, Wi-Fi only, 59 rue St. Louis-en-l'Ile, tel. 01 43 26 13 35, fax 01 43 29 60 25, www.2iles.com, hotel.2iles@free.fr).

$$$ Hôtel Saint-Louis*** has less personality but good rooms with parquet floors and comparatively good rates (Db-€145–160, extra bed-€50, Wi-Fi only, 75 rue St. Louis-en-l'Ile, tel. 01 46 34 04 80, fax 01 46 34 02 13, www.hotelsaintlouis.com, slouis@noos.fr).

In the Historic Core, on Ile de la Cité

$$ Hôtel Dieu Hospitel Paris is the only Paris hotel with an Ile de la Cité address. It's located in the oldest city hospital of Paris, on the square in front of Notre-Dame (find the hospital on the map on page 75.) Originally intended to receive families of patients, it now offers rooms for tourists, too. To get a spot in this prime location in front of Notre-Dame, with only 14 rooms, you'll need to book well in advance. You'll be surprised by the modern, comfortable decor and may even forget you're in a hospital (Sb-€104, Db-€115, some rooms have peek-a-boo views of Notre-Dame, 1 place du Parvis, tel. 01 44 32 01 00,

Hotels and Restaurants on Ile St. Louis

View
Metro Station
Batobus Boat Stop

MARAIS
SEINE RIVER
Notre Dame
Deportation Memorial
Pont Marie
TO BASTILLE
Sully Morland

100 YARDS
100 METERS

1. Hôtel du Jeu de Paume
2. Hôtel de Lutèce & Grocery
3. Hôtel des Deux-Iles
4. Hôtel Saint-Louis
5. Le Tastevin Rest.
6. Café Med
7. La Brasserie de l'Ile St. Louis

8. Rests. Nos Ancêtres les Gaulois & La Taverne du Sergeant Recruteur
9. Berthillon Ice Cream (3)
10. Amorino Gelati
11. Good Picnic Spot

www.hotel-hospitel.com, hospitelhoteldieu@wanadoo.fr). Enter the hotel's main entrance, turn right, follow signs to wing B2, and take the elevator to the sixth floor.

LUXEMBOURG GARDEN AREA (ST. SULPICE TO PANTHEON)

(5th and 6th arrondissements, Mo: St. Sulpice, Mabillon, Odéon, and Cluny–La Sorbonne; RER: Luxembourg)
This neighborhood revolves around Paris' loveliest park and offers quick access to the city's best shopping streets and grandest café-hopping. Sleeping in the Luxembourg area offers a true Left Bank experience without a hint of the low-end commotion of the nearby Latin Quarter tourist ghetto. The Luxembourg Garden, boulevard St. Germain, Cluny Museum, and Latin Quarter are all at your doorstep. Here you get the best of both worlds: youthful Left Bank energy and the classic trappings that surround the monumental Panthéon and St. Sulpice Church. Hotels in this central area are more expensive than in other neighborhoods I list.

Having the Luxembourg Garden at your back door allows strolls through meticulously cared-for flowers, a great kids' play area (see Paris with Children chapter, page 403), and a purifying escape from city traffic. Place St. Sulpice offers an elegant, pedestrian-friendly square and quick access to some of Paris' best boutiques (see Shopping chapter, page 407). Sleeping in the Luxembourg area also puts several movie theaters at your fingertips (at Métro stop: Odéon), as well as lively cafés on boulevard St. Germain, rue de Buci, rue des Canettes, place de la Sorbonne, and place de la Contrescarpe, all of which buzz with action until late.

While it takes only 15 minutes to walk from one end of this neighborhood to the other, I've located the hotels by the key monument they are close to (St. Sulpice Church, the Odéon Theater, and the Panthéon). Most hotels are within a five-minute walk of the Luxembourg Garden (and none is more than 15 minutes away).

Services: The nearest **TI** is across the river in Gare de Lyon (Mon–Sat 8:00–18:00, closed Sun, all-Paris TI tel. 08 92 68 30 00). There are two useful **SNCF boutiques** for easy train reservations and ticket purchase: at 79 rue de Rennes and at 54 boulevard Saint-Michel (Mon–Sat 8:30–18:00, closed Sun).

Markets: The colorful street market at the south end of rue Mouffetard is a worthwhile 10- to 15-minute walk from these hotels (Tue–Sat 8:00–12:00 & 15:30–19:00, Sun 8:00–12:00, closed Mon, five blocks south of place de la Contrescarpe, Mo: Place Monge).

Bookstore: The **Village Voice** bookstore carries a full selection of English-language books (including mine), and is near St. Sulpice (Mon 14:00–19:00, Tue–Sat 10:00–19:00, Sun 12:00–18:00, 6 rue Princesse, tel. 01 46 33 36 47, www.villagevoicebookshop.com).

Internet Access: You'll find it at **Le Milk** (always open, between the Luxembourg Garden and Panthéon at 17 rue Soufflot).

Métro Connections: Métro lines 10 and 4 serve this area (10 connects to the Austerlitz train station, and 4 runs to the Montparnasse, Est, and Nord train stations). Neighborhood stops are Cluny-La Sorbonne, Mabillon, Odéon, and St. Sulpice. RER-B (Luxembourg station is handiest) provides direct service to Charles de Gaulle airport and Gare du Nord trains, and access to Orly airport via the Orlybus (transfer at Denfert-Rochereau).

Bus Routes: Buses #63, #86, and #87 run eastbound through this area on boulevard St. Germain, and westbound along rue des Ecoles, stopping on place St. Sulpice. Lines #63 and #87 provide direct connections west to the rue Cler area. Line #63 also serves the Orsay, Army, Rodin, and Marmottan museums to the west and Gare de Lyon to the east. Lines #86 and #87 run east to the Marais, and #87 continues to Gare de Lyon.

Hotels near St. Sulpice Church

These hotels are all within a block of St. Sulpice Church and two blocks from famous boulevard St. Germain. This is nirvana for boutique-minded shoppers—and you'll pay extra for the location. Métro stops St. Sulpice and Mabillon are equally close.

$$$ Hôtel de l'Abbaye**** is a lovely refuge just west of Luxembourg Garden; it's a find for well-heeled connoisseurs of this area. The hotel's four-star luxury includes refined lounges inside and out, with 44 sumptuous rooms and every amenity at surprisingly reasonable rates (Db-€220, bigger Db-€335, suites and apartments available for €390–425, includes breakfast, 10 rue Cassette, tel. 01 45 44 38 11, fax 01 45 48 07 86, www.hotel-abbaye.com, hotel.abbaye @wanadoo.fr).

$$$ Hôtel Relais St. Sulpice***,** on the small street just behind St. Sulpice Church, is a dark little boutique hotel with a cozy lounge and 26 pricey and stylish rooms, most surrounding a leafy glass atrium. Top-floor rooms get more light and are worth requesting (Db-€180–215 depending on size, sauna free for guests, Wi-Fi only, 3 rue Garancière, tel. 01 46 33 99 00, fax 01 46 33 00 10, www.relais -saint-sulpice.com, relaisstsulpice@wanadoo.fr).

$$$ Hôtel la Perle***** is a spendy pearl in the thick of the lively rue des Canettes, a block off place St. Sulpice. At this snappy, modern, business-class hotel, sliding glass doors open onto the traffic-free street, and you're greeted by a fun lobby built around a central bar and atrium (standard Db-€185, bigger Db-€205, luxury Db-€235, check website or call for last-minute deals within five days of your stay, 14 rue des Canettes, tel. 01 43 29 10 10, fax 01 46 34 51 04, www.hotel laperle.com, booking@hotellaperle.com).

$$ Hôtel Bonaparte**,** an unpretentious place wedged between boutiques, is a few steps from place St. Sulpice. While the 29 Old World rooms don't live up to the handsome entry, they're adequately comfortable and generally spacious, with big bathrooms and molded ceilings (Sb-€100–120, Db-€133–155, big Db-€165, Tb-€175, includes breakfast, 61 rue Bonaparte, tel. 01 43 26 97 37, fax 01 46 33 57 67, www.hotelbonaparte.fr, reservation@hotelbonaparte.fr, helpful Fréderic and Eric at reception).

$$ Hôtel le Récamier**,** romantically tucked in the corner of place St. Sulpice, feels like grandma's house—but it has a new owner with big plans. For now, it has flowery wallpaper, dark halls, and clean, simple rooms, but all this should change in 2009. Regardless, the location is ideal (pre-renovation rates: S-€100, Sb-€120, D-€100, Db-€125, bigger Db-€140–150, Tb-€165, Qb-€190, no air-con, no Internet access, 3 bis place St. Sulpice, tel. 01 43 26 04 89, fax 01 46 33 27 73, hotelrecamier@wanadoo.fr).

Hotels and Restaurants near St. Sulpice and the Odéon Theaters

200 YARDS
200 METERS

Ⓑ BUS STOP
Ⓜ METRO STATION

❶ Hôtel Relais St. Sulpice	❿ Le Bistrot Henri IV
❷ Hôtel la Perle	⓫ Lou Pescadou-Chez Julien Rest.
❸ Hôtel Bonaparte	⓬ Chez Georges
❹ Hôtel le Récamier	⓭ Le Café de Flore & Les Deux Magots
❺ Hôtel Michelet Odéon	⓮ Café Bonaparte
❻ Hôtel de l'Abbaye	⓯ Café le Procope
❼ Hôtel Relais Médicis	⓰ SNCF Boutique
❽ La Méditerranée Restaurant	⓱ Village Voice Books
❾ La Crêpe Rit du Clown	⓲ Launderette

SLEEPING

Near the Odéon Theater

These two hotels are between the Odéon Métro stop and Luxembourg Garden (five blocks east of St. Sulpice), and may have rooms when others don't. In addition to the Odéon Métro stop, the RER-B Luxembourg stop is a short walk away.

$$$ Hôtel Relais Médicis*** is perfect in every way—if you've always wanted to live in a Monet painting and can afford it. Its 16 rooms surround a fragrant little garden courtyard and fountain, giving you a countryside break fit for a Medici in the heart of Paris. This delightful refuge is tastefully decorated with floral Old World charm, and is permeated with thoughtfulness (Sb-€172, Db-€208–228, deluxe Db-€258, Tb-€298, €30 cheaper mid-July–Aug and Nov–March, includes extravagant continental breakfast, faces the Odéon Theater at 23 rue Racine, tel. 01 43 26 00 60, fax 01 40 46 83 39, www.relais medicis.com, reservation@relaismedicis.com, eager-to-help Isabelle runs reception).

$$ Hôtel Michelet Odéon** sits shyly in a corner of place de l'Odéon with big windows on the world. It's a decent value in this pricey area, with 24 spacious-but-simple rooms with modern decor and views of the square (Db-€105–130, Tb-€165, Qb-€185, no air-con, pay Wi-Fi, 6 place de l'Odéon, tel. 01 53 10 05 60, fax 01 46 34 55 35, www.hotelmicheletodeon.com, hotel@micheletodeon.com).

Near the Panthéon and Rue Mouffetard

The last two listings below are cheap dives, but in a great area.

$$ Hôtel des Grandes Ecoles*** is idyllic. A private cobbled lane leads to three buildings that protect a flower-filled garden courtyard, preserving a sense of tranquility rare in this city. Its 51 rooms are French-countryside-pretty, spotless, and reasonably spacious, but have no air-conditioning. This romantic spot is deservedly popular, so call well in advance (Db-€115–140 depending on size, extra bed-€20, parking garage-€30, Wi-Fi only, 75 rue du Cardinal Lemoine, Mo: Cardinal Lemoine, tel. 01 43 26 79 23, fax 01 43 25 28 15, www.hotel -grandes-ecoles.com, hotel.grandes.ecoles@wanadoo.fr, mellow Marie speaks English, Mama does not).

$$ Hôtel des 3 Collèges** greets clients with a sterile lobby, claustrophobic hallways, and unimaginative rooms with low ceilings... but decent rates (small Sb-€80, small Db-€110, bigger Db-€130–150, Tb-€132–165, pay Wi-Fi only, 16 rue Cujas, tel. 01 43 54 67 30, fax 01 46 34 02 99, www.3colleges.com, hotel@3colleges.com).

$ Hôtel Cluny Sorbonne** is welcoming and a good deal. It's located in the thick of things across from the famous university and below the Panthéon. Rooms are clean and comfortable, with wood furnishings (standard Db-€95, really big Db-€160, no air-con, 8 rue Victor Cousin, tel. 01 43 54 66 66, fax 01 43 29 68 07, www.hotel -cluny.fr, cluny@club-internet.fr).

Hotels and Restaurants near the Panthéon

SLEEPING

● Metro Station
ℝ R.E.R. Stop

❶ Hôtel Cluny Sorbonne
❷ Hôtel des 3 Collèges
❸ Hôtel des Grandes Ecoles
❹ Port-Royal-Hôtel
❺ Hôtel de L'Espérance
❻ Hôtel de France
❼ Hôtel Central
❽ Young & Happy Hostel
❾ Hotel des Mines
❿ Restaurant Perraudin
⓫ Le Soufflot Café
⓬ Place de la Sorbonne Eateries
⓭ Restaurant Polidor
⓮ Brasserie Bouillon Racine

⓯ Café Delmas
⓰ Le Mouffetard Café
⓱ Les Papillons Restaurant
⓲ Cave de Bourgogne
⓳ Internet Café
⓴ SNCF Boutique

Luxembourg Musts for Temporary Residents

- Pass oodles of time at Luxembourg Garden, sitting in a green chair with your feet propped up on the pond's edge.
- Observe Daniel Roth's Sunday organ mastery up close at St. Sulpice Church (see page 54).
- Join the locals at the only café on place St. Sulpice for a morning coffee or afternoon drink.
- Stroll rue Mouffetard day or night, and stop for a drink on place de la Contrescarpe.
- Window-shop the boutiques between Sèvres-Babylone and St. Sulpice (described on page 412).
- Spend too much for a coffee at a grand café and watch the world go by (see "Les Grands Cafés de Paris," page 397).
- Wander the rue de Buci and find Voltaire's favorite café (see Left Bank Walk, page 233).
- Ponder the history of France in the Panthéon (see page 57).

$ Hôtel Central*, wedged between two cafés, has a smoky, dingy reception, a steep, slippery stairway, dumpy beds, and mildewed rooms. Bottom line: It's youth-hostel cheap, but with a charm only romantic hobos will appreciate. All rooms have showers, but toilets are down the hall (Ss-€33–38, Ds-€46–51, cash only, no elevator, no air-con, no Internet access, 6 rue Descartes, Mo: Cardinal Lemoine, tel. 01 46 33 57 93). Do your best to get a smile out of Madame Pilar, who doesn't speak English.

$ Young & Happy Hostel is easygoing, well-run, and English-speaking, with Internet access, kitchen facilities, and acceptable hostel conditions. It sits dead-center in the rue Mouffetard bar, café, and people action...which can be good or bad (all rates per person: bunk in 4- to 10-bed dorms-€24, in 3- to 5-bed dorms-€26, in double rooms-€28, includes breakfast, sheets-€2.50, credit cards accepted, no air-con, no lockers but safety box at reception, rooms closed 11:00–16:00 but reception stays open, no curfew, 80 rue Mouffetard, Mo: Place Monge, tel. 01 47 07 47 07, fax 01 47 07 22 24, www.youngandhappy.fr, smile@youngandhappy.fr).

Farther Away from the Seine, at the Bottom of Rue Mouffetard

These hotels, away from the Seine and other tourists in an appealing workaday area, offer more room for your euro. They require a longer walk or Métro ride to sights, but often have rooms when

SLEEPING

other accommodations are booked up. Rue Mouffetard is the bohemian soul of this area, running south from its heart—place de la Contrescarpe—to rue de Bazeilles. Two thousand years ago, it was the principal Roman road south to Italy. Today, this small, meandering street has a split personality. The lower half thrives in the daytime as a pedestrian shopping street. The upper half sleeps during the day but comes alive after dark, teeming with bars, restaurants, and nightlife. Use Métro stop Censier-Daubenton or Les Gobelins.

$$ Hôtel de France**, on a busy street, offers modest but comfortable rooms. It's scheduled for a complete makeover that will add air-conditioning, so the information below may change. Currently, the best and quietest rooms are *sur la cour* (on the courtyard), though streetside rooms are acceptable (Sb-€95, Db-€100–115, Tb-€140, 108 rue Monge, Mo: Censier-Daubenton, tel. 01 47 07 19 04, fax 01 43 36 62 34, www .hotelfrancequartierlatin.com, hotel.de.fce@wanadoo.fr).

$ Port-Royal-Hôtel* has only one star, but don't let that fool you. Its 46 rooms are polished top to bottom and have been well-run by the same proud family for 68 years. You could eat off the floors of its spotless, comfy rooms...but you won't find air-conditioning, Internet access, or Wi-Fi. Ask for a room away from the street (S-€41–55, D-€55, Db-€79–89 depending on size, big shower down the hall-€3, cash only, nonrefundable cash deposit required, on busy boulevard de Port-Royal at #8, Mo: Les Gobelins, tel. 01 43 31 70 06, fax 01 43 31 33 67, www.hotelportroyal.fr, portroyalhotel@wanadoo.fr).

$ Hôtel de L'Espérance** is a terrific two-star value. It's quiet, pink, and cushy, with feminine rooms and canopy beds (Sb-€75–80, Db-€80–90, Tb-€107, no Internet access, 15 rue Pascal, Mo: Censier-Daubenton, tel. 01 47 07 10 99, fax 01 43 37 56 19, www.hoteldel esperance.fr, hotel.esperance@wanadoo.fr).

On the South Side of Luxembourg Garden

$ Hôtel des Mines** is less central but worth the walk. Its 50 well-maintained rooms are a good value and come with updated bathrooms and a welcoming lobby (standard Db-€100, bigger Db-€100–120, Tb-€144, Qb-€170, check for Web deals, between Luxembourg and Port-Royal stations on the RER-B line, a 10-min walk from Panthéon, one block past Luxembourg Garden at 125 boulevard St. Michel, tel. 01 43 54 32 78, fax 01 46 33 72 52, www.hoteldesminesparis.com, hotel@hoteldesminesparis.com).

NEAR PLACE DE LA REPUBLIQUE

(10th and 11th arrondissements, Mo: République, Oberkampf)
The three budget accommodations below are in the neighborhood north of the Marais, between place de la République and Canal St. Martin. This area is untouristy, young, and *très* international (read

Budget Hotels Near Place de la République

- ❶ Hôtel de Nevers
- ❷ Auberge de Jeunesse Jules Ferry (Hostel)
- ❸ Hostel Absolute Paris
- ❹ La Marine Restaurant

"melting pot"). It's definitely unpolished (and edgy to some) and more remote—but if you can put up with some rough edges and don't mind using the Métro and buses for all your sightseeing, you'll find some good deals here.

$ Hôtel de Nevers* is a cheap one-star hotel with a historic elevator and pretty good rooms for the price, despite the dim room lighting (D-€44–50 with free shower down the hall, Ds-€55, Db-€65, Tb-€75, Qb-€84, 53 rue de Malte, tel. 01 47 00 56 18, fax 01 43 57 77 39, www.hoteldenevers.com, reservation@hoteldenevers.com).

$ Auberge de Jeunesse Jules Ferry is a relaxed youth hostel right on the parkway that runs above Canal St. Martin. Arrive before 10:00 or book online to be assured a room (€22 per bunk in pleasant, sink-equipped 2-, 4-, or 6-bed rooms, higher rates for non-members; small lockers available, rooms closed 10:30–14:00, 8 boulevard Jules Ferry, tel. 01 43 57 55 60, fax 01 43 14 82 09, www.hihostels.com).

$ Hostel Absolute Paris is part two-star hotel, part four-beds-per-room hostel. It faces the canal and is filled with backpackers. The rooms are industrial-strength clean and adequate—but only worth considering if you want dorm-style accommodations (€24 each in 4-bed room with private bathroom, Db-€85, Tb-€100, includes breakfast, Internet access, 1 rue de la Fontaine du Roi, tel. 01 47 00 47 00, fax 01 47 00 47 02, www.absolute-paris.com, bonjour@absolute -paris.com).

FOR LONGER STAYS

Staying a week or longer? Consider the advantages that come with renting a furnished apartment. Complete with a small, equipped kitchen and living room, this option is also great for families on shorter visits. Among the many English-speaking organizations ready to help, the following have proven most reliable. Their websites are generally excellent, and essential to understanding your options. Read the conditions of rental carefully.

Most of the agencies listed below are middlemen, offering an ever-changing selection of private apartments for rent on a weekly basis (or longer). If staying a month or longer, save money by renting directly from the apartment owners. Check the housing section in the ad-filled paper *France-USA Contacts* (available at the American Church and elsewhere in Paris), or check out www.fusac.fr. Some readers have reported good success using Craig's List (www.craigslist.org).

Paris Perfect is a French-owned, London-based business that seeks the "perfect apartment" for its clients, and is selective about what they offer. Their pricey apartments (which run about €300/night) are named for wines, and their service gets rave reviews (to reach their British tel. & fax from the US, call 011-44-20-7938-2939, fax 011-44-20-7937-2115, www.parisperfect.com).

Paris Appartements Services rents studios (€100–170/night) and one-bedroom apartments (€140–230/night) in central neighborhoods (20 rue Bachaumont, tel. 01 40 28 01 28, fax 01 40 28 92 01, www.paris-apts.com).

Home Rental Service has been in business for 14 years and offers a big selection of apartments throughout Paris with no agency fees (120 Champs-Elysées, tel. 01 42 25 65 40, fax 01 42 25 65 45, www.homerental.fr).

Locaflat offers accommodations ranging from studios to five-room apartments, with occasional specials online (63 avenue de la Motte-Picquet, tel. 01 43 06 78 79, fax 01 40 56 99 69, www.locaflat.com).

Immo Marais has over 100 apartments in all sizes in the Marais (60 rue Roi de Sicile, tel. 01 42 74 06 17, www.immomarais.fr).

Paris Home is a small outfit with only two studios, but both are located on rue Amélie in the heart of the rue Cler area. Each has modern furnishings and laundry facilities. Friendly Slim, the owner, is the best part (€490/week, one-week minimum, special rates for longer stays, credit cards accepted, free Internet access and US or France telephone calls, free maid service, tel. 06 19 03 17 55, http://parishome2000.free.fr, parishome2000@yahoo.fr).

EATING

The Parisian eating scene is kept at a rolling boil. Entire books (and lives) are dedicated to the subject. Paris is France's wine-and-cuisine melting pot. While it lacks a style of its own (only French onion soup is truly Parisian), it draws from the best of France. Paris could hold a gourmet Olympics and import nothing.

Parisians eat long and well. Relaxed lunches, three-hour dinners, and endless hours of sitting in outdoor cafés are the norm. Local cafés, cuisine, and wines become a highlight of any Parisian adventure—sightseeing for your palate. Even if the rest of you is sleeping in a cheap hotel, let your taste buds travel first-class in Paris. (They can go coach in London.)

You can eat well without going broke, but choose carefully—you're just as likely to blow a small fortune on a mediocre meal as you are to dine wonderfully for €20. Follow the suggestions offered in this chapter, and you'll have a better dining experience.

The no-smoking revolution hit France last year, when a new law mandated that all café and restaurant interiors be smoke-free. Today the only smokers you'll find are outside (under space heaters in cool weather).

Waiters probably won't overwhelm you with friendliness. Notice how hard they work. They almost never stop. Cozying up to clients (French or foreign) is probably the last thing on their minds. To get a waiter's attention, say, "*S'il vous plaît*" (see voo play)—"please."

Breakfast

You'll almost always have the option of breakfast at your hotel, which is pleasant and convenient. *Petit déjeuner* (puh-tee day-zhuh-nay) is typically café au lait, hot chocolate, or tea; a roll with butter and marmalade; and a croissant. Some hotels offer only this classic continental breakfast for about €8–15, while others offer buffet breakfasts for a few euros more (cereal, yogurt, fruit, cheese, croissants, juice, and the occasional hard-boiled egg)—which I usually spring for.

If all you want is coffee or tea and a croissant, the corner café is cheaper (though you get more coffee at your hotel). It's fine to buy a croissant or roll at a bakery and eat it with your cup of coffee at a café. Better still, some bakeries offer worthwhile breakfast deals with juice, croissant, and coffee or tea for about €4. If you crave eggs for breakfast, drop into a café and order *une omelette* or *œufs sur le plat* (fried eggs). You could also buy or bring from home plastic bowls and spoons, buy a box of cereal and a small box of milk, and eat in your room before heading out for coffee.

Picnics and Snacks

Great for lunch or dinner, Parisian picnics can be first-class affairs and adventures in high cuisine. Be daring. Try the smelly cheeses, ugly pâtés, sissy quiches, and minuscule (usually drinkable) yogurts. Local shopkeepers are accustomed to selling small quantities of produce. Try the tasty salads-to-go, and ask for a plastic fork *(une fourchette en plastique)*. A small container is *une barquette*.

Gather supplies early for a picnic lunch; you'll probably visit several small stores to assemble a complete meal, and many close at noon for their lunch break. Look for a *boulangerie*, a *crémerie* or *fromagerie* (for cheeses), a *charcuterie* (for deli items, meats, and pâtés), an *épicerie* or *magasin d'alimentation* (small grocery store with veggies, drinks, and so on), and a *pâtisserie* (for delicious pastries). For fine picnic shopping, check out the street market recommendations in the Shopping chapter. While wine is taboo in public places in the US, it's *pas de problème* in France.

Supermarchés offer less color and cost, more efficiency, and adequate quality. Department stores often have supermarkets in the basement, along with top-floor cafeterias offering not-really-cheap but low-risk, low-stress, what-you-see-is-what-you-get meals. For a quick meal to go, look for food stands and bakeries selling take-out sandwiches and drinks. For an affordable sit-down meal, try a *crêperie* or café.

In stores, unrefrigerated soft drinks and beer are half the price of cold drinks. Milk and boxes of fruit juice are the most inexpensive. Avoid buying drinks to go at streetside stands; you'll find them far cheaper in a shop. Try to keep a water bottle with you. Water quenches your thirst better and cheaper than anything you'll find in a store or café. I drink tap water in Paris and use that to refill my bottle. You'll pass many fountains on Paris streets with good water (but if it says *non potable*, it's not drinkable).

For good lunch picnic sites, consider these suggestions: The Palais Royal (across place du Palais Royal from the Louvre) is a good spot for a peaceful, royal picnic, as is the little triangular Henry

IV park on the west tip of Ile de la Cité. The pedestrian pont des Arts bridge, across from the Louvre, has great views and plentiful benches, as does the Champ de Mars park below the Eiffel Tower. For great people-watching, try the Pompidou Center (by the *Homage to Stravinsky* fountains), the elegant place des Vosges (closes at dusk), the gardens behind Les Invalides, and the Tuileries and Luxembourg gardens (parks close at dusk).

Sandwiches, Quiche, and Pizza

Across Paris, you'll find bakeries and small stands selling baguette sandwiches, quiche, and pizza-like items to go for €4–6. Usually filling and tasty, they also streamline the picnic process. (If you don't want your sandwich drenched in mayonnaise, ask for it *sans mayonnaise;* sahn my-oh-nehz). Here are some sandwiches you'll see:

Jambon beurre (zhahn-bohn bur): Ham and butter (boring for most).

Fromage beurre (froh-mahzh bur): Cheese and butter (white on white on beige).

Poulet crudités (poo-lay krew-dee-tay): Chicken with tomatoes, lettuce, carrots, and cucumbers.

Thon crudités (tohn krew-dee-tay): Tuna with tomatoes, lettuce, carrots, and cucumbers.

Jambon crudités (zhahn-bohn krew-dee-tay): Ham with tomatoes, lettuce, carrots, and cucumbers.

Jambon or **Poulet à la provençal** (zhahn-bohn/poo-lay ah lah proh-vehn-sahl): Ham or chicken, usually with marinated peppers, tomatoes, and eggplant. I love these.

Look also for grilled panini sandwiches *à la italienne.*

Café Culture

French cafés (and brasseries) provide budget-friendly meals and a relief from museum and church overload. At a café, you can feel free to order only a bowl of soup and a salad or *plat* (main course) for lunch or dinner.

Cafés generally open by 7:00, but closing hours vary. Unlike restaurants, which open only for lunch and dinner, most cafés serve food throughout the day (though with a more limited menu than at restaurants)—making them the best option for a late lunch or an early dinner. In general, head for a café if you're hungry when restaurants are closed (late afternoon).

If you're a novice, it's easier to sit and feel comfortable when you know the system. Check the price list first, which by law must be posted prominently. You'll see two sets of prices; you'll pay more for the same drink if you're seated at a table *(salle)* than if you're seated at the bar or counter *(comptoir)*. At large cafés, outdoor tables are most expensive, and prices can rise after 22:00. For tips on beverages, see the next page.

Coffee and Tea Lingo

By law, the waiter must give you a glass of tap water with your coffee or tea if you request it; ask for *"un verre d'eau, s'il vous plaît"* (uhn vayr doh, see voo play).

Coffee

French	Pronounced	English
un express	uh nex-press	shot of espresso
une noisette	oon nwah-zeht	espresso with a shot of milk
café au lait	kah-fay oh lay	coffee with lots of steamed milk (closest to an American latte)
un grand crème	uhn grahn krehm	big café au lait
un petit crème	uhn puh-tee krehm	small café au lait
un café allongé (a.k.a. *café longue)*	uhn kah-fay ah-lohn-zhay (kah-fay lohn)	closest to an American cup of coffee
un décaffiné	uhn day-kah-fee-nay	decaf—available for any of the above drinks

Tea

French	Pronounced	English
un thé nature	uhn tay nah-tour	plain tea
un thé au lait	uhn tay oh lay	tea with milk
un thé citron	uhn tay see-trohn	tea with lemon
une infusion	oon an-few-see-yohn	herbal tea

Standard Menu Items: *Croque monsieur* (grilled ham and cheese sandwich) and *croque madame* (*monsieur* with a fried egg on top) are generally served day and night. Sandwiches are least expensive, but

plain—and much better—at the *boulangerie* (bakery). To get more than a piece of ham *(jambon)* on a baguette, order a sandwich *jambon crudité*, which means garnished with veggies. Omelets come lonely on a plate with a basket of bread. The daily special—*plat du jour* (plah dew zhoor), or just *plat*—is your fast, hearty, and garnished hot plate for €13–18. At most cafés, feel free to order only *entrées* (which in French means the starter course); many find these lighter and more interesting than a main course. A vegetarian can enjoy a tasty, filling meal by ordering two *entrées.* Regardless of what you order, bread is free; to get more, just hold up your bread basket and ask, *"Encore, s'il vous plaît."*

Salads: They're typically large—one is perfect for lunch or a light dinner, or split between two people as a first course. The classics include:

Salade niçoise (nee-swahz), a specialty from Nice, usually features green salad topped with green beans, boiled potatoes, tomatoes, anchovies, olives, hard-boiled eggs, and lots of tuna.

Salade au chèvre chaud is a mixed green salad topped with warm goat cheese and toasted croutons.

Salade composée is "composed" of any number of ingredients, such as *lardons* (bacon), *comté* (a Swiss-style cheese), *roquefort* (blue cheese), *œuf* (egg), *noix* (walnuts), and *jambon* (ham, generally thinly sliced).

Salade paysanne usually comes with potatoes *(pommes de terre)*, walnuts *(noix)*, tomatoes, ham, and egg.

Salade aux gesiers has chicken livers.

To get salad dressing on the side, order *la sauce à part* (lah sohs ah par).

Wine and Beer: House wine at the bar is cheap (about €3 per glass, cheapest by the pitcher—*pichet,* pee-shay), and the local beer is cheaper on tap *(une pression;* oon pres-yohn) than in the bottle *(bouteille;* boo-teh-ee). France's best beer is Alsatian; try Kronenbourg or the heavier Pelfort (even heavier is the Belgian beer Leffe). *Une panaché* (oon pan-a-shay) is a refreshing French shandy (7-Up and beer).

Soft Drinks: For a fun, bright, nonalcoholic drink of 7-Up with mint syrup, order *un diablo menthe* (uhn dee-ah-bloh mahnt). Kids love the local lemonade *(citron pressé;* see-trohn preh-say, you'll need to add sugar) and the flavored syrups mixed with bottled water *(sirops à l'eau;* see-roh ah loh). The ice cubes melted after the last Yankee tour group left.

Tipping

All cafés and restaurants include a service charge in the bill (usually 15 percent, referred to as *service compris* or *prix net*), but it's polite to round up for a drink or meal well-served. This bonus tip is usually about five percent of the bill (e.g., if your bill is €19, leave €20). If you want the waiter to keep the change when you pay, say, *"C'est bon"* (say bohn), meaning, "It's good." Tipping is not necessary if you order food at a counter.

Restaurants

Choose restaurants filled with locals. Consider my suggestions and your hotelier's opinion, but trust your instinct. If a restaurant doesn't post its prices outside, move along. Refer to my restaurant recommendations to get a sense of what a reasonable meal should cost.

Restaurants open for dinner around 19:00, and small local favorites get crowded after 21:00. To minimize crowds, go early (around

Why French Women Don't Get Fat

Americans are recognized by their large rear ends. And French women just don't get fat. At least those are the popular images. If it's true that French women aren't fat, the reason is lifestyle and what is—to them—common sense: They eat small quantities. Rather than snack, they smoke. They avoid processed food and fast food. They drink lots of water. Their lifestyle—less time in cars and in front of TVs—just naturally includes lots of exercise. And they fall in love with abandon.

But recently, the French have measured a 20 percent increase in obesity, especially among children. The government has begun a propaganda campaign to promote eating fruits and vegetables. And, in a bold move, they're taking vending machines out of schools.

19:30). Many restaurants close Sunday and Monday.

If a restaurant serves lunch, it generally begins at 11:30 and goes until 14:00, with last orders taken at about 13:30. If you're hungry when restaurants are closed (late afternoon), go to a café—most offer a minimal menu (or more) all day; for more information, see "Café Culture," page 372.

If you ask for the *menu* (muh-noo) at a restaurant, you won't get a list of dishes; you'll get a fixed-price meal. *Menus*, which include three or four courses, are generally a good value if you're hungry: You get your choice of soup, appetizer, or salad; your choice of three or four main courses with vegetables; plus a cheese course and/or a choice of desserts. Service is included (*service compris* or *prix net*), but wine and other drinks are generally extra. Restaurants that offer a *menu* for lunch often charge about €5 more for the same *menu* at dinner.

Many restaurants offer cheaper versions of their *menu*, with a choice of two courses, rather than three or four. These pared-down *menus* are commonly called *formules* and feature an *entrée et plat* (first course and main dish), or *plat et dessert* (main dish and dessert). Most restaurants offer a reasonable *menu-enfant* (kids' menu).

Ask for *la carte* (lah kart) if you want to see a menu and order à la carte, as the locals do. Request the waiter's help in deciphering the French. Consider his or her recommendations and anything *de la maison* (of the house), as long as it's not an organ meat *(tripes, rognons, or andouillette)*. Galloping gourmets should bring a menu translator; the *Marling Menu-Master* is good. The *Rick Steves' French Phrase Book*, with a Menu Decoder, works well for most travelers. The wines are often listed in a separate *carte des vins*.

Remember that in France, an *entrée* is the appetizer, and *le plat* or *le plat du jour* (plate of the day) is the main course with vegetables (usually €13–18). If all you want is a salad or soup, find a café instead.

French Specialties by Region

Alsace

The German influence is obvious: sausages, potatoes, onions, and sauerkraut. Look for *choucroute garnie* (sauerkraut and sausage—although it seems a shame to eat it in a fancy restaurant), the more traditionally Alsatian *Baeckeoffe* (potato, meat, and onion stew), *Rösti* (an oven-baked potato-and-cheese dish), fresh trout, foie gras, and *flammekueche* (a paper-thin pizza topped with bacon, onions, and sour cream).

Burgundy

Considered by many to be France's best, Burgundian cuisine is peasant cooking elevated to an art. This wine region excels in *coq au vin* (chicken with wine sauce), *bœuf bourguignon* (beef stew cooked with wine, bacon, onions, and mushrooms), *œufs en meurette* (eggs poached in red wine), *escargots* (snails), and *jambon persillé* (ham with garlic and parsley).

Basque

Mixing influences from the mountains, sea, Spain, and France, it's dominated by seafood, tomatoes, and red peppers. Look for anything *basquaise* (cooked with tomatoes, eggplant, red peppers, and garlic), such as *thon* (tuna) or *poulet* (chicken). Try *piperade,* a dish combining peppers, tomatoes, garlic, and eggs (ham optional), and *ttoro,* a seafood stew that is the Basque answer to bouillabaisse.

Languedoc and Périgord

The cuisine of these regions is referred to in Paris as "Southwest cuisine" *(cuisine du sudouest)*. This hearty peasant cooking uses full-bodied red wines and lots of duck. Try the hearty *cassoulet* (white bean, duck, and sausage stew), *canard* (duck), *pâté de*

Parisians are willing to pay for bottled water with their meal (*eau minérale;* oh mee-nay-rahl) because they prefer the taste over tap water. If you prefer a free pitcher of tap water, ask for *une carafe d'eau* (oon kah-rahf doh). Otherwise, you may unwittingly buy bottled water. To get inexpensive wine at a restaurant, order table wine in a pitcher (*un pichet;* uhn pee-shay), rather than a bottle (though finer restaurants usually offer only bottles of wine). If all you want is a glass of wine, ask for *un verre de vin* (uhn vehr duh van). A half carafe of wine is *un demi-pichet* (uhn duh-mee pee-shay), a quarter carafe (ideal for one) is *un quart* (uhn kar).

PARISIAN CUISINE

There is no "Parisian cuisine" to speak of. The fun part of dining in Paris is that you can sample fine cuisine from throughout France. Many restaurants specialize in a particular region's cuisine (I list foie gras (goose-liver pâté), *pommes sarladaise* (potatoes fried in duck fat), *truffes* (truffles, earthy mushrooms), and anything with *noix* (walnuts).

Normandy and Brittany
Normandy specializes in cream sauces, sea salt, organ meats (sweetbreads, tripe, and kidneys—the "gizzard salads" are great), and seafood *(fruits de mer)*. Dairy products are big here. Munch some *moules* (mussels) and *escalope normande* (veal in cream sauce). Brittany is famous for its oysters and crêpes. Both regions use lots of *cidre* (hard apple cider) in their cuisine.

Provence
The almost extravagant use of garlic, olive oil, herbs, and tomatoes makes Provence's cuisine France's liveliest. To sample it, order anything *à la provençale*. Among the area's spicy specialties are ratatouille (a thick mixture of vegetables in an herb-flavored tomato sauce), *brandade* (a salt cod, garlic, and cream mousse), aioli (a garlicky mayonnaise often served atop fresh vegetables), tapenade (a paste of puréed olives, capers, anchovies, herbs, and sometimes tuna), *soupe au pistou* (vegetable soup with basil, garlic, and cheese), and *soupe à l'ail* (garlic soup).

Riviera
The Côte d'Azur gives Provence's cuisine a Mediterranean flair. Local specialties are bouillabaisse (the spicy seafood stew/soup that seems worth the cost only for those with a seafood fetish), *bourride* (a creamy fish soup thickened with aioli garlic sauce), and *salade niçoise* (nee-swahz; a tasty tomato, potato, olive, anchovy, and tuna salad).

restaurants specializing in food from Provence, Burgundy, Alsace, Normandy, Dordogne, Languedoc, and the Basque region). So be a galloping gourmet and try a few of these regional restaurants (see "French Specialties by Region," above).

The French eat dinner in courses, rather than all on one plate. For general, classic, anywhere-in-France dishes, consider these suggestions:

First Course *(Entrée)*
Soupe à l'oignon: Hot, salty, and filling, French onion soup is a beef broth served with cheesy croutons floating on top.

Salade au chèvre chaud: A mixed green salad topped with warmed goat cheese and croutons.

Salade niçoise: While famous as a specialty from Nice (in southern France), this classic salad is served throughout the country. There are many versions, though most include a base of green salad topped with green beans, boiled potatoes (sometimes rice), tomatoes (sometimes corn), anchovies, lots of tuna, and hard-boiled eggs.

Crudités: A mix of raw and lightly cooked fresh vegetables, usually including grated carrots, celery root, tomatoes, and beets, often with a hefty dose of vinaigrette dressing. If you want the dressing on the side, say, *"La sauce à côté, s'il vous plaît"* (lah sohs ah koh-tay, see voo play).

Escargots: Snails cooked in parsley-garlic butter. You don't even have to like the snail itself. Just dipping your bread in garlic butter is more than satisfying. Prepared a variety of ways, the classic is *à la bourguignon* (served in their shells).

Huîtres: Oysters served raw any month and delivered fresh from nearby Brittany. This food is particularly popular at Christmas and New Year's, when every café seems to have overflowing baskets lining the storefront.

Pâtés and Terrines: Slowly cooked ground meat (usually pork, though chicken and rabbit are also common) that is highly seasoned and served in slices with mustard and *cornichons* (little pickles). Pâtés are smoother than the similarly prepared but chunkier *terrines*.

Foie gras: Rich and buttery in consistency, this pâté is made from the swollen livers of force-fed geese (or ducks, in *foie de canard*). Spread it on bread with your knife, and do not add mustard to this pâté dish.

Main Course *(Plat Principal)*

Coq au vin: This Burgundian dish is rooster marinated ever so slowly in red wine, then cooked until it melts in your mouth. It's served (often family-style) with vegetables.

Bœuf bourguignon: Another Burgundian specialty, this classy beef stew is cooked slowly in red wine, then served with onions, potatoes, and mushrooms.

Steak: Referred to as *pavé, bavette,* or *entrecôte,* French steak is usually thinner than American steak and is always served with sauces (*au poivre* is a pepper sauce, *une sauce roquefort* is a cheese sauce). You will also see *steak haché,* which is a lean, gourmet hamburger patty served *sans* bun. By American standards, the French undercook meats: rare, or *saignant* (seh-nyahn), is close to raw; medium, or *à point* (ah pwan), is rare; and well-done, or *bien cuit* (bee-yehn kwee), is medium.

Steak tartare: This wonderfully French dish is for adventurous types only. It's very lean, raw hamburger served with spices (usually Tabasco, onions, salt, and pepper on the side) and topped with a raw egg.

Gigot d'agneau: Leg of lamb served in many styles, often with white beans. The best lamb is *pré salé*, which means the lamb has been raised in salt-marsh lands (like at Mont St. Michel).

Confit de canard: This Southwest favorite is duck that has been preserved in its own fat, then cooked in its fat, and often served with potatoes cooked in the same fat. Not for dieters.

Saumon: You'll see salmon dishes served in various styles. The salmon usually comes from the North Sea and is always served with sauce, most commonly a sorrel *(oseille)* sauce.

Cheese Course *(Le Fromage)*

In France, the cheese course is served just before (or instead of) dessert. It not only helps with digestion, it gives you a great opportunity to sample the tasty regional cheeses. There are more than 400 different French cheeses to try. Some restaurants will offer a cheese platter, from which you select a few different cheeses. A good cheese plate has four types: hard cheese (like Emmentaler—a.k.a. Swiss cheese), a flowery cheese (like Brie or Camembert), a bleu or Roquefort cheese, and a goat cheese.

Cheeses most commonly served in Paris are *brie de Meaux* (mild and creamy, from just outside Paris), Camembert (semi-creamy and pungent, from Normandy), *chèvre* (goat cheese with a sharp taste, usually from the Loire), and Roquefort (strong and blue-veined, from south-central France).

If you'd like a little of several types of cheese from the cheese plate, say, *"Un assortiment, s'il vous plaît"* (uhn ah-sor-tee-mahn, see voo play). If you serve yourself from the cheese plate, observe French etiquette and keep the shape of the cheese. It's best to politely shave off a slice from the side or cut small wedges.

Dessert *(Le Dessert)*

Crème brulée: A rich, creamy, dense, caramelized custard.

Tarte tatin: This is apple pie like grandma never made, with caramelized apples cooked upside down, but served upright.

Mousse au chocolat: Chocolate mousse.

Ile flottante: This lighter dessert consists of islands of meringue floating on a pond of custard sauce.

Profiteroles: Cream puffs filled with vanilla ice cream, smothered in warm chocolate sauce.

Tartes: Narrow strips of fresh fruit, baked in a crust and served in thin slices (without ice cream).

Sorbets: Known to us as sherbets, these light, flavorful, and fruity ices are sometimes laced with brandy.

Café: If you order espresso, it will always come after dessert. To have coffee with dessert, ask for *"café avec le dessert"* (kah-fay ah-vehk luh day-sayr). See the list of coffee terms on page 373.

RESTAURANTS

My recommendations are centered on the same great neighborhoods listed in the Sleeping chapter; you can come home exhausted after a busy day of sightseeing and find a good selection of restaurants right around the corner. And evening is a fine time to explore any of these delightful neighborhoods, even if you're sleeping elsewhere.

To save piles of euros, review the budget eating tips above and restaurant recommendations below. Remember that service is almost always included (so little or no tipping is required—although it's nice to round up for good service), and consider dinner picnics (great take-out dishes available at charcuteries). Smokers dominate outdoor tables.

In the Rue Cler Neighborhood

The rue Cler neighborhood caters to its residents. Its eateries, while not destination places, have an intimate charm. I've provided a full range of choices from cozy ma-and-pa diners, to small and trendy boutique restaurants, to classic, big, and boisterous bistros. You'll generally find great dinner *menus* for €20–30, *plats du jour* for around €14–18, and meal-sized salads for €10–12. Eat early with tourists or late with locals. For all restaurants listed in this area, use the Ecole Militaire Métro stop (unless another station is listed).

Close to Ecole Militaire, Between Rue de la Motte-Picquet and Rue de Grenelle

$$$ **Le Florimond** is good for a special occasion. The setting, while spacious and quiet, is also intimate and welcoming. Locals come for classic French cuisine with elegant indoor or breezy streetside seating. Friendly English-speaking Laurent—with his playful ties changing daily—serves one small room of tables gracefully and loves to help with suggestions. Try the explosively tasty stuffed cabbage (€36 *menu*, closed Sun, reservations smart, good house wine by the carafe, afford-able wine selection, 19 avenue de la Motte-Picquet, tel. 01 45 55 40 38).

$$ **Restaurant Pasco,** perched elegantly overlooking Les Invalides, is semi-dressy, with a special enthusiasm for fish. The owner, Pasco Vignes, attracts a local clientele with his modern Mediterranean cuisine, generously endowed with olive oil. While there's some outdoor seating, I'd come here for the cozy redbrick interior (€20 *plats*, €20–34 *menus*, daily, reservations smart, 74 boulevard de la Tour Maubourg, Mo: La Tour Maubourg, tel. 01 44 18 33 26).

$$ **La Terrasse du 7ème** is a sprawling, happening café with grand outdoor seating and a living room–like interior with comfy love seats. Located on a corner, it overlooks a busy intersection with a constant parade of people. Chairs are set up facing the street, as a meal here is like dinner theater—and the show is slice-of-life Paris. Consider their Spring Plate for an adventurous gourmet starter (€16

> # Restaurant Price Code
>
> To help you choose among these listings, I've divided the res-
> taurants into three categories, based on the price for a typical
> meal without wine.
>
> **$$$** **Higher Priced**—Most meals €35 or more.
> **$$** **Moderately Priced**—Most meals between €20–35.
> **$** **Lower Priced**—Most meals under €20.

daily *plats*, no fixed-price *menu*, good €13 *salade niçoise*, daily until
at least 24:00 and sometimes until 2:00 in the morning, at Ecole
Militaire Métro stop, tel. 01 45 55 00 02).

$$ Café le Bosquet is a modern, chic Parisian brasserie with
dressy waiters and your choice of the mod-elegant interior or sidewalk
tables on a busy street. Come here for a bowl of French onion soup, or
a full three-course *menu* with good fish and meat choices. Say *bonsoir*
to owner Jean-François, who likes to be called Jeff. Escargots are great
here; the house red wine is plenty good, too (€15 *plats*, closed Sun, res-
ervations smart Fri–Sat, fun menu includes vegetarian options, corner
of rue du Champ de Mars and avenue Bosquet, 46 avenue Bosquet,
tel. 01 45 51 38 13).

$ Café du Marché boasts the best seats, coffee, and prices on
rue Cler. The owner's philosophy: Brasserie on speed—crank out
good food at great prices to trendy locals and savvy tourists. It's high-
energy, with waiters who barely have time to smile...*très* Parisian. This
place is ideal if you want to eat an inexpensive, one-course meal among
a commotion of people and are willing to go with the small, fresh
menu. The chalkboard lists your choices: good, hearty €10 salads or
more filling €10 *plats du jour* (Mon–Sat 11:00–23:00, Sun 11:00–17:00,
arrive before 19:30 for dinner—it's packed at 21:00, and service can be
slow; free water served without a grimace, at the corner of rue Cler
and rue du Champ de Mars, at 38 rue Cler, tel. 01 47 05 51 27).

$ Tribeca Italian Restaurant, next door to Café du Marché, is
run by the same people with essentially the same formula. They offer
similar (if not even better) value and more space, a calmer ambience,
and more patient service. This family-friendly eatery offers €12 pizzas
and €12 Italian *plats*.

$ Crêperie Ulysée en Gaule offers the best cheap seats on rue
Cler. Their crêpes are €3–10 to go, with no extra charge to sit for read-
ers of this book if you buy a drink. The Ulysée family—Stephanos,
Chrysa, Marcos, and English-speaking Vassilis—seem to make
friends with all who drop by for a bite. The family loves to serve Greek
dishes, and their excellent crêpes are your least expensive rue Cler hot
meal (open daily, 28 rue Cler, tel. 01 47 05 61 82).

Between Rue de Grenelle and the River

$$$ **Altitude 95** is in the Eiffel Tower, 95 meters (about 300 feet) above the ground. Reserve a month in advance for a view table (€21–31 lunches, €50 dinners, daily 12:00–21:45, dinner seatings nightly at about 19:00 and 21:00, bar open until 23:00; before you ascend to dine, drop by the booth between the north/*nord* and east/*est* pillars to buy your Eiffel Tower ticket and pick up a pass that enables you to skip the line; Mo: Bir-Hakeim or Trocadéro, RER: Champ de Mars-Tour Eiffel, tel. 01 45 55 20 04, fax 01 47 05 94 40). Also in the Eiffel Tower is the even more expensive **Jules Verne Restaurant,** described on page 174.

$$$ **Au Petit Tonneau** is a souvenir of old Paris. Fun-loving owner-chef Madame Boyer prepares everything herself, wearing her tall chef's hat like a crown as she rules from her family-style kitchen. The small, plain dining room doesn't look like it's changed in the 26 years she's been in charge. Her steaks and lamb are excellent (€8–10 starters, €18 *plats*, open daily, 20 rue Surcouf, Mo: La Tour Maubourg, tel. 01 47 05 09 01).

$$$ **La Fontaine de Mars** is a longtime favorite for locals, charmingly situated on a classic, tiny Parisian street and jumbled square. It's a happening scene, with tables jammed together for the serious business of good eating. Reserve in advance for a table on the ground floor (or in summer on the square), or eat upstairs without the fun street-level ambience (€20 *plats du jour*, superb foie gras, open nightly, where rue de l'Exposition and rue St. Dominique meet, 129 rue St. Dominique, tel. 01 47 05 46 44).

$$ **Le P'tit Troquet,** a petite eatery taking you back to the Paris of the 1920s, is gracefully and earnestly run by Dominique. The fragile elegance here makes you want to hug a flapper. Dominique is particularly proud of her foie gras and lamb, and of her daughter's breads and pastries. The delicious, three-course €32 *menu* comes with traditional choices. Its delicate charm and gourmet flair make this restaurant a favorite of connoisseurs (opens at 18:00, closed Sun, reservations smart, 28 rue de l'Exposition, tel. 01 47 05 80 39).

$$ **Billebaude,** run by patient Pascal, is an authentic Parisian bistro where the focus is on what's fresh and meats from the hunt (€29 *menu*, closed Sun–Mon, 29 rue de l'Exposition, tel. 01 45 55 20 96).

$$ **Chez Agnès,** the smallest of my recommended Paris restaurants, is not for everyone. It's tiny, flowery, family-style, and filled with kisses on the cheek. Eccentric but sincere Agnès (a French-Tahitian Rosie O'Donnell) does it all—cooking in her minuscule kitchen and serving, too. Agnès, who cooks "French with an exotic twist" and clearly loves her work, makes children feel right at home. Don't come for a quick dinner (€23 *menu*, closed Mon, 1 rue Augereau, tel. 01 45 51 06 04).

$$ **L'Ami Jean** offers excellent Basque specialties at fair prices. The chef has made his reputation on the quality of his cuisine. Arrive

Rue Cler Restaurants

5 MIN. WALK TO SEINE RIVER + AMERICAN CHURCH

RUE DE L'UNIVERSITE

RUE MALAR

RUE NICOT

ST. PIERRE

AVENUE

ST. DOMINIQUE

RUE AMELIE

RUE CLER

RUE NICOT

COMTE

MAUBOURG

La Tour-Maubourg

RUE DE BOSQUET

R. DE L'EXPO

RUE

RUE

AUGEREAU

LA BOURDONNAIS

DE GRENELLE

RUE VALADON

DE MARS

RUE DU CHAMP

RUE DUVIVIER

RUE PSICHARI

ST. JEAN

LA MOTTE PICQUET

TOUR MAUBOURG

BLVD. DE LA TOUR

CHEVET

RUE

DE LA MOTTE PICQUET

POST

Ecole Militaire

ARMY MUSEUM + NAPOLEONS TOMB

TO EIFFEL TOWER +

CHAMP DE MARS

KIDS' PLAY AREA

AVENUE DUQUESNE

AVE DE TOURVILLE

DCH

M METRO STATION

200 YARDS
200 METERS

① Le Florimond	⑫ Billebaude Bistro
② Restaurant Pasco	⑬ Chez Agnès
③ La Terrasse du 7ème	⑭ L'Ami Jean
④ Café le Bosquet	⑮ Chez Pierrot
⑤ Café du Marché & Tribeca Italian Rest.	⑯ Café Constant
⑥ Crêperie Ulysée en Gaule	⑰ La Varangue
⑦ Petite Brasserie PTT	⑱ La Gourmandise Pizzeria
⑧ To Altitude 95 Rest. & Jules Verne Restaurant	⑲ Real McCoy
⑨ Au Petit Tonneau	⑳ Late-Night Groceries (2)
⑩ La Fontaine de Mars	㉑ Julien's Bakery
⑪ Le P'tit Troquet	㉒ Café la Roussillon
	㉓ O'Brien's Pub

by 19:30 or call ahead (€33 *menu*, closed Sun–Mon, 27 rue Malar, Mo: La Tour Maubourg, tel. 01 47 05 86 89).

$$ Chez Pierrot is a warm, welcoming bistro with 12 tables served by smiling Linda. On a quiet street, it offers large portions of traditional fare—try the beef stew (€18 *plats*, €12 big salads, daily, 9 rue Amélie, tel. 01 45 51 50 08).

$ Café Constant is a tiny, cool two-level place that feels more like a small bistro–wine bar than a café. They serve delicious and affordably priced dishes in a fun setting to a well-established clientele (€14 *plats,* closed Sun–Mon, corner of rue Augereau and rue St. Dominique, next to recommended Hôtel Londres Eiffel).

$ La Varangue is an entertaining one-man show featuring English-speaking Philippe, who ran a French catering shop in Pennsylvania for three years. He lives upstairs, and has found his niche serving a mostly American clientele, who are all on a first-name basis. The food is cheap and basic (don't come here for high cuisine), the tables are few, and he opens early (at 17:30). Norman Rockwell would dig his tiny dining room—with the traditional kitchen sizzling just over the counter. Philippe is so fun and accessible that you are welcome to join him in the kitchen and help cook your meal. Try his snails and chocolate cake...but not together (€12 *plats*, €17.50 *menu,* always a vegetarian option, closed Sun, 27 rue Augereau, tel. 01 47 05 51 22).

$ La Gourmandise is a tiny, friendly pizzeria across the street from La Varangue. Its good, cheap pizza is ideal for kids (closed Sun, eat in or take out, 28 rue Augereau, tel. 01 45 55 45 16).

Picnicking

Rue Cler is a moveable feast that gives "fast food" a good name. The entire street is clogged with connoisseurs of good eating. Only the health-food store goes unnoticed. A festival of food, the street is lined with people whose lives seem to be devoted to their specialty: polished produce, rotisserie chicken, crêpes, or cheese.

✪ For a self-guided tour of all the temptations, see the Rue Cler Walk on page 164.

For a magical picnic dinner at the Eiffel Tower, assemble it in no fewer than five shops on rue Cler. Then lounge on the best grass in Paris, with the dogs, Frisbees, a floodlit tower, and a cool breeze in the parc du Champ de Mars.

Asian delis (generically called *Traiteur Asie*) provide tasty, low-stress, low-price take-out treats (€6 dinner plates, the one on rue Cler near rue du Champ de Mars has tables). **Crêperie Ulysée en Gaule,** the Greek restaurant on rue Cler across from Grand Hôtel Lévêque, sells take-away crêpes (described above). **Real McCoy** is a little shop selling American food and sandwiches (closed Sun, 194 rue de Grenelle). There's a small **late-night grocery** at 197 rue de Grenelle (open daily until midnight), and another where rues Cler and Grenelle cross. For excellent baguettes and sandwiches, try **Julien's** bakery at 85 rue St. Dominique.

Breakfast

Hotel breakfasts, while convenient, are generally not a good value. For a great rue Cler start to your day, drop by the **Petite Brasserie PTT,** where Jerome and Alexi promise Rick Steves readers a *deux pour douze* breakfast special (2 "American" breakfasts—juice, a big coffee, croissant, bread, ham, and eggs—for €12; closed Sun, 2-min walk from most area hotels, opposite 53 rue Cler).

Nightlife

This sleepy neighborhood is not ideal for night owls, but there are a few notable exceptions. **Café du Marché** and **La Terrasse du 7ème** (both listed above) are busy with a Franco-American crowd until at least midnight, as is the younger **Café la Roussillon** (occasional happy hours from 18:00–20:00—but every hour seems happy, €10 salads, €13 *plats*, fine for a French pub atmosphere, corner of rue de Grenelle and rue Cler). **O'Brien's Pub** is a relaxed Parisian rendition of an Irish pub, full of Anglophones (77 avenue St. Dominique, Mo: La Tour Maubourg).

In the Marais Neighborhood

The trendy Marais is filled with locals enjoying good food in colorful and atmospheric eateries. The scene is competitive and changes all the time. I've listed an assortment of eateries—all handy to recommended hotels—that offer good food at decent prices, plus a memorable experience.

On Romantic Place des Vosges

On this square, which offers Old World Marais elegance, you'll find several different eateries (use Bastille or St. Paul Métro stops). Enjoy a square stroll around the entire arcade—fun art galleries alternate with enticing restaurants. Choose the restaurant that best fits your mood and budget; all have arcade seating and provide big space-heaters to make outdoor dining during colder months an option. Also consider a drink or dessert on the square at Café Hugo or Nectarine after eating elsewhere.

　　$$$ Ma Bourgogne is a classic old eatery where you'll sit under warm arcades in a whirlpool of Frenchness, as bow-tied and black-aproned waiters serve you traditional French specialties: blood-red steak, lots of French fries, escargot, and great red wine. While service comes with few smiles, the staff of this venerable Marais fixture enjoy their work and care about your experience. Monsieur Cougourou (koo-gah-roo), who's run this place since de Gaulle was sniveling at Americans, offers anyone with this book a free *amuse-bouche* ("amusement for your mouth") of steak tartare. This is your ideal chance to try this "raw spiced hamburger" delicacy without dedicating an entire meal to it...and the quality here is famous (€35 *menu*, daily, dinner reservations smart, cash only, at northwest corner at #19, tel. 01 42 78 44 64).

$$ At **Les Bonnes Soeurs,** barely off the square, Cecile and Alexandra cater to a somewhat younger and more local clientele by mixing modern and traditional fare with fun ambience (*plats* from €16, no *menu*, daily, 8 rue du pas de la Mule, tel. 01 42 74 55 80).

$ Nectarine is small and demure—with a wicker, pastel, and feminine atmosphere. This peaceful teahouse serves healthy €10 salads, quiches, and €12–14 *plats du jour* day and night. Its menu lets you mix and match omelets and crêpes, and the huge desserts are splittable (daily, at #16, tel. 01 42 77 23 78).

$ Café Hugo, named for the square's most famous resident, is best for drinks only, as the cuisine does not live up to its setting (daily, at #22).

Near the Bastille

To reach these restaurants, use the Bastille Métro stop.

$$ Brasserie Bofinger, an institution for over a century, is famous for fish and traditional cuisine with Alsatian flair. You're surrounded by brisk, black-and-white-attired waiters. The sprawling interior features elaborately decorated rooms reminiscent of the Roaring Twenties. Eating under the grand 1919 *coupole* is a memorable treat (as is using the "historic" 1919 WC downstairs). Check out the boys shucking and stacking seafood platters out front before you enter. Their €32 three-course *menu*, while not top cuisine, is a good value. If you've always wanted one of those picturesque seafood platters, this is a good place—you can take the standard platter or create one à la carte (open daily and nightly, fun kids' menu, 5 rue de la Bastille, don't be confused by the lesser "Petite" Bofinger across the street, tel. 01 42 72 87 82).

$$ Chez Janou, a Provençal bistro, tumbles out of its corner building and fills its broad sidewalk with happy eaters. At first glance, you know this is a find. Don't let the trendy and youthful crowd intimidate you—it's relaxed and charming, with helpful and patient service. While the curbside tables are inviting, I'd sit inside (with very tight seating) to immerse myself in the happy commotion. The style is French Mediterranean, with an emphasis on vegetables (€15–18 *plats du jour* that change with the season, daily from 19:45, 2 blocks beyond place des Vosges at 2 rue Roger Verlomme, tel. 01 42 72 28 41). They're proud of their 81 different varieties of *pastis* (licorice-flavored liqueur, €3.50 each, browse the list above the bar).

$$ La Bastoche (Parisian slang for "the Bastille") is cozy and welcoming. Step down into an 18th-century building with exposed timbers and a great mural of the storming of the old prison, and choose from a nice selection of traditional French fare at good prices. Caring

Marais Restaurants

1. Ma Bourgogne
2. Nectarine & Café Hugo
3. Brasserie Bofinger
4. Chez Janou
5. Les Bonnes Soeurs
6. La Bastoche

7. Vins des Pyrénées
8. Au Temps des Cerises
9. Au Bourguignon du Marais
10. L'Ebouillanté
11. Restaurante Sant Antonio
12. BHV Cafeteria
13. Place du Marché Ste.
    Catherine Eateries
14. L'Enoteca Wine Bar
15. Camille Brasserie
16. Le Rouge Gorge
17. Chez Marianne
18. L'As du Falafel
19. Bistrot les Sans Culottes
20. Au Petit Fer à Cheval &
    La Belle Hortense
21. La Perla Bar
22. Le Pick-Clops Bar Rest.

owners Sylvie and Lise work hard to please (€23 3-course *menu*, daily, 7 rue St. Antoine, one block away from the Bastille, tel. 01 48 04 84 34).

$$ Vins des Pyrénées ("Wines of the Pyrenees") is a fun bistro that attracts a young, lively crowd with its convivial setting, varying *menus* with lots of choices, reasonable wine list, and hardworking, English-speaking owner, Olivier. Don't come here for a romantic dinner (€15–20 *plats*, daily, 25 rue Beautreillis, tel. 01 42 72 64 94).

$ Au Temps des Cerises is a *très* local wine bar, with a woody 1950s atmosphere, tight seating, and wads of character. While they serve three-course, €15 lunch *menus*, I'd come here for wine and heavy munchies pre- or post-dinner—or even for dinner. "Dinner" is limited to bread, dry sausage, cheese, and wine served by goateed Yves and his wife, Michele. While full plates of cold cuts run around €13, a small mixed plate of cheese (€5), meat (€5), and a carafe of good wine (€4–8) surrounded by the intimate Old World ambience can make a good light meal (Mon–Sat until about 22:00, closed Sun, at rue du Petit-Musc and rue de la Cerisaie).

Closer to Hôtel de Ville

These eateries, near the Pompidou Center, appear on the map on page 387. To reach them, use the Hôtel de Ville Métro stop.

$$$ Au Bourguignon du Marais is an attractive wine bar–bistro for Burgundy-lovers, where excellent wines (available by the glass) blend with a good selection of well-designed dishes and efficient service (Philippe is clearly in charge). The *œufs en meurette* were the best I've ever had, and the *bœuf bourguignon* could feed two (€10–14 starters, €18–22 *plats*, closed Sun–Mon, indoor and outdoor seating, 52 rue Francois Miron, tel. 01 48 87 15 40).

$ L'Ebouillanté is a breezy crêperie-café, romantically situated near the river on a broad, cobbled lane behind a church. With great outdoor seating and an artsy, cozy interior, it's ideal for an inexpensive and relaxing tea, snack, or lunch—or for dinner on a warm evening. Try a *brick*, the light-hearted chef's specialty (think beefy crêpe). The salads and desserts are also good (€13 *plats,* €15 2-course *menu*, Tue–Sun 12:00–22:00, closed Mon, 6 rue des Barres, tel. 01 42 71 09 69).

$ Restaurante Sant Antonio is bustling and cheap, serving up €10 pizzas and salads on a fun Marais square (daily, barely off rue de Rivoli on place du Bourg Tibourg).

$ BHV Department Store's fifth-floor cafeteria provides nice views, an escape from the busy streets below, and no-brainer, point-and-shoot cafeteria cuisine (Mon–Sat 11:30–18:00, closed Sun, at intersection of rue du Temple and rue de la Verrerie, one block from Hôtel de Ville).

In the Heart of the Marais

These are closest to the St. Paul Métro stop.

$$ *On place du Marché Ste. Catherine:* This small, romantic square, just off rue St. Antoine, is an international food festival cloaked in extremely Parisian, leafy-square ambience. On a balmy evening, this is clearly a neighborhood favorite, with a handful of restaurants offering €20–30 meals. Study the square, and you'll find two popular French bistros (**Le Marché** and **Au Bistrot de la Place,** each with €23 3-course *menus*, tight seating indoors and out, both open daily) and other inviting eateries serving a variety of international food—Russian, Korean, Italian, and so on. You'll eat under the trees, surrounded by a futuristic-in-1800 planned residential quarter.

$$ L'Enoteca is a high-spirited, half-timbered spot serving affordable Italian cuisine (no pizza) with a tempting *antipasti* bar. It's a relaxed, open setting with busy, blue-aproned waiters serving two floors of local eaters (€15 pastas, €20 *plats*, €30 3-course *menu*, open daily, across from L'Excuse at rue St. Paul and rue Charles V, 25 rue Charles V, tel. 01 42 78 91 44).

$ Camille, a traditional corner brasserie, is a neighborhood favorite with great indoor and sidewalk seating. Its waiters serve €13 salads and very French *plats du jour* (€20) from the chalkboard list to a down-to-earth but sophisticated clientele (daily, 24 rue des Francs Bourgeois at corner of rue Elzévir, tel. 01 42 72 20 50).

$ Le Rouge Gorge's relaxed wine bar and bistro is 10-table cozy. Come for a meal (€16–20 dinner *plats* based on monthly themes), a coffee, or a glass of wine. Friendly François, the owner, will send you downstairs to the *cave* (cellar) to choose your wine; there are different prices for take-out wine purchases (closed Sun, 8 rue St. Paul, tel. 01 48 04 75 89).

$ Several hardworking **Asian fast-food eateries,** great for a €6 meal, line rue St. Antoine.

On Rue des Rosiers in the Jewish Quarter

To reach the Jewish Quarter, use the St. Paul Métro stop.

$ Chez Marianne, a neighborhood fixture, offers classic Jewish meals and Parisian atmosphere. Choose from several indoor zones with a cluttered wine shop/deli ambience, or sit outside. You'll select from two dozen "Zakouski" elements to assemble your €15 plate (great vegetarian options, eat cheap with a €6 falafel sandwich, or even cheaper with takeout, long hours daily, corner of rue des Rosiers and rue des Hospitalieres St. Gervais, tel. 01 42 72 18 86). For takeout, pay inside first and get a ticket before you order outside.

$ L'As du Falafel rules the falafel scene in the Jewish quarter. Monsieur Isaac, the "Ace of Falafel" here since 1979, brags he's got "the biggest pita on the street...and he fills it up." Apparently, it's Lenny Kravitz's favorite, too. Your inexpensive meal comes on plastic plates, in a bustling setting that seems to prove he's earned his success. While the €6.50 "special falafel" is the big hit, many Americans enjoy his lighter chicken version *(poulet grillé)* or the tasty and filling *assiette de falafel.* Their take-out service draws a constant crowd; the interior is air-conditioned (day and night until late, closed Sat, 34 rue des Rosiers).

Picnicking

Picnic at peaceful place des Vosges (closes at dusk) or on the Ile St. Louis *quais* (see below). Stretch your euros at the basement supermarket of the **Monoprix** department store (closed Sun, near place des Vosges on rue St. Antoine). You'll find a small **grocery** open until 23:00 near 48 rue St. Antoine.

Nightlife

The best scene for hard-core night owls is the dizzying array of wacky eateries, bars, and dance halls on **rue de Lappe.** This street is what the Latin Quarter aspires to be. Just east of the stately place de la Bastille, it's one of the wildest nightspots in Paris and not for everyone. Sitting amid the chaos like a Van Gogh painting is the popular, old-time **Bistrot les Sans Culottes.**

Trendy cafés and bars—popular with gay men—also cluster on rue Vieille du Temple, rue des Archives, and rue Ste. Croix de la Bretonnerie (closing at about 2:00 in the morning). You'll find a line of bars and cafés providing front-row seats for the buff parade on rue Vieille du Temple, a block north of rue de Rivoli (the horseshoe-shaped **Au Petit Fer à Cheval** bar-restaurant and the atmospheric **La Belle Hortense** bookstore/wine bar are the focal points of the action). Nearby, rue des Rosiers bustles with youthful energy, but there are no cafés to observe from. **Vins des Pyrénées** (described earlier) is young and fun—find the small bar in the back. **La Perla** is full of Parisian yuppies in search of the perfect margarita (26 rue François Miron).

$ Le Pick-Clops bar-restaurant is a happy peanuts-and-lots-of-cocktails diner with bright neon, loud colors, and a garish local crowd. It's perfect for immersing yourself in today's Marais world— a little boisterous, a little edgy, a little gay, fun-loving, easygoing... and no tourists. Sit inside, on old-fashioned diner stools, or streetside to watch the constant Marais parade. The name means "Steal the Cigarettes"—but you'll pay €10 for your big salad (daily 7:00–24:00, 16 rue Vieille du Temple, tel. 01 40 29 02 18).

The most enjoyable peaceful evening may be simply donning your floppy "three musketeers" hat and slowly strolling around place des Vosges, window-shopping the art galleries.

On Ile St. Louis

Ile St. Louis is a romantic and peaceful neighborhood where you can amble around for plenty of promising dinner possibilities. Cruise the island's main street for a variety of options, from cozy *crêperies* to

Italian eateries (intimate pizzerias and upscale) to typical brasseries (a few with fine outdoor seating facing the bridge to Ile de la Cité). After dinner, sample Paris' best sorbet and stroll across to the Ile de la Cité to see Notre-Dame illuminated, or enjoy a scenic drink on the deck of a floating café moored under Notre-Dame's right transept. All these listings line the island's main drag, rue St. Louis-en-l'Ile (see map on page 359; to get here, use the Pont Marie Métro stop). Consider skipping dessert to enjoy a stroll licking the best ice cream in Paris (described under "Ice-Cream Dessert," on the next page).

$$$ Le Tastevin is an intimate mother-and-son-run restaurant serving top-notch traditional French cuisine with white-tablecloth, candlelit, gourmet elegance under heavy wooden beams. The romantic setting (and the elegantly romantic local couples enjoying the place) makes you naturally whisper. The three-course *menus* start at about €38 and offer plenty of classic choices that change with the season to ensure freshness (daily, reserve for late-evening dining, good wine list, 46 rue St. Louis-en-l'Ile, tel. 01 43 54 17 31; owner Madame Puisieux and her gentle son speak just enough English).

$$$ *Medieval Theme Restaurants:* **La Taverne du Sergeant Recruteur,** famous for its rowdy, medieval-cellar atmosphere, is ideal for hungry warriors and their wenches who like to swill hearty wine. For as long as anyone can remember, they've served up a rustic all-you-can-eat buffet with straw baskets of raw veggies and bundles of sausage (cut whatever you like with your dagger), massive plates of pâté, a meat course, and all the wine you can stomach for €41. The food is just food; burping is encouraged. If you want to eat a lot, drink a lot of wine, be surrounded with tourists, and holler at your friends while receiving smart-aleck buc caneer service, this food fest can be fun. And it comes with an historic twist: The "Sergeant Recruiter" used to get young Parisians drunk and stuffed here, then sign them into the army (daily from 19:00, #37 rue St. Louis-en-l'Ile, tel. 01 43 54 75 42). Next door, **Nos Ancêtres les Gaulois** is a bit goofier and grittier, and serves the same basic formula. As the name implies ("Our Ancestors the Gauls"), this place makes barbarians feel right at home (tel. 01 46 33 66 07). You might swing by both and choose the..."ambience" is not quite the right word...that fits your mood.

$$ La Brasserie de l'Ile St. Louis is situated at the prow of the island's ship as it faces Ile de la Cité, offering purely Alsatian cuisine (try the *choucroute garni* for €18), served in a Franco-Germanic setting with no-nonsense brasserie service. This is a good balmy-evening perch for watching the Ile St. Louis promenade—or, if it's chilly, the interior is plenty characteristic for a memorable night out (closed Wed, no reservations, 55 quai de Bourbon, tel. 01 43 54 02 59).

$ Café Med, near the pedestrian bridge to Notre-Dame at #77, has inexpensive salads, crêpes, and a €13–20 *menu* served in a tight but cheery setting (open daily, limited wine list, tel. 01 43 29 73 17). Two similar *crêperies* are just across the street.

Riverside Picnic for Impoverished Romantics

On sunny lunchtimes and balmy evenings, the *quai* on the Left Bank side of Ile St. Louis is lined with locals who have more class than money, spreading out tablecloths and even lighting candles for elegant picnics. And tourists can enjoy the same budget meal. There's the handy grocery store at #67 on the main drag (Wed-Mon until 22:00, closed Tue) that has tabouli and other simple, cheap take-away dishes for your picnicking pleasure.

Ice-Cream Dessert

Half the people strolling Ile St. Louis are licking an ice-cream cone, because this is the home of *les glaces Berthillon*. The original **Berthillon** shop, at 31 rue St. Louis-en-l'Ile, is marked by the line of salivating customers (closed Mon–Tue). Another Berthillon shop is across the street, and there's one more around the corner on rue Bellay (all are located on map on page 359). The three shops are so popular that the wealthy people who can afford to live on this fancy island complain about the congestion they cause. For a less famous but at least as tasty treat, the homemade Italian gelato a block away at **Amorino Gelati** is giving Berthillon competition (no line, bigger portions, easier to see what you want, and they offer little tastes—Berthillon doesn't need to, 47 rue St. Louis-en-l'Ile, tel. 01 44 07 48 08). Having some of each is not a bad thing.

In the Luxembourg Garden Area

Sleeping in the Luxembourg neighborhood puts you near many appealing dining and after-hours options. Because my hotels in this area cluster around the Panthéon and St. Sulpice Church (see Sleeping chapter), I've organized restaurant listings the same way. Restaurants near the Panthéon tend to be calm, those around St. Sulpice more boisterous; it's a short walk from one area to the other. Anyone sleeping in this area is close to the inexpensive eateries that line the always-bustling rue Mouffetard. You're also within a 15-minute walk of the *grands cafés* of St. Germain and Montparnasse (with Paris' first café and famous artist haunts; see "Les Grands Cafés de Paris," page 397).

Near the Panthéon

For locations, see the map on page 364. These eateries are served by the Cluny-La Sorbonne Métro stop and the RER-B Luxembourg station.

$$ Restaurant Perraudin is a welcoming, family-run, red-checkered-tablecloth eatery understandably popular with tourists. Friendly Monsieur Correy serves classic *cuisine bourgeoise* with an emphasis on Burgundian dishes in air-conditioned comfort. The decor is vintage turn-of-the-20th-century, with big mirrors and old wood paneling (€19 lunch *menus*, €30 dinner *menus*, *bœuf bourguignon* is a specialty here, between the Panthéon and Luxembourg Garden at 157 rue St. Jacques, tel. 01 46 33 15 75).

$ Le Soufflot Café, between the Panthéon and Luxembourg Garden, is well-positioned for afternoon sun. It has a nifty library-like interior, lots of outdoor tables, point-blank views of the Panthéon, and friendly service (Frédéric and Serge are owners). The cuisine is café-classic: good €10 salads, omelets, and *plats du jour* (daily, a block below the Panthéon on the right side of rue Soufflot as you walk toward Luxembourg Garden, tel. 01 43 26 57 56).

$ *Place de la Sorbonne:* This cobbled and green square, with a small fountain facing the Sorbonne University just a block from the Cluny Museum, offers several opportunities for a quick outdoor lunch or light dinner. At the tiny **Baker's Dozen,** you'll pay take-away prices for salads and sandwiches you can sit down to eat (€5 salad and quiche special, Mon–Sat until 17:00, closed Sun). **Café de l'Ecritoire** is a typical, lively brasserie with happy diners enjoying €11 salads, €13 *plats,* and fine square seating (daily, tel. 01 43 54 60 02). **Patios,** with appealing decor inside and out, seems more popular. It serves inexpensive Italian fare, including pizza (daily until late).

Near the Odéon Theater

To reach these, use the Odéon Métro stop. In this same neighborhood is Café le Procope, listed under "Les Grands Cafés de Paris," later in this chapter.

$$ Brasserie Bouillon Racine takes you back to 1906 with an Art Nouveau carnival of carved wood, stained glass, and old-time lights reflected in beveled mirrors. The over-the-top decor, energetic waiters, and affordable menu combine to give it an inviting conviviality. Check upstairs before choosing a table. Their roast suckling pig (€18) is a house favorite. There's good beer on tap and a fascinating history on the menu (€18 *plats,* €29 *menu,* traditional French with lots of fish and meat, daily 12:00–14:00 & 19:00–23:00, 3 rue Racine, tel. 01 44 32 15 60, Phillipe).

$$ La Méditerranée is all about fish in a pastel and dressy setting...with similar clientele. The scene and the menu are sophisticated while accessible, and the view of the Odéon is *formidable.* The sky-blue tablecloths and the lovingly presented dishes add to the romance (€18–27 *plats,* €32 3-courses *menus,* open daily, smart to book ahead, facing the Odéon at 2 place de l'Odéon, tel. 01 43 26 02 30).

$ Restaurant Polidor, a bare-bones neighborhood fixture since the 19th century, is much-loved for its unpretentious quality cooking, fun old-Paris atmosphere, and fair value. Stepping inside, you know this is a winner—noisy, happy diners sit tightly at shared tables as waiters chop and serve fresh bread. The selection features classic bourgeois *plats* from every corner of France; their *menu fraicheur* is designed for lighter summer eating (€12–15 *plats,* €20–30 3-course *menus*, daily 12:00–14:30 & 19:00–23:00, cash only, no reservations, 41 rue Monsieur-Le-Prince, tel. 01 43 26 95 34, Amelia).

On Rue Mouffetard

Lying several blocks behind the Panthéon, rue Mouffetard is a conveyer belt of comparison-shopping eaters with wall-to-wall budget options (fondue, crêpes, Italian, falafel, and Greek). Come here to sift through the crowds and eat a less expensive meal (you get what you pay for). This street stays up late and likes to party (particularly around place de la Contrescarpe). The gauntlet begins on top, at thriving place de la Contrescarpe, and ends below where rue Mouffetard stops at St. Médard Church. Both ends offer fun cafés where you can eat, drink, and watch the action. The upper stretch is pedestrian and touristic; the bottom stretch is purely Parisian. Anywhere between is no-man's land for consistent quality. Still, strolling with so many fun-seekers is enjoyable, whether you eat or not. To get here, use the Censier-Daubenton Métro stop.

$ Café Delmas, at the top of rue Mouffetard on picturesque place de la Contrescarpe, is *the* place to see and be seen. Come here for a before- or after-dinner drink on the broad outdoor terrace, or for typical but pricey café cuisine (€15 salads, €20 *plats*, great chocolate ice cream, open daily).

$ Le Mouffetard, a traditional café with a lively location in the heart of rue Mouffetard, is good for an inexpensive lunch or dinner (€13 lunches, €16 2-course *menus*, closed Sun evening and all day Mon, 116 rue Mouffetard, tel. 01 43 31 42 50).

$ Bar-restaurant **Les Papillons** is a down-and-dirty local diner where a few outdoor tables tangle with pedestrians and no one seems to care (€12 *plats*, closed Sun–Mon, 129 rue Mouffetard, tel. 01 43 31 66 50).

$ Cave de Bourgogne is *très* local and serves reasonably priced café fare at the bottom of rue Mouffetard. Outside has picture-perfect tables on a raised terrace; inside is warm and cozy (€13–16 *plats*, specials listed on chalkboards, daily, 144 rue Mouffetard).

Near St. Sulpice Church:
Rue des Canettes and Rue Guisarde

For an entirely different experience, roam the streets between the St. Sulpice Church and boulevard St. Germain, abounding with restaurants, *crêperies*, wine bars, and jazz haunts (use Mo: St. Sulpice). Find rue des Canettes and rue Guisarde, and window-shop the many French and Italian eateries—most with similar prices, but each with a slightly different feel. For tasty crêpes, try **$ La Crêpe Rit du Clown** (Mon–Sat 12:00–23:00, closed Sun, 6 rue des Canettes, tel. 01 46 34 01 02). For good ambience and above-average bistro fare in a zone where every restaurant looks the same, consider **$$ Le Bistrot Henri**

IV (daily, only indoor seating, 6 rue Princesse, tel. 01 46 33 51 12) or **$$ Lou Pescadou-Chez Julien** (daily, some outdoor seating, 16 rue Mabillon, tel. 01 43 54 56 08).

And for a bohemian pub lined with black-and-white photos of the artsy and revolutionary French '60s, have a drink at **Chez Georges.** Sit in a cool little streetside table nook, or venture downstairs to find a hazy, drippy-candle, traditionally French world in the Edith Piaf–style dance cellar (cheap drinks from old-fashioned menu, Tue–Sat 14:00–2:00 in the morning, closed Sun–Mon and in Aug, 11 rue des Canettes).

Elsewhere in Paris
In the Galerie Vivienne, Behind the Palais Royal
$$ Le Grand Colbert, appropriately located in the elegant Galerie Vivienne (see page 419 in the Shopping chapter), gives its clients the feel of a luxury restaurant at moderate prices. It's a stylish, grand brasserie with hurried waiters, leather booths, and brass lamps, serving all the classic dishes from steak *frites* to escargots (*menus* from €41, daily, 4 rue Vivienne, Mo: Palais Royal/Musée du Louvre or Pyramides, tel. 01 42 86 82 38).

Along Canal St. Martin, North of République
Escape the crowded tourist areas and enjoy a breezy canalside experience. Take the Métro to place de la République and walk down rue Beaurepaire to Canal St. Martin. There you'll find a few worthwhile cafés with similarly reasonable prices. **$ La Marine** is a good choice (daily, 55 bis quai de Valmy, tel. 01 42 39 69 81). In the summertime, most bars and cafés offer beer and wine to go (*à emporter*), so you can take it to the canal's edge and picnic there with the young locals.

Near Opéra Garnier
$ Bouillon Chartier is a noisy, old, classic eatery. It's named for the bouillon it served the neighborhood's poor workers back in 1896, when its calling was to provide an affordable warm meal for those folks. Workers used to eat *à la gamelle* (from a tin lunchbox). That same spirit—complete with surly waiters and a cheap menu—survives today. Among more than 300 simple seats and 15 frantic waiters, you can still see the restaurant's napkin drawers for its early regulars (€18 *menus*, daily 11:30–15:00 & 18:00–22:00, east of the Opéra Garnier near boulevard Poissonniere, 7 rue de Faubourg-Montmartre, Mo: Grands Boulevards, tel. 01 47 70 86 29).

Montmartre
Montmartre is extremely touristy, with many mindless mobs following guides to cancan shows. But the ambience is undeniably fun, and an evening up here overlooking Paris is a quintessential experience

in the City of Light. The steps in front of Sacré-Cœur are perfect for a picnic with a view. Along the touristy main drag (near place du Tertre and just off it), several fun piano bars serve crêpes with great people-watching. To reach this area, use the Anvers Métro stop. More eateries are mentioned in the Montmartre Walk on page 323.

$$ Restaurant Chez Plumeau, just off jam-packed place du Tertre, is touristy yet moderately priced, with formal service but great seating on a tiny, characteristic square (elaborate €16 salads, €16–20 *plats,* closed Wed, place du Calvaire, tel. 01 46 06 26 29).

$ L'Eté en Pente Douce hides under generous branches below the crowds on a classic neighborhood corner. It features fine indoor and outdoor seating, €10 *plats du jour* and salads, vegetarian options, and good wines (daily, 23 rue Muller, many steps below Sacré-Cœur to the left as you leave, down the stairs below the WC, tel. 01 42 64 02 67).

Dinner Cruises

The following companies all offer dinner cruises (reservations required). Bateaux Mouches and Bateaux Parisiens have the best reputations and the highest prices. They offer multicourse meals and music in aircraft carrier–size dining rooms with glass tops and good views. For both, proper dress is required—no denim, shorts, or sport shoes; Bateaux Mouches requires a jacket and tie for men. The main difference between these companies is the ambience: Bateaux Mouches offers violin and piano to entertain your romantic evening, while Bateaux Parisiens boasts a lively atmosphere with a singer, band, and dance floor.

Bateaux Mouches, started in 1949, is hands-down the most famous. You can't miss its sparkling port on the north side of the river at Pont de l'Alma. The boats usually board 19:30–20:15, depart at 20:30, and return at 22:45 (€130/person, RER: Pont de l'Alma, tel. 01 42 25 96 10, www.bateauxmouches.com).

Bateaux Parisiens leaves from Port de la Bourdonnais, just east of the bridge under the Eiffel Tower. Begin boarding at 19:45, leave at 20:30, and return at 23:00 (€100–145/person, 3 price tiers, depends on seating, tel. 08 25 62 75 13, www.bateauxparisiens.com). The middle level is best. Pay the few extra euros to get seats next to the windows—it's more romantic and private, with sensational views.

Le Capitaine Fracasse offers the budget option (€50/person, €70 with wine; tables are first-come, first-serve, so get there early; boarding times vary by season and day of week, closed Mon, walk down stairs in the middle of Bir Hakeim bridge near the Eiffel Tower to Iles aux Cygne, Mo: Champs de Mars Tour Eiffel, tel. 01 46 21 48 15, www.croisiere-paris.com).

LES GRANDS CAFES DE PARIS

Here's a short list of grand Parisian cafés, worth the detour only if you're not in a hurry nor on a tight budget (some ask outrageous prices for a shot of espresso). Think of these cafés as monuments to another time. Try to understand why they matter as much today as they did yesterday (see sidebar). For tips on enjoying Parisian cafés, see "Café Culture" on page 372.

St. Germain-des-Prés

For locations, see the map on page 362. Use the St. Germain-des-Prés Métro stop.

Where the boulevard St. Germain meets rue Bonaparte, you'll find two famous cafés (both open daily). **Les Deux Magots** offers prime outdoor seating and a warm interior. Once a favorite of Ernest Hemingway (in *The Sun Also Rises,* Jake met Brett here) and Jean-Paul Sartre (he and Simone de Beauvoir met here), today the café is filled with international tourists. **Le Café de Flore,** next door, feels much more literary—wear your black turtleneck. Pablo Picasso was a regular at the time he painted *Guernica.*

For scenic outdoor seating and the same delightful view for less just a block away, set up for coffee or a light lunch at **$ Café Bonaparte** (on the sunny side of the street, from Les Deux Magots, one block up rue Bonaparte toward river, tel. 01 43 26 42 81).

Paris' first and most famous, **$ Café le Procope** (1686), lies an enchanting five-minute stroll away. This was a *café célèbre*, drawing notables such as Voltaire, Rousseau, Honoré de Balzac, Emile Zola, Maximilien de Robespierre, Victor Hugo, and two Americans, Benjamin Franklin and Thomas Jefferson (beautiful restaurant and café but average cuisine, daily 10:00–24:00, 13 rue de l'Ancienne Comédie, tel. 01 40 46 79 00). To reach it from Café Bonaparte, walk down rue de l'Abbaye, then continue onto rue de Bourbon-le-Château. Veer left on the picturesque rue de Buci (more cafés), and turn right on rue de l'Ancienne Comédie.

Boulevard du Montparnasse

An eclectic assortment of historic cafés gathers along the busy boulevard du Montparnasse near its intersection with boulevard Raspail (Mo: Vavin). Combine these historic cafés with a visit to the Luxembourg Garden, which lies just a few blocks away, down rue Vavin (next to Le Select).

$$$ Le Dôme, right at the intersection of boulevard Raspail and boulevard du Montparnasse, is small, elegant, and refined, with green leather booths and polished wood paneling—Le Dôme makes me want to dress up and look better than I do (allow €80 with wine, daily, 108 boulevard du Montparnasse, tel. 01 43 35 25 81).

History of Cafés in Paris

The first café in the Western world was in Paris—established in 1686 at Le Procope (still a restaurant today; see page 397). The French had just discovered coffee, and their robust economy was growing a population of pleasure-seekers and thinkers looking for places to be seen, to exchange ideas, and to plot revolutions—both political and philosophical. And with the advent of theaters such as La Comédie-Française, the necessary artsy, coffee-sipping crowds were birthed. By 1700, more than 300 cafés had opened their doors; at the time of the Revolution (1789), there were over 1,800 cafés in Paris. Revolutionaries from Jean-Paul Marat and Napoleon to Salvador Dalí enjoyed the spirit of free-thinking that the cafés engendered.

Café society took off in the early 1900s. Life was changing rapidly, with new technology and wars on a global scale. Many retreated to Parisian cafés to try to make sense of the confusion. Vladimir Lenin, Leon Trotsky, Igor Stravinsky, Ernest Hemingway, F. Scott Fitzgerald, James Joyce, Albert Einstein, Jean-Paul Sartre, Gene Openshaw, and Albert Camus were among the devoted café society. Some virtually lived at their favorite café, where they kept their business calendars, entertained friends, and ate every meal. Parisian apartments were small, walls were thin (still often the case), and heating (particularly during war times) was minimal, making the warmth of cafés all the harder to leave.

There are more than 12,000 cafés in Paris today, though their numbers are shrinking. They're still used for business meetings, encounter sessions, political discussions, and romantic interludes. Most Parisians are loyal to their favorites and know their waiter's children's names. And the new smoking ban could draw an ever-more health conscious French population back to its café roots.

$$ La Coupole, built in the 1920s, was decorated by aspiring artists (Fernand Léger, Constantin Brancusi, and Marc Chagall, among others) in return for free meals. It still supports artists with regular showings on its vast walls. This cavernous café feels like a classy train station, with acres of seating, brass decor, and tuxedoed waiters by the dozen. Bring your friends and make noise. The food is fine; the service can be impersonal, but that's not the reason you came (€30 *menu*, daily, food served from 12:00 until the wee hours, come early to get better service, 102 boulevard du Montparnasse, tel. 01 43 20 14 20).

$$ Le Select, more relaxed and traditional, was popular with the more rebellious types...Leon Trotsky, Jean Cocteau, and Pablo Picasso loved it. It feels more conformist today, with good outdoor seating

EATING

and pleasant tables just inside the door—though the locals hang out at the bar further inside (€10–12 salads, €16 *plats*, daily, 99 boulevard du Montparnasse, across from La Coupole, tel. 01 45 48 38 24).

Avenue des Champs-Elysées

To reach these two cafés, use the George V Métro stop. These are also described in more detail on page 257 of the Champs-Elysées Walk.

$$$ Fouquet's, which opened in 1899, has played host to coachmen, biplane fighter pilots, artists, today's celebrities...and tourists. While the intimidating interior is impressive, the outdoor setting is Champs-Elysées great, with pay-for-view €6 espresso (daily, 99 avenue des Champs-Elysées).

$$ Ladurée, two blocks downhill, is a classic on Paris' grandest boulevard (daily, a block below avenue George V at #75).

On Place de la Concorde

$$$ Hôtel Crillon's four-star elegance can be yours for an afternoon. Considered the most exclusive (and expensive) hotel in Paris (and the last of the great hotels to be French-owned), it gives you a taste of château life. Wear the best clothes you packed, arrive after 15:00, let the bellhop spin the door, and settle into the royal chairs in the *salon du thé*. You'll be surrounded by famous people you won't recognize (€9 for a pot of tea or double *café au lait*, about €32 for high tea served daily, €47 if you toss in a glass of champagne, 15:30–18:00, 10 place de la Concorde, Mo: Concorde).

Near the Louvre

$ Café le Nemours, a staunchly Parisian fixture serving pricey but good light lunches, is tucked into the corner of the Palais Royal adjacent to the Comédie Française. With elegant brass and Art Deco style, and outdoor tables under an arcade two minutes from the pyramid, it's a great post-Louvre retreat (fun and filling €11 salads, open daily; leaving the Louvre, cross rue de Rivoli and veer left to 2 place Colette—see Louvre map on page 103; Mo: Palais Royal, tel. 01 42 61 34 14).

At Gare de Lyon

$$$ Le Train Bleu is a grandiose restaurant with a low-slung, leather-couch café-bar area built right into the train station for the Paris Exhibition of 1900 (which also saw the construction of the pont Alexandre III and the Grand and Petit Palais). It's simply a grand-scale-everything experience, with over-the-top, belle époque decor that speaks of another age, when going to dinner was an event—a chance to see and be seen—and intimate dining was out. Forty-one massive paintings of scenes along the old rail lines tempt diners to consider a short getaway. Many films have featured this restaurant.

EATING

Reserve ahead for dinner, or drop in for a drink before your train leaves (€50 *menu*, €7 beer, €5 espresso, open daily, up the stairs opposite track L, tel. 01 43 43 09 06, www.le-train-bleu.com). If you're in a rush (a pity), you can have the €50 *menu TGV*—two gourmet courses served in less than 45 minutes, with coffee.

Honorable Mention

$ Café de la Mosque, behind the Jardins des Plantes and attached to Paris' largest mosque, beams you straight to Morocco, with outdoor courtyards and an interior room, all in North African tearoom decor with a full menu to match (€16–18 couscous, daily 10:00–24:00, 39 rue Geoffroy St. Hilaire, Mo: Place Monge, tel. 01 43 31 38 20). Consider an afternoon tea-and-pastry stop (€2 pastries, to eat in or take out).

$ Café la Palette, on *le* Left Bank, is across the river and a few blocks from the Louvre. Over 100 years old, this café feels real and unaffected by the passage of time (reasonably priced drinks, 43 rue de Seine, Mo: Mabillon). For more on this café, see page 237 in the Left Bank Walk.

PARIS WITH CHILDREN

Paris works surprisingly well with children—smart adults enjoy the "fine art" of simply being in Paris' great neighborhoods, parks, and monuments while watching their kids uncover the City of Light. After enjoying so many family-friendly sights, your children may want to return to Paris before you do. Consider these tips:

- Hotel selection is critical. Stay in a kid-friendly area near a park. The rue Cler and Luxembourg neighborhoods are both good. If you're staying a week or more, rent an apartment (see "For Longer Stays," page 368).

- Before you go, get your kids into the Parisian spirit by reading (see "Kids' Reading List," next page). Bring along plenty of kids' books; they're harder to find and expensive in Paris. If you run out, visit one of the English-language bookstores listed on page 25.

- If traveling with infants, pack a light stroller and a child backpack. Strollers are tough in the Métro (piles of stairs) and not allowed at some sights, but are ideal for neighborhood walks. Backpacks are easier on the Métro and buses, but prohibited at many museums (in which case strollers are generally allowed and sometimes even provided).

- Don't overdo it. Tackle one key sight each day (Louvre, Orsay, Versailles), and mix it with a healthy dose of fun activities. To minimize unnecessary travel, try to match kid activities with areas where you'll be sightseeing (e.g., the Louvre is near the kid-friendly Palais Royal's courtyards and Tuileries Garden). Kids prefer the Louvre after dark, when it's very quiet (Wed and Fri only).

- The double-decker bus tours (see page 33) are a good way to start your visit.

- Follow this book's crowd-beating tips to the letter. Kids despise long lines more than you do.

- Eat dinner early, before the sophisticated local crowd dines (aim for 19:00–19:30 at restaurants, earlier at cafés). Skip romantic places. Try relaxed cafés (or fast-food restaurants) where kids can move around without bothering others. Picnics work well.
- The cheapest toy selection is usually in the large department stores, such as Bon Marché (see Shopping chapter, page 410).
- French marionette shows, called *guignols*, are fun for everyone. They take place in several locations in Paris, mostly in big parks. See *Pariscope* or *L'Officiel des Spectacles* (sold at newsstands), under "Marionettes," for times and places. Even in French, the plots are easy to follow, and the price is right (€2–5). Arrive 20 minutes early for good seats.
- Involve your children in the trip. Let them help choose daily activities, lead you through the Métro, and so on.
- The best thing we did on a recent trip was buy a set of *boules* (a form of outdoor bowling—for the rules, see the sidebar on page 346). We'd play *boules* before dinner, side by side with real players at the neighborhood field. Buy your *boules de pétanque* at the BHV store in the Marais (next to Hôtel de Ville) or at any sporting-goods store. The *boules* make great (if weighty) souvenirs and are fun to play back at home.
- Some Paris parks host temporary amusement parks. The summer Ferris wheel and rides in the Tuileries Garden are the best—my daughter preferred it to Disneyland Paris (for Disneyland Paris details, see page 525). Consider visiting an amusement park as an end-of-trip reward.
- Note that Wednesdays can be busy days at children's sights, since school lets out early.
- Consider hiring a babysitter for a night or two—check www .babychou.com (click on "Babysitting in Paris Hotels") and www .paris-anglo.com (click on "Classifieds").

Kids' Reading List

Pick up books at the library and rent videos. Watch or read the Madeline stories by Ludwig Bemelmans, *The Hunchback of Notre-Dame* by Victor Hugo, *The Three Musketeers* by Alexandre Dumas, or Dumas' *The Man in the Iron Mask*. *Anni's Diary of France*, by Anni Axworthy, is a fun, picture-filled book about a young girl's trip; it could inspire your children.

How Would You Survive in the Middle Ages?, by Fiona MacDonald, is an appealing "guide" for kids. Serious kid historians will devour *The Kingfisher History Encyclopedia*. *Cathedral* by David Macauley re-creates the building of a French Gothic cathedral in detailed pen-and-ink sketches. If your children are interested in art, get your hands on *The History of Art for Young People* by Anthony Janson and *Discovering Great Artists: Hands-On Art for Children in the Styles of the*

Great Masters by MaryAnn Kohl. (Also see "Recommended Books and Movies," including some good choices for teenagers, on page 538 of the appendix.)

TOP 10 SIGHTS AND ACTIVITIES

Luxembourg Garden

This is my favorite place to mix kid business with pleasure. This perfectly Parisian park has it all—from tennis courts to cafés—as well

as an extensive big-toys play area with imaginative slides, swings, jungle gyms, and chess games (see map on page 243). To find the big-toys play area, head to the southwest corner (small fee, entry good all day, many parents watch from chairs outside the play area, open daily, usually 10:00–19:00 in summer, until 16:00 in winter). Kids also like the speedy merry-go-round (small fee), the pony rides (by the tennis courts), and the toy rental sailboats in the main pond (activities open daily in summer, otherwise only Wed and Sat–Sun). Near the main building is a toddler wading pool (summer only) and sand pit (both free). Adults and kids enjoy the terrific puppet shows *(guignols)* held in the afternoons near the children's play area, also located in the southwest corner of the park (€2–5, times listed in *Pariscope* as "Marionnettes du Luxembourg" under "Enfants" section). The park has big, open areas perfect for kicking a ball. Kids can even play in the grass opposite the palace (Mo: St. Sulpice, Odéon, or Notre-Dame-des-Champs, tel. 01 43 26 46 47).

Eiffel Tower, Champ de Mars Park, and Trocadéro

You could fill an entire kid-fun day here. Come early and ride the elevator up the tower before crowds appear, or ride it above the lights at night (see Eiffel Tower Tour, page 172). The Champ de Mars park stretches out from the tower's base, with picnic-perfect benches, big toys, sand pits, pony rides, puppet shows, and pedal go-carts. Big toys are located at the non-river end of the park (with your back to the tower, it's to the right). The pony rides, puppet shows, and go-carts are in the center in the park (after 11:00 Wed, Sat–Sun, and on all summer days; after 15:00 otherwise, Mo: Ecole Militaire; RER-C: Champ de Mars-Tour Eiffel stop; or bus #69).

All ages enjoy the view from Trocadéro across the river to the Eiffel Tower, especially after dark (Mo: Trocadéro). There's a terrific **National Maritime Museum** (Musée National de la Marine) docked at Trocadéro, with all things nautical and many ship models (kids-€4.50, adults-€6.50, covered by Museum Pass, Wed–Mon 10:00–18:00, closed Tue, unfortunately very little in English, the museum is to your right as you face the tower from Trocadéro Square). See page 51 for more information. The Musée de l'Homme, next door, is an anthropological museum, but has zero information in English.

Notre-Dame, Towers, and Crypt

Paris' famous Gothic cathedral doesn't have to be dry and dull. Replay Quasimodo's stunt and climb the tower (go early to avoid long lines). Kids love being on such a lofty perch with a face-to-face look at a gargoyle. The crypt on the square in front of Notre-Dame is quick and interesting (covered by Museum Pass). Kids can push buttons to highlight remains of Roman Paris and leave with a better understanding of how different civilizations build on top of each other. In-line skaters perform amazing stunts just to the right of the cathedral as you face it. (What's more amazing is that the city permits such an activity at this location.) The small but beautiful park along the river outside Notre-Dame's right transept has sandboxes, picnic benches, and space to run (Mo: Cité).

    ❖ See Historic Paris Walk, page 74.

Riverboat Rides

A variety of companies offer one-hour Seine cruises on huge glass-domed boats, with departures until 22:30 (best at sunset or after dark). Or hop on a Batobus, a river bus connecting eight stops along the river: Eiffel Tower, Champs-Elysées, Orsay/place de la Concorde, Louvre, Notre-Dame, St. Germain-des-Prés, Hôtel de Ville, and Jardin des Plantes. Longer boat trips ply the tranquil waters of Canal St. Martin between the Bastille and Bassin de la Villette (see "Tours—By Boat," page 34).

Arc de Triomphe and Champs-Elysées

This area is popular with teenagers, day and night. Mine couldn't get enough of it. Watch the crazy traffic rush around the Arc de Triomphe for endless entertainment, then stroll avenue des Champs-Elysées with its car dealerships (particularly Renault's space-age café), Virgin Megastore (music), Disney store, and the river of humanity that flows along its broad sidewalks. Take your teenager to see a movie on the Champs-Elysées ("v.o." next to the showtime means it's shown in the original language).

    ❖ See Champs-Elysées Walk, page 251.

Versailles

This massive complex of palaces, gardens, fountains, and forest can be a good family getaway if well planned. Do the gardens first and the interior late, when crowds subside. Rent a bike or (even better) a golf cart to explore the gardens. Driving around the grounds in a golf cart, while pricey (€28/hr), is great fun and extremely easy. (They'll want parents to do the driving for liability reasons, but once away from the palace, you're on your own.) Or you can row row row a boat on the canal. The Hamlet has barnyard animals. Be careful of crowds on weekends, when the fountains are flowing.

✪ See Versailles Day Trip, page 456.

Jardin des Plantes

These colorful gardens are a must for gardeners and good for kids. Located across the river from the Marais, the park is short on grass but tall on kid activities, including a small *ménagerie* (zoo) near the river (kids-€5, adults-€7, daily 9:00–18:00), several play areas, and two kid-friendly natural science museums (both closed Tue).

Young kids enjoy the dinosaur exhibit at the **Galerie d'Anatomie Comparée et de Paléontologie;** there are no English explanations, but they're not really needed (kids-€4, adults-€6, Wed–Mon 10:00–17:00, until 18:00 on April–Sept weekends, closed Tue, busiest on weekends, entrance faces river next to McDonald's).

The **Grande Galerie de l'Evolution,** at the non-river end of the park, is a dazzling museum describing the evolution of animals, with huge models and fun exhibits. English explanations are not provided, so you'll need the well-done guidebook (*Grande Galerie de l'Evolution,* €10) available in English at the museum's bookstore (kids-€6, adults-€8, not covered by Museum Pass, Wed–Mon 10:00–18:00, closed Tue, busiest on weekends, tel. 01 40 79 30 00, www.mnhn.fr/evolution). From the park entrance on place Valhubert, the museums line the left side of the park (Mo: Gare d'Austerlitz or Jussieu).

Outside the park, just behind Grande Galerie de l'Evolution, is the Moroccan-themed Café de la Mosque (see page 400 in the Eating chapter).

Pompidou Center

Teens like the Pompidou Center for its crazy outdoor entertainers, throngs of young people, happening cafés, and fun fountains next door (dead on Tue, when museum is closed). Inside, the temporary exhibits and gift shops on the main floor are visually impressive. The *Star Wars*–esque escalator to the top is fun for all ages, but you need a Museum Pass or Pompidou combo-ticket to escalate (Mo: Rambuteau).

✪ See Pompidou Center Tour, page 273.

Jardin des Enfants aux Halles

This is a terrific place to drop your child for an hour (ages 7–11 only, no adults allowed inside, call at least an hour ahead to reserve, tel. 01 45

08 07 18). It's outdoors, in front of Les Halles shopping center near St. Eustache church. Kids get one supervised hour (that's it) to negotiate a great play area filled with clever activities, including a small toboggan ride, a maze, a volcano, and much more. The staff speaks enough English and is accustomed to non-French-speaking kids (free, Tue and Thu–Fri 9:00–12:00 & 14:00–18:00, Wed and Sat 10:00–18:00, Sun 13:00–18:00, closed Mon and if rainy, 105 rue Rambuteau, Mo: Les Halles).

Aquaboulevard

Paris' best pool/water slide/miniature golf complex is easy to reach and a timely escape from the museum scene. Indoor and outdoor pools with high-flying slides, waves, geysers, and whirlpool tubs draw kids of all ages. It's pricey (and steamy inside), but a fun opportunity to see soaked Parisians at play. Ride the Métro to the end of line 8 (Balard stop), walk two blocks under the elevated freeway, veer left across the traffic circle, and find Aquaboulevard in a complex of theaters and shops (kids under 12-€10/6 hrs, adults-€25/6 hrs, much cheaper rates for more than one visit, daily 9:00–23:00, English-speaking staff, keep a €1 coin for lockers, boys and men need Speedo-style swimsuits—€6–10 at the Decathlon sporting-goods store right there, see map on page 411 for location, tel. 01 40 60 10 00).

SHOPPING

Shopping provides a break from Paris' heavyweight museums and monuments. And, if approached thoughtfully, boutique browsing can be a culturally enlightening experience. In this chapter, you'll find information on shopping for souvenirs, clothing, food, and bargains.

Most travelers are interested in finding a few souvenirs and maybe an article of clothing. Here's a simple approach that works for most:

- If you need just souvenirs, find a souvenir shop or consult your neighborhood supermarket for that Parisian box of tea, jam, or cookies—perfect for tucking into your suitcase at the last minute.
- For more elaborate purchases, large department stores provide painless one-stop shopping in elegant surroundings.
- Neighborhood boutiques offer the greatest reward at the highest risk. While clerks and prices can be intimidating, the selection is more original, and the experience is purely Parisian.

For information on VAT refunds and customs regulations, see page 11 in the Introduction.

Tips on Shopping

Before you enter a Parisian store, remember the following points:

- In small stores, always say, *"Bonjour, Madame/Mademoiselle/Monsieur"* when entering and *"Au revoir, Madame/Mademoiselle/Monsieur"* when leaving.
- The customer is not always right. In fact, figure the clerk is doing you a favor by waiting on you.
- Except in department stores, it's not normal for the customer to handle clothing. Ask first before you pick up an item.
- For clothing size comparisons between the US and France, see page 552 of the appendix.
- Forget returns (and don't count on exchanges).
- Saturday afternoons are busiest.

Key Phrases

English	French	Pronounced
Just looking.	*Je regard.*	zhuh ruh-gar
How much is it?	*Combien?*	kohm-bee-ehn
Too big/small/ expensive	*Trop grand/ petit/cher*	troh grahn/ puh-tee/sher
May I try it on?	*Je peux l'essayer?*	zhuh puh luh-say-yay
Can I see more?	*Auriez vous autre chose à me proposer?*	oh-ree-ay voo zoh-truh shohz ah muh proh-poh-zay?
I'd like this.	*Je voudrais ça.*	zhuh voo-dray sah
On sale	*Solde*	sold
Discounted price	*Prix réduit*	pree ray-dwee
Big discounts	*Prix choc*	pree shock

- Observe French shoppers. Then imitate.
- Stores are generally closed on Sunday, except at the Carrousel du Louvre (underground shopping mall at the Louvre), and some shops near Sèvres-Babylone, along the Champs-Elysées, and in the Marais.
- Don't feel obliged to buy. The expression for "window-shopping" in French is *faire du lèche-vitrines* ("window-licking").

Souvenir Shops

Avoid souvenir carts in front of famous monuments. Prices and selection are better in shops and department stores. Look around the Pompidou Center, on the streets of Montmartre, and in department stores (see below). The riverfront stalls near Notre-Dame sell a variety of used books, old posters and postcards, magazines, and tourist paraphernalia in the most romantic setting; see "*Les Bouquinistes* (Riverside Vendors)" sidebar. You'll find some good deals at the souvenir shops that line rue d'Arcole between Notre-Dame and Hôtel de Ville. Rue de Rivoli, running alongside the Louvre, is filled with hawkers selling knickknacks to tourists.

Department Stores (Les Grands Magasins)

Like cafés, department stores were invented here (surprisingly, not in America). While the stores seem overwhelming at first, they generally work like ours, and those listed here are accustomed to wide-eyed foreign shoppers and have English-speaking staff. These stores are

Les Bouquinistes (Riverside Vendors)

The used-book sellers *(bouquinistes)* you see along the Seine around Notre-Dame are a Parisian fixture. They've been here since the mid-1500s, when shops and stalls lined most of the bridges in Paris. In 1557, these merchants were tagged as thieves for selling forbidden Protestant pamphlets during the Wars of Religion (Parisians were staunchly Catholic).

The term *bouquinistes* (boo-keen-eest) probably comes from the Dutch word *boeckin*, meaning "small book." First using wheelbarrows to transport and sell their goods, these hardy entrepreneurs eventually fastened trays to the parapets of the bridges with thin leather straps. After the Revolution, business boomed when entire libraries were liberated from nobles or clergymen and wound up for sale cheap on the banks of the Seine. In 1891, *bouquinistes* received permission to permanently attach their boxes to the quaysides. Today, the waiting list to become one of Paris' 250 *bouquinistes* is eight years.

Each *bouquiniste* is given four boxes, all of a specified size, and rent is paid only for the stone on which the boxes rest (less than €100 per year). The most coveted spots are awarded based on seniority. Maintenance costs, including the required *vert* wagon paint (the green color of old train cars), are paid by the *bouquinistes*. With little overhead, prices are usually cheaper than in most shops. While these days tourists prefer magnets and posters over vintage books, the city "officially" allows no more than one box of souvenirs for every three boxes of books.

Bouquinistes must be open at least four days a week, or they lose their spot. Wednesdays are best (when school is out), and warm, dry days are golden (notice that every item is wrapped in protective plastic). And yes, they do leave everything inside when they lock up at night; metal bars and padlocks keep things safe.

not only beautiful monuments to a more relaxed, elegant era, but also a great lesson in how others live. It's instructive to see what's in style, check out Parisians' current taste in clothes and furniture, and compare the selection with stores back home.

Parisian department stores begin with their showy perfume sections, almost always central on the ground floor, and worth a visit to see how much space is devoted to pricey, smelly water. Helpful information desks are usually near the perfume section (handy floor plans in English). Most stores have a good selection of souvenirs and toys at fair prices, plus reasonable restaurants; some have view terraces. Stores are generally open Monday through Saturday from 10:00–19:00, some are open later on Thursdays, and all are jammed on Saturdays and closed on Sundays.

Galeries Lafayette and Printemps

You'll find both Galeries Lafayette and Printemps (pran-tom) department stores in several Parisian neighborhoods. The most convenient and best sit side by side behind the old Opéra, complementing that monument's similar, classy era (Mo: Chaussée d'Antin-La Fayette, Havre-Caumartin, or Opéra). Both stores sprawl over three buildings (with one being the venerable and domed original) and consume entire city blocks. The selection is huge, crowds can be huger (especially on summer Saturdays), and the prices are considered pretty high.

At the Galeries Lafayette near the Opéra Garnier, don't miss the belle époque dome (enjoy from the railing on the third or fourth floor) or the stunning, open-air rooftop view on the seventh floor (free, open daily May–Sept, climb there from the cafeteria on the sixth floor). Fashion shows for the public take place year-round at Galeries Lafayette on Fridays at 15:00 (call 01 42 82 30 25 to confirm time and to reserve—they speak English, in auditorium on seventh floor). Beware the *"mode seduction"* on the third floor. Continue your shopping by walking from this area to place Vendôme (see "Boutique Strolls," later in this chapter).

Bon Marché

Combine a visit to Paris' oldest department store with a great neighborhood shopping experience. Take the Métro (or bus #87) to Sèvres-Babylone and find the Bon Marché behind a small park. The Bon Marché ("inexpensive") opened in 1852, when fascination with iron and steel construction led to larger structures (like train stations, exhibition halls, and Eiffel Towers). The Bon Marché was the first large-scale store to offer fixed prices (no bargaining) and a vast selection of items under one glass roof. This rocked the commercial world and forever changed the future of shopping. High-volume sales allowed low prices and created loyal customers—can you say "Costco"?

Start your tour at the perfume section in the center—check out the fine scarf selection next to this area—then escalate up a few floors for a better perspective. Consider a new couch (furniture on top floor), then review the toy selection in the basement. Graze the gourmet groceries in the store's second building (La Grande Epicerie, behind the main building), ideal for food souvenirs such as mustards, teas, and chocolates. I buy a small picnic here for the park in front.

To find my favorite boutique-store streets, walk through the small park and down rue de Sèvres, passing the grand Hôtel Lutetia—which was built for shoppers by the Bon Marché's owners—on your right (see "Sèvres-Babylone to St. Sulpice," on page 412).

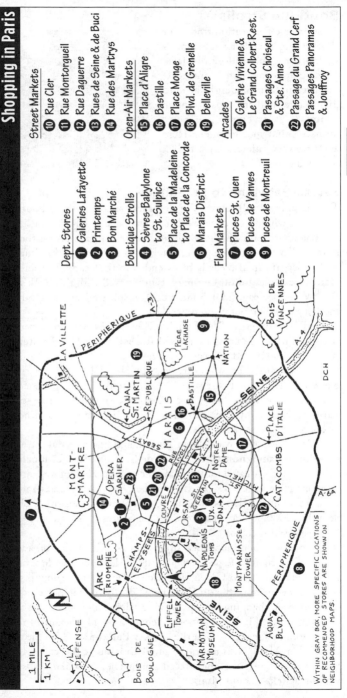

Shopping in Paris

Dept. Stores
- ❶ Galeries Lafayette
- ❷ Printemps
- ❸ Bon Marché

Boutique Strolls
- ❹ Sèvres-Babylone to St. Sulpice
- ❺ Place de la Madeleine to Place de la Concorde
- ❻ Marais District

Flea Markets
- ❼ Puces St. Ouen
- ❽ Puces de Vanves
- ❾ Puces de Montreuil

Street Markets
- ❿ Rue Cler
- ⓫ Rue Montorgueil
- ⓬ Rue Daguerre
- ⓭ Rues de Seine & de Buci
- ⓮ Rue des Martrys

Open-Air Markets
- ⓯ Place d'Aligre
- ⓰ Bastille
- ⓱ Place Monge
- ⓲ Blvd. de Grenelle
- ⓳ Belleville

Arcades
- ⓴ Galerie Vivienne & Le Grand Colbert Rest.
- ㉑ Passages Choiseul & Ste. Anne
- ㉒ Passage du Grand Cerf
- ㉓ Passages Panoramas & Jouffroy

SHOPPING

WITHIN GRAY BOX, MORE SPECIFIC LOCATIONS OF RECOMMENDED STORES ARE SHOWN ON NEIGHBORHOOD MAPS.

1 MILE
1 KM

Boutique Strolls

Allow yourself a vacation from your
sightseeing-focused vacation by
sifting through window displays,
pausing at corner cafés, and feeling the rhythm of neighborhood
life. While smaller shops are more
intimate, sales clerks are more
formal—mind your manners. Here
are three very different areas to lick
some windows.

Sèvres-Babylone to St. Sulpice

This shopping stroll allows you to sample smart clothing boutiques
and clever window displays while enjoying one of Paris' more attrac-
tive neighborhoods. This leisurely, one-hour saunter starts at the Bon
Marché department store (described above) and ends at the church of
St. Sulpice. It can also easily be extended to the nearby Luxembourg
Garden or boulevard St. Germain, tying in well with this book's Left
Bank Walk (see page 233). Some stores on this walk are open Sunday,
though the walk is better on other days.

After visiting the Bon Marché (Mo: Sèvres-Babylone), walk by
the small park and cross boulevard Raspail, with Hôtel Lutetia to
your right, and start down rue de Sèvres.

La Maison du Chocolat, next to Hôtel Lutetia (19 rue de
Sèvres), makes a good first stop. The shop sells handmade chocolates
in exquisitely wrapped boxes and delicious ice-cream cones in season.
Parisians commonly offer chocolates when invited over, and no gift
box better impresses than this.

Cross the street, walk down a block, and find a seat at the atmospheric **Au Sauvignon Café** (10 rue de Sèvres), ideal for lunch or a
drink, and well-situated for watching the conveyor belt of well-dressed
shoppers glide by. Check out the zinc bar and picture-crazy interior.
If your feet hurt, relief is at hand—a **Mephisto** shoe store is almost
next door. A block farther down rue de Sèvres, a wicked half-man,
half-horse statue stands guard.

From here, boutique-lined streets fan out like spokes on a wheel
(from left to right): rue de Grenelle, rue du Dragon, rue du Cherche
Midi, and rue du Vieux Colombier. Each street merits a detour if shopping matters to you. Rue du Cherche Midi (follow the horse's fanny)
offers an ever-changing but always chic selection of shoe, purse, and
clothing stores. Find Paris' most celebrated bread—beautiful round
loaves with designer crust—at the low-key **Poilane** at #8 (on the right,
closed Sun–Mon). Next door, the small **Cuisine de Bar** café—which
is a *bar à pains*—serves open-faced sandwiches *(tartines)* and salads
with bread (closed Sun–Mon).

When back at the horse, turn right and continue down rue du Vieux Colombier. You'll pass the Théâtre du Vieux-Colombier (1913), one of three key venues for La Comédie-Française, a historic state-run troupe. At **Longchamps** (#21), you can hunt for a stylish bag in any color. Cross busy rue de Rennes, gasping at the dreadful Montparnasse Tower, and continue down rue du Vieux Colombier. Many stores in this area offer just one or two items, but in a variety of colors and patterns. Check out **Vilebrequin** if the man or *petit-garçon* in your life needs a swimsuit. St. Sulpice Church awaits a block farther down. The **Café de la Mairie** has a privileged location on this lovely square. From here, you can visit St. Sulpice (see page 240) and either cross the square to Luxembourg Garden (page 242) or backtrack to rue Bonaparte, turning right to reach boulevard St. Germain (and more shopping and several *grands cafés*, described on page 397). If you need a bookstore, take a detour left on rue Mabillon, another left on rue Guisarde, then find the **Village Voice** at 6 rue Princesse).

For Paris' best pastries—according to local shopkeepers and my wife—continue along rue St. Sulpice, with the church on your right, passing **Café Estrella** (closed Sun, 34 rue St. Sulpice, excellent teas and coffee with *real* French roast, and a friendly owner, Jean-Claude). A few blocks beyond, take the second left on rue de Seine (marked *rue du Tournon* to the right) and find **Gérard Mulot's Pâtisserie/Bakery.** Ogle the window display and try his chocolate macaroons and savory quiches—oh, baby (closed Wed, 76 rue de Seine, tel. 01 43 26 85 77).

From here, the closest Métro station is Odéon. To get there, continue on rue de Seine up to boulevard St. Germain and walk a couple of blocks to the right. You can also continue down rue de Seine to the river and follow my Left Bank Walk (page 233).

Place de la Madeleine, Rue Royale, Place Vendôme, and Place de la Concorde

The ritzy streets connecting these high-priced squares form a magnificent mile of gourmet food shops, jewelry stores, four-star hotels, exclusive clothing boutiques, and people who are better dressed than you. This area offers the best illustration of the value Parisians place on outrageously priced products. If you include the place Vendôme detour (with brief stops to shop), this walk takes about two hours. For most, the one-hour walk *sans* detour, ending on place de la Concorde, offers a sufficient sample of conspicuous consumption.

Place de la Madeleine: Start at place de la Madeleine for a gourmet food fantasy (see map on page 411; Mo: Madeleine). From the Métro, follow *sortie* signs to the back of the Madeleine and circumnavigate counterclockwise around the square, starting at the black-and-white awnings of...

Fauchon: This bastion of over-the-top food products has faded from its glory days, and today caters to a largely tourist clientele—though it can still make your mouth water and your pocketbook ache. Fauchon outposts were found all over Paris until competitor Le Nôtre snapped them up. Now the only Fauchon that remains is this mothership store—the place where it all began.

Two separate pink-streaked shops are necessary to meet demand. The *Boulangerie-Traiteur* (Mon–Sat 8:00–19:00, closed Sun, tel. 01 70 39 38 96) is like a delicatessen with prepared foods—meats, meals, *pâtisseries* (pastries), breads, and cookies (of course, there are always *madeleines* on this square). Peruse the sumptuous desserts and take-away dinner *plats* that cost more than most restaurant meals. Above the *Traiteur,* you can have a meal or a drink in the *Salon de Thé* (Mon–Sat 8:00–19:00, closed Sun, tel. 01 70 39 38 78).

The *Confiserie et Epicerie* (candies and grocery) is Fauchon's more impressive shop, across the small street (Mon–Sat 9:00–21:00, closed Sun). This razzle-dazzle store makes me feel like a movie star when I enter. It's all about style, branding, and packaging. Tourists gobble up anything wrapped in pink and black—provided Fauchon's name is emblazoned on it. Stroll downstairs and find a vast wine bar with seats surrounding an imprisoned wine steward. Look for the €4,000 bottles of century-old Cognac on shelves to the back—who buys this stuff? The floor above the *Epicerie* is a fashionable restaurant with view tables of La Madeleine and supermodel hostesses.

More Shops on Place de la Madeleine: Turn right out of Fauchon's and find **Marquise de Sévígné** next door, where well-coiffed chocolate consultants are just waiting to match you with the perfect box of chocolate (Mon–Sat 10:00–19:00, closed Sun).

Hédiard lies across the square at #21 (Mon–Sat 9:00–21:00, closed Sun, tel. 01 43 12 88 85). This older, more appealing, and more accessible gourmet food shop was founded in 1854. It features elegantly displayed produce and meats, a slick atrium wine shop, and a nifty café above (take the glass elevator up for a coffee or lunch). The small red containers make good souvenirs, with flavored mustards, jams, coffee, candies, and tea. Anyone can enter the glass doors of the wine cellar, marked *Le Chais,* and be greeted by the sommelier (find the €2,000 bottles of Petrus), but you need special permission to access *Les Vénérables* wines.

Next to Hédiard at #19 is the **house of truffles** (Mon–Sat 9:30–21:00, closed Sun, tel. 01 42 65 53 22). Ponder the window display of ugly black mushrooms that sell for up to €1,000 a pound. Inside, you'll find a small shop and a sharp little restaurant serving a variety of dishes, all with truffles. Find the surprisingly reasonable *menu* and consider a truffle omelet (€22), or maybe chocolate cake with truffles (€14). You'll also see every possible food that can be made with truffles—even Armagnac brandy—as well as white truffles from Italy that sell for €2,500 a pound. Small jars of black truffles sell for €40.

At #17, **Caviar Kaspia,** you can add Iranian caviar, eel, and vodka to your truffle collection. Find the price list on the counter: The stronger caviars are cheaper (€110 for a small tin); the "finer" caviars sell for up to €16,000 a kilo (I have a hard time visualizing 2.2 pounds of caviar, and a harder time visualizing paying for it). The restaurant upstairs serves what you see downstairs—at exorbitant prices (Mon–Sat 10:00–24:00, closed Sun). A caviar competitor recently opened next door (Caviar Prunier)—demand must be strong.

Rue Royale: Pass the snazzy Baccarat crystal shop on your right and keep straight, cross three crosswalks, and trade expensive food for expensive stuff (I'm not sure how Toto landed a storefront here). Strut one block down rue Royale (consider a dip into the classy Village Royale mini-mall). At rue du Faubourg St. Honoré, cross rue Royale to your left—pausing in the middle for a great view both ways—and find **Ladurée** at 16 rue Royale, an out-of-this-world pastry break in an 1800s setting (look for the green awning, Mon–Sat 8:30–19:00, Sun 10:00–19:00).

Place Vendôme: A detour left on rue du Faubourg St. Honoré leads several blocks past clothing boutiques to the *très* elegant square, place Vendôme, home to the Hôtel Ritz (Hemingway liberated the bar in World War II) and upper-crust jewelry stores—Van Cleef & Arpels, Dior, Chanel, Cartier, and others (if you have to ask how much...). Only jewelry stores are allowed on place Vendôme. The square was created by Louis XIV during the 17th century as a setting for a statue of himself. One hundred and fifty years later, Louis XIV was replaced by a statue of Napoleon.

Leave place Vendôme by walking up rue de la Paix—strolling by still more jewelry, high-priced watches, and crystal—and enter place de l'Opéra, where you'll find the *Paris Story* film, the Opéra Garnier (see page 61), and Galeries Lafayette and Printemps—if you're not shopped out yet (see descriptions earlier in this chapter). Or return to our walk on rue Royale.

Place de la Concorde: If you skip the place Vendôme detour, continue two more blocks down rue Royale to its end at place de la Concorde. Browse the crystal and jewelry shops, then end your stroll at **Hôtel Crillon** for the appropriate finish to this walk (see "Les Grands Cafés de Paris," page 397).

Marais

For more eclectic, avant-garde stores, peruse the artsy shops between the Pompidou Center and place des Vosges. Stick to the west–east axes formed by rue Ste. Croix de la Bretonnerie, rue des Rosiers, rue des

Francs Bourgeois, and rue St. Antoine. (These streets are part of the Marais Walk; see map on page 263.) This area is rich with jewelry, shoes, and trendy clothing boutiques. On Sunday afternoons, when the rest of Paris naps, this area buzzes with shoppers and café crowds.

Don't miss the luxurious tea extravaganza at **Mariage Frères,** just off rue Ste. Croix de la Bretonnerie at 30 rue du Bourg Tibourg (daily 10:30–19:30, serving tea from 12:00).

The next three places are on **rue Vieille du Temple:** For an assortment of tasty eats to nibble between shops, duck into **Tout au Beurre** ("Everything made with butter")—you just can't go wrong with a name like that (at #29). **La Belle Hortense** is a bookstore/ wine bar oozing with atmosphere (at #31; daily 17:00–24:00). Get your *chocolat* fix (the movie and the candy) at **Cacao et Chocolat,** which serves deliciously beautiful chocolates in a place that feels right out of the movie *Chocolat* (at #36).

Between place des Vosges and the Carnavalet Museum, **rue des Francs Bourgeois** is the epicenter of Marais chic, with hyper-trendy boutiques. Pop in and out of shops to find the ultimate little black dress, silk scarf, or dangly earrings. At #47, check out *l'art du buro* with Parisian-cool office supplies.

Drop into **Un Chien dans le Marais** to experience how much the French love their pets, and peruse the bejeweled doggie collars and clothes (at 35 bis rue du Roi de Sicile).

Puces St. Ouen—The Flea Market at Porte de Clignancourt

Paris' sprawling flea markets (*marché aux puces;* mar-shay oh-poos; *puce* is French for "flea") are oversized garage sales. They started in the Middle Ages, when middlemen sold old, flea-infested clothes and discarded possessions of the wealthy at bargain prices to eager peasants. Buyers were allowed to rummage through piles of aristocratic garbage.

Today **Puces St. Ouen** (poos sahn-wahn), at Porte de Clignancourt, carries on that tradition. This is the mother of all flea markets, with more than 2,000 vendors selling everything from flamingos to faucets, but mostly antiques (Sat 9:00–18:00, Sun 10:00–18:00, Mon 11:00–17:00, closed Tue–Fri, pretty dead the first 2 weeks of Aug, tel. 01 58 61 22 90, www.st-ouen-tourisme.com and www.parispuces .com).

This market shows off Paris' gritty, seamy underbelly and can be intimidating. No event brings together the melting-pot population of Paris better than this carnival-like market. Some find it claustrophobic, over-crowded, and threatening; others find French *diamants*-in-the-rough and return happy. You can bargain a bit (best deals are made with cash at the end of the day), though don't expect swinging deals here.

The St. Ouen "market" is actually a collection of individual markets. Most of these are a covered alley, each with a different

Puces St. Ouen Flea Market

name and specializing in a particular angle on antiques, bric-a-brac, and junk. You'll see *marchés* Vernaison, Dauphine, Biron, Serpette (classy antiques), and Paul Bert by walking down rue des Rosiers. Look for a map (at shops or the TI) that tries to explain the general character of each.

Space for this flea market was created in the 1800s, when the city wall was demolished (now a freeway), leaving large tracts of land open. The vacuum eventually was filled by street vendors, then antique dealers. The hodgepodge pattern of markets reflects their unplanned evolution. Strolling the markets can feel more like touring a souk in North Africa, a place of narrow alleys packed with people and too much to see.

Even if antiques, African objects, and T-shirts aren't your thing, you can still find this market worth the Métro ride. Pretend you just rented a big, empty apartment...and need to furnish it. Come for lunch in one of the many lively and reasonable cafés and receive a reality check, away from the beautiful people and glorious monuments of Paris. You'll get a dose of life in "the 'burbs." **La Chope des Puces bar,** on rue des Rosiers, has live Gypsy music concerts on Saturday and Sunday afternoons, complete with a questionable clientele (open

14:00–19:00, tel. 01 40 11 02 49).

To get to the Puces St. Ouen, take Métro line 4 to the end of the line at Porte de Clignancourt, then carefully follow *Sortie, Marché aux Puces* signs. Walk straight out of the Métro down avenue de la Porte de Clignancourt, passing by leather stores and through blocks of trinkets and cheap clothing stalls. Your destination is just beyond the elevated freeway (white bridge). Cross under the freeway, leaving Paris and entering the suburb of St. Ouen, veering left on the angled street. Turn left onto rue des Rosiers, the spine that links the many markets of St. Ouen. If you buy a large item, note that shipping is very expensive (Camard company has the best reputation, tel. 01 49 46 10 82).

Wear your money belt; pickpockets and scam artists thrive in these wall-to-wall-shopper events. Don't use ATM machines here if you can help it, as many are tampered with by con artists.

Other Flea Markets: Puces de Vanves is comparatively tiny and civilized, and preferred by many flea-market connoisseurs who find better deals at less famous markets (Sat–Sun 7:00–17:00, closed Mon–Fri, Mo: Porte de Vanves). The mega–**Puces de Montreuil** is the least organized and most traditional of them all, with chatty sellers and competitive buyers (Sat–Mon 8:00–18:00, closed Tue–Fri, Mo: Porte de Montreuil).

Open-Air Markets

Browse these markets for picnics, or find a corner café from which to appreciate the scene. I've listed Paris' most appealing markets below.

Street Markets

Several traffic-free street markets overflow with flowers, produce, fish vendors, and butchers, illustrating how most Parisians shopped before there were supermarkets and department stores. Markets are open daily except Sunday afternoons, Monday, and lunchtime throughout the week (13:00–15:00).

Rue Cler—a wonderful place to sleep and dine as well as shop—is a refined street market serving an upscale neighborhood near the Eiffel Tower (Mo: Ecole Militaire; for details, see Rue Cler Walk, page 338, and the Sleeping and Eating chapters).

Rue Montorgueil is a thriving and less touristed market street. Ten blocks from the Louvre and five blocks from the Pompidou Center, rue Montorgueil (mohn-tor-go-ee) is famous as the last vestige of the once massive Les Halles market (just north of St. Eustache church, Mo: Etienne Marcel). Once the home of big warehouses and wholesale places to support the market, these have morphed into retail outlets to survive. Other traffic-free streets cross rue Montorgueil—don't miss the nearby covered arcade, passage du Grand Cerf (down rue Marie Stuart at the Les Halles end of rue Montorgueil).

Rue Daguerre, near the Catacombs and off avenue du Général Leclerc, is the least touristy of the street markets listed here (Mo: Denfert-Rochereau; for Catacombs description, see page 59).

Rue de Seine and rue de Buci combine to make a central and colorful market within easy reach of many sights (Mo: Odéon; see also "Les Grands Cafés de Paris," page 397, and Left Bank Walk, page 233).

Rue des Martyrs near Montmartre makes Paris feel like a village. Consider exploring this lively market scene as part of the Montmartre Walk (see page 323).

Larger, Morning-Only Markets

Offering cheaper prices and more selection, these markets take over selected boulevards and squares throughout Paris generally from 8:00–12:30. Expect a lively combination of flea- and street-market atmosphere and items.

Marché de la place d'Aligre, 10 blocks behind the Opéra Bastille down rue de Faubourg St. Antoine, is an intimate open-air market where you'll see few tourists (daily 9:00–12:00, place d'Aligre, Mo: Ledru-Rollin).

Marché de la Bastille is huge, with a vast selection of products (Thu and Sun, Mo: Bastille); consider combining either of these two markets with a stroll through Promenade Plantée park (see page 70) and the Marais Walk (page 263).

Marché place Monge is comparatively minuscule, specializing in high-quality foods (Wed, Fri, and Sun; near rue Mouffetard, Mo: Monge).

Marché boulevard de Grenelle, a few blocks southwest of Champ de Mars park and the rue Cler area, is packed with produce, nonperishable goods, and Parisians in search of a good value (Wed and Sun, between Dupleix and La Motte Picquet-Grenelle Métro stops).

Marché Belleville is big and very untouristy (Tue and Fri, Mo: Belleville).

Arcaded Shopping Streets (Passages)

More than 200 of these covered shopping streets once crisscrossed Paris, providing much-needed shelter from the rain. The first were built during the American Revolution, though the ones you'll see date from the 1800s. Today, only a handful remain to remind us where shopping malls got their inspiration, although they now sell things you would be more likely to find in flea markets than at JCPenney. Here's a short list to weave into your sightseeing plan. (They're found on the map in this chapter and on the "East Paris" color map at the beginning of this book.)

Galerie Vivienne, behind the Palais Royal off rue des Petits-Champs and a few blocks from the Louvre, is the most refined and accessible of the *passages* for most, though they don't reflect the typical, more funky *passages* (Mo: Pyramides or Palais Royal). Check out Le Grand Colbert, a surprisingly affordable yet elegant restaurant with decent cuisine (2 rue Vivienne, see page 395).

Passage Choiseul and **Passage Ste. Anne,** four blocks west of Galerie Colbert and Galerie Vivienne, are fine examples of most Parisian *passages,* selling used books, paper products, trinkets, and snacks (down rue des Petits-Champs toward avenue de l'Opéra, same Métro stops).

Passage du Grand Cerf is a more elegant arcade, easily combined with a visit to the nearby rue Montorgueil street market described earlier (Mo: Etienne Marcel).

Passage Panoramas and **Passage Jouffroy** are long galleries that connect with several other smaller *passages* to give you the best sense of the elaborate network of arcades that once existed (on both sides of boulevard Montmartre, between Métro stops Grands Boulevards/rue Montmartre and Richelieu Drouot).

NIGHTLIFE

Paris is brilliant after dark. Save energy from your day's sightseeing and experience the City of Light lit. Whether it's a concert at the Sainte-Chapelle, a boat ride on the Seine, a walk in Montmartre, a hike up the Arc de Triomphe, or a late-night café, you'll see Paris come alive. Night walks in Paris are wonderful. Any of the self-guided walking tours in the book are fun after dark.

The *Pariscope* magazine (€0.40 at any newsstand, in French) offers a complete weekly listing of music, cinema, theater, opera, and other special events—I decipher this useful periodical for you below. The *Paris Voice* website, in English, has a helpful monthly review of Paris entertainment (www.parisvoice.com).

Pariscope

The weekly *Pariscope* (€0.40, comes out on Wed) or *L'Officiel des Spectacles* (€0.35) is essential if you want to know what's going on in Paris. I prefer *Pariscope*. Pick one up at a newsstand and page through it. The order of the contents changes periodically, but the basics described below are always there...somewhere.

The magazine, all in French, begins with a listing of "Théâtre" and what's playing at all key theater venues. "Musique and Concerts Classiques" follow, listing each day's events (program, location, time, price), including both opera houses if performances are scheduled. Remember that some concerts are free *(entrée libre)*.

A third of the magazine is devoted to *cinéma*—a Parisian forte. While a code marks films as "Comédie," "Documentaire," "Drame," "Karaté," "Erotisme," and so on, the key mark for non-French-speakers is "v.o.," for *version originale* (original-language version)—this means the movie hasn't been dubbed in French. Films are listed alphabetically, by neighborhood ("Salles Paris"), and by genre. To find a showing near your hotel, simply look for a cinema in the same arrondissement.

"Salles Périphérie" means the cinema is located out in the suburbs. Many cinemas offer discounts on Monday or Wednesday nights.

The "Arts" section lists current hours for temporary expositions and all of the museums (*tlj* = daily, *sf* = except, *Ent* = entry price, *TR* = reduced price—usually for students and children).

The "Enfants" section covers a myriad of possible children's activities. "Spectacles" are shows (like magic shows); you'll also see many "Marionettes" (puppet) shows and "Cirques" (circuses)—both are fun, even for non-French-speakers.

"Promenades et Loisirs" covers outdoor events and sights, including open-air theater, flea markets, sound-and-light shows *(son et lumières),* key monuments such as the Eiffel Tower and Arc de Triomphe, river cruises, parks, zoos, and aquariums.

For cancan mischief, look under "Paris la Nuit."

Music

Jazz Clubs

With a lively mix of American, French, and international musicians, Paris has been an internationally acclaimed jazz capital since World War II. You'll pay €12–25 to enter a jazz club (may include one drink; if not, expect to pay €5–10 per drink; beer is cheapest). See *Pariscope* magazine under "Musique" for listings, or, even better, the American Church's *Paris Voice* website for a good monthly review, or drop by the clubs to check out the calendars posted on their front doors. Music starts after 21:00 in most clubs. Some offer dinner concerts from about 20:30 on. Here are several good bets:

Caveau de la Huchette, a characteristic, old, jazz/dance club, fills an ancient Latin Quarter cellar with live jazz and frenzied dancing every night (admission about €11 on weekdays, €13 on weekends, €6 drinks, Tue–Sun 21:30–2:30 in the morning or later, closed Mon, 5 rue de la Huchette, Mo: St. Michel, recorded info tel. 01 43 26 65 05, www.caveaudelahuchette.fr).

For a spot teeming with late-night activity and jazz, go to the two-block-long rue des Lombards, at boulevard Sébastopol, midway between the river and the Pompidou Center (Mo: Châtelet). **Au Duc des Lombards** is one of the most popular and respected jazz clubs in Paris, with concerts nightly in a great, plush, 110-seat theater-like setting (admission about €20, cheap drinks, shows at 20:00 and 22:00, 42 rue des Lombards, tel. 01 42 33 22 88, www.ducdeslombards.fr). **Le Sunside,** run for 15 years by Stephane Portet, is just a block away. The club offers two little stages (ground floor and downstairs); one stage is devoted to contemporary world jazz, while the other features more traditional jazz—Dixieland and big band (concerts generally at 21:00, 60 rue des Lombards, tel. 01 40 26 21 25, www.sunset-sunside.com).

Cabaret

Old-Time Parisian Cabaret on Montmartre: Au Lapin Agile—This historic cabaret maintains the atmosphere of the heady days when bohemians would gather here to enjoy wine, song, and sexy jokes. For €24, you gather with about 25 French people in a dark room for a drink and as many as 10 different performers—mostly singers with a piano. Performers range from sweet and innocent Amélie types to naughty Maurice Chevalier types. While tourists are welcome, it's exclusively French, with no accommodation for English-speakers (and non-French-speakers will be lost). You sit at carved wooden tables in a dimly lit room, taste the traditional drink (brandy with cherries), and are immersed in a true Parisian ambience. The soirée covers traditional French standards, love ballads, sea chanteys, and more. The crowd sings along, as it has here for a century (Tue–Sun 21:00–2:00 in the morning, closed Mon, best to reserve ahead, 22 rue des Saules, tel. 01 46 06 85 87, www.au-lapin -agile.com; also see ✪ Montmartre Walk, page 323).

A Modern Cabaret near Canal St. Martin: Chez Raymonde—This club proves that the art of dinner cabaret is still alive in Paris. Your evening begins with a good three-course dinner (including apéritif, wine, a half-bottle of champagne, and coffee) in an intimate dining room, where you get to know your neighbors. Around 22:00, the maître d'hôtel and the chef himself kick off the performance with a waltz together. Then it's feather boas, song, and dance—audience participation is encouraged (€85–100/person, Fri–Sun evenings only, dinner starts at 20:00 and performance usually finishes about 23:00, reservations necessary, 119 avenue Parmentier, Mo: Goncourt, Parmentier, or République, tel. 01 43 55 26 27, www.chez-raymonde .com). On Sunday afternoons, you can also attend a performance over lunch (€70–85, starts at 12:30).

Beyond Cabaret in the Latin Quarter: Rocky Horror Picture Show—For a splash of cross-cultural cross-dressing, join the local Rocky Horror club for a goofy evening at the Studio Galande theater near the church of St. Julien-le-Pauvre (see ✪ Historic Paris Walk, page 74). For 25 years, this artsy little theater has hosted *Rocky Horror Picture Show* enthusiasts every weekend (€8, Fri and Sat at 22:00, drop by to get tickets in advance, 42 rue Galande, Mo: St. Michel, www .rocky.fr).

Concerts and Operas

Classical Concerts—For classical music on any night, consult *Pariscope* magazine; the "Musique" section under "Concerts Classiques" lists concerts (both free and for a fee). Look for posters at tourist-oriented churches.

From March through November, these churches regularly host concerts: St. Sulpice, St. Germain-des-Prés, Ste. Madeleine, St.

Eustache, St. Julien-le-Pauvre, and Sainte-Chapelle. It's well worth the €25 entry for the pleasure of hearing Mozart or Vivaldi while surrounded by the stained glass of the tiny Sainte-Chapelle (unheated—bring a sweater). Pick up concert schedules and tickets during the day at the small ticket booth to the left of the chapel entrance. Or call 01 42 77 65 65 to reserve ahead; you can leave your message in English (just speak clearly and spell your name). Seats are unassigned, so arrive 30 minutes early to snare a good view. There are often two concerts per evening, at 19:00 and 20:30; specify which one you want when you buy or reserve your ticket.

The **Salle Pleyel** hosts world-class artists, from string quartets and visiting orchestras to international opera stars. Tickets are usually expensive and hard to come by, so it's best to order online in advance (252 rue du Faubourg Saint-Honoré, Mo: Ternes, tel. 01 42 56 13 13, www.sallepleyel.fr).

Look also for daytime concerts in parks, such as the Luxembourg Garden. Even the Galeries Lafayette department store offers concerts. Many concerts are free *(entrée libre),* such as the Sunday atelier concert sponsored by the American Church (generally Sept–June at 17:00 but not every week, 65 quai d'Orsay, Mo: Invalides, RER: Pont de l'Alma, tel. 01 40 62 05 00).

Opera—Paris is home to two well-respected opera venues. The **Opéra Bastille** is the massive modern opera house that dominates place de la Bastille. Come here for state-of-the-art special effects and modern interpretations of classic ballets and operas. In the spirit of this everyman's opera, unsold seats are available at a big discount to seniors and students 15 minutes before the show. Standing-room-only tickets for €15 are also sold for some performances (Mo: Bastille, tel. 01 43 43 96 96). The **Opéra Garnier,** Paris' first opera house, hosts opera and ballet performances. Come here for less expensive tickets and grand belle époque decor (Mo: Opéra). To get tickets for either opera house, call 08 92 89 90 90, or easier, reserve online at www.opera-de-paris.fr. You can also go direct to each opera's ticket office (open daily 11:00–18:00).

Art in the Evening

Various **museums** are open late on different evenings, offering the opportunity for more relaxed, less crowded visits: the Louvre (Wed and Fri until 21:45), Orsay (Thu until 21:45), Orangerie (Fri until 21:00), Grand Palais (Wed until 22:00), and Pompidou Center (Wed–Mon until 21:00).

Art gallery openings are a fun way to check out new work by contemporary artists. Opening night receptions *(vernissage)* are classy and free. Check upcoming events listed on the *Paris Voice* website (www.parisvoice.com), or just follow my ✪ Left Bank Walk (on page 233) and see what's happening.

Seine River Cruises

Several companies offer dinner cruises on huge glass-domed boats (or open-air decks in summer) with departures along the Seine, including from the Eiffel Tower; see page 396 in the Eating chapter.

Night Walks

Go for an evening walk to best appreciate the City of Light. Break for ice cream, pause at a café, and enjoy the sidewalk entertainers as you join the post-dinner Parisian parade. Use any of this book's self-guided walking tours as a blueprint, and remember to avoid poorly lit areas and stick to main thoroughfares. Consider the following suggestions; most are partial versions of this book's longer walking tours.

▲▲▲**Trocadéro and Eiffel Tower**—This is one of Paris' most spectacular views at night. Take the Métro to the Trocadéro stop and join the party on place du Trocadéro for a magnificent view of the glowing Eiffel Tower. It's a festival of gawkers, drummers, street acrobats, and entertainers. Pass the fountains and cross the river to the base of the tower, worth the effort even if you don't go up (daily June–Aug until 24:45, Sept–mid-June until 23:45). See "Eiffel Tower," page 50.

From the Eiffel Tower, you can stroll through Champ de Mars park past Frisbees, soccer balls, and romantic couples, and take the Métro home (Ecole Militaire stop, across avenue de la Motte-Picquet from far southeast corner of park). Or there's a handy RER stop (Champ de Mars Tour Eiffel) two blocks west of the Eiffel Tower.

▲▲**Champs-Elysées and the Arc de Triomphe**—The avenue des Champs-Elysées glows after dark (see ☻ Champs-Elysées Walk, page 251). Start at the Arc de Triomphe (observation deck open daily, April–Sept until 23:00, Oct–March until 22:30), then stroll down Paris' lively grand promenade. A right turn on avenue George V leads to the Bateaux-Mouches river cruises. A movie on the Champs-Elysées is a fun experience (weekly listings in *Pariscope* under "Cinéma").

▲**Ile St. Louis and Notre-Dame**—Take the beautiful ☻ Historic Paris Walk (see page 74) after dinner on Ile St. Louis (see page 86).

To get to Ile St. Louis, take the Métro (line 7) to the Pont Marie stop, then cross pont Marie to Ile St. Louis. Turn right up rue St. Louis-en-l'Ile, stopping for dinner—or at least a Berthillon ice cream at #31 or Amorino Gelati at #47. At the end of Ile St. Louis, cross pont St. Louis to Ile de la Cité, with a great view of Notre-Dame. Wander to the Left Bank on quai de l'Archevêché, and drop down to the river to the right for the best floodlit views. From May through September, you'll find several permanently moored barges *(péniches)* that operate as bars. While I wouldn't eat dinner here, the atmosphere is great for a drink, often including live music on weekends (daily until 2:00 in the morning, closed Oct–April, live music often Thu–Sun from 21:00). End your walk on place du Parvis Notre-Dame in front of

Notre-Dame (on Sat–Sun in July–Aug, tower open until 23:00), or continue across the river to the Latin Quarter.

Place de la Concorde, Place Vendôme, and Place de l'Opéra—These three squares tie together nicely for an elegant post-dinner walk (see ✪ Shopping, page 413). Take the Métro to place de la Concorde and splurge for a pricey drink at the most expensive hotel in Paris (Hôtel Crillon, see "Les Grands Cafés de Paris," page 397). Get out to the obelisk for a terrific view of the Champs-Elysées and the beautifully lit, Greek-looking National Assembly building (to your left looking up the Champs-Elysées). Then walk up rue Royale toward the Madeleine church, turn right on rue St. Honoré, then left after several blocks on rue Castiglione. The sumptuous place Vendôme makes me wish I were rich. Exit place Vendôme at the opposite end and walk up rue de la Paix to find Opéra Garnier, stunning at night (see page 61; Mo: Opéra is right there to take you home).

Montmartre—Take the Métro to the area near Sacré-Cœur (church open daily until 23:00) and join the party (see ✪ Montmartre Walk, page 323). Follow the walking tour as far as you like, but keep to the top of the hill (avoid place Pigalle and boulevard de Rochechouart). Have a drink on place du Tertre and get your portrait sketched. Montmartre was a nighttime destination for Parisians in search of a lively evening even before the Impressionists arrived. For some old-time cabaret music, consider Au Lapin Agile (described earlier in this chapter). Sit in front of the Sacré-Cœur church (to leave the rabble, jump the fence for a spot on the grass) and marvel at the glorious city view.

Rue de Lappe—Take a walk on Paris' wild side along the three-block stretch of rue de Lappe behind the Bastille, from boulevard Richard Lenoir to rue de Charonne (Mo: Bastille). Nightclubs, bouncer-staffed bars, and youthful, boy-meets-girl energy power this late-night scene.

Marais—This artsy neighborhood is a hotbed for nightlife, full of cafés and tiny bars catering to locals and tourists alike. The action centers around rue Vieille du Temple (Mo: St. Paul), which offers something for every taste and attracts all age groups and sexual persuasions. Look for the Au Petit Fer à Cheval bar and the bookstore/winebar La Belle Hortense (daily 17:00–24:00, 31 rue Vieille du Temple, tel. 01 48 04 71 60).

Place St. Germain-des-Prés and Odéon—These areas are close to each other, worth combining for evening fun. Place St. Germain-des-Prés, along the Left Bank's main east–west route, hosts street theater and musicians that are better than ones you'll hear in the Métro. The church of St. Germain-des-Prés is often lit up and open at night, and Parisians sip drinks at two famous nearby cafés: Les Deux Magots and Le Café de Flore (see page 397; Mo: St. Germain-des-Prés). Nearby, night owls prowl along rues des Canettes and Guisarde (see "Near St. Sulpice Church" on page 394 of the Eating chapter). The Odéon, a few blocks away, is home to several movie theaters and still more lively cafés.

After-Dark Bus Tour

Several companies offer evening tours of Paris. I've described the company offering the most tours below. These trips are sold through your hotel (brochures in lobby) or directly at the offices listed below. You save no money by buying direct. (For the cost of two after-dark bus tickets, you can more than pay for my private taxi tour of floodlit Paris, described below.)

Paris Illumination Tours, run by Paris Vision, connect all the great illuminated sights of Paris with a 100-minute bus tour in 12 languages. The double-decker buses have huge windows, but the most desirable front seats are sometimes reserved for customers who've bought tickets for the overrated Moulin Rouge. Left-side seats are better. Visibility is fine in the rain.

You'll stampede on with a United Nations of tourists, get a set of headphones, dial up your language, and listen to a tape-recorded spiel (which is interesting, but includes an annoyingly bright TV screen and a pitch for the other, more expensive excursions). Uninspired as it is, the ride provides an entertaining, first-night overview of the city at its floodlit and scenic best. Bring your city map to stay oriented as you go. You're always on the bus, but the driver slows for photos at viewpoints (€26/person, kids under 12 ride free, 1.5 hours, departures 19:00–22:00 depending on time of year, usually April–Oct only, reserve 1 day in advance, arrive 30 min early to wait in line for best seats, departs from Paris Vision office at 214 rue de Rivoli, across the street from Mo: Tuileries, tel. 01 42 60 30 01, fax 01 42 86 95 36, www.parisvision.com). Skip their pricier minivan night tours.

▲▲Floodlit Paris Taxi Tour

Seeing the City of Light floodlit is one of Europe's great travel experiences and a great finale to any day in Paris. For less than the cost of two seats on a big bus tour, you can hire your own cab (maximum four passengers) and have a glorious hour of illuminated Paris on your terms and schedule. The downside: You don't have the high vantage point and big windows. The upside: it's cheaper, you go when and where you like, and you can jump out anywhere to get the best views and pictures.

Tour Overview: This is a circular one-hour route—from Notre-Dame to the Eiffel Tower along the Left Bank, then back along the Right Bank. Start at the taxi stand at Notre-Dame or any convenient point along the route and make any stops you like. Suggested stops are listed in bold on the list in "Taxi Instructions" (*"petit arrêt"* means "little stop"). To make it more of a party, bring a bottle of red wine

Taxi Instructions

Greetings, Monsieur/Madame. We are tourists and would like a tour of Paris at night. Are you willing to take us on the following route? We expect to be with you an hour, with a few short stops. We will pay the metered rate. How much do you expect this to cost?

Bonjour, Monsieur/Madame. Nous sommes des touristes et nous voulons faire un circuit touristique de Paris illuminé. Est-ce que c'est possible de suivre la route suivante? Nous resterions avec vous une heure, avec quelques petits arrêts. Nous paierons le montant indiqué sur le compteur. Combien cela va t-il coûter approximativement?

1. Notre-Dame
2. Hôtel de Ville
3. Pont Marie
4. Pont de la Tournelle (arrêt)
5. Quai de la Tournelle
6. Musée d'Orsay
7. Esplanade des Invalides
8. Invalides
9. Place Vauban/Eglise du Dome (arrêt)
10. Champ de Mars (place Jacques Rueff—arrêt)
11. Tour Eiffel
12. Pont d'Iena
13. Place du Trocadéro (arrêt)
14. Avenue Kléber
15. Arc de Triomphe (2 revolutions)
16. Champs-Elysées
17. Place de la Concorde (1 revolution)
18. Quai François Mitterrand
19. Musée du Louvre/Place du Carrousel/Pyramide (arrêt)
20. Quai du Louvre
21. Notre-Dame

Floodlit Paris Taxi Tour

Stops

1. Notre-Dame View from Pont de la Tournelle
2. Les Invalides View from Place Vauban
3. Eiffel Tower View from Champ de Mars
4. Eiffel Tower View from Place du Trocadéro
5. Champs-Elysées View from Place de la Concorde
6. Louvre Museum & Pyramid View

ILE ST. LOUIS

PONT MARIE

HOTEL DE VILLE

PONT DE LA TOURNELLE

1

CONCIERGERIE

LOUVRE MUSEUM + PYRAMID

6

PLACE ST. MICHEL

FINISH

NOTRE-DAME
START

QUAI-DES-TUILERIES

ORSAY MUSEUM

PLACE DE LA CONCORDE

5

SEINE RIVER

NAT'L. ASSEMBLY

NAPOLEON'S TOMB

PLACE VAUBAN

2

CHAMPS-ELYSEES

PONT ALEX. III

EIFFEL TOWER

BOULEVARD DE LA BOURDONNAIS

CHAMP DE MARS PARK

ARC DE TRIOMPHE

AVE. KLEBER

PLACE DU TROCADERO

4

PONT D'IENA

3

½ MILE
1 KM

N

DCH

NIGHTLIFE

and some chocolate to enjoy each time you hop out of the taxi (not in the taxi).

Taxi Logistics: Taxis have a strict meter (€26/hr plus about €1 per kilometer). This suggested loop takes an hour and costs around €40 (a bit more on Sunday). If your cabbie was easy to work with, add a 10 percent tip; if not, tip just five percent. Traffic is sparse and lights are bright between 22:00 and 24:00 every night. Your only timing concern: The Eiffel Tower twinkles for only the first five minutes of each hour after dark. If you start at Notre-Dame at half past the hour, you should be right on time for the sparkles. You might talk the driver into taking four people in a cab, though this is tight for decent sight-seeing (with three, everyone gets a window).

Give the driver the instructions on page 428. Before you go, photocopy it (ask at your hotel) or rip the page out (but trace the route on another map so that you can follow along). Make sure the driver understands the plan—and enjoys the challenge. Review with the driver exactly where you hope to stop before you start.

And you're on your way. Roll the windows down, learn your driver's name and use it, work with him to select a good radio station, and turn the cab light on to read if you like (this is no problem for the driver). Let the cabbie add a few little deviations (which can be great) as long as he understands your general plan. Stop when you want (but remember that the meter runs at about €0.50 per minute when stopped). Some cabbies might speak a little English; if not, learn and use the following key words:

English	French	Pronounced
Slower, please.	*Lentement, s'il vous plaît.*	lawn-tuh-mohn see voo play
Stop, please.	*Arrêtez, s'il vous plaît.*	ah-ret-tay see voo play
Wait, please.	*Patientez, s'il vous plaît.*	pah-see-yahn-tay see voo play
I love Paris!	*J'aime Paris!*	zhem pah-ree

The Tour Begins: Start at Notre-Dame (taxi stand just in front, on left). Drive over pont d'Arcole to Hôtel de Ville, then turn right along the Seine (the white stripe of light is a modern bridge connecting the two islands).

Cross Ile St. Louis on pont Marie. Stop on the next bridge (pont de la Tournelle) just after the island, get out, and giggle with delight at the city and illuminated Notre-Dame. Then turn right along the Seine on quai de la Tournelle, motoring scenically past Notre-Dame.

Drive west along the entire length of the long Louvre—once the world's biggest building (across the river), then under the Orsay Museum (above you, on left). The National Assembly (on left) faces place de la Concorde (on right). The ornate pont Alexandre comes next (on right).

Turn left down Esplanade des Invalides to the gilded dome of Les Invalides, marking Napoleon's Tomb. As you approach the grand building, watch the illusion of the fancy dome sinking behind the facade. Circle left around Invalides for a close-up view. Get out at place Vauban (behind the dome) and marvel at its symmetry.

Take avenue de Tourville to avenue de la Bourdonnais, which runs alongside the Champ de Mars park (former military training grounds that now serve as the Eiffel Tower's backyard). Turn left onto avenue Joseph Bouvard, leading to a circle made to order for viewing the Eiffel Tower. Get out and gasp.

Pont d'Iéna leads from directly in front of the tower across the Seine to place du Trocadéro for another grand Eiffel view (get out again and walk toward the tower to get the best photos and to enjoy the night scene here).

Avenue Kléber leads through one of Paris' ritziest neighborhoods to the Arc de Triomphe. Battle twice around the eternal flame marking the Tomb of the Unknown Soldier and Paris' craziest traffic circle. Notice the rules of the road: Get to the center ASAP, those entering have the right-of-way, and any accidents are no-fault (insurance companies just split the costs down the middle). As you circle, notice the uniform boulevards reaching out like spokes from this hub. Try to find the huge and modern La Grande Arche in the distance opposite the Champs-Elysées.

When ready to continue, say the rhyme, "Champs-Elysées, *s'il vous plaît*" (shahnz ay-lee-zay see voo play). Cruise down Europe's grandest boulevard—past fancy restaurants, car dealerships, and theaters—to the bold white obelisk marking the former site of the guillotine, place de la Concorde.

Circle once (maybe twice) around place de la Concorde, picking out all the famous landmarks near and far. Stop at the center to look up the Champs-Elysées. Then continue east (reminding your cabbie the next stop is "Pyramide") along the Seine on quai des Tuileries (the two train-station clocks across the river mark the Orsay Museum) and sneak (via a taxi/bus-only lane) into the courtyard of the Louvre for a close look at the magically glowing pyramid. Stop here.

Return to the riverfront along the Right Bank and pass the oldest bridge in Paris, pont Neuf, and the impressive Conciergerie with its floodlit medieval turrets (this is where Marie-Antoinette was imprisoned during the Revolution). Turn right on pont de Notre-Dame and you complete the loop back where you (and Paris) started, at place du Parvis, facing Notre-Dame on the Ile de la Cité.

Montmartre Extra: For an extra €15, you can extend your night drive to Montmartre and end your taxi tour there. You'll pass many more floodlit sights, and you'll experience the night scene on Paris' rollicking hill. The steps in front of Sacré-Cœur are filled with tourists and pickpockets. The café scene on and around place du Tertre is always lively. It's touristy and fun for those with the right mindset. (For more information, see ✪ Montmartre Walk on page 323.) After you finish exploring, you can catch any taxi back to your hotel.

Here's the Montmartre side-trip route: Start at the pyramid at the Louvre and drive through place Vendôme (with Hôtel Ritz on your left) to the Opéra Garnier. Then go up rue de la Chaussée past the Trinity Church; then head up rue Jean Baptiste to rue Pigalle. Drive up rue Pigalle (slowly, to peek into the many bars strewn with prostitutes). At place Pigalle, head left, past the sex shows and Moulin Rouge nightclub (with a mile-long line of tour buses marking the touristy cancan shows), to place Clichy, then drive up, up, up to the top of Montmartre. Say *au revoir* to your cabbie at the steps of the Sacré-Cœur, with the City of Light spreading out before you forever.

TRANSPORTATION CONNECTIONS

This chapter covers Paris' two main airports, one smaller airport, six train stations, and its main bus station, and includes parking tips for drivers.

When leaving Paris, get to your departure point early to allow time for waiting in lines. Figure on three hours for an overseas flight; 1–2 hours for flights within Europe (particularly if flying with a budget airline—they often have long check-in lines); and one hour for a train trip or bus ride, if you're doing anything beyond simply boarding (Eurostar trains require you to check in at least 30 minutes early). Whether arriving or departing, keep your luggage near you at all times. Pickpockets have their eyes peeled for travelers who let down their guard.

AIRPORTS

Charles de Gaulle Airport

The airport has three terminals: T-1, T-2, and T-3. Most flights from the US use T-1 or T-2. To see which terminal serves your airline, check your ticket, or contact the airport (toll tel. 3950, www.adp.fr).

The RER (Paris suburban train, connecting to Métro) stops at T-2 and near T-1 and T-3. The TGV (high-speed train) station is at T-2. The new CDGVAL automated shuttle train connects the terminals with the TGV and RER stations and parking garages (free, every 10 min, 24/7).

Pickpockets prey on jet-lagged tourists on shuttles between terminals, and on RER trains. Don't take an unauthorized taxi from the men greeting you on arrival; official taxi stands are well-signed.

Charles de Gaulle Airport

TERMINAL 1

UNDERGROUND WALKWAYS

CONTROL TOWER

TERMINAL 3

Ⓡ RER Stop
Ⓟ Parking

TO LILLE & BRUSSELS

TERMINAL 2

TO ROISSY-EN-FRANCE, ❸, A-1 FREEWAY & PARIS

2 B   2 D   2 F

2 A   2 C   2 E

CONTROL TOWER

TRAIN STATION (TGV & Ⓡ) & SHERATON HOTEL

TO DISNEYLAND PARIS, DIJON, LYON & AVIGNON

DCH

❶ Hôtel Ibis
❷ Novotel
❸ To Hôtel Campanile, Hôtel Kyriad Prestige & B&B Hôtel

Terminal 1 (T-1)

This circular terminal has one main entry and covers three floors—arrival (*arrivées*, top floor), departure (*départs*, one floor down) and shops/boutiques (basement level). For information on getting to Paris, see "Transportation Between Charles de Gaulle Airport and Paris," next page.

Arrival Level: You'll find a variety of services at the gates listed below. Expect changes during construction.

- Gate 36: Called "Meeting Point" (Point de Rencontre), this gate has an information counter with English-speaking staff, a café, and an ATM.
- Gate 34: Outside are Air France buses to Paris (see "Transportation Between Charles de Gaulle Airport and Paris" later in this chapter) and Orly Airport (see "Connecting Paris Airports" later in this chapter).
- Gate 30: Outside are Roissy-Buses to Paris (buy tickets from driver) and hotel shuttle buses *(navettes hôtels)*.
- Gates 24–30: Car rental desks.
- Gate 18: Taxis outside.
- Gates 12–14: Baggage storage (open daily, drop-off 10:00–16:00, pickup 8:30–19:30, tel. 01 48 16 34 90).

TRANSPORTATION

Departure Level *(niveau 3)*: Flight check-in, restaurants, a PTT (post office), a pharmacy, boutiques, and a handy grocery store one floor below the ticketing desks (*niveau 2* on the elevator).

Terminal 2 (T-2)

This long, horseshoe-shaped terminal is dominated by Air France and is divided into six subterminals (or halls), each identified by a letter (A through F). Baggage storage in T-2 is at both 2A (door 3, daily 8:00–20:00, tel. 01 48 16 20 61) and 2F (arrival level, door 4, daily 7:00–19:00, tel. 01 48 16 20 64). Free shuttle buses constantly circle, connecting the halls with the RER and the TGV station every seven minutes. The RER and TGV stations are below the Sheraton Hotel (and are within walking distance of some of the halls). Stops for shuttle buses, Air France buses, and Roissy-Buses are all well-marked and near each hall (see "Transportation Between Charles de Gaulle Airport and Paris," below). ADP's orange information desks are located near Gate 6 in each hall. Car-rental offices, post offices, pharmacies, and ATMs *(point d'argent)* are also well-signed.

Transportation Between Charles de Gaulle Airport and Paris

Three efficient public-transportation routes, airport vans, and taxis link the airport's terminals with central Paris. If you're traveling with one or two companions, carrying lots of baggage, or are just plain tired, taxis are worth the extra cost (avoid the airport vans going in the airport-to-Paris direction; I'll explain why later in this section).

RER line B (RER-B) trains stop at T-2 and near T-1, then stop in central Paris at Gare du Nord, Châtelet-Les Halles, St. Michel, and Luxembourg (€8.50, 4/hr, runs 5:00–24:00, 30 min to Gare du Nord). Buy tickets from the machines (requires €8.50 in coins, some machines take bills) or at the often-crowded ticket windows.

To get out to the airport from the city, take RER line B, and make sure the sign over the platform shows *Roissy-Charles de Gaulle* as a stop served (the line splits, not every line B train serves the airport). If you're not clear, ask another rider *(air-o-por sharl duh Gaul?)*. Beware of pickpockets on these trains; wear your money belt. The other transportation options described below have far fewer theft problems.

Roissy-Buses run every 15–20 minutes to the Opéra Métro stop (€8.50, runs 6:30–21:00, 50 min, buy ticket on bus). You'll arrive at a bus stop on rue Scribe on the left side of the Opéra building. To get to the Métro entrance, turn left out of the bus and walk counterclockwise around the Opéra to the front. The Métro station entrance is on the island in the middle of the square. For rue Cler hotels, take Métro line 8 (direction: Balard) to La Tour Maubourg or Ecole Militaire. For hotels in the Marais neighborhood, take line 8 (direction: Créteil

(sidebar) TRANSPORTATION

Public Transportation to Recommended Hotels

The following public-transportation options are recommended, and are all described below in greater detail.

Rue Cler Area: Roissy-Bus to Opéra, then take Métro line 8 (direction: Balard) and get off at the La Tour Maubourg or Ecole Militaire stop.

Marais: Air France bus to the Gare de Lyon, with a quick trip on Métro line 1 (direction: La Défense) to the Bastille, St. Paul, or Hôtel de Ville stop.

Luxembourg Garden: RER-B to the Luxembourg stop.

Préfecture) to the Bastille stop. You can also take a taxi (about €12) to any of my listed hotels from behind the Opéra (the stand is in front of Galeries Lafayette department store).

Air France buses serve central Paris and continue to Orly Airport (at least 2/hr, 5:45–23:00). Allow 45 minutes to the Arc de Triomphe and Porte Maillot; 45 minutes to the Gare de Lyon train station; and 60 minutes to Montparnasse Tower/train station. To reach Marais hotels from the Gare de Lyon, take Métro line 1 (direction: La Défense) to the Bastille, St. Paul, or Hôtel de Ville stops; or walk 10 minutes up rue de Lyon to place de la Bastille. A ticket costs €14 one-way, €20 round-trip (pay driver).

Taxis run about €50 for up to three people (more if traffic is bad). Your hotel can call for a taxi to the airport. Specify that you want a real taxi *(un taxi normal)*, and not a limo service that costs €20 more (and gives your hotel a kickback).

Airport vans also go straight to and from your hotel, but are not a good option to take from the airport to Paris; you have to book them in advance even though you don't know exactly when you'll arrive (getting baggage, going through customs). However, they are a good budget option *to* the airport (particularly for single travelers or families of four or more, as that's too many for a taxi). If your hotel does not work with a van service, reserve directly (book at least a day in advance—most hoteliers will make the call for you). Airport vans cost about €35 for one person, €45 for two, and €55 for three. **Golden Air** is reliable (from Paris to Charles de Gaulle: €27 for one person, €17 per person for two; from Charles de Gaulle to Paris: €35 for one person, €20 per person for two; these special prices promised with this book in 2009, tel. 01 34 10 12 92, fax 01 34 10 93 89, www.paris-airport-shuttle-limousine.com, goldenair @wanadoo.fr).

A **Disneyland shuttle** is at each terminal (€17, every 45 min, daily 8:30–19:45).

Sleeping at or near Charles de Gaulle Airport

Hôtel Ibis**, outside the Charles de Gaulle-1 RER stop, is huge and offers standard and predictable accommodations (Db-€95–120, near *navette* stop, free and fast shuttle bus to all terminals, tel. 01 49 19 19 19, fax 01 49 19 19 21, www.ibishotel.com, h1404@accor.com). **Novotel***** is next door and the next step up. Book early for the best rates (Db-€120–170, can rise to €260 for last-minute rooms, tel. 01 49 19 27 27, fax 01 49 19 27 99, www.novotel.com, h1014@accor.com). Both have simple restaurants.

The small village of **Roissy en France** (you'll see signs just before the airport as you come from Paris), which gave its name to the airport (Roissy Charles de Gaulle), has better-value chain hotels with free shuttle service to and from the airport and the RER Roissy Rail station (4/hr, 15 min, look for *navettes hôtels* signs). Hotels have reasonably priced restaurants with long hours. Choose between **Hôtel Campanile** (Db-€90, tel. 01 34 29 80 40, fax 01 34 29 80 39, www.campanile.fr, roissy@campanile.fr) and **Hôtel Kyriad Prestige** (Db-€90–140, tel. 01 34 29 00 00, fax 01 34 29 00 11, www.kyriad.fr, roissy@kyriadprestige .fr). The cheapest option is **B&B Hôtel,** where many flight attendants stay (Db-€55, tel. 01 34 38 55 55, www.hotelbb.com).

To avoid rush-hour traffic, drivers can consider sleeping north of Paris in either **Auvers-sur-Oise** (30 min west of airport, see accommodations on page 522) or in the pleasant medieval town of **Senlis** (15 min north of airport). The **Ibis Senlis Hôtel** is a few minutes from town (Db-€80-100, Wi-Fi, route nationale A1, tel. 03 44 53 70 50, fax 03 44 53 51 93, www.ibishotel.com, h0709@accor.com). If you don't have a car, sleep elsewhere.

Orly Airport

This airport feels small. It's good for rental-car pickup and drop-off, as it's closer to Paris and far easier to navigate than Charles de Gaulle Airport.

Orly has two terminals: Ouest (west) and Sud (south). Air France flights arrive at Ouest, and all others use Sud. At the Sud terminal, you'll exit the baggage claim (near Gate H) and see signs directing you to city transportation, car rental, and so on. Turn left to enter the main terminal area, where you'll find exchange offices with bad rates, an American Express office, an ATM, the ADP counter (*Espace Tourisme*, a quasi-tourist office that offers free city maps and basic sightseeing information, open until 24:00), and an SNCF rail desk (next to ADP, daily 7:45–12:00 & 13:00–20:00, sells train tickets and even Eurailpasses). Downstairs is a sandwich bar, WCs, a bank (same bad rates), a newsstand (buy a phone card), and a post office. Car-rental offices are located in the parking lot in front of the terminal opposite Gate C. For flight info on any airline serving Orly, call 3950. For information on either of Paris' airports, visit www.adp.fr.

Transportation Between Orly Airport and Paris

Several efficient public-transportation routes, taxis, and a couple of airport vans link Orly with central Paris. The gate locations listed below apply to Orly Sud, but the same transportation services are available from both terminals.

Air France buses (outside Gate K) run to Montparnasse train station (with many Métro lines) and to the Invalides Métro stop (€9 one-way, €14 round-trip, 4/hr, 40 min to Invalides). These buses are handy for those staying in or near the rue Cler neighborhood (from Invalides bus stop, take the Métro to La Tour Maubourg or Ecole Militaire to reach recommended hotels; see also "RER trains," below). Remember that to continue on the Métro, you'll need to buy a separate ticket (for ticket types and prices, see "Getting Around Paris" in the Orientation chapter, page 26).

Jetbus (outside Gate H, €5.70, 4/hr) is the quickest way to the Paris Métro and a good way to the Marais and Luxembourg Garden neighborhoods. Take the Jetbus to the Villejuif-Louis Aragon Métro stop. To reach the Marais neighborhood, take the Métro to the Sully-Morland stop. For the Luxembourg area, take the same train to the Censier-Daubenton or Place Monge stop. If taking the Jetbus from the Marais to the airport, make sure before you board the Métro that your train is going to Villejuif-Louis Aragon (not Mairie d'Ivry), as the route splits at the end of the line.

The **Orlybus** (outside Gate H, €6.20, 3/hr) takes you to the Denfert-Rochereau RER-B line and the Métro, offering Métro access to central Paris, including the Luxembourg area and Notre-Dame Cathedral, as well as the Gare du Nord train station.

Shuttle Buses to Disneyland depart from Gate H (€17, daily 8:30–19:45, confirm gate and schedule at ADP *Espace Tourisme* office—described earlier).

These two routes provide access to Paris via **RER trains:** an ADP shuttle (**Orly Rail bus**) takes you to RER-C (Pont d'Orly stop), with connections to Gare d'Austerlitz, St. Michel/Notre-Dame, Musée d'Orsay, Invalides, and Pont de l'Alma stations and is handy for some rue Cler hotels (outside Gate G, 4/hr, €6). **Orlyval trains** take you to the Antony stop on RER-B (serving Luxembourg, Châtelet-Les Halles, St. Michel, and Gare du Nord stations in central Paris, €9.50, includes RER ticket).

Taxis are to the far right as you leave the terminal, at Gate M. Allow €28–38 with bags for a taxi into central Paris.

Airport vans are good for single travelers or families of four or more (too many for a taxi) if going from Paris to the airport (see page 436 for a company to contact; from Orly, figure about €23/1 person, €30/2 people, less per person for larger groups and kids).

Sleeping near Orly Airport

Two chain hotels, owned by the same company, are your best option near Orly. **Hôtel Ibis**** is reasonable, basic, and close by (Db-€70–90, tel. 01 56 70 50 60, fax 01 56 70 50 70, www.ibishotel.com, h1413 @accor.com). **Hôtel Mercure***** provides more comfort for a higher price; check its website for special discounts (Db-€130–200, book early for better rate, tel. 01 49 75 15 50, fax 01 49 75 15 51, www.accorhotel .com, h1246@accor.com). Both have free shuttles to the terminal.

Beauvais Airport

Budget airlines such as Ryanair use this airport, offering dirt-cheap airfares but leaving you 50 miles north of Paris. Still, this small airport has direct buses to Paris (see below). It's ideal for drivers who want to rent a car here and head to Normandy or north to Belgium. The airport is basic (the terminal for departing passengers and baggage claim is under a tent, and waiting areas are crowded and have few services), but it's being improved as it deals with an increasing number of passengers (airport tel. 08 92 68 20 66, www.aeroportbeauvais.com; Ryanair tel. 08 92 68 20 73, www.ryanair.com).

Transportation Between Beauvais Airport and Paris: Buses depart from the airport about 20 minutes after flights arrive and take 90 minutes to reach Paris. Buy your ticket at the little kiosk to the right as you exit the airport (€14). Buses wait nearby and depart once they are full (baggage goes underneath), and arrive at Porte Maillot on the west edge of Paris, which has a Métro and RER stop. The closest taxi stand is across the street at Hôtel Concorde LaFayette.

Buses depart Paris for Beauvais Airport three hours and 15 minutes before scheduled flight departures. Catch the bus at Porte Maillot in the parking lot on boulevard Pershing next to Hôtel Concorde LaFayette. Arrive with enough time to purchase your bus ticket before boarding (Beauvais Airport tel. 08 92 68 20 66, www .aeroportbeauvais.com).

Trains connect Beauvais' city center and Paris' Gare du Nord (20/day, 80 min).

Taxis run from Beauvais Airport to Paris: €130 to central Paris, €12 to Beauvais' train station or city center.

Connecting Paris Airports

Air France buses directly and conveniently link Charles de Gaulle and Orly airports (roughly 2/hr, 5:45–23:00, 80 min, €17).

RER line B also connects Charles de Gaulle and Orly but requires a transfer to the Orlyval train and isn't as easy as the Air France bus (5/hr, 90 min, €18). This line splits at both ends: Heading to Orly, take trains that serve the Antony stop (then tranfer to Orlyval train); heading to Charles de Gaulle, take trains that end at the airport ("Roissy-CDG"), not Mitry-Claye.

Connect to and from the Beauvais Airport train at Gare du Nord (see previous section, "Beauvais Airport").

Taxis are easiest, but pricey (€80 between Charles de Gaulle and Orly, €115 between Charles de Gaulle and Beauvais, €135 between Orly and Beauvais).

Cheap Flights

If you're visiting one or more French cities on a longer European trip—or linking up far-flung French cities (such as Paris and Nice)—you might consider intra-European airlines. While trains are still the best way to connect places that are close together, a flight can save both time and money on long journeys. When comparing a flight versus a train trip, consider the time it takes to get to the airport and how early you'll need to arrive to check in before the flight. Most flights make sense only as an alternate to a train ride five or more hours in length.

One of the best websites for comparing inexpensive flights is www.skyscanner.net. Other comparison search engines include www.kayak.com, www.mobissimo.com, www.sidestep.com, and www.wegolo.com.

Well-known cheapo airlines include easyJet (www.easyjet.com) and RyanAir (www.ryanair.com). Be aware of the potential drawbacks of flying on the cheap: nonrefundable and nonchangeable tickets, rigid baggage restrictions (and fees if you have more than what's officially allowed), use of airports far outside town, tight schedules that can mean more delays, little in the way of customer assistance if problems arise, and, of course, no frills. To avoid unpleasant surprises, read the small print—especially baggage policies—before you book.

TRAINS

Station Overview

Paris is Europe's rail hub, with six major stations and one minor one, each serving different regions:

- Gare du Nord (northern France and Europe)
- Gare Montparnasse (northwestern France and TGV service to France's southwest)
- Gare de Lyon (southeastern France and Italy)
- Gare de l'Est (northeastern France and eastbound trains)
- Gare St. Lazare (northwestern France)
- Gare d'Austerlitz (southwestern France and Europe)
- Gare de Bercy (smaller station, departure point for most night trains to Italy)

Any train station has schedule information, can make reservations, and can sell tickets for any destination. Buying tickets is handier

Paris' Train Stations

1 MILE
1 KM

TO LA DEFENSE

RING ROAD PERIPHERIQUE

MONTMARTRE
SACRE-CŒUR

PERIPHERIQUE

BOIS DE BOULOGNE

ARC DE TRIOMPHE

❻ OPERA GARNIER

❶

❺

PLACE DE LA REPUBLIQUE

PERE LACHAISE CEM.

[A-1] TO DE GAULLE AIRPORT

CHAMPS-ELYSEES

RIGHT BANK

Louvre

POMPIDOU CTR.

MARAIS

[A-3] TO NORMANDY ROUEN

RUE CLER

ORSAY ●

CITE ●

LEFT BANK

NOTRE-DAME

SEINE

EIFFEL TOWER

ARMY MUSEUM

LUX. GDN.

RODIN MUSEUM

❷

MONT-PARNASSE TOWER

❼

❸

❹

PLACE DE LA BASTILLE

BOIS DE VINCENNES

RER-C TRAIN TO VERSAILLES

PLACE D'ITALIE

[A-6] TO ORLY AIRPORT & SOUTH

[A-4] TO REIMS

Paris Train Stations & Destinations

❶ Gare Nord: To London, Brussels, Amsterdam & N. France (also Chantilly & Auvers-sur-Oise)

❷ Gare Montparnasse: To SW France (Languedoc & Dordogne), Loire Valley, Brittany (also Chartres) & Mont St. Michel

❸ Gare de Lyon: To Italy & SE France (Burgundy, Alps, Provence & Riviera; also Fontainebleau & Melun/Vaux-le-Vicomte)

❹ Gare de Bercy: Night trains to Italy

❺ Gare de l'Est: To NE France (Reims, Champagne & Alsace), S. Germany, Switzerland & Austria

❻ Gare St. Lazare: To Normandy (also Vernon/Giverny)

❼ Gare d'Austerlitz: To SW France, Loire Valley & Spain

from an SNCF neighborhood office. See "SNCF Boutiques" on page 450 for a more extensive list.

Schedules change by season, weekday, and weekend. Verify train schedules shown in this book—on the Web, check Germany's excellent all-Europe schedule site, http://bahn.hafas.de/bin/query.exe/en. The French rail website (www.sncf.com) shows ticket prices and sells some tickets online (worth checking if you're traveling on one or two long-distance trains without a railpass, as advance-purchase discounts can be a great deal).

While there's no deadline to buy any train ticket, the fast, reserved TGV trains can fill up. It's wise to book ahead for any TGV you cannot afford to miss. Tickets go on sale 90 days in advance, and the cheapest tickets sell out early. You can buy tickets online at www .raileurope.com (a US company that delivers tickets to your home but doesn't always have the lowest rates), or better, at www.tgv.com (if you select English as your language and any country other than the US or France, you'll be able to print tickets at home or pick up in the station; if instead you choose France, the site will be in French, and if you choose the US, you'll be redirected to www.raileurope.com).

All six main train stations have banks or change offices, ATMs, train information desks, telephones, cafés, newsstands, and clever pickpockets. Because of security concerns, not all have baggage checks, though those with this service are identified below.

Métro and RER trains, as well as buses and taxis, are well-marked at every station. When arriving by Métro, follow signs for *Grandes Lignes-SNCF* to find the main tracks.

Each station offers two types of rail service: long distance to other cities, called *Grandes Lignes* (major lines); and suburban service to outlying areas, called *Banlieue* or RER. Both *Banlieue* and RER trains serve outlying areas and the airports; the only difference is that *Banlieue* lines are operated by SNCF (France's train system, called Transilien) and RER lines are operated by RATP (Paris' Métro and bus system). You may also see ticket windows identified as *Ile de France*. This is for Transilien (SNCF) trains serving destinations outside Paris in the Ile de France region (usually no more than an hour from Paris).

Paris train stations can be intimidating, but if you slow down, avoid peak times, take a deep breath, and ask for help, you'll find them manageable and efficient. Bring a pad of paper for clear communication at ticket/info windows. All stations have helpful information booths *(accueil);* the bigger stations have roving helpers, usually wearing red or blue vests. They're capable of answering rail questions more quickly than the information or ticket windows. I make a habit of confirming my track number and departure time with these helpers.

Gare du Nord

The granddaddy of Paris' train stations serves cities in northern France and international destinations north of Paris, including Copenhagen, Amsterdam (see "To Brussels and Amsterdam by Thalys Train," page 451), and the Eurostar to London (see "To London by Eurostar Train," page 451), as well as two of the day trips described in this book (Chantilly and Auvers-sur-Oise).

Arrive early to allow time to navigate this station. From the Métro,

France's Public Transportation

RAIL
EUROSTAR RAIL
BUS
BOAT
AIRPORTS (NOT ALL SHOWN)

100 MILES
200 KM

GREAT BRITAIN
LONDON
PORTSMOUTH
NEW-HAVEN
DOVER
FOLKE-STONE
CALAIS
OSTENDE
BRUGES
BRUSSELS
ENGLISH CHANNEL
BOUL.
LILLE
AUL.
BELG.
LIEGE
GER-
TO AMSTERDAM
LE HAVRE
TRIER
LUX.
TO IRELAND
CHERBOURG
HONFLEUR
DIEPPE
BEAUVAIS
ROUEN
REIMS
DE GAULLE
VERDUN
TO FRANKFURT + RHINE
ROSCOFF
MONT ST. MICHEL
BAYEUX
CAEN
VER.
PARIS
METZ
NANCY
STRAS-BOURG
KEHL
DINAN
AVRANCHES
PONTORSON
CHARTRES
ORLY
SEMUR
CUL.
MUL-HOUSE
COLMAR
QUIMPER
RENNES
LE MANS
ORLEANS
BLOIS
MONT-BORD
DIJON
BASEL
TO MILAN
ANGERS
LANG.
AMBOISE
BEAUNE
BES.
DOLE
BERN
QUIBERON
NANTES
CHINON
AZAY
TOURS
VIER-ZON
CHAGNY
CHALONS
FRASNE
LAUSANNE
MARTIGNY
POITIERS
ORA-DOUR
CLER. FER.
MACON
GENEVA
ANNECY
CHAMONIX
S. GERVAIS
LA ROCHELLE
ANG.
LIMOGES
LYON
ITALY
TO TURIN
ATLANTIC OCEAN
LES EYZIES
PERIGUEUX
GRENOBLE
CHAMB.
S.E.M.
SARLAT
SOUILLAC
AVIGNON
ISLE-SUR-SORGUE
DIGNE
VENTI-MIGLIA
BORDEAUX
LE BUISSON
BEY-NAC
CAHORS
PONT DU GARD
S. REMY LES BAUX
ST. PAUL
AGEN
ALBI
NIMES
ARLES
NICE
MONACO
ANTIBES
CANNES
BAYONNE
ST. JEAN
HENDAYE
DAX
TOULOUSE
CARCA-SSONNE
NARBONNE
TOULON
CASSIS
MARSEILLE
SAN SEB.
PAU
IRUN
LOURDES
LA TOUR
COLLIOURE
PORT BOU
TO MADRID
AND.
PUIGCERDA
SPAIN
TO BARCELONA
MEDITERRANEAN SEA

DCH

TRANSPORTATION

follow *Grandes Lignes* signs (main lines) and keep going up until you reach the tracks at street level. *Grandes Lignes* depart from tracks 3–21 (tracks 20 and 21 are around the corner), suburban *Banlieue/Transilien* lines from tracks 30–36, and RER trains from tracks 37–44 (tracks 41–44 are one floor below). Glass train information booths *(accueil)* are scattered throughout the station, and information-helpers circulate (all rail staff are required to speak English).

The tourist information kiosk is opposite track 19 (Mon–Sat 8:00–18:00, closed Sun). Information booths for the **Thalys** trains (high-speed trains to Brussels and Amsterdam) are opposite track 8. All non-Eurostar ticket sales are opposite tracks 13–18. Passengers departing on **Eurostar** trains (London via Chunnel) can buy tickets and must check in at least 30 minutes early on the second level, opposite track 6 (check-in is similar to an airline—you'll fill out a "landing

Key Transportation Phrases

French	Pronounced	English
accueil	ah-koy	information/ assistance
niveau	nee-voh	level
billets	bee-yay	tickets
départs	day-par	departures
arrivées	ah-ree-vay	arrivals
aller simple	ah-lay sam-pluh	one-way
aller-retour	ah-lay ruh-toor	round-trip
a l'heure	ah loor	on time
fenêtre/couloir	fuh-neh-truh/ kool-wahr	window/aisle seat
fenêtre isolée	fuh-neh-truh ee-zoh-lay	single seat by window (first class only)
voyageurs munis de billets	voh-yah-zhoor moo-nee duh bee-yay	travelers with tickets
navette	nah-veht	shuttle bus
Grandes Lignes	grahnd leen	major domestic and international lines
RER	air ay air	suburban lines
Transilien	trahn-seel-ee-yehn	suburban lines
RATP	air ah tay pay	Paris' Métro and bus system
SNCF	es en say ef	France's country-wide train system
TGV	tay zhay vay	high-speed lines
banlieue	bahn-lee-yuh	suburban
quai	kay	platform
accès aux quais	ahk-seh oh kay	access to the platforms
voie	vwah	track
retard	ruh-tar	delay
salle d'attente	sahl dah-tahnt	waiting room
consigne	kohn-seen	baggage check (also called espaces bagages)
consigne automatique	kohn-seen oh-toh-mah-teek	storage lockers
première classe	pruhm-yair klahs	first class
deuxième classe	duhz-yehm klahs	second class
point d'argent	pwan dar-zhahn	ATM
PTT	pay tay tay	post office

TRANSPORTATION

card" and go through security). Monet-esque views over the trains and peaceful, air-conditioned cafés hide on the upper level, past the Eurostar ticket windows (find the cool view WCs down the steps in the café). Other WCs are down the stairs across from track 10 (€1). Baggage check and rental cars are at the far end, opposite track 3 and down the steps. Taxis are at the door past track 3. Steps down to the Métro are opposite tracks 10 and 19.

Key Destinations Served by Gare du Nord *Grandes Lignes:* **Chantilly-Gouvieux** (hourly, fewer on weekends, 25 min, also served by slower RER lines), **Brussels** (about 2/hr, 1.5 hrs, see "To Brussels and Amsterdam by Thalys Train," page 451), **Bruges** (about 2/hr, 2.5 hrs, change in Brussels), **Amsterdam** (nearly hourly, 4–5 hrs, change in Brussels, see "To Brussels and Amsterdam by Thalys Train," page 451), **Copenhagen** (7/day, 14–18 hrs, two night trains), **Koblenz** (9/day, 5 hrs, most change in Köln), and **London** via Eurostar Chunnel train (12–15/day, 2.5 hrs, tel. 08 36 35 35 39, see "To London by Eurostar Train," page 451).

By *Banlieue*/**RER Lines**: **Chantilly-Gouvieux** (3/day, 45 min), **Charles de Gaulle Airport** (4/hr, 30 min, runs 5:00–24:00, track 4), **Auvers-sur-Oise** (2/hr, 1 hr, transfer at Pontoise or St. Ouen).

Gare Montparnasse

This big and modern station covers three floors, serves lower Normandy and Brittany, and has TGV service to the Loire Valley and southwestern France, as well as suburban service to Chartres. At street level, you'll find a bank, *Banlieue* trains (you can also reach the *Banlieue* trains from the second level), and ticket windows for Ile de France trains in the center, just past the escalators. TER trains to Chartres depart mostly from level 2.

Most services are provided on the second (top) level, where the *Grandes Lignes* arrive and depart. Ticket windows and an information booth are to the far left (with your back to glass exterior). *Banlieue* trains depart from tracks 10–19. The main rail information office *(accueil)* is opposite track 15. WCs and baggage check are on the mezzanine level. Taxis and car rentals are to the far left as you leave the tracks. Air France buses to Orly and Charles de Gaulle Airports stop in front of the station, down the escalators and outside. City buses are outside to the left (#28 connects conveniently to the rue Cler area).

Key Destinations Served by Gare Montparnasse: Chartres (10/day, 1 hr, *Banlieue* lines), **Amboise** (12/day in 1.5 hrs with change in St. Pierre-des-Corps, requires TGV reservation; non-TGV trains leave from Gare d'Austerlitz), **Pontorson/Mont St. Michel** (7/day, 3.5–4 hrs, via Rennes or Dreux, some with bus from Rennes), **Dinan** (6/day, 4 hrs, change in Rennes and Dol), **Bordeaux** (20/day, 3.5 hrs), **Sarlat** (7/day, allow 6 hrs; 3/day with change in Bordeaux-St. Jean or Libourne, then TGV; 4/day to Souillac, then bus), **Toulouse** (13/day,

Train Tips

- Arrive at the station with plenty of time before your departure to find the right platform, confirm connections, and so on. In small towns, your train may depart before the station opens; if so, go directly to the tracks and find the overhead sign that confirms your train stops at that track.

- Larger stations have platforms with monitors showing each car's layout (numbered forward or backward) so you can figure out where your *voiture* will stop on the long platform and where to board each car. Notice the low baggage area placed every two cars—people use it to avoid hoisting their suitcases to the high overhead rack.

- Check schedules in advance if possible. Upon arrival at a station, learn your departure possibilities. Large stations have a separate information window or office; at small stations, the ticket office gives information.

- If you have a rail flexipass, write the date on your pass each day you travel.

- Validate tickets (not passes) and reservations in yellow machines before boarding. If you're traveling with a pass and have a reservation for a certain trip, you must validate the reservation.

- Reservations for all TGV trains are required, and often sell out. You can reserve any train at any station or through SNCF Boutiques (small offices in city centers). A limited number of reservations are allocated for railpass users during peak times—reserve as far ahead as you can for Friday and Sunday afternoons and Saturday mornings.

- Before getting on a train, confirm that it's going where you think it is. For example, if you want to go to Chartres, ask the conductor or any local passenger, "A Chartres?" (ah shart-ruh; meaning, "To Chartres?").

- Some longer trains split cars en route. Make sure your train car is continuing to your destination by asking, "Cette voiture va à Chartres?" (seht vwah-toor vah ah shart-ruh; meaning, "This car goes to Chartres?").

- If a non-TGV train seat is reserved, it will usually be labeled *réservé,* with the cities to and from which it is reserved.

- Verify with the conductor all of the transfers you must make ("Correspondance à?"; meaning, "Transfer to where?").

- To guard against theft, keep your bags right overhead. If you must store them at the end of the car, make sure you can see them from your seat (they're most vulnerable to theft when the train stops).

- Note your arrival time, so you'll be ready to get off.

- Use the train's free WCs before you get off (but not while the train is stopped).

5–7 hrs, most require change, usually in Bordeaux or Montpellier), **Albi** (6/day, 6–7.5 hrs, change in Toulouse, also night train), **Carcassonne** (14/day, 6.5 hrs, most require changes in Toulouse or Montpellier, direct trains take 8 hrs, night train also available), **Tours** (18/day, 1 hr), **Madrid** (3/day, 13.5 hrs, one overnight via Irun, more night trains from Gare d'Austerlitz), and **Lisbon** (1/day, 21.5 hrs via Irun or Madrid).

Gare de Lyon

This huge and bewildering station offers TGV and regular service to southeastern France, Italy, and other international destinations (for more trains to Italy, see "Gare de Bercy," page 448). Frequent *Banlieue* trains serve Melun (near Vaux-le-Vicomte) and Fontainebleau (some depart from the main *Grandes Lignes* level, more frequent departures are from one level down, follow RER-D signs, and ask at any information booth or ticket window where the next departure leaves from). Don't leave this station without relaxing in Le Train Bleu Restaurant lounge, up the stairs opposite track G (see page 399).

Grande Ligne trains arrive and depart from street level, but are divided into two areas (tracks A–N in the blue area, and 5–23 in the yellow area). Monitors will show either yellow or blue even before the track is posted, so you know which general area your train leaves from. The two areas are connected by the long platform along tracks A and 5, and by the hallway adjacent to track A and opposite track 9. This hallway has all the services, including ticket windows, ticket information, WCs, banks, and shops (Virgin Records/Books sells some books in English). Transilien ticket windows are just inside the hall adjacent to track A *(billets Ile de France). Grandes Lignes* and *Banlieue* lines share the same tracks.

A tourist office (Mon–Sat 8:00–18:00, closed Sun) and a train information office are both opposite track L. From the RER or Métro, follow signs for *Grandes Lignes Arrivées* and take the escalator up to reach the platforms. Train information booths are opposite tracks A and 11 and downstairs. Baggage check (daily 6:15–22:00, €4–10) is down the stairs opposite track 13. Taxi stands are well-signed in front of, and underneath, the station. If you need a quiet waiting area, here are two to choose from: Le Train Bleu's pricey but way-cool bar-lounge opposite track G; or opposite track 13, follow *consigne* (baggage check) signs down one floor and make a U-turn to the right.

Air France buses to Montparnasse (easy transfer to Orly Airport) and direct to Charles de Gaulle Airport stop outside the station's main entrance (opposite tracks A to L, walk across the parking lot—the stop is opposite the Café Européen on the right; €13, 2/hr, normally at :15 and :45 after the hour).

Key Destinations Served by Gare de Lyon: Vaux-le-Vicomte (train to Melun, 2/hr by train and RER, 30 min), **Fontainebleau**

(nearly hourly, 45 min), **Disneyland** (RER line A-4 to Marne-la-Vallée-Chessy, at least 3/hr, 45 min), **Beaune** (nearly hourly, 2.5 hrs, most require change in Dijon), **Dijon** (nearly hourly, 1.5 hrs), **Chamonix** (8/day, daily July–Aug and Dec–April, Fri–Sun only May–June and Sept–Nov, may be more frequent in May, 6–8 hrs, night train possible), **Annecy** (13/day, 4–5 hrs, many with change in Lyon), **Lyon** (at least hourly, 2 hrs), **Avignon** (9/day in 2.5 hrs to Avignon TGV station, 5/day in 3.5 hrs to Avignon Centre-Ville station, more connections with change—3–4 hrs), **Arles** (17/day, 2 direct TGVs in 4 hrs, 15 with change in Avignon in 5 hrs), **Nice** (10/day, 6 hrs, may require change, 11-hr night train possible out of Gare d'Austerlitz), **Venice** (3/day, 4/night, 10–13 hrs with change in Milan; 1 direct overnight, 13 hrs, important to reserve ahead), **Rome** (3/day, 13–16 hrs, plus several overnight options, important to reserve ahead), **Bern** (11/day, 5–5.5 hrs, 1 direct train in morning and 1 in evening, otherwise 1–2 changes), **Interlaken** (nearly hourly, 6.5 hrs, night train possible via Basel from Gare de l'Est), and **Barcelona** (3/day, 9 hrs, 1–2 changes; night train possible from Gare d'Austerlitz).

Gare de Bercy: This smaller station handles some night train service to Italy (Mo: Bercy, one stop east of Gare de Lyon on line 14).

Gare de l'Est

This two-floor station (with underground Métro), is relatively easy to navigate. All trains depart at street level from tracks 1–30. Ticket sales are in the hall opposite track 12. All other services are down the escalator through the hall opposite track 16 (baggage check, car rental, WC, small grocery store, and Métro access). A Virgin Records store with some books in English is at the top of the escalator, in the hall opposite track 16. Access to taxis and buses is out the front of the station (exit with your back to the tracks).

Key Destinations Served by Gare de l'Est: Colmar (12/day with TGV, 3.5 hrs, change in Strasbourg), **Strasbourg** (hourly with TGV, 2.5 hrs), **Reims** (12/day with TGV, 45 min), **Verdun** (2/day, 1.75 hrs with TGV and shuttle bus; non-TGV 6/day, 3–3.5 hrs, change in Metz or Chalon), **Munich** (4/day, 6–7 hrs, some require changes), **Interlaken** (night train possible via Basel with changes at 5:00 and 8:00), **Vienna** (7/day, 12–17 hrs, 1–3 changes, night train), **Zürich** (2/day direct, 4 hrs; 7/day with changes, 5–6.5 hrs; night train), **Berlin** (6/day, 8–9 hrs, 1–2 changes, many via Belgium; 1 direct night train, 11.25 hrs) and **Prague** (5/day, 12–18 hrs, night train possible via Berlin).

Gare St. Lazare

This relatively small station serves upper Normandy, including Rouen and Giverny. All trains arrive and depart one floor above street level. The station is undergoing renovation, so be prepared for the temporary displacement of shops and services.

Coping with Strikes

Going on strike *(en grève)* is a popular pastime in this revolution-happy country. President Sarkozy is pushing unions to their limits, and since bargaining between management and employees is not standard procedure, workers strike to get attention. Truckers and tractors block main roads and autoroutes (in a movement called Opération Escargot: "Operation Snail's Pace"); baggage handlers bring airports to their knees; museum workers make Mona Lisa off-limits to tourists; and Métro and train personnel seem to strike every year—perhaps during your trip. What does the traveler do? You could *jetter l'éponge* (throw in the sponge) and go somewhere less strike-prone (Switzerland's nice), or learn to accept certain events as being out of your control. Strikes in France generally last no longer than a day or two, and if you're aware of them, you can usually plan around them. Your hotelier will know the latest (or can find out). Make a habit of asking your hotel receptionist about strikes, and check online for English-language updates at www.americansinfrance.net/dailylife/strike.cfm.

TRANSPORTATION

From the Métro, follow signs to *Grandes Lignes* to reach the tracks (long walk). The ticket office and car rental are near track 27. *Grandes Lignes* depart from tracks 17–27; *banlieue* trains depart from 1–16. Train information offices *(accueil)* are scattered about the station. Taxis, the Métro, and buses are well-signed. This station has no baggage check.

Key Destinations Served by Gare St. Lazare: Giverny (train to Vernon, 6/day, more on Sat, get there in time to visit the gardens, 45 min—see schedule in Giverny day trip on page 518—then bus or taxi 15 min to Giverny), **Rouen** (hourly, 1–1.5 hrs), **Honfleur** (13/day, 2–3.5 hrs, via Lisieux, then bus), **Bayeux** (11/day, 2.5 hrs, some change in Caen), **Caen** (14/day, 2 hrs), and **Pontorson/Mont St. Michel** (2/day, 4–5.5 hrs, via Caen; more trains from Gare Montparnasse).

Gare d'Austerlitz

This small station provides non-TGV service to the Loire Valley, southwestern France, and Spain. All tracks are at street level. The information booth is opposite track 17, and all ticket sales are in the hall opposite track 10. Baggage check, WCs (with €6 showers that include towel, soap, and the works), and car rental are along the side of the station, opposite track 21. To get to the Métro and RER, you must walk outside and along either side of the station.

Key Destinations Served by Gare d'Austerlitz: Versailles (via RER line C, 4/hr, 30–40 min), **Amboise** (10/day direct in 2 hrs; faster TGV connection from Gare Montparnasse—see page 445), **Cahors**

(5/day, 5 hrs, 1 direct night train; other slower trains from Gare Montparnasse), **Barcelona** (1/night, 12 hrs; day trains from Gare de Lyon), and **Madrid** (2/night, 13 hrs direct, 16 hrs via Irun; day trains from Gare Montparnasse).

SNCF Boutiques

You can save time and stress by buying train tickets or making train reservations at an SNCF boutique. These small branch offices of the French National Rail Company are conveniently located throughout Paris, with offices near most of my recommended hotels and museums and at Orly and Charles de Gaulle Airports. Arrive when they open to avoid lines (generally open Mon–Sat 8:30–19:00 or 20:00, closed Sun).

Historic Core
- 18 rue du Pont Neuf, Mo: Pont Neuf

Marais
- 2 rue de Turenne, Mo: St. Paul
- 5 rue de Lyon, Mo: Gare de Lyon

Near Major Museums
- Musée d'Orsay RER station, below Orsay Museum
- Forum des Halles Shopping Mall, 4th floor, returns office *(Salle d'Echanges)*, Mo: Châtelet-Les Halles

Champs Elysées
- 229 rue du Faubourg Saint-Honoré, Mo: St Philippe du Roule

Farther North on the Right Bank
- 53 rue Chaussée d'Antin, Mo: Chaussée d'Antin (near Opéra Garnier and Galeries Lafayette)
- 32/34 rue Joubert, Mo: Haussman-St. Lazare (near Gare St. Lazare)
- 71/73 boulevard Magenta, Mo: Gare du Nord (Gare du Nord)
- 82 avenue de la Grande Armée, Mo: Porte Maillot (near Hôtel Concorde-Lafayette and Beauvais Airport bus stop)

Montmartre
- 27 rue Lepic, Mo: Blanche

Eiffel Tower/Rue Cler
- 80 rue Saint Dominique, Mo: La Tour Maubourg
- 19 rue de Passy, Mo: Passy (near Marmottan Museum)
- Invalides Métro/RER station

Latin Quarter/Luxembourg Garden
- 54 boulevard Saint-Michel, Mo: Cluny-Sorbonne
- 79 rue de Rennes, Mo: St. Sulpice

Farther South on the Left Bank
- 17 rue Littré, Mo: Montparnasse-Bienvenüe (near Luxembourg Garden and Grand Cafés)
- 68 avenue du Maine: Mo. Montparnasse-Bienvenüe (near Grand Cafés)

- 30 avenue d'Italie, in Centre Commerciale Galaxie, Mo: Place d'Italie

You'll also find quieter SNCF offices in train stations of the towns I suggest for day trips from Paris, such as Versailles, Fontainebleau, Melun (for Vaux-le-Vicomte), Chartres, Chantilly, Vernon (for Giverny), and Pontoise (for Auvers-sur-Oise).

To Brussels and Amsterdam by Thalys Train

The pricey Thalys train has the monopoly on the rail route between Paris and Brussels (for a cheaper option, try the Eurolines bus; see page 453). Without a railpass, you'll pay about €80–100 second class for the Paris–Amsterdam train (compared to €45 by bus) or about €60–80 second class for the Paris–Brussels train (compared to €25 by bus). Even with a railpass, you need to pay for train reservations (second class-€14.50; first class-€27, includes a meal). Book at least a day ahead, as seats are limited (www.thalys.com). Or hop on the bus, Gus.

CROSSING THE CHANNEL

To London by Eurostar Train

The fastest and most convenient way to get from the Eiffel Tower to Big Ben is by rail. Eurostar, a joint service of the Belgian, British, and French railways, is the speedy passenger train that zips you (and up to 800 others in 18 sleek cars) from downtown Paris to downtown London (at least 15/day, 2.5 hrs) faster and more easily than flying. The actual tunnel crossing is a 20-minute, black, silent, 100-mile-per-hour nonevent. Your ears won't even pop.

Eurostar Fares

Channel fares are reasonable but complicated. Prices vary depending on how far ahead you reserve, whether you can live with restrictions, and whether you're eligible for any discounts (children, youths, seniors, and railpass holders all qualify). Rates are lowest for round-trips.

Fares can change without notice, but typically a **one-way, full-fare ticket** (with no restrictions on refundability) runs about $425 first-class and $310 second-class. Accepting more restrictions lowers the price substantially (figure $90–200 for second class, one-way), but these **cheaper seats** sell out quickly. Those traveling with a railpass that covers France or Britain should look first at the **passholder** fare (about $90–160 for second-class, one-way Eurostar trips). For more details, visit www.ricksteves.com/eurostar.

Buying Eurostar Tickets

Since only the most expensive (full-fare) ticket is refundable, don't reserve until you're sure of your plans. But if you wait too long, the cheapest tickets will get bought up.

Once you're confident about the time and date of your crossing, you can check and book fares by phone or online in the US, and pay to have your ticket delivered to you in the US. (Order online at www.ricksteves.com /rail/eurostar, prices listed in dollars; order by phone at US tel. 800-EUROSTAR). Or you could order from a French company (French tel. 08 92 35 35 39, www .eurostar.com, prices listed in euros) and pick up your ticket at the train station. In Europe, you can buy your Eurostar ticket at

any major train station in any country, at neighborhood SNCF offices (see "SNCF Boutiques," above), or at any travel agency that handles train tickets (expect a booking fee). Passholder discount tickets can be purchased at Eurostar departure stations, online, or by phone, but may be harder to get at other train stations and travel agencies.

Note that the arrival and departure times printed on your ticket are local times, and that France's time zone is one hour later than Britain's. For example, your departure from Paris is listed in French time, and the arrival in London is British time.

Taking the Eurostar

Check in at Gare du Nord (see page 442) at least 30 minutes in advance for your Eurostar trip. It's very similar to an airport check-in: You pass through airport-like security, fill out a customs form, show your passport to customs officials, and find a TV monitor to locate your departure gate. The currency-exchange booth here has rates about the same as you'll find on the other end.

Crossing the Channel by Ferry

Ferries are cheaper than the Eurostar train, but twice as complicated and time-consuming. They're a good idea, however, if you're traveling on the fly and haven't booked a Eurostar ticket in advance. See www .posl.com and www.aferry.to for routes and fares.

BUSES

The main bus station is the Gare Routière du Paris-Gallieni (28 avenue du Général de Gaulle, in suburb of Bagnolet, Mo: Gallieni, tel. 01 49 72 51 51). Buses provide cheaper—if less comfortable and more

Driving in France: Distance and Time

ENGLAND

Calais
(Ferry to Britain)

Lille

BELGIUM

GERMANY

LUX.

Arromanches
(D-Day Beaches)

Honfleur

20m 45m 55m
.5h .75h 1h

Bayeux
80m • 1.5h

Reims
Verdun

Mont St.
Michel

80m • 1.5h Caen
Rouen

80m • 1.5h

90m • 1.5h

150m • 2.75h

Dinan

Paris

75m • 1.25h

305m • 4.5h Strasbourg

195m • 3h

285m • 5.5h Colmar

225m • 4.5h

40m • .75h Chartres

55m
1h

155m • 2.5h

50m
1h

85m • 2h

140m • 2.25h

Amboise

Semur-
en-Auxois

50m
.75h

165m • 2.5h

50m • 1.5h

250m • 4h

Chinon

270m • 5.5h

Beaune

135m • 3h

SWITZ.

m = miles
h = hours

360m • 5.25h

220m • 4.5h

FRANCE

Oradour-
sur-Glane

145m • 2.25h

85m
1.5h

Chamonix

100m
2.25h

Lyon

260m • 5h

Annecy

55m • 1h

St. Emilion

80m • 2h

140m • 2h

235m • 5h

ITALY

Sarlat

30m • 1.25h

Rocamadour

Nice

St. Jean-
de-Luz

155m • 2.5h

125m • 2.5h

Albi

25m
.5h

Avignon

160m • 2.5h

20m • .5h

210m • 4.75h

170m • 3h

70m
1.75h

150m • 2.25h

Arles

10m
.5h

San
Sebastián

250m • 3.5h

Carcassonne

165m • 2.5h

105m • 1.5h

10m
.5h

SPAIN

95m
1.5h

Collioure

80m
1.25h

Cassis

Antibes

.5h

MONACO

Note: Your times may vary
based on traffic, construction,
and road conditions.

TRANSPORTATION

time-consuming—transportation to major European cities. The bus is also the cheapest way of crossing the English Channel; book at least two days in advance for the best fares. Eurolines' buses depart from here (tel. 08 36 69 52 52, www.eurolines.com). Look on their website for offices in central Paris.

DRIVING

Parking in Paris

Street parking is free 19:00–9:00 on Sunday, and in August. To pay for streetside parking, you must go to a *tabac* and buy a parking card *(une carte parking)*, sold in €10, €20, and €30 denominations. Insert the card into the meter and punch the desired amount of time (generally €1–2/hour), then take the receipt and put it inside your windshield. Meters limit street parking to a maximum of two hours. For a longer stay, park for less at an airport (about €10/day) and take public transport or a taxi into the city. You'll pay more to park in a downtown lot (about €20–27/day, €55/3 days, and €10/day more after that). There are underground lots at St. Sulpice, the Panthéon, and Bastille (www .vincipark.com). Otherwise, ask your hotelier for suggestions.

DAY TRIPS
FROM PARIS

VERSAILLES DAY TRIP

Château de Versailles

If you've ever wondered why your American passport has French writing in it, you'll find the answer at Versailles (vehr-"sigh")—every king's dream palace. The powerful court of Louis XIV at Versailles set the standard of culture for all of Europe, right up to modern times. Today, if you're planning to visit just one palace in all of Europe, make it Versailles.

Versailles offers three blockbuster sights. The main attraction is the palace itself, called the **Château.** Here you walk through dozens of lavish, chandeliered rooms once inhabited by Louis XIV and his successors. Next come the expansive **Gardens** around the palace, a landscaped wonderland dotted with statues and fountains. Finally, at the far end of the Gardens, is the **Domaine de Marie-Antoinette,** a pastoral area featuring several small palaces—perfect for getting away from the mobs at the Château.

Visiting Versailles can seem daunting because of its size and hordes of visitors. But it's easy. Arm yourself with a pass to skip ticket-buying lines; arrive early to avoid the crowds; and use this self-guided tour to focus on the highlights. I've provided all the details in "Orientation," next. First-timers can simply follow my recommended strategy in "Planning Your Time at Versailles" on page 460.

Note that the entire complex is undergoing extensive renovation in 2009, so expect some closures and changes. Restoration projects may close the Opera House through June 2009; the newly renovated Petit Trianon is now open.

ORIENTATION

Cost: I recommend buying either a Paris Museum Pass or Versailles' "Le Passeport" Pass, both of which give you access to the most important parts of the complex (see "Passes" on next page).

You can also buy individual tickets to each of the three different sections:

1. The **Château,** the main palace, costs €13.50 (€10 after 15:00, under 18 always free, includes audioguide). Your Château ticket includes the King's and Queen's State Apartments (with the famous Hall of Mirrors), the Royal Chapel, the Opera House (closed through June 2009), and several lesser rooms.

2. The **Domaine de Marie-Antoinette,** the estate of the queen, costs €9 April–Oct; €5 after 16:00 and Nov–March; under 18 always free. This ticket gives you access to the far part of the Gardens and entry into several small palaces: the queen's Hamlet, the Grand and Petit Trianons, and a smattering of nearby buildings.

3. The **Gardens** are free, except on weekends April–Sept, when the fountains blast and the price is €8 (see "Fountain Spectacles," page 462).

Passes: Smart travelers arrive at Versailles with one of these two passes in hand. Either pass can save you money—and allows you to skip the long ticket-buyer lines (though everyone must endure the security check before entering the palace).

The **Paris Museum Pass** covers the Château and the Domaine de Marie Antoinette (a €22.50 value). The Paris Museum Pass does not include audioguides and does not cover the Gardens on Fountain Spectacle weekends. For Paris Museum Pass pricing and details, see page 38.

The **Le Passeport** one-day pass is a good deal if you don't have a Paris Museum Pass and you want to see the whole shebang. Le Passeport covers your entrance to the Château, Domaine de Marie-Antoinette, and Gardens. It also covers several things not covered by the Paris Museum Pass: audioguides and weekend Fountain Spectacles. You can buy a Le Passeport at a FNAC department store in Paris, or at the Versailles TI or Château box office. From April–Oct, Le Passeport costs €20 Mon–Fri, €25 Sat–Sun; from Nov–March it's €16 Tue–Sun. This pass is a poor value on Mon, when only the Domaine de Marie-Antoinette and Gardens are open.

Hours: The **Château** is open Tue–Sun April–Oct 9:00–18:30, Nov–March 9:00–17:30, closed Mon. The **Domaine de Marie Antoinette** is open daily April–Oct 12:00–18:30, Nov–March 9:00–17:30. The **Gardens** are generally open daily from 9:00 to sunset (17:30 to 21:30), except on Sat in summer when they close at 18:00 to prepare for evening events. Last entry to all of these areas is one hour before closing.

Crowd Control: From May through September, Versailles is a zoo between 10:00–13:00, and all day Tue and Sun. For fewer crowds,

Versailles

WALKING TIMES
Train Station to Château = 10 min.
Château to Grand Trianon = 30 min.
Grand Trianon to the Hamlet = 15 min.
The Hamlet to Château = 30 min.

DOMAINE DE MARIE ANTOINETTE

PETIT CANAL

GRAND CANAL

SUMMER HOUSE

GRAND TRIANON

PETIT TRIANON

THE HAMLET

CAFÉ & KIOSK

TRAM STOP

WC

MAIN ENTRY

BOAT RENTAL

APOLLO BASIN

TEMPLE OF LOVE

ROUTE DE ST. CYR (N-10)

GAR·DENS

BIKE & GOLF CART RENTAL

WC

TAPIS VERT

AVE. DE TRIANON

BLVD. DE

BIKE RENTAL

COLONNADE

WC

WC

LATONA BASIN

ORANGERIE

TRAM STOP

NEPTUNE BASIN

GOLF-CART RENTAL

CHATEAU

— ROADS & PATHS
P PARKING
⤏ VIEW

500 METERS
500 YARDS

KING'S VEGETABLE GARDEN

❸ P PLACE D'ARMES

❽

SATORY

ST. LOUIS

AVE. DE GAULLE

❺

❹

STABLES

❾

AVE. DE SCEAUX

AVE. DE L'EUROPE

AVE. DE PARIS

❶

AVE. DE ST. CLOUD

CARNOT

PLACE HOCHE

NOTRE DAME

PLACE DU MARCHÉ

❼ ❻

LA

REINE

❷

RIVE DROITE TRAIN STN.

RER TRAIN STATION (RIVE GAUCHE)

❿

TO PARIS

TO WN

TO VERSAILLES CHANTIERS STN. (TO PARIS MONTPARNASSE STN. & CHARTRES)

TO PARIS (ST. LAZARE STN.)

❶ Hôtel de France
❷ Hôtel le Cheval Rouge
❸ Hôtel d'Angleterre
❹ Hôtel Ibis Versailles
❺ Hôtel du Palais
❻ La Bœuf à la Mode Rest.
❼ A la Côte Bretonne Rest.
❽ Chez Lazare Restaurant
❾ Equestrian Performances
❿ City of Versailles TI: Pass Sales, Hotel Info, etc.
⓫ Apollo Basin/Grand Canal Rests.

VERSAILLES

go early or late. If you go early, arrive by 9:00 (when the palace opens), and tour the Château first, then the Gardens. If you arrive later, tour the Gardens first and the Château after 13:00 when crowds dissipate (except on Tue and Sun, when the place is packed from open to close). Note that the last guided tours of the day generally depart by 15:00.

Avoid ticket-buying lines altogether by using a Paris Museum Pass or Le Passeport, or by booking a guided tour (see below). Everyone must wait in the security-check line to enter the Château.

Pickpockets: Assume pickpockets are working the tourist crowds.

Getting There: The town of Versailles is 30 minutes southwest of Paris. The palace is a 10-minute walk from the train station.

Take the **RER-C train** (4/hr, 30–40 min one-way, €6 round-trip) from any of these RER stops: Gare d'Austerlitz, St. Michel, Musée d'Orsay, Invalides, Pont de l'Alma, and Champ de Mars. Scan the list of departing trains. Any train whose name starts with a V (e.g., "Vick") goes to Versailles; don't board other trains. Get off at the last stop, which is Versailles R.G., or "Rive Gauche." Exit through the turnstiles by inserting your ticket. To reach the palace, turn right out of the train station, then left at the first boulevard, and walk 10 minutes.

All trains leaving Versailles from the Rive Gauche station serve all downtown Paris RER stops on the C line. (To visit Versailles and Chartres on the same day using public transportation, see page 483.)

Taxis for the 30-minute ride between Versailles and Paris cost about €55.

By **car,** it's a 30-minute drive to reach Versailles from Paris, if the traffic's not bad. Get on the *périphérique* freeway that circles Paris, and take the toll-free A13 autoroute toward Rouen. Follow signs into Versailles, then look for *château* signs and park in the huge pay lot (€4.50/2 hrs, €8/4 hrs, €12/8 hrs, free 19:30–8:30).

Information: Visit Versailles' good website before you go: www .chateauversailles.fr. Versailles has two information offices: the town's official TI (helpful, less crowded), and one at the palace. Both sell Paris Museum Passes and Le Passeport. You'll pass the town TI on your walk from the main RER station to the palace; it's just past the Pullman Hôtel (daily April–Sept 9:00–19:00, Oct–March 9:00–18:00, tel. 01 39 24 88 88). The Château's information office is on the left side of the Château courtyard (as you face the Château, tel. 08 10 81 16 14). The useful *Versailles Orientation Guide* brochure (free at either information office) explains your sightseeing options.

Planning Your Time at Versailles

Here's what I'd do on a first visit to Versailles:

In Paris, buy a Paris Museum Pass or Le Passeport (see "Passes," page 457).

Leave Paris by 8:00 and arrive at the palace just before it opens at 9:00. Tour the Château following my self-guided tour, which hits the highlights (Opera House, Chapel, King's and Queen's State Apartments, and the Hall of Mirrors). Consider supplementing the tour in this chapter with an audioguide (free with Le Passeport).

Have lunch in the Gardens, at one of the sandwich kiosks or cafés. Spend the afternoon touring the Gardens and the Domaine de Marie-Antoinette. On spring or summer weekends, catch the Fountain Spectacles in the Gardens. Stay for dinner in Versailles town (see recommended restaurants on page 481), or head back to Paris.

Guided Tours: For a basic visit, this chapter's self-guided tour works great. But the primary 90-minute English guided tour does have a few extras: commentary from trained guides, access to a few extra rooms (the interior of the Royal Chapel, some private apartments—the line-up varies), plus it's a good way to skip ticket-buying lines if you don't have a pass. The guided tours are long, but those with an appetite for palace history enjoy them.

Skip the tours hawked as you leave the train station; book directly at the Château. Reserve your tour upon arrival (tours can sell out by 13:00) at the information office in the Château courtyard (€7.50 plus Château admission or pass, 90 min, departing roughly every 45 min 10:00–15:00). Don't wait in the ticket-buying line—instead, walk to the front of the line, where you'll find the guided tour desk to the right.

Audioguide Tours: Audioguides are available at the entrances to the Château and Domaine de Marie-Antoinette. They're free with Le Passeport or individual Château or Domaine tickets. With the Paris Museum Pass, the Château audioguide costs €6 (€10 on Fountain Spectacle weekends); the Domaine audioguide is €4.

A free Rick Steves audioguide tour of the most important rooms of the King's and Queen's State Apartments is available for users of iPods and other MP3 players at www.ricksteves.com.

Versailles' Entrances

GARDENS ❸.

TO ORANGERIE

HALL OF MIRRORS

TO DOMAINE DE MARIE-ANTOINETTE

KING'S & QUEEN'S STATE APARTMENTS

TO GARDENS

START

HISTORY OF FRANCE GALLERIES

FINISH

WC

CHAPEL & OPERA HOUSE

CAFE & WC

ACCESS TO GARDENS

❷

ℹ ❶

CHATEAU ENTRANCE

DCH

FROM TRAIN STATION

❶ Chateau Ticket & Pass Sales
❷ Guided Tour Reservations & Departure Point
❸ Tram (Petit Train)
❹ Golf-Cart Rental (Voitures Eléctrique) & Fountain Spectacles Ticket Booth (weekends only)

••• Self-Guided Tour of State and Private Apartments

You may also want to check out the podcasts at www.podibus .com/versailles.

Length of This Day Trip: With the usual lines, allow 90 minutes for the Château, two hours for the Gardens, and another hour for the Domaine de Marie-Antoinette. Add another two hours for round-trip transit, plus another hour for lunch...and Versailles is a full day trip from Paris.

Baggage Check: There's a free checkroom at the main entrance—use it to check forbidden items (food, big bags, baby carriages, and so on). Strollers are not allowed inside the Château, so today's a good day for parents to either hire a babysitter (see page 402) or carry their toddler in a backpack with a child-seat.

Services: Reminiscent of the days when dukes urinated behind the potted palm trees, WCs at the Château are few and far between, and come with long lines. Use the public WC just before the palace gates, or find one of several in the Gardens.

Cuisine Art: A cafeteria and WCs are to the right of the Château's main entrance. Sandwich kiosks and cafés are scattered about the Gardens, including a good range of restaurants near the Apollo Basin and canal.

In the **town,** restaurants are on the street to the right of the parking lot (as you face the Château), though the best eateries line the lively market square, place du Marché, in the town center. A handy McDonald's is immediately across from the train station (WC without crowds, Internet café next door). An appealing assortment of reasonable restaurants line rue de Satory between the station and the palace (see "Eating," page 481).

Photography: Allowed indoors without a flash.

Fountain Spectacles: On spring and summer weekends, loud classical music fills the king's backyard, and the Garden's fountains are in full squirt. Louis XIV had his engineers literally reroute a river to fuel these gushers. Even by today's standards, they are impressive.

The fountains run April–Sept Sat–Sun 11:00–12:00 & 15:30–17:00, with the finale from 17:20–17:30. On these "spray days," the Gardens cost €8. (Pay at the ticket booth near the golf-cart rental in the Gardens; covered by Le Passeport but not Paris Museum Pass; not included in individual Château ticket.) Pick up the helpful *Les Grandes Eaux Musicales* brochure and ask about the various evening spectacles (Sat in July–Aug).

Starring: Louis XIV, Marie-Antoinette, and the *ancien régime*.

Overview

The main sights to see at Versailles—all covered by this self-guided tour—are the Château (the palace), the landscaped Gardens in the "backyard," and the small palaces of the Domaine de Marie-Antoinette. If your time is limited, stick to the Château and the Gardens just outside. It's a 30-minute walk from the Château, through the Gardens to the heart of the Domaine at the far end (longer if you stop along the way).

In the Château, the highlights are the King's and Queen's State Apartments, the Opera House, and the Chapel. (These rooms are labeled the "Red Itinerary" and "Blue Itinerary" by Versailles' curators.) We'll see all these on our self-guided tour.

THE TOUR BEGINS

• *Stand in the courtyard and face the palace. If you need to buy a ticket (or want to book a tour), go to the box office on the far left side of the court-yard. If you already have a ticket or pass, enter the Château through the modern glass entry just left of center (expect a line). The original golden Royal Gate in the center of the courtyard, nearly 260 feet long and decorated with 100,000 gold leaves, "disappeared" during the Revolution. This rep-lica (which cost €5 million to build) was installed in 2008—and definitely makes a statement.*

Exterior—
The Original Château and the Courtyard

The section of the palace with the clock is the original château, once a small hunting lodge where little Louis XIV spent his happiest boy-hood years. Naturally, the Sun King's private bedroom (the three arched windows beneath the clock) faced the rising sun. The palace and grounds are laid out on an east–west axis.

Once king, Louis XIV expanded the lodge by attaching wings, creating the present U-shape. Later, the long north and south wings were built. The total cost of the project has been estimated at half of France's entire GNP for one year.

Think how busy this courtyard must have been 300 years ago. There were as many as 5,000 nobles here at any one time, each with an entourage. They'd buzz from games to parties to amorous rendezvous in sedan-chair taxis. Servants ran about delivering secret messages and roast legs of lamb. Horse-drawn carriages arrived at the fancy gate with their finely dressed passengers, having driven up the broad boulevard that ran directly from Paris (the horse stables still line the boulevard). Incredible as it seems, both the grounds and most of the palace were public territory, where even the lowliest peasants could come to gawk (so long as they followed a dress code). Then, as now, there were hordes of tourists, pickpockets, palace workers, and men selling wind-up children's toys.

• *Enter the Château. (In 2009, the exact path you follow may change, due to renovation.) Once inside, follow the crowds (and signs for the Red and Blue Itineraries). You'll walk to the end of a lo-o-ong sculpture-lined hall, where you'll find our first stop—the Opera House.*

OPERA HOUSE AND CHAPEL

Versailles Royal Opera House (Opéra Royale)

Note: The Opera House is likely to be closed through June 2009.

The 700-seat, oval-shaped theater is a dizzying mix of pink, green, and blue, dazzling with mirrors and chandeliers, and all laced with gold.

Kings and Queens and Guillotines

• *You could read this on the train ride to Versailles. Relax...the palace is the last stop.*

Come the Revolution, when they line us up and make us stick out our hands, will you have enough calluses to keep them from shooting you? A grim thought, but Versailles raises these kinds of questions. It's the symbol of the *ancien régime*, a time when society was divided into rulers and the ruled, when you were born to be rich or to be poor. To some, it's the pinnacle of civilization; to others, the sign of a civilization in decay. Either way, it remains one of Europe's most impressive sights.

Versailles was the residence of the king and the seat of France's government for a hundred years. Louis XIV (r. 1643–1715) moved out of the Louvre in Paris, the previous royal residence, and built an elaborate palace in the forests and swamps of Versailles, 10 miles west. The reasons for the move were partly personal—Louis XIV loved the outdoors and disliked the sniping environs of stuffy Paris—and partly political.

Louis XIV was creating the first modern, centralized state. At Versailles, he consolidated Paris' scattered ministries so that he could personally control policy. More importantly, he invited France's nobles to Versailles in order to control them. Living a life of almost enforced idleness, the "domesticated" aristocracy couldn't interfere with the way Louis ran things. With 18 million people united under one king (England had only 5.5 million), a booming economy, and a powerful military, France was Europe's number-one power.

Around 1700, Versailles was the cultural heartbeat of Europe, and French culture was at its zenith. Throughout Europe, when you said "the king," you were referring to the French king... Louis XIV. Every king wanted a palace like Versailles. Everyone learned French. French taste in clothes, hairstyles, table manners, theater, music, art, and kissing spread across the Continent. That cultural dominance continued, to some extent, right up to the 20th century.

Louis XIV

At the center of all this was Europe's greatest king. He was a true Renaissance man, a century after the Renaissance: athletic, good-looking, a musician, dancer, horseman, statesman, art-lover, lover. For all his grandeur, he was one of history's most polite and approachable kings, a good listener who could put even commoners at ease in his presence.

Louis XIV called himself the Sun King because he gave life and warmth to all he touched. He was also thought of as Apollo, the Greek god of the sun. Versailles became the personal temple of this god on earth, decorated with statues and symbols of Apollo, the sun, and Louis XIV himself. The classical themes throughout underlined the divine right of France's kings and queens to rule without limit.

Louis XIV was a hands-on king who personally ran affairs of state. All decisions were made by him. Nobles, who in other countries were the center of power, became virtual slaves dependent on Louis XIV's generosity. For 70 years, he was the perfect embodiment of the absolute monarch. He summed it up best himself with his famous rhyme—"L'état, c'est moi!" (lay-tah say-mwah): "The state, that's me!"

Another Louis or Two to Remember

Three kings lived in Versailles during its century of glory. Louis XIV built it and established French dominance. Louis XV, his great-grandson (Louis XIV reigned for 72 years), carried on the tradition and policies, but without the Sun King's flair. During Louis XV's reign (1715–1774), France's power abroad was weakening, and there were rumblings of rebellion from within.

France's monarchy was crumbling, and the time was ripe for a strong leader to reestablish the old feudal order. They didn't get one. Instead, they got Louis XVI (r. 1774–1792), a shy, meek bookworm, the kind of guy who lost sleep over Revolutionary graffiti... because it was misspelled. Louis XVI married a sweet girl from the Austrian royal family, Marie-Antoinette, and together they retreated into the idyllic gardens of Versailles while Revolutionary fires smoldered.

The entire structure is made of wood, carved to look like Ionic columns or painted to simulate marble. When Marie-Antoinette married the future Louis XVI in 1770, they had their reception here in this building, which was built specifically for the occasion by architect Ange-Jacques Gabriel. It was used not only as a theater, but could also be quickly converted into a ballroom or audience hall by machinery that raised the auditorium floor to the same level as the stage. Look up above the double balconies to the chandeliers: It took thousands of candles to light the place for a single night, so performances were rare and treasured.

• *Our tour continues upstairs, in the room that overlooks the lavish Royal Chapel, with its pipe organ. (You can enter the chapel itself only on a guided tour.)*

Royal Chapel

Every morning at 10:00, the organist and musicians struck up the music, these big golden doors opened, and Louis XIV and his family walked through to attend Mass. While Louis XIV sat here on the upper level and looked down on the golden altar, the lowly nobles below knelt with their backs to the altar and looked up—worshipping Louis worshipping God. Important religious ceremonies took place here, including the marriage of young Louis XVI to Marie-Antoinette.

In the vast pagan "temple" that is Versailles—built to glorify one man, Louis XIV—this Royal Chapel is a paltry tip of the hat to that "other" god...the Christian one. It's virtually the first, last, and only hint of Christianity you'll see in the entire complex. Versailles celebrates Man, not God, by raising Louis XIV to almost godlike status, the personification of all good human qualities. In a way, Versailles is the last great flowering of Renaissance humanism and revival of the classical world.

• *Take a map flyer and enter the next room, a large space with a fireplace and a colorful painting on the ceiling.*

Hercules Drawing Room

Pleasure ruled. The main suppers, balls, and receptions were held in this room. Picture elegant partygoers in fine silks, wigs, rouge, lipstick, and fake moles (and that's just the men), as they dance to the strains of a string quartet.

On the wall opposite the fireplace is an appropriate painting showing Christ in the middle of a Venetian party. The work—by Paolo Veronese, a gift from the Republic of Venice—was one of Louis XIV's favorites, so they decorated the room around it. (Stand by the fireplace for the full effect: The room's columns, arches, and frieze match the height and style of Veronese's painted architecture, which makes the painting an extension of the room.)

The ceiling painting of Hercules being crowned a god gives the room its name. Hercules (with his club) hurries up to heaven on a chariot, late for his wedding to the king of the gods' daughter. Louis XIV built the room for his own daughter's wedding reception in the style of the day—pure Baroque. As you wander, the palace feels bare, but remember that entire industries were created to furnish and decorate the place with carpets, mirrors, furniture, and tapestries.

• *From here on, it's a one-way tour—getting lost is not allowed. Follow the crowds into the small green room with a goddess in pink on the ceiling. The names of the rooms generally come from the paintings on the ceilings.*

THE KING'S AND QUEEN'S STATE APARTMENTS

The King's Wing

Salon of Abundance

If the party in the Hercules Room got too intense, you could always step in here for some refreshments. Silver trays were loaded up with liqueurs, exotic stimulants (coffee), juice, chocolates, and, on really special occasions, three-bean salad.

The ceiling painting shows the cornucopia of riches poured down on invited guests. Around the edges of the ceiling are painted versions of the king's actual dinnerware and treasures. The two black chests of drawers are from Louis' furniture collection (most of it was lost in the Revolution). They rest on heavy bases and are heavily ornamented—the so-called Louis XIV style.

Louis himself might be here. He was a gracious host who enjoyed letting his hair down at night. If he took a liking to you, he might sneak you through those doors there (in the middle of the wall) and into his own private study, or "cabinet of curiosities," where he'd show off his collection of dishes, medals, jewels, or...the *Mona Lisa*, which hung on his wall. Louis' favorite show-and-tell items are now in the Louvre.

The paintings on the walls are of Louis XIV's heirs. He reigned for more than 70 years and outlived three of them, finally leaving the crown to his pink-cheeked, five-year-old great-grandson, Louis XV (on the right).

Venus Room

Love ruled at Versailles. In this room, couples would cavort beneath the Greek goddess of love (on the ceiling), who sends down a canopy of golden garlands to ensnare mortals in delicious *amour*. Notice how a painted garland goes "out" the bottom of the central painting, becomes a golden garland held by a satyr, transforms into a gilded wood garland, and then turns back into a painting again. Baroque artists loved to mix their media to fool the eye. Another illusion is in the paintings at both ends of the room—the painted columns match the room's real ones, and so extend this grand room into mythical courtyards.

Don't let the statue of a confident Louis XIV as a Roman emperor fool you. He started out as a poor little rich kid with a chip on his shoulder. His father died before Louis was old enough to rule, and, during the regency period, the French Parliament treated little Louis and his mother like trash. They were virtual prisoners, humiliated in their home (at that time, the Royal Palace was the Louvre in Paris) with bland meals, hand-me-down leotards, and pointed shoes. Once Louis XIV attained power and wealth, there was one topic you never discussed in his presence—poverty. Maybe Versailles was his way of saying, "Living well is the best revenge."

Diana Room

Here in the billiards room, Louis and his men played on a table that stood in the center of the room, while ladies sat surrounding them on Persian-carpet cushions, and music wafted in from next door. Louis was a good pool player, a sore loser, and a king—he rarely lost.

The famous bust of Louis by Giovanni Lorenzo Bernini (in the center) shows a handsome, dashing, 27-year-old playboy-king. His gaze is steady amid his windblown cloak and hair. Young Louis loved life. He hunted animals by day (notice Diana the Huntress on the ceiling) and chased beautiful women at night.

Games were actually an important part of Louis' political strategy, known as "the domestication of the nobility." By distracting the nobles with the pleasures of courtly life, he was free to run the government his way. Billiards, dancing, and concerts were popular, but the biggest distraction was gambling, usually a card game similar to blackjack. Louis lent money to the losers, making them even more indebted to him. The good life was an addiction, and Louis kept the medicine cabinet well-stocked.

As you move into the next room, notice the fat walls that hid thin servants, who were to be at their master's constant call—but out of sight when not needed.

Mars Room

Also known as the Guard Room (as it was the room for Louis' Swiss bodyguards), it's decorated with a military flair. On the ceiling, there's Mars, the Greek god of war, in a chariot pulled by wolves. The bronze cupids in the corners are escalating from love arrows to heavier artillery. But it's not all war. The painting of David playing his harp is a reminder that Louis loved music and played his guitar or enjoyed a concert here nearly every evening.

Out the window are sculpted gardens in the style of a traditional Italian villa—landscaped symmetrically, with trimmed hedges and cone-shaped trees lining walkways that lead to fountains.

Mercury Room

Louis' life was a work of art, and Versailles was the display case. Everything he did was a public event designed to show his subjects how it should be done. This room served as Louis' official (not actual) bedroom, where the Sun King would ritually rise each morning to warm his subjects.

From a canopied bed (like this 18th-century one), Louis would get up, dress, and take a seat for morning prayer. Meanwhile, the nobles would stand behind a balustrade, in awe of his piety, nobility, and clean socks. At breakfast, they murmured with delight as he deftly decapitated his boiled egg with a knife. And when Louis went to bed at night, the dukes and barons would fight over who got to hold the candle while he slipped into his royal jammies. Bedtime, wakeup, and meals were all public rituals.

Apollo Room

This was the grand throne room. Louis held court from a 10-foot-tall, silver-canopied throne on a raised platform placed in the center of the room. (Notice the metal rings in the ceiling that once supported the canopy.)

Everything in here reminds us that Louis XIV was not just any ruler, but the Sun King, who lit the whole world with his presence. On the ceiling, the sun god Apollo drives his chariot, dragging the sun across the heavens to warm the four corners of the world (counterclockwise from above the exit door): 1) Europe, with a sword; 2) Asia, with a lion; 3) Africa, with an elephant; and 4) good old America, an Indian maiden with a crocodile. Notice the ceiling's beautifully gilded frame and *Goldfinger* maidens.

The famous portrait by Hyacinthe Rigaud over the fireplace gives a more human look at Louis XIV. He's shown in a dancer's pose, displaying the legs that made him one of the all-time dancing fools of kingery. At night, they often held parties in this room, actually dancing around the throne.

Louis XIV (who was 63 when this was painted) had more than 300 wigs like this one, and he changed them many times a day. This fashion first started when his hairline began to recede, then sprouted all over Europe, and even to the American colonies in the time of George Washington.

Louis XIV may have been treated like a god, but he was not an overly arrogant man. His subjects adored him because he was a symbol of everything a man could be, the fullest expression of the Renaissance Man. Compare the portrait of Louis XIV with the one across the room of his last successor, Louis XVI—same arrogant pose, but without the inner confidence to keep his head on his shoulders.

The War Room

"Louis Quatorze was addicted to wars," and France's success made other countries jealous and nervous. At the base of the ceiling (in semi-

circular paintings), we see Germany (with the double eagle), Holland (with its ships), and Spain (with a red flag and roaring lion) ganging up on Louis XIV. But Lady France (center of ceiling), protected by the shield of Louis XIV, hurls thunderbolts down to defeat them. The stucco relief on the wall shows Louis XIV on horseback, triumphing over his fallen enemies.

Versailles was good propaganda. It showed the rest of the world how rich and powerful France was. A visit to the palace and Gardens sent visitors reeling.

And Louis XIV's greatest triumph may be the next room, the one that everybody wrote home about.

The Hall of Mirrors

No one had ever seen anything like this hall when it was opened. Mirrors were still a great luxury at the time, and the number and size of these monsters were astounding. The hall is nearly 250 feet long. There are 17 arched mirrors, matched by 17 windows letting in that breathtaking view of the Gardens. Lining the hall are 24 gilded candelabra, eight busts of Roman emperors, and eight classical-style statues (seven of them ancient). The ceiling decoration chronicles Louis' military accomplishments, topped off by Louis himself in the central panel (with cupids playing cards at his divine feet), doing what he did best—triumphing. Originally, two huge carpets mirrored the action depicted on the ceiling.

Imagine this place lit by the flames of thousands of candles, filled with ambassadors, nobles, and guests dressed in silks and powdered wigs. At the far end of the room sits the king, on the canopied throne

moved in temporarily from the Apollo Room. Servants glide by with silver trays of hors d'oeuvres, and an orchestra fuels the festivities. The mirrors reflect an age when beautiful people loved to look at themselves. It was no longer a sin to be proud of good looks and fine clothes, or to enjoy the good things in life: laughing, dancing, eating, drinking, flirting, and watching the sun set into the distant canal.

From the center of the hall, you can fully appreciate the epic scale of Versailles. The huge palace (by architect Louis Le Vau), the fantasy interior (by Charles Le Brun), and the endless Gardens (by André Le Nôtre) made Versailles *le* best. In 1871, after the Prussians defeated the French, Otto von Bismarck declared the establishment of the German Empire in this room. And in 1919, Germany and the Allies signed the Treaty of Versailles, ending World War I (and, some say, starting World War II) right here, in the Hall of Mirrors.

• *From the Hall of Mirrors, a short detour takes you to the heart of the palace...*

King's Bedroom and Council Rooms

Look out the window and notice how this small room is at the exact center of the immense horseshoe-shaped building, overlooking the main courtyard and—naturally—facing the rising sun in the east. Imagine the humiliation on that day in 1789 when Louis XVI was forced to stand here and acknowledge the angry crowds that filled the square demanding the end of the divine monarchy. While this was his bedroom, he also worked here and the rooms on either side were for top council meetings.

• *Return to the Hall of Mirrors. At the far corner, enter the small...*

Peace Room

By the end of the Sun King's long life, he was tired of fighting. In this sequel to the War Room, peace is granted to Germany, Holland, and Spain as cupids play with the discarded cannons, armor, and swords. Louis XIV advised his great-grandson to "be a peaceful king."

The oval painting above the fireplace shows 19-year-old Louis XV bestowing an olive branch on Europe. Beside him is his Polish wife, Marie Leszczynska, cradling their baby twin daughters.

The Peace Room marks the beginning of the queen's half of the palace. The Queen's Wing is a mirror image of the King's Wing. While the King's Wing was mostly ceremonial and used as a series of reception rooms, the Queen's Wing is more intimate. For instance, on Sundays, the queen held chamber-music concerts in this room for family and friends (notice the gilded music motifs).

• *Enter the first room of the Queen's Wing, with its canopied bed.*

The Queen's Wing
The Queen's Bedchamber

It was here that the queen rendezvoused with her husband. Two queens died here, and this is where 19 princes were born. The chandelier is where two of them were conceived. (Just kidding.) Royal babies were delivered in public to prove their blue-bloodedness.

True, Louis XIV was not the most faithful husband. There was no attempt to hide the fact that the Sun King warmed more than one bed, for he was above the rules of mere mortals. Adultery became acceptable—even fashionable—in court circles. The secret-looking door on the left side of the bed was for Louis' late-night liaisons—it led straight to his rooms.

Some of Louis XIV's mistresses became more famous and powerful than his rather quiet queen, but he was faithful to the show of marriage and had genuine affection for his wife. Louis XIV made a point of sleeping with the queen as often as possible, regardless of whose tiara he tickled earlier in the evening.

This room looks like it did in the days of the last queen, Marie-Antoinette, who substantially redecorated the entire wing. That's her bust over the fireplace, and the double eagle of her native Austria in the corners. The big chest to the left of the bed held her jewels.

The queen's canopied bed is a reconstruction. The bed, chair, and wall coverings switched with the seasons. This was the cheery summer pattern.

Salon of the Nobles

The wife of Louis XV and her circle of friends met here, seated on the stools, under paintings by Boucher—popular with the queen for their pink-cheeked Rococo exuberance. Discussions ranged from politics to gossip, food to literature, fashion to philosophy. All three of Versailles' rulers considered themselves enlightened monarchs who promoted the arts and new ideas. Louis XIV laughed at the anti-authoritarian plays of Molière, and Louis XV gave free room and board here to the political radical Voltaire. Ironically, these discussions planted the seeds of liberal thought that would grow into the Revolution.

Queen's Antechamber

The royal family dined here publicly, while servants and nobles fluttered around them, admired their table manners, and laughed at the king's jokes like courtly Paul Shaffers. A typical dinner consisted of four different soups, two whole birds stuffed with truffles, mutton, ham slices, fruit, pastries, compotes, and preserves.

The central portrait is of luxury-loving, "let-them-eat-cake" Marie-Antoinette, who became a symbol of decadence to the peasants. The portrait at the far end is a public-relations attempt to soften her image by showing her with three of her children.

VERSAILLES

Queen's Guard Room

On October 5, 1789, a mob of Revolutionaries—appalled by their queen's taste in wallpaper—stormed the palace. They were fed up with the ruling class leading a life of luxury in the countryside while they were starving in the grimy streets of Paris.

The king and queen locked themselves in. Some of the Revolutionaries gained access to this upper floor. They burst into this room where Marie-Antoinette was hiding, overcame her bodyguards, and dragged off her and her husband. (Some claim that, as they carried her away, she sang, "Louis, Louis, oh-oh...we gotta go now.")

The enraged peasants then proceeded to ransack the place as revenge for the years of poverty and oppression they'd suffered. (The stripped palace was refurnished a decade later under Napoleon and turned into a national museum.) Marie-Antoinette and Louis XVI were later taken to the place de la Concorde in Paris, where they knelt under the guillotine and were made a foot shorter at the top.

Did the king and queen deserve it? Were the Revolutionaries destroying civilization or clearing the decks for a new and better one? Was Versailles a symbol of progress or decadence?

Coronation Room

No sooner did the French throw out a king than they got an emperor. The Revolution established democracy, but it was shaky in a country that wasn't used to it. In the midst of the confusion, the upstart general Napoleon Bonaparte took control and soon held dictatorial powers. This room captures the glory of the Napoleon years, when he conquered most of Europe. In the huge canvas on the left-hand wall, we see him crowning himself emperor of a new, revived "Roman" Empire. (While also painted by the master, Jacques-Louis David, this is a lesser-quality version of the famous one hanging in the Louvre.)

Turn and face the windows to see the portrait (between the windows) of a dashing, young, charismatic Napoleon in 1796, when he was just a general in command of the Revolution's army in Italy. Compare this with the adjacent portrait from 10 years later—looking less like a revolutionary and more like a Louis. Above the young Napoleon is a portrait of Josephine, his wife and France's empress. In David's *Distribution of Eagles* (opposite the *Coronation*), the victorious general, in imperial garb, passes out emblems of victory to his loyal troops. In *The Battle of Aboukir* (opposite the window), Joachim Murat, Napoleon's general and brother-in-law, looks bored as he slashes through a tangle of dark-skinned warriors. His horse, though, has a look of, "What are we doing in this mob? Let's get out of here!" Let's.

• Before leaving, stop by the **Hall of Battles** (not always open, in the History of France Galleries—the Yellow Itinerary). This nearly 400-foot-long hall

All the King's Veggies & Horses: Lesser Sights near the Palace

Two sights located a few minutes' walk from the Château give a different take on life in royal times. For the locations, see the map on page 458.

The King's Vegetable Garden (Le Potager du Roi)

When Louis XIV demanded fresh asparagus in the middle of winter, he got it, thanks to his vegetable garden. The 22-acre garden—still productive—is open to visitors. Stroll through symmetrically laid-out plots planted with vegetables both ordinary and exotic, among thousands of fruit trees. The garden is surrounded by walls and sunk below street level to create its own microclimate. Overseeing the central fountain is a statue of the agronomist Jean de la Quintinie, who wowed Louis XIV's court with Versailles-sized produce. Even today, the garden sprouts 20 tons of vegetables and 50 tons of fruit a year, which you can buy in season (€4.50 on weekdays, €6.50 on weekends, April–Oct daily 10:00–18:00, closed Nov–March, 10 rue du Maréchal Joffre).

The Equestrian Performance Academy (Academie du Spectacle Equestre)

The art of horseback riding has returned to Versailles. On most weekends from May through mid-December, you can watch rigorous training sessions, or enjoy choreographed performances—including "equestrian fencing"—performed to classical music (training sessions-€11, 60 min, Sat-Sun only at 11:15; musical shows-€25, Sun and some Thu at 15:00 plus Sat at 20:00 May–July and at 18:00 Sept–Dec, maybe also Tue-Sun mid-Feb–mid-March and April, but schedule is sporadic—check website for closure dates and extra performances). The stables (Grandes Ecuries) are across the parking square from the Château, next to the post office. For information, call 01 39 02 07 14. For reservations, call 08 92 68 18 91 or visit www.acadequestre.fr.

(even longer then the Hall of Mirrors) celebrates the great French battles from the sixth century to 1830, with 33 grand paintings and piles of busts of military big shots. It's worth a wander for historians.

The exit staircase puts you outside on the left (south) side of the palace, opposite the WC. Turn left under the colonnade to enter the Gardens, or turn right to leave the Château.

Now might be a good time to break for lunch (see "Cuisine Art" on page 462). When you're ready for the Gardens, plan your time with the "Getting Around the Gardens" sidebar on page 476.

THE GARDENS

Controlling Nature

Louis XIV was a divine-right ruler. One way he proved it was by controlling nature like a god. These lavish grounds—elaborately planned, pruned, and decorated—showed everyone that Louis was in total command. Louis loved his Gardens and, until his last days, presided

over their care. He personally led VIPs through them and threw his biggest parties here. With their Greco-Roman themes and incomparable beauty, the Gardens further illustrated his immense power (well-explained in the free *Garden and Groves* flier, available at the TIs and also at the garden entry on Fountain Spectacle weekends).

• *Entering the Gardens, with the palace to your back, go to the far left to reach the stone railing. You'll pass through flowers and cookie-cutter patterns of shrubs and green cones. Stand at the railing overlooking the courtyard below and the Louis-made lake in the distance.*

The Orangerie

The warmth from the Sun King was so great that he could even grow orange trees in chilly France. Louis XIV had a thousand of these to amaze his visitors. In winter, they were kept in the greenhouses (beneath your feet) that surround the courtyard. On sunny days, they were wheeled out in their silver planters and scattered around the grounds.

• *Make an about-face and walk back toward the palace. Sit on the top stairs and look away from the palace.*

View Down the Royal Drive

This, to me, is the most stunning spot in all of Versailles. With the palace behind you, it seems as if the grounds stretch out forever. Versailles was laid out along an eight-mile axis that included the grounds, the palace, and the town of Versailles itself, one of the first instances of urban planning since Roman times and a model for future capitals, such as Washington, D.C., and Brasilia.

Getting Around the Gardens

On Foot: It's a 30-minute walk from the palace, down to the Grand Canal, and past the two Trianon palaces to the Hamlet—the heart of the Domaine de Marie-Antoinette. Allow more time if you stop along the way.

By Bike: A rental bike gives you the most freedom to explore the Gardens economically (€6.50/hr, near the Grand Canal, kid-size bikes available).

By *Petit Train:* The fast-looking, slow-moving tram leaves from behind the Château (north side) and serves the Grand Canal and the Domaine. You can hop on and off as you like (€6, 4/hr, three stops, worthless commentary).

By Golf Cart: This makes for a fun drive through the Gardens, complete with music and a relaxing commentary. But you can't go wherever you want—the cart shuts off automatically if you diverge from the prescribed route. Be warned: To make it out to the Hamlet and back within your allotted hour, you'll need to put the pedal to the metal without stops...or you'll pay extra (€28/hr, audioguide-€1.20, rent at Orangerie side of palace or down by the canal).

Looking down the Royal Drive (also known as "The Green Carpet"), you see the round Apollo fountain far in the distance. Just beyond that is the Grand Canal. The groves on either side of the Royal Drive were planted with trees from all over, laid out in an elaborate grid, and dotted with statues and fountains. Of the original 1,500 fountains, 300 remain.

Looking back at the palace, you can see the Hall of Mirrors—it's the middle story, with the arched windows.

• *Stroll down the steps to get a good look at the frogs and lizards that fill the round...*

Latona Basin

Everything in the garden has a symbolic meaning. The theme of Versailles is Apollo, the god of the sun, associated with Louis XIV. This round fountain tells the story of the birth of Apollo and his sister, Diana. On top of the fountain are Apollo and Diana as little kids with their mother, Latona (they're facing toward the Apollo fountain). Latona, an unwed mother, was insulted by the local peasants. She called on the king of the gods, Zeus (the children's father), to avenge the insult. Zeus swooped down and turned all the peasants into the frogs and lizards that ring the fountain.

• *As you walk down past the basin toward the Royal Drive, you'll pass by "ancient" statues done by 17th-century French sculptors. The Colonnade is hidden in the woods on the left-hand side of the Royal Drive, about three-fourths of the way to the Apollo Basin (you'll spot it off the main path through an opening).*

The Colonnade

Versailles had no prestigious ancient ruins, so the king built his own. This prefab Roman ruin is a 100-foot circle of 64 marble columns supporting arches. Beneath the arches are small birdbath fountains (imagine them all spouting water). Nobles would picnic in the shade to the tunes of a string quartet and pretend that they were the enlightened citizens of the ancient world.

The Apollo Basin

The fountains of Versailles were its most famous attraction, a marvel of both art and engineering. This one was the centerpiece, showing the sun god—Louis XIV—in his sunny chariot, as he starts his journey across the sky. The horses are half-submerged, giving the impression, when the fountains play, of the sun rising out of the mists of dawn. Most of the fountains were only turned on when the king walked by, but this one played constantly for the benefit of those watching from the palace.

All the fountains are gravity-powered. They work on the same principle as blocking a hose with your finger to make it squirt. Underground streams (pumped into Versailles by Seine River pressure) feed into smaller pipes at the fountains, which shoot the water high into the air.

Looking back at the palace from here, realize that the distance you just walked is only a fraction of this vast complex of buildings, gardens, and waterways. Be glad you don't have to mow the lawn.

The Grand Canal

Why visit Venice when you can just build your own? In an era before virtual reality, this was the next best thing to an actual trip. Couples in gondolas would pole along the waters accompanied by barges with orchestras playing "O Sole Mio." The canal is actually cross-shaped; you're looking at the longest part, one mile from end to end. Of course, this, too, is a man-made body of water with no function other than to please. Originally, authentic gondoliers, imported with their boats from Venice, lived in a little settlement next to the canal.

• *To enter the Domaine de Marie-Antoinette—the Queen's playground— you'll need to pay a separate €9 entry fee (€5 after 16:00 and Nov–March), unless you have a Paris Museum Pass or Le Passeport. You can enter/exit the Domaine at several spots: near the palace known as the Grand Trianon (where we'll enter), near the Petit Trianon, or near The Hamlet.*

You can rent a bike or golf cart, or catch the pokey tourist train, but the walk is half the fun. It's about a 30-minute walk from here to the end of the tour, plus another 30-minute walk back to the palace.

To get to the Grand Trianon, face the Grand Canal and turn right, walking down a long straight road marked with signs to the Domaine. After about five minutes, turn left on Avenue de Trianon, which leads to the Grand Trianon.

DOMAINE DE MARIE-ANTOINETTE

The Trianon Area—Retreat from Reality

Versailles began as an escape from the pressures of kingship. But in a short time, the palace became as busy as Paris ever was. Louis XIV needed an escape from his escape and built a smaller palace out in the boonies. Later, his successors retreated still farther into the garden and built a fantasy world of simple pleasures, allowing them to ignore the real world that was crumbling all around them.

Grand Trianon

This was the king's private residence away from the main palace. Louis XIV usually spent a couple of nights a week here, but the two later Louises spent more and more time retreating. While the main palace of Versailles was a screen separating French reality from the royal utopia, the Trianon palaces were engulfed in the royals' fantasy world, and therefore favored.

The facade of this one-story building is a charming combination of pink, yellow, and white, a cheery contrast to the imposing Baroque facade of the main palace. Ahead, you can see the Gardens through the columns. The king's apartments were to the left of the columns.

The flower gardens were changed daily for the king's pleasure—for new color combinations and new "nasal cocktails."

Walk around the palace (to the right), if you'd like, for a view of the Gardens and rear facade.

• *Facing the front, do an about-face. The Summer House is not down the driveway but about 200 yards away, along the smaller pathway at about 10 o'clock.*

French Pavilion—Summer House

This small, white building with four rooms fanning out from the center was one more step away from the modern world. Here, Marie-Antoinette spent summer evenings with family and a few friends, listening to music or playing parlor games. She and her friends explored all avenues of *la douceur de vivre*, the sweetness of living. To the left are the buildings of the menagerie, where her servants kept cows, goats, chickens, and ducks.

• *Continue frolicking along the path until you run into the...*

Petit Trianon

Louis XV developed an interest in botany. He wanted to spend more time near the French Gardens, but the Summer House just wasn't big

enough. He constructed the Petit Trianon ("Small Trianon") at the urging of his first mistress, Madame de Pompadour, and it later became home to his next mistress, Madame du Barry.

This gray, cubical building is a masterpiece of Neoclassical architecture, built by the same architect who created the Opera House in the main palace. The Petit Trianon reopened in 2009 following renovation. It has four distinct facades, each a perfect and harmonious combination of Greek-style columns, windows, and railings. Walk around it and find your favorite.

When Louis XVI became king, he gave the building to his new bride, who made this her home base. Despite her bad reputation with the public, Marie-Antoinette was a sweet girl from Vienna who never quite fit in with the fast, sophisticated crowd at Versailles. Here at the Petit Trianon, she could get away and re-create the simple home life she remembered from her childhood. On the lawn outside, she installed a merry-go-round.

• *Five minutes more will bring you to the...*

Temple of Love

A circle of 12 marble Corinthian columns supports a dome, decorating a path where lovers would stroll. Underneath, there's a statue of Cupid making a bow (to shoot arrows of love) out of the club of Hercules. It's a delightful monument to a society where the rich could afford that ultimate luxury, romantic love. When the Revolution came, I bet they wished they'd kept the club.

• *And finally, you'll reach...*

The Hamlet (Le Hameau)

Marie-Antoinette longed for the simple life of a peasant—not the hard labor of real peasants, who sweated and starved around her—but the fairytale world of simple country pleasures. She built this complex of 12 buildings as her own private village.

This was an actual working farm with a dairy, a water mill, and domestic animals. The harvest was served at Marie-Antoinette's table.

Marie-Antoinette didn't do much work herself, but she "supervised," dressed in a plain white muslin dress and a straw hat.

The Queen's House is the main building, actually two buildings connected by a wooden gallery. Like any typical peasant farmhouse, it had a billiard room, library, elegant dining hall, and two living rooms.

Nearby was the small theater. Here, Marie-Antoinette and her friends acted out plays, far from the rude intrusions of the real world.

• *The real world and the main palace are a 30-minute walk to the southeast (longer with stops). Along the way, check out the Neptune Basin near the palace, an impressive miniature lake with fountains, and indulge your own favorite fantasy.*

SLEEPING

For a less-expensive and laid-back alternative to Paris, within easy reach of the big city by RER train (4/hr, 40 min), Versailles can be a good overnight stop, especially for drivers. Park in the palace's main lot while looking for a hotel, or leave your car there overnight (€4.50/2 hrs, free 19:30–8:30). Get a map of Versailles at your hotel or at the TI.

$$$ Hôtel de France*,** in an 18th-century townhouse, offers Old World class, with mostly air-conditioned, appropriately royal rooms, a pleasant courtyard, elaborate public spaces, a bar, and a restaurant (Db-€141, Tb-€180, Qb-€240, Wi-Fi, just off parking lot across from Château at 5 rue Colbert, tel. 01 30 83 92 23, fax 01 30 83 92 24, www .hotelfrance-versailles.com, hotel-de-france-versailles@wanadoo.fr).

$$ Hôtel le Cheval Rouge,** built in 1676 as Louis XIV's stables, now houses tourists. It's a block behind the place du Marché in a quaint corner of town on a large, quiet courtyard with free parking and crisp, sufficiently comfortable rooms, many with open beams (Db with shower-€78, Db with tub-€95, Tb-€115, Qb-€125, 18 rue André Chénier, tel. 01 39 50 03 03, fax 01 39 50 61 27, www.chevalrouge.fr.st, chevalrouge@club-internet.fr).

$$ Hôtel d'Angleterre,** away from the frenzy, is a tranquil, homey place with smiling, Polish-born Madame Kutyla in control. Rooms are modest, comfortable, and spacious. Park in the nearby Château lot (D-€52, Db-€80–92, family Qb-€100–125, extra bed-€15, Wi-Fi, just below palace to the right as you exit, 2 rue de Fontenay, tel. 01 39 51 43 50, fax 01 39 51 45 63, www.hotel-angleterre-versailles .com, hotel.angleterre.versailles@wanadoo.fr).

$ Hôtel Ibis Versailles** offers a good weekend value and modern comfort, with 85 air-conditioned rooms but no character (Db-€75 Fri–Sun, €110 Mon–Thu, extra bed-€10, parking-€10, across from RER station, 4 avenue du Général de Gaulle, tel. 01 39 53 03 30, fax 01 39 50 06 31, www.ibishotel.com, h1409@accor.com).

Sleep Code

(€1 = about $1.50, country code: 33)
S = Single, **D** = Double/Twin, **T** = Triple, **Q** = Quad, **b** = bathroom,
s = shower only. Everyone speaks English and accepts credit
cards.

To help you easily sort through these listings, I've divided
the rooms into three categories, based on the price for a
standard double room with bath.

$$$ Higher Priced—Most rooms €125 or more.
$$ Moderately Priced—Most rooms between €80-125.
$ Lower Priced—Most rooms €80 or less.

$ Hôtel du Palais, facing the RER station, rents 24 clean, basic rooms—the cheapest I list in this area. Ask for a quiet room off the street (Db-€60–68, piles of stairs, 6 place Lyautey, tel. 01 39 50 39 29, fax 01 39 50 80 41, hotelpalais@ifrance.com).

EATING

In the pleasant town center, around place du Marché Notre-Dame, you'll find a thriving open market (Sun, Tue, and Fri mornings until 13:00) and a variety of reasonably priced restaurants, cafés, and a few cobbled lanes (see map on page 458). The square is a 15-minute walk from the Château (veer left when you leave the Château).

On or near Place du Marché Notre-Dame: This square is lined with colorful and inexpensive eateries. Troll the intriguing options or try one of these: **La Bœuf à la Mode,** right on the square, is a bistro with traditional cuisine and a passion for red meat (€18 *plats*, €30 three-course dinner *menu*, open daily, 4 rue au Pain, tel. 01 39 50 31 99). **A la Côte Bretonne** is your best bet for crêpes in a friendly, cozy setting. Yann-Alan and his family have served up the cuisine of their native Brittany region since 1951 (€4–10 crêpes from a fun and creative menu, Tue–Sun 12:00–14:30 & 19:00–22:30, closed Mon, fine indoor and outdoor seating, a few steps off the square on traffic-free rue des Deux Portes at #12, tel. 01 39 51 18 24).

On Rue Satory: This pedestrian-friendly street is on the south side of the Château, near Hôtel d'Angleterre (10-min walk, angle right out of the Château). The street is lined with a rich variety of restaurants, ranging from cheap ethnic to more pricey and formal French. Friendly **Chez Lazare** is a good value inside or out, with €13–16 *plats* (closed Sun–Mon, 18 rue de Satory, tel. 01 39 50 41 45).

VERSAILLES

CHARTRES CATHEDRAL DAY TRIP

Some of the children who watched the old church burn to the ground on June 10, 1194, grew up to build Chartres Cathedral and attend the dedication Mass in 1260. That's astonishing, considering that other Gothic cathedrals, such as Paris' Notre-Dame, took hundreds of years to build. Having been built so quickly, Chartres is arguably Europe's best example of pure Gothic, with a unity of architecture, statues, and stained glass that captures the spirit of the Age of Faith.

Chartres itself, an easy day trip from Paris, offers a pleasant small-town break. Its pleasing, cobbled old center is overshadowed by its great cathedral. Discover the picnic-friendly park behind the cathedral and wander the quiet alleys and peaceful squares. For accommodations and eateries, see the end of this chapter.

ORIENTATION

Cost: Church entry free; climbing the 300-step north tower costs €6.50 (free on first Sun of the month, and for those under 18). Skip the Chartres Pass sold at the TI.

Hours: Church open daily 8:30–19:30. Tower open May–Aug Mon–Sat 9:30–12:30 & 14:00–18:00, Sun 14:00–18:00; Sept–April closes at 16:30 (entrance inside church after bookstore on left). Mass held Mon–Fri at 11:45 (in the crypt) and 18:15; Sat at 11:45 (in the crypt) and 18:00; Sun at 9:15 (Gregorian) and 11:00.

Getting There: Chartres is a one-hour train trip from Paris' Gare Montparnasse (about €13 one-way, 10/day, buy tickets at Ile-de-France ticket windows in center of station, street level). Figure on a round-trip total of three hours from Paris to cathedral doorstep and back.

Upon arrival at the Chartres train station, plan ahead and jot down times when the train returns to Paris (last train generally departs Chartres around 21:00). Exiting the Chartres station, you'll see the spires of the cathedral dominating the town, a five-minute walk uphill. On your way to the cathedral, stop at the TI (see "Information," below).

Combining with Versailles: TER trains link Versailles and Chartres frequently (up to 30/day), on the route from Paris to Le Mans. In Versailles, this train stops at the Chantiers station (that's "Versailles C.H.")—not the Versailles R.G., or Rive Gauche, station listed in this book's Versailles visit (see page 459). The Versailles C.H. station is a 25-minute walk to the palace (just ask locals, "Château?").

Bring: Binoculars, if you got 'em. You can rent binoculars at a souvenir shop near the south porch of the church (€1.50/hr, €20 deposit, at 10 cloître Notre-Dame).

Information: At the **TI,** pick up the good free map with basic information on the town and cathedral. The TI has specifics on cathedral tours with Malcolm Miller, and also rents audioguides for the old town—both are described below (open April–Sept Mon–Sat 9:00–19:00, Sun 9:30–17:30; Oct–March Mon–Sat 9:00–18:00, Sun 9:30–17:00; located 100 yards in front of church, tel. 02 37 18 26 26, www.chartres-tourisme.com).

The church has two **bookstores**. One is inside near the entrance; the other—called La Crypte—is outside near the south porch (church tel. 02 37 21 59 08, www.diocese-chartres.com).

Cathedral Tours by Malcolm Miller: This fascinating English scholar, who moved here 50 years ago, has dedicated his life to studying this cathedral—and sharing its wonder through his guided lecture tours. His 75-minute tours are worthwhile, even if you've taken my self-guided tour (below). No reservation is needed—just show up (€10, offered Mon–Sat at 12:00 and 14:45, no tours last half of Aug and Jan–Feb). Some take both of his tours, as every tour is different. Tours begin inside the church at the orange-and-purple *Cathedral Tours* sign by the bookstore. Consult this sign for changes or cancellations. He also offers private tours (private tour info tel. 02 37 28 15 58, fax 02 37 28 33 03, millerchartres@aol.com). For a detailed look at Chartres' windows, sculpture, and history, pick up Malcolm Miller's two guidebooks (sold at cathedral).

Audioguides: You can rent audioguides from the bookstore inside the cathedral near the entrance. Routes include the cathedral (€4.20, 45 min), the choir only (€3.20, 25 min), or both (€6.20, 70 min). The TI offers an audioguide for the often-missed old town (€5.50, €8.50/double set, about 2 hours, available only at the TI, leave passport as a deposit).

Crypt Tours: The crypt (which means "hidden") is the foundation of the previous, ninth-century church. Today, these foundations can be visited only as part of a very boring guided tour in French (with an English handout). You'll see remnants of the earlier churches, a modern copy of the old wooden Mary-and-baby statue, and hints of the old well and Roman wall (€2.70; April–Oct at 11:00, 14:15, 15:15, and 16:30; June–July also at 17:15, 2/day Nov–March, 30-min tours start in La Crypte bookstore, located outside church near south porch, tel. 02 37 21 75 02).

Length of This Tour: One hour—plus three hours in transit—means that Chartres is effectively an all-day excursion from Paris.

THE CHARTRES GENERATION— THE 1200S

• *Kill train time by reading this.*

From king to bishop and knight to pawn, French society was devoted to the Christian faith. It inspired knights to undertake the formidable Crusades, artists to re-create heaven in statues and stained glass, and architects to build skyscraping cathedrals filled with the mystic light of heaven. They aimed for a golden age, blending faith and reason. But misguided faith often outstripped reason, resulting in very un-Christian intolerance and violence.

Timeline

c. 1194 The old cathedral burns down.

1200 The University of Paris is founded, using human reason to analyze Christian faith. Borrowing from the pagan Greek philosopher Aristotle, scholars described the Christian universe as a series of concentric rings spinning around the Earth in geometrical perfection.

1202 The pope calls on all true Christians to rescue the Holy Land from Muslim "infidels" in the Fourth Crusade (1202–1204). This crusade ends disastrously in the sacking of Constantinople, a Christian city.

1206 Chartres' cornerstone is laid. The style is *opus francigenum* ("French-style work")—which is what the people in Gothic times called Gothic. Chartres is just one of several great cathedrals under construction in Europe.

1207 Francis of Assisi, a rebellious Italian youth, undergoes a conversion to a life of Christian poverty and love. His open spirit inspires many followers, including France's King Louis IX (a generation later).

1209 France's King Philip Augustus, based in Paris, invades southern France and massacres fellow Christians (the Cathars or Albigensians) as heretics.

1212 Thousands of boys and girls idealistically join the Children's Crusade to save the Holy Land. Most die in transit or are sold into slavery.

1220 The external structure of Chartres Cathedral is nearly finished. Work begins on the statues and stained glass.

1226 Eleven-year-old Louis IX is crowned as *rex et sacerdos,* "King and Priest," beginning a 45-year Golden Age combining church and state. His mother, Blanche of Castile (granddaughter of Eleanor of Aquitaine), is his lifelong mentor.

1230 Most of Chartres' stained glass is completed.

1244 At age 30, Louis IX falls sick and sees a vision while in a coma that changes his life. His personal integrity helps unify the nation. He reforms the judicial system along Christian lines, helping the poor.

1245 The last Albigensian heretics are burned at Montségur, in a crusade ordered by Louis IX and his mother, Blanche.

1248 Louis IX personally leads the Seventh Crusade by walking barefoot from Paris to the port of departure. During the fighting, he is captured and ransomed. He later returns home a changed man. Humbled, he adopts the poverty of the Franciscan brotherhood. His devotion earns him the title of St. Louis.

1260 Chartres Cathedral is dedicated. The church is the physical embodiment of the Age of Faith, with architecture as mathematically perfect as God's Creation, sculpture serving as sermons in stone, and stained glass lit by the light of God.

Mary's Church and Mary's Veil ("Notre Dame" = "Our Lady" of Chartres)

The church is (at least) the fourth church on this spot dedicated to Mary, the mother of Jesus, who has been venerated here for some 1,700 years. There's even speculation that the pagan Romans dedicated a temple here to a mother-goddess. In earliest times, Mary was honored next to a natural spring of healing waters (not visible today).

In 876, the church acquired the torn, 2,000-year-old veil (or birthing gown) supposedly worn by Mary when she gave birth to Jesus. The veil (now on display—see below) became the focus of worship at the church. By the 11th century, Mary (a.k.a. "Queen of All Saints") was hugely popular. God was obscure and scary, but motherhood was accessible, and Mary provided a handy go-between for Christians and their Creator. Chartres, a small town of 10,000 with a prized relic, found itself big time on the pilgrim circuit.

When the fire of 1194 incinerated the old church, the veil was feared lost. Lo and behold, several days later, they found it miraculously unharmed in the crypt (beneath today's choir). The people were so stoked, they worked like madmen to erect this grand cathedral in which to display it. The small town built a big-city church, one of the most impressive structures in all of Europe. Thinkers and scholars gathered here, making it a leading center of learning in the Middle Ages (until the focus shifted to Paris' university).

The Book of Chartres

Historian Malcolm Miller calls Chartres a picture book of statues, stained glass, and symbolic architecture, telling the entire Christian story—from Creation to Christ's birth (the north side of the church), from Christ and his followers up to the present (south entrance), to the end of time when Christ returns as judge (west entrance).

The Christian universe is a complex web of heaven and earth, angels and demons, and prophets and martyrs. Much of the medieval symbolism is obscure today. Expect to be overwhelmed by the thousands of things to see, but appreciate the perfect unity of this Gothic masterpiece.

You don't go to the library to read all the books, and you don't go to the cathedral to read all the windows. Think of it as the world's biggest comic strip, or the best and most intact library of medieval religious iconography in existence.

THE TOUR BEGINS

❶ The Main Entrance (West Facade), c. 1150

Chartres' soaring (if mismatched) steeples announce to pilgrims that they've arrived. For centuries, pilgrims have come here to see holy relics, to honor "Our Lady," and to feed their souls.

The facade is about the only survivor of the intense, lead-melting fire that incinerated the rest of the church in 1194. The church we see today was rebuilt behind this facade in a single generation (1194–1260).

Towers: The right (south) tower, with a Romanesque stone steeple, survived the fire. The left (north) tower lost its wooden steeple in the 1194 fire. In the 1500s, it was topped by a steeple bigger than the tapered lower half was meant to hold.

The West Doors: The emaciated column-like statues flanking the three doors are pillars of the faith. These kings of Judah, prophets, and Old Testament big shots foretold the coming of Christ. With solemn gestures and faces, they patiently endure the wait.

What they predicted came to pass. History's pivotal event is shown above the **right door,** where Mary (seated) produces baby Jesus from her loins. This Mary-and-baby sculpture is a 12th-century stone

Chartres Cathedral

1. Main Entrance (West Facade)
2. Nave
3. Labyrinth
4. View of 3 Rose Windows
5. Blue Virgin Window
6. Choir Screen Sculptures
7. Mary's Veil
8. Chapel of Our Lady on the Pillar
9. Noah Window & Tower Climb
10. Flying Buttresses
11. South Porch & To Crypt
12. North Porch

NORTH PORCH   SOUTH PORCH

WEST FACADE

BOOK-SHOP   ★ MEET GUIDED TOURS HERE

1. MAIN ENTRANCE

20 YARDS
20 METERS

DCH

version of an even older wooden statue that burned in 1793. Centuries of pilgrims have visited Chartres to see Mary's statue, gaze at her veil,

and ponder the mystery of how God in Heaven became Man on Earth, as He passed through immaculate Mary like sunlight through stained glass.

Over the **central door** is Christ in majesty, surrounded by animals symbolizing Matthew, Mark, Luke, and John. Over the **left door,** Christ ascends into heaven after his death and resurrection.

• *Enter the church (from a side entrance, if the main one is closed) and wait for your pupils to enlarge.*

❷ Nave

The place is huge—the nave is 427 feet long, 20 feet wide, and 120 feet high. Notice the height of the entrance doors compared to the tourists...the doors are 24 feet tall!

The long, tall central nave is lined with 12 pillars. These support pointed, crisscrossed arches on the ceiling, which lace together the heavy stone vaulting. The pillars themselves are supported by flying buttresses on the outside of the church (which we'll see later). This skeleton structure was the miracle of Gothic, making it possible to build tall cathedrals with ribbed walls and lots of stained-glass

CHARTRES CATHEDRAL

windows (see the big saints in the upper stories of the nave). Chartres has 28,000 square feet of stained glass. The narrow nave is flanked by raised side aisles. This design was for crowd flow, so pilgrims could circle the church without disturbing worshippers.

Try to picture the church in the Middle Ages—painted in greens, browns, and golds. It was full of pilgrims, a rough cross between a hostel, a soup kitchen, and a flea market. The floor of the nave slopes in to the center, for easy drainage when hosing down dirty pilgrims who camped here. Looking around the church, you'll see stones at the base of the columns smoothed by centuries of tired pilgrim butts. With all the hubbub in the general nave, the choir (screened-off central zone around the high altar) provided a holy place with a more sacred atmosphere.

· On the floor, midway up the nave, find the...

❸ Labyrinth

The round maze inlaid in black marble on the floor is a spiritual jour-

ney. Mazes like this were common in medieval churches. Pilgrims enter from the west rim by foot or on their knees and wind inward, meditating, on a metaphorical journey to Jerusalem. About 900 feet later, they hope to meet God in the middle. (The chairs are removed on Fridays. To let your fingers do the walking, you'll find a small model of the maze just outside the gift shop, where the tours begin.)

· Walk up the nave to where the transept crosses. As you face the altar, north is to the left.

❹ The Rose Windows— North, South, and West

The three big, round "rose" (flower-shaped) windows over the entrances receive sunlight at different times of day. All three are predominantly blue and red, but each has different "petals," and each tells a different part of the Christian story in a kaleidoscope of fragmented images.

As we've all read, stained glass was a way to teach Bible stories to the illiterate medieval masses...who apparently owned state-of-the-art binoculars. The windows were used many ways: They tell stories, allow parents to teach children simple lessons, help theologians explain complex lessons, enable worshippers to focus on images as they meditate or pray...and, of course, they light a dark church in a colorful and decorative way.

Surviving the Centuries

Chartres contains the world's largest collection of medieval stained glass, with over 150 early 13th-century windows, about 80 percent still the original glass. Through the centuries, much of the rest of France's stained glass was destroyed by various ideologues: Protestant puritans who disapproved of papist imagery, Revolutionaries who turned churches into "temples of reason" (or stables), Baroque artists who preferred clear windows and lots of light, and the bombs of World War II.

Chartres was spared many (but not all) of these ravages. In World War II, the citizens removed all the windows and piled sandbags to protect the statues. Today, Chartres survives as Europe's best-preserved medieval cathedral.

The brilliantly restored **north rose window** charts history from the distant past up to the birth of Jesus. On the outer rim, murky, ancient (barely visible) prophets foretell Christ's coming. Then (circling inward), there's a ring of red squares with kings who are Jesus' direct ancestors. Still closer, a circle of white doves and winged angels zero in on the central event of history—Mary, the heart of the flower, with her newborn baby, Jesus.

This window was donated by King Louis IX, who built Paris' stained-glass masterpiece of a church, Sainte-Chapelle (see page 91). See his coat of arms (yellow fleur-de-lis on a blue background) just below the rose, alongside his mom's coat of arms, Blanche of Castile (gold castles on a red background).

The **south rose window** (possibly under renovation in 2009) tells how the Old Testament prophecies were fulfilled. Christ sits in the center (dressed in blue, with a red background), setting in motion radiating rings of angels, beasts, and instrument-playing apocalyptic elders who labor to bring history to its close. The five lancet windows below show Mary flanked by four Old Testament prophets (Isaiah, Daniel, Jeremiah, and Ezekiel) lifting New Testament writers (Matthew, Mark, Luke, and John) on their shoulders. (In the first window on the left, see white-robed Luke riding piggyback on dark-robed Jeremiah.) These demonstrated how the ancients prepared the way for Christ—and how the New Testament evangelists had a broader perspective from their lofty perches.

In the center of the **west rose window,** a dark Christ rings in history's final Day of Judgment. Around him, winged angels blow their trumpets and the dead rise, face judgment, and are sent to hell or raised to eternal bliss. The frilly edge of this glorious "rose" is flecked with tiny clover-shaped dewdrops.

• *Now walk around the altar to the right (south) side and find the window with a big, blue Mary (second one from the right).*

GOD = LIGHT

You can try to examine the details, but a better way to experience the mystery of Chartres is to just sit and stare at these enormous panels as they float in the dark of empty space like holograms or space stations or the Queen of Heaven's crown jewels. Ponder the medieval concept that God is light.

To the Chartres generation, the church was a metaphor for how God brings his creation to life, like the way light animates stained glass. They were heavy into mysticism, feeling a oneness with all creation in a moment of enlightenment. The Gospel of John (as well as a writer known to historians as the Pseudo-Dionysus) was their favorite. Here are select verses from John 1:1–12 (loosely translated):

In the beginning was The Word.
Jesus was the light of the human race.
The light shines in the darkness, and the darkness cannot resist it.
It was the real light coming into the world, the light that enlightens everyone.
He was in the world, but the world did not recognize Him. But to those who did,
He gave the power to become the children of God.

❺ The Blue Virgin Window

Mary, dressed in blue on a rich red background, cradles Jesus, while the dove of the Holy Spirit descends on her. This very old window

(from 1150) was the central window behind the altar of the church that burned in 1194. It survived and was reinserted into this frame in the new church around 1230. Mary's glowing dress is an example of the famed "Chartres blue," a sumptuous color made by mixing cobalt oxide into the glass (before cheaper materials were introduced). The Blue Virgin was one of the most popular stops for pilgrims—especially pregnant ones—of the cult of the Virgin-about-to-give-birth.

Devotees prayed, carried stones to repair the church, and donated to the church coffers; Mary rewarded them with peace of mind, easy births, and occasional miracles.

Below Mary (bottom panel), see **Christ being tempted** by a red-faced, horned, smirking devil.

The **Zodiac Window** (two windows to the left) shows the 12 signs of the zodiac (in the right half of the window; read from the bottom up—Pisces, Aries, Gemini in the central cloverleaf, Taurus, Cockroach, Leo, Virgo, etc.). On the left side are the corresponding months (February warming himself by a fire, April gathering flowers, and so on).

• *Now turn around and look behind you.*

❻ The Choir Screen—Life of Mary

The choir (enclosed area around the altar where church officials sat) is the heart *(coeur)* of the church. A stone screen rings it with **41 statue groups** illustrating Mary's life. Although the Bible says little about the mother of Jesus, legend and lore fleshed out her life. Take some time to learn about the Lady this church is dedicated to.

Scene #1 (south side) shows Mary's dad hearing the news that Mary is on the way. In #4, Mary is born, and maidens bathe the new baby. In #6, Mary marries Joseph (sculpted with the features of King François I). In scene #7, an angel announces to Mary she'll be the mother of the Messiah, and (#10) she gives birth to Jesus in a manger. In #12, the Three

Kings—looking like the three musketeers—arrive. In #14, Herod orders all babies slaughtered, but Mary's son survives to begin his mission.

Next come episodes from the life of Jesus. On the other side of the choir screen, in #27, Jesus is crucified, and in #28, lays lifeless in his mother's arms. Scene #34 depicts the Ascension, as Jesus takes off, Cape Canaveral–style, while his awestruck followers look up at the bottoms of his rocketing feet. In #39, Mary has died and is raised by angels into heaven, where (#40) she's crowned Queen of Heaven by the Father, Son, and Holy Ghost.

The **plain windows** surrounding the choir date from the 1770s, when the dark mystery of medieval stained glass was replaced by the open light of the French Enlightenment. The plain windows and the choir are some of the only "new" features. Most of the 13th-century church has remained intact, despite style changes, Revolutionary vandals, and war bombs.

• *Continue around the ambulatory to the very back of the church. In the next chapel you encounter (Chapel of the Sacred Heart of Mary—see map), you'll find a gold frame holding a fragment of Mary's venerated veil. These days it's kept—for its safety and preservation—out of the light and behind bulletproof glass.*

❼ Mary's Veil

This **veil** (or tunic) was supposedly worn by Mary when she gave birth to Jesus. It became the main object of adoration for the cult of the Virgin.

The great King of the Franks, Charlemagne (742/47–814), received the veil as a present from Byzantine Empress Irene. Charlemagne's grandson gave the veil to Chartres in 876. In A.D. 911, with the city surrounded by Vikings, the bishop hoisted the veil like a battle flag and waved it at the invaders. It scared the bejeezus out of them, and the town was saved.

In the frenzy surrounding the fire of 1194, the veil mysteriously disappeared, only to reappear three days later (recalling the Resurrection). This was interpreted by church officials and the townsfolk as a sign from Mary that she wanted a new church, and thus the building began. Recent tests confirm that the material itself and the weaving technique used to make the cloth date to the first century A.D., lending support to claims of the relic's authenticity.

• Continue on a few more chapels until you find the one with Mary on a pillar.

❽ Chapel of Our Lady on the Pillar

A 16th-century **statue of Mary and baby**—draped in cloth, crowned and sceptered—sits on a 13th-century column in a wonderful carved-wood alcove. This is today's pilgrimage center, built to keep visitors from clogging up the altar area. Modern pilgrims (including lots of new moms pushing strollers) honor the Virgin by leaving flowers, lighting candles, and kissing the column.

• Return to the west end and find the last window on the right (near the tower entrance).

❾ The Noah Window and Tower Climb

Read Chartres' windows in the medieval style: from bottom to top. In the bottom diamond, God tells Noah he'll destroy the earth. Next, Noah hefts an axe to build an ark, while his son hauls wood (diamond #2). Two by two, he loads horses (cloverleaf, above left), purple elephants (cloverleaf, right), and other animals. The psychedelic ark sets sail (diamond #3). Waves cover the earth and drown the wicked (two cloverleaves). The ark survives (diamond #4), and Noah releases a dove. Finally, up near the top (diamond #7), a rainbow (symbolizing God's promise never to bring another flood) arches overhead, God drapes himself over it, and Noah and his family give thanks.

Chartres was a trading center, and its merchant brotherhoods donated money to make 42 of the windows. For 800 years, these panes have publicly thanked their sponsors. In the bottom left is a man making a wheel. More workers are to the right. The panels announce that, "These windows are brought to you by..." the wheel, axe, and barrel-making guilds.

• *If you'd like to climb the north tower, the entrance is nearby. Then exit the church (through the main entrance or the door in the south transept) to view its south side.*

❿ South Exterior—Flying Buttresses

On the south side, six flying buttresses (the arches that stick out from the upper walls) push against six pillars lining the nave inside,

helping to hold up the heavy stone ceiling and sloped, lead-over-wood roof. The ceiling and roof push down onto the pillars, of course, but also outward (north and south) because of the miracle of Gothic: the pointed arch. The flying buttresses push back, channeling the stress outward to the six vertical buttresses, then down to the ground. The result is a tall cathedral held up by slender pillars buttressed from the outside, allowing the walls to be opened up for stained glass.

The church is built from large blocks of limestone. Peasants trod in hamster-wheel contraptions to raise these blocks into place—a testament to their great faith.

⓫ South Porch

The south porch may be covered by scaffolding when you visit (it's being cleaned, a process that could take several years). The three doorways of the south entrance show the world from Christ to the present, as Christianity triumphs over persecution.

Center Door—Christ and Apostles: Standing between the double doors, **Jesus** holds a book and raises his arm in blessing. He's a simple, itinerant, bareheaded, barefoot rabbi, but underneath his feet he tramples symbols of evil, the dragon and lion. Christ's face is among the most noble of all Gothic sculpture.

Christ is surrounded by his **apostles,** who spread the good news to a hostile world. **Peter** (to the left as you face Jesus), with curly hair and beard, holds the keys to the kingdom of heaven and the slender upside-down cross on which he was crucified. **Paul** (to the right of Jesus) fingers the sword of his martyrdom and contemplates the inevitable loss of his head and the hair upon it. In fact, all of these apostles were killed or persecuted, and their faces are humble, with sad eyes. But their message prevailed, and under their feet, they crush the squirming rulers who once persecuted them.

The final triumph comes above the door in the **Last Judgment.** Christ sits in judgment, raising his hands, while Mary and John beg him to take it easy on poor humankind. Beneath Christ, the souls are judged—the righteous on our left, and the wicked on the right, who are thrown into the fiery jaws of hell. Farther to the right (above the statues of Paul and the apostles), horny demons subject wicked women to an eternity of sexual harassment.

Left Door—Martyrs: Eight martyrs flank the left door. **St. Lawrence** (second from left) cradles the grill (it looks like a book) on which he was barbecued alive. His last brave words to the Romans actually were: "You can turn me over—I'm done on this side." **St. George** (far right) wears the knightly uniform of the 1200s, when Chartres was built and King Louis IX was crusading. Depicted beneath the martyrs are gruesome **methods of torture,** such as George stretched on the wheel. Many of these techniques were actually used in the 1200s against heretics, Muslims, Jews, and Albigensians, the Cathar sect of southern France.

• *Reach the north side by circling around the back end of the church (great views) or by cutting through the church.*

⑫North Porch

In "the Book of Chartres," the north porch is chapter one, from the Creation up to the coming of Christ.

Look between the double doors to see **Baby Mary** (headless), in the arms of her mother Anne, marking the end of the Old Testament world and the start of the New.

History begins in the tiny details in the

concentric arches over the doorway. **God creates Adam** (at the peak of the outermost arch) by cradling his head in his lap like a child.

Next look at the statues that flank the doors. **Melchizedek** (far-thest to the left of Mary and Anne), with the cap of a king and the cup of communion, is the Biblical model of the *rex et sacerdos* (king-priest), the title bestowed on King Louis IX.

Abraham (second from left) holds his son by the throat and raises a knife to slit him for sacrifice. Just then, he hears something and turns his head up to see God's angel, who stops the bloodshed. The drama of this frozen moment anticipates Renaissance natu-ralism by 200 years.

John the Baptist (fourth to the right from Mary/Anne), the last Old Testament prophet who prepared the way for Jesus, holds a lamb, the symbol of Christ. John is skinny from his diet of locusts and honey. His body and beard twist and flicker like a flame.

All these prophets, with their beards turning down the corners of their mouths, have the sad, wise look of having been around since the beginning of time and having seen it all—from Creation to Christ to Apocalypse. Over the door is the culmination of all this history: **Christ on his throne,** joined by Mary, the Queen of Heaven. They are some of the last work done on the church, completing the church's stone-and-glass sermon.

Imagine all this painted and covered with gold leaf in preparation for the dedication ceremonies in 1260, when the Chartres genera-tion could finally stand back and watch as their great-grandchildren, carrying candles, entered the cathedral.

CHARTRES TOWN

Chartres is worth a quick stroll. You can rent an audioguide or just wander, following the route marked on the free tourist map (audioguide and map at TI—see "Information," on page 483). The walk takes you on a one-hour loop from the cathedral down along the river and back.

In medieval times, Chartres was actually two towns—the pil-grims' town around the cathedral, and the industrial town along the river, which powered the mills.

You'll start by walking to the right of the cathedral, down rue des Changes. Notice the streets with evocative names, including rue des Changes (pilgrims needed to change money), rue au Lait (milk), and rue aux Herbes (folks smoked hemp). A half-block to the

CHARTRES CATHEDRAL

Chartres

- ❶ Hôtel Châtelet
- ❷ Hôtel Jehan de Beauce
- ❸ Hôtel le Boeuf Couronné
- ❹ Le Pichet Restaurant
- ❺ Le Café des Arts
- ❻ Les Picholines Restaurant
- ❼ Le Bistrot de la Cathédrale
- ❽ Trois Lys Crêperie
- ❾ Access to Crypt (Through "La Crypte" Bookstore)
- ❿ To Internet Café & Launderette
- ⓫ Launderettes (2)

left is place de la Poissonnerie (fish market), today marked by a fine half-timbered building.

Continuing along rue des Changes, you'll pass today's open-air produce market on place Billard. Several blocks later, you'll run into a classic, old, half-timbered house. As the population grew, so did the fire hazard, and the town required half-timbered buildings to be plastered over for safety. Today, the town government—interested in pumping up the touristic charm—pays folks to peel away the plaster and re-expose those timbers. You can see that this building is one of the oldest—note the tilting lintel and the asymmetrical windows.

Turn left at the house and go down the *tertre,* a series of stair-step terraces that link the upper and lower towns. At the bottom, turn right, heading past the Church of St. Pierre (great photo-op of flying buttresses). A block past the church, turn left, and you're at the river.

The Eure River is another photogenic spot, with old buildings, humpback bridges, and the cathedral steeples in the distance. The river was once lined with busy mills and warehouses. This was the industrial town. The worst polluters were kept downstream (dyeing, tanning, slaughterhouses). Notice the names of the riverside lanes: rue du Massacre, rue de la Tannerie.

When the industry moved out to make room for Chartres' growing population, laundry places replaced the old mills. These were two-story structures—the wash cycle downstairs at the river, then the dry cycle upstairs, where vents allowed the wind to blow through. The last riverside laundry closed in the 1960s.

As you double back to the cathedral along the river, stop at Queen Bertha's Staircase (Escalier de la Reine Berthe), a spiral staircase hugging a half-timbered house on rue des Ecuyers.

Back at the cathedral, consider a stop at the nearby International Stained Glass Center to learn the techniques behind the mystery of this fragile but enduring art (Centre International du Vitrail, €4, Mon–Fri 9:30–12:30 & 13:30–18:00, Sat 10:00–12:30 & 14:30–18:00, Sun 14:30–18:00, just 50 yards from cathedral, tel. 02 37 21 65 72, www.centre-vitrail.org).

Near Chartres: La Maison Picassiette

If you have time to burn and enjoy oddities, walk about 20 minutes (or take the bus) to the home created by local artist Raymond Isidore. La Maison Picassiette is covered wall-to-wall (inside and out) with broken-pottery mosaics (€4.50, April–Nov Wed–Sat and Mon 10:00–11:45 & 14:00–17:45, Sun 14:00–18:00, closed Tue and Dec–March, tel. 02 37 34 10 78).

Getting There: Leave the old town downhill (behind the cathedral, direction: Porte Guillaume). Walk straight on rue Faubourg Guillaume, which becomes rue Ste. Chernon. Take a right on rue du Repos. It's at #22. You can also take bus #4 (direction: La Madeleine, €1, buy ticket from driver, no bus on Sun or holidays).

SLEEPING

Chartres, a good getaway from Paris, can also be a first or last overnight stop for those flying to or from Orly Airport.

Chartres has three **launderettes.** One is in the lower town (across from recommended Trois Lys Crêperie, near pont Boujou, 15-min walk from cathedral). Another is in the upper town by the market (daily 7:00–21:00, 16a place de la Poissonerie). The third is at 32 rue St. Michel (daily 7:00–20:00), just down the street from **Internet access** at Tout va Bien (Mon–Sat 8:00–21:00, closed Sun, 2 rue de la Mairie, 5-min walk from cathedral down rue des Changes).

Sleep Code

(€1 = about $1.50, country code: 33)
S = Single, **D** = Double/Twin, **T** = Triple, **Q** = Quad, **b** = bathroom,
s = shower only. Everyone speaks English and accepts credit cards.

In Chartres

The first two hotels face each other (200 yards straight out of train station, 300 yards below cathedral).

$$ Hôtel Châtelet*,** run by friendly Chantal, Marilou, Franck, and Nathalie, is comfortable, from its welcoming lobby to its spotless, spacious, well-furnished rooms. Choose between plush, modern, recently renovated "privilege" rooms with air-conditioning, or the cheaper "standing" rooms with Old World charm (Sb-€88–118, Db-€102–130, extra bed-€22, parking-€7.50, 6 avenue Jehan de Beauce, tel. 02 37 21 78 00, fax 02 37 36 23 01, www.hotelchatelet.com, reservation@hotelchatelet.com).

$ Hôtel Jehan de Beauce** is basic, clean (despite the shabby hallways), and quiet. Some of its rooms have tiny bathrooms (S-€38, Ss-€52–58, Sb-€60, D-€49, Ds-€57–63, Db-€68, Tb-€72, 19 avenue Jehan de Beauce, tel. 02 37 21 01 41, fax 02 37 21 59 10, jehandebeauce @club-internet.fr).

$ Hôtel le Boeuf Couronné** is warmly run by Madame Vinsot, with 21 clean but slightly worn rooms and a handy location (S-€32, Sb-€50, D-€37, Db-€60–70, elevator, 15 place Châtelet, tel. 02 37 18 06 06, fax 02 37 21 72 13).

Near Chartres

$ Chambres d'Hôte Brossollet, practical only for drivers, is a pleasant haven of tranquility in Saint-Prest, about four miles from Chartres. This spacious property has an enclosed garden, thatched roofs, two rooms to rent, and kind hosts, Claire and Etienne Brossollet (Db-€55, includes breakfast, tel. 02 37 22 25 31, claire.etienne.brossollet@gmail .com). Leave Chartres to the north and follow signs to Saint-Prest. Once in the village, continue just over a mile straight through on the main road until you see the thatched roof on your left-hand side.

EATING

Le Pichet, run by friendly Marie-Sylvie and Xavier, is reasonable and homey, with good daily specials (€12–18 *plats*, €12–15 daily *menu*, closed Tue and Sun evenings and all day Wed, 19 rue du Cheval Blanc, near TI, tel. 02 37 21 08 35).

Le Café des Arts is a sleek, modern place just a block from the cathedral. It's perfect for a quick, reasonably priced three-egg omelet or salad. Yvon, the owner, prides himself on the delicious €6–14 *tartines*—warm, open-faced sandwiches served with a small salad (€16–18.50 *menus*, 45–47 rue des Changes, tel. 02 37 21 07 05).

Les Picholines is a favorite for Mediterranean-inspired cuisine. Come here to get your fix of tapas and olives, or to feast on €11–14 pastas and salads (€14–19 lunch *menu*, €23–28 dinner *menu*, open daily, rue du Cheval Blanc, tel. 02 37 36 85 84).

Le Bistrot de la Cathédrale is fine for salads and traditional bistro fare, but you'll pay for the view (*menus* from €20, open daily, south side of cathedral at 1 cloître Notre-Dame, tel. 02 37 36 59 60).

Trois Lys Crêperie makes good, cheap crêpes just across the river on pont Boujou (closed Sun–Mon, 3 rue de la Porte Guillaume, across from one of the recommended launderettes, tel. 02 37 28 42 02).

CHARTRES CATHEDRAL

REIMS
DAY TRIP

With its Roman gate, Gothic cathedral, Champagne caves, and vibrant pedestrian zone, Reims (pronounced "rance," which rhymes with France) feels both historic and youthful. And thanks to the TGV bullet train, it's just a 45-minute ride from Paris.

Reims has a turbulent history: This is where 26 French kings were crowned, where Champagne first bubbled, where WWI devastation (all but 70 buildings were damaged in 1918) met miraculous reconstruction during the Art Deco age, and where the Germans officially surrendered in 1945, bringing World War II to a close in Europe. The town's sights give you an entertaining peek at the entire story.

Planning Your Time

You can see Reims' essential sights in less than a day (either as a day trip from Paris or a stop en route to or from Paris). Twelve daily TGV trains make the trip from Paris a breeze. Take a morning train from Paris and explore the cathedral and city center before lunch, then spend your afternoon below ground, in a cool, chalky Champagne cellar. You can be back at your Parisian hotel in time for a rest before dinner.

To best experience contemporary Reims, explore the busy shopping streets between the cathedral and the train station. Rue de Vesle, rue Condorcet, and place Drouet d'Erlon are most interesting.

ORIENTATION

Reims' hard-to-miss cathedral marks the city center and makes an easy orientation landmark. Most sights of interest are within a 15-minute walk from the Reims-Centre train station. Easy-to-use loop bus routes connect the harder-to-reach Champagne *caves* with the train station and cathedral. The city is ambitiously renovating its downtown, and is converting the square and streets around the cathedral into pedestrian zones.

Tourist Information

At the TI outside the cathedral's left transept, pick up a free map of the town center and a map of the Champagne *caves* (TI open Easter–mid-Oct Mon–Sat 9:00–19:00, Sun 10:00–18:00; mid-Oct–Easter Mon–Sat 9:00–17:00, Sun 11:00–16:00; public WCs across street, tel. 03 26 77 45 00, www.reims-tourisme.com). The TI can book a visit to any *cave* that accepts visitors, and can call a taxi to get you there. Better yet, go by *cyclopolitain* (tricycle taxi) or bus (for more on both, see "Getting Around Reims," next page). The TI also rents pricey audioguide tours covering the cathedral, city center, and Art Deco architecture (single-€5, each additional set-€4).

Arrival in Reims

By Train: From Paris, you'll arrive at the easy-to-navigate Reims-Centre station (no baggage check). You can reach the cathedral by foot in 15 minutes: Walk straight out of the station (passing Avis), cross the tree-lined boulevards Joffre and Foch, and stroll up the pedestrian place Drouet d'Erlon. Turn left on rue Condorcet, then right on rue de Talleyrand. The time-saving Citadine bus runs from the station (see "Getting Around Reims," next page) to the cathedral and to the Taittinger and Martel *caves* (described in "Champagne Tours," page 507).

By Car: Follow *Centre-Ville* and *Cathédrale* signs and park on the street approaching the cathedral (rue Libergier) or in the well-signed Parking Cathédrale structure (€1.40/hour).

Helpful Hints

Internet Access: You can surf and snack at **Clique et Croque** (€4/hr, Mon–Sat 10:00–24:00, Sun 14:00–20:00, near the cathedral at 19 rue Chanzy, tel. 03 26 86 93 92).

Laundry: **Laverie Chanzy** is a few blocks in front of the cathedral (daily 7:00–21:30, 59 rue Chanzy).

Taxi: Call 03 26 47 05 05. A taxi from the train station to the farthest Champagne *cave* will cost about €8.

Car Rental: Avis is at the train station (cours de la Gare, tel. 08 20 05 05 05); **Europcar** is at 76 boulevard Lundy (tel. 08 25 04 52 82); and **Hertz** is at 26 boulevard Joffre (tel. 03 26 47 98 78; all three usually open Mon–Sat 8:00–12:00 & 14:00–19:00, closed Sun).

Local Guide: British expat Jon Catt can show you around the city, its champagne *caves,* and the battlefields near Reims. Jon does not drive so you must have your own transport if you go beyond Reims (€120/half-day, €200/day, plus expenses, tel. & fax 03 25 73 74 52, mobile 06 17 44 49 67, http://tourguidechampagne.blog spot.com, Jon.Catt@wanadoo.fr).

Getting Around Reims

By Citadine Bus: While most sights are close, two Champagne *caves* (Taittinger and Martel) are a 30-minute walk from the station. Two Citadine bus lines link the historic center with these far-flung cellars, with circular routes starting and ending at the Reims-Centre train station (every 12 min, none on Sun, €1, pay driver). Line #1 does the route clockwise; line #2 does it counterclockwise. To catch the bus, cross the parking lot in front of the train station and look for the yellow Citadine bus stop before crossing the boulevard. From in front of the station, Citadine #1 runs to the cathedral and TI (stop: Cathédrale) in five minutes, and to Taittinger and Martel (stop: St. Niçaise) in 10 minutes. To return, board the same bus and continue the loop back to the station. Bus line #K also runs from the station (catch it just across the street from Hertz car rental, direction Béthany), getting you close to the Mumm Champagne *cave* (stop: Justice).

By *Cyclopolitain* Tricycle: These modern lightweight electric tricycles carry one or two passengers and function like taxis, but for shorter trips. The young drivers (called Cyclonautes) speak English and are happy to take you anywhere within the city limits (€2 per person per kilometer, €20 for 30-min tour; flag one down, have the TI call for you, or call direct at 06 27 95 54 72). If you take a tour, it'd be nice to tip €2–3; otherwise there's no need to tip for simple transport from point to point.

SIGHTS

▲▲▲Reims Cathedral

The cathedral of Reims, begun in 1211, is a glorious example of Gothic architecture, and one of Europe's greatest churches (free, daily 7:30–19:30). Clovis, the first king of the Franks, was baptized at a church on this site in A.D. 496, establishing France's Christian roots that hold firm today. Since Clovis' baptism, Reims' cathedral has served as *the* place for the coronation of 25 French kings and queens—allowing it to play

a more important role in France's political history than Paris' Notre-Dame cathedral. A self-assured Joan of Arc led a less-assured Charles VII to be crowned here in 1429. The French rallied around their new king to push the English out of France and to finally end the Hundred Years' War. During the French Revolution, the cathedral was converted to a temple of reason (as was Notre-Dame in Paris). After the restoration of the monarchy, the cathedral hosted the crowning of Charles X in 1825—the last coronation in France. During World War I, it was devastated by severe bombing. Then it was

REIMS

Reims

B Citadine Bus Stops
P Parking
Pedestrian Zone

PLACE ARISTIDE BRIANDE

CATHEDRAL
PALAIS DU TAU
& CARNEGIE LIBRARY

TAITTINGER

MARTEL

ST. REMI BASILICA

CATHEDRALE EXIT

400 YARDS
400 METERS

ST. REMI EXIT

PL. DROITS L'HOMME

PCH

REIMS

1. Grand Hôtel Continental &
   Micro Brasserie les 3 Brasseurs
2. Latino Hôtel
3. Bénédicte et Claude
   Philippon B&B
4. Grand Hôtel du Nord &
   L'Apostrophe Rest.
5. Brasserie du Boulingrin
6. Au Plat du Jour
7. Café du Palais
8. Europcar Car Rental
9. Hertz Car Rental
10. Museum of the Surrender
11. Parking Cathédrale
12. Launderette & Internet Café

completely rebuilt, thanks in large part to John D. Rockefeller...just in time for the start of World War II.

Stand on the square in front of the cathedral and admire perhaps the best west portal anywhere, with more than 2,000 statues festooning its walls inside and out. (Since medieval churches face east, toward the Holy Land, you enter through the west portal.) Like the cathedrals in Paris and in Chartres, this church is dedicated to "Our Lady" (Notre-Dame). Statues depicting the crowning of the virgin take center-stage on the facade. For eight centuries, Catholics have prayed to the "Mother of God," kneeling here to ask her to intervene with God on their behalf. In 1429, Joan of Arc received messages from Mary encouraging her to rally French troops against the English at the Siege of Orléans.

Notice the flying buttresses soaring from the sides of the church. These massive "beams" are critical to supporting this structure. The pointed arches inside the church push the weight of the roof outward, rather than downward. The "flying" buttresses support the roof by pushing back inward, creating a delicate balance between the two forces. Gothic architects learned by trial and error—many church roofs caved in as they tested their theories and strove to build ever higher. Work on this cathedral began decades after the Notre-Dame cathedrals in Paris and Chartres, allowing architects to take advantage of what they'd learned from those magnificent earlier structures.

Contemplate the lives of the people who built this huge building, starting in 1211. Construction on a scale like this required a wholesale community effort—all hands on deck. Most townsfolk who participated donated their money or their labor knowing that neither they, nor their children, nor their children's children, would ever see it completed—such was their pride, dedication, and faith. Imagine the effort it took to raise the funds and manage the workforce. Master masons supervised, while the average Jean did much of the sweat work. Labor was something even the poorest medieval peasant could donate generously.

Walk inside. The weight of the roof is supported by a few towering columns that seem to sprout crisscrossing pointed arches. This technique allowed the church to grow higher, and liberated the walls to become window frames. Now, look back at the entry wall with 120 statues filling the niches. The rose window (high above on this wall) contains the best original stained glass in the church (from 1255, removed during World War I to be spared destruction). Most of the windows are clear and newer: 18th- and 19th-century tastes called for more light, and the original, dark stained glass was replaced.

The south transept windows, destroyed in World War I, were replaced in 1954 by the local Champagne-makers. The windows show the connection of the Champagne industry to this town and its church with scenes portraying the tending of vines (left), the harvest (center), and the time-honored double-fermentation process (right). Notice, around the edges, the churches representing all the grape-producing villages in the area.

The apse (east end, behind the altar) holds a luminous set of Marc Chagall stained-glass windows from 1974. Chagall's inimitable style

lends itself to stained glass and he enjoyed opportunities to adorn great churches with his windows. The left window shows scenes from the Old Testament, and the center features the resurrection of Christ. On the right the tree of Jesse is extended to symbolically include the royalty of France—both affirming the divine power of the monarchs and stressing the responsibility to rule with wisdom and justice. Helpful English explanations offer historical detail.

Palais du Tau—This former Archbishop's Palace houses artifacts from the cathedral (with scant English information). You'll look into the weathered eyes of original statues from the cathedral's facade (taken in from the acidic open air for their own preservation). A set of precious tapestries, telling stories from the life of Mary, are the originals that warmed the walls of the cathedral's choir in the 16th century. As mentioned earlier, Reims hosted the last French coronation—that of Charles X in 1825. Since the coronation jewels, vestments, and other garb were lost a generation earlier in the French Revolution, what you see here was mostly made especially for this event (€6.50; May–Aug Tue–Sun 9:30–18:30, closed Mon; Sept–April Tue–Sun 9:30–12:30 & 14:00–17:30, closed Mon; tel. 03 26 47 81 79).

More Sights

▲Museum of the Surrender (Musée de la Reddition)—World War II buffs enjoy visiting the historic room where the Germans signed

the document of surrender of all German forces in the early morning of May 7, 1945. The news was announced the next day, turning May 8 into Victory in Europe (V-E) Day. Anyone interested in World War II will find the extensive collection of arti-

facts fascinating (particularly the ticker tape with the happy news, old photos, and a 10-minute video shown on request). The room of the signing still has the maps with troop positions on the walls and the 13 chairs with name tags, each in their original spots (€3, Wed–Mon 10:00–12:00 & 14:00–18:00, closed Tue, 12 rue Franklin Roosevelt, tel. 03 26 47 84 19).

REIMS

Porte de Mars—The last vestige of Reims' ancient Roman heritage—an entry gate—is a short walk from the Reims-Centrale train station. The Porte de Mars, built in the second century A.D., was one of four principal entrances into the ancient Gallo-Roman town and the only one still standing. Inspired by triumphal arches that Rome built to herald war victories, this one was constructed to celebrate the Pax Romana (a period of peace and stability—after all of Rome's foes were vanquished). Unlike most of the rest of town, the Porte was undamaged in World War I but bears the marks of other eras, such as its integration into the medieval ramparts. Find the ruts under the arcade which guided chariots, and look for the depiction of the legend of Romulus and Remus (extremely faint on ceiling under left arch), complete with suckling she-wolf, from which Reims gets its name (free, always open, place du Boulingrin).

▲Carnegie Library (Bibliotheque Carnegie)—The legacy of the Carnegie Library network, funded generously by the 19th-century American millionaire Andrew Carnegie and his steel fortune (notice the American flag above the main entrance on the left), extends even

to Reims. Built in the flurry of inter-war reconstruction, this beautiful Art Deco building still houses the city's public library. Since entrance is free and it's just behind the cathedral, it's worth a quick look. Visitors are welcome to admire the mosaics, onyx-laden entrance hall, and Jacque Simon chandelier, but are
asked not to enter the reading room (some come here to study). Peek through the reading room door to admire the stained-glass windows of this temple of thinking. The gorgeous wood-paneled card-catalogue room takes older visitors back to their childhoods (notice how each card is tediously typed), or even back to 1928, the year the library was inaugurated (free, Tue–Sat 10:00–13:00 & 14:00–19:00, closed Thu morning and Sun–Mon, place Carnegie).

Art Deco on Place Drouet d'Erlon—Place Drouet d'Erlon is a long street-like square marking the commercial center of town. (From the train station, it's directly across the park-like boulevards.) The square's centerpiece, a fountain with a winged figure of victory at the top, celebrates the major rivers of this district. It hasn't worked as a fountain since WWI bombings—a reminder of the devastation brought on this city. All around you'll see the stylized features—geometric reliefs, motifs in iron work, rounded corners, and simple concrete elegance—of Art Deco. The only hints that this was once a Middle Ages town are the narrow lots that struggle to fit today's buildings. Pop into the Waida Patisserie (3 place Drouet d'Erlon) for a pure,

REIMS

typical Art Deco interior. As you stroll about, keep an eye open for "Biscuits Roses"—light, rose-colored egg-and-sugar cookies that date from 1756. They're the locals' favorite munchie to accompany a glass of Champagne (most places that sell the treat offer free samples).

Champagne Tours and Sights

In Reims

▲▲**Champagne Tours**—Reims is the capital of the Champagne region. While the bubbly stuff's birthplace is closer to Epernay, you can tour several interesting Champagne *caves* right in Reims. All charge for tastings and are open daily. Most have daily English tours (often booked for groups) and sometimes allow individuals to join these tours. Call in advance for the schedule and to secure a spot on a tour (Martel offers the most personal and best-value tour). Bring a sweater, even in summer, as the *caves* are cool and clammy.

Mumm (pron. moome) is closest to the train station (15-minute walk) and welcomes the public. Its "traditional visit" (€8, 1 hour) includes a good 10-minute video, a small museum of old Champagne-making contraptions, and a tour of its industrial-size, modern-feeling chalk cellars where 25 million bottles are stored. The video explains the place's history back to 1827 and the Champagne-making process with the enthusiasm of an advertisement ("Cordon Rouge is dedicated to the audacity and passion of exceptional men and women, with a subtle balance between freshness and intensity"). The tour ends with a glass of bubbly Cordon Rouge. You can pay more for the same tour with extra "guided" tastings—€14 for two tastes, or €20 for three (tours depart March–Oct daily 9:00–11:00 & 14:00–17:00, Nov–Feb weekend afternoons and weekdays by reservation, tel. 03 26 49 59 69, www.mumm.com, guides@mumm.com). Mumm is four blocks left out of the train station, on the other side of place de la République at 34 rue du Champ de Mars (also accessible by bus line #K from the train station). Visits begin in the building on the right, #34, at the end of the courtyard. Follow *Visites des Caves* signs.

Taittinger (tay-tan-zhay) is one of the biggest, priciest, and most renowned of Reims' *caves*. They run three morning and three afternoon tours in English through their impressive cellars (call for times and to reserve a spot, about 20–30 people per tour). After seeing their 10-minute promo-movie (hooray for Taittinger!), follow your guide—mine reminded me of an old-time airline hostess—for 45 chilly minutes and 80 steps down to a chalky underworld of *caves*, the deepest of which were dug by ancient Romans. You'll tour part of the three miles of *caves*, pass some of the three million bottles stored here, and learn all you need to know about the Champagne process from your well-informed guide. Popping corks signal when the tour's done and the tasting's begun (€10, includes tasting, 1 hour, tours daily mid-March–mid-Nov 9:30–12:00 & 14:00–16:30, closed weekends off-season, 9 place St. Nicaise, tel. 03 26 85 84 33, www.taittinger.com).

Martel gives a homey contrast to Taittinger's big-business style. It's a small operation with less extensive *caves* and is *sans* doubt the best deal in town. Call to set up a visit and expect a small group that might be yours alone. Friendly Emmanuel runs the place with a relaxed manner. Only 20 percent of their product is exported (mostly to Europe), so you won't find much of their Champagne in the US. Their €8, 45-minute visit focuses on the basics and includes an informative 10-minute film and a tour of their small cellars peppered with rusted, old wine-making tools. It culminates with a tasting of three different Champagnes in a casual living-room atmosphere (daily 10:00–19:00, open through lunch, 17 rue des Créneaux, tel. 03 26 82 70 67, www.champagnemartel.com).

Getting to Taittinger and Martel: These two places are a few blocks apart, about 30 minutes by foot southeast of the cathedral. It's easiest and cheap (€1) to get there by Citadine bus (see "Getting Around Reims," page 502). A handy Citadine stop is just behind the cathedral (find the yellow stop a block to the left at the rear of the cathedral and take #1). Get off at the stop St. Nicaise (stops are digitally displayed on the bus or ask driver) and you'll see the long walls of Taittinger and the green sign to little Martel. If you take a taxi from the train station, figure on €8 one-way (cellars will call a cab for you after the tour). By *cyclopolitain* tricycle, it's €6 per person. If you walk, take rue de l'Université (from behind the cathedral's right transept), then rue du Barbâtre.

Near Reims

Epernay—Champagne purists may want to visit Epernay (16 miles away, well-connected to Paris and Reims), where the granddaddy of Champagne companies, **Moët et Chandon,** offers tours with three pricey tasting possibilities (€13 for single tasting, €18 for 2 tastes, €25 for 3, no reservation needed, daily mid-March–mid-Nov 9:30–11:30 & 14:00–16:30, closed weekends off-season, tel. 03 26 51 20 20, www.moet.com). From the Epernay train station, walk five minutes straight up rue Gambetta to place de la République, and take a left on avenue de Champagne (how fitting). According to the story, it was near here in about 1700 that the monk Dom Perignon, after much fiddling with double fermentation, stumbled onto this bubbly treat. On that happy day, he ran through the abbey shouting, "Brothers, come quickly...I'm drinking stars!"

Route de la Champagne—Drivers can joyride through the scenic and prestigious vineyards just south of Reims (the TI has maps). Follow D-9 south to Cormontreuil, then Louvois, then Bouzy, to see the chalky soil and vines that produce Champagne's costly wines. Many of the villages have small hotels if you'd like to sleep surrounded by vineyards.

SLEEPING

(€1 = about $1.50, country code: 33)

The first three of my listings are on place Drouet d'Erlon.

$$ Grand Hôtel Continental*** is a fine old hotel with well-priced, three-star comfort; stay-awhile public spaces; and helpful Maxeme at the desk (standard Db-€63–76, "junior suite" Db-€98–112, "superior suite" Db-€165–185, apartments for 3–8 available, 10 percent discount for Rick Steves readers on all but standard rooms, some non-smoking rooms, air-con, elevator, laundry service, pricey Wi-Fi, parking-€6, 5-min walk from the train station at 93 place Drouet d'Erlon, tel. 03 26 40 39 35, fax 03 26 47 51 12, www.grand hotelcontinental.com, grand-hotel-continental@wanadoo.fr).

$$ Latino Hôtel lives up to its name with spicy music and 11 colorful, funky rooms at fair rates. It's above a bar so it can be noisy on weekends. Rooms facing the back are quieter but smaller and face the adjacent building (Db-€54–74, 33 place Drouet d'Erlon, tel. 03 26 47 48 89, fax 03 26 86 92 67, www.latinocafe.fr, latinocafe@latinocafe.fr).

$$ Grand Hôtel du Nord** delivers basic two-star comfort in high-ceilinged rooms (Db-€65, 75 place Drouet d'Erlon, tel. 03 26 47 39 03, fax 03 26 40 92 26).

$ Bénédicte et Claude Philippon Chambres d'Hôte is Reims' best lodging value. This delightful couple offers two comfortable, homey, and centrally located rooms on place du Chapitre (#21), 100 yards from the cathedral's left transept. Look for the yellow *Chambres d'Hôte* sign (S-€40, D-€50, T-€65, shared bathroom, includes French breakfast, fourth floor with elevator, parking on square, tel. 03 26 91 06 22, mobile 06 77 76 20 13, claude.philippon@tele2.fr).

EATING

Find good people-watching opportunities—if not high cuisine—with the scads of restaurants on place Drouet d'Erlon. All of these recommendations make good lunch or dinner options.

L'Apostrophe, an appealing place with a snazzy-cozy interior, offers a well-presented, creative cuisine that draws a loyal clientele (€15 *plats*, €26 *menu*, look for specials, daily, 59 place Drouet d'Erlon, tel. 03 26 79 19 89).

Micro Brasserie les 3 Brasseurs is a rollicking, Alsatian-flavored microbrewery with copper vats and a young, inviting feel. You'll get good brasserie fare and (rare in France) more beer than wine (€8 salads, €10–13 *plats*, €16 choucroute, 73 place Drouet d'Erlon, tel. 03 26 47 86 28).

Brasserie du Boulingrin is the oldest brasserie in town, gushing with Art Deco. A Reims institution, it serves traditional French cuisine at blue-collar prices (€15–18 *plats*, €18–25 *menus*, closed Sun;

10-min walk north of the TI or central train station at 49 rue de Mars, or take the Citadine bus #2, stop Boulingrin; tel. 03 26 40 96 22).

Au Plat du Jour, near the Martel and Taittinger *caves,* makes a useful pre- or post-Champagne-tasting option. Casually elegant, with old posters and Champagne labels adorning the walls, this is a good spot to enjoy hearty, classic French cuisine (€14–19 *plats*, €16–21 *menus*, closed Sun, 219 rue Barbâtre, tel. 03 26 85 27 60).

Café du Palais is appreciated by older locals who don't mind paying a premium to eat a meal or sip coffee wrapped in 1930s ambience. Reims' most venerable café-bistro stands across from the Grand Theater (14 place Myron Herrick, tel. 03 26 47 52 54).

TRANSPORTATION CONNECTIONS

There are two train stations in Reims (Reims-Centre and Gare Champagne-Ardennes). All trains to/from Paris (TGV and other) use the Reims-Centre station, while TGV trains to/from points east (i.e., Strasbourg or Colmar) use Gare Champagne-Ardennes (3 miles from the center of Reims, frequent shuttle-train connections to Reims-Centre station).

From Reims by Train to: Paris' Gare de l'Est (via TGV: 12/day, 45 min), **Epernay** (non-TGV: 12/day, 30 min), **Verdun** (via TGV to nearby Gare Meuse: 1/day, 30 min, plus 30-min shuttle bus from Gare Meuse to Verdun's city center; via non-TGV train: 3/day, 2–4 hrs, most with change in Châlons or Metz), **Strasbourg** (via TGV: 10/day, 2 hrs, change at Gare Champagne-Ardennes), **Colmar** (via TGV: 10/day, 3 hrs, most change at Gare Champagne-Ardennes and in Strasbourg).

MORE DAY TRIPS

- *Grand Châteaux near Paris*
- *Impressionist Excursions: Giverny and Auvers-sur-Oise*
- *Disneyland Paris*

Efficient trains bring dozens of day trips within the grasp of temporary Parisians. Châteaux, flowery gardens, riverfront villages, and an amusement park await the traveler looking for a refreshing change from urban Paris.

Grand Châteaux near Paris

The region around Paris (Ile de France) is littered with sumptuous palaces. Paris' booming upper class made it the heartland of European château building in the 16th and 17th centuries. Most of these châteaux were lavish hunting lodges—getaways from the big city. The only things they defended were noble and royal egos. Try to avoid visiting on weekends, when they are most crowded.

Consider four very different châteaux:

▲▲▲**Versailles**—For its history, grandeur, and accessibility (closed Mon); see page 456.

▲▲▲**Vaux-le-Vicomte**—For sheer beauty and intimacy (open daily, closed Nov–late March); see next page.

▲▲**Fontainebleau**—For its history, fine interior, and pleasant city (closed Tue); see page 515.

▲**Chantilly**—For its beautiful setting and fine collection of paintings (closed Tue); see page 516.

If you only have time for one château, choose between Vaux-le-Vicomte and Versailles. Except for Versailles, these châteaux are quiet on weekdays. Versailles, Fontainebleau, and Chantilly are covered by the Paris Museum Pass (see page 38).

Vaux-le-Vicomte

While Versailles is most travelers' first choice for its sheer historic weight, Vaux-le-Vicomte (voh luh vee-komt) offers an intimate interior and a better sense of 17th-century château life. Located in a huge forest, with magnificent gardens and no urban sprawl in sight, Vaux-le-Vicomte gave me just a twinge of palace envy.

Vaux-le-Vicomte was the architectural inspiration for Versailles and set the standard for European châteaux to come. The proud owner, Nicolas Fouquet (Louis XIV's finance minister), threw a château-warming party. Louis XIV was so jealous that he arrested his host; took his architect (Louis Le Vau), artist (Charles Le Brun), and landscaper (André Le Nôtre); and proceeded with the construction of the bigger and costlier (but not necessarily more splendid) palace of Versailles. Monsieur Fouquet's party, and later arrest, feature prominently in the third Musketeer book by Alexandre Dumas, and at least two versions of *The Man in the Iron Mask* were filmed here.

Vaux-le-Vicomte is more difficult to visit than Versailles (because of transportation), but it's a joy to tour. Most rooms have some English explanations. For more information, rent an audioguide (with a pro-Fouquet perspective) or get a souvenir booklet at the gift shop. Outside the gift shop is a reasonably priced café (limited menu, daily 11:30–18:00, until 24:00 during candlelit visits).

Start your tour with the fine exhibit of carriages *(équipages)* in the old stables. Wax figures and an evocative soundtrack get you in the proper mood. Next, stroll like a wide-eyed peasant across the stone bridge (any fish down there?) and up the front steps into the château. Turn around to admire the symmetry and elegance of the stables; horses lived well here.

As you wander through Fouquet's dream home, you'll understand Louis XIV's jealousy. Versailles was a simple hunting lodge when this was built. The furniture in Vaux-le-Vicomte is not original—Louis XIV confiscated the real stuff for Versailles. You'll see cozy bedrooms upstairs and grand living rooms downstairs (billiards room, library, card room, and dining room; feel free to fast-forward the 90-min audioguide tour—the first few rooms set the scene). The kitchen and wine cellar are in the basement. Climb the cupola for a great view (€2, check out the build-your-own-dome sketches on the way up). An interesting exhibit on Le Nôtre's gardens should be in place in the basement, a good finish to your visit.

Survey the garden from the palace's back steps. Landscaper

Day Trips from Paris

One-Way Travel Times From Appropriate Train Station in Paris

Chartres – 60 min	Vernon (Giverny) – 60 min
Versailles – 40 min	Auvers-sur-Oise – 90 min
Vaux-le-Vicomte – 45 min	Orly Airport – 30 min
Fontainebleau – 60 min	Charles de Gaulle Airport – 30 min
Chantilly – 45 min	Disneyland Paris – 45 min
Reims – 45 min	

Le Nôtre's first claim to fame, this garden was the cutting edge of sculpted French gardens. He integrated ponds, shrubbery, and trees in a style that would be copied in palaces all over Europe. Take the 30-minute walk (one-way) to the viewpoint atop the grassy hill far in the distance. Rentable golf carts (Club Cars, 45 min–€15, €5 extra for recorded commentary, ID required) make the trip easier.

Cost and Hours: €13 for gardens, château, and carriage museum, not covered by Museum Pass, audioguide-€2.50. Open late-March–early-Nov daily 10:00–17:30, gardens until 19:00, closed early-Nov–late-March, tel. 01 64 14 41 90, www.vaux-le-vicomte.com. The château closes for lunch weekdays (generally 13:00–14:00). From April through Oct, the impressive fountains run from 15:00–18:00 on the second Sat and last Sat of each month.

Candlelit Visits: Two thousand candles and piped-in classical music illuminate the palace early May to early Oct on Sat and holiday nights, and July–Aug on Fri nights as well, open 20:00–24:00); call to ask about any upcoming holidays. Note that the gardens are hard to see by candlelight. These *visites aux chandelles* re-create the party thrown in Louis XIV's honor in 1661 but it doesn't get really dark until 22:00 in late May, June, and July, and the last train to Paris leaves Melun at about 22:00. Skip it if you're not driving.

Getting to Vaux-le-Vicomte: To reach Vaux-le-Vicomte by a **train-and-taxi** combination, take the RER-D train to Melun (direction Montereau) from Paris' Gare du Nord or Châtelet–Les Halles stations. Faster SNCF *Banlieue* trains to Melun leave from the Gare de Lyon (about €7.50 one-way, 2/hr, 30 min). From Melun's train station, taxis make the 15-minute drive to Vaux-le-Vicomte (€15 one-way Mon–Sat, €18 eves and Sun, taxi tel. 01 64 52 51 50, other numbers posted above taxi stand). Ask a staff person at the château to call a cab for your return, or schedule a pickup time with your driver. In either direction, seek others to split the fare with (regular taxis can take three people maximum, minivan taxis can take four). On Saturdays and Sundays (April–Oct), a **shuttle bus** *(navette)* provides limited service between Melun's train station and the château (€7 round-trip, call château or check website for schedule, extra trips on Sat eves July–Aug for candlelight visits). With time to kill before your return train, or to make more of your excursion, consider exploring Melun's small medieval center, 10 easy minutes on foot from the station (walk down avenue Gallieni past the ugly concrete buildings, then turn right on rue Thiers and cross the river).

The Paris Vision **tour** company offers minibus excursions to Vaux-le-Vicomte (www.parisvision.com; see page 33). Many travelers find these worthwhile given the tricky train access.

By **car** from Paris, take the A-6 autoroute toward Lyon, then follow signs to Melun. In Melun, follow signs to Meaux (N-36), then Vaux-le-Vicomte.

Adding Fontainebleau: Vaux-le-Vicomte and Fontainebleau can be combined into a full, though manageable, day trip by car, taxi, or train from Paris (except on Tue, when Fontainebleau is closed). Fontainebleau is 12 minutes by train from Melun (allow €40 by taxi).

Sleeping near Vaux-le-Vicomte: Drive 15 minutes to Fontainebleau and sleep at one of the recommended hotels (see page 516).

Château of Fontainebleau

Fontainebleau's history rivals that of more modern Versailles. Many French kings have called this glamorous hunting lodge home. Louis XIII was born here, Louis XV married here, and Napoleon was baptized here. The little emperor also welcomed the pope to this château during his coronation celebration, and it was here that he abdicated his rule when exiled to Elba in 1814. Many years later, General Patton set up headquarters at this château on his way to Berlin.

While Vaux-le-Vicomte and Versailles are French-designed, Fontainebleau was built a century earlier by an Italian. The palace you see today was largely financed by Renaissance King François I. Inspired by his travels through Renaissance Italy, he hired Italian artists to build his palaces. He even encouraged one artist to abandon his native Italy and settle in France for the last eight years of his life—Leonardo da Vinci.

Visit the information room to orient yourself using its huge model of the château (first door on your right in the grand courtyard, look for blue "I"). The palace entry/

ticket office is 50 yards farther down. Regular entry provides access to the Chinese rooms and the main rooms of the château, called *les grands appartements*. Free audioguides give good room-by-room descriptions (allow one hour), and basic English explanations are posted throughout. Napoleon buffs will enjoy the interesting little museum of Napoleonic history, or a visit to his *petits appartements*. Unfortunately, both can be visited only with a guided tour in French, including one with a Napoleon III Second Empire theme (price and hours vary, call ahead or ask on arrival).

In the main château, start downstairs with the small but impressive Chinese collection of Napoleon III's empress, then climb to the main rooms of the palace. Highlights include the stunning Renaissance hall of François I, the opulent dance hall with piped-in music *(salle de bal)*, Napoleon's throne room, and Diana's Gallery (library). The gardens, designed a century later by the landscaper André Le Nôtre, are worth a stroll.

Cost and Hours: €8, includes audioguide, covered by Museum Pass, free first Sun of the month. Open June–Sept Wed–Mon 9:30–18:00, Oct–May closes at 17:00, last entry 45 minutes before closing, closed Tue.

Information: Tel. 01 60 71 50 70, www.musee-chateau-fontaine bleau.fr.

Getting to Fontainebleau: Catch a train at the *Grande Ligne* tracks from Paris' Gare de Lyon in the direction of Montereau (about €7.50 one-way, nearly hourly, 45 min) to the Fontainebleau-Avon station. Cross under the tracks and catch the *Cars Aerial* bus to the château (about €1.50, every 20 min). Check return train times before leaving the station, as there can be big gaps—note that your train might make an unscheduled stop in the middle of the forest to drop off hikers. Taxis to the château cost about €7; to nearby Vaux-le-Vicomte, about €40 (taxi tel. 01 64 22 00 06).

Town of Fontainebleau: Turn right out of the château courtyard and keep right to reach the town center, where cafés and restaurants abound. The helpful **TI** is two blocks across from the château behind Hôtel Londres, has hiking maps and bikes for rent, and posts train/bus schedules (Mon–Sat 10:00–18:00, Sun 10:00–13:00 & 14:00–17:30, Nov–March closed Sun afternoon, 4 rue Royale, tel. 01 60 74 99 99, www.fontainebleau-tourisme.com). When you're ready to catch the bus back to the train station, you'll find bus stops across the street from the TI next to Chez Bernard café, and at the post office in the city center.

English Bookstore: Check out **ReelBooks** at 9 rue de Gerrare, and say hi to Sue and Judy (Tue–Sat 11:00–19:00, closed Sun–Mon, tel. 01 64 22 85 85).

SLEEPING AND EATING

$$ Hôtel de Londres*** is run by gentle Philippe and Mama, who have left no stone unturned in their zeal to make everything perfect. The 15 rooms are big, immaculate, and *très* country French. Many have point-blank views of the château, and most have air-conditioning (smaller Db-€122, spacious Db with château view-€155–185, no elevator, 1 place du Général de Gaulle, tel. 01 64 22 20 21, fax 01 60 72 39 16, www.hoteldelondres.com, hdelondres1850@aol.com).

There are eating options at all prices in Fontainebleau's old city. Here are two of many: **Croquembouche** (*menus* from €25, closed Wed and Sun, 43 rue de France, tel. 01 64 22 01 57) or dine by candlelight under the arches at **Caveau des Ducs** (€13–19 lunch special Mon–Sat, good €24–41 dinner *menus*, open daily, 24 rue de Ferrare, tel. 01 64 22 05 05).

Château of Chantilly

Chantilly (shahn-tee-yee), 30 minutes north of Paris, floats serenely on a reflecting pond amid grand gardens. This extravagant hunting palace is the quintessence of a château—filled with great art, surrounded by a luxurious garden and a moat, and accessed by a drawbridge.

While there are better châteaux to tour, Chantilly's claim to fame is its art collection. Because of the social upheaval in France during the Revolution of 1848, the château's owner, Prince de Condé, fled to England. Twenty years later, when blue blood was safe again in France, he returned to his château with a fabulous art collection (800 paintings, including three Raphaels) and book collection. He turned his palace into the museum you see today and willed it to France on the condition that it would be maintained as he left it, and the collections would never be loaned to any other museum.

As most of the château was destroyed during the French Revolution, today's château is largely rebuilt in a fanciful 19th-century

style. It's divided into two parts: apartments and art gallery. The plush-but-nothing-really-special private apartments require an included guided tour (20 min, leaving every few minutes, generally in French). The painting gallery and library are impressive, and the €2 audioguide gives them meaning. Gallery highlights are paintings by Raphael, Titian, Nicolas Poussin, and Eugène Delacroix. Of the 13,000 books in the prince's library, the most exquisite is the 40-page *Book of Hours* by Jean Fouquet (c. 1460).

The gardens immediately behind the château are formal and austere. With your back to the château, follow the signs to the right to *le Hameau*. This little hamlet, with an enchanting garden café, was the prototype for the more famous *hameau* at Versailles. Just beyond is a small kiosk offering boat trips along the canals.

Cost and Hours: €9, covered by Museum Pass, March–Oct Wed–Mon 10:00–18:00, closed Tue; Nov–Feb Wed–Fri and Mon 10:30–12:45 & 14:00–17:00, Sat–Sun 10:00–18:00, closed Tue; tel. 03 44 62 62 62, www.chateaudechantilly.com.

Live Horse Stables (Les Ecuries Vivant): The Prince de Condé believed he'd be reincarnated as a horse, so he built this opulent horse château for his next go-round (a 5-min walk from château). The stable museum—with displays on everything from horse medicine to racing to circuses—includes 40 live horses in their stables and daily demonstrations (€9, Mon and Wed–Fri 14:00–17:00, Sat–Sun 10:30–17:30, last ticket sold one hour before closing, closed Tue; tel. 03 44 57 40 40, www.museevivantducheval.fr). On the first Sunday of each month there's a grand one-hour show where horses prance to music; call or check the website for times and prices (about €22).

Getting to Chantilly: Leave from Paris' Gare du Nord for Chantilly-Gouvieux (on the Creil line). While the RER serves Chantilly, service is faster on the main lines at the *Grandes Lignes* level. Ask any information desk for the next departure (about €8 one-way, covered by railpass, hourly, 25 min). Upon arrival in Chantilly, confirm return times (fewer trips on weekends). The **TI** is across from the station (Mon–Sat 9:30–12:30 & 14:30–17:30, closed Sun, tel. 03 44 67 37 37). To get to the château, ask at the TI about the bus heading toward Senlis (1/hr); get lucky and catch the shuttle bus (marked *le Duc,* 4/day); walk 30 minutes (get a map from TI and follow signs, stay on path, turn right before gas station, cross grassy field, "château" in distance is stables, real château is beyond that); or take a taxi (about €7, ask at TI, they extort people with €17 château pickups).

Impressionist Excursions: Giverny and Auvers-sur-Oise

Giverny

Claude Monet's gardens at Giverny are like his paintings—brightly colored patches that are messy but balanced. Flowers were his brush-

strokes, a bit untamed and slapdash, but part of a carefully composed design. Monet spent his last (and most creative) years cultivating his garden and his art at Giverny (zhee-vayr-nee), the Camp David of Impressionism (1883–1926).

In 1883, middle-aged Claude Monet, his wife Alice, and their eight children from two families set-tled into a farmhouse here, 50 miles west of Paris (for more on Monet's family, see sidebar on page 229). Monet, at that point a famous artist and happiest at home, would spend 40 years in Giverny, traveling less with each passing year. He built a pastoral paradise complete with a Japanese garden and a pond full of floating lilies.

In the last half of his life (beginning in 1912), Monet—the great-est visionary, literally, of his generation—began to go blind with cataracts. He used larger canvases and painted fewer details. The true subject is not really the famous water lilies, but the changing reflec-tions on the pond's surface—the blue sky, white clouds, and green trees that line the shore.

All kinds of people flock to Giverny. Gardeners admire the earth-moving landscaping and layout, botanists find interesting new plants, and art lovers can see paintings they've long admired come to life.

Giverny

NOT TO SCALE

PARKING LOT
ENTRANCE
EXIT

WATER LILY STUDIO
GIFT SHOP & EXIT

RUE   CLAUDE

TO MUSEUM OF AMERICAN ART & ⑥

HOUSE

WALLED GARDEN
(CLOS NORMAND)

MONET

④

TO VERNON (4 MILES) & BIKE PATH

D-5 ROAD

PATH

① ② ③

WATER GARDEN

DCH

- ① Pedestrian Tunnel
- ② Japanese Bridge
- ③ Water Lily Pond
- ④ Hôtel la Musardière
- ⑤ Café & Sandwich Stand
- ⑥ To Café at Museum of American Art & Hôtel Baudy

Fans enjoy wandering around the house where Monet spent half his life and seeing the boat he puttered around in, as well as the henhouse where his family got the eggs for their morning omelets.

There are two gardens, split by a busy road, plus the house, which displays Monet's prized collection of Japanese prints.

Try to arrive before it opens and be first in line, or arrive at this busy place late (see "Avoiding Crowds," page 521). Buy your ticket and go directly to the Walled Garden (Clos Normand) by the house. Monet cleared this land of pine trees and laid out symmetrical beds, split down the middle by a "grand alley" covered with iron trellises of climbing roses. He did his own landscaping: flowerbeds of lilies, irises, and clematis, and arbors of climbing roses. The arched trellises form a natural tunnel that leads your eye down the path—an effect exploited in his *Rose Trellis* paintings (on display in Paris at the Marmottan Museum, page 225). In his careless manner, Monet throws together hollyhocks, daisies, and poppies. But each flowerbed has an overall color scheme that contributes to the look of the whole garden.

Impressionism

Impressionism was a revolutionary movement in European art—all the rage in the 1880s. Artists abandoned photorealism in favor of a wispy style that captured light, glimmers, feelings, and impressions. Impressionists—capturing nature as a mosaic of short brushstrokes of different colors placed side by side, suggesting shimmering light—were committed to conveying the subtleties of nature. And there is no better nature for an Impressionist ready to paint than Monet's delightful mix of weeping willows, luminous clouds, delicate bridges, reflecting ponds...and lush water lilies.

In the far corner of the Walled Garden, you'll find a pedestrian tunnel that leads under the road to the Water Garden. Cross under the road and follow the path leading to the Japanese bridge, under weeping willows, over the pond filled with water lilies, and past countless scenes that leave artists aching for an easel. Monet landscaped like he painted—he built an Impressionist pattern of blocks of color. Once he planted the gardens, he painted them, from every angle, at every time of day, in all kinds of weather. Assisted by his favorite step-daughter, Blanche (also a painter, who married Monet's son Jean from an earlier marriage), he worked on several canvases at once, moving with the sun from one to the next. In a series of canvases, you can watch the sunlight sweep over the gardens from early dawn to twilight.

Back on the other side, continue your visit with a wander through his mildly interesting home. The jammed gift shop at the exit is the actual skylighted studio where Monet painted his water-lily masterpieces (displayed at the Orangerie Museum in Paris, page 155).

Cost and Hours: €5.50, €4 for gardens only, April–Oct Tue–Sun 9:30–18:00, last entry 17:30, closed Mon and Nov–March, open some Mon holidays—check website, tel. 02 32 51 28 21, www.fondation-monet.com.

Nearby Sights: The Museum of American Art (Musée d'Art Américain, turn left when leaving Monet's place and walk 100 yards) is devoted to American artists who followed Claude to Giverny (same price and hours as Monet's home). Monet and his garden had a great influence on American artists of his day. This bright, modern gallery—

with good information in English, though its most appealing feature might be its garden café (good if a bit pricey salads and quiches).

If you miss your train back to Paris, spend an hour in pleasant little Vernon while you wait for the next train.

Avoiding Crowds: While lines may be long and tour groups may trample the flowers, true fans still find magic in the gardens. Minimize crowds by arriving by 9:15 (get in line, it opens at 9:30), during lunchtime, or after 16:00. If you're traveling by train, take the first departure from Paris listed below.

SLEEPING AND EATING

(€1 = about $1.50, country code: 33)

$$ Hôtel la Musardière** is nestled in the village of Giverny two blocks from Monet's home (exit home and go right). It's cute and welcoming, with a reasonable and homey *crêperie*-restaurant (Db-€72–82, 123 rue Claude Monet, tel. 02 32 21 03 18, fax 02 32 21 60 00, www .lamusardiere.fr, hotelmusardieregiverny@wanadoo.fr).

You'll find a **café and sandwich stand** near the entrance to Monet's home and a peaceful **garden café** at the Museum of American Art (surrounded by gardens Monet would appreciate, but a little pricey).

The rose-colored **Hôtel Baudy** was the American artists' hangout and offers an appropriately pretty setting for lunch or dinner (*menus* from €23, popular with tour groups, closed Sun eve and Mon, 5-min walk past Museum of American Art at 81 rue Claude Monet, tel. 02 32 21 10 03).

TRANSPORTATION CONNECTIONS

By Tour: Big tour companies do a Giverny day trip from Paris for around €70; ask at your hotel.

By Car: From Paris's Périphérique ring road, follow A-13 toward Rouen, get off at Vernon, follow *Centre Ville* signs, then signs to Giverny.

By Train: Take the Rouen-bound train from Paris' Gare St. Lazare station to Vernon (about €23 round-trip, 45 min one-way, 4 miles from Giverny, no baggage check). The schedule from 2008 follows (a few departures require an easy transfer in Mantes la Jolie, verify 2009 schedule before going!):

Leave Paris for Vernon: Weekdays at 8:16, 11:03, 12:04, 12:40, 14:23, 15:42; Saturday 8:39, 10:32, 12:04, 12:34, 13:45, 14:23, 17:09,

18:48; Sunday 8:07, 9:32, 10:44, 13:20, 14:25, 17:09.

Leave Vernon for Paris: Weekdays at 7:51, 8:03, 8:44, 9:04, 10:53, 12:55, 14:59, 15:09, 17:12, 17:49; Saturday 8:44, 10:53, 12:55, 14:59, 17:32, 18:00, 19:30; Sunday 10:53, 12:42, 15:35, 17:33, 18:00, 19:27.

From Vernon's Train Station to Giverny: From the Vernon train station to Monet's garden (4 miles one-way), you have four good options: by bus, taxi, bike, or on foot.

The Vernon–Giverny **bus** meets every train listed above for the 15-minute run to Giverny (no buses on Mon) and takes you back to every return train to Paris. If you miss the last bus, find others to share a taxi (see below). The stop to Giverny is in front of Vernon's train station, facing Café du Chemin de Fer (don't dally, the bus leaves soon after your train arrives). The ticket office at Monet's home in Giverny has bus schedules for the return trip. The bus stop for the return trip is in the bus parking lot on the opposite side of the main road, by the roundabout. The stop is the first one on your right. Look for the white #18 bus marked *Vernon–Giverny Car.*

If you take a **taxi,** allow €12 for up to three people, €13 for four (tel. 06 77 49 32 90, 06 76 08 50 78, or 02 32 21 31 31). With buses meeting every train, taxis are unnecessary (unless you miss the bus). Taxis wait in front of the station in Vernon.

You can rent a **bike** at Café du Chemin de Fer opposite the train station (€12, tel. 02 32 21 16 01), and follow a paved bike path *(piste cyclable)* that runs from near Vernon along an abandoned railroad right-of-way (figure about 30 min to Giverny). Get the easy-to-follow map to Giverny with your bike and leave the train station paralleling tracks to your right, take the first left and follow that to the river, cross the river, turn right and meet the bike trail. There's a lovely riverside park on the left side of the bridge after crossing the Seine (where you turn right for the bike path).

Hikers can go on **foot** to Giverny, following the bike instructions above, and take a bus or taxi back.

Auvers-sur-Oise

There's no better place to get a feel for life during the Impressionist era than on the banks of the lazy Oise River, about a 45-minute drive (or 1.5-hour train ride) northwest of Paris.

Auvers-sur-Oise (oh-vehr soor wahz) is famous as the village where Vincent van Gogh committed suicide after relocating from southern France to be near his sympathetic doctor (Paul Gachet). But many other artists enjoyed this peaceful rural retreat, including Charles-François Daubigny, Jean-Baptiste-Camille Corot, Camille Pissarro, and Paul Cézanne.

Today, this modest little town opens doors to visitors with a few sights, walking trails leading to scenes painted by the artists (some with copies of the paintings posted), and a tranquil break from the big city. Come for the afternoon (some sights are closed in the morning) and avoid weekends if you can. Auvers has cafés, restaurants, and bakeries with sandwiches. Most sights are closed Mondays and Tuesdays and from November to Easter.

Start at the eager-to-help **TI,** which has good information on all village sights, bus and RER train schedules, a few picnic tables, a rustic WC, and a helpful €0.50 map of Auvers showing the walking routes, with famous art scenes posted (Tue–Sun 9:30–12:30 & 14:00–18:00, Nov–March closes at 17:00, closed Mon, tel. 01 30 36 10 06).

The skippable **Musée Daubigny,** one floor up from the TI, houses a small collection of works from artists who came to work with Monsieur Daubigny, an ardent defender of the Impressionists (€4, Wed–Sun 14:00–18:00, Nov–March closes at 17:00, closed Mon–Tue, tel. 01 34 48 03 03).

The best way to spend a few hours in Auvers is to wander the streets between the TI and the château and find locations where paintings were set, and to visit the dazzling château.

The town's most worthwhile sight is **Château d'Auvers** (follow *Château* signs along the small road that runs above the TI, 15 min on foot). The entire château has been transformed into a re-creation of life during the Impressionist years. Elaborate multi-media displays use an audioguide, video screens, and lasers to guide you along the Impressionist route that led from Montmartre to the sea, giving you a keen appreciation of life's daily struggles and pleasures during this time (€12, family rates available, April–Sept Tue–Sun 10:30–18:00, closed Mon; Oct–March Tue–Sun 10:30–16:30, until 17:30 Sat–Sun, closed Mon; tel. 01 34 48 48 45, www.chateau-auvers.fr).

Loyal van Gogh enthusiasts can visit the home of Dr. Gachet (**Maison du Docteur Gachet**), Vincent's personal physician in Auvers-sur-Oise. The doctor was also a painter himself, and entertained famous artists such as Cézanne, Monet, Renoir, and Pissarro (€4, Wed–Sun 10:30–18:30, closed Mon–Tue, 78 rue du Dr. Gachet, tel. 01 30 36 81 27).

You can walk through the same crow-infested wheat fields Vincent did. From the château, return to Auvers along the same road, but veer left when you reach rue Daubigny, then turn right on rue du Montier, and turn right again up a dirt trail. As you stroll through the wheat fields (can be muddy), ponder how amazed the artist would be at his popularity today. You can go as far as the cemetery and visit the tombs of Vincent and his brother Theo (15 min on trail; as you enter cemetery, tombs on left wall halfway down), or take the dirt-trail shortcut a few hundred yards before the cemetery down to the **Church at Auvers** (see van Gogh's painting at Paris' Orsay Museum, page 130). From here, it's a short walk down to the train station and bus stop to Pontoise.

Some van Gogh fans make a pilgrimage to **Auberge Ravoux** (also called "Maison de van Gogh"), where Vincent died after shooting himself. Informative English-information plaques in the free courtyard explain Vincent's tragic life. Wooden steps lead to his small room (€5, March–Oct Wed–Sun 10:00–18:00, closed Mon–Tue and Nov–Feb, includes 12-min slideshow and possible English commentary, otherwise tour on your own). Food connoisseurs can skip the visit and have a tasty lunch in the *auberge*'s perfectly preserved restaurant (€35 *menus*).

SLEEPING AND EATING

(€1 = about $1.50, country code: 33)
Auvers is a handy first or last stop for drivers using Charles de Gaulle Airport.

$$$ Hostellerie du Nord*** is small, friendly, and polished—a treat for those who want to sleep in luxury. It has modern, spacious rooms and a seriously good restaurant that requires reservations (Db-€98–128, suites-€188, *menus* from €58, a block from train station at 6 rue du Général de Gaulle, tel. 01 30 36 70 74, fax 01 30 36 72 75, www.hostelleriedunord.fr).

The place to eat in Auvers is **Auberge Ravoux,** unchanged (except for its prices) since 1876, when painters would meet here over a good meal (€28–35 *menus*, closed Mon–Tue, below TI on place de la Mairie, tel. 01 30 36 60 60).

TRANSPORTATION CONNECTIONS

Between Paris and Auvers-sur-Oise

Frequent trains to Auvers (with a transfer in Pontoise or St. Ouen) leave from Gare du Nord and Gare St. Lazare. The easiest trip is via RER-C to Pontoise (2/hr, 1 hour, catch in Paris at St. Michel, Orsay, Invalides, or Pont de l'Alma stops). Pontoise is the end of the line.

To get from Pontoise to Auvers, a 10-min ride away, take the train in direction: Creil (if it's leaving soon), or hop on bus #95 (runs more frequently than train, catch it to the right out of the station; look for the posted schedule—you're at "Chemin de la Gare" in Pontoise, and you want the "Marie" stop in Auvers). Taxis wait outside the

Pontoise station to the left (€10 to Auvers, tel. 01 30 75 95 95; for a bit more money, the same taxi can pick you up in Auvers for the return).

If you arrive in Auvers by train, you can reach the **TI** by turning left on the main road leaving Auvers' station (look for signs, TI has bus schedules to Pontoise). For a taxi in Auvers, call 06 71 60 50 06 or 06 08 24 54 88.

By **car,** Auvers is about 45 minutes northwest of Paris, off Autoroute A-15 (exit #7 to N-184, then follow direction: Beauvais).

Disneyland Paris

Europe's Disneyland is a remake of California's, with most of the same rides and smiles. The main difference is that Mickey Mouse

speaks French, and you can buy wine with your lunch. My kids went ducky.

Disneyland is easy to get to, and worth a day, if Paris is handier than Florida or California. Saturday, Sunday, Wednesday, public holidays, and any day in July and August are the most crowded. After dinner, crowds are gone. Food is fun and not outrageously priced. (Still, many smuggle in a picnic.) The free FASTPASS system is a worthwhile timesaver (get FASTPASS card at entry, good for five most popular rides, at ride insert card in machine to get a window of time to enter—often within about 45 min). You'll also save time by buying your tickets ahead (at airport TIs, some Métro stations, or along the Champs-Elysées at the TI, Disney Store, or Virgin Megastore). Disney brochures are in every Paris hotel. For Disneyland information and reservations, call 08 25 30 60 30 (€0.15/min) or try www.disneylandparis.com or www.mickey-mouse.com.

Walt Disney Studios: This zone, which opened in 2002 next to the original 16-year-old amusement park, has a Hollywood focus geared for an older crowd, with animation, special effects, and movie magic "rides." The Aerosmith Rock 'n' Roller Coaster is nothing special. The highlight is the Stunt Show Spectacular, filling a huge backlot stadium five times a day for 45 minutes of car chases and thriller filming tips. An actual movie sequence is filmed with stunt drivers, audience bit players, and brash MTV-style hosts.

Cost: Disneyland Paris and Walt Disney Studios charge the same. You can pay separately for each or buy a combined ticket for both, called a "Hopper" ticket. A one-day pass to either park is about €60 for adults and €50 for kids aged 3–11 (check their website for special offers). There's no charge for kids under 3. In the summer, save 25 percent by going after 17:00.

For entry to both parks, adults pay about €80 for one day, €120 for two days, and €138 for three days (less for kids). Regular prices are discounted about 25 percent Nov–March and promotions are offered occasionally (check www.disneylandparis.com).

Hours: Disneyland is open daily mid-July–Aug 10:00–23:00, Sept–mid-July 10:00–19:00, some weekends have longer hours—check website or at ticket office. Walt Disney Studios is open summer daily 9:00–18:00; winter Mon–Fri 10:00–18:00, Sat–Sun 9:00–18:00.

Sleeping at Disneyland: Most are better off sleeping in reality (Paris), though with direct buses and freeways to both airports, Disneyland makes a convenient first- or last-night stop. Seven different Disney-owned hotels offer accommodations at or near the park in all price ranges. Prices are impossible to pin down, as they vary by season and by the "package deal" you choose (deals that include park entry are usually a better value). The cheapest is **Davy Crockett's Ranch,** but you'll need a car. **Hôtel Santa Fe**** offers the best midrange value, with frequent shuttle service to the park. The most expensive is **Disneyland Hotel****,** right at the park entry, about twice the price of the Santa Fe. To reserve any Disneyland hotel, call 01 60 30 60 30, fax 01 60 30 60 65, or check www.disneylandparis.com. The prices you'll be quoted include entry to the park.

TRANSPORTATION CONNECTIONS

Between Paris and Disneyland Paris

By Train: Pricey TGV trains connect Disneyland directly with **Charles de Gaulle airport** (10 min), the **Loire Valley** (1.5 hrs, Tours-St. Pierre des Corps station, 15 min from Amboise), **Avignon** (3 hrs, TGV station), **Lyon** (2 hrs, Part Dieu station), and **Nice** (6 hrs, main station).

By RER: The slick 45-minute RER trip is the best way to get to Disneyland from downtown Paris. Take RER line A-4 to Marne-la-Vallée-Chessy; check the signs over the platform to be sure Marne-la-Vallée-Chessy is served, because the line splits near the end (catch RER line A-4 from Paris' Charles de Gaulle-Etoile, Auber, Châtelet-Les Halles, or Gare de Lyon stations, about €8 each way, 3/hr, drops you 45 min later right in the park). The last train back to Paris leaves shortly after midnight. When returning, remember to use your same RER ticket for your Métro connection in Paris.

By Bus: Both of Paris' major airports have direct shuttle buses to Disneyland Paris (about €17, daily 8:30–19:45, every 45 min).

By Car: Disneyland is about 40 minutes (20 miles) east of Paris on the A-4 autoroute (direction Nancy/Metz, exit #14). Parking is about €10 per day at the park.

FRENCH HISTORY AND CONTEMPORARY POLITICS

HISTORY

Celts and Romans (52 B.C.–A.D. 500)

Julius Caesar conquered the Parisii, turning Paris from a tribal fishing village into a European city. The mix of Latin (southern) and Celtic (northern) cultures, with Paris right in the middle, defined the French character.

Sights
- Cluny Museum (Roman baths)
- Louvre (Roman antiquities)
- Paris Archaeological Crypt (in front of Notre-Dame)

Dark Ages (500–1000)

Roman Paris fell to German pirates ("Franks" = France), and later to the Vikings ("Norsemen" = Normans). During this turbulent time, Paris was just another island state ("Ile de France") in the midst of many warring kingdoms. The lone bright spot was the reign of Charlemagne (A.D. 768–814), who briefly united the Franks, giving a glimpse of the modern nation-state of France.

Sights
- Cluny Museum (artifacts)
- Statue of Charlemagne (near Notre-Dame)

Border Wars with England (1066–1500)

In 1066, the Norman duke William the Conqueror invaded and conquered England. This united England, Normandy, and much of what is today western France; sparked centuries of border wars; and produced many kings of England who spoke French. In 1328 King

A Typical Medieval Church

History comes to life when you visit a medieval church. Knowing a few simple terms will enrich your experience. Note that not every church will have every feature, and that a "cathedral" isn't a type of church architecture, but rather a governing center for a local bishop.

Nave: The long, central section of the church (running east to west, from the entrance to the altar) where the congregation stood through the service.

Transept: The north–south part of the church, which crosses (perpendicularly) the east–west nave. In a traditional Latin cross-shaped floor plan, the transept forms the "arms" of the cross.

Aisles: The long, generally low-ceilinged arcades that flank the nave.

Altar: The raised area with a ceremonial table (often adorned with candles or a crucifix), where the priest prepares and serves the bread and wine for Communion.

Choir: A cozy area, often screened off, located within the church nave and near the high altar where services are sung in a more intimate setting.

Apse: The space beyond the altar, generally bordered with small chapels.

Narthex: The area (portico or foyer) between the main entry and the nave.

West Portal: The main entry to the church (on the west end, opposite the main altar).

Facade: The outer wall of the church's main (west) entrance, viewable from outside and generally highly decorated.

Groin Vault: An arched ceiling formed where two equal barrel vaults meet at right angles. Less common usage: term for a medieval jock strap.

Charles IV died without an heir, and the Norman king of England tried to claim the throne of France, which led to more than 100 years of Franco-Anglo battles, called the Hundred Years' War. Rallied by the teenage visionary Joan of Arc in 1429, the French finally united north and south, and drove the English across the Channel in 1453. Modern France was born, with Paris as its capital.

Sights
- Notre-Dame Cathedral
- Sainte-Chapelle
- Cluny Museum (tapestries)
- Carnavalet Museum
- The Sorbonne
- The Latin Quarter

Renaissance and Religious Wars (1500s)

A strong, centralized France emerged, with French kings setting Europe's standard. François I made Paris a cultural capital, inviting Leonardo and *Mona Lisa* to visit. Catholics and Protestants fought openly, with 2,000 Parisians slaughtered in the St. Bartholomew's Day Massacre in 1572. The Wars of Religion subsided for a while when the first Bourbon king, Henry IV, took the throne in 1589 after converting to Catholicism. (In 1598, he signed the Edict of Nantes, which instituted freedom of worship.)

Sights
- Louvre (palace and Renaissance art)
- Pont Neuf
- Place des Vosges
- Fontainebleau

Louis XIV, the Absolute Monarch (1600s)

Louis XIV solidified his power, neutered the nobility, revoked the Edict of Nantes, and moved the capital to Versailles, which also became the center of European culture. France's wealth sparked "enlightened" ideas that became the seeds of democracy.

Sights
- Versailles
- Vaux-le-Vicomte
- Hôtel des Invalides
- Paintings by Nicolas Poussin and Claude Lorrain

Decadence and Revolution (1700s)

This was the age of Louis XV, Louis XVI, Marie-Antoinette, Voltaire, Jean-Jacques Rousseau, Maximilien de Robespierre, and Napoleon. A financial crunch from wars and royal excess drove the French people to revolt. On July 14, 1789, they stormed the Bastille. A couple of years later, the First French Republic arrested and then beheaded the king and queen. Thousands lost their heads—guillotined if suspected of hindering progress. A charismatic commoner rose amid the chaos, promising stability—Napoleon Bonaparte.

Sights

- Versailles
- Place de la Concorde
- Place de la Bastille
- Conciergerie
- Paintings by Antoine Watteau, François Boucher, Jean-Honoré Fragonard, and Jacques-Louis David

Elected Emperors and Constitutional Kings (1800s)

Napoleon conquered Europe, crowned himself emperor, invaded Russia, was defeated on the battlefields of Waterloo, and ended up exiled to an island in the Atlantic. The monarchy was restored, but rulers toed the democratic line—or were deposed in the popular uprisings of 1830 and 1848. The latter resulted in the Second French Republic, whose first president was Napoleon's nephew. He rewrote the constitution with himself as Emperor Napoleon III, and presided over a wealthy, middle-class nation with a colonial empire in slow decline. The disastrous Franco-Prussian War in 1870 ended his reign, leading to the Third Republic. France's political clout was fading, even as Paris remained the world's cultural center during the belle époque, or beautiful age.

Sights

- Arc de Triomphe
- Baron Haussmann's wide boulevards
- Eiffel Tower
- Les Invalides and Napoleon's Tomb
- Pont Alexandre III
- Grand Palais
- Petit Palais
- Montmartre
- Opéra Garnier
- Paintings by Jean-Auguste-Dominique Ingres and Eugène Delacroix (Louvre)
- Impressionist and Postimpressionist paintings (Edouard Manet,

Claude Monet, Pierre-Auguste Renoir, Edgar Degas, Henri de Toulouse-Lautrec, Paul Cézanne, and so on) at the Orsay, Marmottan, and Orangerie museums.

War and Depression (1900–1950)

France began the turn of the 20th century as top dog, but two world wars with Germany (and the earlier Franco-Prussian War) wasted the country. France lost millions of men in World War I, sank into an economic depression, and was easily overrun by Hitler in World War II. Paris, now dirt cheap, attracted foreign writers and artists.

This was the age of Pablo Picasso, Maurice Ravel, Claude Debussy, Erik Satie, Igor Stravinsky, Vaslav Nijinsky, Ernest Hemingway, F. Scott Fitzgerald, Gertrude Stein, Ezra Pound, Jean-Paul Sartre, Edith Piaf, and Maurice Chevalier.

Sights
• Picasso Museum
• Deportation Memorial
• Holocaust Memorial
• Pompidou Center (art from this period)

Postwar France (1950–Present)

After the war, France reestablished a democracy with the Fourth Republic. But France's colonial empire dissolved after bitter wars in Algeria and Vietnam, which helped mire an already unsteady government. Wartime hero Charles de Gaulle was brought back in 1958 to assist with France's regrowth. He rewrote the constitution, beginning the Fifth (and current) Republic. Immigrants from former colonies flooded Paris. The turbulent '60s, progressive '70s, socialist-turned-conservative '80s, and the middle-of-the-road '90s bring us to the *début de siècle*, or the beginning of the century.

Sights
• Montparnasse Tower
• La Défense
• Louvre's pyramid
• Pompidou Center (modern art)

CONTEMPORARY POLITICS IN FRANCE

The key political issues in France today are high unemployment (about 8 percent), high taxes (about 44 percent of the gross domestic product), a steadily increasing percentage of ethnic minorities (almost 10 percent of France's population is Muslim), the extent of the European Union's power, and the balancing act between maintaining cushy workers' benefits with the need to compete in a global marketplace. The challenge is to address these issues while maintaining the social benefits the French expect from their government.

Today, France is part of the 27-member European Union (a kind of "United States of Europe") that has successfully dissolved borders and implemented a single currency, the euro. However, while France's governments have been decidedly pro-EU, its people are somewhat skeptical. In 2005, the French voted against ratifying an EU constitution that would have increased the EU's political powers. Many French fear that a more powerful EU would ultimately result in a loss of job security and social benefits (a huge issue in France).

French national politics are complex but fascinating. While only two parties dominate American politics, France has seven major parties and several smaller ones. From left to right, the major parties include the Ligue Communiste Révolutionnaire (LCR), which is as far left as you get in France; the more moderate reformed Communists (PCF: Parti Communiste Français); the environmental party (Les Verts, "The Greens"); the middle-of-the-road Socialists (PS: Parti Socialiste); the aristocratically conservative MoDem (Mouvement Démocrate, formerly the Union pour la Démocratie Française); the center right UMP (Union pour la Majorité Présidentielle); and the racist, isolationist Front National. In general, the UDF and UMP split the conservative middle ground, and the Socialists dominate the liberal middle ground. But in France, unlike in the US, informal coalitions are generally necessary for any party to "rule."

You've likely read about the Front National party, led by Jean-Marie Le Pen. Le Pen's "France for the French" platform calls for the expulsion of ethnic minorities and broader police powers. The situation was especially tense in the fall of 2005, when Muslim youths rioted in Parisian suburbs protesting discrimination. Although the Front National has a staunch voter base of about 15 percent, the recent rise in unemployment and globalization worries have increased its following, allowing Le Pen to nudge the political agenda to the right. On the far left, the once powerful Communists (PCF) draw only about 5 percent of the popular vote, forcing them to work more flexibly with the less radical Socialists and the environmental party (Les Verts). This left end of the political spectrum in France sees its fortunes rise when the economy is strong, and fall when it's weak.

While the French president is elected by popular vote every five years, he is more of a figurehead than his American counterpart. The more powerful prime minister is chosen by the president, then confirmed by the parliament (Assemblée Nationale). With five major parties, a single majority is rare, so it takes a coalition to elect a prime minister. Over the past 12 years, the right has been more successful in marshaling its supporters than the left. Previous President Jacques Chirac (two terms) and current President Nicolas Sarkozy (elected in

2007) are both conservatives.

Sarkozy is pro-America (though he doesn't speak English) and pro–European Union. He is tough on crime and on unchecked immigration. To address a sluggish economy, he proposes a tough-love, carrot-and-stick approach—limiting the power of unions and cutting workers' benefits, while offering tax incentives to workers who put in overtime (above the current 35–39-hour work week). His policies are generating predictable resistance from unions—expect at least one major strike somewhere in France during your trip.

It's his personal life, however, that has raised more French eyebrows. Sarkozy likes to jog, and wears sweats when relaxing *(quelle horreur!)*. Moreover, within a year of becoming president, he divorced his wife of 11 years and married sexy Italian model-turned-singer Carla Bruni (who has been linked romantically with Mick Jagger, Eric Clapton, and one of your co-authors). The press has nicknamed Sarkozy "Bling Bling" for his love of celebrities and celebrity status.

APPENDIX

CONTENTS

Resources 535
Telephones, Email, and Mail 540
Holidays and Festivals 550
Conversions and Climate 552
Essential Packing Checklist 554
Hotel Reservation Form 555
French Pronunciation
    Guide for Paris 556
French Survival Phrases 559

RESOURCES

Tourist Office in the US

France has a helpful national tourist information office (abbreviated **TI** in this book). Before you go, you can contact the TI to briefly describe your trip and request any information (such as city maps and schedules of upcoming festivals). To ask questions and request tourist materials (for a small shipping fee), email info.us@franceguide.com or call 514/288-1904. You can download many brochures free of charge at their website, www.franceguide.com, but read the options carefully to avoid signing up for promotional emails.

Websites: Paris' tourist information offices all share an official website (www.parisinfo.com) offering practical information on hotels, special events, museums, children's activities, fashion, nightlife, and more. Two other websites that are entertaining and useful are www.bonjourparis.com (which claims to offer a virtual trip to Paris—featuring interactive French lessons, tips on wine and food, and news on the latest Parisian trends) and the similar www.paris-anglo.com (with informative stories on visiting Paris, plus a directory of over 2,500 English-speaking businesses). For a preview of special art exhibitions in Paris, check www.rmn.fr.

Resources from Rick Steves

Guidebooks and Online Updates

This book is updated every year in person. The telephone numbers and hours of sights listed in this book are accurate as of mid-2008—but even with annual updates, things change. For the very latest, visit www.ricksteves.com/update. Also at my website, you'll find a valuable list of reports and experiences—good and bad—from fellow travelers (www.ricksteves.com/feedback).

Paris 2009 is one of more than 30 titles in my series on European travel, which includes country guidebooks (including France), city

and regional guidebooks (including Provence and the French Riviera), and my budget-travel skills handbook, *Rick Steves' Europe Through the Back Door*. My phrase books—for French, Italian, German, Spanish, and Portuguese—are practical and budget-oriented. My other books are *Europe 101* (a crash course on art and history, newly expanded and in full color), *European Christmas* (on traditional and modern-day celebrations), and *Postcards from Europe* (a fun memoir of my travels). For a complete list of my

books, see the inside of the last page of this book.

Public Television and Radio Shows

My TV series, *Rick Steves' Europe*, covers European destinations in 70 shows, with six episodes on France. My weekly public radio show, *Travel with Rick Steves*, features interviews with travel experts from around the world, including several hours on France and French culture. All the TV scripts and radio shows (which are easy and free to download to an iPod or other MP3 player) are at www.ricksteves .com.

Free Audiotours of Paris

Rick Steves and Gene Openshaw (one of the co-authors of this book) have produced free self-guided audiotours of Paris—for the Louvre, Orsay, Versailles, and Historic Paris—as well as Florence, Rome, and Venice. Created for users of iPods and other MP3 players, the tours allow you to focus on what you're seeing rather than

Begin Your Trip at www.ricksteves.com

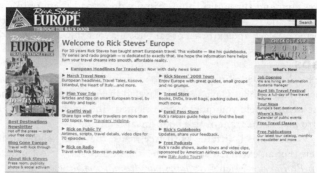

At our travel website, you'll find a wealth of free information on European destinations, including fresh monthly news and helpful tips from thousands of fellow travelers.

Our **online Travel Store** offers travel bags and accessories specially designed by Rick Steves to help you travel smarter and lighter. These include Rick's popular carry-on bags (wheeled and rucksack versions), money belts, totes, toiletries kits, adapters, other accessories, and a wide selection of guidebooks, planning maps, and DVDs.

Choosing the right **railpass** for your trip—amidst hundreds of options—can drive you nutty. We'll help you choose the best pass for your needs, plus give you a bunch of free extras.

Rick Steves' Europe Through the Back Door travel company offers **tours** with more than two-dozen itineraries and about 450 departures reaching the best destinations in this book...and beyond. Our France tours include Paris and the South of France in 15 days, Paris and the Heart of France in 11 days (focusing on the best of the north; a kid-friendly version of this tour is also available), the Best of Paris and London in eight days, and the one-week Paris city tour. You'll enjoy great guides, a fun bunch of travel partners (with small groups of generally around 26), and plenty of room to spread out in a big, comfy bus. You'll find European adventures to fit every vacation length. For all the details, and to get our Tour Catalog and a free Rick Steves Tour Experience DVD (filmed on location during an actual tour), visit www.ricksteves.com or call the Tour Department at 425/608-4217.

what you're reading.

These free tours are available through iTunes and at www.rick steves.com and through iTunes. Simply download them onto your computer and transfer them to your iPod or MP3 player. (Remember to bring a Y-jack and extra set of ear buds for your travel partner.)

Maps

The black-and-white maps in this book, drawn by Dave Hoerlein, are concise and simple. Dave is well-traveled in Paris and has designed these maps to help you quickly get oriented. The color city maps and Métro map at the front of this book are also useful.

While Paris is littered with free maps, they don't show all the streets. For an extended stay, I prefer the pocket-size, street-indexed *Paris Pratique* or Michelin's *Paris par Arrondissement* (each about €6, sold at newsstands and bookstores in Paris). Take a look before you buy to be sure the map has the level of detail you want.

Other Guidebooks

If you're like most travelers, this book is all you need. But if you'll be exploring beyond my recommended neighborhoods and destinations, $25–35 for extra maps and books can be money well-spent. The readable *Paris Access* guide and the more scholarly *Michelin Green Guide* are informative. Also recommended are *Paris: The Collected Traveler* (Barrie Kerper) and *The Paris Mapguide* (Michael Middleditch). Of the multitude of other guidebooks on France and Paris, many are high on facts and low on opinion, guts, or personality.

If you'll be traveling elsewhere in France, consider the 2009 editions of *Rick Steves' France* and *Rick Steves' Provence and the French Riviera*.

Recommended Books and Movies

To get the feel for Paris past and present, consider reading some of these books or seeing these films:

Non-Fiction

For a better understanding of French politics, culture, and people, check out *Sixty Million Frenchmen Can't Be Wrong* (Nadeau and Barlow), *Culture Shock: France* (Taylor), *French or Foe*, and *Savoir-Flair!* (both by Polly Platt). *The Course of French History* (Goubert) provides a basic summary of French history, while *The Cambridge Illustrated History of France* (Jones) comes with coffee-table-book pictures and illustrations.

A Moveable Feast is Ernest Hemingway's classic memoir of 1920s Paris. In *I'll Always Have Paris*, Art Buchwald meets Hemingway, among others. *Suite Francaise* (Nemirovsky) is by a Jewish writer who eloquently describes how life changed after the Nazi occupation. *Is*

Paris Burning? (Collins) brings post-WWII Paris to life on its pages. *Paris Noir: African Americans in the City of Light* (Stovall) explains why African-Americans found Paris so freeing in the first half of the 20th century.

Paris to the Moon is Adam Gopnik's charming collection of stories about life as a New Yorker in Paris (his literary anthology, *Americans in Paris,* is also recommended). *A Corner in the Marais* (Karmel) is a detailed account of one Parisian neighborhood, while Diane Johnson's *Into a Paris Quartier* tells tales about the sixth arrondissement. The memoir *The Piano Shop on the Left Bank* (Carhart) captures Paris' sentimental appeal. *Almost French* (Turnbull) is a funny take on living as a Parisian native. Reading *The Flaneur* is like wandering with author Edmund White through his favorite finds. *The Authentic Bistros of Paris* (Thomazeau), a pretty picture book, will have you longing for a *croque monsieur.* A mix of writers explore Parisian culture in *Travelers Tales: Paris* (O'Reilly).

Fiction

Dickens' *A Tale of Two Cities* shows the pathos and horror of the French Revolution, as does Victor Hugo's *Les Misérables* (his *The Hunchback of Notre-Dame* is also set in Paris).

The anthology *A Place in the World Called Paris* (Barclay) includes essays by literary greats from Truman Capote to Franz Kafka. The characters in Marge Piercy's *City of Darkness, City of Light* storm the Bastille. While it relies on some stereotypes, *A Year in the Merde* (Clarke) is a lighthearted look at life as a *faux* Parisian.

George Simenon was a Belgian, but he often set his *Inspector Maigret* detective series in Paris; *The Hotel Majestic* is particularly good. Mystery fans should also consider *Murder in Montparnasse* (Engel), *Murder in the Marais* (Black), and *Sandman* (Janes), set in Vichy-era Paris.

For kids, there's the beloved *Madeline* series (Bemelmans), where "in an old house in Paris that was covered with vines, lived twelve little girls in two straight lines."

Films

Children of Paradise (1946), a melancholy romance, was filmed during the Nazi occupation of Paris. In *The Red Balloon* (1956), a small boy chases his balloon through the city streets, symbolizing that beauty can be found even in the simplest toy. *The 400 Blows* (1959) and *Jules and Jim* (1962) are both classics of French New Wave cinema by director François Truffaut. *Charade* (1963) combines a romance between Audrey Hepburn and Cary Grant with a crime story.

Blue/White/Red (1990s) is a stylish trilogy of films, each featuring a famous French actress as the lead (*Blue*, with Juliette Binoche, is the best of the three). *Ridicule* (1996), set in the opulent court of Louis

XVI, shows that survival then depended on a quick wit and an acid tongue. In the crime caper *Ronin* (1998), Robert De Niro and Jean Reno lead a car chase through the city.

Moulin Rouge! (2001) is a fanciful musical set in the legendary Montmartre night club. *Amélie* (2001), a crowd-pleasing romance, features a charming young waitress searching for love and the meaning of life. No Disney flick, *The Triplets of Belleville* (2003) is a surreal, creepy-yet-heartwarming animated film about a very Parisian fictional city.

For over-the-top, schlocky fun, watch *The Phantom of the Opera* (2004), about a disfigured musical genius hiding in the Paris Opera House, and *The Da Vinci Code* (2006), a blockbuster murder mystery partly filmed inside the Louvre.

If you'll be heading to Versailles, try *Marie Antoinette* (2006), a delicate little bonbon of a film about the misunderstood queen.

TELEPHONES, EMAIL, AND MAIL

Telephones

Smart travelers learn the phone system and use it daily to reserve or reconfirm rooms, get tourist information, reserve restaurants, confirm tour times, or phone home. When spelling out your name on the phone, you'll find that some letters are pronounced differently in French: *a* is pronounced "ah," *e* is pronounced "eh," and *i* is pronounced "ee." To avoid confusion, say "*a*, Anne," "*e*, euro," and "*i*, Isabelle."

Types of Phones

You'll encounter various kinds of phones in France:

Card-operated phones—in which you insert a locally bought phone card into a public pay phone—are common in Europe.

Coin-operated phones, the original kind of pay phone, are rare in France. (You may see coin-operated phones at gas stations and in big hotel lobbies.)

Hotel-room phones are sometimes cheap for local calls (confirm at the front desk first), but can be a rip-off for long-distance calls ($1–2/ minute unless you use an international phone card—described below). But incoming calls are free, making this a cheap way for friends and family to stay in touch, provided they have a good long-distance plan for calls to Europe.

American mobile phones work in Europe if they're GSM-enabled, tri-band or quad-band, and on a calling plan that includes international calls. They're convenient, but pricey. For example, with a T-Mobile phone, you'll pay $1 per minute for calls and about $0.35 for text messages.

European mobile phones run about $40–75 (for the most basic models) and come without contracts. These phones are loaded with prepaid calling time that you can recharge as you use up the minutes. As long as you're not "roaming" outside the phone's home country, incoming calls are free. On my last trip I bought a good phone for €40 (that came with five minutes of time) and added 30 minutes for €25. For a total of €65, I had more than enough time for making daily calls and receiving calls from home during my three weeks in and around Paris. If you're traveling to multiple countries within Europe, make sure the phone is electronically "unlocked," so that you can swap out its SIM card (a fingernail-sized chip that holds the phone's information) for a new one in other countries. For more information on mobile phones, see www.ricksteves.com /phones.

APPENDIX

Using Phone Cards

Get a phone card for your calls. Prepaid phone cards come in two types: international and insertable (both described below). Look for these cards at any post office and most newsstands and tobacco shops *(tabacs),* which you'll find everywhere, including at train stations and airports.

Both types of phone card work only in France. While traveling in France, you can share either type of card with your companions (and, in the case of an international phone card, your buddy doesn't even need the actual card—just the numbers on it). If you have time left on a card when you leave the country (as you likely will), simply give it to another traveler—anyone can use it.

International phone cards, called *cartes à code international* (cart ah code ahn-tehr-nah-see-oh-nahl) enable you to make calls to the US for as little as three cents per minute. They come with a dial-up code that can be used from nearly any phone, including the one in your hotel room (if it's set on "pulse," switch it to "tone"). Cards are marked as national (for France) or international. All cards work for domestic or international calls, but you get far better rates if you use the card for the purpose it was intended—so if you plan to use your card mostly for calls home, ask for an international card (denominations in €7 and €15 amounts). They're all good values—my €15 international card lasted for four weeks of regular calls home.

These *cartes à code* are simple to use, generally all work the same way, and come with English instructions. Scratch to get your code (though some shops also sell cardless codes, printed right on your receipt). Dial the free number; if the four-digit access code on the card doesn't work from your hotel-room phone, try the card's 10-digit, toll-free code that starts with 08. A voice in French (but sometimes followed by English) tells you to enter your code. Before or after entering your code, you may need to press (or "*touche,*" pronounced toosh) either the pound key (#, *dièse,* dee-ehz) or the star key (*, *étoile,* eh-twahl)—this varies per card. At the next message, dial the number you're calling (possibly followed by pound or star key; you don't have to listen through the entire sales pitch).

Insertable phone cards, called *télécartes* (tay-lay-kart), can only be used at pay phones. While international per-minute rates are much cheaper with an international phone card than with an insertable phone card, the international cards are slower to use (more numbers to dial). Use a *télécarte* for quick local calls from a phone booth. There are two denominations: *une petite* costs about €7.50; *une grande* about €15. While you can use a *télécarte* to call anywhere in the world, it's only a good deal for making local calls.

Using Hotel-Room Phones, VoIP, or US Calling Cards

The best way to call home is to use an international phone card, but here are some other alternatives.

The phone in your **hotel room** is convenient...but expensive. While incoming calls (made by folks back home) can be the cheapest way to keep in touch, charges for *outgoing* calls can be a very unpleasant surprise. Before you dial, get a clear explanation from the hotel staff of the charges, even for local and (supposedly) toll-free calls.

If your family has an inexpensive way to call Europe, either through a long-distance plan or prepaid calling card, have them call you in your hotel room. Give them a list of your hotels' phone numbers before you go. Then, as you travel, send them an email or cell-phone text message, or make a quick pay-phone call to set up a time for them to give you a ring.

If you're traveling with a laptop, consider trying **VoIP (Voice over Internet Protocol).** With VoIP, two computers act as the phones, allowing for a free Internet-based call. The major providers are Skype (www.skype.com) and Google Talk (www.google.com/talk).

US Calling Cards (such as the ones offered by AT&T, MCI, and Sprint) are the worst option. You'll nearly always save a lot of money by paying with a phone card (see above).

How to Dial

Calling from the US to Europe, or vice versa, is simple—once you break the code. The European calling chart on page 544 will walk you through it.

Dialing Within France

France has a direct-dial 10-digit phone system (no area codes). To call anywhere within France, just dial the number. (All Paris numbers start with 01.)

France's toll-free numbers start with 0800 (like US 800 numbers, though in France you don't dial a 1 first). In France, these 0800 numbers—called *numéro vert* (green number)—can be dialed free from any phone without using a phone card. But you can't call France's toll-free numbers from America, nor can you count on reaching America's toll-free numbers from France.

Note that any 08 number that does not have a 00 directly following is a toll call, generally costing €0.10–0.50 per minute.

Dialing Internationally

If you want to make an international call, follow these steps:

Dial the international access code (00 if you're calling from Europe, 011 from the US or Canada). If you see a phone number that begins with +, you have to replace the + with the international access code.

Then dial the country code of the country you're calling (33 for France, or 1 for the US or Canada).

Then dial the local number. If you're calling France, drop the initial zero of the 10-digit number.

So, to call a recommended Parisian hotel from the US, dial 011 (the US international access code), 33 (France's country code), then 1 47 05 49 15. To call my office in Edmonds, Washington, from France, I dial 00 (Europe's international access code), 1 (the US country code), 425 (Edmonds' area code), and 771-8303.

Useful Phone Numbers
Consulates/Embassies

US Consulate and Embassy: tel. 01 43 12 22 22, passport services open Mon–Fri 9.00-12:00, closed Sat–Sun (4 avenue Gabriel, to the left as you face Hôtel Crillon, Mo: Concorde, http://france.us embassy.gov)

Canadian Consulate and Embassy: tel. 01 44 43 29 00, open Mon–Fri 14:30–16:00, closed Sat–Sun (35 avenue Montaigne, Mo: Franklin D. Roosevelt, www.amb-canada.fr)

Australian Consulate: tel. 01 40 59 33 00, Mon–Fri 9:00–12:00 & 14:00–16:00, closed Sat–Sun (4 rue Jean Rey, Mo: Bir-Hakeim, www .france.embassy.gov.au)

Emergency Needs

Police: tel. 17

Emergency Medical Assistance: tel. 15

American Hospital: tel. 01 46 41 25 25 (63 boulevard Victor Hugo, in Neuilly suburb, Mo: Porte Maillot, then bus #82)

Ambulance: tel. 01 45 67 50 50 (message asks for your address and name)

English-Speaking Pharmacy (Pharmacie les Champs): tel. 01 45 62 02 41, open 24 hours every day of the year (84 avenue des Champs-Elysées, Mo: Georges V)

SOS Doctors: tel. 01 47 07 77 77 or 01 48 28 40 04

European Calling Chart

Just smile and dial, using this key:
AC = Area Code, LN = Local Number.

European Country	Calling long distance within ...	Calling from the US or Canada to ...	Calling from a European country to ...
Austria	AC + LN	011 + 43 + AC (without the initial zero) + LN	00 + 43 + AC (without the initial zero) + LN
Belgium	LN	011 + 32 + LN (without initial zero)	00 + 32 + LN (without initial zero)
Bosnia-Herzegovina	AC + LN	011 + 387 + AC (without initial zero) + LN	00 + 387 + AC (without initial zero) + LN
Britain	AC + LN	011 + 44 + AC (without initial zero) + LN	00 + 44 + AC (without initial zero) + LN
Croatia	AC + LN	011 + 385 + AC (without initial zero) + LN	00 + 385 + AC (without initial zero) + LN
Czech Republic	LN	011 + 420 + LN	00 + 420 + LN
Denmark	LN	011 + 45 + LN	00 + 45 + LN
Estonia	LN	011 + 372 + LN	00 + 372 + LN
Finland	AC + LN	011 + 358 + AC (without initial zero) + LN	999 + 358 + AC (without initial zero) + LN
France	LN	011 + 33 + LN (without initial zero)	00 + 33 + LN (without initial zero)
Germany	AC + LN	011 + 49 + AC (without initial zero) + LN	00 + 49 + AC (without initial zero) + LN
Greece	LN	011 + 30 + LN	00 + 30 + LN
Hungary	06 + AC + LN	011 + 36 + AC + LN	00 + 36 + AC + LN
Ireland	AC + LN	011 + 353 + AC (without initial zero) + LN	00 + 353 + AC (without initial zero) + LN

European Country	Calling long distance within …	Calling from the US or Canada to …	Calling from a European country to …
Italy	LN	011 + 39 + LN	00 + 39 + LN
Montenegro	AC + LN	011 + 382 + AC (without initial zero) + LN	00 + 382 + AC (without initial zero) + LN
Netherlands	AC + LN	011 + 31 + AC (without initial zero) + LN	00 + 31 + AC (without initial zero) + LN
Norway	LN	011 + 47 + LN	00 + 47 + LN
Poland	LN	011 + 48 + LN (without initial zero)	00 + 48 + LN (without initial zero)
Portugal	LN	011 + 351 + LN	00 + 351 + LN
Slovakia	AC + LN	011 + 421 + AC (without initial zero) + LN	00 + 421 + AC (without initial zero) + LN
Slovenia	AC + LN	011 + 386 + AC (without initial zero) + LN	00 + 386 + AC (without initial zero) + LN
Spain	LN	011 + 34 + LN	00 + 34 + LN
Sweden	AC + LN	011 + 46 + AC (without Initial zero) + LN	00 + 46 + AC (without initial zero) + LN
Switzerland	LN	011 + 41 + LN (without initial zero)	00 + 41 + LN (without initial zero)
Turkey	AC (if no initial zero is included, add one) + LN	011 + 90 + AC (without initial zero) + LN	00 + 90 + AC (without initial zero) + LN

APPENDIX

- The instructions above apply whether you're calling a land line or mobile phone.
- The international access codes (the first numbers you dial when making an international call) are 011 if you're calling from the US or Canada, or 00 if you're calling from virtually anywhere in Europe (except Finland, where it's 999).
- To call the US or Canada from Europe, dial 00, then 1 (the country code for the US and Canada), then the area code and number. In short, 00 + 1 + AC + LN = Hi, Mom!

SOS Help: tel. 01 46 21 46 46 (anonymous telephone hotline with crisis/suicide prevention listening service in English, daily 15:00–23:00)
Chiropractic Centers: tel. 01 43 54 26 25 or 01 43 87 81 62
Lost Property (Bureau des Objets Trouvés, at police station): tel. 08 21 00 25 25, €0.12/min, open Tue and Thu 8:30–20:00 (36 rue des Morillons, Mo: Convention)

Travel Advisories
US Department of State: tel. 202/647-5225, www.travel.state.gov
Canadian Department of Foreign Affairs: Canadian tel. 800-267-6788, www.dfait-maeci.gc.ca
US Centers for Disease Control and Prevention: tel. 877-FYI-TRIP, www.cdc.gov/travel

Directory Assistance
Directory Assistance for Paris and France (some English spoken): tel. 12
Collect Calls to the US: tel. 00 00 11

Tourist Info, Transportation, and Banking
Paris Tourist Information: tel. 08 92 68 30 00 (recorded info with long menu, €0.34/min)
Ile de France Tourist Information (covers Paris area, including Fontainebleau, Vaux-le-Vicomte, and Chantilly): tel. 01 42 60 28 62
Booking Service (for hotels, transportation, restaurants, and other tourist activities): tel. 01 53 62 02 29 for **Paris Concierge Services** (111 avenue Victor Hugo, www.pariswebservices.com, contactpws@pariswebservices.com, helpful Gérard)

Airports
Charles de Gaulle and Orly: tel. 3950 (€0.34/min), www.adp.fr
Beauvais: tel. 08 92 68 20 66, www.aeroportbeauvais.com

Airlines
The following 08 numbers are toll calls; the per-minute fee generally ranges from €0.10–0.50.
Aer Lingus: tel. 08 21 23 02 67
Air Canada: tel. 08 25 88 29 00
Air France: tel. 08 20 82 08 20 or 08 20 82 36 54
Alitalia: tel. 08 20 31 53 15
American Airlines: tel. 01 55 17 43 41
Austrian Airlines: tel. 08 02 81 68 16
BMI British Midlands: tel. 08 90 71 00 81
British Airways: tel. 08 25 82 54 00
Continental: tel. 01 71 23 03 35
Delta: tel. 08 11 64 00 05

Easy Jet: tel. 08 26 10 33 20
Iberia: tel. 08 25 80 09 65
Icelandair: tel. 01 44 51 60 51
KLM: tel. 08 90 71 07 10
Lufthansa: tel. 08 26 10 33 34
Northwest: tel. 08 90 71 07 10
Olympic: tel. 01 44 94 58 58
Royal Air Maroc: tel. 08 20 82 18 21
SAS: tel. 08 25 32 53 35
Swiss: tel. 08 20 04 05 06
United: tel. 08 10 72 72 72
US Airways: tel. 08 10 63 22 22

Hotel Chains

Huge Chain of Hotels: www.accorhotels.com (handles Ibis, Mercure, and Novotel hotels); US tel. 800-515-5679
Ibis Hotels: www.ibishotel.com, tel. 08 92 68 66 86; from US, dial 011 33 8 92 68 66 86 (message tells you to push the star button).
Mercure Hotels: www.mercure.com, toll tel. 08 25 88 33 33; US tel. 800-221-4542
Kyriad Hotels: www.kyriad.com, tel. 08 25 02 80 38; from US, dial 011 33 1 64 62 59 70
Best Western Hotels: www.bestwestern.com, tel. 08 00 90 44 90; US tel. 800-780-7324
Country Home Rental: www.gites-de-france.fr/eng or www.gite.com

Youth Hostels

Hostelling International, US Office: www.hiayh.org
Hostelling International, Canada Office: www.hostellingintl.ca

English-Language Churches in Paris

American Church (interdenominational): tel. 01 40 62 05 00, reception open Mon–Sat 9:30–13:00 & 14:00–22:30, Sun 9:00–14:00 & 15:00–19:00 (65 quai d'Orsay, Mo: Invalides, www.acparis.org; for more information, see page 24)
American Cathedral (Episcopalian): tel. 01 53 23 84 00 (23 avenue George V, Mo. George V, www.americancathedral.org)
Unitarian Universalist Fellowship: tel. 01 30 82 75 33 (7 bis rue du Pasteur Wagner, Mo: Bastille, www.uufp.info)
Scots Kirk (Church of Scotland): tel. 01 48 78 47 94 (17 rue Bayard, Mo: Franklin D. Roosevelt, www.scotskirkparis.com)
St. George's Anglican Church: tel. 01 47 20 22 51 (7 rue Auguste Vacquerie, www.stgeorgesparis.com)
St. Joseph's Church (Roman Catholic): tel. 01 42 27 28 56 (50 avenue Hoche, www.stjoeparis.org)

The Language Barrier and That French Attitude

You've no doubt heard that Parisians are "mean and cold and refuse to speak English." This is an out-of-date preconception left over from the days of Charles de Gaulle. Parisians are as friendly as any other people, and no more disagreeable than New Yorkers. Like many big cities, Paris is a massive melting pot of international cultures; your evening hotel receptionist is just as likely to speak French with an accent as not. Without any doubt, Parisians speak more English than Americans speak French. Be reasonable in your expectations: Waiters are paid to be efficient, not chatty. And Parisian postal clerks are every bit as speedy, cheery, and multilingual as ours are back home.

The biggest mistake most Americans make when traveling in France is trying to do too much with limited time. Hurried, impatient travelers who miss the subtle pleasures of people-watching from a sun-dappled café often misinterpret French attitudes. By slowing your pace and making an effort to understand French culture, you're much more likely to have a richer experience. With five weeks' paid time off each year, your hosts can't comprehend why anyone would rush through a vacation.

Parisians take great pride in their customs, clinging to their belief in cultural superiority. Let's face it: It's tough to keep on smiling when you've been crushed by a Big Mac, Mickey-Moused by Disney, and drowned in instant coffee. Your hosts are cold only if you decide to see them that way. Polite and formal, the

St. Michael's Church (Anglican): tel. 01 47 42 70 88 (5 rue d'Aguesseau, Mo: Concorde or Madeleine)

Multi-Subject Classes in English
WICE: tel. 01 45 66 75 50, offers a variety of well-run short- and longer-term classes in English on art, food, and more (20 boulevard du Montparnasse, www.wice-paris.org)

French-Language Classes
Ecole France Langue: tel. 01 45 00 40 15, provides intensive classes on weekly basis with business-language options (www.france-langue.fr)
Institut Parisien: tel. 01 40 56 09 53, offers general conversational courses (www.institut-parisien.com)
OISE: tel. 01 42 22 01 98, has total-immersion French classes (www.oise.com/paris)
Le Français Face à Face: tel. 02 40 71 99 47, runs intensive French courses with total immersion and full-board options (www.lefrancais faceaface.com)

French respect the fine points of culture and tradition. In Paris, strolling down the street with a big grin on your face and saying hello to strangers is a sign of senility, not friendliness (seriously). Parisians think that Americans, while friendly, are hesitant to pursue more serious friendships. Recognize sincerity and look for kindness. Give them the benefit of the doubt.

Communication difficulties are exaggerated. To hurdle the language barrier, bring a phrase book (or use the French Survival Phrases—see page 559), a small English/French dictionary, a menu reader, and a good supply of patience. In transactions, a small notepad and pen minimize misunderstandings about prices; have vendors write the price down.

If you learn only five phrases, learn and use these: *bonjour* (good day), *pardon* (pardon me), *s'il vous plaît* (please), *merci* (thank you), and *au revoir* (goodbye). The French place great importance on politeness. Begin every encounter with *"Bonjour, madame/monsieur,"* or *"s'il vous plaît"* and end every encounter with *"Au revoir, madame/monsieur."*

The French are language perfectionists—they take their language (and other languages) seriously. Often they speak more English than they let on. This isn't a tourist-baiting tactic, but timidity on their part to speak another language less than fluently. Start any conversation with, *"Bonjour, madame/monsieur. Parlez-vous anglais?"* and hope they speak more English than you speak French.

Cooking Schools
These schools have demonstration courses.
Le Cordon Bleu: tel. 01 53 68 22 50 (8 Rue Léon Delhomme, www.lcbparis.com)
Ritz Escoffier Ecole de Gastronomie: tel. 01 43 16 30 50 (15 place Vendôme, Mo: Madeleine, www.ritzparis.com)
Ecole Superieure de Cuisine Francaise: tel. 01 45 27 09 09 (www.escf.ccip.fr)

Wine Tasting
Ô Château: tel 08 00 80 11 48 (fun and informative, €20 one-hour class, €65 for wine-and-cheese lunch, at private apartment in Paris, www.o-chateau.com, young and enthusiastic Olivier Magny)

Email and Mail
Email: Many travelers set up a free email account with Yahoo, Microsoft (Hotmail), or Google (Gmail). Email use among European hoteliers is quite common.

In Paris you'll find plenty of coffee shops offering wireless connections (Wi-Fi, pronounced "wee-fee" by the French) to travelers with laptop computers. Little hole-in-the-wall Internet-access shops, while common in the rest of Europe, are not prevalent in France. Post offices are a good solution in smaller towns offering Internet access *(cyberposte)*; buy a chip-card (for about same prices as phone cards) and you're in business.

More and more hotels now offer their guests Internet access in their lobbies from a terminal (which may be free or operated with coins or a telephone card); the access is usually slow, though you'll probably be slow, too, getting used to a French keyboard. Every year, more hotels offer Wi-Fi (usually free, sometimes for a charge). And some even have laptop loaners. Ask if your hotel has access. If it doesn't, your hotelier will direct you to the nearest place to get online. Given the number of locations currently offering free Wi-Fi in Paris, you should not have to pay to get online.

Mail: French post offices are sometimes called PTT, for "Post, Telegraph, and Telephone"—look for signs for *La Poste*. Hours vary, though most are open weekdays 8:00–19:00 and Saturday morning 8:00–12:00. Stamps and phone cards are also sold at *tabac* (tobacco) shops. It costs about €1 to mail a postcard to the US. While you can arrange for mail delivery to your hotel (allow 10 days for a letter to arrive), phoning and emailing are so easy that I've dispensed with mail stops altogether. Federal Express makes pricey two-day deliveries.

One convenient, if pricey, way to send packages home is by using the PTT's Colissimo XL postage-paid mailing box. It costs about €33 for the International version, which allows you to send home all the goodies you can stuff into an 18" × 12" × 8" box (no weight limit).

HOLIDAYS AND FESTIVALS

Holidays and Festivals in Paris

Paris is lively with festivals throughout the summer and fall. Kicking off the season in late May is the month-long **Festival of St. Denis** in that Parisian suburb, featuring musicians from around the world at various venues (tel. 01 48 13 06 07, www.festival-saint-denis.fr).

Paris celebrates the solstice (June 21) with its **Music Festival** (Fête de la Musique), with concerts throughout the city.

On July 26, the **Tour de France** bicycle race ends on the Champs-Elysées (www.letour.fr). **Bastille Day,** France's National Day (July 14), brings fireworks, dancing, and revelry countrywide (see sidebar on page 266).

From mid-July to mid-August, the **Paris Neighborhoods Festival** features theater, dance, and concerts around the city. At the same time,

2 0 0 9

JANUARY

S	M	T	W	T	F	S
				1	2	3
4	5	6	7	8	9	10
11	12	13	14	15	16	17
18	19	20	21	22	23	24
25	26	27	28	29	30	31

FEBRUARY

S	M	T	W	T	F	S
1	2	3	4	5	6	7
8	9	10	11	12	13	14
15	16	17	18	19	20	21
22	23	24	25	26	27	28

MARCH

S	M	T	W	T	F	S
1	2	3	4	5	6	7
8	9	10	11	12	13	14
15	16	17	18	19	20	21
22	23	24	25	26	27	28
29	30	31				

APRIL

S	M	T	W	T	F	S
			1	2	3	4
5	6	7	8	9	10	11
12	13	14	15	16	17	18
19	20	21	22	23	24	25
26	27	28	29	30		

MAY

S	M	T	W	T	F	S
					1	2
3	4	5	6	7	8	9
10	11	12	13	14	15	16
17	18	19	20	21	22	23
24/31	25	26	27	28	29	30

JUNE

S	M	T	W	T	F	S
	1	2	3	4	5	6
7	8	9	10	11	12	13
14	15	16	17	18	19	20
21	22	23	24	25	26	27
28	29	30				

JULY

S	M	T	W	T	F	S
			1	2	3	4
5	6	7	8	9	10	11
12	13	14	15	16	17	18
19	20	21	22	23	24	25
26	27	28	29	30	31	

AUGUST

S	M	T	W	T	F	S
						1
2	3	4	5	6	7	8
9	10	11	12	13	14	15
16	17	18	19	20	21	22
23/30	24/31	25	26	27	28	29

SEPTEMBER

S	M	T	W	T	F	S
		1	2	3	4	5
6	7	8	9	10	11	12
13	14	15	16	17	18	19
20	21	22	23	24	25	26
27	28	29	30			

OCTOBER

S	M	T	W	T	F	S
				1	2	3
4	5	6	7	8	9	10
11	12	13	14	15	16	17
18	19	20	21	22	23	24
25	26	27	28	29	30	31

NOVEMBER

S	M	T	W	T	F	S
1	2	3	4	5	6	7
8	9	10	11	12	13	14
15	16	17	18	19	20	21
22	23	24	25	26	27	28
29	30					

DECEMBER

S	M	T	W	T	F	S
		1	2	3	4	5
6	7	8	9	10	11	12
13	14	15	16	17	18	19
20	21	22	23	24	25	26
27	28	29	30	31		

the fun **Paris Plage,** a riverside ersatz beach, is set up in the middle of the city (see page 45).

La Villette Jazz Festival brings a week of outdoor jazz concerts to this Parisian park in early- to mid-September. The first Saturday of October, Montmartre celebrates the **grape harvest** with a parade and festivities. The **Festival of Autumn** (www.festival-automne.com) runs through autumn, with theater, dance, film, and opera performances.

For more information, you can contact the France TI (listed at the beginning of the appendix) and visit the websites www.parisinfo.com and www.franceguide.com.

French Holidays in 2009

These national holidays (when many sights close) are observed throughout France. Note that this isn't a complete list; holidays can strike without warning.

Jan 1	New Year's Day
Jan 6	Epiphany
April 12	Easter Sunday
May 1	Labor Day and
May 8	V-E Day
May 21	Ascension
May 31	Pentecost
July 14	Bastille Day
Aug 15	Assumption of Mary
Nov 1	All Saints' Day
Nov 11	Armistice Day
Dec 25	Christmas Day

CONVERSIONS AND CLIMATE

Numbers and Stumblers

- Europeans write a few of their numbers differently than we do. 1 = 1, 4 = 4, 7 = 7.
- In Europe, dates appear as day/month/year, so Christmas is 25/12/09.
- Commas are decimal points and decimals commas. A dollar and a half is 1,50, and there are 5.280 feet in a mile.
- When pointing, use your whole hand, palm down.
- When counting with fingers, start with your thumb. If you hold up your first finger to request one item, you'll probably get two.
- What Americans call the second floor of a building is the first floor in Europe.
- On escalators and moving sidewalks, Europeans keep the left "lane" open for passing. Keep to the right.

Metric Conversions (approximate)

1 foot = 0.3 meter	1 square yard = 0.8 square meter
1 yard = 0.9 meter	1 square mile = 2.6 square kilometers
1 mile = 1.6 kilometers	1 ounce = 28 grams
1 centimeter = 0.4 inch	1 quart = 0.95 liter
1 meter = 39.4 inches	1 kilogram = 2.2 pounds
1 kilometer = 0.62 mile	32°F = 0°C

Clothing Sizes

When shopping for clothing, use these US-to-France comparisons as general guidelines (but note that no conversion is exact).

- Women's dresses and blouses: Add 30 (US size 10 = French size 40)
- Men's suits and jackets: Add 10 (US size 40 regular = French size 50)

- Men's shirts: Multiply by 2 and add about 8 (US size 15 collar = French size 38)
- Women's shoes: Add about 31 (US size 8 = French size 39)
- Men's shoes: Add 32–34 (US size 9 = French size 43; US size 11 = French size 45)

Paris' Climate

First line, average daily high; second line, average daily low; third line, days of no rain. For more detailed weather statistics for destinations in this book (as well as the rest of the world), check www .worldclimate.com.

J	F	M	A	M	J	J	A	S	O	N	D
43°	45°	54°	60°	68°	73°	76°	75°	70°	60°	50°	44°
34°	34°	39°	43°	49°	55°	58°	58°	53°	46°	40°	36°
14	14	19	17	19	18	19	18	17	18	15	15

Temperature Conversion:

Fahrenheit and Celsius

Europe takes its temperature using the Celsius scale, while we opt for Fahrenheit. For a rough conversion from Celsius to Fahrenheit, double the number and add 30. For weather, remember that 28°C is 82°F—perfect. For health, 37°C is just right.

Essential Packing Checklist

Whether you're traveling for five days or five weeks, here's what you'll need to bring. Remember to pack light to enjoy the sweet freedom of true mobility. Happy travels!

- ❏ 5 shirts
- ❏ 1 sweater or lightweight fleece jacket
- ❏ 2 pairs pants
- ❏ 1 pair shorts
- ❏ 1 swimsuit (women only—men can use shorts)
- ❏ 5 pairs underwear and socks
- ❏ 1 pair shoes
- ❏ 1 rain-proof jacket
- ❏ Tie or scarf
- ❏ Money belt
- ❏ Money—your mix of:
    - ❏ Debit card for ATM withdrawals
    - ❏ Credit card
    - ❏ Hard cash in US dollars
- ❏ Documents (and back-up photocopies)
- ❏ Passport
- ❏ Airplane ticket
- ❏ Driver's license
- ❏ Student ID and hostel card
- ❏ Railpass/car rental voucher
- ❏ Insurance details
- ❏ Daypack
- ❏ Sealable plastic baggies
- ❏ Camera and related gear
- ❏ Empty water bottle
- ❏ Wristwatch and alarm clock
- ❏ Earplugs
- ❏ First-aid kit
- ❏ Medicine (labeled)
- ❏ Extra glasses/contacts and prescriptions
- ❏ Sunscreen and sunglasses
- ❏ Toiletries kit
- ❏ Soap
- ❏ Laundry soap (if liquid and carry-on, limit to 3 oz.)
- ❏ Clothesline
- ❏ Small towel
- ❏ Sewing kit
- ❏ Travel information
- ❏ Necessary map(s)
- ❏ Address list (email and mailing addresses)
- ❏ Postcards and photos from home
- ❏ Notepad and pen
- ❏ Journal

Hotel Reservation

To: _____   _____
               hotel   *email or fax*

From: _____   _____
               name   *email or fax*

Today's date: _____ / _____ / _____
                         day   *month*   *year*

Dear Hotel _____ ,
Please make this reservation for me:

Name: _____

Total # of people: _____   # of rooms: _____   # of nights: _____

Arriving: _____ / _____ / _____   My time of arrival (24-hr clock): _____
                 day   *month*   *year*   (I will telephone if I will be late)

Departing: ____ / ____ / ____
                  day   *month*   *year*

Room(s): Single ___   Double ___   Twin ___   Triple ___   Quad ___

With: Toilet ___   Shower ___   Bath ___   Sink only ___

Special needs: View ___   Quiet ___   Cheapest ___   Ground Floor ___

Please email or fax confirmation of my reservation, along with the type of
room reserved and the price. Please also inform me of your cancellation
policy. After I hear from you, I will quickly send my credit-card information
as a deposit to hold the room. Thank you.

_____
Name

_____
Address

_____
City   *State*   *Zip Code*   *Country*

*Before hoteliers can make your reservation, they want to know the informa-
tion listed above. You can use this form as the basis for your email, or you can
photocopy this page, fill in the information, and send it as a fax (also available
online at www.ricksteves.com/reservation).*

French Pronunciation Guide for Paris

Nasalize the underlined "n" if you can (let the sound come through your nose).

Arc de Triomphe
  ark duh tree-oh<u>n</u>f

arrondissement
  ah-roh<u>n</u>-dees-moh<u>n</u>

Art Nouveau art noo-voh

Auvers-sur-Oise
  oh-vehr-sur-wahz

Bateaux Mouches
  bah-toh moosh

Bon Marché boh<u>n</u> mar-chay

boulangerie
  boo-lah<u>n</u>-zheh-ree

Carnavalet kar-nah-val-eh

Champ de Mars shah<u>n</u> duh mar

Champs-Elysées
  shah<u>n</u>-zay-lee-zay

Chantilly shah<u>n</u>-tee-yee

charcuterie shar-koo-tuh-ree

Chartres shar-truh

château(x) shah-toh

Cité see-tay

Cité des Sciences
  see-tay day see-ah<u>n</u>s

Conciergerie
  kon-see-ehr-zhuh-ree

Contrescarpe koh<u>n</u>-truh-scarp

droguerie droh-guh-ree

Ecole Militaire
  eh-kohl mee-lee-tehr

Egouts ay-goo

Fauchon foh-shoh<u>n</u>

Fontainebleau foh<u>n</u>-tehn-bloh

fromagerie froh-mah-zhuh-ree

Galeries Lafayette
  gah-luh-ree lah-fay-yet

gare gar

Gare d'Austerlitz
  gar doh-stehr-leets

Gare de l'Est gar duh lest

Gare de Lyon gar duh lee-oh<u>n</u>

Gare du Nord gar dew nor

Gare St. Lazare
  gar sah<u>n</u> lah-zar

Garnier gar-nee-ay

Giverny zhee-vehr-nee

Grand Palais grah<u>n</u> pah-lay

Grande Arche de la Défense
  grah<u>n</u>d arsh duh lah
  day-fah<u>n</u>s

Hôtel de Sully
  oh-tehl duh soo-lee

Hôtel Salé oh-tehl sah-lay

Ile de la Cité
  eel duh lah see-tay

Ile St. Louis eel sah<u>n</u> loo-ee

Jacquemart-André
  zhahk-mar-ah<u>n</u>-dray

jardin zhar-da<u>n</u>

Jardin des Plantes
  zhar-da<u>n</u> day plahnt

Jeu de Paume juh duh pohm

La Madeleine
  lah mah-duh-lehn

La Marseillaise
  lah mar-seh-yehz

Le Hameau luh ah-moh

Les Halles lay ahl

Les Invalides lay-za<u>n</u>-vah-leed

Loire lwar

L'Orangerie loh-rah<u>n</u>-zhuh-ree

Louvre loov-ruh

Marais mah-ray

marché aux puces
  mar-chay oh poos

Marmottan mar-moh-tah<u>n</u>

Métro may-troh

Monge moh<u>n</u>zh

Montmartre moh<u>n</u>-mart

Montparnasse moh<u>n</u>-par-nas

Moulin Rouge moo-la<u>n</u> roozh

musée mew-zay

Musée de l'Armée
mew-zay duh lar-may

Musée d'Orsay
mew-zay dor-say

Notre-Dame noh-truh-dahm

orangerie oh-rahn-zhuh-ree

Orsay or-say

palais pah-lay

Palais de Justice
pah-lay duh zhew-stees

Palais Garnier
pah-lay gar-nee-ay

Palais Royal pah-lay roh-yahl

Parc de la Villette
park duh la vee-leht

Parc Monceau park mohn-soh

Père Lachaise pehr lah-shehz

Petit Palais puh-tee pah-lay

Pigalle pee-gahl

place plahs

Place Dauphine
plahs doh-feen

Place de la Bastille
plahs duh lah bah-steel

Place de la Concorde
plahs duh lah kohn-kord

Place de la République
plahs duh lah ray-poo-bleek

Place des Vosges
plahs day vohzh

Place du Tertre
plahs dew tehr-truh

Place St. André-des-Arts
plahs sahn tahn-dray
day zart

Place Vendôme
plahs vahn-dohm

Pompidou pohn-pee-doo

pont pohn

Pont Alexandre III
pohn ah-leks-ahn-druh twah

Pont Neuf pohn nuhf

Promenade Plantée
proh-mehn-ahd plahn-tay

quai kay

Rive Droite reeve dwaht

Rive Gauche reeve gohsh

Rodin roh-dan

rue rew

Rue Cler rew klehr

Rue Daguerre rew dah-gehr

Rue des Rosiers
rew day roz-ee-ay

Rue Montorgueil
rew mohn-tor-goy

Rue Mouffetard rew moof-tar

Rue de Rivoli
rew duh ree-voh-lee

Sacré-Cœur sah-kray-koor

Sainte-Chapelle
sahnt-shah-pehl

Seine sehn

Sèvres-Babylone
seh-vruh-bah-bee-lohn

Sorbonne sor-buhn

St. Germain-des-Prés
sahn zhehr-man-day-pray

St. Julien-le-Pauvre
sahn zhew-lee-an-luh-
poh-vruh

St. Séverin sahn say-vuh-ran

St. Sulpice sahn sool-pees

Tour Eiffel toor ee-fehl

Trianon tree-ahn-ohn

Trocadéro troh-kah-day-roh

Tuileries twee-lay-ree

Vaux-le-Vicomte
voh-luh-vee-kohnt

Venus de Milo
vuh-news duh mee-loh

Versailles vehr-"sigh"

INDEX

A

Abélard, Peter: 318–319
Abstract art: 278–279
Abstract expressionism: 283–284
Abstract surrealists: 282
Airfare: 3
Airlines: carry-on restrictions, 5;
 phone numbers, 546–547
Airports: Beauvais Airport, 439,
 546; Charles de Gaulle, 433–437;
 Charles de Gaulle Airport, 546;
 connecting to, 439–440; Orly
 Airport, 437–439, 546; tourist
 information (ADP), 23
American Church and Franco-
 American Center: 24
Apartments: 343. *See also* Sleeping
Apollo Gallery, Louvre Museum:
 110
Aquaboulevard: 406
Arc de Triomphe: 42, 60–61, 62,
 251, 252–256, 404, 425
Arcaded shopping streets: 419–420
Archaeological sights: 44, 76, 79
Arearea (Gauguin): 148–149
Army Museum: general information,
 194–195; hours, 42; Louis XIV
 to Napoleon III (East Wing),
 213–216; overview, 196–197; tour,
 200–216; World War I Wing,
 200–204; World War II Wing,
 204–213. *See also* Napoleon's
 Tomb
Arrondissements: 17–18. *See also*
 Neighborhoods
Art galleries: 424
Art Nouveau: 153–154
Assyria: 125, 127
ATMs: 8–9. *See also* Debit cards
Au Lapin Agile Cabaret: 331
Audioguides: 76, 536–538; Chartres
 Cathedral, 483; Rodin Museum,
 183; Versailles, 460–461
Auvers-sur-Oise: 522–525

B

Back Door travel philosophy: 16
Bakeries: 170, 330
Balzac (Rodin): 191

Bargains: 8
Bastille: 68, 290–291. *See also* Place
 de la Bastille
Bastille Day: 266
Beach: 45–46
Beauvais Airport: 439, 546
Bernhardt, Sarah: 321
Bikes: 33; tours, 36–37
The Birth of Venus (Cabanel): 134
Boat cruises/tours: 34–35, 404;
 nightlife, 425
Bonaparte, Louis-Napoleon
 (Napoleon III): 298–299
Bonaparte, Napoleon: 198, 295
Booking service: 546
Books: 538–539
Bookstores: 25–26; Fontainebleau,
 516; Left Bank booksellers,
 86–87, 409; Marais, 353;
 Shakespeare and Company, 76
Boulangeries: 170, 330
Boules: 346
Boulevard du Montparnasse:
 397–399
Boulevard St. Germain: 221
Boulevard St. Michel: 89
Bouquinistes: 409. *See also*
 Bookstores
Brancusi, Constantin: 279
Braque, Georges: 275–276
Bridges: Pont des Arts, 234; Pont
 Neuf, 99
The Burghers of Calais (Rodin): 192
Bus routes: Marais, 353–355; Rue
 Cler neighborhood, 346
Buses: 30–32, 452–453; tours, 33–34,
 217–224, 427
Business hours: 7
Byzantine antiquities: 248

C

Cabaret: 423
Cabaret de Patachou: 328
Café des Deux Moulins: 334
Café du Marché: 169–170
Café La Palette: 237
Café le Procope: 239
Café Roussillon: 165
Cafés: 372–374, 397–400

Cain: 152

Car rental: 5, 501. *See also* Driving

The Card Players (Cézanne): 147

Carnavalet Museum: 70, 263, 268; general information, 286–287; hours, 43; tour, 287–300

Catacombs: 59–60

The Cathedral of Rouen (Monet): 142–143

Celebrities of the Happy Medium (Daumier): 135–136

Cézanne, Paul: 160; Orsay Museum, 146–147

Chagall, Marc: 276–277

Champ de Mars: 218–220, 403

Champagne tours: 507–508

Champs-Elysées: 18, 43, 60, 399, 404, 425; eating, 254, 257–258; and nearby, 60–67; shopping, 257, 258–259; walking tour, 251–262

Chantilly: 516–518

Charcuterie: 169

Charles de Gaulle Airport: 433–437, 546

Charles X: 297

Chartres Cathedral: eating, 498–499; general information, 482–486; labyrinth, 488; map, 496; Mary's veil, 492; sleeping, 497–498; stained glass, 488–491; timeline, 484–485; tour, 486–495; tours, 483; town, 495–497

Chateaux: 511; Chantilly, 516–518; Fontainebleau, 515–516; Vaux-le-Vicomte, 512–514

Cheese shops: 167–168

Children, traveling with: books, 402–403; general information, 401–402; sightseeing, 403–406

Chocolate: 170

Chopin, Frédéric: 317–318

The Church at Auvers-sur-Oise (Van Gogh): 145

Church of St. Pierre-de-Montmartre: 327–328

Churches: Chartres Cathedral, 482–499; Church of St. Pierre-de-Montmartre, 327–328; Notre-Dame Cathedral, 41–44, 62, 74–76, 79–84, 404, 425–426; phone numbers, 547–548; Reims Cathedral, 502–505; Sacré-Cœur, 43, 63, 71, 324, 326–327; Sainte-Chapelle, 42, 45, 76, 91–96; St.

Germain-des-Prés, 54, 233, 239–240; St. Séverin, 88; St. Sulpice Church, 54–55, 56, 234, 240–242; typical medieval church, 528

Cité Métropolitain Stop and Flower Market: 45, 96–97

City info post: 171

Classes: 548

Climate: 4, 553

Clos Montmartre Vineyard: 331

Clothing sizes: 552–553

The Clownesse Cha-U-Kao (Toulouse-Lautrec): 149

Cluny Museum: general information, 54, 244; hours, 43; tour, 245–250

Colette: 319

Communards' Wall: 314

Concerts and operas: 423–424

Concierge services: 546

Conciergerie: 45, 76, 97–98

Conservative art: 133–135

Consulates: 543

Contemporary art: 284–285

Cooking schools: 549

The Coronation of Napoleon (David): 117–118

Costs: 3–4

Credit cards: 5, 9; lost cards, 10

Cubism: 275–276, 303–304

Customs: 12

D

The Da Vinci Code: 56, 241

Dada: 281

Dalí, Salvador: 281–282

Dalí Museum: 71, 324, 329–330

Dance at the Moulin de la Galette (Renoir): 141–142

The Dance Class (Degas): 140

David, Jacques-Louis: 320

Day trips: 37; Auvers-sur-Oise, 522–525; Chantilly, 516–518; Chartres Cathedral, 482–499; Disneyland Paris, 525–526; Fontainebleau, 515–516; Giverny, 518–522; grand chateaux near Paris, 511; Reims, 500–510; Vaux-le-Vicomte, 512–514; Versailles, 456–481

De Gaulle, Charles: 205

Debit cards: 5, 9; lost cards, 10. *See also* ATMs

Declaration of the Rights of Man and the Citizen: 292

Decorative art: 282

Delacroix, Eugène: 320
Delacroix Museum: 55–57, 237–238;
   general information, 233
Delaunay, Robert: 280
Delaunay, Sonia: 280
Department stores: 408–410
Deportation Memorial: 44, 76,
   85–86
Derain, Andre: 162
Design: 279
Dining Room of Adrien Benard
   (Charpentier): 153
Dinner cruises: 396
Directory assistance: 546
Disneyland Paris: 525–526
The Dream: 152
Driving: car rental, 5; map, 453;
   parking, 26, 453–454
Duchamp, Marcel: 281

E
Eating: Auvers-sur-Oise, 524;
   breakfast, 370–371; cafés, 372–
   374, 397–400; Champs-Elysées,
   257–258; Chartres Cathedral,
   498–499; dinner cruises, 396;
   elsewhere, 395–396; general
   information, 370; Giverny, 521; Ile
   St. Louis, 390–392; Luxembourg
   Garden area, 392–395; Marais
   area, 385–390; near the Champs-
   Elysées, 254; Parisian cuisine,
   376–379; picnics and snacks,
   371–372; regional cuisine, 376–
   377; Reims, 509–510; restaurant
   phrases, 560; restaurants,
   374–376, 380–396; Rue Cler area,
   380–385; sandwiches, quiche, and
   pizza, 372; tipping, 10–11, 374;
   Versailles, 481
Ebih-il, the Superintendent of Mari:
   122–123
Eiffel Tower; 62; with children,
   403; general information, 50;
   neighborhood, 18; at night, 425;
   sightseeing tour, 218–220; tour,
   172–182
Electricity: 8
Email: 549–550
Embassies: 543
Emergencies: 6, 543–546
Entertainment costs: 4
Equestrian Performance Academy:
   474

Esplanade des Invalides: 220–221
European calling chart: 544–545
Eurostar trains: 451–452
Exchange rate: 10
*The Excommunication of Robert le
   Pieux*: 152
Excursions from Paris: 37
Expressionism: 280

F
Fat Tire Bike Tours: 33
Fees: credit and debit card, 9
Ferries: 452
Festivals: 550–551
Films: 539–540
Fish markets: 168
Flea markets: 416–418
Fontainebleau: 515–516
Fragonard Perfume Museum: 64
François I: 287–288
French Neoclassical art: 117–119
Fromageries: 167–168

G
Galeries Lafayette: 63
Gallery of Marbles: 193
Gare d'Austerlitz: 449–450
Gare de l'Est: 448
Gare de Lyon: 399–400, 447–448;
   tourist information offices (TIs),
   23
Gare d'Orsay: 132–133. *See also*
   Orsay Museum
Gare du Nord: 442–445; tourist
   information offices (TIs), 23
Gare Montparnasse: 445–447
Gare St. Lazare: 448–449
The Gates of Hell (Rodin): 154,
   192–193
Géricault, Théodore: 320
Giacometti, Alberto: 283
Giverny: 518–522
The Gleaners (Millet): 136
Government buildings: 221
Grand Palais: 66, 259–260
Greek art: 105–108
Gudea, Prince of Lagash: 123
Guidebooks: 536, 538; updates, 6
Guillaume, Paul: 161

H
Haussmann, Georges-Eugène,
   Baron: 64, 298, 321–322
Héloïse: 318–319

Henry IV: 288; statue of, 99
History: Eiffel Tower, 177–178, 179; French, 527–531; Italian Renaissance, 115; of Paris, 78
Holidays: 3, 550–552
Holocaust Memorial: 70, 265, 270–271
Honoré de Balzac (Rodin): 154
Hostels: 342; phone numbers, 547. *See also* Sleeping
Hôtel Concorde-Lafayette: 63, 66
Hôtel de Sully: 267
Hotels: 339–342; phone numbers, 547; reservation form, 555. *See also* Sleeping
Hugo, Victor: house of, 70, 263, 268

I

Ile de la Cité: 18, 222
Ile St. Louis: 45, 86, 425–426; eating, 390–392; map, 85
Impressionism: 520; Marmottan Museum, 228–232; Orsay Museum, 139–143. *See also* Auvers-sur-Oise; Giverny
In a Café (Degas): 140–141
Ingres, Jean-August-Dominique: 320
Internet access: 345, 353, 501
Iraq: ancient places in, 128
Italian Renaissance: 115
Italian Renaissance art: 112–117, 120–121
Itineraries: planning, 4–6, 12–13, 19–23

J

Jacquemart-André Museum: 64–65; hours, 43
Jane Avril Dancing (Toulouse-Lautrec): 149–150
Jardin des Enfants aux Halles: 405–406
Jardin des Plantes: 405
Jardin du Luxembourg. See Luxembourg Garden
Jazz clubs: 422
Jewish Art and History Museum: 68–69, 265; hours, 43
Jewish Quarter: 269–270

K

Kandinsky, Wassily: 278
King Sargon II and a Dignitary: 127
Klee, Paul: 279

L

La Belle Jardinière (Raphael): 114–115
La Défense: 43, 62, 66–67
La Fête de la Féderation: 291
La Grande Arche: 43, 62, 66–67
La Grande Odalisque (Ingres): 118–119
La Maison Rose restaurant: 330
La Tour Eiffel. See Eiffel Tower
La Tour Montparnasse. See Montparnasse Tower
The Lady and the Unicorn tapestries: 249–250
Landscape (Cézanne): 146–147
Language: 6–7; barrier, 548–549; classes, 548; coffee and tea lingo, 373; for the Métro and RER, 28–29; pronunciation guide, 556–557; restaurant phrases, 560; shopping, 408; survival phrases, 559; for taxis, 430; transportation phrases, 444
Latin Quarter: 53–54, 89
Laundry: 345, 353, 501
Laurencin: Marie, 161
Law Codex of Hammurabi, King of Babylon: 124–126
Le Bateau-Lavoir: 332–333
Le Café de Flore: 240
Le Passeport: 457
Left Bank: 18–19, 53–60; booksellers, 86–87, 409; walking tour, 233–243
Léger, Fernand: 280
Les Deux Magots Café: 240
Les Egouts de Paris: 52
L'Espace Dalí. See Dalí Museum
L'espoir du bonheur: 290
Liberty Leading the People (Delacroix): 120
L'Officiel des Spectacles: 23–24
Louis XIV: 288–289, 464–465
Louis XV: 289, 465
Louis XVI: 289, 292, 465
Louis-Philippe: 297
Louvre: The *Da Vinci Code*, 56; eating, 399; general information, 46–48, 101–104; hours, 42; sightseeing tour, 221–222; tour, 105–129
Luncheon on the Grass (Manet): 138
Luxembourg Garden: 57, 234, 242–243, 403
Luxembourg Garden area: eating, 392–395; sleeping, 359

M

The Madonna of the Angels (Cimabue): 111

Mail: 550

Maps: budget hotels near Place de la République, 367; bus #69 tour, 219; Champs-Elysées and nearby, 61; Champs-Elysées walk, 253; Chartres, 496; day trips from Paris, 513; driving in France, 453; Eiffel Tower and nearby, 51; Eiffel Tower area, 173; Eurostar routes, 452; general information, 538; Giverny, 519; historic Paris walk, 75; hotels and restaurants near St. Sulpice and the Odéon Theaters, 362; hotels and restaurants near the Panthéon, 364; Ile St. Louis, 85; Ile St. Louis hotels and restaurants, 359; key bus routes, 31; Left Bank, 55; Left Bank walk, 235; Luxembourg Garden, 242–243; major museums neighborhood, 48; Marais hotels, 354; Marais neighborhood, 69; Marais restaurants, 387; Marais walk, 264; Montmartre walk, 325; Paris sights, 39; Père Lachaise Cemetery, 312; public transportation, 443; Puces St. Ouen flea market, 417; Reims, 503; Rue Cler hotels, 347; Rue Cler restaurants, 383; Sainte-Chapelle, 96; shopping, 411

Marais: 19, 67–71, 222–223; eating, 385–390; at night, 426; sleeping, 352–359; walking tour, 263–272

Marie-Antoinette: 292–293; Trianon, 478–480

Markets: Cité Métropolitain Stop and Flower Market, 45; Marais, 352; open-air markets, 418–419; Rue Cler, 165–171, 345; Rue des Martyrs, 336–337

Marmottan Museum: general information, 53, 225–226; hours, 43; tour, 226–232

The Marriage at Cana (Veronese): 117

Matisse, Henri: 162, 277

Maturity (Claudel): 153–154

Medieval art: 111–112

Mémorial de la Shoah. *See* Holocaust Memorial

Metric system: 7, 552

Métro: 18, 26–29; Cité Métropolitain Stop and Flower Market, 45, 96–97; Marais, 353; Rue Cler neighborhood, 345

Midday (Van Gogh): 145

Modern art: 275–283

Modigliani, Amedeo: 160–161, 320

Molière: 315–316

Mona Lisa (Da Vinci): 116

Mondrian, Piet: 278

Monet, Claude: Marmottan Museum, 226–232; Orangerie Museum 156–159; Orsay Museum, 142–143

Money: 8–12; bargains, 8

Montand, Yves: 321

Montmartre: 19, 71–72; at night, 426; tourist information offices (TIs), 23; walking tour, 323–337

Montmartre Museum: 72, 324, 330

Montparnasse Tower: 59, 63

Morrison, Jim: 316–317

Moulin de la Galette: 333

Moulin Rouge: 334–335

Mur des Fédérés: 314

Musée Carnavalet. See Carnavalet Museum

Musée d'Arte et Histoire du Judaïsme. See Jewish Art and History Museum

Musée Daubigny: 523

Musée de l'Erotisme. See Museum of Erotic Art

Musée de l'Orangerie. See Orangerie Museum

Musée de Montmartre: 72

Musée des Beaux-Arts: 65

Musée d'Orsay. See Orsay Museum

Musée du Louvre. See Louvre

Musée du Quai Branly. See Quai Branly Museum

Musée Jacquemart-Andrè: 64–65

Musée Marmottan Monet. See Marmottan Museum

Musée National de la Marine. See National Maritime Museum

Musée National du Moyen Age. See Cluny Museum

Musée National Eugène Delacroix. See Delacroix Museum

Musée Picasso. See Picasso Museum

Musée Rodin. See Rodin Museum

Musées, Monuments Historiques, et Expositions: 24

Museum of Erotic Art: 72, 324, 335
Museum of the Surrender (Reims):
   505
Museums: Army Museum and
   Napoleon's Tomb, 52, 194-216;
   Carnavalet Museum, 43, 70, 263,
   268, 286–300; Cluny Museum,
   43, 54, 244–250; Dalí Museum,
   71, 324, 329–330; Delacroix
   Museum, 55–57, 233, 237–238;
   Fragonard Perfume Museum, 64;
   free, 47; general information, 18;
   Jacquemart-André Museum, 43,
   64–65; Jewish Art and History
   Museum, 43, 68–69, 265; Louvre,
   42, 46–48, 56, 99–129, 221–222;
   major museums neighborhood,
   46–50; Marmottan Museum,
   43, 53, 225–232; Montmartre
   Museum, 72, 324, 330; *Musée
   des Beaux-Arts*, 65; Museum of
   Erotic Art, 72, 324, 335; Museum
   of the Surrender (Reims), 505;
   National Maritime Museum,
   51–52; nightlife, 424; Orangerie
   Museum, 42, 49, 155–163; Orsay
   Museum, 42, 49–50, 130–154;
   Picasso Museum, 43, 69–70,
   265, 301–309; planning, 13;
   Pompidou Center, 43, 63, 68, 265,
   271–272, 273–285; Quai Branly
   Museum, 51; reduced prices, 47;
   Rodin Museum, 42, 53, 183–193;
   strategy, 25. *See also* Paris Museum
   Pass
Music: cabaret, 423; concerts and
   operas, 423–424; free concerts, 47;
   jazz clubs, 422; national anthem,
   296; Opéra Garnier, 43, 61–63;
   St. Sulpice Church organ concert,
   54–55

N
Napoleon's Tomb: general
   information, 194–195; hours,
   42; tour, 195–199. *See also* Army
   Museum
National Maritime Museum: 51–52
Neighborhoods: 18–19. *See also*
   Arrondissements
New media: 284–285
News: 8
Nightlife: art, 424; bus tours, 427;
   cabaret, 423; concerts and operas,

423–424; jazz clubs, 422; *Pariscope*
   magazine, 23, 421–422; taxi tour,
   427–432; walks, 425–427
Notre-Dame Cathedral: 41–44, 62,
   74–76, 404, 425–426; walking
   tour, 79–84
Numbers: 552

O
The Oath of the Jeu-de-Paume: 290
Odéon Cinemas: 239, 426–427
Odilon Redon: 147
Olive oil: 171
Olympia (Manet): 137
Opéra Bastille: 266
Opéra Garnier: 61–63; hours, 43;
   model in the Orsay Museum, 138
Orangerie Museum: general
   information, 49, 155; hours, 42;
   renovation, 158; tour, 156–163;
   Walter-Guillaume collection, 159
Oriental antiquities: 121–129
Orientation: 17–18; arrondissements,
   17–18
Orly Airport: 437–439, 546
Orsay Museum: 19th Century, 133–
   135; general information, 49–50,
   130–132; hours, 42; tour, 132–154

P
Packing checklist: 554
The Painter's Studio (Courbet): 136
Palace of Sargon II: 126
Palais de Justice: 95
Palais Royal Courts: 48–49
Panthéon: 57–59; hours, 43
Paris Archaeological Crypt: 44, 76,
   79
Paris Museum Pass: 13, 25, 38–41,
   47, 74, 457
Paris Plage: 45–46
Paris Sewer Tour: 52
Paris Story Film: 63–64
Paris Times: 23
Paris Visite pass: 27
Paris Voice: 24
Pariscope magazine: 23, 421–422
Parking: 26, 453–454. *See also*
   Driving
Parks and gardens: Aquaboulevard,
   406; Champ de Mars, 218–220,
   403; Jardin des Enfants aux
   Halles, 405–406; Luxembourg
   Garden, 57, 234, 242–243, 403;

Promenade Plantée Park, 70–71; Rodin Museum gardens, 190–193; Tuileries Garden, 221
Parthenon frieze: 107–108
Passages: 419–420
Passe Navigo Découverte: 26–27
Passports: 5, 6
Payday: 152
Peasant Woman near the Hearth (Van Gogh): 144
Père Lachaise Cemetery: 71, 224, 310–311; hours, 43; tour, 311–322
Petit Bateau: 165–167
Petit Palais: 65, 259–260
Pharmacies: 169
Phone cards: 541–542. *See also* Telephones
Phones. *See* Telephones
Piaf, Edith: 314–315
Picasso, Pablo: 162, 275–276; Cubism, 302–304; early years and Blue Period, 302; family life, 304; last years, 309; residences, 306; Rose Period, 302; in the south of France, 308–309; and Spain, 305–306; studio, 332–333; women, 306–308; World War II, 308
Picasso Museum: 69–70, 265; general information, 301–302; hours, 43; tour, 302–309
Pigalle ("Pig Alley"): 72, 335
Place Dauphine: 98
Place de la Bastille: 223, 265–267. *See also* Bastille
Place de la Concorde: 260–261, 399, 426; nearby, 261–262
Place de la Opéra: 426
Place de la République: 366–368
Place des Vosges: 267–268
Place du Tertre: 328–329
Place St. André-des-Arts: 90
Place St. Germain-des-Prés: 426
Place St. Michel: 90–91
Place Vendôme: 426
Pointillist paintings: 149
Politics: 531–533
Pollock, Jackson: 283
Pompidou Center: 63, 68, 265, 271–272, 405; general information, 273–274; hours, 43; tour, 274–285
Pont des Arts: 234
Pont Neuf: 99
Pop art: 284
Porte de Clignancourt: 416–418

Portrait of the Artist's Mother (Whistler): 140
Post-Impressionism: 143–147
Primitives: 147–150
Promenade Plantée Park: 70–71
Proust, Marcel: 321
Pyramides: tourist information office, 23

Q
Quai Branly Museum: 51
Quartier Latin. See Latin Quarter

R
Radio shows: 536
The Raft of the Medusa (Géricault): 119
Realism: 135–139
Reign of Terror: 293–295
Reims: Carnegie Library, 506; Cathedral, 502–505; champagne tours, 507–508; eating, 509–510; Epernay, 508; general information, 500–501; map, 503; Museum of the Surrender, 505; Palais du Tau, 505; Porte de Mars, 506; Route de la Champagne, 508; sleeping, 509; tourist information offices (TIs), 501; transportation, 501, 502, 510
Renoir, Pierre-Auguste: 159–160
RER: 29–30
Restaurants: 374–376; phrases, 560. *See also* Eating
Restrooms. *See* WCs
Ritz Hotel on Place Vendôme: 56
Robespierre, Maximilien de: 294–295
Rodin Museum: gardens, 190–193; general information, 53, 183–184; hours, 42; tour, 184–193
Roger-Viollet: 236
Roman antiquities: 247–248
Roman art: 108–110
The Romans of the Decadence (Couture): 137
Romanticism: 119–120
Room and board: costs, 3–4. *See also* Sleeping
Rossini, Gioacchino: 319–321
Rouault, Georges: 277
Rousseau, Henri: 160
Rue Cler: eating, 380–385; sleeping, 344–352; walking tour, 164–171

Rue de la Roquette: 223
Rue de Lappe: 426
Rue des Canettes: 240
Rue des Francs Bourgeois: 268
Rue des Martyrs: 336–337
Rue Norvins: 329
Rue Pavée: 269
Rue St. Dominique: 220
Rue Ste. Croix de la Bretonnerie: 271

S

Sacré-Cœur: 63, 71, 324, 326–327;
 hours, 43
Safety: 25
Sainte-Chapelle: 42, 45, 76, 91–96;
 and nearby, 96–100
Sand, George: house of, 236
Satie, Erik: 330
Scams: 24–25. *See also* Theft
The School of Plato: 152
Security: 24–25
Seine River: 99
Self-Portrait (Cézanne): 146
Self-Portrait, Paris (Van Gogh): 144
Self-Portrait, St. Rémy (Van Gogh): 146
Senior discounts: 7
Serenity: 152
Services: tipping for, 11
Seurat, Georges: 320
Shakespeare and Company
 bookstore: 76, 87–88
Shopping: 8; arcaded shopping
 streets, 419–420; bookstores,
 25–26, 76; boutique strolls,
 412–416; Champs-Elysées, 257,
 258–259; clothing sizes, 552–553;
 costs, 4; customs, 12; department
 stores, 408–410; general
 information, 407; language, 408;
 map, 411; open-air markets, 418–
 419; Puces St. Ouen (flea market),
 416–418; souvenir shops, 408;
 tabacs, 26; tips, 407–408; toy store,
 237; VAT refunds, 11–12
Sightseeing: affordability, 47; bus
 #69 tour, 217–224; costs, 4; daily
 schedules, 20–21; freebies, 47;
 general information, 13–14;
 Paris Museum Pass, 13, 25,
 38–41; planning, 12–13. *See also
 individual sights*
Signoret, Simone: 321
Skating: 46

Slaves (Michelangelo): 120–121
Sleeping: air conditioning, 342;
 apartments, 343; Auvers-sur-Oise,
 524; Chartres Cathedral, 497–
 498; costs, 3–4; Fontainebleau,
 516; general information,
 338–339; Giverny, 521; hostels,
 342, 547; hotel reservation form,
 556; hotels, 339–342, 547; longer
 stays, 368–369; Luxembourg
 Garden area, 359–366; making
 reservations, 343–344, 556;
 Marais neighborhood, 352–359;
 near Place de la République,
 366–368; Reims, 509; Rue Cler
 neighborhood, 344–352; sleep
 code, 341; types of rooms, 340;
 Versailles, 480–481
SNCF boutiques: 450–451. *See also*
 Trains
The Source (Ingres): 133–135
Soutine, Chaim: 162–163
Souvenir shops: 408
*St. Francis of Assisi Receiving the
 Stigmata* (Giotto): 111–112
St. Germain-des-Prés: 54, 233,
 239–240, 397
St. Sebastian (Mantegna): 113–114
St. Séverin Church: 88
St. Sulpice Church: 54–55, 56, 234,
 240–242
Stained glass: Chartres Cathedral,
 488–491; Cluny Museum, 245–
 247; Sainte-Chapelle, 92–94
Stein, Gertrude: 313
Stela of Naram-Sin: 124
Stela of the Vulturesi: 122
Street safety: 25
Strikes: 449
Student discounts: 7
Surrealism: 281–282

T

Tabacs: 26, 171
Tapestries: 245, 248–250
Taxis: 32; floodlit Paris taxi tour,
 427–432; Marais, 355; tipping, 11
Telephones: 540; calling France,
 343; dialing, 542–543; European
 calling chart, 544–545; hotel-
 room phones, 542; phone cards,
 541–542; types of, 540–541;
 useful phone numbers, 543–549;
 VoIP, 542

Television shows: 536
Temperature conversion: 553
Thalys train: 451
The Thinker (Rodin): 191
Theft: 24, 28–29, 173, 459. *See also*
    Scams
Time: 7
Time to go: 4
Tipping: 10–11, 374
TIs: 23–24, 352, 501, 535–536, 546
Tobacco stands: 26, 171
Toilets. *See* WCs
Toulouse-Lautrec, Henri de: house
    of, 334
Tour guides: 36; tipping, 11
Tourist information offices (TIs):
    23–24, 352, 535–536, 546; Reims,
    501
Tourist scams: 24–25. *See also* Theft
Tours: bike, 33, 36–37; boat, 34–35;
    bus, 33–34; Chartres Cathedral,
    483; good-value, 47; private tours,
    265; Versailles, 460–461; walking,
    35–36
Trains: to Brussels and Amsterdam,
    451; Eurostar, 451–452; Gare
    d'Austerlitz, 449–450; Gare de
    l'Est, 448; Gare de Lyon, 399–
    400, 447–448; Gare du Nord,
    442–445; Gare Montparnasse,
    445–447; Gare St. Lazare,
    448–449; overnight, 5; SNCF
    boutiques, 450–451; station
    overview, 440–442; strikes, 449;
    tips, 446
Transport of the Cedars of Lebanon:
    127
Transportation: airport connections,
    433–440; Auvers-sur-Oise,
    524–525; *carnets*, 26; costs, 3;
    Disneyland Paris, 526; ferries, 452;
    general information, 14; Giverny,
    521–522; language, 444; passes,
    26–27; public transit tickets, 26;
    to recommended hotels, 436; to
    Reims, 510; to Versailles, 459. *See
    also* Bikes; Buses; Driving; Métro;
    RER; Taxis
Travel advisories: 546
Travel philosophy: 16
Traveling as a temporary local: 15
Trianon: 478–480
Trocadéro Square: 63, 403–404, 425

Tuileries Garden: 221

U
Updates: 6, 536
Utrillo, Maurice: 162, 329

V
Van Gogh, Vincent: house of, 334,
    Orsay Museum, 143–146
Van Gogh's Room at Arles: 145
VAT refunds: 11–12
Vaux-le-Vicomte: 512–514
Vendange Harvest tapestry: 248
Venus de Milo: 106–107
Versailles: 42, 72–73, 404–405;
    eating, 481; Equestrian
    Performance Academy, 474;
    fountain spectacles, 462;
    gardens, 474, 475–477; general
    information, 456–462; hours, 457;
    maps, 458, 461–462; passes, 457;
    sleeping, 480–481; tour, 463–480;
    transportation, 459
Views: 174
Virgin, Child, and St. Anne (Da
    Vinci): 114
VoIP: 542
Voltaire: statue of, 234
Vuitton, Louis: 257

W
Wagner, Richard: house of, 237
The Walking Man (Rodin): 153
Walking tours: 35–36; Champs-
    Elysées, 251–262; historic,
    74–100; Left Bank, 233–243;
    Marais, 263–272; Rue Cler,
    164–171
Walter, Marie-Thérèse: 305
War (Rousseau): 147–148
Warhol, Andy: 284
WCs: 26, 76
Weather: 4, 553
Website: 537
Weekends: 3
Wilde, Oscar: grave, 313; hotel of,
    236
Wine: 167; champagne tours, 507–
    508; tasting, 549
Winged Bulls: 126
Winged Victory of Samothrace:
    109–110

Rick Steves®

EUROPEAN TOURS

Experience Europe the Rick Steves way, with great guides, small groups...and no grumps!

See 30 itineraries at ricksteves.com

▶ Plan Your Trip

Browse thousands of articles and a wealth of money-saving tips for planning your dream trip. You'll find up-to-date information on Europe's best destinations, packing smart, getting around, finding rooms, staying healthy, avoiding scams and more.

▶ Eurail Passes

Find out, step-by-step, if a rail pass makes sense for your trip—and how to avoid buying more than you need. Get a bunch of free extras!

▶ Graffiti Wall & Travelers' Helpline

Learn, ask, share—our online community of savvy travelers is a great resource for first-time travelers to Europe, as well as seasoned pros.

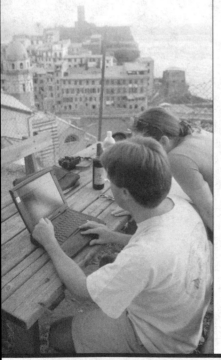

Rick Steves' Europe Through the Back Door, Inc.

ricksteves.com

urn your travel dreams into affordable reality

▶ Free Audio Tours & Travel Newsletter

Get your nose out of this guide-book and focus on what you'll be seeing with Rick's free audio tours of the greatest sights in Paris, Rome, Florence and Venice.

Subscribe to our free *Travel News* e-newsletter, and get monthly articles from Rick on what's happening in Europe.

▶ Great Gear from Rick's Travel Store

Pack light and right—on a budget—with Rick's custom-designed carry-on bags, roll-aboards, day packs, travel accessories, guidebooks, journals, maps and DVDs of his TV shows.

130 Fourth Avenue North, PO Box 2009 • Edmonds, WA 98020 USA
Phone: (425) 771-8303 • Fax: (425) 771-0833 • www.ricksteves.com

Rick Steves

TRAVEL SKILLS
Europe Through the Back Door

EUROPE GUIDES
Best of Europe
Eastern Europe
Europe 101
European Christmas
Postcards from Europe

COUNTRY GUIDES
Croatia & Slovenia
England
France
Germany
Great Britain
Ireland
Italy
Portugal
Scandinavia
Spain
Switzerland

CITY & REGIONAL GUIDES
Amsterdam, Bruges & Brussels
Athens & The Peloponnese NEW IN 2009
Budapest NEW IN 2009
Florence & Tuscany
Istanbul
London
Paris
Prague & The Czech Republic
Provence & The French Riviera
Rome
Venice
Vienna, Salzburg & Tirol NEW IN 2009

PHRASE BOOKS & DICTIONARIES
French
French, Italian & German
German
Italian
Portuguese
Spanish

RICK STEVES' EUROPE DVDs
Austria & The Alps
Eastern Europe
England
Europe
France & Benelux
Germany & Scandinavia
Greece, Turkey, Israel & Egypt
Ireland & Scotland
Italy's Cities
Italy's Countryside
Rick Steves' European Christmas
Spain & Portugal
Travel Skills & "The Making Of"

PLANNING MAPS
Britain, Ireland & London
Europe
France & Paris
Germany, Austria & Switzerland
Italy
Spain & Portugal

JOURNALS
Rick Steves' Pocket Travel Journal
Rick Steves' Travel Journal

Rick Steves' Guidebook Series

Country Guides

Rick Steves' Best of Europe
Rick Steves' Croatia & Slovenia
Rick Steves' Eastern Europe
Rick Steves' England
Rick Steves' France
Rick Steves' Germany
Rick Steves' Great Britain
Rick Steves' Ireland
Rick Steves' Italy
Rick Steves' Portugal
Rick Steves' Scandinavia
Rick Steves' Spain
Rick Steves' Switzerland

City and Regional Guides

Rick Steves' Amsterdam, Bruges & Brussels
Rick Steves' Athens & the Peloponnese (new in 2009)
Rick Steves' Budapest (new in 2009)
Rick Steves' Florence & Tuscany
Rick Steves' Istanbul
Rick Steves' London
Rick Steves' Paris
Rick Steves' Prague & the Czech Republic
Rick Steves' Provence & the French Riviera
Rick Steves' Rome
Rick Steves' Venice
Rick Steves' Vienna, Salzburg & Tirol (new in 2009)

Rick Steves' Phrase Books

French
French/Italian/German
German
Italian
Portuguese
Spanish

Other Books

Rick Steves' Europe Through the Back Door
Rick Steves' Europe 101: History and Art for the Traveler
Rick Steves' European Christmas
Rick Steves' Postcards from Europe

(Avalon Travel)

Avalon Travel
a member of the Perseus Books Group
1700 Fourth Street
Berkeley, CA 94710

ISBN(10) 1-59880-121-X
ISBN(13) 978-1-59880-121-7
ISSN 1522-3299

For the latest on Rick's lectures, guidebooks, tours, public radio show, and public television
series, contact Europe Through the Back Door, Box 2009, Edmonds, WA 98020, tel.
425/771-8303, fax 425/771-0833, www.ricksteves.com, or rick@ricksteves.com.

Europe Through the Back Door Managing Editor: Risa Laib
ETBD Lead Editor: Cameron Hewitt
ETBD Editors: Gretchen Strauch, Jennifer Madison Davis, Tom Griffin, Cathy Lu, Sarah
    McCormic
Avalon Travel Senior Editor and Series Manager: Madhu Prasher
Avalon Travel Project Editor: Kelly Lydick
Avalon Travel Editorial Assistant: Jamie Andrade
Copy Editor: Ellie Behrstock
Proofreader: Lotta Eyestrane
Indexer: Claire Splan
Production & Typesetting: McGuire Barber Design
Cover Design: Kimberly Glyder Design
Maps & Graphics: David C. Hoerlein, Laura VanDeventer, Lauren Mills, Barb Geisler,
    Mike Morgenfeld
Photography: Rick Steves, Steve Smith, David C. Hoerlein, Gene Openshaw, Barb
    Geisler, Rob Unck
Front Cover Image: © Carl Valiquet/Masterfile
Front Matter Color Photos: p. i, The Louvre at Night © Laura VanDeventer; p. viii, Place
    du Tertre © FOLIO, Inc.